INVESTMENTS

INVESTMENTS

FRANK · K · REILLY

BERNARD · J. · HANK PROFESSOR
UNIVERSITY OF NOTRE DAME

THE DRYDEN PRESS CHICAGO NEW YORK PHILADELPHIA SAN FRANCISCO MONTREAL TORONTO
LONDON SYDNEY TOKYO MEXICO CITY RIO DE JANEIRO MADRID

Acquisitions Editor: Glenn Turner
Developmental Editor: Paul Psilos
Project Editor: Kathy Richmond
Design Director: Alan Wendt
Cover and Text Design by Alan Wendt
Copy Editing by Madelyn Roesch

Address orders to:
383 Madison Avenue
New York, New York 10017

Address editorial correspondence to:
901 North Elm Street
Hinsdale, Illinois 60521

Library of Congress Catalog Card Number:
ISBN: 0-03-056712-2
Printed in the United States of America
 23-144 · 98765432

CBS College Publishing
The Dryden Press
Holt, Rinehart and Winston
Saunders College Publishing

To my fabulous wife, Therese, and our children who have given us so much joy, Frank K. III, Clarence R. II, Therese B., and Edgar B.

PREFACE

The pleasure of writing a textbook comes in writing on a subject that you enjoy and find exciting. You hope that you can pass on to the reader not only knowledge, but also the excitement that you feel. In addition, when writing about investments there is an added stimulant because you know that you are dealing with a subject that can affect the reader during his entire business career and beyond. It is hoped that what you derive from this course will help you enjoy a better life because you will learn to manage your resources properly. There is nothing sadder than to hear about a great athlete or entertainer who earned large salaries for a few years, but is discovered to be destitute during his or her later years. When one hears about such cases, the standard comment is, "if only they had managed their money properly."

The purpose of this book is to help you, the reader, learn how to manage your money so that you will derive the maximum benefit from what you earn. To accomplish this purpose, it is necessary to learn what investment alternatives are available today, and, more important, to develop a way of thinking about investments that will remain with you in the years ahead when new and different investment opportunities become available. Because of its dual purpose, the book is a mixture of description and theory. The descriptive material involves a discussion of available investment instruments and considers how the capital markets currently work. The theoretical portion takes into consideration how you should evaluate current investments and future investment opportunities.

With these goals in mind, the text is intended to be used in a beginning course in investments by those who have had a basic course in financial management and the normal prerequisites of accounting and economics. Any technical tools required beyond this are discussed in one of the several appendices.

One of the innovations in this text is the inclusion of a number of profiles of individuals who have made and are making significant contributions to the field of investments. I feel that it is important for you to "know" the people behind the names you see in footnotes and references. I have also included some individuals whom you might hear about in the contemporary investment world. I hope you enjoy learning about these people as much as I did writing about them. I sincerely appreciate the help they provided in terms of biographical information and pictures.

A student Study Guide prepared by Eugene F. Drzycimski of the University of Wisconsin–Oshkosh is available for the book. For each chapter there is a four-part presentation which includes:

1. A brief discussion of purpose of the main purpose of the chapter

2. The highlights and major points of the chapter

3. Extensive exercises including true-false, fill in the blank, multiple-choice questions, and some short answer questions

4. Answers to all the exercises in Part 3.

Reprints of some recent articles that can be used in class discussion also appear in the Study Guide.

During the period that I was writing this book I received help and support from the College of Commerce and Business Administration at the University of Illinois and from a number of individuals. My friend Kenneth Carey at the University of Illinois provided substantial input into the portfolio chapters and Michael Joehnk of the University of Tulsa was a big help on the bond chapters. In addition, I had some excellent reviewers who commented on the total manuscript:–Brian Belt, University of Missouri, Kansas City; Eugene F. Dryzycimski, University of Wisconsin–Oshkosh; Stephen Goldstein, University of South Carolina; Ronald Hoffmeister, University of Wyoming; Ron Hutchins, Eastern Michigan University; Ali Jahankhani, University of Illinois; John Mathys, DePaul University; Dennis McConnell, University of Maine; Douglas Southard, Virginia Polytechnic Institute; and Harold Stevenson, Arizona State University. I also received help on an earlier manuscript from Robert Angell, East Carolina University; Joseph E. Finnerty, University of Massachusetts; Mary Lindahl, University of Tennessee; and George Pinches, University of Kansas.

During the time the text was being written and used in classes, I received excellent suggestions from students, especially Paul Fellows, R. H. Gilmer, Jr., and Daniel Lehmann at the University of Illinois. The most extensive help came from Wenchi Wong, my very talented, dedicated, and delightful research assistant. I also received comments from C. F. Lee, University of Illinois, Don Panton, University of Kansas; Donald Tuttle, Indiana University; and John M. Wachowicz, University of Tennessee. The greatest thoughts and suggestions on the book and many other topics came from my very good friend, Jim Gentry, during our long runs through the farms and apple orchards of the University of Illinois.

I have been fortunate to have a number of good friends in the investment community who gracefully answered my questions about the "real world" and made sure I didn't stray too far from reality: Ray Dixon, Goldman Sachs & Co.; John Maginn, Mutual of Omaha; Robert Milne, Duff and Phelps Investment

Management Co.; Arthur Rockwell, Security Pacific National Bank; Stanley Ryals, Investment Counselor; Barry Schnepel, Merrill Lynch, Pierce, Fenner and Smith, Inc.; Robert Murray, First National Bank of Oregon; and Thomas V. Williams, Kemper Financial Services.

Glenn Turner and Paul Psilos of the Dryden Press provided guidance and a fair amount of prodding in preparing this manuscript. Kathy Richmond was the project editor who gracefully pulled it together at the end. Again, I was fortunate to get Madelyn Roesch as my copy editor. She has that rare talent to provide meaningful suggestions, make you laugh, and build a friendship at the same time. Carol Carrillo typed good copy from illegible scribbling with patience and good humor.

As always, my greatest debt is to my family. This includes my own parents who gave of themselves and my wonderful in-laws who gave me their daughter. Most important is my wife and children who gave their love and understanding which provided a support system that is crucial to a project such as this.

Frank K. Reilly
University of Notre Dame
Notre Dame, Indiana

OPPORTUNITIES IN INVESTMENTS

Most students take this course because they want to learn how to invest excess earnings. In addition, some students may consider the investments field as an area for future employment. Over the years many students have asked me, "What are the job opportunities in the investments area?" Here is a brief discussion of some specific investment positions with various financial institutions.

1. **Registered Representative with a Brokerage Firm**   (Also referred to as a broker.) The registered representative is involved in the sale of stocks, bonds, options, commodities, and other investment instruments to individuals or institutions. If you decide to buy or sell stock, you call your broker at the investment firm where you have an account and he or she arranges the purchase or sale. If you are a regular customer, your broker may call you and suggest that you buy or sell some stock; if you agree, he or she will arrange it. It typically takes several years for a broker to build a clientele, but once you do, it can be an exciting profession and very rewarding—both financially and in terms of what you do for your clients.

2. **Investment Analysis: Brokerage Firms and/or Investment Bankers**   This involves analysis of alternative industries, the companies in the industry, and their securities as support for registered representatives. For example, as an employee for Merrill Lynch Pierce Fenner and Smith, you do an analysis of the computer industry and all the major companies in the industry and prepare a report. This report is used by the registered representatives at Merrill Lynch offices all over the country.

    Alternatively, if your firm is an investment banking firm that underwrites new stock or bond issues, you may analyze the industry and stocks of an issue your firm will underwrite to determine its needs and the characteristics of the issue. Also investment bankers are heavily involved in finding merger partners for their clients and helping negotiate terms. An analyst would help answer these questions: how much is the potential merger firm worth and what are reasonable terms?

3. **Investment Analysis: Banks**   Banks require investment analysis in two major areas—loans and trust departments. Obviously firms that are being considered for commercial loans must be analyzed to find out why the firm needs money, how much the firm needs, and when and how will it be able to pay the loan back.

    Bank trust departments manage trust accounts for individuals and pension funds for companies, and the capital is invested in various combinations of stocks and bonds. Again, they need analysts to examine various industries and the individual companies and recommend what securities should be bought, sold or held in the trust accounts.

4. **Investment Analysis: Investment Counselors and Mutual Funds**   Both groups manage large portfolios of stocks, bonds, and other assets for clients. Investment counselors manage pension funds and individual accounts (over $1 million) for wealthy individuals. As an investment analyst you would examine various industries and the companies within them and make recommendations regarding what stocks and bonds should be included in the portfolios.

   In mutual funds (also referred to as investment companies), investors pool their money and acquire a portfolio of stocks. The investment company that manages the portfolio will hire analysts to examine industries and companies and to help select securities for the portfolio.

5. **Investment Analysis: Insurance Companies**   Insurance companies typically have large investment portfolios that they manage in order to derive returns for policyholders. While the asset mix of the portfolios differs depending upon the type of insurance (life versus property and casualty), the normal emphasis is on fixed-income securities.

6. **Portfolio Managers**   For each of the latter financial firms (banks, investment counselors, mutual funds, insurance companies), there are portfolio managers in addition to the analysts. The portfolio managers are responsible for gathering the information and recommendations from the analysts and for making the final decision about the securities in the portfolio.

Some Factors to Consider

Many firms only want to hire investment analysts who have three or four years of experience. How do you get the experience if nobody will hire you for that first job? The only solution is to contact a lot of firms in the field, show a willingness to apply yourself, and accept a relatively low beginning salary. Assuming you can get the initial position and get the necessary experience, the long-run income range for an experienced analyst is quite high.

Even if you get a job as an analyst, it is very likely that your beginning salary will be low relative to other jobs. Most investment firms believe that the first few years are almost entirely a training program. This training period is very costly to the firm. Once you acquire this experience, though, your salary can rise rapidly.

For some analyst jobs, there is a tendency to hire individuals with graduate degrees. Often firms will hire undergraduates and encourage them to go on for graduate degrees in evening programs.

Almost anyone who considers a career in investment analysis or portfolio management should attempt to become a Chartered Financial Analyst (CFA). This is a professional designation similar to the CPA in accounting. It is based upon three examinations. The designation is becoming greatly valued by financial institutions. The program and its requirements are described in an appendix to Chapter 23.

CONTENTS

PART · TWO

PART · FOUR

INVESTMENTS

The Investment Background

PART·ONE

The chapters in this section are meant to give the reader a background in the total area of investments by answering the following questions:

Why do people invest?

What are some of the investments available?

How do securities markets function?

How and why are these securities markets changing?

How can you determine what common stocks are doing?

Where do you get relevant information on various potential investments?

In the first chapter we will consider why individuals invest and discuss in detail the factors that determine a person's required rate of return on an investment. The lat-

ter point will be very important in subsequent analyses. Because one of the most important tenets of investment theory is the need to diversify, in the second chapter we will briefly discuss a number of alternative investment instruments and consider several studies of the rates of return and risk some of them involve.

In Chapter 3 we examine the function of markets in general, and of the securities markets specifically, concentrating on the markets for bonds and common stocks. There have been significant changes in the operation of the securities market since 1965 and these are dealt with in Chapter 4, where we will also consider what the future may hold for these markets, and the implications for investors.

The behavior of the stock market is often measured in terms of changes in various stock market series. Because these series are used in a number of ways, in Chapter 5 we will examine them in depth, and compare several of them. The final chapter contains a description of sources of information on various aspects of investments.

The Investment Setting

✥ 1 ✥

It's easy to dream that at some point in our lives we will accumulate an estate that will enable us to enjoy certain luxuries and retire at the end of our working days in comfort and security. For some people, this dream may easily be a reality, either because they inherited a large amount of money or property or because they worked in an occupation that paid very large salaries. For most of us, though, the accumulation of an estate is going to require substantial knowledge, planning, and effort. Even those who inherited wealth or receive large salaries over short periods (professional athletes, entertainers) or over longer periods (doctors, lawyers, partners in accounting firms) need to work at preserving their wealth from the ravages of taxes and inflation. The whole process of building and preserving an estate is described as investments, which is the subject of this book. Specifically, the intent is to provide you with the knowledge necessary to be an intelligent investor and to help in the planning required. Such knowledge involves a grasp of the investment process, acquiring information on what investment instruments are available, and determining how to acquire these alternative investments. Even though you may know how to invest, it is necessary to *plan* so that you have the funds available to invest at the appropriate time. The final ingredient in building or preserving an estate is *effort,* which can only be provided by the individual. It is hoped that having the knowledge and the understanding of the planning process will provide the motivation.

In this chapter we are initially concerned with a definition of investments. Because investing involves the tradeoff between the expected rate of return on an investment alternative and the risk or uncertainty of the return, the second section briefly deals with alternative ways of measuring return and risk. The bulk of the chapter involves a discussion of the general factors that one should consider in determining the rate of return required on an investment; e.g., why would you want a 7 percent return on government bonds at one point in time and 11 percent on those same bonds at a later time? Why would you want a higher rate of return on common stock than on treasury bills?

The Concept of Investment

For most of our lives, we will be earning money. Also, we will want to purchase certain things. Usually, though, there will be an imbalance between our current money income and our consumption desires at any given point in time, and also in the future. We will have more money than we need to spend, or we will want more things than we can afford based upon our current wealth or income. In most cases, these imbalances will cause us to save either negative or positive amounts in order to maximize the benefits (utility) from our income.

When your current money income exceeds your current consumption desires, you will save the excess. You can put the savings under your mattress or bury them in the backyard until some future time when your consumption desires exceed current income. Or you may feel that it is worthwhile to give up the immediate possession of these savings for a future larger amount of money that will be used for consumption. This tradeoff of *present* consumption for a higher level of *future* consumption is the essence of saving and investment. In contrast, when your current money income is less than your current consumption desires, you will attempt to trade part of your *future* money income stream for a higher level of *current* consumption. Where current consumption desires exceed current money income, you engage in *negative saving*, commonly referred to as *borrowing*. The funds borrowed can be used for consumption *or* invested at rates of return above the cost of borrowing.

Obviously the individual who foregoes part of his current money income stream, and thereby defers current consumption, will want more than the current amount in the future. At the same time, the individual attempting to consume or invest more than his current income is willing to pay back more than a dollar in the future for a dollar today. The rate of exchange between *certain* future consumption (future dollars) and *certain* current consumption (current dollars) is the *pure rate of interest* or the *pure time value of money*. The rate of exchange between current and future consumption is established in the capital market and is influenced by the supply of excess income available to be invested at a point in time and the demand for excess consumption (borrowing). If the cost of exchanging $100 of certain income today is $104 of certain income one year from today, the pure rate of exchange on a risk-free investment is said to be 4 percent (104/100 − 1).

The pure time value of money is a "real" rate in that it indicates the increase in "real" goods and services desired. The investor is giving up $100 of consumption today in order to consume $104 of goods and services *at today's prices*. If investors expect a change in the prices of the goods and services they want to consume, they will adjust their required rate of exchange to compensate. If they expect prices to increase at the rate of 2 percent during the period of investment, one would expect them to increase their rate of exchange by this 2 percent (from 4 percent to 6 percent).

Finally, if you feel that the future payment is not certain, you will require a return that exceeds the pure time value of money plus the inflation rate. The amount required in excess of the pure time value of money plus the inflation rate is called a *risk premium*. Extending the example, when you are not certain about future repayment, you would require something in excess of $106 one year from today, possibly $110. In this example, you are requiring a $4, or 4 percent, risk premium.

Investment Defined

Following from the previous discussion, an investment may be defined as *the current commitment of funds for a period of time to derive a future flow of funds that will compensate the investing unit for the time the funds are committed, for the expected rate of inflation, and also for the uncertainty involved in the future flow of funds.* This encompasses all types of investments, whether they be corporate investments in machinery, plant, and equipment; government investments in flood control; or investments by individuals in stocks, bonds, commodities, or real estate. In all cases the investor is trading a *known* dollar amount today for some *expected* future stream of payments or benefits that will exceed the current outlay by an amount which will compensate the investor for the time the funds are committed, for the expected changes in prices during the period, and the uncertainty involved in expected future cash flows.[1] The alternative investments that are considered by various investing units (i.e., corporations, governments, and individuals) only differ with regard to the institutional characteristics of the investment and some unique factors which must be considered in the analysis (e.g., differential taxes).

Measures of Return and Risk

In our discussion we referred to the return derived from an investment and contended that this return is influenced by various factors. Prior to discussing the specific factors that determine the required rate of return in greater detail, it is necessary to briefly discuss how return is measured. In addition, it is important to generate an operational definition of risk and determine how it is measured.

Measure of Return

The purpose of investing is to defer current consumption and thereby add to our wealth so that it will be possible to consume more in the future. Therefore, when we talk about a return on an investment, we are concerned with the increase in wealth resulting from this investment. As an example, if you commit

---

[1]It is recognized that the uncertainty involved is a function of (1) the asset's unique uncertainty, and (2) its relationship with all other assets in the investing unit's portfolio. The exact nature of this uncertainty is considered in detail in a later chapter. At this point it is only necessary to recognize that the investor requires that the expected cash flows compensate him for this uncertainty, however defined.

$100 to an investment at the beginning of a year and get back $110 at the end of the year, it can be said that the return on the investment (i.e., increase in wealth) is $10. Because the actual dollar amount committed to alternative investments differs, it is typical to express the return in terms of a relationship between the amount invested and the amount returned, i.e., to express it as a *rate of return*:

$$\frac{\text{Rate of}}{\text{Return}} = \frac{\text{Ending Wealth} - \text{Beginning Wealth}}{\text{Beginning Wealth}}$$

$$= \frac{\$110 - \$100}{\$100} = \frac{\$10}{\$100} = 10\%$$

Many investments provide the investor with a flow of cash in addition to changing value while the funds are invested. These cash flows must also be considered an addition to wealth. And, because a particular investment may only be a portion of your wealth, it is appropriate to consider the rate of return on each investment. Therefore, a more general specification of rate of return is:

$$\text{Rate of Return} = \frac{\text{Ending Value} - \text{Beginning Value} + \text{Cash Flows}}{\text{Beginning Value}}$$

If we consider the earlier example and add a three-dollar cash flow to it, the rate of return would be:

$$\text{Rate of Return} = \frac{\$110 - 100 + 3}{100}$$

$$= \frac{10 + 3}{100} = \frac{13}{100} = 13\%$$

The rate of increase in wealth for this portion of your portfolio would therefore be 13 percent. This *total* rate of return of 13 percent can be broken down into capital appreciation (the change in price), which was 10 percent, and dividend income, which was 3 percent.

Risk and Uncertainty

Although in a formal sense, there is a difference between risk and uncertainty, in the discussion that follows such a distinction will not be made because, in fact, there is a tendency to use the terms interchangeably or to use one term to explain the other. Risk is thought of as *uncertainty regarding the expected rate of return from an investment*. When an investor is considering an investment, it is possible to ask what rate of return he "expects." The answer might be 10 percent, which is really a point estimate of his total expectation. If you were to press him further, he might acknowledge that he is not certain of this return, and he recognizes that, under certain conditions, the return might go as low as minus 10 percent or as high as plus 25 percent. The point is, the larger the range of possible returns, the more uncertain the investor is regarding the actual return, and, therefore, the greater the risk.

It is possible to determine how certain an investor is regarding the expected rate of return on an investment by analyzing the probability distribution of expected returns. A probability distribution indicates the *possible* returns and assigns probabilities to each of them. The probabilities of a specified return range from zero (no chance of this return) to one (complete certainty). The probabilities that can be assigned to a particular return are either subjective estimates by the investor or are based upon past frequencies (e.g., about 30 percent of the time the return on this particular investment was 10 percent). Let us begin with an example of perfect certainty; i.e., the investor is supposedly certain of a return of 5 percent. This expectation can be schematized as:

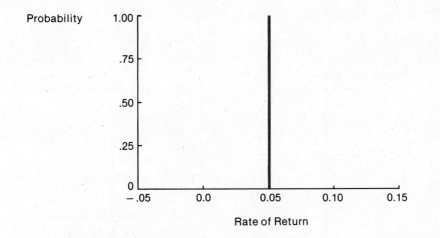

In the case of certainty there is only one possible return and the probability of receiving that return is 1.0. The *expected* return from an investment is defined as:

$$\text{Expected Return} = \Sigma(\text{Probability of Return})(\text{Possible Return})$$
$$= \Sigma(\text{Pi})(\text{Ri})$$

In this case it would be:

$$\text{Expected Return} = (1.0)(.05) = .05$$

An alternative example would be a case in which an investor felt several rates of return were possible under different conditions. If there is a strong economic environment with high corporate profits and little or no inflation, the investor may feel that his return on common stock could be as high as 20 percent. In contrast, if there is an economic decline and a higher than average rate of inflation as was the case during 1974 and 1977, he might feel that the return on common stock could be a negative 20 percent. Finally, the investor may feel that, if there is no major change in the economic environment, the return on common stock will approach the long-run average of 10 percent. The investor's estimated probabilities for each of these potential states, based upon past experience, are as follows:

State of Nature	Probability	Rate of Return
Strong Economy—No Inflation	.15	.20
Weak Economy—Above-Average Inflation	.15	−.20
No major change	.70	.10

This set of potential outcomes can be visualized as follows:

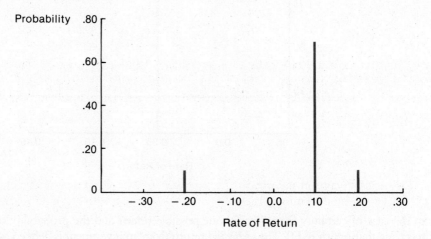

The computation of the expected rate of return is as follows:

$$\text{Expected Rate of Return} = (.15)(.20) + (.15)(-.20) + (.70)(.10)$$
$$= (.03) + (-.03) + (.07)$$
$$= .07$$

Obviously, the investor is more uncertain regarding this investment than he was with the previous investment with a single possible return. One can visualize an investment with ten possible outcomes ranging from minus 40 percent to plus 50 percent with equal probabilities for each rate of return. A graph of such a set of expectations would look like this:

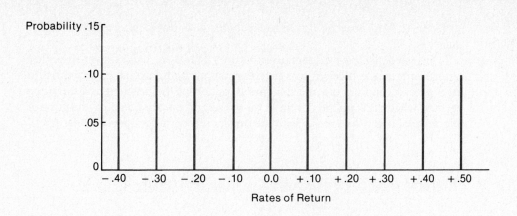

In this case there are numerous outcomes from a wide range of possibilities. The expected return would be:

$$
\begin{aligned}
\text{Expected Rate of Return} ={}& (.10)(-.40) + (.10)(-.30) + (.10)(-.20) \\
& + (.10)(-.10) + (.10)(0.0) + (.10)(.10) \\
& + (.10)(.20) + (.10)(.30) + (.10)(.40) + (.10)(.50) \\
={}& (-.04) + (-.03) + (-.02) + (-.01) \\
& + (.00) + (.01) + (.02) + (.03) + (.04) + (.05) \\
={}& .05
\end{aligned}
$$

Note that the *expected* rate is the same as it was in the certainty case, but the investor is obviously not very certain about what the *actual* return will be. This would be considered a high-risk investment; i.e., the investor is very uncertain as to what the actual realized return will be.

Measure of Risk

The previous discussion indicated that the uncertainty or risk of an investment can be derived by determining the range of possible outcomes and the probability of each occurring. What is needed now is a *measure* of the dispersion of returns. There are several possible measures, including simply the range of the distribution. Another possible measure that has been suggested in some theoretical work on portfolio theory is the *variance* of the estimated distribution of expected returns, or the square root of the variance, i.e., the *standard deviation* of the distribution. These statistical calculations would serve as indicators of the deviations of possible returns from the expected return.[2]

The larger the variance, everything else remaining constant, the greater the dispersion of expectations and the greater the uncertainty or risk the investment entails. Note that in the case of perfect certainty, there is *no variance of return* be-

---

[2]The appendix to this chapter contains a more detailed discussion of variance and standard deviation, including a sample computation.

cause there is *no deviation from expectations* and, therefore, *no risk or uncertainty*.

It is generally assumed that investors are *risk averse*. This means that, if they are given a choice between two investments that both have an expected return of 5 percent, and for one the standard deviation of the probability distribution is .001, while the standard deviation for the second distribution is .1, the investor would choose the investment with the smaller standard deviation (smaller risk).

Determinants of Required Rates of Return

Once an individual has excess income (savings), and decides that he wants to invest it, the required rate of return on the investment instrument selected (savings account, bond, stock, real estate, etc.) becomes a crucial question. There are two important points to consider regarding required rates of return. First, *the overall level of required rates of return for all investments changes dramatically over time.* An example of such changes is the promised yield on Moody's Aaa corporate bonds (the highest grade corporate bonds), which was over 5 percent during the 1930s, declined to about 3 percent in the 1940s, and rose to over 9 percent in the 1970s.[3] Obviously, it is important to understand why the required rate of return on *all* investments changes over time. The second point is that *there is a wide range of required returns for alternative investments.* As an example, Table 1.1 contains a list of promised yields on different bonds:

Type of Bond	1975	1976	1977	1978	1979	1980
U.S. Govt.—3-month treasury bills	5.80	4.98	5.27	7.19	10.07	11.43
U.S. Govt.—long-term	6.98	6.78	7.06	7.89	8.74	10.81
Aaa Utility	9.41	8.49	8.19	8.96	10.03	12.74
Aaa Corporate	8.83	8.43	8.02	8.73	9.63	11.94
Baa Corporate	10.61	9.75	8.97	9.45	10.69	13.67

Table 1.1   Promised Yields on Alternative Bonds
Source: *Federal Reserve Bulletin,* various issues

The point is, all of these are bonds and yet the yields differ significantly. One could detect even greater differences in expected returns if one could observe promised yields on common stock, real estate, etc.

[3]For a graph of the long-term rates extending back to the 1920s see *Historical Chart Book* *(Washington, D.C: Board of Governors of the Federal Reserve System, 1980).*

Because the required returns on all investments change over time, and because of the large differences in required rates of return for alternative investments, you should be aware of what determines the required return. In the following discussion, the components of the required rate of return are considered.

The Risk-Free Rate

The risk-free rate (RFR) is the basic exchange rate assuming no uncertainty of future flows; i.e., the investor knows with certainty what cash flows he will receive and when he will receive them. There is no probability of default on the investment. Earlier this was referred to as the pure time value of money because the only sacrifice on the part of the lender was that he give up the use of the money (consumption) for a period of time. The pure rate of interest is the price charged for the exchange between current goods (consumption) and future goods. There are two factors, one psychological and one objective, that influence this price. The subjective factor is the *time preference of individuals for the consumption of income*. When individuals give up $100 of consumption this year, how much consumption do they want a year from now to compensate for this sacrifice? The level of this human desire for consumption influences the rate of compensation required. The time preference will vary among individuals with a composite rate determined by the market. While this composite time preference rate will change over time, one would expect any aggregate changes to be gradual and slow.

The objective factor influencing the risk-free rate is the *investment opportunities available in the economy*. These investment opportunities are a function of the *long-run real growth rate of the economy*. Therefore, a change in the economy's long-run growth rate causes a change in all investment opportunities, and a change in the required returns on all investments. There are three factors that influence the real growth rate of the economy: (1) the long-run growth rate of the labor force; (2) growth in the average number of hours worked by the labor force; and (3) growth in the productivity of the labor force. When examining these variables, the investor should emphasize *long-run* trends and not be mislead by short-run changes caused by cyclical fluctuations. The overall performance of these factors has generally suggested a real growth rate of about 3 percent as follows: the long-run growth rate of the labor force has been 1.5 to 2 percent a year. At the same time, the average number of hours worked has been constant or declining at the rate of .5 percent a year. Finally, the rate of growth in labor productivity was between 2 and 3 percent prior to the 1970s, but apparently has declined to about 1.5 percent during the past decade. Therefore, the real growth rate was probably between 3 and 3.5 percent during the 1950s and '60s, and about 2.5 percent during the 1970s.

As the investment opportunities in an economy increase or decrease due to changes in the long-run real growth rate, the risk-free rate of return should likewise increase or decrease; i.e., there is a *positive* relationship between the investment opportunities in an economy and the RFR. Again, while investment opportunities and, therefore, the RFR can change over time, one would expect these changes to be slow and gradual.

Factors Influencing the Nominal (Money) Rate on Risk-Free Investments

Because the factors that determine the level of the risk-free rate are long-term variables that change only gradually, one might expect the required rate on a risk-free investment to be quite stable over time. As noted previously, this has *not* been true for long-term government bonds over the period from 1930 through 1980. A more specific example can be derived from an analysis of the average yield on U.S. Government Treasury Bills for the period 1967–1980 given in Table 1.2. This analysis is appropriate because government T-Bills are a prime example of a default-free investment, owing to the government's unlimited ability to derive income from taxes or the creation of money.

1967	4.29	1972	4.07	1977	5.27
1968	5.34	1973	7.03	1978	7.19
1969	6.67	1974	7.84	1979	10.07
1970	6.39	1975	5.80	1980	11.43
1971	4.33	1976	4.98		

Table 1.2   Average Yields on U.S. Government Three-Month Treasury Bills
Source: *Federal Reserve Bulletin*, various issues.

Especially notable is the steady increase in 1968 and 1969, followed by a sharp decline in 1971 and a mammoth increase (75 percent) in 1973. Again, following a decline to below 5 percent in 1976, rates increased to 7 percent in 1978 and to over 11 percent in 1980; i.e., these rates more than doubled in a period of three years. The nominal (money) rate of interest on a default-free investment is definitely *not* stable in the long run or the short run, even though the underlying determinants of the RFR *are* quite stable. Therefore, it is important to consider the other factors that influence the *nominal* risk-free rate. Recall that these nominal rates are also referred to as money rates or market rates. The two factors that influence the *market* rates are relative ease or tightness in the capital market, and the expected rate of inflation.

Relative Ease or Tightness
This is a short-run phenomenon that is caused by temporary changes in the supply and demand of future income streams or capital. As an example, starting

from a point of equilibrium in the capital market, one can visualize a disruption caused by a change in monetary policy as evidenced by a sharp decrease in the growth rate of the money supply. In the short run, assuming no immediate adjustment in demand, there would be relative tightness and interest rates would increase. An alternative example would be a relatively stable supply of funds and a sudden increase in the government's demand for capital because of an increase in the deficit. Again, there would be an increase in money rates reflecting the relative tightness. Therefore, the market rate on risk-free investments can change in the short run because of temporary ease or tightness in the capital market. One would expect this to be a short-term effect because, in the long run, the higher or lower rates would affect supply and demand.

Expected Inflation

Up to this point the discussion has been in "real" terms, unaffected by changes in the price level. In discussing the rate of exchange between current consumption and future consumption, it was assumed that the 4 percent required return meant that the investor was willing to give up one dollar of consumption today in order to consume $1.04 worth of goods and services one year from now. The exchange rate assumed *no change in prices,* so a 4 percent increase in money wealth would mean a 4 percent increase in potential consumption of goods and services. If the price level is going to increase during the period of investment, investors should increase their required rate of return by the rate of inflation to compensate. Assume that an investor wants a 4 percent rate of return on a risk-free investment. The 4 percent required return is a "real" required rate of return. Assuming the investor expects prices to increase by 3 percent during the period of the investment, we would expect him to increase his required rate of return by approximately the same amount, to about 7 percent $[(1.04 \times 1.03) - 1]$. If the investor does not increase his required return, he will receive $104 at the end of the year. But because prices have increased by 3 percent during the year, what cost $100 at the beginning of the year now costs $103 and the investor can only consume about one percent more at the end of the year ($104/103 - 1$). His ability to consume "real" goods and services has only increased by about one percent, and his "real" return (i.e., his "real" increase in wealth) is only one percent, not 4 percent. If he had required a 7 percent nominal return (in current dollars), his real consumption would have increased by 4 percent ($107/103 - 1$). Therefore, an investor's *nominal* required rate of return (in current dollars) on a risk-free investment is:

$$\text{Nominal RFR} = (1 + \text{RFR})(1 + \text{Expected Rate of Inflation}) - 1$$

In summary, the nominal RFR is affected by the real RFR and by changes in the expected rate of inflation. It can also be influenced in the short run by temporary ease or tightness in the capital market. Clearly, the major changes in the average yield on T-bills shown in Table 1.2 were due to the large changes in the expected rate of inflation during this period.

The Common Effect

Note that all the factors discussed thus far regarding the required rate of return *affect all investments equally.* Irrespective of whether the concern is with stocks, bonds, real estate, or machine tools, if the expected rate of inflation increases from 2 percent to 6 percent, the required return on all investments should increase by 4 percent. On the other hand, if there is a general easing in the capital market because of an increase in the rate of growth of the money supply that causes a one percent decline in the market RFR, then the required return on all investments will decline by one percent.

A Risk Premium

A risk-free investment was defined as one for which the investor is certain of the amount and timing of his income stream. In contrast, an investor in the "real world" is not certain of the amount of income he will receive, when he will receive it, or if he will receive it. Not only is there uncertainty involved in most investments, but the uncertainty also encompasses a wide spectrum running from basically risk-free items, such as government T-Bills, to highly uncertain items like the common stock of small companies engaged in speculative operations such as oil exploration. Because most investors do not like uncertainty, they will require an additional return on the latter investment to compensate for the uncertainty. This additional required return is referred to as a *risk premium* that is added to the nominal RFR.

While the risk premium is determined by a composite of all uncertainty, it is possible to consider several major sources of uncertainty. The three most frequently discussed are: business risk, financial risk, and liquidity risk.

Business Risk   This uncertainty of income flows is caused by the nature of the firm's business. When someone, a firm or an individual, borrows money, his ability to repay the loan and pay interest on it is a function of the certainty of his income flows. As the income flows of the borrower become more uncertain, the uncertainty of the flows to the lender increases. Therefore, the lender will consider the basic pattern of income flows the borrower receives and assign a risk premium on the basis of this distribution of flows. An example of a borrower with no uncertainty of income flows is the U.S. Government because of its power to tax. In contrast, a small oil drilling firm has a potential range of returns from a large probability of no income to a small probability of a very large income. This uncertainty of income caused by the basic business of the firm is typically measured by the distribution of the firm's operating income over time, i.e., the more volatile the firm's operating income over time relative to its mean income, the greater the business risk.

In turn, the firm's operating income volatility is a function of its sales volatility and its operating leverage. Assuming a constant profit margin, if sales fluctuate over time, operating income will fluctuate. Hence, one can consider sales volatility to be the prime determinant of operating earnings volatility (business risk). One must also consider the production function of the firm; if all production costs are variable costs, then operating income will vary according to sales variability. In contrast, if some costs are fixed, (e.g., depreciation, administration, research), then operating income will be more volatile than sales. Depending upon where the firm is operating relative to its break-even point, its earnings can increase by more than sales during good times and decline by more than sales during bad times. This effect of fixed costs on the volatility of operating earnings is referred to as *operating leverage*. Therefore, a firm's business risk is measured in terms of the coefficient of variation of operating earnings. In turn, operating-earnings volatility is a function of sales volatility and operating leverage.

Business Risk = f(Volatility of Operating Earnings)

Operating Earnings Volatility = f(Sales Volatility; Operating Leverage)

Financial Risk   This is the uncertainty introduced by the method of financing an investment. If a firm uses common stock to finance a project, there is only business risk involved; the variability of income to the ultimate owner is the same as the variability of operating income (assuming a constant tax rate). If, in addition to using equity, a firm borrows money to help finance an investment, it introduces fixed financing charges (interest) that must be paid before the owners (the stockholders) are paid. As a result, the uncertainty of returns (variability) increases because of the method of financing the investment. This increase in uncertainty due to fixed-cost financing is referred to as *financial risk* and causes investors to increase their risk premium.[4]

Liquidity Risk   This is the uncertainty introduced by the secondary market for an investment. When an investor gives up current consumption (commits funds) by investing, there is an expectation that, at some future time, the investment will mature (as with a bond), or that the investor will be able to sell it to someone else (convert it into cash) and use the proceeds for current consumption or other investments. Given a desire to liquidate an investment (convert it into the most liquid of all assets—cash) the investor is faced with two uncertainties: (1) how long will it take to make the conversion?; and (2) what price will be received? There is similar uncertainty for a buyer: how long will it take to acquire the asset and what will be the price? *The ability to buy or sell an investment quickly without making a substantial price concession is known as liquidity.*[5] The greater the uncertainty regarding whether the investment can be bought or sold, or the greater the price concession required to buy or sell it, the greater the liquidity risk. An example of an asset with almost no liquidity risk would be a

[4]A more detailed discussion of business risk and financial risk may be found in most financial management texts.

[5]See William L. Fouse, "Risk and Liquidity: The Keys to Stock Price Behavior," *Financial Analysts Journal* 32 (1976) 35–45.

United States Government Treasury Bill. A treasury bill can be bought or sold in minutes at a price almost identical to the quoted price. Purchase or conversion into cash is almost instantaneous and the price is known with almost perfect certainty. In contrast, an example of an illiquid asset would be a specialized machine or a parcel of real estate in a remote area. In both cases it might take a considerable period of time to find a potential seller or buyer, and the expected selling price could vary substantially from expectations; i.e., the selling price is uncertain because it is a "unique" investment.

The risk premium on an investment is, therefore, determined by the basic uncertainty of income flows to the investor. The specific factors influencing this uncertainty are sales volatility and operating leverage (business risk), any added uncertainty of flows caused by how the investment is financed (financial risk), and the uncertainty involved in buying or selling the investment (liquidity risk).[6]

Risk Premium = f(Business Risk; Financial Risk; Liquidity Risk)

Summary of Required Return

The overall required rate of return on alternative investments is determined by three major sets of variables. The first is the economy's RFR which is influenced by the investment opportunities in the economy (i.e., the long-run real growth rate) and investors' time preferences for consumption. These factors are generally quite stable and change only gradually. The second set of variables influences the market rate on risk-free investments and includes short-run ease or tightness in the capital market and expected changes in the price level (inflation). *The first two sets of variables are the same for all investments.* The final set are those variables that influence the risk premium on investments, which is the factor that causes differences among investments. One can visualize the risk premium as being affected by business risk, financial risk, and liquidity risk. Therefore:

Required Rate of Return
A. Risk-Free Rate
   1. Time Preference for Consumption
   2. Investment Opportunities (Long-run real growth rate)
     a. Growth of Labor Force
     b. Growth in Hours Worked
     c. Growth in Worker Productivity
B. Factors Influencing the Market RFR
   1. Ease or Tightness of Capital Market
   2. Expected Rate of Inflation

---

[6]It is possible to show that the risk premium should be related to relative stock returns over time. This alternative view is discussed in detail in the chapter on portfolio theory.

C. Risk Premium
   1. Business Risk
   2. Financial Risk
   3. Liquidity Risk

Relationship between Risk and Return

To better illustrate the foregoing material, this section contains a graph of the relationship between risk and return with an emphasis on what causes changes in required returns over time. The basic relationship is shown in Figure 1.1.

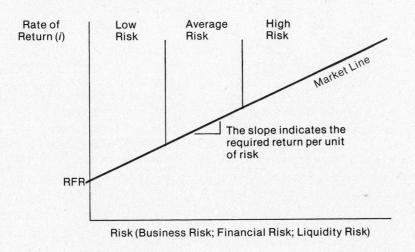

Figure 1.1   Relationship between Risk and Return

This graph indicates that investors want the risk-free return on riskless investments and that they increase their required rate of return as perceived uncertainty increases. As noted, the slope of the market line indicates the composite return per unit of risk required by all investors. One could conceive of the slope of this line changing if there were a change in the aggregate attitude towards risk; i.e., the slope would increase if investors became more risk averse.

Given the market line indicating the average risk-return relationship, investors select investments that are consistent with their risk preferences. Some will only consider low risk, while others will welcome high-risk investments.

Figure 1.2 indicates what happens to the market line when the notion of ease or tightness in the capital market or expected inflation is considered. The dotted line indicates a parallel *shift* in the market line that is caused by either temporary tightness in the capital market or an increase in the expected rate of inflation. The parallel shift in the line reflects the fact that these changes affect all investments, irrespective of their level of risk.

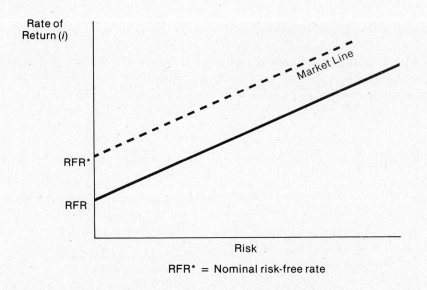

Figure 1.2   Effect of a Shift in the Capital Market Line on Required Rates of Return
RFR* = nominal risk-free rate

Summary

Individuals have expected income streams and patterns of desired consumption. Except in rare cases, these streams of income and desired consumption do not match. Therefore, there are certain economic units that have more income than they want to consume (savings) and that are willing to trade current consumption for a larger amount of future consumption. In contrast, others have more current consumption desires than income and want to dis-save (borrow future income). The rate of exchange between current and future consumption, assuming no risk, is the time value of money.

Because the required rate of return differs substantially between alternative investments, and the required return on specific investments changes over time, it is important to examine the factors that influence the required rate of return on investments. The three major variables affecting it are the RFR, factors that influence the market rate on risk-free investments (most notably inflation), and the risk premium. The required rate of return on all investments is changed by changes in the RFR, by market ease or tightness, or by changes in the expected rate of inflation. Therefore, the factor causing all differences *between* investments at a point in time is the risk premium.

Questions

1. Why do people invest? Be specific regarding when they are willing to invest and what they are looking for in the future.

2. Define an investment.

3. Why do people engage in negative saving, i.e., dis-save? Be specific.

4. As a student are you saving or dis-saving? What do you expect to derive from this activity?

5. Divide a person's life from ages 20 to 70 into ten-year segments and discuss what the saving or dis-saving patterns during each of these periods are likely to be and why.

6. Would you expect the saving–dis-saving pattern to differ by occupation, e.g., for a doctor versus a plumber? Why or why not?

7. It was reported in the *Wall Street Journal* that the yield on common stocks is about 4 percent, while a study at the University of Chicago contends that the rate of return on common stocks has averaged about 9 percent. Reconcile these statements.

8. What are the three *major* determinants of an investor's required rate of return on an investment? Discuss each of these briefly.

9. Discuss the two major factors that determine the market's risk-free rate (RFR). Which of these factors would you expect to be more volatile over the business cycle? Why?

10. Discuss the three internal factors that contribute to the risk premium of an investment.

11. You own stock in the Edgar Company and you notice that after a recent bond offering, the firm's debt/equity ratio has gone from 30 percent to 45 percent. What effect will this change have on the variability of the net income stream, other factors being constant? Discuss. Would you change your required rate of return on the common stock of the Edgar Company? Why?

12. Draw a properly labeled graph of the capital market line and indicate where you would expect to plot the following investments along that line. Discuss your reasoning for this placement.

    a. Common stock of large firms

    b. U.S. Government bonds

    c. Low-grade corporate bonds

    d. Common stock of a new, small firm.

13. Discuss in nontechnical terms why you would change your nominal required

rate of return if you expected the rate of inflation to go from zero (no inflation) to 7 percent. Give an example of what would happen if you did not change your required rate of return under these conditions.

14. Assume the long-run growth rate of the economy increased by one percent, and the expected rate of inflation increased by 4 percent. What would happen to the required rate of return on government bonds, common stocks, and real estate? How would the effect differ? Show this graphically.

15. Discuss an example of a liquid investment asset and an illiquid asset. Indicate specifically why they are liquid or illiquid.

References

Arditti, Fred D. "Risk and the Required Return on Equity." *Journal of Finance* 22 (1967).

Ben-Zion, Uri, and Shalit, Sol S. "Size, Leverage and Dividend Record as Determinants of Equity Risk." *Journal of Finance* 30 (1975).

Fisher, Irving. *The Theory of Interest.* New York: Macmillan, 1930; reprinted by August M. Kelley, New York, 1961.

Fisher, Lawrence. "Determinants of Risk Premiums on Corporate Bonds." *Journal of Political Economy* (1959).

Fouse, William L. "Risk and Liquidity: The Keys to Stock Price Behavior." *Financial Analysts Journal* 32 (1976).

Appendix A to Chapter 1

Computation of Variance and Standard Deviation

The variance or standard deviation is a measure of how the actual values (Rates of Return) differ from the expected value (mean) of a given series of values. As noted, it is possible to conceive of other measures of this difference (dispersion), but the variance and standard deviation are the best known because of their uses in statistics and probability theory. Variance is defined as follows:

$$\text{Variance } (\sigma^2) = \Sigma(\text{Probability})(\text{Possible Return} - \text{Expected Return})^2$$
$$= \Sigma(P_i) (R_i - E(\overline{R}))^2$$

Consider the following example discussed in the chapter:

Probability of Possible Return (Pi)	Possible Return (Ri)	Pi Ri
.15	.20	.03
.15	−.20	−.03
.70	.10	.07
		$\Sigma = .07$

Therefore, the expected return ($\overline{R}$) is 7 percent. The dispersion of this distribution in terms of the variance is as follows:

Probability (Pi)	Return (Ri)	Ri − $\overline{R}$	(Ri − $\overline{R}$)²	Pi(Ri − $\overline{R}$)²
.15	.20	.13	.0169	.002535
.15	−.20	−.27	.0729	.010935
.70	.10	.03	.0009	.000630

$$\Sigma = .014100$$

Thus, the variance (σ^2) is equal to .014100, i.e., 1.41 percent. The standard deviation is equal to the square root of the variance as follows:

$$\text{Standard Deviation } (\sigma) = \sqrt{\Sigma Pi(Ri - \overline{R})^2}$$

Therefore, the standard deviation for the example above would be:

$$\sigma_i = \sqrt{.0141} = .11874$$

This would indicate a standard deviation of approximately 11.87 percent. Therefore, one could describe this distribution as having a mean (expected value) of 7 percent and a standard deviation of 11.87 percent.

In many instances an investor might want to compute the variance or standard deviation for a historical series. As an example, assume that you are given the following information on annual rates of return for common stocks listed on the New York Stock Exchange (NYSE):

Year	Annual Rate of Return
19_1	.07
19_2	.11
19_3	−.04
19_4	.12
19_5	−.06

In this case, we are not dealing with expected rates of return, but actual returns. Therefore, we can assume equal probabilities, and the expected value of the series is simply the sum of the series divided by the number of observations. In this example it is .04 (.20/5). The variance and standard deviation would be as follows:

Year	Ri	Ri − $\overline{R}$	(Ri − $\overline{R}$)²	
19_1	.07	.03	.0009	$\sigma^2 = .0286/5$
19_2	.11	.07	.0049	$= .00572$
19_3	−.04	−.08	.0064	
19_4	.12	.08	.0064	$\sigma = \sqrt{.00572}$
19_5	−.06	−.10	.0100	$= .0756$
			$\Sigma = .0286$	

Therefore, regarding the performance of stocks during this period of time, one would say that the average rate of return was 4 percent and the standard deviation of annual rates of return was 7.56 percent.

Coefficient of Variation

In some instances one might want to compare the dispersion of two different series. A problem with the variance or the standard deviation is that they are *absolute* measures of dispersion, and, therefore, they can be influenced by the magnitude of the original numbers. When it is necessary to compare series with very different values, it is desirable to have a *relative* measure of dispersion. A potential measure that indicates this relative dispersion is the coefficient of variation which is defined as follows:

$$\text{Coefficient of Variation (CV)} = \frac{\text{Standard Deviation}}{\text{Expected Return}}$$

The larger this value, the greater the dispersion *relative* to the expected return. For the previous example, the CV would be:

$$CV = \frac{.0756}{.0400} = 1.89$$

It would be possible to compare this value to a comparable figure for a very different distribution. Assume you wanted to compare this to another investment alternative that had a mean return of 10 percent and a standard deviation of 9 percent. On the basis of the standard deviations alone, the second series has greater dispersion and might be considered higher risk (i.e., 9 percent versus 7.56 percent). In fact, the relative dispersion is much less:

$$CV_1 = \frac{.0756}{.0400} = 1.89$$

$$CV_2 = \frac{.0900}{.1000} = 0.90$$

Considering the relative dispersion and the total distribution, most investors would probably prefer the second series.

ALTERNATIVE INVESTMENTS: A BRIEF OVERVIEW

⇒ 2 ⇐

In any book on investments, the emphasis is usually on common stocks. Although this is also true, to a great extent, of the book in your hands, at the outset you should be aware that *there are numerous investment instruments available, and the astute investor should consider a broad range of alternatives.* The principles of valuation and portfolio management discussed here are applicable to a variety of investments with which we will deal. In some cases there may be problems in deriving data for the valuation models, but the concept will be the same.

One of the main reasons that investors should consider numerous different investments is that they can derive substantial benefits from *diversification.* In the context of investments, diversification means *owning alternative investments with different return patterns over time* such that when one investment is yielding a low or negative rate of return, another investment, hopefully, will be enjoying above-normal returns. The overall result is relatively stable earnings for the collection of investments (also referred to as the *portfolio*). Several subsequent chapters contain a discussion of the principle of diversification in greater detail. At this point it is important only to recognize that proper diversification results in less variability in the rates of return for a portfolio over time and, therefore, helps reduce the uncertainty or risk of the portfolio.

Types of Investments

The purpose of this chapter is to briefly discuss some of the major investment alternatives that all investors should consider for their portfolios. It will become apparent that some of these investments are not appropriate for particular investors given their individual risk or liquidity preferences. Hopefully, though, exposure to the numerous alternatives will ensure that an investor considers the full range and does not miss some very worthwhile and interesting investment opportunities. We will begin our discussion with the most obvious alternatives, bonds and stocks, but will eventually consider some rather unusual possibilities. We conclude the chapter with a historical analysis of different risk and return measures for several investment instruments and consider the relationships among returns.

Fixed-Income Investments

Within this category are investments that have a *fixed payment schedule*. With securities of this type, the owner is promised specific payments at predetermined times, although the legal force behind the promise varies. At one extreme, if the contractual payment is not made at the appointed time, the issuing firm can be declared bankrupt. In other cases, the payments must be made only if they are earned (an income bond); while in some instances the payment does not have to be made unless the board of directors votes for it (preferred stock).

Savings Accounts

It is probably not necessary to describe savings accounts except to indicate that they are an example of a fixed-income investment. When an individual deposits funds in a savings account at a bank or savings and loan association, he is really lending money to the institution to derive a fixed payment. Such investments are considered very low risk (almost all are insured), convenient, and liquid. Therefore, the rate of return is generally low compared to that for other alternatives.

Banks and savings and loan associations have created several new savings account instruments that should also be considered. The *passbook savings account* is the basic account; no minimum amount is required to open such an account and no minimum balance must be maintained at any point in time. In addition, it is generally possible to withdraw funds at any time with very little loss of interest. (Generally the loss is of interest for the current quarter only on the amount withdrawn). Due to the flexibility involved, the promised interest on passbook accounts is lower than on the other types of accounts to be discussed.

For investors with larger amounts of funds who are willing to give up the use of the money for a specified period (i.e., give up liquidity), banks and S & Ls developed *certificates of deposits* (CDs) which involve minimum amounts (typically $500) and specified time periods (e.g., three months, six months, one year, two-and-a-half years). The promised rates on these CDs are higher than those for passbook savings, and the rate increases with the length of deposit of the CD. As an example, assume the rate on passbook savings is 5.25 percent; the rates on alternative CDs might be as follows: three month, 5.75 percent; six month, 6.00 percent; one year, 6.35 percent; two-and-a-half year, 9.25 percent. As stated, an investor can receive a higher rate because he makes a higher initial deposit, and also mainly because he is willing to forgo the use of the money for a definite period of time. The longer the time period, the higher the rate. If the investor wants to cash in a CD prior to its stated expiration date, there is a heavy penalty in terms of the interest received on the money.

For investors with large sums of money (a minimum of $10,000), it has always been possible to invest in treasury bills (T-bills), which are short-term obligations (three or six months) of the United States Government. The T-bills are sold at auction each week by the government, and the rate is determined by the current supply and demand for short-term money. To compete for the funds that might be invested in T-bills, banks and S & Ls developed *money market certificates* which are similar to CDs, but involve a minimum investment of $10,000 and a minimum maturity of six months. A unique feature is that the promised rate on these certificates fluctuates at some premium over the weekly rate on six-month T-bills. As an example, if the rate on six-month T-bills were 8.50 percent, the rate on six-month money market certificates would be about 8.75 percent. These certificates are like regular CDs since they can only be redeemed at the bank that issued them and there is a penalty for early withdrawal of funds.

Government Securities[1]

All government securities are fixed-income instruments that generally differ in terms of the time to maturity when they are initially issued. Specifically, bills are for less than a year, notes are from 1 to 10 years, and bonds are for over 10 years. Because these are obligations of the U.S. Government, they are riskless in terms of default, and they are very liquid in terms of the ability to buy or sell them quickly at a known price.

Municipal Bonds   These are similar to the bonds mentioned above, but they are issued by municipalities (states, cities, towns, etc.). Municipal bonds can be *general obligation* bonds wherein the full taxing power of the municipality is used to pay for them. Also there are municipal *revenue* bonds for which the revenue comes from a particular project (e.g., sewer bonds for which the revenue comes from water taxes).

A major feature distinguishing municipal bonds is that they are *tax-exempt,* which means that the interest earned is exempt from taxation by the federal government and by the state that issued the bond, if the investor is a resident of that state. This feature is important to investors in high tax brackets. Assume that an individual has an income such that his marginal tax rate is 60 percent. If he buys a regular bond with an interest rate of 8 percent, because he must pay 60-percent tax on this income, his net return after taxes is only 3.2 percent (.08 × [1 − .60]). Such an investor would be better off with a tax-free bond that has a yield of 5 percent. As a result, yields on municipal bonds are below yields on comparable taxable bonds. (The yield is generally about 60−70 percent of the yield on taxable bonds[2]).

---

[1]Chapter 14 contains a detailed discussion of marketable bonds including government securities, municipal bonds, and corporate bonds. For a readable discussion of bonds see the latest edition of *The Bond Book* (New York: Merrill Lynch, Pierce, Fenner & Smith).

[2]A readable article on the subject is "Investing in Tax-Exempts," *Business Week,* 25 July 1977, pp. 127−129.

Corporate Bonds

Corporate bonds can be broken down in terms of issuer (industrial corporations, public utility corporations, or railroads), in terms of quality (i.e., the rating assigned by an agency on the basis of probability of default), or in terms of maturity (short term, intermediate term, or long term). In addition, they can be considered on the basis of their internal characteristics or the contractual promise to the investor implied, e.g., whether a bond is a debenture, a mortgage bond, an income bond, or a convertible bond, as described below.

Debentures   These are promises to pay interest and principal, but typically there is no collateral put up and the lender is dependent upon the success of the borrower to receive the promised payment. Debenture owners usually have first call on the earnings and assets of a firm. If an interest payment is not made, the debenture owners can declare the firm bankrupt and claim the assets of the firm to pay off the bonds. The reader should recognize that a bond can take an almost unlimited variety of potential forms.

Mortgage Bonds   These bonds are similar to debentures, but in case of bankruptcy, there are specific assets pledged as backing for them. Examples would include land, buildings, or equipment.

Income Bonds   These have a stipulated coupon and interest payment schedule, but the interest is only due and payable *if the company earns the interest payment* by a stipulated date. If the required amount is not earned, the interest payment does not have to be made, and the firm cannot be declared bankrupt. Instead, the interest payment is considered in arrears and, if subsequently earned, must be paid off. Given the lack of legal guarantees, an income bond is not considered as safe as a debenture or a mortgage bond.

Convertible Bonds   These bonds have all the characteristics of other bonds with the added feature that *they can be converted into the common stock of the company that issued the bond.* A firm could issue a $1,000 face value bond and stipulate that owners of the bond could, at their discretion, convert the bond into 40 shares of common stock. Such bonds are considered very attractive, especially when issued by growth firms. In this case, investors acquire an investment with a fixed income feature, but also have the potential opportunity to convert the bond into the common stock of the firm and become an owner if the company does well. The interest rates on convertible bonds are generally lower than those on comparable straight debentures of the firm. The greater the potential of the company, the greater the yield differential because the conversion potential is of greater value.[3]

[3]For further discussion of bonds see Chapters 14 and 15, and David M. Darst, *The Complete Bond Book* (New York: McGraw–Hill, 1975); and Marcia Stigum, *The Money Market: Myth, Reality and Practice* (Homewood, IL: Dow–Jones–Irwin, 1978).

Preferred Stock

Preferred stock is a fixed-income security because a yearly payment is stipulated that is either a coupon (e.g., 5 percent of the face value) or a stated dollar amount (e.g., $5 preferred). The major difference between preferred stock and bonds is that the preferred stock payment (which is a dividend) is not legally binding and, for each period, must be voted on by the firm's board of directors as is a common stock dividend. Even if the firm earned enough money to pay the preferred stock dividend, the board of directors could vote to withhold it and, because most preferred stock is cumulative preferred, the dividend would accumulate.

Although preferred dividends are not legally binding, they are considered binding in a practical sense because of the credit implications of a missed dividend. Because preferred stock payments cannot be deducted from the taxes of the issuing firm, as the interest on bonds can, preferred stock has not been a very popular source of financing for most corporations except utilities. Ignoring the latter category, preferred stocks constitute less than 3 percent of all new corporate financing. At the same time, because corporations can legally exclude 85 percent of dividends from taxable income, preferred stocks have become popular investments for some financial corporations. The demand by these corporations has been such that, during many periods, the yield on high-grade preferred stock has been *below* the yield on high-grade bonds.[4]

Equity Instruments

Common stock

When considering investing, many persons think of common stock. Such stock represents *ownership* of a firm, and, therefore, an investor who buys shares in a company is basically buying part of the company. Like any owner of a business, he will share in the company's successes and problems. If, like IBM or Xerox, the company does very well, the value of his common stock will increase tremendously, and the investor can become very wealthy. In contrast to such success stories, one can think of several instances in which the firms went bankrupt (e.g., Penn Central) or eventually were forced to liquidate their assets. The point is, common stock entails all the advantages *and* disadvantages of ownership, and is a relatively risky investment compared to fixed-income securities.

Other Common Stock Classifications

In addition to classifying equity investments according to the risk involved, the nature of the firm invested in should also be considered, both in terms of the type of business it represents and in terms of its earnings potential.

---

[4]For a detailed analysis of trends regarding preferred stock, see Donald E. Fischer and Glenn A. Wilt, Jr., "Non-Convertible Preferred Stock As a Financing Instrument, 1950–1965," *Journal of Finance* 23 (1968): 611–624.

Classification by Business Line

Common stocks can be categorized in a number of ways. An obvious broad classification is by function or general business line: industrial firms, utilities, transportation, or financial institutions.

The best-known firms are the *industrial* companies such as General Motors, General Electric, and IBM, a category which includes a wide variety of specific industries. In fact, Standard & Poor's has constructed a stock price index for 400 industrial firms and has broken these 400 firms down into about 80 separate industries including autos, electrical equipment, retail stores, and computers. Clearly, the industrial category includes a wide variety of different economic groups.

The *utility* category includes companies providing telephone service, electricity, gas, etc. Major factors differentiating these firms from industrial companies are their monopoly position, the regulation involved, and their geographical limitations.

The *transportation* group includes the railroads that, at one point, were the only companies in this category. In recent years airlines have been added along with trucking companies and shipping firms.

Finally, the *financial* category includes banks, savings and loan companies, loan companies, and insurance firms.

Classification by Operating Performance

Another technique for classifying companies is in terms of their internal operating performance, e.g., growth companies, cyclical companies, and defensive companies. Such a classification helps the investor analyze the companies and subsequently make a valuation of the stock.

Growth Company   This is a company that has opportunities to invest capital at rates of return that exceed the firm's required cost of capital. As a result of these opportunities, such firms retain a large amount of earnings (have low dividend payments), and their earnings grow rapidly—almost certainly faster than the average firm's. Growth firms can provide outstanding opportunities, but they can also be very risky if their growth rates decrease.

Cyclical Companies   These are closely tied to cyclical fluctuations in the economy and typically experience changes in earnings over the business cycle that are *greater* than the earnings changes for the aggregate economy. The industries that fall into this category are automotive, steel, and industrial machinery.

Defensive Companies   These are firms whose sales and earnings are expected to move countercyclically to the economy, especially during recessions. These firms are not expected to feel the effects of a recession. Typically these companies produce or sell products that are considered necessities. A prime example is retail food stores. These firms are also generally defensive during expansions, which means that they do not feel the full benefits of an expansion because consumers generally reduce the proportion of income spent on necessities during expansions.

Investment Companies

Up to this point we have been discussing individual securities that can be acquired from the government, a state or municipality, or a corporation. However, rather than buy an individual stock or bond issued by one of these sources, an investor may choose to acquire shares in an investment company that owns a number of individual stocks and/or bonds. Specifically, an investment company sells shares in itself and uses the proceeds (the money invested in the investment company) to acquire bonds, stocks, or other investment instruments. As a result, an investor who acquires shares in an investment company is a partial owner of the investment company that, in turn, owns the stock or bonds. Therefore, the investor owns part of the *portfolio* of stocks or other investment instruments.

Investment companies are usually identified by the types of investment instruments they acquire. Some of the major types are as follows:[5]

Money Market Funds These are companies that generally invest in high-quality money market instruments like T-bills, high-grade commercial paper (public short-term loans) from various corporations, and large CDs from the major money center banks. The yields on the money market portfolios is always above that on normal bank CDs because the investment is larger and there is a longer maturity than the typical individual CD involves. In addition, the returns on the commercial paper the fund acquires are above the prime rate. The typical minimum initial investment is $1,000 and there is no sales commission. Minimum additions are $250–$500. Notably, it is possible to withdraw the money invested in a money market fund at any time without any penalty; you receive the current interest to the day of withdrawal. Because of the high yields available and the extreme flexibility and liquidity, these funds have experienced phenomenal growth since 1975 to over $118 billion in 1981.

Bond Funds These generally invest in various long-term government, corporate, or municipal bonds. The funds differ in terms of the quality ratings assigned by various rating services to the bonds the funds invest in.

Common Stock Funds These invest in a variety of common stocks depending upon the stated investment objective of the fund. As a result of these objectives, a fund may invest in a range of stocks from income stocks to growth stocks to gold-mining stocks.

Balanced Funds These invest in a combination of bonds and stocks of various sorts depending on the stated objective of the fund.

Because the basic concept of an investment company is to pool the money of a number of individuals and have a group of professionals invest the money in a portfolio of investment instruments for a variety of objectives, it is possible to

---

[5]There is a detailed discussion of investment companies in Chapter 19.

conceive of an investment company for almost every investment instrument discussed. We will see that this is true not only for the instruments discussed, but also for foreign securities, real estate, and commodities.

Special Equity Instruments

In addition to straight common stock investments, it is also possible to invest in *options* to acquire common stock at a specified price. The two major option instruments available are *warrants* and *puts and calls*.

Warrants

A warrant is an option issued by a corporation that gives the holder the right to acquire the common stock of the company, from the company, at a specified price within a designated time period. The warrant does not constitute ownership of the stock, only the option to buy the stock.

Warrants are generally issued by corporations in conjunction with fixed-income instruments (bonds) to increase the appeal of the bonds. A firm with common stock selling at $45 a share can issue a $1,000 bond with 10 warrants attached that will allow the bondholder to buy shares of the company's common stock from the company at $50 a share for the next five years. Assuming that investors have confidence in the growth prospects of the firm, these common stock warrants could become very valuable.

Quantities of warrants are currently available from large, well-known firms. We will deal in depth with the valuation of warrants in a subsequent chapter. For now, the reader should be aware merely of their availability and their usefulness in creating a well-balanced portfolio.[6]

Puts and Calls

A call option is somewhat similar to a warrant in that it is an option to buy the common stock of a company at a specified price (referred to as the *striking price*) within a certain period. The difference is that the call option is *not* issued by the company but by another investor willing to "write" such an option and stand behind it. It also differs because it is typically for a much shorter period (less than a year compared to an initial term of over five years for warrants).

A put is an option that allows the holder to sell a given stock at a specified price during a designated time period. It is used by investors who expect the stock price to decline during the period, or by investors who own the stock and want to have downside protection (i.e., protection from a price decline).

Prior to 1973, the put and call market was very small and was not used by the typical individual investor or by institutions because it did not have enough volume and liquidity. In April 1973, this changed dramatically with the establishment of the Chicago Board Options Exchange (CBOE). The CBOE introduced

---

[6]For further discussion and references, see Chapter 17.

many features that helped to standardize this market. The numerous articles and books on the subject indicate that the options market is certainly a viable investment alternative and allows a wide range of risk for those who want to buy or sell options.[7]

Initial Stock Issues

An investor can occasionally acquire shares of a stock that was not public prior to the sale; an example was Coor's Brewing in 1975. Because there is no public market for the stock when it is sold, the initial pricing is uncertain, so the risk of these stocks is quite high. The new-issue market was very active during 1968 and 1969 and almost disappeared during 1974. There was some recovery after 1976 that has continued.[8] Therefore, investors should be aware of the risks and returns of this investment alternative.[9]

Foreign Securities

American citizens think nothing of buying TV sets and automobiles produced by companies in Japan, Germany, and France, but seldom consider the common stock of these firms. This is a mistake because the earnings of many foreign firms have grown substantially as a result of increasing sales to the U.S. market.

In addition to the potential rates of return, foreign securities are attractive because of the diversification possibilities. Specifically, foreign companies have sales and earnings patterns that are substantially different from those of U.S. firms. Hence, the correlation between the returns on foreign stock and those on U.S. stocks is much lower than is among alternative U.S. stocks. Therefore, even leaving aside the possibility of superior returns from the stocks of fast-growing foreign companies, there are substantial diversification advantages to be derived from foreign stocks.[10]

Commodities Trading

Almost all individuals who have excess funds to invest will consider buying either stocks or bonds. In contrast, very few potential investors ever consider trading commodities. While some characteristics of commodities trading probably justify this attitude, there are many aspects of this trading that are very similar to buying

---

[7]Further discussion and extensive references are contained in Chapter 16.

[8]For a discussion of the revivals, see Peter C. DuBois, "Hot-and-Cold Issues," *Barron's,* 19 July 1976, p. 3; John C. Boland, "Avantek to Xidex," *Barron's,* 30 October 1978, p. 7.

[9]For a more detailed analysis of the historical short-run returns on initial stock issues, see Frank K. Reilly, "New Issues Revisited," *Financial Management* 6 (1977): 28–42, and Stanley Block and Marjorie Stanley, "The Financial Characteristics and Price Movement Patterns of Companies Approaching the Unseasoned Securities Market in the Late 1970s," *Financial Management,* 9 (1980): 30–36.

[10]Chapter 22 contains a detailed analysis of international diversification. Also see Anna Merjos, "How to Invest Abroad," *Barron's* 24 July 1978, p. 9. Also see, Jill Bertner, "Foreign Stocks Catch on with Small Investors; Gains are Bigger Lure Than Diversification," *Wall Street Journal,* 20 April 1981, p. 36.

and selling stock.[11] Investors should be aware of the similarities between stocks and commodities and not be intimidated by some of the unique characteristics of commodity trading.

Spot Contracts

In one sense, the commodity exchanges function like any other market, simply dealing in the purchase and sale of commodities (corn, wheat, etc.) for current delivery and consumption. This is obviously a very necessary function, bringing together those who produce commodities (farmers), and those who consume them (food processors). When someone wants to buy a commodity for current delivery, he goes to a "spot" market and acquires the available supply. There is a spot market for each commodity and prices fluctuate depending upon current supply and demand.

Future Contracts

The bulk of trading on the commodity exchanges is in future contracts, which are contracts for the delivery of a commodity at some future date, usually within nine months. The price reflects what the participants feel the future will be for the commodity. In July of a given year one could speculate on the future prices for wheat on the Chicago Board of Trade in September, December, March, and May of the next year. If investors expected that eventually the price would rise, they could buy contracts now and sell them later; if they expected the prices to fall, they could sell contracts now and buy similar contracts later to cover the sale when the price declines. The number of commodities available for trading is quite large and increasing over time, as shown by the quotations in the *Wall Street Journal*.

There are several factors that distinguish investing in commodities from investing in stocks.[12] One of these is the greater use of leverage which increases the volatility of returns. Specifically, because an investor only puts up a small proportion of the contract (10–15 percent), when the price of the commodity changes, the change in the *total* value of the contract is large compared to the amount invested. Another unique aspect is the term of the investment. While stocks can have an infinite maturity, commodity contracts are almost never for more than a year.

Real Estate

Real estate investments are somewhat like commodities in that most investors consider this area "interesting" and probably profitable, but feel that it is limited to a select group of experts with large capital bases. The fact is, there are real

---

[11]For a discussion of some of these similarities, see Charles V. Harlow and Richard J. Teweles, "Commodities and Securities Compared," *Financial Analysts Journal* 28 (1972): 64–70.

[12]For a detailed discussion of these differences, see Richard J. Teweles, Charles V. Harlow, and Herbert L. Stone, *The Commodity Futures Trading Guide* (New York: McGraw-Hill, 1969), and Chapter 18.

estate investments that are feasible for all investors because they do not require large capital commitments. We will begin our discussion by considering low-capital alternatives.

Real Estate Investment Trusts (REIT)

An REIT is basically a closed-end mutual fund (these terms are defined in Chapter 19) designed to invest in various real estate properties. The idea is similar to a common stock mutual fund except that the purpose is to invest in property and buildings rather than in stocks and bonds. There are several types.

Construction and Development Trusts and Mortgage Trusts   Construction and development trusts lend the money required during the initial construction of a building, shopping center, etc. Mortgage trusts are involved in long-term financing of various properties, acquiring the long-term mortgage once the construction is completed.

Equity Trusts   Equity trusts own various income-producing properties such as office buildings or apartment houses. As a result, an investor who buys an equity trust is buying a portfolio of income-producing properties.

REITs were very popular during the period 1969–1970 and grew substantially. They experienced problems during 1973–1974 due to general economic and money market conditions. While they are subject to unique risks, it appears that the concept is viable for investors interested in real estate investments.[13]

Direct Real Estate Investments

The most common type of direct real estate investment is the purchase of a home. It is often said that this will be the largest investment you will make in your career. This is certainly possible when you consider that the purchase of a single-family house will probably cost a minimum of over $60,000.[14] The purchase of a home is considered an investment because the buyer is committing a sum of money for a number of years and hopes to get that money back along with some excess return when the house is sold. The financial commitment includes a down payment and specific payments made over a 20- to 30-year period.

Raw Land   Another form of direct real estate investment is the purchase of raw land with the intent of selling it in the future at a profit. From purchase to sale it is necessary to make payments on the mortgage and pay all taxes until the time

---

[13]For a general description of REITs, see Peter A. Schulkin, "Real Estate Investment Trusts," *Financial Analysts Journal* 27 (1971): 33–40. More recent appraisals are contained in Mary Greenebaum, "Searching for Bargains Among the REITs," *Fortune,* 12 March 1979, pp. 153–156; Michael Brody, "Sounder Ground," *Barron's,* 21 May 1979, pp. 4–5; James Carberry, "Many REITs Stage Comeback, Aided by an Attraction of Foreign Investors," *Wall Street Journal,* 6 August 1979, p. 6.

[14]The average price of a new home in early 1981 was in excess of $90,000 according to the Federal Home Loan Bank.

at which someone will want to buy the lot. Obviously, a major risk is the general lack of liquidity of such an asset compared to that of most stocks and bonds.[15]

Apartment Buildings   It is possible to acquire a building with rental apartments with a low down payment. Once the initial down payment is made, the intent is to derive enough from the rents to pay the expenses of the building, including the mortgage payments. For the first few years following the purchase, there is generally no reported income from the building because of deductible expenses. Subsequently, there is a cash flow and an opportunity to profit from the sale of the building after the equity has been increased.[16]

Land Development   The idea of buying raw land, splitting it into individual lots, and building houses on it is a feasible form of investment, but such an undertaking requires a substantial commitment of capital and time, and also extensive expertise. Clearly, the returns from a successful development can be significant.[17]

Low-Liquidity Investments

All of the investment alternatives mentioned thus far are generally traded on national markets and have good liquidity. The investments briefly discussed in this section are certainly viable alternatives for individual investors, but they have never been considered by financial institutions because they have low liquidity and high transaction costs. Many of these assets are sold at auctions and there is substantial uncertainty regarding the expected price under such conditions. It may take a long time to get the "right" price for some of them. The transaction cost on these investments is usually very high compared to that on bonds and stocks. This is because there is no national market for these investments, so local dealers must be compensated for the added carrying costs and the cost of searching for buyers or sellers. Given these two attributes, many observers consider these investment alternatives to be more in the nature of hobbies, although the returns have often been substantial.

Antiques
The most obvious antique investors are antique dealers who specifically acquire antiques in order to refurbish them and sell them at a profit. From the few specific instances in which the value of antiques can be established based upon sale

[15]Some indication of the returns on this form of investment can be derived from Frank K. Reilly, Raymond Marquardt, and Donald Price, "Real Estate as an Inflation Hedge," *Review of Business and Economic Research* 12 (1977): 1–19.

[16]A well-known articles on this topic is Paul F. Wendt and Sui N. Wong, "Investment Performance: Common Stocks Versus Apartment Houses," *Journal of Finance* 20 (1965): 633–646.

[17]For a general review of studies of returns on real estate see Stephen E. Roulac, "Can Real Estate Returns Outperform Common Stocks?" *Journal of Portfolio Management* 2 (1976): 26–43; and C. F. Sirmans and James R. Webb, "Investment Yields in the Money, Capital and Real Estate Markets: A Comparative Analysis for 1951–1976," *The Real Estate Appraiser and Analyst* 44 (1978): 40–46. Several other articles in this issue should also be of interest.

prices at large public auctions, it can be estimated that returns to serious collectors may be substantial.[18]

Art

There are many examples of paintings that have subsequently increased in value and the implied rates of return could be significant. The returns are generally realized on the works of well-known artists which enjoy some liquidity. Therefore, art can be used as an investment vehicle, but it typically requires a large capital base to acquire the work of known artists.[19]

Coins and Stamps

The market for coins and stamps is fragmented compared to the stock market, but is more liquid than most of the market for art and antiques. The reason is that the volume of coins and stamps traded has prompted the publication of several price lists on a weekly and monthly basis.[20] These areas are therefore much more amenable to investment because the investor can use a grading specification to determine the correct market price on most coins or stamps. Once graded, a coin or stamp can usually be disposed of quite quickly through a dealer.[21]

Historical Returns on Alternative Investments

Given the previous discussion of some of the investments available, it seems appropriate to examine the historical performance of some of them. Therefore, this section contains a discussion of several studies that have dealt with the rates of return for some of these investment instruments. This should provide the reader with a better background on the returns that are possible, and the relationship among returns. As noted, information about the relationship among returns is important for optimal diversification.

During the past two decades a number of studies have been done on the rates of return available on common stocks. These studies were prompted by the interest in common stocks as an investment and because the data on stocks, as com-

---

[18]Richard H. Rush, *Antiques as an Investment* (New York: Bonanza Books, 1968).

[19]Richard H. Rush, *Art as an Investment* (Englewood Cliffs, NJ: Prentice Hall, 1961). Also, James Winjum and Joanne Winjum, "The Art Investment Market," *Michigan Business Review,* November 1974, pp. 1–5; and Gigi Mahon, "Investing in Art," *Barron's,* 16 July 1979, p. 1 ct seg.

[20]There are several monthly coin magazines including *Coinage* (Encino, Calif.: Behn-Miller Publications, Inc.). Besides providing current prices for a wide range of coins, the magazine contains articles on investing in specific types of coins. Several articles indicate a growing interest in the area: Nicholas Ronalds, "While Money in Your Pocket Loses Value, Rare Old Coins are Appreciating Smartly," *Wall Street Journal,* 27 August 1979, p. 28; Ray Vicker, "The Search for Sanctuary by Scared-Stiff Investors," *Wall Street Journal,* 13 November 1980, p. 29.

[21]For a discussion of grading stamps, see Richard Cabeem, *Standard Handbook of Stamp Collecting* (New York: Thomas Y. Crowell, 1957). For a discussion of a stamp auction see Myron Keller, "Above Catalog," *Barron's,* 12 April 1976, p. 11; and Donald Moffitt, "Prices on Collectible Stamps Soar as Cash Flows into Market; IRAs, Keoghs in Stamps," *Wall Street Journal,* 2 April 1979, p. 40.

pared to other investments, were readily available. Recently there has been a growing interest in bonds, and their performance has been dealt with in several studies. The impact of inflation has also been a subject of growing interest, and studies have examined the computed nominal and "real" rates of return on investments. Finally, a few studies have examined the performance of other assets, e.g., real estate, foreign stocks, commodities. In this section we will review results of some of the major studies.

The Fifty-Year Fisher–Lorie Study

The most famous work on the historical performance of common stocks was the Fisher-Lorie studies done at the University of Chicago.[22] These studies were substantially more complete than previous studies had been in that they included *all* common stocks listed on the NYSE since 1926 and considered all capital changes such as splits and mergers. In addition, they included consideration of taxes and commissions as well as showing the effect of reinvesting dividends. The results were widely publicized and became a new bench mark for all portfolio managers. Subsequently, the authors updated the returns through 1976.[23] The later study expanded the earlier work in three ways: (1) in addition to computing rates of return for an equal-weighted portfolio (there is an equal dollar amount invested in each stock), the authors computed rates of return for a value-weighted portfolio (the amount of each stock in the portfolio is proportional to the market value of that particular stock); (2) besides computing rates of return on a current-dollar basis, the rates of return are adjusted for changes in the price level (inflation); and (3) rates of return for long-, intermediate-, and short-term government bonds are included.

The rates of return reported in Table 2.1 were taken from over 20 tables and were limited to three time intervals considered to be of interest: the longest period available (12/25 to 12/76); the latest 20-year period (12/56 to 12/76); and the latest 10-year period (12/66 to 12/76).

An analysis of the first block of returns, which are based on the assumption that all dividends are reinvested and that the portfolio is held at the end of the period, allows for several interesting observations. The first figure in the upper left-hand corner (9.0) is of prime interest because it is widely quoted as the long-run rate of return on common stocks. This figure does not take into account any taxes, the effects of inflation, or commissions or taxes entailed in selling the portfolio. The long-run effect of inflation over the 50-year period can be seen by comparing the returns in current dollars to the same returns in deflated dollars.

[22]Lawrence Fisher and James H. Lorie, "Rates of Return on Investment in Common Stock," *Journal of Business* 37 (1964): 1–17; ibid., "Rates of Return on Investment in Common Stock: The Year-by-Year Record, 1926–1965," *Journal of Business* 40 (1968): 219–316; Lawrence Fisher, "Outcomes for Random Investments in Common Stocks Listed on the New York Stock Exchange," *Journal of Business* 38 (1965): 149–161.

[23]Lawrence Fisher and James H. Lorie, *A Half Century of Returns on Stocks and Bonds* (Chicago: The University of Chicago Graduate School of Business, 1977).

	12/25 to 12/76		12/56 to 12/76		12/66 to 12/76	
	Equal Weighted	Value Weighted	Equal Weighted	Value Weighted	Equal Weighted	Value Weighted
Dividend Reinvested; Cash to Portfolio:						
Tax Exempt; Current Dollars	9.0	9.1	9.6	8.5	8.4	7.4
Tax Exempt; Deflated Dollars	6.5	6.6	5.6	4.5	2.4	1.4
Lower Tax Rate; Current Dollars	8.3	8.3	8.7	7.5	7.4	6.2
Lower Tax Rate; Deflated Dollars	5.8	5.9	4.7	3.6	1.5	0.3
Higher Tax Rate; Current Dollars	7.2	7.1	7.4	6.1	6.2	4.9
Higher Tax Rate; Deflated Dollars	4.7	4.7	3.5	2.2	0.4	−0.9
Without Dividend Reinvested; Cash to Portfolio:						
Tax Exempt: Current Dollars	7.3	7.9	9.9	8.6	8.4	7.1
Tax Exempt; Deflated Dollars	5.8	6.7	6.4	5.1	2.5	1.3
Lower Tax Rate; Current Dollars	7.0	NA[a]	9.0	NA[a]	7.5	NA[a]
Lower Tax Rate; Deflated Dollars	5.4	NA[a]	5.4	NA[a]	1.6	NA[a]
Higher Tax Rate; Current Dollars	6.4	6.8	7.6	6.2	6.3	4.8
Higher Tax Rate; Deflated Dollars	4.6	5.3	3.9	2.6	0.4	−0.9
Rates of Change in Prices; Cash to Portfolio:						
Tax Exempt: Current Dollars	4.6	4.3	5.9	4.5	4.9	3.4
Tax Exempt; Deflated Dollars	2.2	1.9	2.0	0.7	−0.9	−2.3

Table 2.1   Long-Run Rates of Return for Common Stocks Listed on the
New York Stock Exchange under Various Assumptions

[a]Not available.

Source: Lawrence Fisher and James H. Lorie, *A Half Century of Returns on Stocks and Bonds* (Chicago: The University of Chicago Graduate School of Business, 1977). Reprinted by permission.

Such a comparison will show that the difference was about 2.5 percent for the total period 1925–1976 (e.g., 9.0 to 6.5). Subsequently, the difference increased to about 4 percent for the last 20 years (1956–1976), and approached 6 percent during the last 10 years. Because of the increase in the rate of inflation, Fisher and Lorie felt it was appropriate to report two sets of returns (i.e., nominal and "real").

You can see the effect of taxes by examining the difference between returns for a hypothetical tax-exempt investor compared to returns for an investor with a lower tax rate, and to returns for an investor subject to a higher tax rate. The data indicate that the difference between tax exempt and lower tax rates was about one percent, with another one percent due to higher tax rates. Finally, the effect of weighting the stocks in the portfolio also had a changing impact. For the longest period (51 years) there was *very little difference* in returns due to the weighting. In contrast, during the last 20 years and 10 years the rates of return differed by at least one percent. This indicates that stocks with a higher market value did not do as well as other stocks.

A comparison of the rates of return in the first and second blocks indicates the effect of reinvesting dividends as compared to those of consuming dividends. Finally, the last set of returns indicates the effect of dividends on the total rates of return in that the rate of change is the difference in dividends. In general, the impact was significant. Between 4 and 5 percent a year and over 50 percent of the total return is due to the dividend return.

The total listing of common stock results clearly shows that investors in common stock listed on the NYSE have received positive rates of return during the great majority of periods since 1926. Also investors have received fairly substantial positive returns during most periods, even when considering commissions and taxes.

Table 2.2 contains selected annual rates of return on U.S. Treasury securities of different maturities for different time intervals (51 years, 20 years, 10 years). All of these securities are considered to be risk-free in the sense that there is no probability of default.

An analysis of the rates of return *across* a line indicates the influence of maturity on rates of return. (The long-term bonds have a maturity of at least 10 years, the intermediate bonds have maturities of between 5 and 10 years, and it was assumed that the short-term bonds were acquired when they had about a year left to maturity and were sold after 6 months.) For the 51-year period, the intermediate securities consistently provided the highest rates of return. The effect of taxes on bond returns was similar to the effect on stock returns, about one percent for lower taxes and an additional 1 percent for the higher tax rates. The most important effect was that of inflation. For the total period the returns adjusted for inflation were about 2 percent lower, but were typically positive. For the last 20 years, the "real" returns (returns adjusted for inflation, i.e., deflated dollars) were only about 1 percent without taxes and were negative after taxes. During the last 10 years, *almost all* deflated returns were negative. Therefore, individuals who invested in government securities during the last 10 years were not able to increase their consumption of goods and services as a result of this investment.

The rates of return on U.S. Treasury securities have generally been consistent with expectations over the long-run (51 years). In contrast, recent experience has been unique because of the effect of inflation on relative returns. This indicates the importance of considering the effect of inflation when analyzing individual investments and constructing portfolios; i.e., the returns from an investment must be adjusted for inflation.

Interest Reinvested	12/25 to 12/76			12/56 to 12/76			12/66 to 12/76		
	Long	Inter-mediate	Short	Long	Inter-mediate	Short	Long	Inter-mediate	Short
Tax Exempt; Current Dollars	3.4	3.6	3.0	4.2	4.7	5.3	5.4	5.7	7.0
Tax Exempt; Deflated Dollars	1.1	1.2	0.7	0.4	0.8	1.4	−0.4	−0.1	1.0
Lower Tax; Current Dollars	2.7	2.9	2.4	2.8	3.3	3.9	3.5	3.8	5.0
Lower Tax; Deflated Dollars	0.4	0.6	0.1	−1.0	−0.5	0.1	−2.2	−1.9	−0.8
Higher Tax; Current Dollars	1.7	2.0	1.6	1.0	1.5	2.1	1.3	1.6	2.7
Higher Tax; Deflated Dollars	−0.6	−0.3	−0.7	−2.7	−2.2	−1.6	−4.3	−4.0	−3.0

Table 2.2   Long-Run Rates of Return on U.S. Treasury Securities
For Different Maturities Under Various Assumptions

Source: Lawrence Fisher and James H. Lorie, *A Half Century of Returns on Stocks and Bonds* (Chicago: The University of Chicago Graduate School of Business, 1977). Reprinted by permission.

Ibbotson-Sinquefield Study[24]

A second major study dealing with the nominal and real rates of return on common stocks, bonds, and bills for the period 1926–1974 was done by Ibbotson and Sinquefield at the University of Chicago.[25] The authors present year-by-year historical rates of return for five major classes of assets in the United States: 1) common stocks, 2) long-term U.S. Government bonds, 3) long-term corporate bonds, 4) U.S. Treasury bills, and 5) consumer goods (a measure of inflation). For each asset, the authors present total rates of return that reflect dividend or interest income as well as capital gains or losses. None of the returns is adjusted for taxes or transaction costs.

Given the monthly and annual rates of return, the authors computed geometric mean returns over longer periods and the arithmetic mean returns on the assets analyzed. In addition to the five basic series, the authors computed seven additional returns series derived from the basic series. The first three of these were net returns reflecting different premiums. The first was a net return from investing in common stocks rather than in U.S. Treasury bills. This net return is referred to as the *risk premium* involved in investing in a risky alternative, rather

[24]Results were originally published in Roger G. Ibbotson and Rex A. Sinquefield, "Stocks, Bonds, Bills and Inflation: Year-by-Year Historical Returns (1926–1974)," *Journal of Business* 49 (1976): 11–47.

[25]Idem, *Stock, Bonds, Bills, and Inflation: The Past (1926–1976) and the Future (1977–2000)* (Charlottesville, Virginia: Financial Analysts Research Foundation, 1977; and *Stocks, Bonds, Bills, and Inflation: Historical Returns (1926–1978)* (Charlottesville, Virginia: Financial Analysts Research Foundation, 1979).

than in something basically risk-free like treasury bills. The second net return was the difference in investing in long-term government bonds rather than U.S. Treasury bills. This is referred to as a *maturity premium* because in both cases the securities are considered default-free and the only difference between them is their maturity dates. Finally, the difference in net returns from long-term corporate bonds and long-term government bonds was determined. This is referred to as a *default premium* because the difference between the two long-term bond series is that the corporate bonds involve a possibility of default. The final four series derived are basically inflation-adjusted returns for the initial four. The authors ascertained the *real* rates of return on common stocks, treasury bills, long-term government bonds, and long-term corporate bonds. After the original article was published, the results were updated in 1977 and 1979.[26]

A summary of the results for the basic and derived series is contained in Table 2.3. The geometric mean returns are always lower than the arithmetic returns, and the difference increases with the standard deviation of returns.[27]

Over the period 1926–1978, common stocks returned 8.9 percent a year, compounded annually. For the total period, the risk premium on common stocks was 6.2 percent, and the inflation adjusted "real" returns were 6.1 percent per year. Although common stocks outperformed the other assets in the study, the returns on stocks were also far more volatile as measured by the range and the standard deviation of returns.

Long-term U.S. Government bonds experienced a 4.0 percent annual return over the period 1926–1978. During the same period, the real return on these bonds was one percent and the maturity premium for these bonds, compared to treasury bills, was 0.7 percent. The returns on these bonds were far less volatile than the annual returns on common stocks.

The annual compound rate of return on long-term corporate bonds was 3.2 percent over the total period. The default premium on these bonds, compared to that on long-term government bonds, was only 0.6 percent. The inflation adjusted return was 1.4 percent. The volatility of these bonds was similar to the volatility on government bonds.

During the entire period, U.S. Treasury bills returned 2.5 percent a year, which was equal to the rate of inflation for the total period. As a result, the inflation-adjusted return on T-bills for the entire period was 0.0 percent. The return on T-bills was not very volatile; the standard deviation was the lowest for all of the series examined. In contrast, the inflation-adjusted T-bill series was much more volatile.

This study generally confirmed the results of the Fisher-Lorie studies and extended the analysis to other alternatives. The returns were as expected and were generally consistent with the uncertainty measured using the standard deviation of annual returns.

[26]Ibid.

[27]There is a discussion of the difference between the arithmetic and geometric mean in the appendix to this chapter. Readers not familiar with the difference are encouraged to read this before proceeding further.

Series	Annual Geometric Mean Rate of Return	Arithmetic Mean of Annual Returns	Standard Deviation of Annual Returns	Number of Years Returns are Positive	Number of Years Returns are Negative	Highest Annual Return (and year)	Lowest Annual Return (and year)
Common Stocks	8.9%[a]	11.2%	22.2%	35	18	54.0% (1933)	−43.3% (1931)
Long-Term Government Bonds	4.0	4.1	5.6	39	14	16.8 (1932)	− 9.2 (1967)
Long-Term Corporate Bonds	3.2	3.4	5.7	42	11	18.6 (1976)	− 8.1 (1969)
U.S. Treasury Bills	2.5	2.5	2.2	52	1	8.0 (1974)	− 0.0 (1940)
Consumer Price Index	2.5	2.6	4.8	43	10	18.2 (1946)	−10.3 (1932)
Risk Premiums on Common Stocks	6.2	8.7	22.3	33	20	53.5 (1933)	−43.7 (1931)
Maturity Premiums on Long-Term Govt. Bonds	0.7	0.9	6.0	27	26	15.7 (1932)	−12.8 (1967)
Default Premiums on Long-Term Corp. Bonds	0.6	0.7	3.2	32	21	10.5 (1933)	− 7.2 (1974)
Common Stocks—Inflation Adjusted	6.1	8.8	23.5	33	20	53.3 (1954)	−37.4 (1931)
Long-Term Government Bonds—Inflation Adjusted	1.0	1.3	8.0	31	22	30.2 (1932)	−15.5 (1946)
Long-Term Corporate Bonds—Inflation Adjusted	1.4	1.7	7.7	33	20	23.5 (1932)	−13.9 (1946)
U.S. Treasury Bills—Inflation Adjusted	0.0	0.0	4.6	32	21	12.6 (1932)	−15.2 (1946)

Table 2.3   Basic and Derived Series: Historical Highlights (1926–1978)

[a]The annual geometric mean rate of return for capital appreciation exclusive of dividends was 3.5 percent over the entire period.

Source: Roger G. Ibbotson and Rex A. Sinquefield, *Stocks, Bonds, Bills, and Inflation: Historical Returns (1926–1978)* (Charlottesville, VA: Financial Analysts Research Foundation, 1979).

Robichek–Cohn–Pringle Study

The R–C–P Study deals with the rates of return on a number of investments, including stocks, bonds, commodities, real estate, and foreign securities.[28] In the study *ex post* rates of return and correlation coefficients are computed for 12 investment media for the period 1949–1969, inclusive, and the implications of the results for portfolio construction are analyzed. The purpose of the study was to show the difference in returns for alternative investments. The specific media considered were: (1) Standard & Poor's Industrial Common Stock Index, (2) S&P Utility Index, (3) U.S. Government 2 percent bonds of 1970–65, (4) Bethlehem Steel 2¾ percent bonds due in 1970, (5) Canadian Pacific Perpetual 4 percent bonds, (6) farm real estate, (7) cotton future contracts, (8) wheat future contracts, (9) copper future contracts, (10) Japanese common stocks, (11) Australian common stocks, and (12) Treasury bill yields. A summary of the mean returns and the standard deviation of returns for the total period 1949–1969 are contained in Table 2.4.

The authors felt that the returns on U.S. equities were as expected. Industrials had a higher mean return and a higher standard deviation than did utilities. The returns on Japanese stocks indicated that the mean annual return for the 20, one-year periods was a surprising 24.07 percent. The holding period return over the entire time was 18.94 percent. The coefficient of variation of returns for Japanese stocks was higher than it was for U.S. stocks. Returns from Australian common stocks, at 6.8 percent, were considerably lower than returns from other groups. On the other hand, the relationship between the instability of returns and the mean return was about the same for Australian stocks as for Japanese issues and somewhat higher than it was for American stocks.

The *ex post* compound rates of return over the 20-year period for the three bonds studied were 2.4 percent for the U.S. government 2 percent bonds, 2.0 percent for the Bethlehem Steel bonds, and 1.4 percent for the Canadian Pacific Perpetual 4 percent bonds. All of these *ex post* returns exhibited a high degree of variance in relation to the mean return, and all three bonds produced negative returns during many years. The *ex post* returns on these bonds were lower than the average rate of return on treasury bills, which was 3 percent.

The most notable characteristic of the results on farm real estate was the apparent stability of returns over time. The geometric mean rate of return was 9.47 percent and the standard deviation was only 4.5 percent, resulting in a coefficient of variation of only .48. This relative measure of volatility was considerably lower than that of any other long-term investment medium.

Returns on commodity futures showed very large year-to-year variations. Comparison of the returns on futures contracts in the three different commodities shows that wheat provided a high negative mean return (minus 22.88 percent), copper a high positive rate of return (26.60 percent), and cotton a very low mean return (3.8 percent).

---

[28]Alexander A. Robichek, Richard A. Cohn, and John J. Pringle, "Returns on Alternative Media and Implications for Portfolio Construction," *Journal of Business* 45 (1972): 427–443.

	Arithmetic Mean	Geometric Mean	Standard Deviation[a]	Coefficient of Variation[b]
S&P Industrials	12.97	11.63	17.55	1.51
S&P Utilities	9.31	8.60	12.43	1.45
Japanese Stocks	24.07	18.94	41.30	2.18
Australian Stocks	7.80	6.82	14.22	2.09
Treasury Bill Yields	3.01	3.00	1.60	0.53
U.S. Government 2 percent bonds, 1970–65	2.48	2.37	4.68	1.97
Bethlehem Steel, 2³/₄ percent bonds (maturity 1970)	2.06	2.00	3.40	1.70
Canadian Pacific Perpetual 4 percent bonds	1.56	1.40	5.71	4.08
Farm Real Estate	9.56	9.47	4.50	0.48
Cotton Futures	17.10	3.80	66.77	17.57
Wheat Futures	−0.49	−22.88	64.07	2.80
Copper Futures	121.02	26.60	244.02	9.17

Table 2.4   Mean Rates of Return and Variability of Annual Returns for Alternative Investment Media: 1949–1969

[a]Standard deviation about geometric mean

[b]Coefficient of Variation = Standard Deviation ÷ Geometric Mean

Source: Reprinted from "Returns on Alternative Investment Media and Implications for Portfolio Construction," by Alexander A. Robichek, Richard A. Cohn, and John J. Pringle, *Journal of Business*, vol. 45, no. 3 (July 1972), by permission of The University of Chicago Press. Copyright © 1972 by The University of Chicago Press.

The authors examined the correlation among the rates of return over time for the alternative investment media (for a discussion of covariance and correlation, see Appendix B to Chapter 2). The matrix of correlation coefficients is contained in Table 2.5.

The correlation coefficients among the various media were generally low, and the signs of the coefficients were almost equally divided between positive and negative values. The common stock returns for the different countries had very low correlation coefficients. This is especially true for the Japanese stocks, which are negatively correlated with U.S. industrial stocks and Australian stocks. Given the high rates of return on Japanese stocks, the negative correlations indicate that they would have been very desirable additions to the portfolio of a U.S. investor.

The returns from real estate were very stable and not significantly correlated with any other media. Commodity futures, on the other hand, were extremely volatile year-to-year and variability among the commodities were quite different from other media. These general findings indicate that enlarging the universe of investment alternatives would be of benefit in portfolio construction in

	S&P Industrial	S&P Utilities	U.S. Government	Bethlehem Steel	Canadian Pacific	Farm Real Estate	Cotton Futures	Wheat Futures	Copper Futures	Japanese Stocks	Australian Stocks
S&P Utilities	.59[a]	...									
U.S. Govt. 2s of March 15, 1970–65	–.54[b]	–.17	...								
Bethlehem Steel 2¾s of July 15, 1970	–.30	–.08	.81[a]	...							
Canadian Pacific Perpetual 4s	.23	.34	.02	.10	...						
Farm Real Estate	–.13	–.15	–.19	–.26	–.13	...					
Cotton Futures	.29	–.04	–.21	–.12	–.01	–.09	...				
Wheat Futures	.29	.06	–.31	–.41	.14	–.24	.67[a]	...			
Copper Futures	.32	–.24	–.20	–.10	.12	–.21	.23	.38	...		
Japanese Stocks	–.07	.11	–.21	–.19	.05	.48[b]	–.31	–.09	–.13	...	
Australian Stocks	.22	–.17	–.28	–.05	–.44[b]	–.29	.33	.04	.13	–.15	...
Treasury Bill Yields	–.55[a]	–.66[a]	.26	.20	–.40	.06	–.41	–.35	.05	–.02	.14

Table 2.5   Matrix of Correlation Coefficients

[a]Significant at the .01 level. Critical values and corresponding significance levels as follows: .55 (1 percent), .43 (5 percent), .37 (10 percent), and .29 (20 percent).

[b]Significant at the 0.5 level.

Source: Reprinted from "Returns on Alternative Investment Media and Implications for Portfolio Construction," by Alexander A. Robichek, Richard A. Cohn, and John J. Pringle, *Journal of Business*, vol. 45, no. 3 (July 1972), by permission of The University of Chicago Press. Copyright © 1972 by The University of Chicago Press.

terms of the risk-return opportunities. Given the correlation coefficients, the authors specifically constructed a number of portfolios and found that there was a significant improvement in their risk-return characteristics based upon the multimedia diversification. The authors contended that *the results support the arguments that investors should look beyond common stocks and treasury bills in constructing investment portfolios.*

Summary

The purpose of this chapter was to brie/y describe some of the major investment alternatives available to individuals. In addition, we want to help you become aware of *the vast variety of these alternatives.*[29] You should be aware of *all* of the alternatives for two reasons. The first is that they provide a wide variety of risk and return choices that may be of interest to different investors. One man's garbage may be another man's feast. As an example, one reader, after becoming familiar with commodities trading, may decide that it is much too speculative for him and would not consider it at all, while another reader may feel that it is very exciting and decide to commit a large share of his resources to this area.

In addition, it is widely acknowledged that considering several areas in terms of risk can benefit the investor's portfolio. Assuming that the alternatives are not highly correlated, it can be shown that the variance of returns for an investor's total portfolio can be substantially reduced through diversification.

The chapter finished with a discussion of three studies concerned with the historical rates of return on common stocks and a number of other investment alternatives including bonds, commodities, and real estate. The results of these studies pointed toward two generalizations:

1. There was typically a positive relationship between the rates of return on an investment medium and the variability of the rate of return over time. This is consistent with expectations in a world of risk-averse investors who require a higher return to assume more uncertainty.

2. The correlation of the rates of return for alternative investments were typically quite low, which indicates that there are definite benefits to diversification among investments in order to reduce the variability of the investor's total portfolio.

Questions

1. What are the major advantages to investing in the common stock rather than the corporate bonds of the same company? What are the major disadvantages?

---

[29]There are obviously a number of investment alternatives we are not able to cover. For a collection of articles on alternative investments by a number of authors, see Leo Barnes and Stephen Feldman, eds., *Handbook of Wealth Management* (New York: McGraw-Hill, 1977).

2. Discuss briefly why an investor might prefer utility common stocks to industrial common stocks.

3. Would you expect the returns on industrial common stocks to have the same pattern over time as the common stock of financial firms? Why or why not?

4. Assume that the returns from transportation stocks are not correlated with the returns from financial stocks. Will this benefit an investor who has both types of stock in his portfolio? Why or why not?

5. How does a bond differ from a common stock in terms of the certainty of returns over time? Draw a simple time-series graph to demonstrate the pattern of returns you might imagine from these two alternative investments.

6. Assume that you had the opportunity to acquire a convertible bond from a growth company or a utility. Both firms have straight debentures that yield 9 percent. Given the conversion feature, which convertible bond would have the lower yield? Why?

7. Define a spot commodity contract and a future commodities contract.

8. A contract involves 5,000 bushels of wheat. Assuming wheat is selling for $3.50 a bushel, the total value of the contract is $17,500. Given a margin of 15 percent, an investor would have to put up $2,625 to purchase such a contract. Ignoring commissions, if the price of wheat increases to $3.75 a bushel, what is the percent of change in the value of the contract, and what is the investor's return on his investment? Assuming a decline in price to $3.35, what is his return? Show all calculations.

9. Define an REIT and briefly discuss the alternative types.

10. Discuss the difference in liquidity between an investment in raw land and an investment in common stock. Be specific as to why there is a difference and how they differ. (Hint: begin by defining liquidity.)

11. Define a stock warrant. Define a call option. Discuss how a warrant differs from a call option.

12. What has the CBOE contributed to the call option market that has caused significant growth in the market since 1973? Be specific.

13. Would you expect the price of an initial public offering to fluctuate more when it is first offered than would the price of a listed stock involved in a new offering? Why or why not?

14. It is contended that the returns on foreign stocks should have low correlation with the returns on U.S. stocks. What is the rationale behind such an assumption?

15. Why is it contended that antiques and art are generally illiquid investments? Be specific in your discussion. Why are coins and stamps considered to be more liquid than antiques and art? Again be specific and consider what it would require to sell the various assets.

16. Look up in the *Wall Street Journal* the current *maturity premium* on U.S. Government securities. The long-term security should have a maturity of at least 20 years.

17. Each week in *Barron's* on the last two or three pages there is a set of stock indexes for foreign countries. For a recent week, determine the percent of change in the index for Japanese and Australian stock and compare this to the percent of change in the Dow-Jones Industrial Average for the same period. Do the results of the comparison indicate any benefits to diversification among securities from these countries? Why or why not?

References

Barnes, Leo, and Feldman, Stephen, eds. *Handbook of Wealth Management.* New York: McGraw-Hill, 1977.

The Bond Book. New York: Merrill Lynch, Pierce, Fenner, and Smith, 1975.

Cabeem, Richard. *Standard Handbook of Stamp Collecting.* New York: Thomas Y. Crowell Company, 1957.

Darst, David M. *The Complete Bond Book.* New York: McGraw-Hill, 1975.

Fisher, Lawrence, and Lorie, James H. *A Half Century of Returns on Stocks and Bonds.* Chicago: University of Chicago Graduate School of Business, 1977.

Ibbotson, Roger G., and Sinquefield, Rex A. *Stocks, Bonds, Bills, and Inflation: Historical Returns (1926–1978).* Charlottesville, VA: Financial Analysts Research Foundation, 1979.

Reilly, Frank K. "New Issues Revisited." *Financial Management* 6, (1977).

Robichek, Alexander A.; Cohn, Richard A.; and Pringle, John J. "Returns on Alternative Investment Media and Implications for Portfolio Construction." *Journal of Business* 45 (1972).

Roulac, Stephen E. "Can Real Estate Returns Outperform Common Stocks?" *Journal of Portfolio Management* (1976).

Rush, Richard H. *Antiques as an Investment.* New York: Bonanza Books, 1968.

Rush, Richard H. *Art as an Investment.* Englewood Cliffs, NJ: Prentice-Hall, 1961.

Schulkin, Peter A. "Real Estate Investment Trusts." *Financial Analysts Journal* 27 (1971).

Sirmans, C. F., and Webb, James R. "Investment Yields in the Money, Capital and Real Estate Markets: A Comparative Analysis for 1951–1976." *The Real Estate Appraiser and Analyst* (1978).

Teweles, Richard J.; Harlow, Charles V.; and Stone, Herbert L. *The Commodity Futures Trading Guide.* New York: McGraw-Hill, 1969.

Appendix A to Chapter 2
Geometric Mean Returns

When examining the average returns on an investment over an extended period of time, the typical measure used is the arithmetic average of annual rates of return. As will be shown, the arithmetic average return can be biased upward if there is substantial variability in the returns over time. An alternative measure of the central tendency is the geometric mean of the annual returns. This measure is considered superior by some investigators because it is the same formulation that is used to derive compound interest and provides a proper measure of the true ending wealth position for the investment involved.

Arithmetic Mean Bias

As is known, the arithmetic mean (designated $\overline{X}$) is the sum of each value in a distribution divided by the total number of values.

$$\overline{X} = \Sigma X/n$$

A problem occurs if there are large changes in the annual returns over time. Consider the example in which a nondividend paying stock goes from $50 to $100 during year one and back to $50 during year two. The annual returns would be:

Year 1: 100%
Year 2:−50%

Obviously, during the two years there was *no* return on the investment. Yet the arithmetic mean return would be:

$$(+100) + (-50)/2 = 50/2 = 25\%$$

In this case, although there was *no* change in wealth and, therefore, no return, the arithmetic mean return is computed at 25 percent.

Geometric Mean

The geometric mean (designated G) is the nth root of the product arrived at by multiplying the values in the distribution by each other. Specifically, it is:

$$G = \Pi X^{1/n}$$

where Π stands for "product." When calculating the geometric mean returns, it is customary to use holding-period returns, which are the yield plus 1.0 (e.g., a positive 10 percent return is designated 1.10; a negative 15 percent return is designated 0.85). This is done because a negative yield causes the geometric mean calculation to be meaningless. As an example, consider the extreme example used in the previous discussion of the arithmetic mean:

	Yield	Holding-Period Return
Year 1:	100%	2.00
Year 2:	−50%	0.50

$$G = (2.00 \times 0.50)^{1/2} = (1.00)^{1/2} = 1.00 - 1.00 = 0\%$$

To get the yield, 1.00 is subtracted from the geometric holding-period return. As can be seen, this answer is consistent with the ending wealth position of the investor. He ended where he began and had a 0 percent return during the period.

Extended Example

Consider the following, more complete example using actual rounded percent of price changes for the Dow-Jones Industrial Average (DJIA) during the period 1970–1979:

	Percent of Price Change	Holding Period Change
1970	5.00	1.05
1971	6.00	1.06
1972	15.00	1.15
1973	−17.00	0.83
1974	−28.00	0.72
1975	38.00	1.38
1976	18.00	1.18
1977	−17.00	0.83
1978	−3.00	0.97
1979	4.00	1.04

$$\overline{X} = \Sigma X/n = 21/10 = 2.1\%$$

$$G = \Pi X^{1/n}$$

$$= 1.0429^{1/10} = 1.004209 - 1.00 = 0.4\%$$

As shown, the arithmetic mean price change is more than five times as large as the geometric mean price change. Because of the upward bias in the arithmetic mean, it will *always* be larger than the geometric mean (except where all returns are equal), and the discrepancy will be wider with a more volatile series. If there is a large difference between the arithmetic mean and the geometric mean, it can be inferred that the returns were very volatile.

Appendix B to Chapter 2
Covariance and Correlation

Covariance

It is assumed that almost all students have been exposed to the concept of covariance, so the following discussion is set forth in intuitive terms with an example that will, hopefully, help the reader recall the concept.[1]

Covariance is an absolute measure of the extent to which two sets of numbers move together over time, i.e., move up or down together. In this regard

---

[1] For a more detailed, rigorous treatment of the subject the reader is referred to any standard statistics text including Ya–lun Chou, *Statistical Analysis* (New York: Holt, Rinehart, and Winston, Inc., 1975). pp. 152–156.

"move together" means they are generally above their means or below their means at the same time. Covariance between i and j is defined as:

$$Cov_{ij} = \frac{\Sigma(i - \bar{i})(j - \bar{j})}{N}$$

If we define $(i - \bar{i})$ as i' and $(j - \bar{j})$ as j', then

$$Cov_{ij} = \frac{\Sigma i' j'}{N}$$

Obviously, if both numbers are consistently above or below their individual means at the same time, their products will be positive, and the average product (covariance) will be a large positive value. In contrast, if the i value is below its mean when the j value is above its mean or vice versa, their products will be large negative values and you would find negative covariance. The following example should make this clear.

Obs.	i	j	$i - \bar{i}$	$j - \bar{j}$	$i'j'$
1	3	8	−4	−4	16
2	6	10	−1	−2	2
3	8	14	+1	+2	2
4	5	12	−2	0	0
5	9	13	+2	+1	2
6	11	15	+4	+3	12
Σ	= 42	72			34
Mean =	7	12			

$$Cov_{ij} = \frac{34}{6} = +5.67$$

Table 2B.1   Calculation of Covariance

In this example the two series generally moved together, so there was positive covariance. As noted, this is an *absolute* measure of their relationship and, therefore, can range from $+\infty$ to $-\infty$. Note that the covariance of a variable with itself is its *variance*.

Correlation

To obtain a relative measure of a given relationship we use the correlation coefficient (r_{ij}) which is a normalized measure of the relationship:

$$r_{ij} = \frac{Cov_{ij}}{\sigma_i \, \sigma_j}$$

The reader will recall from the appendix in Chapter 1 that $\sigma_i = \sqrt{\dfrac{\Sigma(i - \bar{i})^2}{N}}$ so, if the two series move *completely* together, then the covariance would equal $\sigma_i\sigma_j$ and

$$\frac{Cov_{ij}}{\sigma_i\sigma_j} = +1.0$$

The correlation coefficient would equal unity, and we would say the two series are perfectly correlated. Because we know that

$$r_{ij} = \frac{Cov_{ij}}{\sigma_i\sigma_j}$$

we also know that $Cov_{ij} = r_{ij}\sigma_i\sigma_j$, which is a relationship that may be useful when computing the standard deviation of a portfolio because, in many instances, the relationship between two securities is stated in terms of the correlation coefficient rather than the covariance.

Continuing the example given in Table 2B.1, the standard deviations are computed in Table 2B.2 as is the correlation between i and j. As shown, the two standard deviations are rather large and similar but not the same. Finally, when the positive covariance is normalized by the product of the two standard deviations, the results indicate a correlation coefficient of .898, which is obviously quite large and close to 1.00. Apparently these two series are highly related.

Obs.	$i - \bar{i}$*	$(i - \bar{i})^2$	$j - \bar{j}$ª	$(j - \bar{j})^2$
1	-4	16	-4	16
2	-1	1	-2	4
3	$+1$	1	$+2$	4
4	-2	4	0	0
5	$+2$	4	$+1$	1
6	$+4$	16	$+3$	9
		42		34

$$\sigma_i^2 = 42/6 = 7.00 \qquad\qquad \sigma_j^2 = 34/6 = 5.67$$
$$\sigma_i = \sqrt{7.00} = 2.65 \qquad\qquad \sigma_j = \sqrt{5.67} = 2.38$$
$$r_{ij} = Cov_{ij}/\sigma_i\sigma_j = \frac{5.67}{(2.65)\,(2.38)} = \frac{5.67}{6.31} = .898$$

Table 2B.2 Calculation of Correlation Coefficient

*from Table 2B.1

Adam Smith

In one of your economics classes you may have heard of the great economist Adam Smith who advocated free markets and the invisible hand of competition. The Adam Smith of free markets died in 1790. The Adam Smith pictured here is alive and well and writing about the current monetary environment and its impact on investments. Because his writing style blends facts, historical anecdotes, and analysis of facts in an entertaining and useful way, his three books have been widely read. Specifically, Adam Smith is the author of The Money Game and Supermoney. Both of these books were number one on the New York Times bestsellers list. His most recent book is Paper Money published in 1981. It is destined to be very successful, since it deals with the impacts of OPEC and inflation on alternative investments.

Adam Smith is the pseudonym of George J. W. Goodman, chairman of a private investment group, a former member of the editorial board of The New York Times, and a co-founder of three regional magazines, New York Magazine, New New Jersey Monthly plus the financial journal, Institutional Investor. His unique combination of financial and literary talent has won an international audience of investment professionals. Adam Smith himself has been a securities analyst and fund manager. Among his corporate directorships are those of a worldwide hotel chain and a major airline.

Louis Rukeyser

While a few national news commentators have become well-known, seldom has a financial commentator become a celebrity. Louis Rukeyser is the clear exception. He has become a national celebrity as the host of Wall Street Week, a weekly television show devoted to the discussion and analysis of national and international events and their impact on our securities markets.

Wall Street Week began on November 20, 1970, with Rukeyser as the host for a limited audience. In October 1972 the Public Broadcasting Service broadcast the series nationally, and it has been growing in popularity ever since. The series' success can be directly correlated to the television and economic expertise of Louis Rukeyser whose skillful and witty approach has attracted a large following to the current topics that Wall Street Week covers. A panel of 17 top investment experts appears on the show at various intervals. Specifically, every week three individuals from this panel discuss their short- and long-term outlooks for the market. Besides the weekly forecasts, Rukeyser periodically reviews the earlier predictions that one or more of his panelists have made, then he compares those predictions to what actually happened and elicits comments (good or bad) on the comparison. As a result, the viewer not only hears opinions that are not generally available to the public, but he also witnesses a review of the experts' opinions. In addition, each week there is a "guest expert" who is questioned by Rukeyser and by the panelists. The result is a very interesting and stimulating show.

After graduating in 1954 from Princeton's Woodrow Wilson School of Public and International Affairs, he spent 11 years as a political and foreign correspondent for the Baltimore Sun. Rukeyser's next stop was ABC News where he served eight years as a senior correspondent and commentator. In 1968 he returned to New York as a national economic commentator. During the past ten years he has received numerous awards for his television commentaries and also for his newspaper columns.

Beyond his nationally acclaimed TV show, his book How to Make Money in Wall Street (New York: Doubleday, 1976) was chosen "best investment book of the year," by the Literary Guild, and the book was selected twice to be included in the Literary Guild's list. His newspaper column of economic commentary is nationally distributed by the McNaught Syndicate and appears three times a week in several hundred newspapers. For several years he has been a popular speaker on the national lecture circuit.

ORGANIZATION AND FUNCTIONING OF SECURITIES MARKETS

⇒ 3 ⇐

The stock market, Wall Street, the Dow-Jones Industrials are part and parcel of our everyday experience. Each evening we find out how they fared on the television news broadcasts; each morning we read about their prospects for a rally or decline in the pages of our daily newspaper. Yet the operation of the securities market remains a given to most investors. What this market is, how it functions, and who is involved in it are imperfectly understood, at best. It is the purpose of this chapter to define the securities market, both primary and secondary, and to indicate those persons who are key to its operation, particularly the specialists.

Financial Markets

What Is a Market?

Prior to discussing the organization and functioning of the stock and bond markets, it seems appropriate to consider the general question of what a market is, or, more specifically, what is its purpose. Most people have been exposed to numerous markets in their lives, without really being aware of what markets do and why they exist. Basically, we take markets for granted. *A market is the means through which buyers and sellers are brought together to aid in the transfer of goods and/or services.* Several aspects of this general definition seem worthy of emphasis. First, it is not necessary for a market to have a physical location. It is only necessary that the buyers and sellers can communicate regarding the relevant aspects of the purchase or sale.

Second, the market does not necessarily own the goods or services involved. When we discuss what is required for a "good" market, the reader will note that ownership is not involved; the basic criterion is the smooth, cheap transfer of goods and services. In the case of most financial markets, those who establish and administer the market do not own the assets, but simply provide a location for potential buyers and sellers to meet, and those who administer the market help the market to function by providing information and transfer facilities.

Finally, a market can deal in any variety of goods and services. For any commodity with a diverse clientele, a market should develop to aid in its transfer. Both buyers and sellers will benefit from its existence.

Factors That Determine a "Good" Market

A buyer or seller of goods or services enters a market to buy or sell the commodity quickly, at a price justified by the prevailing supply and demand in the market. So the buyer or seller would like to have timely and accurate information on past transactions in terms of volume and price, and on all currently outstanding bids and offers. Therefore, one attribute of a good market is *availability of information regarding price and volume for past transactions and on current market conditions.*

Another prime requirement is a liquid market, where we define liquidity as *the ability to buy or sell an asset quickly, at a known price,* i.e., a price not substantially different from the previous price, assuming no new information is available. Therefore, there are two aspects of liquidity: *the time involved to complete the transaction* and *the certainty of the price.* An instance in which a broker can assure the owner of a specified price, but indicates that it might take six months to sell the asset at that price would not be considered a very liquid market because the time involved is excessive. In contrast, if a broker tells an owner that he can sell an asset very quickly, but at a substantial discount from the previous market price for a comparable asset, this, likewise, is not a very liquid market because of the significant price change that accompanies a quick transaction. The latter case, in which it is possible to sell *quickly* is sometimes referred to as *marketability;* i.e., *the asset can be turned into cash quickly,* but there is nothing certain about price. Therefore, marketability is a necessary, but *not* a sufficient, condition for liquidity.

One of the factors that contributes to liquidity is *price continuity.* Continuity refers to prices that do not change much from one transaction to the next, unless substantial new information becomes available. Given a case in which new information is not forthcoming, and the last transaction was at a price of $20, if the next trade were at $20\frac{1}{8}$,[1] it would probably be considered a reasonably continuous market. Obviously, *it is necessary to have a continuous market without large price changes between trades in order to have a liquid market.*

A continuous market also requires *depth.* There must be numerous potential buyers and sellers who are willing to trade at prices above and below the current-market price. These buyers and sellers enter the market when there are small price changes and thereby ensure that there are no major price moves.

Another factor contributing to a good market is the *cost of a transaction.*

---

[1]The reader should be aware that common stocks are sold in increments of eighths which are equal to $0.125. Therefore, $20\frac{1}{8}$ means the stock sold at $20.125 per share.

The lower the cost of the transaction (in terms of the percentage of the value of the trade), the more efficient is the market. Assuming that an individual is comparing two markets, if the cost of a transaction on one were 2 percent of the value of the trade, while the other market charged 5 percent, the individual would trade in the 2 percent market. Most microeconomic textbooks define an "efficient" market as *one in which the cost of the transaction is minimized.* Papers by West and Tinic define this attribute of a market as "internal" efficiency.[2]

Finally, a buyer or seller would want the prevailing market price to adequately reflect all the available supply and demand factors in the market. If supply and demand conditions change as a result of new information, participants would want this information to be reflected in the price of the commodity. Therefore, another requirement for a good market is that *prices adjust quickly to new information regarding supply or demand.* This attribute is referred to as "external" efficiency.

In summary, a good market for goods and services would have the following characteristics:

1. Timely and accurate information on the price and volume of past transactions and similar information on prevailing supply and demand.

2. Liquidity—a buyer or seller of a good or service can buy or sell the asset quickly, at a price that is close to the price of previous transactions, assuming no new information has been received. In turn, a liquid market requires price continuity; i.e., prices do not change very much from transaction to transaction. Price continuity itself requires depth. There must be a number of buyers and sellers willing and able to enter the market at prices above and below those prevailing.

3. Low transaction cost. This "internal" efficiency means that all aspects of the transaction entail low costs, including the cost of reaching the market, the actual brokerage cost involved in the transaction, as well as the cost of transferring the asset after the purchase or sale.

4. Rapid adjustment of prices to new information. This "external" efficiency ensures that the prevailing price reflects all available information regarding the asset.

Organization of the Securities Market

Before discussing the specific operation of the securities market, it is important that we understand the overall organization of the market. This understanding will provide insight into the purpose of the different segments of the securities market and their interrelationships. In this context, the principal distinction is

[2]Richard R. West and Seha M. Tinic, "Corporate Finance and the Changing Stock Market," *Financial Management* 3 (1974) 14–23; Richard R. West, "On the Difference Between Internal and External Market Efficiency," *Financial Analysts Journal* 31 (1975): 30–34.

between *primary* markets, where new securities are sold, and *secondary* markets, where outstanding securities are bought and sold. Within each of these markets there is a further division based upon the economic unit that issued the security, e.g., the U.S. Government, local municipalities, or corporations. In the following discussion, we will consider each of these major segments of the securities market with an emphasis on the individuals involved and the functions they perform.

Primary Markets

Primary Offerings

The primary market for securities is the one in which *new* issues of bonds, preferred stock, or common stock are sold by various economic units to acquire *new* capital. The important factor in this definition is that the proceeds of the sale of securities go to the issuing economic unit as new capital. Examples would include a new bond issue by the U.S. Treasury to finance some portion of the U.S. Government deficit; a municipal bond issue by the state of California to finance the construction of roads, schools, or state buildings; a debenture issue by International Business Machines (IBM) to finance the computers that they lease to customers; or a common stock issue by Anheuser-Busch to finance the construction of a new brewery.[3]

Primary issues are typically underwritten by investment bankers who acquire the total issue from the company and, in turn, sell the issue to interested investors. The underwriter gives advice to the economic unit selling the security on the general characteristics of the issue, its pricing, and the timing of the offering. He also accepts the risk of selling the new issue after he acquires it from the economic unit.[4]

After the bond or stock is sold by the economic unit through its underwriter, the security is traded (bought and sold) in the *secondary* securities market.

Secondary Markets

In secondary markets there is trading in outstanding issues. In this case, an issue has already been sold to the public, and it is traded between current and potential owners. Again, there are secondary markets for bonds, preferred stock, and

---

[3]An extensive analysis of this segment of the new issues market is contained in I. Friend, J. R. Longstreet, M. Mendelson, E. Miller, and A. P. Hess, Jr., *Investment Banking and the New Issues Market* (Cleveland, OH: World Publishing, 1967).

[4]For a detailed discussion of the underwriting process, see J. Fred Weston and Eugene F. Brigham, *Managerial Finance,* 6th ed. (Hinsdale, IL: Dryden Press, 1978), chapter 12.

common stock. The proceeds from a sale in the secondary market do *not* go the company but to the current owner of the security.

Before discussing the various segments of the secondary market, we must consider its overall importance. As noted, the secondary market involves trading securities initially sold in the primary market. Therefore, the secondary market provides *liquidity* to individuals who acquired securities in the primary markets. After you have acquired securities in the primary market, you want to be able to sell them at some point in the future to acquire other securities, buy a house, or go on a vacation. Such a sale takes place in the secondary market. Your ability to convert the asset into cash (your liquidity) is heavily dependent upon the secondary market. *The primary market would be seriously hampered in its function of helping firms acquire new capital without the liquidity provided by the secondary market.* Investors would be hesitant to acquire securities in the primary market if they felt they would not subsequently have the ability to sell the securities quickly, at a known price, in the secondary market.

Secondary markets are also important to a corporation because the prevailing market price of any security the firm issues is determined by action in the secondary market. Therefore, any seasoned new issue (i.e., additional shares of an outstanding issue) sold in the primary market will necessarily be priced in line with the current price of that firm's issues in the secondary market. As a result, the firm's current capital costs are determined in the secondary market.

Secondary Bond Markets

Types of Bonds

When considering the secondary markets for bonds, the distinction that should be made is the division between the vast number of bonds issued by the government, bonds issued by state and local government units, and bonds issued by individual business firms.

Government bond issues can be divided into several groups. The first group are those issued by the federal government and include long-term bonds and notes that have maturities of from one year to 25 years. In addition, there are short-term treasury bills that have maturities, at the time of issue, of from 90 to 180 days. There are a number of governmental agencies that likewise are authorized to issue their own bonds. Examples would include the Federal Home Loan Banks, the Federal Land Bank, the Federal National Mortgage Association (FNMA), and the World Bank. There is a more detailed discussion of these bonds in later chapters.

There is also a large market for bonds issued by state and local government units known as municipal bonds. These issues are typically broken down into general obligation securities (GOs) that are backed by the full taxing power of the municipality, and revenue issues that are backed by the expected revenues generated from a particular governmental service.

Corporate bonds are issued by industrial companies, railroads, and utilities.

There can be a large difference in the quality of these bonds depending upon the firm that issued them. Quality in this case refers to the ability of the firm to meet all required interest payments and the face value at maturity and is indicated by alternative bond ratings.[5]

Secondary Government and Municipal Bond Markets

All government bonds are traded by bond dealers specifically concerned with government bonds. These dealers are typically distinguished by the type of government bonds they handle. Some deal almost wholly in federal bonds, others are involved in agency bonds, and there is a virtually completely separate group of municipal bond dealers. Some of the most active government bond dealers are large banks in major cities like New York and Chicago and some of the large investment banking firms.

Banks are likewise active in municipal bond trading because a large part of their investment portfolios are committed to them. Many large investment banking firms also have municipal bond departments because such firms are active in underwriting these issues.

Secondary Corporate Bond Market

The secondary market for corporate bonds has two major segments, the exchanges and the over-the-counter market. The major exchange for bonds is the New York Stock Exchange (NYSE). As of the end of 1980 there were over 2,900 bond issues listed on the NYSE with a par value of over $500 billion and a market value of approximately $460 billion.[6] On a typical day about 1,000 of the issues are traded, and the volume of trading is about $25 million. In addition, there are about 200 issues listed on the American Stock Exchange (ASE) which has a typical daily volume of about $2 million. All corporate bonds not listed on one of the exchanges are traded over-the-counter by dealers who buy and sell for their own account. The majority of trading in corporate bonds is done on the over-the-counter market.

Secondary Equity Markets

Secondary equity markets are usually broken down into three major groups: the major national exchanges, including the New York Stock Exchange and the American Stock Exchange; what are usually called "regional exchanges" in cities like Chicago, San Francisco, Boston, Philadelphia, and Washington; and the over-the-counter market where securities not listed on an organized exchange are traded. The first two groups are similar in that they are referred to as listed securities exchanges; they differ in terms of size and geographic emphasis.

The listed securities exchanges are formal organizations that have a specified

---

[5]For a discussion of bond ratings, see Hugh C. Sherwood, *How Corporate and Municipal Debt is Rated* (New York: John Wiley & Sons, 1976), and the discussion in Chapter 14.

[6]*Fact Book* (New York: New York Stock Exchange, 1980), p. 71.

Pre-Tax Income Last Year	$ 2,500,000
Pre-Tax Income Last 2 Years	$ 2,000,000
Net Tangible Assets	$16,000,000
Shares Publicly Held	1,000,000
Market Value Publicly Held Shares[a]: Maximum	$16,000,000
Minimum	8,220,000
Number of Round-Lot Holders (100 shares or more)	2,000

Table 3.1   Listing Requirements for NYSE

[a]This required market value depends upon the value of the NYSE Common Stock Index. For specifics see the 1981 *Fact Book,* p. 29–31.

Source: *Fact Book* (New York: New York Stock Exchange, 1981). Reprinted by permission.

group of members that may use the facilities of the exchange, and a specified group of securities (stocks or bonds) that have qualified for "listing." In addition to limitations on membership and the securities eligible for trading, these exchanges are similar in that the prices of securities listed on them are determined via an auction process, whereby interested buyers and sellers submit "bids" and "asks" for a given stock at a central location for that stock. The bids and asks are recorded by a "specialist" assigned to that stock. Shares of stock are then sold to the highest bidder and bought from the investing unit (individual, institution, etc.) with the lowest asking price (the lowest offering price).

National Securities Exchange

Two securities exchanges are generally referred to as national in scope: the New York Stock Exchange (NYSE) and the American Stock Exchange (ASE). They are considered national because of the large number of securities they list, the geographic dispersion of the firms listed, and their clientele of buyers and sellers.

The New York Stock Exchange (NYSE)   This is the largest organized securities market in the United States. The initial constitution that formally established the exchange was adopted in 1817. The NYSE was originally named the "New York Stock and Exchange Board." This was changed to the New York Stock Exchange in 1863.

At the end of 1980, there were 1,565 companies with stock listed on the NYSE, and 2,192 stock issues (common and preferred) with a total market value of $961 billion. The specific listing requirements for the NYSE as of 1980 are contained in Table 3.1.

The average number of shares traded on the exchange has increased steadily as has the number of issues listed and the turnover of shares. The average daily volume in recent years is contained in Table 3.2. These figures indicate that prior to the 1960s, the average daily volume was less than 3 million shares. Daily volume increased to about 5 million shares in the early 1960s, increased again to about 10 million shares in the second half of the 1960s, and averaged

1940	751	1971	15,381
1945	1,422	1972	16,487
1950	1,980	1973	16,084
1955	2,578	1974	13,904
1960	3,042	1975	18,551
1961	4,085	1976	21,186
1962	3,818	1977	20,928
1963	4,567	1978	28,591
1964	4,888	1979	32,233
1965	6,176	1980	44,867
1966	7,538		
1967	10,080		
1968	12,971		
1969	11,403		
1970	11,564		

Table 3.2   Average Daily Reported Share Volume Traded
on the NYSE (thousands)

Source: *Fact Book* (New York: New York Stock Exchange, various years). Reprinted by permission.

about 15 million during the period 1970–1974. Starting in 1975 there was an increase to about 18–20 million shares a day. During 1978 trading increased to the 30 million share range that continued in 1979. Finally, in 1980 the average approached 45 million shares a day.

The domination of other listed exchanges by the NYSE is indicated by Table 3.3, which contains the percentage breakdown of share volume and the value of trading on that exchange. The NYSE has consistently accounted for about 75 percent of all shares traded on listed exchanges, as compared to about 10 to 20 percent for the ASE, and about 10 percent for all regional exchanges combined (the "other" category). Because the price of shares on the NYSE tends to be higher than that of shares on the ASE, the percentage of value of trading on the NYSE has averaged from 80 to 85 percent with lower figures for the ASE, while the regional exchanges are typically comparable in shares traded and the value of trading.

Based upon this clearly dominant position and the history of the NYSE, the exchange has been called a monopolist.[7] The volume of trading and dominant position are also reflected in the price of membership on the exchange (referred to as a "seat"). As shown in Table 3.4, the price of membership has fluctuated in line with trading volume and other factors that influence the profitability of membership.

[7]Robert W. Doede, "The Monopoly Power of the New York Stock Exchange" (Ph.D, University of Chicago, June 1967).

	Number of Shares Traded (Percent of Total)			Market Value of Shares Traded (Percent of Total)		
	NYSE	ASE	Other	NYSE	ASE	Other
1935	77.6	12.8	9.6	87.3	7.9	4.8
1940	76.0	12.9	11.1	85.3	7.7	7.0
1945	66.6	20.5	12.9	83.0	10.6	6.4
1950	76.5	13.4	10.1	86.0	6.8	7.2
1955	67.7	20.1	12.2	86.5	6.8	6.7
1960	69.0	21.6	9.3	83.9	9.2	6.8
1965	69.9	22.5	7.5	82.0	9.7	8.3
1970	70.8	19.4	9.8	78.7	10.9	10.4
1971	72.1	17.7	10.2	79.5	9.6	10.9
1972	71.4	17.5	11.1	78.3	10.0	11.7
1973	75.7	12.9	11.4	82.3	5.9	11.9
1974	79.0	9.8	11.2	83.9	4.3	11.9
1975	81.1	8.7	10.2	85.2	3.6	11.2
1976	80.3	9.1	10.7	84.4	3.8	11.8
1977	79.9	9.3	10.8	84.0	4.6	11.4
1978	80.3	10.5	9.2	84.4	6.1	9.5
1979	79.9	10.7	9.4	83.7	6.9	9.4
1980	80.0	10.7	9.3	83.6	7.3	9.1

Table 3.3   Shares Sold on Registered Exchanges

Source: Securities and Exchange Commission, *Annual Report* (Washington, D.C.: U.S. Government Printing Office); *Fact Book* (New York: New York Stock Exchange, various years). Reprinted by permission.

The American Stock Exchange (ASE)   The ASE was begun by a group of persons who traded unlisted shares at the corner of Wall and Hanover Streets in New York and was referred to as the Outdoor Curb Market. It made several moves along the streets of the financial district and, in 1910, formal trading rules were established and the name was changed to the New York Curb Market Association. The members moved inside a building in 1921 and continued to trade mainly in unlisted stocks (i.e., stocks not listed on one of the registered exchanges). The predominance of unlisted stocks continued until 1946, when listed stocks finally outnumbered unlisted stocks. The current name was adopted in 1953.[8]

[8]For a further discussion of the development of the ASE, see Robert Sobel, *The Curbstone Brokers: The Origins of the American Stock Exchange* (New York: Macmillan, 1970).

	NYSE		ASE			NYSE		ASE	
	High	Low	High	Low		High	Low	High	Low
1925	150	99	38	9	1971	300	145	150	65
1935	140	65	33	12	1972	250	150	145	70
1945	95	49	32	12	1973	190	72	100	27
1955	90	80	22	18	1974	105	65	60	27
1960	162	135	60	51	1975	138	55	72	34
1961	225	147	80	52	1976	104	40	68	40
1962	210	115	65	40	1977	95	35	52	21
1963	217	160	66	53	1978	105	46	65	25
1964	230	190	63	52	1979	210	82	90	40
1965	250	190	80	55	1980	275	175	270	95
1966	270	197	120	70					
1967	450	220	230	100					
1968	515	385	315	220					
1969	515	260	350	150					
1970	320	130	185	70					

Table 3.4   Membership Prices on the NYSE and the ASE
(in thousands of dollars)

Source: *Fact Book* (New York: New York Stock Exchange, various issues); *Amex Databook* (New York: American Stock Exchange, various issues). Reprinted by permission of the New York Stock Exchange and the American Stock Exchange.

    The ASE is distinct because of its desire to be different from the NYSE. A major factor in this uniqueness was that, prior to August 1976, no stocks were listed on the NYSE and ASE at the same time. This was changed in August 1976 when a request by the ASE to abolish "The New York Rule" was approved by the SEC.[9] This rule was an agreement between the two exchanges that no stock would be listed on both. Subsequently several firms listed on the ASE applied for listing on the NYSE but retained their ASE listing. Subsequently, most of them gave up their ASE listing because the great majority of trading was on the NYSE.[10]

    The ASE has been quite innovative in listing foreign securities over the years. There were over 70 foreign issues listed in 1980, and trading in these issues constituted over 10 percent of total volume.[11] Further, there were warrants listed on the ASE for a number of years before the NYSE would list them. The most recent

[9]"SEC Clears Trading on Amex of Stocks Listed on Big Board," *Wall Street Journal,* 23 August 1976, p. 3.

[10]The topic of dual listing on the NYSE and ASE is discussed further in the next chapter.

[11]American Stock Exchange Research Department.

1940	171	1966	2,741	1976	2,565
1945	583	1967	4,544	1977	2,514
1950	435	1968	6,353	1978	3,622
1955	912	1969	4,963	1979	4,182
1960	1,113	1970	3,319	1980	6,377
1961	1,948	1971	4,233		
1962	1,225	1972	4,454		
1963	1,262	1973	3,003		
1964	1,479	1974	1,908		
1965	2,120	1975	2,150		

Table 3.5   Average Daily Reported Share Volume Traded
on the American Stock Exchange (thousands)

Source: *Amex Databook* (New York: American Stock Exchange, various issues). Reprinted by permission.

innovation by the ASE has been the trading of call options on listed securities, introduced after option trading became wide spread with the establishment of the Chicago Board Options Exchange (CBOE). Again, because options are not traded on the NYSE (as of mid-1981) almost all options traded on the ASE are for stocks listed on the NYSE.

At the end of 1980, there were approximately 1,400 stock issues listed on the ASE.[12] As can be seen from the figures in Table 3.5 average daily trading volume has fluctuated substantially over time as the demand for smaller and younger firms, which are mainly traded on the ASE, has changed. Prior to 1955, average daily volume was below 500,000 shares. Average daily volume reached 1 million shares in 1959, almost 2 million in 1961, and exceeded 2 million in 1965 and 1966. In 1967, the average daily volume increased to 4.5 million and reached its highest level up to that time of 6.3 million shares a day in 1968. Trading volume declined to between 3 and 4 million shares a day during 1970–1973 and declined further to about 2 million shares a day during the period 1974–1977. This decline in volume is also reflected in the percent of trading as reported in Table 3.3. During 1978 and 1979 the exchange enjoyed an increase in trading volume similar to that of the NYSE and daily volume consistently exceeded four million shares. The resurgence carried into 1980 when the Exchange's average daily volume was over 6 million shares. Note that this figure exceeded the 1968 peak.

The American Stock Exchange is national in scope and, although also located in New York, is distinct from the NYSE. The companies listed on the ASE are almost completely different from those listed on the NYSE. In addition, ASE

[12]The requirements for listing on the ASE are contained in Table 3.6. The reader will note that the requirements are clearly less stringent than those for listing on the NYSE. As a result, the average firm on the ASE is substantially smaller than the typical firm on the NYSE in terms of sales, earnings, and assets.

Pre-Tax Income Last Year	$ 750,000
Pre-Tax Income Last 2 Years	—
Net Income Last Year	$ 400,000
Net Tangible Assets	$4,000,000
Shares Publicly Held	400,000
Market Value Publicly Held Shares	$3,000,000
Number of Round-Lot Holders	1,200

Table 3.6   Listing Requirements for ASE

Source: *Amex Databook* (New York: American Stock Exchange, 1980). Reprinted by permission.

firms are generally smaller and younger than the firms listed on the NYSE, which is consistent with the difference in listing requirements. To prosper and compete against the NYSE, the ASE has had a history of innovation. Because of the differences, most of the large brokerage firms are members of both the NYSE and the ASE.

Regional Securities Exchanges

Regional Exchanges have basically the same operating procedures as the NYSE and ASE, but differ in terms of their listing requirements and the geographic distribution of the firms listed. There are two main reasons for the existence of regional stock exchanges. First, they provide trading facilities for local companies that are not large enough to qualify for listing on one of the national exchanges. Second, they list national firms that are also listed on one of the national exchanges for local brokers who are not members of a national exchange. As an example, American Telephone and Telegraph and General Motors are both listed on the NYSE, but they are *also* listed on several regional exchanges. This dual listing of national firms allows a local brokerage firm that is not large enough to purchase a membership on the NYSE (for $55,000 or more) to buy and sell shares of a dual listed stock (e.g., General Motors) using his membership on a regional exchange. As a result, the broker will not have to go through the NYSE and give up part of his commission. Currently, about 90 percent of the volume on regional exchanges is attributable to trading in dual listed issues.[13]

The major regional exchanges are:

Midwest Stock Exchange (Chicago)

Pacific Stock Exchange (San Francisco—Los Angeles)

[13]For an extended discussion of the regional exchanges, see James E. Walter, *The Role of Regional Security Exchanges* (Berkeley: University of California Press, 1957). In the next chapter we will discuss more extensively the current and future status of the regional stock exchanges.

PBW Exchange (Philadelphia–Pittsburgh)

Boston Stock Exchange (Boston)

Spokane Stock Exchange (Spokane, Washington)

Honolulu Stock Exchange (Honolulu, Hawaii)

Intermountain Stock Exchange (Salt Lake City)

The first three exchanges (Midwest; Pacific; PBW) account for about 90 percent of all regional exchange volume. In turn, total regional volume is about 10 percent of total exchange volume as shown in Table 3.3 (regional stock exchange volume is the "other" category).

The Over-the-Counter (OTC) Market

The over-the-counter market encompasses trading in all stocks not listed on one of the exchanges. It can also include trading in stocks that are listed. This latter arrangement, referred to as the "third market," is discussed in the following section. The OTC market is not a formal market organization with membership requirements or a specific list of stocks deemed eligible for trading. In theory, it is possible to trade *any* security on the OTC market as long as someone is willing to "take a position" in the stock. This means an individual or firm is willing to buy or sell (i.e., "make a market" in the stock).

Size   The OTC market is the largest segment of the secondary market in terms of the number of issues traded and is also the most diverse in terms of quality. As noted earlier, there are about 2,000 issues traded on the NYSE, and about 1,400 issues on the ASE. In terms of active issues, there are about 2,500 traded on the OTC quotation system (NASDAQ described in the following section), inclusion in which requires certain size and at least two active market-makers. In addition, there are at least another 3,000–4,000 stocks that are traded fairly actively, but are not on NASDAQ. Therefore, there are between 5,500 and 6,500 issues traded on the OTC market—more issues than are traded on the NYSE and ASE combined. While the OTC is dominant in terms of the numbers of issues, the NYSE is still dominant in terms of the total *value* of the stocks.

There is tremendous diversity in the OTC because there are no minimum requirements for a stock to be traded. Therefore, it is possible for OTC listings to range from the smallest, most unprofitable company, to the largest, most profitable firm. On the upper end, all U.S. Government bonds are traded on the OTC market, as are the vast majority of bank stocks and insurance stocks. Finally, the 150 listed stocks that are *also* traded on the OTC (the third market), include AT&T, General Motors, IBM, Xerox, and a host of other stocks with active third markets.

Operation of the OTC   As noted, any stock can be traded on the OTC as long as someone indicates he is willing to "make a market" in the stock, i.e., buy or sell it for his own account. Therefore, *participants in the OTC market act as dealers* *because they buy and sell for their own accounts.*[14] This is in contrast to the situation on the listed exchanges where there is a "specialist", whose function will be defined later, and who is generally acting as an agent for other investors. Because of this, the OTC market is referred to as a *negotiated* market in which investors directly negotiate with dealers. Exchanges are *auction* markets with the specialist acting as the intermediary (auctioneer).

The NASDAQ System   NASDAQ is an acronym for the National Association of Securities Dealers Automatic Quotations. It is an electronic quotation system that serves the vast OTC market. Because any number of dealers can elect to make a market in an OTC stock, it is possible to have 10, 15, or more market-makers for a given stock, and it is common to have 3 to 5. A major problem has always been determining the current quotations offered by specific market-makers. Prior to the introduction of NASDAQ, it was necessary for a broker to make phone calls to three or four dealers to determine the prevailing market and then, after such a "survey," go back to the one with the best market for his client (i.e., the one with the highest bid or lowest asking price). With NASDAQ, all quotes by market-makers are available immediately, and the broker can make one phone call to the dealer with the best market, verify that the quote has not changed, and make the sale or purchase.

The National Association of Securities Dealers (NASD) has specified three levels for the NASDAQ system to serve firms with different needs and interests.[15] Level 1 is for firms that want current information on OTC stocks, but do not consistently buy or sell OTC stocks for their customers and are not market-makers. For these brokerage firms, a current quote on alternative OTC stocks is most important. Level 1 provides a single *median* ("representative") *quote* for all stocks in the system that takes into account all the market-makers (half the quotes are higher and half the quotes are lower). This composite quote is changed constantly to adjust for any changes by individual market-makers.

Level 2 is for firms that seriously trade in OTC stocks for themselves or their customers. For this clientele, Level 2 provides *instantaneous current individual quotations by all market-makers in a stock*. Given a desire to buy or sell, the broker examines all the individual quotations on the video screen and simply calls the market-maker with the best market for his purpose (highest bid if he is selling or lowest offer if he wants to buy) and consummates the deal.

Level 3 is for investment firms that make markets in OTC stocks. Such firms want to know what everyone else is quoting (Level 2), but they also need the capability to enter their own quotations and the ability to *change* their quotations. This is what Level 3 provides, everything in Level 2 plus the ability to enter the system and change quotes.

---

[14]Dealer and market-maker are synonymous.

[15]A detailed description of the NASDAQ system is contained in *NASDAQ and the OTC* (Washington, D.C.: National Association of Securities Dealers), or *The NASDAQ Revolution: How Over-the-Counter Securities are Traded* (New York: Merrill Lynch, Pierce, Fenner & Smith, 1978).

A Sample Trade   Assume an investor is considering the purchase of 100 shares of Wendy's International. Although Wendy's is large enough and profitable enough to be eligible for listing on a national exchange, the company has never applied for listing because it enjoys a very active market on the OTC (daily volume is typically above 50,000 shares and often exceeds 100,000 shares). Therefore, when the individual contacts his broker, the broker will consult the NASDAQ electronic quotation machine to determine the current markets for WNDY (the trading symbol for Wendy's).[16] The display screen on his Level 2 machine would indicate that about 10 dealers are making a market in WNDY. An example of differing markets might be as follows:

Dealer	Bid	Ask
1	$14^1/_4$	$14^3/_4$
2	$14^3/_8$	$14^3/_4$
3	$14^1/_4$	$14^5/_8$
4	$14^1/_2$	15
5	$14^1/_8$	$14^3/_4$

If we assume for the moment that these are the best markets available from the total group, the investor's broker would then call dealer number 3 because he had the lowest offering price; i.e., he was willing to sell at the lowest price. He would verify the quote and then tell dealer number 3 that he wants to buy 100 shares of WNDY at $14^5/_8$ (14.625 a share). Because the investor's firm was not a market-maker in the stock, the firm would probably act as a broker for the customer and charge $1,462.50 plus a commission for the trade. If the customer had been interested in selling 100 shares of Wendy's, the broker would have contacted dealer number 4 because he had the highest bid, i.e., dealer 4 was willing to pay the most to buy the stock. If the broker was also a market-maker in WNDY and had the quote of $14^1/_4 - 14^5/_8$, then he would have sold the stock to the customer at $14^5/_8$ "net" (without commission).

Changing Dealer Inventory   It seems useful at this point to consider the quotation an OTC dealer would give if he wanted to change his inventory on a given stock. For example, assume dealer number 2 with a current quote of $14^3/_8 - 14^3/_4$ decides that he wants to *increase* his holdings of WNDY. An examination of the quotes on his NASDAQ quote machine indicates that the highest bid is currently

[16]Trading symbols are one- to four-letter codes used to designate stocks. Whenever a trade is reported on a stock ticket the trading symbol is used. Many are obvious, like GM (General Motors), F (Ford Motors), GE (General Electric), or T (American Telephone and Telegraph).

$14\frac{1}{2}$. He can increase his bid to $14\frac{1}{2}$ and get some of the business currently going to dealer number 4, or, if he wants to be very aggressive, he can raise his bid to $14\frac{5}{8}$ and buy all of the stock that is offered, including some from dealer number 3 who is offering it at $14\frac{5}{8}$. In this example, the dealer raises his bid but does not change his asking price, which was above another dealer's. Thus he is going to buy stock, but probably will not sell any. If the dealer had more stock than he wanted, he would keep his bid below the market (lower than $14\frac{1}{2}$) and reduce his asking price to $14\frac{5}{8}$ or less. Dealers are constantly changing their bid and/or asking price, depending upon their current inventory or the outlook for the stock.

The Third Market

The term third market is used to describe *over-the-counter trading of shares listed on an exchange*. Most of the activity on this market is conducted by large financial institutions trading in large, well-known stocks like AT&T, General Motors, and IBM. This segment of the market grew dramatically from 1965 through 1972 because it provided a means for large institutions to avoid the high commissions charged for large transactions on the NYSE. As will be discussed in Chapter 4, when negotiated commissions were introduced, there was a decline in third market activity because this market no longer provided a cost savings relative to prices on the NYSE.

The Fourth Market   The term fourth market is used to describe *the direct trading of securities between two parties* with no broker intermediary. In almost all cases, both parties involved are institutions.

The fourth market evolved because the brokerage fee charged institutions with large orders is substantial. At some point it becomes worthwhile for institutions to attempt to deal directly with each other and save the brokerage fee. Consider an institution that decides to sell 40,000 shares of AT&T. Assuming that AT&T is selling for about $50 a share, the value of the 40,000 shares is $2 million. The average commission on such a transaction, before negotiated rates were introduced (see Chapter 4), was about one percent of the value of the trade which, for this trade, would be $20,000. Given this cost, it becomes attractive for the selling institution to spend some time and effort finding another institution interested in increasing its holding of AT&T and attempting to negotiate a direct sale. Because of the diverse nature of the fourth market and the lack of reporting requirements, there are no data available regarding its specific size or growth, although it is generally conceded that is has grown, especially in trading of the large institutional favorites, such as IBM and AT&T.

Detailed Analysis of the Exchange Market

Because of the importance of the listed exchange market, it must be dealt with at some length. In this section we will discuss the types of membership on the exchanges, the major types of orders used, and finally the function of the specialist who is considered the main determinant of a "good" exchange market.

Exchange Membership

Listed securities exchanges typically have five major categories of membership: (1) specialist, (2) odd-lot dealer, (3) commission broker, (4) floor broker, and (5) registered trader.

Specialists   They constitute about 25 percent of the total membership on exchanges. Specialists are considered by some observers to be the most important group because, as will be discussed, they are responsible for maintaining a fair and orderly market in the securities listed on an exchange.

Odd-Lot Dealers   These dealers stand ready to buy or sell less than a round lot of stock (a round lot is typically a multiple of 100 shares). When an individual wants to buy fewer than 100 shares, the order is turned over to an odd-lot dealer who will buy or sell from his own inventory. Note that the dealer is *not* a broker, and that he is buying and selling from his own inventory. Prior to 1976, all odd-lot transactions were handled by odd-lot houses. Since then, the NYSE has taken over the function. On most other exchanges, the specialist in a stock is also the odd-lot dealer for the stock. Some large brokerage firms (most notably Merrill Lynch, Pierce, Fenner & Smith, Inc.) have been acting as odd-lot dealers for their own customers.

Commission Brokers   They are employees of a member firm who buy or sell for the customers of the firm. When an investor places an order to buy or sell stock through a registered representative of a brokerage firm, and the firm has a membership on an exchange, it will contact its commission broker who will go to the appropriate post on the floor of the exchange to buy or sell the stock as instructed.

Floor Brokers   These are members of an exchange who act as brokers on the floor for other members. They are typically not connected with a member firm but own their own seats. When the commission broker for Merrill Lynch becomes too busy to handle all of his orders, he will ask one of the floor brokers to help. At one time they were referred to as "$2 brokers" because that is what they received for each order. Currently, they receive about $4 per 100 share order.

Registered Traders   They are allowed to use their membership to buy and sell for their own account. They therefore save the commission on their own trading, and observers feel they have an advantage because they are on the floor and can react quickly to new information. The exchanges and others feel they should be allowed these advantages because registered traders provide the market with added liquidity. Because of possible abuses, there are regulations regarding how registered traders can trade and how many registered traders can be in a trading crowd around a specialists' booth at a point in time.

Types of Orders

The reader should have a full understanding of the different types of orders used by individual investors and by the specialist in his dealer function. The most frequent type is a market order. A *market order* is an order to buy or sell a stock at the best price currently prevailing. An investor who wants to sell some stock using a market order indicates that he would be willing to sell *immediately* at the highest bid available at the time the order reaches the specialist on the exchange. A market buy order indicates the investor is willing to pay the lowest offering price available at the time the order reaches the floor of the exchange. Market orders are used when an individual wants to effect a transaction *quickly* (wants immediate liquidity), and is willing to accept the prevailing market price. Assume an investor is interested in American Telephone and Telegraph (AT&T) and called his broker to find out the current "market" on the stock. Using a quotation machine, the broker determines that the prevailing market is 52 bid—$52^{1}/4$ ask. This means that currently the highest bid on the books of the specialist, i.e., the most that anyone has offered to pay for AT&T, is 52. The lowest offer is $52^{1}/4$, which is the lowest price someone is willing to accept for selling the stock. If an investor placed a market buy order for 100 shares, he would buy 100 shares at $52.25 a share (the lowest ask price) for a total cost of $5,225 plus commission. If an investor submitted a market sell order for 100 shares, he would sell the shares at $52 each and receive $5,200, less commission.

The second major category is a *limit order,* which means that the individual placing the order has specified the price at which he will buy or sell the stock. An investor might submit a bid to purchase 100 shares of stock at $48 a share, when the current market is 52 bid—$52^{1}/4$ ask, with the expectation that the stock will decline to $48 in the near future. Such an order must also indicate *how long* the limit order will be outstanding. The alternatives, in terms of time, are basically without bounds—they can be instantaneous ("fill or kill"—fill instantly or cancel it), for part of a day, for a full day, for several days, a week, a month, or open ended, which means the order is good until cancelled (GTC). Rather than wait for a given price on a stock, a broker will give the limit order to the specialist, who will put it in his book and act as the broker's representative. When and if the market reaches the limit order price, the specialist will execute the order and inform the broker. The specialist receives a small part of the commission for rendering this service.

While most investors purchase stock with the expectation that they will derive their return from an increase in value, there are instances in which an investor believes that a stock is overpriced, and wants to take advantage of an expected decline in the price. The way to do this is to *sell the stock short.* A *short sale* is the sale of stock that is not owned, with the intent of purchasing it later at a lower price. The investor *borrows* the stock from another investor through his broker and sells it in the market. He will subsequently repurchase the stock (hopefully, at a price lower than the one at which he sold it) and thereby replace it. The investor who lent the stock has the use of the money paid for it, because it is left with him as collateral on the stock loan. While there is no time limit on a short sale, the lender can indicate that he wants to sell his shares, in which case the broker must find another investor willing to lend his stock.

Two technical points in connection with short sales are important. First, a short sale can only be made on an uptick trade (the price of the sale must be higher than the last trade price). The reason for this restriction is that the exchanges do not want traders to be able to *force* a profit on a short sale by pushing the price down through continually selling short. Therefore, the transaction price for a short sale must be an uptick or, if there is no change in price, the previous price must have been higher than its previous price (a zero uptick). An example of a zero uptick would be the following set of transaction prices: 42, 42$\frac{1}{4}$, 42$\frac{1}{4}$. You could sell short at 42$\frac{1}{4}$ even though the price is unchanged from the previous trade at 42$\frac{1}{4}$. Second, the short seller is responsible for the dividends to the investor who lent the stock. The purchaser of the short-sale stock receives the dividend from the corporation, so the short seller must pay a similar dividend to the lender.

In addition to these general orders, there are several special types of orders. One is a *stop-loss order,* which is a conditional market order, whereby the investor indicates that he wants to sell a stock *if* the stock drops to a given price. Assume an individual buys a stock at 50 and expects it to go up. If he's wrong, he wants to minimize or limit his losses. Therefore, he would put in a stop-loss order at 45, in which case, *if* the stock price dropped to 45, his stop-loss order would become a *market sell order,* and the stock would be sold at the prevailing market price. Another example would be if the investor bought the stock at 50 and it increased to 100. At that point the investor might want to hold the stock for further possible gains, but might also want to protect the profit already realized. To do this he might put in a stop-loss order at 90, in which case, if the price began to decline, he would automatically sell out at about $90. The order does not guarantee that the investor will get the specified price; he can get a little bit more or a little bit less. Because of the possibility of market disruption caused by a large number of stop-loss orders, the stock exchanges, on occasion, have canceled all stop-loss orders on certain stocks and have not allowed brokers to accept further stop-loss orders on the issues involved.

Another type of stop loss, but on the other side, is a *stop-buy order.* These are used by an investor who has sold stock short and wants to minimize any loss if the stock begins to increase in value. This order makes it possible to place a conditional buy order at a price above the price at which he sold the stock short. Assume you had sold a stock short at 50, expecting it to decline to 40. To protect yourself from an increase, you could put in a stop-buy order to purchase the stock if it reached a price of 55. This would limit any loss on the short sale to approximately $5 a share.

Margin Transactions   Given any type of order, the investor can pay for the stock with cash or can borrow part of the cost, i.e., can *leverage* the transaction. Leverage is accomplished by *buying or selling on margin* which means that the investor pays some cash and borrows the rest through his broker, putting up the stock for collateral. The determination of the maximum proportion that can be borrowed is set by the Federal Reserve Board under Regulations T and U. These regulations were enacted during the 1930s because it was contended that the excessive credit extended for stock acquisition was a reason for the stock market collapse of 1929. Since the enactment of the regulations, the margin requirement (the proportion of total value that must be paid for in cash) has varied from 40 percent (you could borrow 60 percent of the value) to 100 percent (no borrowing allowed). As of June 1981, the *initial margin requirement* is 50 percent. After the initial purchase, the market price of the stock will vary such that the proportion of *equity* will change (equity equals the market value of the collateral stock minus the amount borrowed). Obviously, if the stock price increases, the investor's equity as a proportion of the total value of the stock will increase (i.e., the investor's margin will exceed the initial margin requirement). In contrast, if the stock price declines, the investor's equity will decline. At this point, the relevant criterion is the *maintenance margin,* the proportion of equity to the total value of the stock. At present, the maintenance margin is 25 percent. If the stock price declines to the point where the investor's equity drops below 25 percent of the total value of the stock position, the account is considered undermargined, and the investor must provide more equity (the investor will receive a margin call), or the stock will be sold to pay off the loan.

It is important to recognize that buying on margin provides all the advantages *and* disadvantages of leverage; i.e., the *lower* the margin, the more you can borrow and the *greater* the percentage gain or loss on your investment when the stock price increases or decreases. The leverage factor is equal to 1/percent margin. Thus, if the margin is 50 percent, the leverage factor is two. This means that if the rate of return on the stock is plus or minus 10 percent, the return on the equity for an investor who borrowed 50 percent of the purchase price would be plus or minus 20 percent. If the margin declines to 33 percent, you can borrow more (67 percent) and the leverage factor is three (1/.33). Therefore, when you acquire stock or other investments using margin, you are increasing the financial risk of the investment beyond that which is inherent in the security itself, and you should increase your required return accordingly.

The Specialist

With justification, the stock exchange specialist has been referred to as the center of the auction market for stocks. As noted, a major requirement for a "good" market is liquidity which necessitates price continuity and depth. The existence of these characteristics is heavily dependent upon how the specialist does his job.

The specialist is a member of the exchange who applies for his position by asking the exchange to assign stocks to him. The typical specialist will handle about 15 stocks. He must possess substantial capital to carry out this function, either $500,000 or enough to purchase 5,000 shares of the stock, whichever is greater. He must also have the knowledge to fulfill the functions of a specialist.

Functions of the Specialist

The specialist has two major functions. The first is that of a *broker* who handles the limit orders or special orders placed with member brokers. An individual broker who receives a limit order to purchase a stock at five dollars below the current market does not have the time or inclination to constantly watch the stock to determine when and if the decline takes place. Therefore, he leaves the limit order (or a stop-loss or stop-buy order) with the specialist who enters it in his book and executes it when appropriate. For this service the specialist receives a portion of the broker's commission on the trade.

The second major function is to act as a *dealer* in the stocks assigned to him to maintain a "fair and orderly market." He is expected to buy and sell *for his own account* when there is insufficient public supply or demand to provide a continuous, liquid market. In this function he is acting like a dealer on the OTC market. If a stock is currently selling for about $40 per share, one could envision a situation in an auction market in which the current bid and ask (without the intervention of the specialist) might be a 40 bid—41 ask. Assuming this spread is considered too large for the stock involved, the specialist is expected to provide an alternative bid and/or ask that will narrow the spread and thereby provide greater price continuity over time. In the above example this would entail either entering a bid of $40\frac{1}{2}$ or $40\frac{3}{4}$ or an ask of $40\frac{1}{2}$ or $40\frac{1}{4}$ to narrow the spread to one-half or one-quarter point. The specialist can enter *either* side of the market or *both* sides (e.g., he could enter a bid of $40\frac{1}{4}$ and an ask of $40\frac{3}{4}$). Which side he enters will depend upon several factors. The first is *the trend of the market*. Because he is committed to being a stabilizing force in the market, he is expected to buy or sell *against* the market when prices are clearly moving in one direction; i.e., he is expected to buy stock for his own inventory when there is an excess of sell orders and the market is definitely declining, or to sell stock from his inventory or sell it short when there is an excess of buy orders and the market is rising. He is not expected to prevent the price from rising or declining, but only to ensure that the price changes in an orderly fashion.

Another factor is *his current inventory position in the stock*. If a specialist has a large inventory, he will enter on the ask side to reduce his inventory. In contrast, if he has very little inventory or if he is currently short stock, he will enter a bid to acquire stock.

Finally, *the position of his book* (i.e., the specialist's information on all limit orders for a stock) will influence his actions, assuming there are no current trends to which he must react. If the specialist notes a large number of limit buy orders (bids) close to the current market, and very few limit sell orders (asks), he might surmise that the most likely future move for the stock, in the absence of any new information, is toward a higher price because there is apparently heavy demand and limited supply. Under such conditions, one would expect the specialist to attempt to accumulate some stock in anticipation of an increase.

Income

The specialist derives income from both of his major functions. The actual breakdown between income from acting as a broker for limit orders, and income from acting as a dealer to maintain an orderly market will depend upon the specific stock. In the case of a very actively traded stock (e.g., American Telephone and Telegraph), there is not much need for the specialist to act as a dealer because substantial public interest in the issue creates a tight market. The major concern of the specialist (and his main source of income for this stock) is maintaining the limit orders for the stock. In contrast, in the case of a stock with low trading volume and substantial price volatility, the specialist would constantly have to enter his own bid and/or ask to stabilize the market; i.e., he would be an active dealer, and his income would depend upon his ability to profitably trade in the stock. A major advantage for the specialist in his trading of the stock is his access to the "book" that contains all limit orders for the stock in question. This book should provide the specialist with significant information regarding the probable direction of movement for the stock, at least in the short run.

Therefore, although specialists may be forced to buy or sell against the market for short periods of time, over longer periods they should make substantial profits on their dealer transactions because of the monopoly source of information contained in the specialist's book.[17] In addition, the income derived from acting as a broker for limit orders can be substantial and is basically without risk. Most specialists attempt to balance the stocks assigned to them between the two types: they will have some strong "broker" stocks that provide a steady riskless source of income, and some stocks that require an active dealer role.

Given the capital committed to the specialist function and the risk involved in acting as a dealer, one might wonder about the rate of return that specialists receive on their capital. Based upon the discussion in Chapter 2, we know the long-run returns to investors in the stock market are 10 percent. In contrast, a study by the SEC indicated that although there has been substantial variation, the overall returns to specialists have been substantial. Specifically, returns on investment for specialists have varied from about 80 percent to 180 percent and averaged about 110 percent.[18]

The value of being able to trade using the monopoly information contained in the specialist's book clearly should not be underrated. The specialist performs a very useful function on the exchange, but it also appears that the rate of return he receives is excessive for the risk involved. These excess returns seem to be the result of the very strong position of the NYSE in the secondary exchange market and the monopoly position of the specialists in terms of information regarding their respective stocks. Because of the excess returns the specialist receives, one of the stated goals of the SEC is to introduce more competition into the market-making function. The idea is to maintain the basic structure of the exchange, but introduce more competiton to reduce the costs to the investor. In Chapter 4, we will consider some of the changes that have taken place in the securities markets

[17]In this regard, see Frank K. Reilly and Eugene F. Drzycimski, "The Stock Exchange Specialist and the Market Impact of Major World Events," *Financial Analysts Journal* 31 (1975): 27–32.

[18]United States House Committee on Interstate and Foreign Commerce, subcommittee on Commerce and Finance. *Securities Industry Study: Report and Hearings.* 92nd Congress, 1st and 2nd sessions 1972, Chapter 12.

during the past decade and their effect on the specialist and other members of the securities market.

Summary

This chapter has been concerned with what a market is, why markets exist, and what constitutes a "good" market. It also included a discussion of the division of the securities market into primary and secondary markets, and why secondary markets are important for primary markets. We then considered the major segments of the secondary markets, including listed exchanges (the NYSE, the ASE, and regional exchanges); the over-the-counter market; the third market; and the fourth market. The final section included a detailed analysis of the exchange market and a discussion of the membership on an exchange, a consideration of the types of orders used on the exchange, and an in-depth look at the specialist function.

Questions

1.   Define a market.

2.   You own 100 shares of General Motors stock, and you want to sell it because you need the money to make a down payment on a car. Assume there is *absolutely no secondary market system* in common stocks—how would you go about selling the stock? Discuss what you would have to do to find a buyer, how long it might take, and the price you might receive.

3.   Briefly discuss the major characteristics of a "good" market.

4.   Define liquidity and discuss what factors contribute to liquidity. Give an example of a liquid asset, and illiquid asset, and discuss why they are considered liquid and illiquid.

5.   Define a primary market for securities.

6.   Find an advertisement for a recent primary offering by a corporation in the *Wall Street Journal*. Based upon the information in the ad, indicate the characteristics of the security sold and the major underwriters. How much new capital did the firm derive from the offering before commissions were paid?

7.   What is a secondary market for securities? How does it differ from the primary market?

8.   Some observers would contend that, without a good secondary market for securities, the primary market would be less effective. Discuss the reasoning behind this contention.

9.   In the section of the *Wall Street Journal* on government bonds titled "Treasury Bonds and Notes," what is the current bid and yield on the $8^{1}/_{4}$s of 1990?

10. How do the two national stock exchanges differ from each other?

11. What are the major reasons for the existence of the regional exchanges? How do they differ from the national exchanges?

12. How does the OTC market differ from the listed exchanges?

13. Which segment of the secondary market (listed or OTC) is larger in terms of the number of issues? In terms of the value of the issues traded?

14. Which segment of the secondary market (national exchanges or OTC) has more diversity in terms of the size of the companies and the quality of the issues? Why is this so?

15. What is the NASDAQ system? Discuss the three levels of NASDAQ in terms of what they provide and who would subscribe to each.

16. What are the benefits derived from NASDAQ? What has it done for the OTC market?

17. Define the third market. Give an example of a third-market stock.

18. Why is there a limited number of stocks that are actively traded on the third market?

19. Define the fourth market. Why would a financial institution use the fourth market?

20. What is the major advantage of the fourth market? What is its major disadvantage?

21. Define a market order and give an example for a person selling 100 shares of stock.

22. Briefly define each of the following terms and give an example:
  a. limit order
  b. short sale
  c. stop-loss order

23. The initial margin requirement is 60 percent. You have $30,000 to invest in a stock selling for $75 a share. Ignoring taxes and commissions, show in detail the impact in terms of rate of return if the stock rises to $100 a share and if it declines to $40 a share assuming: (a) you pay cash for the stock; (b) you buy it using the maximum amount of leverage available.

24. Discuss the two major functions of the specialist.

25. Over a long-run period (e.g., six months), would you expect the specialist to make money in his dealer function? Why or why not?

26. What are the two main sources of income for the specialist?

27. Other than the example in the chapter, give an example of a stock that would be a broker stock for the specialist. Why is it a broker stock?

28. What is the high-risk segment of the specialists' dealer function? Why is it high risk? What aspect of the specialist position reduces the risk involved and also increases potential return? Be specific.

References

Amex Databook. New York: American Stock Exchange, published every two or three years.

Baumol, William J. *The Stock Market and Economic Efficiency.* New York: Fordham University Press, 1965.

Doede, Robert W. "The Monopoly Power of the New York Stock Exchange." Dissertation, University of Chicago, June, 1967.

Eiteman, W. J.; Dice, C. A.; and Eiteman, D. K. *The Stock Market.* 4th ed. New York: McGraw-Hill, 1966.

Fact Book. New York: New York Stock Exchange, published annually.

Friend, Irwin, and Winn, W. J. *The Over-the-Counter Securities Markets.* New York: McGraw-Hill, 1958.

Leffler, George L., and Farwell, Loring, *The Stock Market.* 3d ed. New York: Ronald Press, 1963.

Loll, Leo M., and Buckley, Julian G. *The Over-the Counter Securities Markets.* 4th ed. Englewood Cliffs, NJ: Prentice-Hall, 1981.

NASDAQ and the OTC. New York: National Association of Securities Dealers, 1974.

Regan, Donald T. *A View From the Street.* New York: New American Library, 1972.

Robbins, Sidney. *The Securities Markets: Operations and Issues.* New York: Free Press, 1966.

Sobel, Robert. *The Big Board.* New York: Free Press, 1965.

Sobel, Robert. *The Curbstone Brokers: The Origins of the American Stock Exchange.* New York: Macmillan, 1970.

Sobel, Robert. *N.Y.S.E.: A History of the New York Stock Exchange," 1935–1975.* New York: Weybright and Talley, 1975.

Walter, James E. *The Role of Regional Security Exchanges.* Berkeley: University of California Press, 1957.

West, Richard R., and Tinic, Seha M. *The Economics of the Stock Market.* New York: Praeger, 1971.

THE SECURITIES MARKET: PAST AND FUTURE CHANGES

⇒ 4 ⇐

The previous chapter was concerned with a general description of securities markets, what they are intended to do, and how they function. In textbooks written prior to 1970, such a discussion would have completed the analysis of securities markets. In 1965, however, a series of changes began which, by 1970, had profoundly affected these markets. It is necessary, therefore, to add a specific consideration of *what* these changes were and *why* the markets have changed. This analysis will also provide you with an insight into possible future developments.

Changes in the Securities Markets

Why the Market Is Changing

Before we discuss the specific changes in the securities markets that have transpired over the past 16 years, the reader should fully appreciate *why* these changes have occurred. *Almost all the changes have been prompted by the significant and rapid growth of trading by large financial institutions* like banks, insurance companies, pension funds, and investment companies. The amount of trading by these institutions (in both absolute and relative terms) has grown dramatically since 1965. The trading patterns and requirements of institutions are different from those of individual investors. The market mechanism was basically developed and shaped to serve individuals who were the main customers of the securities exchanges. When this mechanism was used by completely different customers whose trading patterns were significantly different, there were problems.

Therefore, regarding the question of why the market changed, the answer is simply that *the changes were prompted by a new, dominant clientele with requirements that were substantially different from those of the original clientele.*

1961—197	1967—257	1973—449	1979—787
1962—204	1968—302	1974—438	1980—872
1963—213	1969—356	1975—495	
1964—218	1970—388	1976—559	
1965—224	1971—428	1977—641	
1966—240	1972—443	1978—717	

Table 4.1   Average Shares Per Sale Printed on the NYSE Tape

Source: *Fact Book* (New York: New York Stock Exchange, various issues). Reprinted by permission.

Evidence of Institutionalization

An indication of the growing impact of large financial institutions can be derived from data on size of trades, block trades, and overall institutional trading. It is assumed, because of the size of institutional portfolios, that the institutional portfolio managers buy and sell large quantities ("blocks") rather than 100–200 share lots. (A "block" is defined as a transaction involving at least 10,000 shares.)

Year	Total Number of Transactions	Total Number of Shares (000)	Percent of Reported Volume	Average Number of Block Transactions per Day
1965	2,171	48,262	3.1	9
1966	3,642	85,298	4.5	14
1967	6,685	169,365	6.7	27
1968	11,254	292,680	10.0	50
1969	15,132	402,063	14.1	61
1970	17,217	450,908	15.4	68
1971	26,941	692,536	17.8	106
1972	31,207	766,406	18.5	124
1973	29,233	721,356	17.8	116
1974	23,200	549,387	15.6	92
1975	34,420	778,540	16.6	136
1976	47,632	1,001,254	18.7	188
1977	54,275	1,183,924	22.4	215
1978	75,036	1,646,905	22.9	298
1979	97,509	2,164,726	26.5	385
1980	133,597	3,311,132	29.2	528

Table 4.2   Block Transactions on the NYSE (10,000 Shares or More)

Source: *Fact Book* (New York: New York Stock Exchange, various issues). Reprinted by permission.

Average Size of Trades   One indication of increased institutional trading, therefore, is an increase in the average size of trades as reflected in the average number of shares per sale printed on the NYSE ticker tape. As shown in Table 4.1, the size of an average trade has grown steadily and has more than tripled during the last 20 years. Note especially the rapid growth since 1967.

Growth of Block Trades   Because financial institutions are the main source of large block trades, further evidence of institutional involvement can be derived from the data on block trades contained in Table 4.2. The number of large block trades grew steadily at a very high rate from 1965 through 1972. There was a slight leveling off in 1973 and a definite decline in 1974 coincident with a decline in stock prices. The growth resumed in 1975 and has continued through 1980. One can derive an appreciation for the tremendous growth in block trades by considering the average number of block trades per day. As recently as 1965 there were only 9 block trades *a day*; obviously they were a relatively rare occurrence. Since 1979, the average has generally exceeded 400 such trades a day. This means that in a six-hour trading day, there are about 65 block trades *an hour*. A block trade is no longer rare. In fact, such trades constitute a major part of the volume on the exchange, consistently in excess of 25 percent.

Public Transactions Studies   As shown in Table 4.3, prior to 1963, individuals accounted for about 70 percent of all trading. The environment began to change in 1965 and 1966, when trading by individuals dropped below 60 percent. The trend continued and is quite noticeable in the 1971 figures which show that *the majority of public trading on the NYSE at that time was done by institutions (62 percent)*. The most recent studies, done during the first quarters of 1974 and 1976, indicate that institutions accounted for about 58 percent of public trading volume.

In summary, the size of trade, number of block trades, and proportion of public volume all indicate substantial growth in trading by financial institutions.

Effects of Institutional Investments on the Securities Markets

The previous discussion indicated that institutions currently dominate the total equity capital market and they differ in how they trade (e.g., they trade 2,000–20,000 shares versus 200–1,000 shares for individuals). This difference in trading patterns has had a profound effect on the functioning of the market in several areas.

Fixed Commission Schedule

Because the securities markets were designed for the individual investor, the system was established to handle transactions involving fewer than 1,000

	Percentage Distribution			Percentage Distribution	
	Individuals	Institutions[b]		Individuals	Institutions[b]
September, 1952	69.2	30.8	First Half, 1969	44.6	55.4
March, 1953	75.0	25.0	Second Half, 1969	43.5	56.5
March, 1954	69.7	30.3	First Quarter, 1971	42.6	57.4
December, 1954	78.7	21.3	Second Quarter, 1971	37.6	62.4
June, 1955	75.5	24.5			
March, 1956	75.0	25.0	First Quarter, 1974	41.1	58.9
October, 1957	71.1	28.9	First Quarter, 1976	42.7	57.3
September, 1958	71.4	28.6			
June, 1959	70.6	29.4			
September, 1960	68.6	31.4			
September, 1961	66.7	33.3			
October, 1963	69.1	30.9			
March, 1965	60.7	39.3			
October, 1966	57.0	43.0			

Table 4.3   Public Volume Shares Bought and Sold on the NYSE[a]

[a]Prior to 1959, data are daily averages for two days (the 1958 data are a projection from a 10 percent sample); for 1959–1966 studies, data are for one day; for 1969 study data are daily averages for the year.

[b]Institutions consist of closed-end investment companies, educational institutions, foundations, guardianships, investment clubs, life and other insurance companies, mutual funds, nonbank administered estates, nonfinancial corporations, nonprofit organizations, partnerships, pension funds, personal holding companies, personal trusts, profit sharing plans having legal ownership of the shares bought and sold, religious groups, saving banks, commercial banks and trust companies, and nonmember broker-dealers.

Source: *Fact Book* (New York: New York Stock Exchange, 1981), p. 52. Reprinted by permission.

shares, and the pricing of trading services was developed to compensate for the handling of small orders. The NYSE developed a *minimum* fixed commission schedule that all exchange members had to abide by. A major effect of heavy institutional trading came in the area of the fixed commission structure because the commissions made no allowance for the substantial economies of scale involved in trading large orders. The increased cost of trading 10,000 shares as opposed to 300 or 400 shares is relatively small. If it costs $20 to sell 300 shares, it probably costs no more than $30 or $40 to sell 10,000 shares, and possibly less. These economies of scale were not adequately taken into account in the commission structure. The commission charged for a 10,000 share block was approximately five times as much as that charged for a 1,000 share trade.[1]

[1]Using the commission schedule in effect in 1970, the commission charge for selling 1,000 shares of a $30 stock would be $262; the commission charge for selling 10,000 shares of this stock would be $1,342.

Reaction to High Commissions

When institutions began trading heavily, the first reaction to the high prices the commission schedule involved was the introduction of "give-ups." The practice of give-ups evolved because brokers acknowledged that they received more for large transactions than was justified by the costs involved. Brokers consequently agreed to pay part of their commissions to other brokerage houses or research firms designated by the institution making the trade. If a brokerage house received $2,000 for a trade by a mutual fund, they were instructed to "give up" some portion of this commission (sometimes as much as 80 percent) to another brokerage house that had been selling the mutual fund, or to a research firm that had provided research to the mutual fund. As a consequence, institutions used part of their excess commission dollars to pay for services other than brokerage. (These commission dollars were referred to as "soft" dollars.)

Another response to the high commissions was the increased use of the third market. One of the advantages of trading in the third market was that commissions were not fixed and regulated as they were on the NYSE. Therefore, institutions could negotiate commissions for trades in the third market. Trading costs for large block trades were generally substantially lower than they were for comparable trades on the NYSE or ASE. The stock was typically acquired for one-quarter point above the last trade on the NYSE *net*, meaning no additional commission was charged. Because of the lower commissions, from 1965 to 1972, the volume of trading on the third market grew steadily in absolute terms and in terms of the percentage of volume on the NYSE. There was a decline after 1972 because of the change in commission structure, as will be discussed in the following section. There was growth after 1965 because using the third market allowed the institution a substantial savings on commissions.

The fixed commission structure also fostered the development and use of the fourth market where two institutions deal directly with one another and, therefore, save the full commission. While it is acknowledged that there was substantial growth in this area, the extent of growth cannot be documented because no published figures are available on these trades.

A final response to the high commission costs was an attempt by some institutions to become members of one of the exchanges. The NYSE and ASE would not allow institutional members, but some of the regional exchanges admitted the institutions to increase trading volume.

Imposition of Negotiated Commissions

All of the aforementioned ploys to offset or avoid commissions were attempted because the institutions felt there was little chance of changing the fixed minimum commission structure. Beginning in 1970, however, the Security and Exchange Commission (SEC) considered implementing negotiated commissions; i.e., for certain specified trades, the fixed commission structure would not hold, and the broker and customer would negotiate the commission involved. The NYSE and almost all member firms vehemently opposed the concept, arguing that negotiated commissions would bring about the demise of the NYSE auction market because members would have no incentive to remain on the exchange if the commissions they received were limited.[2]

This argument was eventually rejected by the SEC, which began a program of allowing negotiated commissions on large transactions and finally allowed negotiated commissions on all transactions. In April 1971, it was ruled that the commission on that part of an order exceeding $500,000 could be negotiated between the broker and the customer. On 24 April 1972, the commission on that part of an order exceeding $300,000 became subject to negotiation. Finally, all commissions became fully negotiated on 1 May 1975 ("May Day").[3] Some of the actual and potential effects of negotiated commissions are discussed in the section on the future of the secondary equity market.

Block Trades, Liquidity, and the Specialist

The increase in institutional trading resulted in a major increase in block trading which is a major test of the market's liquidity because it is obviously difficult to sell a block of 10,000 shares quickly without effecting a major price change.[4] Also, even small price changes due to liquidity are obviously very significant to an institution that wants to buy or sell a "major position" (i.e., a large block of a given security). A half-point price change on a 10,000 share order entails a gain or loss of $5,000; on a 50,000 share order it would constitute a gain or loss of $25,000.

The increase in block trading has had a large impact on specialists because the specialist system had three problems with regard to block trading: *capital, commitment, and contacts* (the three Cs). The first and most obvious problem was that specialists were *undercapitalized* when it came to dealing in large blocks. As the size of blocks has become larger, it has become more difficult for the specialist to come up with the capital needed to acquire the shares involved. Needless to say, large sums would be involved in the acquisition of 10,000 shares, much less the numerous blocks that exceed 20,000 shares. Further, even when the specialist has the capital to finance a position, he may not be willing to *commit* himself because of the risk involved in such an acquisition. Finally, the specialist is not allowed to deal directly with a customer who is not a broker (Rule 113 of the NYSE). Therefore, when an institution brings a block to the exchange, the specialist *cannot contact* another institution to determine whether it would have an interest in some part of the block. He is, therefore, cut off from the major

---

[2]A very insightful discussion of some potential effects of negotiated rates written prior to their imposition is contained in Chris Welles, "Who Will Prosper? Who Will Fail?" *Institutional Investor* 5 (1971): 36–40.

[3]Thomas T. Murphy, ed., *Fact Book* (New York: New York Stock Exchange, 1977).

[4]Recall that we defined liquidity as the ability to convert an asset into cash *quickly* at a known price, i.e., at a price similar to the previous market price.

source of demand for blocks and may be reluctant to take a large position if the stock involved is "thinly" traded; to whom is he going to sell it?

This lack of capital, commitment, and contacts on the part of specialists created a vacuum in the trading of blocks and resulted in the development of a new institution on Wall Street—*block houses*. Block houses evolved because some institutions needed help from institutional brokerage firms in locating other institutions with an interest in buying or selling given stocks. This practice of helping in the movement of blocks eventually became rather widespread.

Block houses are brokerage firms that stand ready to help buy or sell blocks for institutions. They may or may not be members of an exchange. A good block house has the requisites mentioned before in connection with the specialist: it must have the *capital* required to position a large block; it must be willing to *commit* this capital to an individual block; and, finally, it must have *contacts* among institutions.

The following example may help clarify what transpires in a block trade. Assume a mutual fund owns 250,000 shares of Ford Motors and decides that it wants to sell 50,000 shares of this position so that it can establish a position in another stock. Assume further that the fund decides to attempt the sale through Goldman Sachs & Company (GS&Co.), one of the larger, more active block houses, which is a lead underwriter for Ford and "knows" institutions with an interest in the stock. The trader for the mutual fund would contact a block trader at Goldman Sachs, tell him that he wants to sell the 50,000 share block, and ask what GS&Co. can do about it. At this point, several traders at Goldman Sachs would contact some of the institutions that currently own Ford to see if any of them would like to add to their position, and to determine the price the institutions would be willing to bid. After several phone calls, let us assume that GS&Co. receives commitments from four different institutions for a total of 40,000 shares at an average price of $49^5/_8$ (the last sale of Ford on the NYSE was $49^3/_4$). At this point, Goldman Sachs might go back to the mutual fund and bid $49^1/_2$ minus a negotiated commission for the total 50,000 shares. The fund can reject the bid and try another block house. Assuming they accept the bid, Goldman Sachs now owns the block, and will immediately sell 40,000 shares to the four institutions that made prior commitments while "positioning" 10,000 shares themselves. (This means that they own the 10,000 shares and must eventually sell them at the best price possible.) Because GS&Co. is a member of the NYSE, the block will be processed ("crossed") on the exchange as one transaction of 50,000 shares at $49^1/_2$. In the process, a specialist may take some of the stock to fill limit orders on his book at prices between $49^1/_2$ and $49^3/_4$. For working on this trade, Goldman Sachs has received a negotiated commission, but has committed almost $500,000 to position the 10,000 shares. The major risk to GS&Co. is the possibility of a subsequent price change on the 10,000 shares. If the house can sell the 10,000 shares for $49^1/_2$ or more, it will just about break even on the position and have the commission as income. If the price weakens, they may have to sell the position at $49^1/_4$ and take a loss on it. This loss of about $2,500 will offset the income from the commission.

Such an example indicates the importance of having the contacts to quickly find institutions with an interest, the capital to position a certain portion of the block, and the willingness to commit that capital to the block trade. Without all three, the transaction would not have taken place.

Future Developments

Although institutional trading appears to have peaked, the consensus seems to be that the proportion of trading by financial institutions will either stabilize at a high figure (in excess of 60 percent) or continue to grow over time. Therefore, while we may not experience the explosive growth of the past 15 years, financial institutions will continue to be the dominant factor in the securities markets. Given this overriding influence, in this section we must turn our attention to: (1) the impact of fully negotiated commissions, and (2) the makeup and impact of the national market system.

Impact of Fully Negotiated Rates

As noted earlier, many of the changes in the market that occurred during the 1960s and 1970s were a result of the growth of institutional trading and the existence of fixed trading commissions. In the following discussion, we will consider the effect of negotiated commissions on major market participants.[5]

Effect on Commissions

The effect on commissions charged has been dramatic, especially for large trades by institutions. Initially, the new, negotiated commissions were stated in terms of discounts from the fixed rates that prevailed just prior to "May Day." The discounts started at 30 percent and slowly increased to over 40 percent on "no brainers" (i.e., relatively small trades on very liquid stocks, such as 2,000 shares of AT&T). Subsequently, there was a tendency to quote some commissions in cents per share irrespective of price, which could involve a very large discount on high-priced shares.

Initially there was little discounting in trades by individuals, and in some instances the commissions charged on small trades *increased*. Eventually a number of discount brokers appeared who did charge less for individuals wanting only straight transactions (no research advice, no safekeeping, etc.) carried out.[6] As was true for institutional trades, the discounts varied according to the size of

---

[5]An article in which the impact is discussed in some detail is Chris Welles, "Discounting: Wall Street's Game of Nerves," *Institutional Investor* (1976): 27–33.

[6]For a discussion of this development, see Linda Snyder, "Wall Street's Discount Houses are Selling Hard," *Fortune*, March 1977, pp. 117–118.

the trade. The discount firms advertise extensively in the *Wall Street Journal* and *Barron's*.

Effect on Industry Makeup

Because of the lower commissions, there have been numerous mergers and liquidations by smaller investment firms and many observers feel that this consolidation trend will continue, although at a slower pace, for several more years.[7] Therefore, it appears that there will be fewer, but larger and stronger firms in the industry that have a full range of investment services. Even with fewer firms, there is limited concern over the industry's ability to meet the needs of investors and corporations.[8]

Effect on Research Firms

During the period of fixed minimum commissions, institutions used soft dollars to pay for research, and it was cheaper for most institutions to buy research from external sources than to establish extensive in-house research staffs. Therefore, numerous independent research firms were established to serve the institutions, and they were paid with soft commission dollars. With the introduction of competitive rates, there were almost no excess commissions available to "give up," and the institutions concentrated their business with the large brokerage firms that had good trading capability *and* research departments. Given a dearth of excess commissions, the only ways an independent research firm could survive were to develop trading capability or to sell its research for cash. While there are no exact statistics, the general impression is that few of these research firms were able to survive; most of them either disbanded or were merged with full-service brokerage firms that were anxious to acquire analysts and reputation.[9]

Effect on Regional Exchanges

Regional stock exchanges flourished during the early 1970s because they helped institutions distribute soft dollars and because some of them allowed institutions to become members. As a result, many institutions traded some of their blocks on these exchanges. With fully negotiated rates, there were few excess commission dollars to distribute and little incentive to maintain memberships. Therefore, some observers expected regional exchanges to be adversely affected by negotiated commissions. Apparently, the unique trading capability developed by these exchanges, and their ability to implement block trades were relatively effective; a

---

[7]Carol J. Loomis, "The Shakeout of Wall Street Isn't Over Yet," *Fortune,* 22 May 1978, pp. 58–64; "New Round of Wall Street Mergers Due, Say Securities Group's Incoming Chief," *Wall Street Journal,* 21 November 1978, p. 3.

[8]Carol J. Loomis, "Where Does Wall Street's Shakeout Leave Its Customers?" *Fortune,* 19 June 1978, pp. 140–144; Tim Carrington, "Brokerage Firms Urged Again to Stick to Their Basic Capital-Raising Function," *Wall Street Journal,* 5 December 1980, p. 11; Richard E. Rustin, "Wall Street Mergers May Basically Change U.S. Financial System," *Wall Street Journal,* 22 April 1981, p. 1.

[9]An example of such a merger is given in Richard E. Rustin, "Baker Weeks Set to Join Reynolds Securities Unit," *Wall Street Journal,* 16 September 1976, p. 7.

study by Reilly and Perry indicated that overall relative trading on the major regional exchanges during the period 1976–1977 was very similar to what had prevailed prior to 1975.[10] While there were differences between exchanges (e.g., the Detroit exchange went out of existence while the Cincinnati exchange grew substantially), the overall range of relative trading was similar.

Effect on Third Market

The third market expanded rapidly in the late 1960s and early 1970s because of trading by institutions anxious to save on commissions. A major question was whether it would continue to get the business when the commission advantage was lost after May Day. An analysis of the data strongly supported the prophets of doom; relative trading volume peaked in 1972 at over 8.5 percent of NYSE volume (shortly after the second change in commission rates) and declined steadily thereafter to less than 4 percent by 1977. It appears that the third market was still in existence in 1981 but the proportion of trading is clearly below the level that existed in the mid-1970s.

Legal Problems

In a fixed-commission situation in which everyone charged the same price (commission), the only factor to consider was the sale or execution of purchase; i.e., making the best "deal" for the securities. In a world of negotiated commissions, both price and execution must be considered, and institutional investors contended that low commissions are not worthwhile if execution of the trade is poor. As an example, on a 30,000 share block, you might save $2,000 in commissions, but if the sale is made at $1/4$ point below another dealer's price, the loss in value ($7,500) will more than offset the savings in commissions. This is a complex legal issue, because a suit could be brought for poor execution of a trade.

Another legal issue involves payment for research. Many large investment houses still provide research support for their institutional customers, and this is obviously worth some difference in commission. However, the initial feeling was that the SEC would not allow houses to introduce any price difference for such help. Subsequent statements indicate that the SEC would allow a slightly higher price for "service," including research.

Summary of Effects

Clearly the effects of negotiated commissions have been substantial, but they have varied for different segments of the industry. There has been a significant decline in total commissions paid, and a consequent change in the size and structure of the industry. Definite casualties have been numerous independent research firms and the third market. On the other hand, there has apparently been limited

---

[10]Frank K. Reilly and Gladys Perry, "Negotiated Commissions and Regional Stock Exchanges" (Paper presented at Southwest AIDS Meeting, Nashville, Tenn., February 1979). University of Illinois, Faculty Working Paper No. 543 (Urbana, IL).

impact on the regional stock exchanges. Finally, price competition has introduced added legal considerations, but the impact has not been as great as expected.[11]

A National Market System (NMS)

In addition to suggesting that negotiated commissions be introduced, the Institutional Investor Report prepared by the SEC at the request of Congress strongly recommended the creation of a national, competitive market. Although there is no one generally accepted definition of what a national market would constitute, there are four major characteristics that are generally included in a description of such a market:

1. centralized reporting of all transactions
2. a centralized quotation system
3. a centralized limit-order book (CLOB)
4. free and open competition among all qualified market-makers.

A Composite Tape

A central market must involve *centralized reporting of transactions*, i.e., a composite tape on which all transactions in a stock would be reported irrespective of where the transactions took place. As one watched the tape he might see a trade in GM on the NYSE, another on the Midwest, and a third on the OTC. The intent is to report all completed trades on the tape and thereby provide full information on all securities traded. As of 16 June 1975, the NYSE began operating a central tape that includes all NYSE stocks traded on other exchanges and on the OTC.[12] Therefore, this aspect of a National Market System (NMS) has already been introduced for stocks listed on the NYSE.

Centralized Quotations

The second requirement for an NMS is a centralized quotation system that contains the quotes for a given stock from *all* market-makers including those on the national exchanges, the regional exchanges, and the OTC. With a centralized quotation system, a broker who requested the market for GM would be given the prevailing quotes on the NYSE and the Midwest Stock Exchange, those from

---

[11]An article on several of these factors is Seha M. Tinic and Richard R. West, "The Securities Industry Under Negotiated Brokerage Commissions: Changes in the Structure and Performance of New York Stock Exchange Member Firms," *The Bell Journal of Economics and Management Science* 11 (1980): 29–41.

[12]Murphy, *Fact Book,* p. 7.

other regional exchanges on which GM is listed, and the several markets made by OTC dealers. The broker should complete the trade on the market with the best quote for his client.

ITS

Currently there are two centralized quotation systems available. One is the *Intermarket Trading System (ITS)* developed by the American, Boston, Midwest, New York, Pacific, and Philadelphia Stock Exchanges.[13] ITS consists of a central computer facility with interconnected terminals in the participating market centers. Brokers and market-makers in each market center can indicate to those in other centers specific buying and selling commitments by way of a composite quotation display. These displays show the current quote for each eligible stock in that market center, and the current quotes in all other participating market centers. A broker or market-maker in any market center can thus exercise *his own best judgment* in determining, on the basis of current quotations, where to execute a customer's orders. If a better price is available in another market, he simply sends a message to that market center, committing himself to buy or sell at the price shown on the quotation display. When his commitment is accepted, he receives, in return, a message telling him that the transaction has taken place. The following example illustrates how ITS works:

A broker on the NYSE has a market order to sell 100 shares of XYZ stock. The quotation display on the floor of the NYSE shows that the best current bid for XYZ has been entered on the Pacific Stock Exchange (PSE), and he decides to take advantage of that bid. He enters a firm commitment on the NYSE terminal to sell 100 shares at the bid on the PSE. Within seconds, the commitment is flashed on the CRT screen and also printed out at the PSE specialist's post, where it is executed against the PSE bid.

After the commitment is accepted, a short message is entered into the system which immediately reports an execution back to New York, and the trade is reported on the consolidated tape. Brokers on both sides of the transaction receive an immediate confirmation, and a journal of all transactions is transmitted to the appropriate market centers at the end of the day. Thereafter, each broker completes his own clearance and settlement procedure.

As it currently operates, the ITS system provides centralized quotations for the stocks listed, and the NYSE screen specifies whether a bid or ask away from the NYSE market is superior to that on the New York market. Note that there are several characteristics that the system does *not* have. One is that it does not have the capability for automatic execution at the best market; it is necessary to contact the market-maker and indicate that you want to buy or sell at his bid or ask. It is possible that when a NYSE broker goes to "hit" another market, the bid or ask will be withdrawn. Also, it is *not* mandatory that a broker go to the best market. Although the best price is elsewhere, a broker might consider it in-

---

[13]This discussion draws heavily on *ITS: A Cornerstone of the National Market System.* The publication is available from any of the participating exchanges.

convenient to transact on that exchange if the price difference is not substantial. It is almost impossible to audit such actions.

NSTS

Another centralized quotation system that has the capability to become the core of an NMS is the *National Securities Trading System* (NSTS) which is currently operating on the Cincinnati Stock Exchange.[14] With this system it is possible for any qualified broker to enter a bid, ask, or limit order for any of the 16 stocks on NSTS (all are listed on the NYSE). As a consequence, the system encompasses multiple competing market-makers, and all orders are exposed to a national market. Further, once an order is entered and accepted, the trade is executed automatically and subsequent confirmations are automatic.

In contrast to ITS, the NSTS has a public, central limit-order file. All limit orders list a price and time priority, and the system automatically executes the order with the best price and earliest time. The SEC has allowed operation of this system which has been used by Merrill Lynch, Pierce, Fenner, & Smith on an experimental basis.[15]

In summary, there has been substantial progress in development of a central quotation system, which clearly indicates that the required technology is available and operational. The question remaining is, who can use these quotes and who can enter them.

Central Limit Order Book (CLOB)

A major area of controversy has been the establishment of a central limit-order book that would contain all limit orders from *all* exchanges. Ideally, the CLOB would be visible to everyone, and all market-makers and traders could fill orders on the CLOB. Currently, most limit orders are placed with the specialist on the NYSE and, when a transaction *on the NYSE* reaches the stipulated price, the order is filled by the NYSE specialist who receives some part of the commission for rendering this service. The NYSE has opposed a CLOB because the NYSE specialists do not want to share this very lucrative business.

Two versions of CLOB have been proposed. One is a "soft" CLOB that would only be accessible to specialists and specified market-makers, although not limited to those on the NYSE. This version would probably not entail automatic execution of transactions. In contrast, a "hard" CLOB would be available to all market-makers and would involve automatic execution of orders. Generally, advocates of an NMS support the "hard" CLOB with rigid time and price guarantees built into the system. The SEC has proposed a rule that would basically entail creation of a CLOB, and has urged the industry to devel-

---

[14]This discussion draws heavily from the booklet *The National Securities Trading System* (Jersey City, NJ: The Service Bureau Company, 1979).

[15]"Extension of Electronic Trading System at Cincinnati Exchange is Issued by SEC," *Wall Street Journal*, 14 December 1978, p. 9; Tim Carrington, "Securities Industry Group is Urging Plan to Increase Automation for Small Trades," *Wall Street Journal*, 4 December 1980, p. 4.

op the necessary devices.[16] The technology for a CLOB is already available with the NSTS. Given the SEC requirement, it apparently will eventually become a reality.

Competition Between Market-Makers

Competing market-makers have always prevailed on the OTC market, but competition has been opposed by the NYSE. The argument in favor of competition among market-makers is that it forces dealers to make better markets or they will not do any business. Assume dealer A quotes 49–50 for a stock, and dealer B makes a quote of $49\frac{1}{4}$–$49\frac{3}{4}$. Dealer B should do all the business in the stock because he has a higher bid *and* a lower ask. If dealer A wants to do any business, he must at least match the quote by the other market-maker or improve on it by bidding $49\frac{3}{8}$ and/or offering stock at $49\frac{5}{8}$. If competition improves the market for a stock (i.e., reduces the bid-ask spread), this improvement should be reflected in market data. Several studies that examined the relationship between the spread on a sample of stocks and the number of dealers trading those stocks, holding other relevant variables constant, indicated that the more competition (i.e., the more dealers), the smaller the spread.[17]

In contrast, the NYSE argues that a *central* auction market provides the best market because, under such an arrangement, all orders are forced to the one central location and this concentration of orders will ensure the best auction market. The principal device used by the NYSE to create a concentrated market was Rule 394 which was subsequently modified and called Rule 390. This rule states that, unless specifically exempted by the exchange, members must obtain the permission of the exchange before carrying out a transaction in a listed stock off the exchange. The stated purpose of the rule is to ensure that all volume comes to the NYSE so that the exchange can provide the most complete auction market. The exchange contends that Rule 390 is necessary to protect the auction market, arguing that if the rule is eliminated, members will be tempted to trade on or off the exchange and many orders will be *internalized* (i.e., brokers will match orders from the holdings of their own customers and the orders will not come to the exchange at all). In general, a "fragmented" dealer market is envisioned, which the exchange contends is not as good as the central auction market.[18] An alternative view set forth by James Hamilton is that the adverse effects of fragmentation are more than offset by the benefits of competition.[19]

[16]"Two Rules That Move the Securities Industry Nearer National System Proposed by SEC," *Wall Street Journal*, 27 April 1979, p. 4.

[17]Seha M. Tinic and Richard R. West, "Competition and the Pricing of Dealer Service in the Over-the-Counter Stock Market *Journal of Financial and Quantitative Analysis* 7 (1972); 1707–1727; George J. Benston and Rober L. Hagerman, "Determinants of Bid-Asked Spreads in the Over-the-Counter Market," *Journal of Financial Economics* 1 (1974): 353–364.

[18]This is the implication derived from a panel discussion reported in Shelby White, "The New Central Marketplace: The Debate Goes On," *Institutional Investor* 10 (1976); 30–31.

[19]James L. Hamilton, "Marketplace Fragmentation, Competition, and the Efficiency of the Stock Exchange," *Journal of Finance* 34 (1979): 171–187.

The contrasting view is that market-making should be on a *free competitive basis* similar to what occurs on the OTC market where anybody who wants to make a market in a stock and can meet specified basic capital requirements is allowed to do so. In addition, members of the exchange could and *should* trade with the market-maker offering the best market. Advocates of this competitive market contend that such a structure has served well for decades in the OTC market, and several competing dealers would have more capital with which to make markets than does a single specialist.[20]

Competing arguments aside, the SEC contends that its mandate from Congress under the Investment Act of 1975 is to help establish an open competitive market without restrictions like Rule 390. The question is *when* and *how* Rule 390 will be eliminated. The NYSE and a number of brokerage firms have suggested implementing a modified form of Rule 390 *until* the central market is established because they feel that, until the NMS is working, participants will need a strong auction market such as exists on the exchange. The contrasting view is that the abolition is necessary *before* a central market can be established because, as long as Rule 390 exists, about 80 percent of the volume of the NYSE stocks is restricted to the exchange and it is not reasonable to expect a potential market-maker to establish a competitive market under such conditions. Therefore, it is argued that there will not be a truly competitive market *until* this rule is eliminated.

Progress in achieving this final phase of the NMS has been slow due to strong opposition and caution on the part of the SEC.[21] However, changes are being made which indicate that Rule 390 will be eliminated or greatly modified at some point. A step in this direction is a proposal that stocks newly listed on the exchange would *not* be bound by Rule 390; exchange members could trade these newly listed securities away from the exchange.[22]

Impact of NMS Without Rule 390

It is reasonable to assume that the SEC will eventually have its way and establish a true NMS with the characteristics mentioned earlier (consolidated tape and quotes, a CLOB, and no Rule 390). Therefore, let us consider the effect of this on various segments of the industry.

---

[20]For a further discussion of this view, see Seymour Smidt, "Which Road to an Efficient Stock Market?" *Financial Analysts Journal* 27 (1971); 18–20.

[21]Stan Crock and Richard E. Rustin, "Work on a National Stock-Trading System Lags Badly: Some Blame Brokers and SEC," *Wall Street Journal*, 2 February 1979, p. 32; "Chiefs of National Stock Market Hearings Assert Industry, SEC Proceed Too Slowly," *Wall Street Journal*, 25 September 1979, p. 12; "SEC Hit by House Unit for Slow Progress in Creation of National Securities Market," *Wall Street Journal*, 12 September 1980, p. 3; Stan Crock, "SEC's Aim to Start National Stock Market Triggers Partisan Crossfire in Congress," *Wall Street Journal*, 26 February 1981, p. 9; "SEC Delays Test of Electronic Trade Link for OTC, 7 Exchanges to March 1, 1982," *Wall Street Journal*, 22 April 1981, p. 3.

[22]"Two Rules That Move the Securities Industry Nearer National System Proposed by SEC," *Wall Street Journal*, 27 April 1979, p. 4; "SEC Eases Curb on Off-Board Trading by Brokers in Exchange-Listed Issues," *Wall Street Journal*, 6 June 1980, p. 7; Tim Carrington, "Share Trading Away from Exchanges Can Start Tomorrow at Brokerage Firms," *Wall Street Journal*, 17 July 1980, p. 6.

Dealer Markets

One major effect of eliminating Rule 390 would be that any interested market-maker could become a dealer in any stock. Until Rule 390 is eliminated, a member firm of the NYSE obviously cannot make a market in AT&T or GM because all such trades must be made through the exchange, even the large block trades that are matched "upstairs" (away from the floor of the exchange) by block houses like Goldman Sachs and Salomon Bros. Without Rule 390, member firms like GS&Co. and Salomon Bros. will probably not bring the blocks to the exchange, but will simply trade them as dealers off the exchange.

A more significant effect would be the creation of dealer markets for smaller trades by firms such as Merrill Lynch which could begin making dealer markets in stocks like AT&T and GM and make trades for smaller orders in these stocks for their many individual investors. This cannot be done with Rule 390 because all trades must go to the NYSE. As mentioned previously, this practice is referred to as "internalization." If a number of large brokerage firms did this for a large number of stocks, volume on the NYSE could be substantially reduced. However, this line of reasoning appears to be rather drastic and implies that there is little value in the NYSE auction market. The fact is, major firms that have discussed establishing dealer markets when Rule 390 is eliminated have made it quite clear that they will only become dealers in stocks with reasonable spreads from which there is a potential for reasonable returns.[23] These firms have no desire to compete with the NYSE specialists in stocks like AT&T and GM where the typical spread is $1/8$ or $1/4$ point at best, because trading such stocks is not worth their time and effort. They will become dealers in stocks with spreads of $3/8$ or $1/2$ point, because the returns will justify the effort and capital required. Note that the added competition could cause a reduction in the spread, which means the investor will gain. Also, because all trades will be reported on the composite tape, the broker *must* go to the best market or be liable for poor execution.

Effect on the Specialist

Clearly the position of the specialist will change dramatically after Rule 390 is abolished. First, he will lose his protected position as the lone market-maker in many stocks and will have to compete with numerous potential dealers. In some cases, the specialist may choose to stop being the market-maker in less active issues. Assuming that the major order flow for stocks like AT&T and GM will continue to come to the NYSE, the specialist could continue to make this market, but he would lose income that previously came from running the limit book, if we assume that a hard CLOB will be introduced. Therefore, the specialists' returns will clearly be less than those reported in the late 1960s. One contemplated change that will be beneficial to the specialist is the elimination of Rule 113 prohibiting the specialist from dealing with institutions. The elimination of Rule 113

[23]For a discussion of this point and the future without Rule 390, see Chris Welles, "The Showdown Over Rule 390," *Institutional Investor* 11 (1977): 33–38. An article that likewise discusses some of the effects and makes a strong case for the NMS is Julius W. Peake, "The National Market System," *Financial Analysts Journal* 34 (1978): pp. 25–28.

may enable the specialists to be more active in block transactions, although they will no longer be involved in the block trades that are matched "upstairs."

Effect on NYSE

There will be less overall volume because there will no longer be block crosses (i.e., block transactions will no longer be required to be processed on the exchange), the off-exchange dealer markets in stocks with large spreads will increase, and the limit-order book will be replaced by the hard CLOB. The final effect will probably not be as great as some observers envision because the exchange will probably continue to serve as the major auction market in high-volume stocks like AT&T and IBM; i.e., the stocks the exchange will lose are the low-volume stocks with large spreads. The ultimate impact will depend upon how well the specialist is able to compete for the block business in these large-volume stocks.

Effect on Block Houses

The block houses will not be forced to take their trades to an exchange to be crossed. This should save money and make the trades easier, although the block houses will not have the benefit of the specialist in some issues. Still, most blocks are in the large, active stocks in which the specialist will stay active. In fact, the specialist may begin to offer some competition to the block houses after Rule 113 is eliminated.

Effect on Regional Exchanges

The regional exchanges should benefit from wider exposure of their markets on the consolidated quotation machine, and their ability to participate in the limit orders that were formerly restricted to the NYSE. At the same time, they could be seriously affected by the loss of numerous blocks that are crossed on the regionals because block houses will not be required to cross blocks on an exchange.

Summary of Effects of an NMS without Rule 390

Without Rule 390, one should expect the creation of more dealer markets and some internalization of orders. Most new dealer markets will be in stocks with relatively low trading volumes and large spreads, while the specialist will probably retain the large, active stocks with competitive markets. The specialist will lose control of the limit-order book and some of the income from this and from blocks crossed on the exchange, but should benefit from the cancellation of Rule 113. The NYSE may lose some volume but will probably still be the major auction market for the large, active stocks. Block houses will not have to cross blocks on an exchange, but they may lose some liquidity if the specialists stop dealing in small issues, and they may feel competition from the specialist on large issues after Rule 113 is eliminated. Finally, regional stock exchanges will lose most of their block cross business, but gain from greater exposure of their markets and from the hard CLOB.

Summary

In this chapter we considered the many changes in our securities markets since 1965, including a discussion of why the changes transpired and potential future changes. The market changes mainly resulted from the substantial growth of institutional trading, which we documented with empirical evidence. We discussed the effects of the fixed commission schedule, which was eventually eliminated, and the impact of block trading that led to the creation of block houses.

The second half of the chapter was concerned with expected changes. This included a consideration of the ultimate effects of negotiated commissions on various components of the industry and on its overall structure. We discussed what constitutes a national market system and the status of the necessary components. Because the requisites have been accomplished or can be envisioned, we discussed the impact of a NMS on major segments of the securities industry.

As noted initially, this chapter is important because numerous extensive changes have already occurred, but more important, many more changes are yet to come, and the effects will continue to affect the industry and our capital markets. It is hoped that this discussion will provide you with the background to understand these changes and their effects.

Questions

1. The secondary equity market has experienced major changes since 1965. What is the overall reason for these changes?

2. Discuss three pieces of empirical evidence that attest to the growth in institutional trading in an absolute sense; in a relative sense.

3. Briefly discuss *why* trading by financial institutions has grown dramatically since 1965. Why do the institutions own more stock and trade more stock?

4. Would you expect the large financial institutions to continue to dominate trading in the secondary equity market in the future? Why or why not?

5. Describe the fixed commission schedule. Why did it exist and whom did it protect? Why was it a problem for large financial institutions?

6. What were "give-ups" and why did they exist in the fixed commission world?

7. Why did the third market grow so rapidly from 1965 to 1972?

8. Why do you feel the fourth market grew during the period 1965–1974?

9. Why did institutions want to become members of an exchange? Why did some of the exchanges not allow it? Why did some of the exchanges welcome institutions?

10. What is meant by the term "negotiated commissions"? When was "May Day"?

11. Discuss why block trades are considered the ultimate test of the liquidity of a market.

12. In the discussion of block trades and the specialist, it was noted that the specialist is hampered by the three Cs. Discuss each of the three Cs as it relates to block trading.

13. Describe block houses and why they evolved.

14. Describe what is meant by "positioning" part of a block. What is the risk involved?

15. Discuss the impact of fully negotiated rates on each of the following segments of the securities industry. Indicate what you think will happen *and why* you believe it will happen.
   a. research firms
   b. block houses
   c. regional exchanges
   d. the third market

16. Describe the major attributes of a central market.

17. Briefly describe the ITS and what it contributes to a NMS. What are its deficiencies regarding the NMS?

18. Briefly describe the NSTS and how it fits into the requirements for the NMS. What characteristics does it have that are not present with ITS?

19. Briefly discuss Rule 390. What is its purpose?

20. Discuss why the NYSE feels Rule 390 should not be eliminated; i.e., what are the supposed benefits of this rule to the participants (buyers and sellers of stock)?

21. Discuss the free competition argument against Rule 390. What are the supposed advantages of eliminating Rule 390 in terms of market-making and capital?

22. Briefly give the arguments for and against eliminating Rule 390 before a central market is established.

23. What segments of the securities industry will be *most* affected by a central market without Rule 390? Why? What segments will be *least* affected? Why?

References

"Are the Institutions Wrecking Wall Street?" *Business Week,* 2 June 1973.

Black, Fischer. "Toward a Fully Automated Stock Exchange." *Financial Analysts Journal* (1971) 2 parts.

Doede, Robert W. "The Monopoly Power of the New York Stock Exchange." Ph.D dissertation, University of Chicago, 1967.

Farrar, Donald E. "Toward a Central Market System: Wall Street's Slow Retreat into the Future." *Journal of Financial and Quantitative Analysis* 9 (1974).

Farrar, Donald E., ed. *Regional Stock Exchanges in a Central Market System. Explorations in Economic Research,* vol. 2, (1974).

Freund, William C., and Minor, David F. *Institutional Activity on the NYSE: 1975 and 1980. Perspectives on Planning, no. 10.* New York: New York Stock Exchange, June 1972.

Hamilton, James L. "Competition, Scale Economies, and Transaction Cost in the Stock Market." *Journal of Financial and Quantitative Analysis* 11 (1976).

Hamilton, James L. "Marketplace Fragmentation, Competition, and the Efficiency of the Stock Exchange." *Journal of Finance* 34 (1979).

Klemkosky, Robert C. "Institutional Dominance of the NYSE." *Financial Executive* 41 (1973).

Loomis, Carol J. "The Shakeout of Wall Street Isn't Over Yet." *Fortune,* 22 May 1978.

Loomis, Carol J. "Where Does Wall Street's Shakeout Leave Its Customers?" *Fortune,* 19 June 1978.

Lorie, James H. *Public Policy for American Capital Markets.* Washington, D.C.: Department of the Treasury, 1974.

Martin, William McChesney, Jr. *The Securities Markets: A Report with Recommendations.* Submitted to the Board of Governors of the New York Stock Exchange, 1971.

Mendelson, Morris. *From Automated Quotes to Automated Trading: Restructuring the Stock Market in the U.S.* Bulletin of the Institute of Finance, Graduate School of Business Administration, New York University, 1972.

National Bureau of Economic Research. "Regional Stock Exchanges in a Central Market System." *Explorations In Economic Research* 2 (1975).

Peake, Julius W. "The National Market System." *Financial Analysts Journal* 34 (1978).

Reilly, Frank K. "Block Trades and Stock Price Volatility." *Financial Analysts Journal,* forthcoming.

Reilly, Frank K. "Institutions on Trial: Not Guilty." *Journal of Portfolio Management* 3 (1977).

Reilly, Frank K., and Perry, Gladys. "Negotiated Commissions and Regional Exchanges." Urbana, IL.: University of Illinois Working Paper, August 1978.

Reilly, Frank K., and Wachowicz, John. "How Institutional Trading Reduces Market Volatility." *Journal of Portfolio Management* 5 (1979).

Robertson, Wyndham. "A Big Board Strategy for Staying Alive." *Fortune,* March 1977.

Rosenberg, Marvin. "Institutional Investors: Holdings, Prices and Liquidity." *Financial Analysts Journal* 30 (1974).

Smidt, Seymour. "Which Road to an Efficient Stock Market?" *Financial Analysts Journal* 27 (1971).

Soldofsky, Robert M. *Institutional Holdings of Common Stock, 1900–2000.* Ann Arbor, Mich: Bureau of Business Research, University of Michigan, 1971.

Tinic, Seha M., and West, Richard R. "The Securities Industry Under Negotiated Brokerage Commissions: Changes in the Structure and Performance of New York Stock Exchange Member Firms." *The Bell Journal of Economics and Management Science* 11 (1980).

U.S., Congress, House of Representatives, *Securities and Exchange Commission, Institutional Investor Study Report,* 92nd Cong., 1t sess. 1971 [H. Doc. 92–64.]

Weeden, Donald E. "Competition: Key to Market Structure." *Journal of Financial and Quantitative Analysis* 7 (1972).

Welles, Chris. "Discounting: Wall Street's Game of Nerves." *Institutional Investor* 20 (1976).

Welles, Chris. "The Showdown Over Rule 390." *Institutional Investor* 11 (1977).

West, Richard R. "Institutional Trading and the Changing Stock Market." *Financial Analysts Journal* 27 (1971).

West, Richard R., and Tinic, Seha M. *The Economics of the Stock Market.* New York: Praeger, 1972.

Lawrence Fisher & James H. Lorie

When anybody discusses outstanding studies in the area of rates of return for various investment assets, the typical beginning is the several studies carried out at the University of Chicago by Professors Lawrence Fisher and James Lorie. These studies are generally recognized as the first comprehensive and refined measurements of the performance of stocks listed on the New York Stock Exchange. The initial study was done in 1964 with updating and further analysis in 1968 and 1970, and a major analysis of stocks and bonds for the 50-year period 1926–1976 that was published in 1977.

Lawrence Fisher was born in Los Angeles, California on October 19, 1929.

Professor Fisher was at the University of Chicago from 1957 to 1978. During a large part of that time he was the Associate Director of the Center for Research in Security Prices (CRSP). He was mainly responsible for the detailed, meticulous collection of stock price data and for the creation of the CRSP monthly stock price tapes that have become the chief source of data for literally hundreds of studies in finance and accounting. He also created several stock market series for the NYSE that extend back to 1926 and these have likewise been used in numerous academic studies.

Lawrence Fisher is currently a Professor of Finance at the Graduate School of

Management at Rutgers, the State University of New Jersey.

James Lorie was born in Kansas City, MO in 1922, received his A.B. and A.M. degrees from Cornell University and his Ph.D. from the University of Chicago in 1947. Much of his earlier work was in marketing and he published Basic Methods of Marketing Research *in 1951. Professor Lorie was the Director of the University of Chicago Center for Research and Security Prices (CRSP) from its founding in 1961 until 1974. It was during this period that the CRSP tapes for the New York Stock Exchange were developed. These tapes contain month-end prices for every stock on the NYSE and other extensive market information.*

James Lorie has been involved as a consultant or adviser to numerous government committees, foundations, and corporations and is on several boards. Specifically, as a consultant to the Treasury Department he prepared a report, Public Policy for American Capital Markets. *He was a member of the Market Structure Committee of the Midwest Stock Exchange and a member of the National Market Advisory Board, and the Board of the Chicago Board Options exchange. He is editor (with Richard A. Brealey) of* Modern Developments in Investment Management: A Book of Readings *2nd ed. (Dryden Press, 1978) and author (with Mary Hamilton) of* The Stock Market: Theories and Evidence *(Richard D. Irwin, 1973).*

STOCK MARKET INDICATOR SERIES

❧ 5 ❧

A fair statement regarding stock market indicator series is that everybody talks about them, but few people know how they are constructed and what they represent. Although portfolios are obviously composed of individual stocks, there is a tendency on the part of investors to ask, "What happened to the market today?" The reason for this question is that, if an investor owns more than a few stocks, it is cumbersome to follow each stock individually to determine the composite performance of the portfolio. Also there is an intuitive notion that most individual stocks move with the aggregate market. Therefore, if the overall market rose, an individual's portfolio probably also increased in value. To supply investors with a composite report on market performance, some financial publications have developed market indicator series. The general purpose of a market indicator series is to provide an overall indication of aggregate market changes or market movements.

In this chapter we will consider some specific uses of market indicator series, discuss the factors determining what a market indicator series can tell us, and examine some of the major types of indicator series. Finally, we will analyze long- and short-run price movements for some well-known series.

Uses of Market Indicator Series

There are at least four specific uses of stock market indicator series. A primary application is in examining total market returns over a specified time period and using derived returns as a benchmark *to judge the performance of individual portfolios.* A basic assumption is that any investor should be able to derive a rate of return comparable to the "market" return by randomly selecting a large number of stocks from the total market. Hence, it is reasoned that a superior portfolio manager should consistently do better than the market. Therefore, the indicator series are used to judge the performance of professional money managers. In addition to examining the rates of return on the portfolios, however, one should analyze the differential risk for the institutional portfolios compared to the market indicator series; i.e., the evaluation of performance should be on a risk-adjusted basis.

Securities analysts, portfolio managers, and others use the series to examine the *factors that influence aggregate stock price movements.* Studies of the relationship between economic variables and aggregate stock market movements require some measurement of overall stock market movements, i.e., a composite stock market indicator series.

Another group interested in aggregate market series are "technicians," who believe past price changes can be used to predict future price movements. Technicians interested in aggregate market forecasting would obviously want to examine past movements of different market indicator series.

Finally, recent work in portfolio theory has shown that the relevant risk for an individual security is its "systematic" risk with the market. The systematic risk for a stock is determined by the relationship between the rates of return for the security and the rates of return for a market portfolio of risky assets.[1] Therefore, it is necessary for an analyst or portfolio manager attempting to determine the systematic risk for an individual security to relate its returns to the returns for an aggregate market indicator series.

Differentiating Factors in Constructing Market Indicator Series

Because indicator series are intended to indicate the overall movements of a group of stocks, it is necessary to consider which factors are important in computing any average intended to represent a total population.

Sample

Our initial concern is with the sample used to construct the series. When talking about samples, three factors must be considered: *the size of the sample, the breadth of the sample,* and *the source of the sample.*

A small percent of the total population will provide valid indications of the behavior of the total population if the sample is properly selected. In fact, at some point the costs of taking a larger sample will almost certainly outweigh any benefits in terms of generating information that is closer to total market performance. The sample should be *representative* of the total population or the size of the sample will be meaningless; a large, biased sample is no better than a small,

---

[1]William F. Sharpe, "Capital Asset Prices: Theory of Market Equilibrium Under Conditions of Risk," *Journal of Finance* 19 (1964): 425–442.

biased sample. The sample can be generated by completely random selection or by a nonrandom but well-designed selection process in which the characteristics desired are taken into consideration. The *source* of the sample becomes important if there are any differences between alternative segments of the population, in which case samples from each segment are required.

Weighting

Our second concern is with *the weight given to each member in the sample*. In computing stock market indicator series, three principal weighting schemes are used: (1) price weighting, (2) a value weighting, and (3) equal weighting (i.e., an unweighted series).

Computational Procedure

Our final consideration is with *the computational procedure used*. One alternative is to take a simple arithmetic average of the various members in the series. Another is to compute an index and have all changes, whether in price or value, reported in terms of the basic index. Finally, some prefer using a geometric average.

Alternative Indicator Series

Price-Weighted Series

A price-weighted series is an arithmetic average of current prices which means that, in fact, movements are influenced by differential prices.

Dow-Jones Industrial Average

The best-known price-weighted series is also the oldest and certainly the most popular market indicator series, the Dow-Jones Industrial Average (DJIA). The DJIA is a price-weighted average of 30 large, well-known industrial stocks that are generally the leaders in their industry (blue chips) and are listed on the New York Stock Exchange. The index is derived by totaling *the current prices* of the 30 stocks and dividing the sum by a divisor that has been adjusted to take account of stock splits and changes in the sample over time.[2]

$$\text{DJIA}_t = \sum_{i=1}^{30} P_{it}/D_{adj}$$

---

[2]A complete list of all events that have caused a change in the divisor since the DJIA went to 30 stocks on October 1, 1928 is contained in Maurice L. Farrell, ed., *The Dow-Jones Investor's Handbook* (Princeton, NJ: Dow-Jones Books, 1980).

	Before Split	After 3-for-1 Split by Stock A	
	Prices	Prices	
A	30	10	
B	20	20	
C	10	10	
	60 ÷ 3 = 20	40 ÷ X = 20	X = 2 (New Divisor)

Table 5.1   Example of Change in DJIA Divisor When a Sample Stock Splits

where:

$DJIA_t$ = value of the DJIA on day t

P_{it} = closing price of stock i on day t

D_{adj} = adjusted divisor on day t.

In Table 5.1 three stocks are employed to demonstrate the procedure used to derive a new divisor for the DJIA when a stock splits. When stocks split, the divisor becomes smaller. An idea of the cumulative effect of splits can be derived from the fact that the divisor as of July 1981 was 1.314.

The idea is to derive a new divisor that will ensure that the new value for the series is the same as it would have been without the split. In this case, the presplit index value was 20. Therefore, after the split, given the new sum of prices, the divisor is adjusted downward to maintain this value of 20. The divisor is also changed if there is a change in the makeup of the series. This does not happen very often with the series; there were only three changes during the 21 years from 1959 to 1980. In August 1976, Minnesota Mining and Manufacturing (3M) replaced Anaconda. A major change occurred in June 1979, when IBM and Merck & Co. replaced Chrysler and Esmark.[3] Interestingly, IBM was in the sample in 1932, but was deleted in 1939 to make room for American Telephone and Telegraph.

Because the series is price-weighted, a high-priced stock carries more weight in the series than does a low-priced stock; i.e., as shown in the example below, a 10 percent change in a $100 stock ($10) will cause a larger change in the series than a 10 percent change in a $30 stock ($3). In Case A, the $100 stock increases by 10 percent, which causes a 5 percent increase in the average; in Case B, the $30 stock increases by 10 percent and the average only rises by 1.8 percent.

[3]For a discussion of the change, see "Revised Dow-Jones Industrials to Add IBM and Merck, Delete Chrysler and Esmark," *Wall Street Journal* 28 June 1979, p. 31; and H. L. Butler, Jr. and J. D. Allen, "The Dow-Jones Industrial Average Re-Reexamined," *Financial Analysts Journal* 35 (1980): 23–30.

	Period T	Period T + 1	
		Case A	Case B
A	100	110	100
B	50	50	50
C	30	30	33
Sum	180	190	183
Divisor	3	3	3
Average	60	63.3	61
Percent of Change		5.0	1.8

The DJIA has been criticized over time on several counts, the first of which is that the sample used for the series is limited. It is difficult to conceive of how 30 nonrandomly selected blue-chip stocks can be representative of the 1,800 stocks listed on the NYSE. In addition, the stocks included are, by definition, the most important companies in various industries. Therefore, the DJIA probably reflects price movements for large, mature blue-chip firms rather than for the "typical" company listed on the NYSE. Several studies have pointed out that price movements of the DJIA have not been as volatile as they have been for other market indicator series.

In addition, the DJIA is a price-weighted series. Therefore, when a high-priced stock such as DuPont moves even a small percent, it has an inordinate effect on the overall index. In contrast, when companies have a stock split their prices decline and, therefore, their weight in the DJIA is reduced. Therefore, the weighting scheme causes a downward bias in the DJIA because the stocks with higher growth rates will have higher prices; such stocks consistently tend to split, and thereby consistently lose weight within the index.[4] Irrespective of the several criticisms made of the DJIA, a comparison of short-run price movements of the DJIA and of other NYSE indicators, discussed below, shows a fairly close relationship between the daily percentages of price changes for the DJIA and comparable price changes for other NYSE indicators.

In addition to a price series for industrial stocks, Dow-Jones also publishes an average of 20 stocks in the transportation industry and an average for utilities that includes 15 stocks. Detailed reports of the averages are contained in *The Wall Street Journal* and *Barron's*, including hourly figures.[5]

[4]For a discussion of these problems see the following studies: H. L. Butler, Jr. and M. B. Decker, "A Security Check on the Dow-Jones Industrial Average," *Financial Analysts Journal* 9 (1953) 37–45; R. D. Milne, "The Dow-Jones Industrial Average Re-examined," *Financial Analysts Journal* (1966): 83–88; E. E. Carter and K. J. Cohen, "Bias in the DJIA Caused by Stock Splits," *Financial Analysts Journal* 22 (1966): 90–94; Lewis L. Schellbach, "When Did the DJIA Top 1200?" *Financial Analysts Journal* 23 (1967): 71–73.

[5]For a further discussion of the series and extensive historical data for all the averages, see Farrell *The Dow-Jones Investor's Handbook*.

National Quotation Bureau Average

There is another price-weighted series which is, in contrast to the DJIA, probably one of the least-known of all stock market indicator series, the National Quotation Bureau (NQB) Average of 35 over-the-counter industrial stocks. The NQB index, like the DJIA, is composed of only industrial stocks and also includes the large, well-established, blue-chip companies traded on the OTC market.[6]

Value-Weighted Series

A value-weighted index is generated by deriving the initial total market value of all stocks used in the series (market value equals number of shares outstanding times current market price). This figure is typically established as the base and assigned an index value of 100. Subsequently, a new market value is computed for all securities in the index and this is compared to the initial "base" value to determine the percentage of change which, in turn, is applied to the beginning index value of 100.

$$\text{Index}_t = \frac{\Sigma P_t Q_t}{\Sigma P_b Q_b} \times \text{Beginning Index Value}$$

where:

Index_t = index value on day t

P_t = ending prices for stocks on day t

Q_t = number of outstanding shares on day t

P_b = ending prices for stocks on base day

Q_b = number of outstanding shares on base day.

A simple example for a three stock index is shown in Table 5.2.

As can be seen, there is an *automatic adjustment* for stock splits and other capital changes in a value-weighted index because the decrease in the stock price is offset by an increase in the number of shares outstanding. In a value-weighted index, the importance of individual stocks in the sample is dependent on the market value of the stocks. Therefore, a change in the value of a large company has a greater impact than a comparable percentage change for a small company. As an example, consider the figures in Table 5.2. If we begin with a base value of $200 million and there is a 20 percent increase in the value of stock A, which has a beginning value of $10 million, the ending index value will be $202 million or an

---

[6]Since the creation of the NASDAQ price indicator series in 1971 (to be discussed in the next section), it is very difficult to get figures for the NQB series. Apparently they are available daily only in the NQB "pink" sheets; weekly in the *OTC Market Chronicle;* and monthly in the *OTC Securities Review.*

Stock	Share Price	Number of Shares	Market Value
December 31, 1980			
A	$10.00	1,000,000	$ 10,000,000
B	15.00	6,000,000	90,000,000
C	20.00	5,000,000	100,000,000
Total			$200,000,000 –
			Base Value equal to and Index of 100
December 31, 1981			
A	$12.00	1,000,000	$ 12,000,000
B	10.00	12,000,000[a]	120,000,000
C	20.00	5,500,000[b]	110,000,000
Total			$242,000,000

$$\text{New Index Value} = \frac{\text{Current Market Value}}{\text{Base Value}} \times \text{Beginning Index Value}$$

$$= \frac{\$242,000,000}{200,000,000} \times 100$$

$$= 1.21 \times 100$$

$$= 121$$

Table 5.2   Example of Value-Weighted Index

[a]Stock split 2-for-1 during year.

[b]Company paid 10 percent stock dividend during the year.

index of 101. In contrast, if stock C increases by 20 percent from $100 million, the ending value will be $220 million or an index value of 110.

Standard & Poor's Indexes

The first company to widely employ a market value index was Standard & Poor's Corporation. The firm developed an index using 1935–1937 as a base period and computed a market value index for 425 industrial stocks. They also computed an index of 50 utilities and 25 transportation firms. Finally, they developed a 500-stock composite index. The base period was subsequently changed to 1941–1943 and the base value to 10. All the S&P series were again changed significantly on July 1, 1976 when the stocks considered were changed from 425 industrials, 60 utilities, and 15 rails, to 400 industrials, 40 utilities, 20 transportation, and 40 financial. A number of stocks added were listed on the OTC which was necessary because, as noted in Chapter 3, most of the major banks and insurance companies are traded on the OTC market. Therefore, to construct a relevant financial index, it was necessary to break with the tradition of only including NYSE-listed stocks.[7] In addition to their major market indicators, S&P has constructed over 90 individual industry series that include from 3 to 11 companies within an industry group. Daily figures for the major S&P indexes are carried in *The Wall Street Journal* and other newspapers, and weekly data are contained in *Barron's*. Standard & Poor's has a weekly publication titled *The Outlook* that contains weekly values for all the industry groups. Extensive historical data on all these indexes and other financial series are contained in Standard & Poor's *Trade and Securities Statistics*.

New York Stock Exchange Index

In 1966, the NYSE derived 5 market value indexes (industrial, utility, transportation, financial, and composite, which contains the other four) with figures available back to 1940 (The December 31, 1965 figures are equal to 50). In contrast to other indexes, the various NYSE series are not based upon a sample of stocks, but include all stocks listed on the Exchange. Therefore, questions about the number of stocks in the sample or the breadth of the sample do not arise. However, because the index is value-weighted, the issues of large companies still control major movements in the index. For example, the 500 stocks in the Standard & Poor's Composite Index represent 74 percent of the market value of all stocks on the exchange although they are only about 28 percent of exchange listings in terms of numbers.[8]

NASDAQ Series

These constitute a comprehensive set of price indicator series for the OTC market developed by the National Association of Securities Dealers (NASD). The NASDAQ–OTC Price Indicator Series were released to the public on May 17, 1971, with figures available from February 5, 1971 (the index value was 100 as of February 5). Through NASDAQ, the NASD provides daily, weekly, and monthly sets of stock price indicators for OTC securities in different industry categories. All domestic OTC common stocks listed on NASDAQ are included in the indexes, and new stocks are included when they are added to the system. The 2,337 issues contained in the NASDAQ–OTC Price Indexes have been divided into seven categories:[9]

---

[7]For a further discussion of the specific changes see *S&P 500 Stock Index Adds Financial, Transportation Groups* (New York: Standard & Poor's Corporation, 1976). For a detailed discussion of the computation of all the series and all the potential adjustments, see *Trade and Securities Statistics* (New York: Standard & Poor's Corp., 1981).

[8]For a detailed discussion of the index, written shortly after its creation, and including a historical chart, see Stan West and Norman Miller, "Why the New NYSE Common Stock Indexes?" *Financial Analysts Journal* 23 (1967): 49–54.

[9]As of January 1981, securities on the NASDAQ system not included in any of the indexes are warrants, preferred stocks, foreign stocks, and common stocks that are listed on an exchange but traded OTC (third market stocks).

1. composite (2,337 issues)

2. industrials (1,584 issues)

3. banks (53 issues)

4. insurance (125 issues)

5. other finance (449 issues)

6. transportation (51 issues)

7. utilities (75 issues).

The indexes are value-weighted series similar to the S&P series and the NYSE series. Because they are value-weighted, they are heavily influenced by the largest 100 stocks on the NASDAQ system. The NASDAQ series differs from the NQB–OTC series in terms of size of the samples (35 blue-chip stocks versus over 2,000 issues) and method of computation.

Most of the NASDAQ series are reported daily in *The Wall Street Journal* and are contained in *Barron's* on a weekly basis. The daily figures for all years since 1975 are contained in *Barron's Market Laboratory*.[10]

American Stock Exchange

The ASE developed a market indicator series in 1966. As originally developed, it was a price-change series in which the price changes during a given day were added and then divided by the number of issues on the exchange. This average price change was then added to, or subtracted from the previous day's index to arrive at a new index value.[11] As pointed out in two studies published in *Barron's,* this procedure eventually caused a substantial distortion in the value of the series.[12] Because of criticism of the series, the ASE subsequently commissioned the creation of a value-weighted series similar to that used by the NYSE and the NASD. This new series was released in October, 1973 with figures available back to 1969.

Wilshire 5000 Equity Index

This is a value-weighted index published by Wilshire Associates, Inc. (Santa Monica, California) which derives the dollar value of 5,000 common stocks, including all NYSE and ASE issues plus the most active stocks on the OTC market. Because of its sample, one would expect this index to be a weighted composite of the NYSE composite series, the ASE market value series, and the NASDAQ

---

[10]Maurice L. Farrell, ed., *Barron' Market Laboratory* (Princeton, NJ: Dow-Jones Books, annual).

[11]An extended discussion of the original series, including a historical chart, is contained in B. Alva Schoomer, Jr., "The American Stock Exchange Index System," *Financial Analysts Journal* 23 (1967): 57–61.

[12]S. C. Luethold and C. E. Gordon II, "Margin for Error," *Barron's,* 1 March 1971, p. 9; and S. C. Leuthold and K. F. Blaich, "Warped Yardstick," *Barron's,* 18 September 1972, p. 9.

composite, with the NYSE having the greatest influence because of the higher market value of its stocks. Weekly figures for this series are available in *Barron's*.

Unweighted Price Indicator Series

In an unweighted index, all stocks carry equal weight irrespective of their price and/or their value. A $20 stock is as important as a $40 stock, and the total market value of the company is not important. Such an index can be used by an individual who randomly selects stocks for his portfolio. One way to visualize an unweighted series is to assume that equal dollar amounts are invested in each stock in the portfolio (e.g., an equal $1000 investment in each stock). Therefore, the investor would own 50 shares of a $20 stock, 100 shares of a $10 stock, and 10 shares of a $100 stock.

The best-known unweighted (or equal-weighted) stock market series are those constructed by Lawrence Fisher at the University of Chicago.[13] These series were constructed in the course of studies conducted by Fisher and James Lorie that examined the performance of stocks on the NYSE assuming that an investor bought equal amounts of each stock on the exchange.[14] These series are updated periodically and have been used extensively in empirical studies.

Another unweighted price-indicator series that has gained in prominence is the *Indicator Digest* Index of all stocks on the NYSE. It is contended that compared to value-weighted series that are heavily influenced by large firms the *Indicator Digest* series is more representative of all stocks on the Exchange. In several instances, the *Indicator Digest* series reached a trough earlier than other indicator series, and continued to be depressed after some of the "popular" market indicator series resumed rising during a bull market. Such a difference indicates that the market increase only included the large, popular stocks contained in the DJIA or the Standard & Poor's market indicator series.[15]

Comparison of Indicator Series Changes Over Time

In this section we will discuss price movements in the different series with an emphasis on *source* of the samples as opposed to size or selection process. We will also consider price movements for the series in the short run (daily) and over

---

[13]Lawrence Fisher, "Some New Stock Market Indexes," *Journal of Business* 39, Supplement (1966): 191–225.

[14]Lawrence Fisher and James H. Lorie, "Rates of Return on Investments in Common Stock," *Journal of Business* 37 (1964): pp. 1–21; idem, "Rates of Return on Investments in Common Stock: The Year-By-Year Record, 1926–65," *Journal of Business* 41 (1968): 291–316; Lawrence Fisher, "Outcomes for 'Random' Investments in Common Stock Listed on the New York Stock Exchange," *Journal of Business* 38 (1965): 149–161.

[15]Carol J. Loomis, "How the Terrible Two-Tier Market Came to Wall Street," *Fortune*, July 1973, pp. 82–89.

more extended periods (yearly). Our emphasis will be on the difference in results for segments of the total equity market, the NYSE, the ASE, and OTC.

Daily Percentage of Changes

Table 5.3 contains a matrix of the correlation coefficients of the daily percentage of price changes for alternative market indicator series during the period January 4, 1972 through December 31, 1979 (2,019 observations). This recent eight-year period was selected because data were available for all the major series including the new ASE Market Value Series and the NASDAQ series initiated in February 1971.

The results are notable because *almost all of the differences in the correlations of daily percentages of price changes are apparently attributable to differences in the sample of stocks*, i.e., differences in the types of firms listed. All the major series except the DJIA are now total-market value indexes that include a large number of stocks. Therefore, the computational procedure is the same for each, the sample sizes are all quite large (from 400 to 2,400), and the samples represent either a large segment of the total population in terms of value or all members of the population. Thus, the only notable difference between several of the series is the members of the population; i.e., the stocks are from different segments of the aggregate stock market.

The results reported in Table 5.3 indicate that there is *very high positive correlation* between the alternative series that include almost all NYSE stocks (the DJIA, S&P 400, S&P 500, and the NYSE composite). Although there has been criticism of the DJIA because of its sample size and weighting, its correlation with the other major NYSE series ranged from about .89 to .92. This indicates that, on a short-run basis, the DJIA is a very adequate indicator of price movements on the exchange.

In contrast, there is a significantly lower correlation between each of these NYSE series and the ASE series, from an average of about .69 to .75. These results indicate the possibility that the market is segmented between the two exchanges (segmentation being indicated by significant differences in stock price movements).

The average correlation of other series with the NASDAQ Industrial Index is about .68, which is likewise significantly lower than the correlation among alternative NYSE series. In addition, the relationship between the NASDAQ and the ASE series is actually *lower* than it is with any of the NYSE series except the S&P 400. This can probably be explained by the fact that some very large firms are included in the NASDAQ system, such as Coors Company, Tampax Company, and Roadway Express. Several of these companies are larger than the largest firms on the ASE. Therefore, in some respects this index is more closely related to the NYSE than to the ASE.

There is likewise a fairly strong correlation between the NASDAQ Composite Index and the alternative NYSE series because of the difference in the sample for the two series. The NASDAQ composite series, as of 1981, contained

	DJIA	S&P 400	S&P 500	NYSE Composite	ASE Value Index	NASDAQ Industrials	NASDAQ Composite
DJIA	—						
S&P 400	.895	—					
S&P 500	.916	.894	—				
NYSE Composite	.923	.897	.920	—			
ASE Value Index	.716	.695	.727	.752	—		
NASDAQ Industrials	.678	.660	.682	.704	.675	—	
NASDAQ Composite	.794	.772	.800	.829	.788	.785	—

Table 5.3   Correlation Coefficients Between Daily Percentage of Price Changes for Alternative Market Indicator Series January 4, 1972–December 31, 1979 (2,019 Observations)

753 nonindustrial stocks which obviously have a substantial impact on the composite index because they make up a third of the sample in terms of number of issues, but have a much greater effect because of size. The NASDAQ series are value-weighted and some of the very largest OTC companies are insurance and finance firms in the nonindustrial group. These insurance and financial firms obviously have a large impact on the NASDAQ composite series and are, in many cases, similar to NYSE–listed companies.

Annual Price Changes

The annual percentage of price changes for the alternative price indicator series are contained in Table 5.4. The comparison between market segments cannot be made for all years from 1960 through 1979 because the series for the ASE is not available before 1969, while the OTC series was not available prior to February 1971. The four NYSE series, however, can be analyzed for a full 20-year period.

One would expect the DJIA series to be generally less volatile and also to experience lower average returns. The average returns were basically consistent with expectations because the returns for the DJIA were lower than they were for the other three NYSE series. In contrast, all the standard deviations were similar, with a tendency for the DJIA to be the largest.

For the 11-year period 1969–1979 it is possible to compare the results for the NYSE series to the ASE series. One would expect a higher return and a higher risk for the ASE series because of the smaller, more volatile companies listed on this exchange. The total period returns confirmed this, because the risk was higher, as indicated by a higher standard deviation of annual changes. The average price changes were also larger, as expected.

The results for the eight-year period 1972–1979 included all three market segments. The risk-measure results were consistent with expectations; the four

Year	DJIA	S&P[a] 400	S&P 500	NYSE Composite	ASE[b] Value Index	NASDAQ[c] Industrials	NASDAQ[c] Composite
1960	− 9.34	− 4.67	− 2.97	− 3.89			
1961	18.71	23.14	23.13	24.08			
1962	−10.91	−13.00	−11.81	−11.95			
1963	17.12	19.37	18.89	18.07			
1964	14.57	13.96	12.97	14.35			
1965	10.88	9.88	9.06	9.53			
1966	−18.94	−13.60	−13.09	−12.56			
1967	15.20	23.53	20.09	23.10			
1968	5.24	8.47	7.66	10.39			
1969	−15.19	−10.20	−11.36	−12.51	−28.98		
1970	4.82	− 0.58	0.10	− 2.52	−18.00		
1971	6.11	11.71	10.79	12.34	18.86		
1972	14.58	16.10	15.63	14.27	10.33	13.63	17.18
1973	−16.58	−17.38	−17.37	−19.63	−30.00	−36.88	−31.06
1974	−27.57	−29.93	−29.72	−30.28	−33.22	−32.44	−35.11
1975	38.34	31.92	31.55	31.86	38.40	43.38	29.76
1976	17.86	18.42	19.15	21.50	31.58	23.68	26.10
1977	−17.27	−12.35	−11.50	− 9.30	16.43[b]	9.30	7.33
1978	− 3.15	2.39	1.06	2.13	17.73	15.92	12.31
1979	4.19	12.88	12.31	15.54	64.10	38.10	28.11

Average of Annual Changes (Arithmetic Mean)

Year	DJIA	S&P[a] 400	S&P 500	NYSE Composite	ASE[b] Value Index	NASDAQ[c] Industrials	NASDAQ[c] Composite
1960–1979	2.43	4.50	4.23	4.73	—	—	—
1969–1979	0.56	2.09	1.88	2.13	7.93	—	—
1972–1979	1.30	2.76	2.64	3.26	14.42	9.34	6.83

Standard Deviation of Annual Changes

Year	DJIA	S&P[a] 400	S&P 500	NYSE Composite	ASE[b] Value Index	NASDAQ[c] Industrials	NASDAQ[c] Composite
1960–1979	16.33	16.09	15.63	16.35	—	—	—
1969–1979	18.22	17.41	17.28	18.04	30.31	—	—
1972–1979	20.46	19.62	19.43	20.10	30.85	27.69	24.19

Average Annual Compound Rate of Change (Geometric Mean)

Year	DJIA	S&P[a] 400	S&P 500	NYSE Composite	ASE[b] Value Index	NASDAQ[c] Industrials	NASDAQ[c] Composite
1960–1979	1.11	3.19	2.99	3.37	—	—	—
1969–1979	− 1.06	0.54	0.35	0.46	3.51	—	—
1972–1979	− 0.74	0.77	0.70	1.17	9.80	5.23	3.58

Table 5.4   Percentage Changes in Stock Price Indicator Series 1960−1979

[a]S&P 425 prior to July, 1976.

[b]Market-value index started on August 31, 1973 with data back to January 1, 1969.

[c]Index started on February 5, 1971 with no previous data available.

NYSE series all had lower standard deviations than either the ASE or the OTC market. Further, the ASE series was *more* volatile than the NASDAQ composite series, which can be explained by the types of companies on the ASE and by the fact that there are more companies in the NASDAQ series.

The average of the annual changes was consistent with risk: the DJIA had the lowest price changes, followed by the other NYSE series, followed by the NASDAQ series, and, finally the ASE series experienced the highest average price change. The average price changes were generally consistent with the standard deviations for the various series.

Summary

Given the several uses of stock market indicator series, it is important to know how they are constructed and the differences among them in terms of computational and sampling procedures. Because new series for the ASE and OTC have been introduced, the computational differences are slight. A comparison of short-run and long-run price changes for the alternative series indicates that the computational differences are not nearly as important as the differences in the sample of stocks used; i.e., whether the stocks are from the NYSE, the ASE, or the OTC market. Finally, the results were generally consistent with expectations regarding risk and return. The ASE and OTC typically had higher risk (more volatility) and higher returns (larger negative and positive price changes).

Questions

1. Set forth and discuss briefly the several uses that can be made of stock market indicator series.

2. What are the major factors that must be considered when constructing a market indicator series? Put another way, what characteristics differentiate indicator series?

3. What is meant when it is stated that a market indicator series is price weighted? In such a case, would you expect a $100 stock to be more important than a $25 stock? Why?

4. What are the major criticisms made of the Dow-Jones Industrial Average?

5. Describe the procedure used in computing a value-weighted series.

6. Describe how a price-weighted series adjusts for stock splits; how a value-weighted series adjusts for splits.

7. What is meant by an unweighted price-indicator series? How would you construct such a series? Assume a 10 percent price change in IBM and Coor's Brewing; which change will have the greater impact on such an indicator series? Why?

8. If you correlated percentage changes in the Wilshire 5000 Equity Index with

percentage changes in the NYSE Composite, the ASE Index, and the NASDAQ Composite Index, would you expect a difference in the results? Why or why not?

9. The correlation results between the daily percentage of price changes for the alternative NYSE price indicator series indicated substantial correlation among series. What would explain this similarity: size of sample, source of sample, or method of computation?

10. Regarding daily percentage of price changes, what would explain the significantly lower correlation between price changes for the NASDAQ Industrial Index and the various NYSE series? Would it be size of sample, source of sample, or method of construction?

11. Why is the relationship of the NASDAQ composite results with the NYSE series much better than that of the NASDAQ industrial results and the NYSE series?

12. Regarding the historical annual price movements for the various NYSE price indicator series, how did they differ in terms of annual price changes and variability of annual price changes? Were the differences generally consistent with what you would expect based upon economic theory? Discuss.

13. For the period 1972–1979 indicator series for all three market segments can be compared. During this period, were the results in terms of return (price change) and risk (variability of returns) consistent with expectations based upon economic theory? Discuss specifically why or why not.

References

Butler, H. L., Jr., and Allen, J. D. "The Dow-Jones Industrial Average Re-Reexamined," *Financial Analysts Journal* 35 (1979).

Butler, H. L., Jr., and Decker, M. G. "A Security Check on the Dow-Jones Industrial Average." *Financial Analysts Journal* 9 (1953).

Carter, E. E., and Cohen, K. J. "Bias in the DJIA Caused by Stock Splits." *Financial Analysts Journal* 22 (1966).

Carter, E. E., and Cohen, K. J. "Stock Average, Stock Splits, and Bias." *Financial Analysts Journal* 23 (1967).

Cootner, Paul. "Stock Market Indexes—Fallacies and Illusions." *Commercial and Financial Chronicle*, 29 September 1966.

Eubank, A. A., Jr. "Risk-Return Contrasts: NYSE, AMEX, and OTC." *Journal of Portfolio Management* 3 (1977).

Fisher, Lawrence. "Some New Stock Market Indexes." *Journal of Business* 39 Supplement (1966).

Latane, Henry A.; Tuttle, Donald L.; and Jones, Charles P. *Security Analysis and Portfolio Management.* 2d ed. New York: Ronald Press, 1975, Chapter 25.

Latane, Henry A.; Tuttle, Donald L.; and Young, William E. "Market Indexes and Their Implications for Portfolio Management." *Financial Analysts Journal* 27, (1971).

Lorie, James H., and Hamilton, Mary T. *The Stock Market: Theories and Evidence.* Homewood, IL.: Richard D. Irwin, 1973, Chapters 2 and 3.

Milne, R. D. "The Dow-Jones Industrial Average Re-Examined." *Financial Analysts Journal* 22 (1966).

Molodovsky, Nicholas. "Building a Stock Market Measure—A Case Story." *Financial Analysts Journal* 23 (1967.)

Reilly, Frank K. "Evidence Regarding a Segmented Stock Market." *Journal of Finance* 27 (1972).

Reilly, Frank K. "Price Changes in NYSE, AMEX and OTC Stocks Compared." *Financial Analysts Journal* 27 (1971).

Rudd, A. T., "The Revised Dow-Jones Industrial Average: New Wine in Old Bottles?" *Financial Analysts Journal* 35 (1979).

Schellbach, Lewis L. "When Did the DJIA Top 1200? *Financial Analysts Journal* 23 (1967).

Shaw, R. B. "The Dow-Jones Industrials vs. the Dow-Jones Industrial Average." *Financial Analysts Journal* 11 (1955).

West, Stan, and Miller, Norman. "Why the New NYSE Common Stock Indexes?" *Financial Analysts Journal* 23 (1967).

SOURCES OF INFORMATION ON INVESTMENTS

⇥ 6 ⇤

In the chapters that follow, we will discuss the factors that influence aggregate security prices, the prices for securities issued by various industries, and the "unique" factors that influence the returns on individual securities. It is important for the reader to know where to get relevant information to carry out these analyses. To aid in this task, in this chapter some of the major sources of information needed for aggregate economic and market analysis, industry analysis, and individual firm analysis are briefly described.[1] The outline of the presentation is as follows:

Aggregate Economic Analysis

    Government Sources

    Bank Publications

Aggregate Stock Market Analysis

    Government Publications

    Commercial Publications

    Brokerage Firm Reports

Industry Analysis

    S&P Industry Survey

    Trade Associations

    Industry Magazines

---

[1]On several occasions we will discuss *primary* and *secondary* sources of information. A primary source is a source that *generates* the data; e.g., U.S. government publications are a primary source for information on the GNP. A secondary source reprints the data obtained from a primary source.

Individual Stock Analysis

    Company-Generated Information

    Commercial Publications

    Brokerage Firm Reports

    Investment Magazines

    Academic Journals

    Computerized Data Sources

Sources for Aggregate Economic Analysis

This section is concerned with data used in estimating overall economic changes as contrasted to data on the aggregate securities markets (stocks, bonds, etc.).

Government Sources

It should come as no surprise that the main source of information on the economy is the federal government, which issues a variety of publications on the topic.

Federal Reserve Bulletin   This is a monthly publication issued by the Board of Governors of the Federal Reserve System. The magazine contains extensive economic data with thorough coverage of monetary data such as: monetary aggregates; factors affecting member-bank reserves; member-bank reserve requirements; Federal Reserve open-market transactions; and loans and investments of all commercial banks. It is the primary source for almost all monetary data. In addition, it contains figures on financial markets, including interest rates and some stock market statistics; data on corporate finance including profits, assets, and liabilities of corporations; extensive nonfinancial statistics on output, the labor force, and the GNP; and an extensive section on international finance.

Survey of Current Business   A monthly publication issued by the United States Department of Commerce that gives details on national income and production figures. It is an excellent primary source for current, detailed information on all segments of the Gross National Product and national income. It also contains an extensive listing of industrial production for numerous segments of the economy. The Survey is an excellent secondary source for labor statistics (employment and wages), interest rates, and statistics on foreign economic development.

Economic Indicators   A monthly publication prepared for the Congressional Joint Economic Committee by the President's Council of Economic Advisers. It contains monthly and annual data on output, income, spending, employment, production, prices, money and credit, federal finance, and the international economic situation.

Business Conditions Digest (BCD)   A monthly publication issued by the Department of Commerce's Census Bureau that contains data and charts relating to economic indicators derived by the National Bureau of Economic Research (NBER). The NBER has developed a set of economic time series that has consistently indicated future trends in the economy. These series are referred to as leading indicators. The bureau also publishes economic series that turn with the general economy and are used to define business cycles (referred to as coincident series). Finally, it makes available economic series that tend to turn up or down *after* the general economy does, and are referred to as lagging indicators.[2] Basic data for the major series and analytical charts are provided in the BCD. In addition, it contains composite and analytical measures such as diffusion indexes and rate of change series.

The Quarterly Financial Report (QFR)   This is prepared by the Federal Trade Commission and contains up-to-date aggregate statistics on the financial position of U.S. corporations. Based upon an extensive quarterly sample survey, the QFR presents estimated statements of income and retained earnings, balance sheets, and related financial and operating ratios for all manufacturing corporations. Since the third quarter of 1974, the publication has also included data on mining and trade corporations. The statistical data are classified by industry and, within the manufacturing group, by size.

Business Statistics   A biennial supplement to the *Survey of Current Business* that contains extensive historical data for about 2,500 series contained in the survey. The historical data typically include monthly figures for the past four or five years, and quarterly figures for the previous ten years. Annual data typically go back to 1947, if available. A notable feature is a section of explanatory notes for each of the series that describes the series and indicates the primary source for the data.

Federal Reserve Monthly Chart Book   This is a publication of the Federal Reserve Board that presents graphs depicting many of the monetary and economic series contained in the *Federal Reserve Bulletin*. It emphasizes the short-run changes in these series.

Historical Chart Book   A supplement to the *Federal Reserve Monthly Chart Book* that contains long-range financial and business series not included in the monthly book. At the back of the publication is an excellent discussion of the various series that indicates the source of the data for further reference.

---

[2]These series are discussed more extensively in Chapter 10 where they are related to stock market movements.

Economic Report of the President   Each year in January, the President of the United States prepares an economic report that he transmits to the Congress indicating what has transpired during the past year and including a discussion of what he considers will be the major economic problems during the coming year.

This message is published by the federal government and also contains an extensive document titled, "The Annual Report of the Council of Economic Advisers." The report generally runs over 150 pages and contains a detailed discussion of developments in the domestic and international economies gathered by the council (the group that advises the president on economic policy). An appendix contains statistical tables relating to income, employment, and production. Many of the tables provide annual data from the 1940s, in some instances from 1929, to the present.

The Statistical Abstract of the United States   This book, which has been published annually since 1878, is the standard summary of statistics on the social, political, and economic organization of the United States. Prepared by the Bureau of the Census, it is designed to serve as a convenient statistical reference and as a guide to other statistical publications and sources. This volume, which currently runs over 900 pages, includes a selection of data from many statistical publications, both government and private.

Bank Publications

In addition to the material issued by the government, there are data and comments on the economy published by a number of banks. Almost all of these appear monthly and are sent free of charge to individuals requesting them. They can be categorized as publications of Federal Reserve Banks or of commercial banks.

Federal Reserve Banks

The Federal Reserve System is divided into 12 Federal Reserve Districts with a major Federal Reserve Bank in each as follows:[3]

1. Boston	7. Chicago
2. New York	8. St. Louis
3. Philadelphia	9. Minneapolis
4. Cleveland	10. Denver
5. Richmond	11. Dallas
6. Atlanta	12. San Francisco

[3]Specific addresses for each of the district banks and names of major personnel are contained in the *Federal Reserve Bulletin*, published monthly by the board.

Each of the Federal Reserve district banks has a research department that issues periodic reports. Although most of the publications generated by the various banks differ, monthly reviews, which are available to interested parties, are published by all district banks. These reviews typically contain one or several articles of interest to those in the region as well as statistics. A major exception is the St. Louis Federal Reserve Bank which publishes numerous releases weekly, monthly, and quarterly that contain extensive national and international data and comments in addition to its monthly review.[4]

Commercial Banks

A number of large banks prepare weekly or monthly letters that are available to interested individuals. These "letters" are generally comments on the current and future outlook of the economy. Therefore, they typically contain only limited data. Some of the banks publishing letters are:

Chase Manhattan (New York)

Continental Illinois (Chicago)

Harris Trust and Savings (Chicago)

Manufacturers Hanover Trust Company (New York)

Aggregate Stock Market Analysis

There are several government publications that provide useful data on the stock market, but the bulk of detailed information is provided by private firms. Several of the government publications discussed earlier *(Federal Reserve Bulletin; Survey of Current Business)* contain financial market data, such as interest rates and stock prices.

Government Publications

The main source of securities market data is the Securities and Exchange Commission (SEC). The SEC is the federal agency responsible for regulating the operation of the securities markets and collects data in this regard.

Statistical Bulletin   A monthly publication of the SEC that contains data on securities trading in the United States with an emphasis on common stocks. This includes volume of trading on all exchanges and the OTC market; prices on

---

[4]An individual can request to be put on the mailing list for any of these publications (free of charge) by writing to:
    Federal Reserve Bank of St. Louis
    P.O. Box 442
    St. Louis, MO 63166

these exchanges; volatility and liquidity measures; and information on new-issue registrations. In recent years it has also contained data on options trading.

Annual Report of the SEC   This is an annual publication of the SEC for the fiscal year ending in June. It contains a detailed discussion of important developments during the year and comments on the SEC's disclosure system and regulation of the securities markets. Finally, it includes a statistics section containing historical data on many of the items in the *Statistical Bulletin* as well as other annual series.

Commercial Publications

Considering the numerous advisory services in existence, a section dealing with their publications could become voluminous. Therefore, our intent is to list and discuss the *major* services and allow you to develop your own list of "other available sources." An excellent source of advertisements for these services is *Barron's*.

New York Stock Exchange Fact Book   An annual publication of the New York Stock Exchange. The book is an outstanding source of current and historical data on activity on the NYSE, but it also contains comparative data on the ASE, the OTC, institutional trading, and investments in general.

Amex Databook   This is a comparable data book for the American Stock Exchange. The first book was published in 1969, with subsequent editions in 1971, 1973, and 1976. It contains pertinent information on the exchange, its membership, administration, and trading activities.

Wall Street Journal   Published by Dow-Jones and Company, it is the only daily national business newspaper in the United States. It is published five days a week and is clearly the most complete source of daily information on companies and security market prices. It contains complete listings for the NYSE, the ASE, the NASDAQ–OTC market, bond markets, options markets, and commodities quotations. It is recognized worldwide as a primary source of financial and business information.[5]

Barron's   This is a weekly publication of Dow-Jones and Company that typically contains four articles on topics of interest to investors. In addition, this newspaper has the most complete weekly listing of prices and quotes for all financial markets. It provides weekly data on individual stocks, and the latest information on earnings and dividends, as well as including columns on commodities and stock options. Finally, toward the back (typically the last three pages), there

---

[5]A booklet that includes a discussion of many of the features of the *Wall Street Journal* is "A Future Manager's Guide to the *Wall Street Journal*." Copies are available from, *The Wall Street Journal*, Educational Service Bureau, P.O. Box 300, Princeton, NJ 08540.

is an extensive statistical section with detailed information on stock market behavior for the past week.[6]

Dow Jones Booklets

Because of the interest in the statistics contained in Dow-Jones publications, the
company has begun publishing several annual "handbooks."

The Dow-Jones Investor's Handbook   This contains the complete DJIA results
for each year, along with earnings and dividends for the series since 1939. Individual reports on common and preferred stocks and bonds listed on the NYSE
and ASE, including high and low prices, volume, dividends, and the year's most
active stocks, are also included.

The Barron's Market Laboratory   This is an annual compilation of many of
the figures contained in the weekly statistics page of *Barron's*. It contains extensive stock and bond averages (foreign and domestic), and volume of sales,
among other items.

The Dow-Jones Commodities Handbook   This contains a review of price action during the past year for every major futures market and a discussion of the
outlook for these markets. In addition, there are tables of key supply-demand
statistics and cash prices for major markets.

The Dow-Jones Stock Options Handbook   This contains concise financial
sketches of every company whose common stocks underlie options traded on
any of the listed options markets. Tables show how options premiums moved
during the year in relation to prices of underlying securities and to the overall
stock market.

S&P Trade and Security Statistics   This is a service of Standard & Poor's that
includes a basic set of historical data on various economic and security price
series and a monthly supplement that updates the series for the recent period.
There are two major sets of data: (1) business and financial, and (2) security price
index record. Within the business and finance section are long-term statistics on
trade, banking, industry, price, agriculture, and financial trends.

The security price index record contains historical data for all of the Standard & Poor's indexes. This includes 500 stocks broken down into 88 individual groups, from which the four main groups, industrial composite, rails,
utilities, and the 500 composite are derived. There are also four supplementary
group series: capital goods companies, consumer goods, high-grade common
stocks, and low-priced common stocks. In addition to the stock-price series,

---

[6]A booklet that discusses many of the features in *Barron's* and how the series are used by technicians is
Martin E. Zweig, *Understanding Technical Forecasting*. It is likewise available, free of charge, from the
Wall Street Journal, Educational Service Bureau, address above.

Standard & Poor's has derived a quarterly series of earnings and dividends for each of the four main groups. The earnings series includes data from 1946 to the present.

The booklet also contains data on daily stock sales on the NYSE from 1918 on and historical yields for a number of bond series, both corporate and government.

Brokerage Firm Reports

As a means of competing for the investor's business, brokerage firms provide, among other services, information and recommendations on the outlook for securities markets (bonds and stocks). These reports are typically prepared monthly and distributed to customers (or potential customers) of the firm, free of charge. In the competition for institutional business, some of these firms have generated reports that are quite extensive and sophisticated. Among the brokerages issuing these reports are: Goldman Sachs & Company; Merrill Lynch, Pierce, Fenner & Smith; and Salomon Brothers.

Industry Analysis

There is only one publication containing information on a number of industries, the *Standard & Poor's Industry Survey*. Beyond this, the major source of data on a given industry is trade associations or trade magazines.

Standard & Poor's Industry Survey

This is a two-volume reference work that is divided into 34 segments dealing with 69 major domestic industries. Coverage in each area is divided into a current analysis and a basic analysis. The latter begins with an examination of the prospects for that particular industry, followed by an analysis of trends and problems presented in historical perspective. Major segments of the industry are spotlighted and a comparative analysis of the principal companies in the industry is also included. The current analysis provides information on the latest developments in the industry and available industry, market, and company statistics, along with appraisals of the investment outlook for the specific area covered.

Trade Associations

These are organizations set up by those involved in an industry or a general area of business to provide information for others in the area on such topics as: education, advertising, lobbying for legislation, and problem solving. Trade associations gather extensive statistics for the industry. Examples of such organizations include:[7]

Iron and Steel Institute

American Railroad Association

National Consumer Finance Association

Institute of Life Insurance

American Banker's Association

Machine Tool Association

Industry Magazines

These are an excellent source of data and general information. Depending upon the industry, there can be several publications—the computer industry has spawned at least five such magazines. Examples of industry publications include:

Computers

Real Estate Today

Chemical Week

Modern Plastics

Paper Trade Journal

Automotive News

Individual Stocks

Company-Generated Information

An obvious source of information about a company is the company itself. In the case of some small firms, it may be the *only* source of information because there is not enough activity to justify its inclusion in studies issued by commercial services.

Annual Reports
All firms with publicly traded stock are required to prepare and distribute to their stockholders annual reports of financial operations and current financial posi-

---

[7]For a more extensive list see *Encyclopedia of Associations* (Detroit: Gale Research Company, 1977).

tion. In addition to basic information, most reports contain a discussion of what happened during the year and some consideration of future prospects. Most firms also publish a *quarterly financial report* that includes a brief income statement for this interim period and, sometimes, a balance sheet. Both of these reports can be obtained directly from the company. To find an address for a company *Standard & Poor's Register of Corporations, Directors, and Executives* should be consulted. The register is published in three volumes, the most useful of which for the specified purpose is volume one, which contains an alphabetical listing, by business name, of approximately 37,000 corporations.

Security Prospectus

When a firm wants to sell some securities (bonds, preferred stock, or common stock) in the primary market to raise new capital, the Securities and Exchange Commission (SEC) requires that it file a registration statement describing the securities being offered and containing information on the company. The financial information is more extensive than that required in an annual report and such statements also include a substantial amount of nonfinancial information on the firm's operations and personnel. A condensed version of the registration statement, referred to as a *prospectus,* is published by the underwriting firm, and contains most of the relevant information. Copies of a prospectus for a current offering can be obtained from the underwriter or from the company.

Required SEC Reports[8]

In addition to registration statements, the SEC requires three *periodic* statements from publicly held firms. The 8–K form is a report which firms registered with the SEC are required to file each month. In this report, any action that affects the debt, equity, amount of capital assets, voting right, or other changes that would be expected to have a significant impact on the stock is indicated.

The 9–K form is an unaudited report that must be filed every six months, and contains revenues, expenses, gross sales, and special items. This is typically more extensive than the quarterly statements are.

The 10–K form is an annual version of the 9–K but is even more complete. Recently, the SEC has required firms to indicate in their annual reports that a copy of their 10–K is available from the company upon request without charge.

Commercial Publications

There are numerous firms that sell advisory services supplying information on the aggregate market and individual stocks. Therefore, the following is a discussion of only a portion of the information available.

---

[8]For a further discussion of these reports, see Carl W. Schneider, "SEC Filings—Their Use to the Professional," *Financial Analysts Journal* 21 (1965): 33–38.

Standard & Poor's Corporation Records   This is currently a set of seven volumes, the first six of which contain basic information on corporations arranged alphabetically and not according to industry type. The volumes are in binders and are updated throughout the year. The seventh volume is a daily news volume that contains recent data on all companies listed in all the volumes.

Standard & Poor's Stock Reports   These are comprehensive, two-page reports on numerous companies with stocks listed on the NYSE or ASE, or traded OTC. They include the near-term sales and earnings outlook, recent developments, key income statement and balance sheet items, and a chart of stock price movements, and are available in bound volumes arranged by exchange. These reports are revised at least once every three to four months. A sample page is shown in Figure 6.1.

Standard & Poor's Stock Guide   This is a monthly publication that contains, in compact form, pertinent financial data on more than 5,100 common and preferred stocks. A separate section covers over 380 mutual fund issues. The guide contains information for each stock on price ranges (historical and recent), dividends, earnings, financial position, institutional holdings, and ranking for earning and dividend stability. It is a very useful quick reference for almost all actively traded stocks, as is shown by the example in Figure 6.2.

Standard & Poor's Bond Guide   This is likewise published monthly. It contains the most pertinent comparative financial and statistical information on a broad range of domestic and foreign bonds (about 3,900 issues), 200 foreign government bonds, and about 650 convertible bonds.

The Outlook   This is a weekly publication of Standard & Poor's Corporation. It contains advice on the general market environment and also has features on specific groups of stocks or industries (e.g., high-dividend stocks, stocks with low price-to-earnings ratios, high-yielding bonds, stocks likely to increase their dividends, etc.). It also contains weekly figures for 88 industry groups and other market statistics.

Moody's Industrial Manual   This is similar to the S&P service. It is currently published once a year in two bound volumes. It covers industrial companies listed on the NYSE and ASE, as well as companies listed on regional exchanges. There is also a section on international industrial firms and an Industrial News Reports section that contains descriptions of pertinent events that occurred after publication of the basic manual.

Moody's OTC Industrial Manual   This is similar to the *Moody's Industrial Manual* of listed firms, but is limited to stocks traded on the OTC market. Supplementary volumes containing information on recent developments are also published.

Int'l Business Machines   1210

NYSE Symbol IBM   Put & Call Options on CBOE

Price	Range	P-E Ratio	Dividend	Yield	S&P Ranking
May 1'81	1981				
59¹/₈	71¹/₂-58¹/₂	10	3.44	5.8%	A -

Summary

IBM is the world's largest manufacturer of computers and information processing equipment and systems. Earnings increased in 1980, following a rare decline in 1979, although unusual tax adjustments exaggerated the degree of improvement. Further gains are anticipated in 1981. Projected strong demand for improved productivity is expected to fuel long-term growth. A June 1, 1981 deadline has been set for the completion of the company's antitrust trial.

Current Outlook

Earnings for 1981 are estimated at $6.40 a share, versus 1980's $6.10 (which included gains of $0.38 from tax adjustments).

Dividends at $0.86 quarterly are the minimum expectation.

Gross income for the remainder of 1981 should advance at a faster pace than the 12.4% gain of the first quarter, as high backlogs and generally strong new order activity would outweigh a potential softening in some geographic areas. Margins are likely to remain under pressure from rising costs and continued major investments for future growth, but cost control and productivity programs may provide some relief. With demand for information processing and handling products expected to rise steadily, IBM's leading position in the industry, together with its ongoing commitment to technological innovation to meet the need for improved productivity, should enable it to maintain strong growth rates over the longer term.

Gross Income (Billion $)

Quarter	1981	1980	1979	1978
Mar.	6.46	5.75	5.30	4.43
Jun.		6.18	5.35	4.92
Sep.		6.48	5.38	5.28
Dec.		7.81	6.83	6.44
		26.21	22.86	21.07

Gross income for the three months ended March 31, 1981 advanced 12%, year to year, aided by an improved purchase/lease mix and much higher service revenues. Larger cost increases were partially offset by exchange gains of $27 million, versus losses of $30 million; pretax income was up 7.6%. After taxes at 43.9%, against 43.7%, net income rose 7.1%.

TRADING VOLUME
THOUSAND SHARES

Capital Share Earnings ($)

Quarter	1981	1980	1979	1978
Mar.	1.25	1.17	1.14	1.00
Jun.		1.31	1.15	1.19
Sep.		1.51	1.14	1.39
Dec.		2.11	1.73	1.74
		6.10	5.16	5.32

Important Developments

Apr. '81—Judge D.N. Edelstein, U.S. District Court of Manhattan, set June 1, 1981 as the deadline for completion of IBM's antitrust trial.

Apr. '81—Management said that capital spending in 1981 should continue to be heavy, but added that the rate of growth could moderate by 1982.

Next earnings report due in mid-July.

Per Share Data ($)

Yr. End Dec. 31	1980	1979	1978	1977	1976	1975	1974	1973	1972	1971
Book Value	28.18	25.64	23.14	21.39	21.15	19.05	17.05	15.02	13.00	11.50
Earnings	6.10	5.16	5.32	¹4.58	¹3.99	3.34	¹3.12	¹2.70	¹2.21	¹1.88
Dividends	3.44	3.44	2.88	2.50	2.00	1.62¹/₂	1.39	1.12	1.08	1.04
Payout Ratio	56%	67%	54%	54%	50%	49%	45%	42%	49%	56%
Prices—High	72³/₄	80¹/₂	77¹/₂	71¹/₂	72¹/₈	56⁷/₈	63¹/₂	91³/₈	85³/₈	73¹/₄
Low	50³/₈	61¹/₈	58³/₄	61¹/₈	55⁷/₈	37³/₄	37⁵/₈	58⁷/₈	66³/₄	56³/₄
P/E Ratio—	12-8	16-12	15-11	16-13	18-14	17-12	20-12	34-22	39-30	39-30

Data as orig. reptd. Adj. for stk. div(s). of 300% Jun. 1979, 25% May 1973. 1. Ful. dil. 4.57 in 1977, 3.98 in 1976, 3.12 in 1974, 2.69 in 1973, 2.21 in 1972, 1.88 in 1971.

Standard NYSE Stock Reports Vol. 48/No. 88/Sec. 16	**May 8, 1981** Copyright © 1981 Standard & Poor's Corp. All Rights Reserved	Standard & Poor's Corp. 25 Broadway, NY, NY 10004

Figure 6.1   Sample Page from S&P Stock Reports

Source: *Standard & Poor's Stock Reports* (New York: Standard & Poor's Corp., 1981). Reprinted by permission.

1210   International Business Machines Corp.

Income Data (Million $)

Year Ended Dec. 31	Revs.	Oper. Inc.	% Oper. Inc. of Revs.	Cap. Exp.	Depr.	Int. Exp.	Net Bef. Taxes	Eff. Tax Rate	Net Inc.	% Net Inc. of Revs.
1980	26,213	8,102	30.9%	6,592	2,362	¹325	²5,897	39.6%	3,562	13.6%
1979	22,863	7,215	31.6%	5,991	1,970	140	5,553	45.8%	3,011	13.2%
1978	21,076	7,265	34.5%	4,046	1,824	55	5,798	46.3%	3,111	14.8%
1977	18,133	6,657	36.7%	3,395	1,999	40	5,092	46.6%	2,719	15.0%
1976	16,304	5,928	36.4%	2,518	1,858	45	4,519	46.9%	2,398	14.7%
1975	14,437	5,245	36.3%	2,439	1,822	63	3,721	46.5%	1,990	13.8%
1974	12,675	4,871	38.4%	2,913	1,708	69	3,435	46.5%	1,838	14.5%
1973	10,993	4,363	39.7%	2,186	1,589	97	2,946	46.5%	1,575	14.3%
1972	9,533	3,731	39.1%	1,728	1,419	78	2,425	47.3%	1,279	13.4%
1971	8,274	3,228	39.0%	1,882	1,254	70	2,056	47.5%	1,079	13.0%

Balance Sheet Data (Million $)

Dec. 31	Cash	Current Assets	Current Liab.	Ratio	Total Assets	Ret. on Assets	Long Term Debt	Common Equity	Total Cap.	% LT Debt of Cap.	Ret. on Equity
1980	2,112	9,925	6,526	1.5	26,703	13.9%	2,099	16,453	18,734	11.2%	22.7%
1979	3,771	10,851	6,445	1.7	24,530	13.3%	1,589	14,961	16,690	9.5%	21.2%
1978	4,031	10,321	5,810	1.8	20,771	15.7%	286	13,494	13,889	2.1%	24.0%
1977	5,407	10,073	5,209	1.9	18,978	15.0%	256	12,618	12,962	2.0%	21.7%
1976	6,156	9,920	4,082	2.4	17,723	14.4%	275	12,749	13,088	2.1%	19.8%
1975	4,768	8,115	3,363	2.4	15,531	13.4%	295	11,416	11,756	2.5%	18.4%
1974	3,805	7,010	3,210	2.2	14,027	13.9%	336	10,110	10,482	3.2%	19.3%
1973	3,322	5,830	2,555	2.3	12,290	13.6%	652	8,812	9,496	6.9%	19.2%
1972	2,577	4,822	2,259	2.1	10,792	12.5%	773	7,566	8,367	9.2%	17.9%
1971	1,875	3,949	2,088	1.9	9,576	11.9%	676	6,642	7,358	9.2%	17.1%

Data as orig. reptd. 1. Reflects accounting change. 2. Incl. equity in earns. of nonconsol. subs.

Business Summary

IBM is primarily involved in information-handling systems, equipment and services

1980	Gross Inc.	Op. Income
Data processing	82%	91%
Office products	16%	8%
Federal systems	2%	1%

Outright sales provided 42% of revenues in 1980, rentals 41%, and services 17%. Operations outside of the U.S. contributed 53% of both revenues and earnings.

In the data processing segment, IBM provides a wide range of computer products, systems and software, as well as systems engineering, education and related services and supplies.

Office products include electric and electronic typewriters, magnetic media typewriters and systems, information processors, printers, copiers and related supplies and services.

The Federal systems business supplies specialized information handling products and services, primarily for U.S. government space, defense and other agencies.

IBM also offers educational, training and testing materials and services for school, home and industrial use.

Dividend Data

Dividends have been paid since 1916. A dividend reinvestment plan is available.

Amt. of Divd. $	Date Decl.	Ex-divd. Date	Stock of Record	Payment Date
0.86	Jul. 29	Aug. 7	Aug. 13	Sep. 10'80
0.86	Oct. 28	Nov. 5	Nov. 12	Dec. 10'80
0.86	Jan. 27	Feb. 5	Feb. 11	Mar. 10'81
0.86	Apr. 27	May 7	May 13	Jun. 10'81

Next dividend meeting: late Jul. '81.

Finances

Tax adjustments applicable to reductions of tax liabilities in prior periods added $224 million ($0.38 a share) to net income in 1980.

Capitalization

Long Term Debt: $2,099,000,000.

Capital Stock: 583,806,832 shs. ($1.25 par). Institutions hold approximately 49%. Shareholders: 737,230.

Office—Armonk, New York 10504. Tel—(914) 765-1900. Stockholder Relations Dept—717 Fifth Ave. NYC 10022 Tel—(212) 223-4400. Chrmn—F. T. Cary. Pres & CEO—J. R. Opel. Secy—J. H. Grady. Treas—C. A. Northrop. Investor Contact—D. Otis. Dirs—S. D. Bechtel, Jr., G. B. Beitzel, J. E. Burke, F. T. Cary, W. T. Coleman, Jr., J. M. Fox, G. K. Funston, C. A. Hills, A. Houghton, Jr., J. N. Irwin II, N. deB. Katzenbach, T. V. Learson, R. W. Lyman, D. R. McKay, M. McK. Moller, W. H. Moore, J. R. Munro, J. R. Opel, P. J. Rizzo, W. W. Scranton, I. S. Shapiro, C. R. Vance, T. J. Watson, Jr., A. L. Williams. Transfer Agents—Company's NYC & Chicago offices. Registrars—Morgan Guaranty Trust Co., NYC; First National Bank, Chicago. Incorporated in New York in 1911.

Information has been obtained from sources believed to be reliable, but its accuracy and completeness are not guaranteed.   J.R.L.

Figure 6.1   continued

128 Lac-Len **STANDARD & POOR'S CORPORATION**

INDEX	Ticker Symbol	STOCKS NAME OF ISSUE (Call Price of Pfd. Stocks)	Market	Com Rank. & Pfd. Rating	Par Val.	Inst. Hold Cos	Inst. Hold Shs. (000)	PRINCIPAL BUSINESS	Price Range 1960-78 High	1960-78 Low	1979 High	1979 Low	1980 High	1980 Low	Dec. Sales in 100s	December, 1980 Last Sale Or Bid High	Low	Last	% Div. Yield	P-E Ratio
1	LG	**Laclede Gas**	NY,M	B+	4	20	235	Distr nat gas in St. Louis	32⅛	11⅝	23⅝	18⅛	24¼	14⅞	751	24¼	20⅞	23⅝	9.1	7
2	LCLD	**Laclede Steel**	N	B–	20	5	78	Semi & finished steel prods	35¼	3½	15¾	8	14	7⅞	836	10½	9	9B		d
3	LKK	**Lake Shore Mines**	AS,Tc	B–	1	4	130	Investments: custom mill'g	9½	1⅜	5¾	2¼	39½	4½	3137	39½	25¾	29¼		22
4	LAKE	**Lake Superior Dis Pw**	N	B+	10	2	3	Elec util-Wisc & Mich areas	15¼	8	11¾	9	12½	8	83	10	8¾	9½B	12.2	6
5	LMR	**La Maur, Inc**	AS	B	3⅓¢	1	20	Hair care,personal grooming	40	2¼	7¾	4	10½	3⅞	2390	10½	6⅛	9	2.2	11
6	LMS	**Lamson & Sessions**	NY	B+	5	11	546	Freight car eq: fasteners	14	2¼	21	9½	17⅜	7⅛	1598	8	7⅛	7⅝	2.6	d
7	LANC	**Lancaster Colony**	N	B+	1	10	414	Housewares: ind'l products	32	2½	20	11¾	15⅝	9¼	568	14½	12	12⅛B	6.6	7
8	LNCE	**Lance, Inc**	N	A	83⅓¢	19	1387	Snack foods: vending	30	3⅞	23¾	16¼	28	16¾	3090	24¾	20	21¼B	5.5	9
9	LOLS	**Land of Lincoln Sv & Ln**	N	...	1	2	43	Savings & Loan in Illinois	...	...	7½	6⅜	7⅝	4⅝	662	6¾	5½	6⅝B	5.7	6
10	LRES	**Land Resources**	N	NR	10¢	2	108	Real estate interests	13⅜	½	3⅝	2	7⅛	2¼	968	7⅛	5⅛	5½B		10
11	LNDB	**Landmark Bancshrs**	N	...	5	...	...	Multi-bank hldg: Missouri	16½	7½	15½	11½	20	12	42	20	19	20B	5.0	7
12	LBKF	**Landmark Bkg Fla**	N	...	1	11	902	Multiple bank hldg. Fla	22¼	4½	7⅛	5¼	10	5⅞	3397	10	8¼	9¾B	5.1	6
13	LML	**Landmark Land**	AS,M	NR	50¢	1	250	Land develop:bldg mtls dstr	30⅝	1¼	11	4⅛	19	9⅛	644	12⅛	10½	11		9
14	LNY	**Lane Bryant**	NY	A–	No	12	219	Apparel,shoe chain,mail order	34	5⅛	22½	11⅝	20⅜	12⅛	607	18⅞	16	17¾	5.6	7
15	LANE	**Lane Co**	N	A–	5	12	538	Furniture mfr.	59	4⅝	25¾	18¼	29	17¾	297	27¾	27	27B	†5.3	5
16	LAND	**Lane Wood**	N	B–	1	...	...	Mobile hm:handbags:store fix	24⅛	¼	2¾	1¼	2⅛	⅞	933	2⅛	1⅝	1⅝B	...	6
17	LNO	**Laneco, Inc**[60]	AS	B+	1	1	7	Supermkts & department strs	10⅞	1⅛	11	5⅝	11	7⅞	81	9⅜	8⅝	9	s2.7	5
18	LCOR	**Langley Corp**	N	B–	1	1	8	Metal parts,aerosp/electron	14⅞	¼	3¾	1¾	4½	2	727	3⅞	3¼	3½B	...	8
19	LBP	**Lanier Business Pr**	NY,M	NR	1	44	3232	Mfr dictating eq:dstr 3M pr	23⅝	8¾	33½	18	39½	18⅝	1045	36¾	31½	36¼	1.5	15
20	LPI	**La Pointe Indus**	AS	C	1	1	6	Electronic equipment mfr	25	⅝	3¼	2¼	4¼	1⅝	248	2	1⅝	2	...	d
21	LQM	**La Quinta Mtr Inns**	NY,M	B+	10¢	13	1992	Motor inn operator	10⅝	⅜	10½	7½	19¾	8⅜	1747	18⅝	17¼	18⅝		18
22	LARS	**Larsen Co**	N	B+	1	4	44	Canned & frozen vegetables	21	4 1/16	21	16¼	18½	15	135	16	15¼	15¼B	7.9	6
23	LAWH	**Lawhon (J.F.)Furniture**	N	NR	5¢	...	...	Warehouse-showroom retailer	6	2	2¼	⅞	1	½	653	¾	¼	¾B	...	d
24	LAWS	**Lawson Products**	N	B+	No	25	960	Dstr fasteners, maint parts	31½	1⅜	29	19¼	30½	23¼	1076	29	26	27½B	1.5	12
25	LAW	**Lawter Chemicals**	NY	A	1	47	2094	Printing ink vehicles, resin	21¼	¼	15	9⅝	14½	9½	2694	12¼	10⅝	12	5.5	12
26	LKI	**Lazare Kaplan Int'l**	AS	B	1	3	63	Cutter/merchant diamonds	17	2¾	16¼	10⅞	18⅜	11⅛	354	15⅛	13⅛	13⅜	3.7	d
27	LAZB	**La-Z-Boy Chair**	N	B+	1	7	203	Mfr of reclining chairs	46¾	4⅜	12¼	8¾	11½	7¼	998	10¼	9	10B	7.2	5
28	LDBC	**LDB Corp**	N	B–	1	3	19	Floor cov'g: food sv:mob hm	68	1/16	5½	2⅜	4	2½	2223	3¼	2⅞	3B	...	4
29	LPT	**Lear Petroleum**	NY,M	B	10¢	12	242	Gas gathering: oil/gas	6⅞	⅜	24¼	6¼	35½	14½	8245	34⅜	27½	28	0.4	31
30	LSI	**Lear Siegler**	NY,B,M,Ph,P	A	1	57	5286	Vehicle comp:electr/commun	29⅜	3⅜	23⅞	17¼	41¾	18⅛	8999	41⅝	33¾	40⅛	3.1	9
31	Pr	**$2.25 cm Cv Pfd (45)vtg**	NY,P	BB	No	5	14	ind'l,agric,housing prod	72¾	17⅛	57¾	42½	101	45¼	37	100	86	98B	2.3	
32	LRI	**LeaRonal**	AS	A–	1	5	365	Chemicals, electroplat proc	12¾	2½	18	11	47¼	14⅛	386	47¼	39½	46¼	1.3	15
33	LEAS	**Leasco Corp**	N	...	10¢	9	392	Computer leasing	...	...	35½	11¾	60	23½	220	60	43	60B	...	18
34	LTC	**Leaseway Transport**	NY,B	A	1	60	4893	All areas mtr veh transp	34¼	2⅛	24½	18¾	34⅜	19⅜	1677	33¾	27¾	29½	4.7	8
35	LEE	**Lee Enterprises**	NY,M	A–	2	31	1816	Newspaper publish:radio,TV	26½	3⅝	25	19⅝	28⅜	17¼	1584	25⅜	23¼	23¼	4.1	11
36	LPH	**Lee Pharmaceuticals**	AS,P	NR	10¢	1	100	Nail care:orthodontic pr	24	2⅝	6½	3	4⅜	2¾	449	3¼	2⅞	3	...	d
37	LEG	**Leggett & Platt**	NY,M	A–	1	15	682	Mfr springs,etc for furn,bed	18⅜	1⅛	16⅝	10	13½	9⅞	731	12⅜	11⅞	12¼	4.2	7
38	LP	**Lehigh Press**	AS	B+	No	...	...	Commercial printer	28⅜	2	17	12	24	13¾	92	21⅞	20⅜	20½B		5
39	LEH	**Lehigh Valley Ind**	NY,B,M,Ph	C	50¢	3	42	Textiles: castings, shoes	17¼	½	2⅛	1⅛	1⅝	1	2070	1¼	1	1¼	...	d
40	Pr	**$1.50 cm Cv A Pfd (2½) vtg**	NY	C	No	...	...	sales promotion	134	6¼	21	14½	16½	13¼	7	13¾	13¼	13½	...	
41	LEM	**Lehman Corp**	NY,B,M,Ph,P	...	1	35	739	Leading closed-end invest co.	26½	7¼	13⅛	9¼	16⅜	10	3765	16⅜	14	16	3.4	
42	LDYN	**Leisure Dynamics**	N	B–	1	1	24	Games,toys,hobby products	21½	⅛	8	3⅜	5¼	1¼	729	1⅝	1¼	1⅜B	...	d
43	LVX	**Leisure Technology**[73]	AS	NR	10¢	2	120	Retire-recreat'l communit's	34¾	⅝	6¼	2¼	3¾	1⅝	1033	2½	1⅞	2	...	d
44	LTPI	**Leisure Time Prods**	N	NR	No	1	18	Motor homes,delivery trucks	2½	¾	⅞	¼	1½	¼	126	½	½	½B	...	d
45	LEN	**Lennar Corp**	NY,B,Ph	B–	10¢	13	796	Bldr residential communities	16⅜	¾	11 11/16	2⅜	23¼	7 1/16	4725	23¼	16½	22⅛	0.9	8

Uniform Footnote Explanations—See Page 1. Other: [51]□$3.35,'77. [52]□$0.24,'78. [53]□$0.67,'79. [54]□$0.11,'78. [55]Incl pensions. [56]Fiscal Dec,'76 & prior. [57]△$0.82,'80. [58]®$0.65,'79. [59]□$0.05,'76. [60]Oppenheimer group plans acquis, $13. [61]□$0.04,'79. [62]®$0.29,'80. [63]□$0.07,'76. [64]△$0.14,'77. [65]△$0.07,'80. [66]△$0.35,'78. [67]△$0.69,'80. [68]□$0.07,'78. [69]□$1.45,'77. [70]Accum on Pfd. [71]©$1.18,'80. [72]©$0.81,'79. [73]Default on bank debt. [74]■$1.39,'80. [75]®$2.00,'79.

COMMON AND PREFERRED STOCKS **Lac—Len 129**

INDEX	Cash Divs. Ea. Yr. Since	Latest Payment Per $	Latest Payment Date	Ex. Div.	$ So Far 1980	Total Ind. Rate	$ Paid 1979	Cash & Equiv. (Mil-$)	Curr. Assets	Curr. Liabs.	Balance Sheet Date	Long Term Debt Mil-$	Shs. 000 Pfd.	Shs. 000 Com.	Ended	1976	1977	1978	1979	1980	Last 12 Mos.	Interim Period	$ Per Share 1979	1980	INDEX
1	1946	Q0.53½	1-2-81	12-9	1.86	2.14	1.86	36.8	97.4	54.6	6-30-80	115.	362	4363	Sp	2.22	△2.59	3.43	3.75	P3.50	3.50				1
2	.....	0.25	2-25-77	2-7	.....	Nil	.....	5.44	72.6	40.0	9-30-80	30.9	...	1650	Dc	△1.12	d0.53	2.69	0.64	.....	d1.10	9 Mo Sep	0.99	d0.75	2
3	.....	g0.10	11-15-55	10-7	.....	Nil	.....	1.34	2.04	2.81	j12-31-79	.....	...	5104	Dc	△0.18	△0.09	△0.24	△0.26	.....	j1.36	9 Mo Sep	△0.15	△1.25	3
4	1937	Q0.29	12-1-80	11-7	1.14	1.16	1.06	d0.10	9.38	9.77	10-31-80	20.1	30	1336	Dc	1.02	1.49	1.58	1.86	.....	1.51	12 Mo Oct	1.88	1.51	4
5	1965	Q0.05	12-17-80	11-26	0.20	0.20	0.20	1.20	14.5	4.57	9-30-80	.....	...	1404	Dc	0.56	0.56	0.30	0.68	.....	0.81	9 Mo Sep	0.58	0.71	5
6◆	1942	Q0.05	12-10-80	11-17	0.60	0.20	0.733	12.6	129.	40.6	9-30-80	101.	...	5245	Dc	1.16	1.25	1.85	3.03	.....	d0.43	9 Mo Sep	2.68	d0.78	6
7◆	1963	Q0.20	1-2-81	12-4	0.74	0.80	†0.72	3.60	111.	57.9	9-30-80	43.2	...	4794	Je	1.51	1.86	2.46	2.40	1.51	1.64	3 Mo Sep	0.31	0.44	7
8◆	1945	Q0.29	11-15-80	10-27	1.10	1.16	†1.07	23.7	54.5	16.9	9-6-80	3.24	...	8320	Dc	1.53	1.64	1.86	1.95	.....	2.36	9 Mo Sep	1.33	1.74	8
9	1980	0.19	12-19-80	12-3	0.38	0.38	.....	Book Value $18.89			9-30-80	35.3	...	1506	Je	p0.96	p1.01	p1.61	p1.65	1.41	1.13	3 Mo Sep	0.36	0.08	9
10	.....	None Paid			.....	Nil	.....	Equity per shr $9.11			9-30-79	p76.0	p255	p2519	Sp	d0.01	0.21	△0.53	0.31	△P0.53	0.53				10
11	1974	Q0.25	1-2-81	12-9	0.84	1.00	0.72	Book Value $24.17			9-30-80	17.6	*85	900	Dc	△•1.41	△•1.58	2.13	△2.48	.....	2.98	9 Mo Sep	△1.82	2.32	11
12◆	1970	Q0.12½	1-2-81	12-8	0.454	0.50	0.381	Book Value $9.55			9-30-80	18.0	...	7899	Dc	△0.44	△0.74	△0.96	1.23	.....	1.56	9 Mo Sep	•0.89	•1.22	12
13	.....	2.50	10-21-58	10-10	.....	Nil	.....	Equity per shr $5.76			9-30-80	35.0	170	3172	Dc	•0.12	•0.22	1.12	▲0.77	.....	1.17	9 Mo Sep	▲d0.13	0.27	13
14	1941	Q0.25	12-1-80	11-3	1.00	1.00	0.97½	1.98	130.	46.2	8-4-80	14.6	...	4553	Ja	1.78	2.12	2.23	2.25	.....	2.53	9 Mo Oct	1.33	1.61	14
15	1922	†0.30	1-2-81	12-16	†1.42	1.42	†1.22	14.7	77.0	14.9	9-27-80	.....	51	2255	Dc	2.75	2.87	4.11	4.62	.....	5.04	9 Mo Sep	3.37	3.79	15
16	.....	5%Stk	9-13-74	8-12	.....	Nil	.....	Equity per shr $4.26			9-30-80	23.5	...	1380	Dc	d0.95	△•0.19	•0.42	•0.26	.....	0.27	9 Mo Sep	•0.23	•0.24	16
17◆	1975	s0.057	12-18-80	11-24	s0.228	0.24	‡0.235	1.73	15.8	11.0	6-7-80	12.6	...	1119	Sp	0.86	1.22	1.50	1.96	P1.64	1.64				17
18	.....	0.10	1-30-78	1-31	.....	Nil	.....	0.05	3.43	1.53	7-31-80	0.39	...	1303	Oc	0.08	•0.34	0.35	0.32	P0.46	0.46				18
19◆	1977	Q0.14	12-1-80	11-7	0.47	0.56	0.36	3.20	129.	62.2	8-29-80	6.52	...	7414	My	0.92	1.07	1.43	1.88	2.35	2.43	3 Mo Aug	0.42	0.50	19
20	.....	0.15	1-31-78	12-27	.....	Nil	.....	0.30	3.72	1.09	9-30-80	1.66	...	693	Je	0.59	•0.58	d2.91	•0.23	d1.63	d1.82	3 Mo Sep	•0.05	d0.14	20
21◆	.....	None Since Public			.....	Nil	.....	6.88	11.9	12.5	8-31-80	125.	...	*7646	My	0.26	0.38	0.56	0.70	0.91	1.03	6 Mo Nov	0.47	0.59	21
22◆	1936	Q0.30	12-26-80	12-8	1.18	1.20	1.08	1.86	48.2	33.6	8-31-80	13.3	...	758	My	1.65	1.80	2.32	2.91	3.08	2.38	6 Mo Nov	1.55	0.85	22
23	.....	None Paid			.....	Nil	.....	0.03	7.16	8.75	10-31-80	3.85	...	2920	Ja	•0.18	0.26	d0.04	0.06	.....	d1.07	9 Mo Oct	0.06	d1.07	23
24	1973	Q0.10	1-19-81	12-29	0.37	0.40	0.33	4.62	33.2	8.17	9-30-80	.....	...	3321	Dc	1.28	1.55	1.84	▲2.23	.....	2.25	9 Mo Sep	1.53	1.55	24
25◆	1959	Q0.16½	12-1-80	11-7	0.61½	0.66	0.57	13.3	41.2	9.71	9-30-80	0.85	...	11396	Dc	0.63	0.69	0.84	0.98	.....	1.00	9 Mo Sep	0.73	△0.75	25
26	1977	Q0.12½	11-14-80	10-24	0.42½	0.50	0.38	2.31	30.6	12.0	8-31-80	.....	...	1305	My	0.64	1.24	3.48	2.77	0.19	d0.23	3 Mo Aug	d0.25	d0.67	26
27	1963	Q0.18	12-10-80	11-10	0.72	0.72	0.72	10.4	73.9	12.5	10-31-80	14.9	...	4592	Ap	1.88	2.40	1.85	1.65	2.14	1.82	6 Mo Oct	0.79	0.47	27
28	.....	None Since Public			.....	Nil	.....	2.65	41.1	30.0	10-31-80	19.7	3	3258	Jl	△d3.72	△d0.62	•0.18	•0.48	•0.77	0.85	3 Mo Oct	•0.15	•0.23	28
29◆	1977	Q0.03	2-26-81	2-4	0.12	0.12	0.073	2.67	25.0	16.3	9-30-80	52.9	...	7464	Sp	0.11	△0.54	0.61	0.88	0.91	0.91				29
30	1954	Q0.31	12-2-80	11-10	1.19	1.24	0.98	16.5	552.	241.	9-30-80	191	655	15646	Je	1.75	2.70	3.55	4.50	△4.16	4.23	3 Mo Sep	0.81	0.88	30
31	1966	Q0.56¼	12-2-80	11-10	2.25	2.25	2.25	Conv into 2½ shrs com				.....	655	...	Je	.....	.....	b2.94	b3.68	b3.14	.....				31
32◆	1963	Q0.15	11-5-80	10-15	0.60	0.60	0.451	5.75	33.3	11.3	8-31-80	0.59	...	2415	Fb	0.93	1.14	1.75	2.48	.....	3.01	6 Mo Aug	1.07	1.60	32
33	.....	None Since Public			.....	Nil	.....	Equity per shr $9.11			9-30-80	17.2	25	1462	Dc	pd2.35	pd3.67	pd2.25	pd0.89	.....	3.34	9 Mo Sep	pd0.79	3.44	33
34◆	1965	Q0.35	1-7-81	12-9	1.30	1.40	1.20	33.9	140.	228.	9-30-80	295	...	11877	Dc	2.31	2.75	3.34	3.62	E3.70	3.67	9 Mo Sep	2.54	2.59	34
35◆	1960	Q0.24	1-2-81	12-1	0.81	0.96	0.68	4.08	25.8	22.6	6-30-80	31.9	...	7129	Sp	1.25	1.56	△1.81	2.13	P△2.10	2.10				35
36	.....	None Since Public			.....	Nil	.....	0.17	6.97	2.55	6-30-80	.....	...	1964	Sp	0.03	0.08	0.32	0.24	Pd0.39	d0.39				36
37◆	1939	Q0.13	12-15-80	11-17	0.51	0.52	0.44	2.19	57.1	26.1	9-30-80	27.9	...	4018	Dc	1.34	1.63	2.27	■1.70	E1.65	1.61	9 Mo Sep	1.45	1.36	37
38	.....	0.14	10-30-71	10-8	.....	Nil	.....	1.31	24.9	10.1	9-30-80	6.83	1	783	Dc	1.26	1.53	3.41	3.87	.....	4.40	9 Mo Sep	2.82	3.35	38
39	.....	None Paid			.....	Nil	.....	0.68	34.5	21.7	9-27-80	29.7	223	6938	Dc	•0.15	△•0.43	•0.34	d2.36	.....	d2.40	9 Mo Sep	•0.07	•0.03	39
40	.....	0.75	7-3-72	6-16	.....	Nil	.....	Conv into 8 shrs common				.....	160	...	Dc	5.97	16.42	13.17	d72.73	.....	.....	Accum $12.50 to 10-3-80			40
41	1930	0.12	11-13-80	10-28	[71]0.55	•0.55	[72]0.52	Net Asset Val $18.91			12-26-80			34296	Dc	§15.08	§13.12	§13.81	§16.42	.....	.....				41
42	1977	0.10	1-2-80	11-26	0.10	Nil	0.17½	2.88	48.4	30.5	9-30-80	17.1	...	2332	Dc	0.59	0.71	△0.80	0.51	.....	d1.76	12 Mo Sep	0.76	d1.76	42
43	.....	None Paid			.....	Nil	.....	Equity per shr $2.87			9-30-80	50.0	...	3544	Mr	d2.84	•0.75	1.12	■d1.19	.....	d2.42	6 Mo Sep	0.34	d0.89	43
44	.....	None Since Public			.....	Nil	.....	0.33	4.05	2.53	7-31-80	2.59	...	3145	Oc	0.59	0.49	0.19	d0.64	.....	d0.61	9 Mo Jul	d0.40	d0.37	44
45◆	1978	Q0.05	2-16-81	2-2	0.17	0.20	0.14	Equity per shr $9.72			8-31-80	85.8	...	8010	Nv	d0.05	0.34	0.91	2.00	.....	2.64	9 Mo Aug	1.39	2.03	45

◆ **Stock Splits & Divs By Line Reference Index** [6]3-for-2,'78,'79. [7]3-for-2,'78. [8]3-for-2,'78. [12]10%,'80. [17]Adj to 5%,'80. [19]3-for-2,'79. [21]3-for-1,'78:10%,'77 thru,'80. [22]2-for-1,'77. [25]5-for-4,'76. [29]10%,'76,'77:5-for-4,'77,'78,'79;4-for-3,'79:3-for-2,'80. [32]5-for-4,'79:4-for-3,'80. [34]Adj for 4%,'77:3-for-2,'79(ex'78). [35]3-for-2,'76,'78. [37]3-for-2,'78. [45]3-for-2,'79:2-for-1,'80.

Figure 6.2 Example from S&P Stock Guide

Source: *Standard & Poor's Stock Guide* (New York: Standard & Poor's Corp., 1981). Reprinted by permission.

Moody's Public Utility Manual   This provides information on public utilities, including electric and gas, gas transmission, telephone, and water companies. It also contains a news report section.

Moody's Transportation Manual   This covers the transportation industry, including railroads, airlines, steamship companies, electric railway, bus and truck lines, oil pipelines, bridge companies, and automobile and truck leasing companies. A supplementary Transportation News Report is also published.

Moody's Bank and Finance Manual   This is published in two volumes and covers the field of finance represented by banks, savings and loan associations, credit agencies of the United States Government, all phases of the insurance industry, investment companies, real estate firms, real estate investment trusts, and miscellaneous financial enterprises.

Moody's Municipal and Government Manual   The manual is published in two volumes and contains data on the U.S. Government, all the states, state agencies, municipalities (with populations of over 13,500), foreign governments, and international organizations.

The Value Line Investment Survey   The Survey is published in two parts. Part one contains basic historical information on about 1,700 companies, as well as a number of analytical measures of earnings stability, growth rates, and a common stock safety factor (i.e., the relative volatility of the stock price). It also includes extensive two-year *projections* for the given firms and three-year *estimates* of performance. In early 1982, it will include a projection for 1982, 1983, and 1985–1987. The second volume includes a weekly service that provides general investment advice and also recommends individual stocks for purchase or sale. An example of a Value Line company report is shown in Figure 6.3.

The Value Line OTC Special Situations Service   This service is published 24 times a year and is intended for the experienced investor who is willing to accept high risk in the hope of realizing exceptional capital gains. In each issue, past recommendations are discussed and eight to ten new stocks are presented for consideration.

Daily Stock Price Records   These are published quarterly by Standard & Poor's and give individual volumes for the NYSE, the ASE, and the OTC market. Each quarterly bound volume is divided into two parts. Part one, "Major Technical Indicators of the Stock Market," is devoted to market indicators widely followed as technical guides to the stock market and includes price-indicator series, volume series, and data on odd-lots and short sales.

Part two, "Daily and Weekly Stock Action," gives daily high, low, close, and volume information and data on short interest for the stock, insider trading information, a 200-day moving average of prices, and a weekly relative strength series. The books for the NYSE and ASE are available from 1962 on; the OTC books begin in 1968.

SEARS, ROEBUCK & CO. NYSE-S

RECENT PRICE	**19**	
P/E RATIO	**8.0**	(Norm 10.0 / Trail'g 6.3)
DIV'D YIELD	**7.3%**	(Norm 2.0% / Trail'g 7.2%)
		1681

| High | 38.5 | 32.9 | 30.1 | 36.1 | 37.4 | 38.3 | 52.1 | 59.8 | 61.6 | 45.2 | 37.2 | 39.6 | 34.6 | 28.1 | 21.9 | 19.6 | 20.8 |
| Low | 31.0 | 22.3 | 22.1 | 28.1 | 30.1 | 25.5 | 37.4 | 48.7 | 39.1 | 20.8 | 24.2 | 30.8 | 23.8 | 19.8 | 17.8 | 14.4 | 14.9 |

Target Price Range 1983–1984–1985

TIMELINESS **3** Average (Relative Price Performance Next 12 Mos.)
SAFETY **3** (Scale: 1 Highest to 5 Lowest)
BETA .90

June 12, 1981   Value Line

© Arnold Bernhard & Co., Inc.

Insider Decisions 1981
	J	F	M	A	M	J	J	A	S	O	N	D	J	F	M
to Buy	0	0	0	0	0	0	1	0	0	1	0	0	1	0	0
to Sell	0	1	1	0	0	1	1	3	2	0	4	2	1	0	2

Institutional Decisions
	1Q'80	2Q'80	3Q'80	4Q'80	1Q'81
to Buy	64	71	76	60	82
to Sell	161	150	170	176	159
Hldg's(000)	141337	141587	141411	137710	133979

Est'd Ann'l Tot'l Return: 27%-40%
% Due to Yield: 7.3% — 17%-17%
% Due to Growth: 9.7% — 10%-23%
% Due to P/E Change:

	1964	1965	1966	1967	1968	1969	1970	1971	1972	1973	1974	1975	1976	1977	1978	1979	1980	1981			83-85E
Sales per sh	18.86	20.95	22.28	23.95	26.71	28.74	29.98	32.15	35.00	39.12	41.50	43.02	46.86	53.51	55.63	55.19	79.89	87.30	(A)		115.65
"Cash Flow" per sh	1.22	1.32	1.43	1.60	1.70	1.78	1.84	2.11	2.34	2.57	2.09	2.17	2.71	3.21	3.51	3.24	2.81	3.50			5.30
Earnings per sh	1.00	1.06	1.13	1.26	1.37	1.44	1.51	1.78	1.97	2.16	1.62	1.65	2.19	2.62	2.86	2.54	1.92	2.60	(B)		4.20
Div'ds Decl'd per sh	.50	.57	.60	.60	.65	.68	.68	.75	.81	.88	.93	.93	.80	1.08	1.27	1.28	1.36	1.36	(C)		1.75
Tangible Book Value sh	6.62	7.13	7.67	9.51	10.24	11.09	11.96	13.03	14.38	15.85	16.55	16.70	18.58	20.23	21.92	23.48	24.38	25.70			32.80
Common Shs Outst'g	304.40	305.03	305.49	306.05	306.87	308.37	308.97	311.22	314.02	314.56	315.65	317.09	319.01	321.87	322.63	317.33	315.36	315.00			320.00
Avg Ann'l P/E Ratio	29.2	31.3	24.1	22.0	24.2	23.8	22.1	25.1	28.6	22.1	20.8	20.1	15.6	11.2	8.1	7.6	8.6				10.0
Avg Ann'l Div'd Yield	1.7%	1.7%	2.2%	2.2%	2.0%	2.0%	2.1%	1.4%	1.8%	1.8%	2.7%	2.8%	2.4%	3.7%	5.5%	6.7%	8.2%				4.2%

CAPITAL STRUCTURE as of 1/31/80
Total Debt $7402.0 mill. Due in 5 Yrs. $5226.9 mill.
LT Debt $2961.9 mill. LT Interest $282.0 mill.
Incl. $132.2 mill. capitalized leases.
(LT interest earned: 3.5x; total interest coverage: 1.6x) (28% of Cap'l)

Leases, Uncapitalized Annual rentals $117 mill.

Pension Liability $233 mill. vs $136 mill. in 1979

Pfd Stock None

Common Stock 315,357,178 shares (72% of Cap'l)

Sales ($mill)	9262.2	10006	10991	12306	13101	13640	14950	17224	17946	17514	25195	27500			37000
Number of Stores	3137	3343	3485	3625	3750	3776	3779	3763	3727	3680	3062	3600			4000
Net Profit ($mill)	464.2	550.9	614.4	679.9	511.4	522.6	694.5	838.0	921.5	810.1	606.0	600.0			1350
Income Tax Rate	44.0%	42.0%	40.4%	38.9%	37.3%	42.9%	38.5%	29.8%	27.1%	21.3%	12.3%	20.0%			35.0%
Net Profit Margin	5.0%	5.5%	5.6%	5.5%	3.9%	3.8%	4.7%	4.9%	5.1%	4.6%	2.4%	3.0%			3.6%
Inventories ($mill)	1307.7	1429.3	1642.1	1879.1	1979.3	1877.6	2215.1	2626.1	2533.4	2651.5	2721.6	3150			3800
Inventory Turnover	7.1	7.0	6.6	6.6	6.6	7.3	6.8	6.6	7.1	6.6	9.3	6.5			7.0
Working Cap'l ($mill)	2031.2	2059.3	2329.9	2378.6	2352.9	2646.5	3161.8	3582.9	3750.0	3994.8	1174.3	1800			2200
Long-Term Debt ($mill)	630.0	696.0	916.0	980.5	1095.1	1326.3	1563.5	1990.3	2040.2	2473.5	2961.9	3200			3700
Net Worth ($mill)	3708.3	4060.4	4515.4	4993.3	5241.1	5302.4	5936.9	6524.1	7091.6	7467.2	7688.8	8100			10000
% Earned Total Cap'l	11.1%	12.0%	11.9%	11.9%	8.6%	8.5%	9.9%	10.7%	11.0%	9.2%	7.0%	8.5%			11.5%
% Earned Net Worth	12.5%	13.6%	13.6%	13.6%	9.8%	9.9%	11.7%	12.8%	13.0%	10.9%	7.9%	10.0%			13.5%
% Retained to Comm Eq	6.9%	7.9%	8.0%	8.1%	4.2%	4.3%	7.4%	7.4%	7.2%	5.4%	2.4%	5.0%			8.0%
% All Div'ds to Net Prof	45%	42%	41%	40%	57%	56%	37%	42%	44%	50%	70%	52%			41%

CURRENT POSITION
($mill)	1978	1979	(D) 1/31/81
Cash Assets	225.0	283.9	149.4
Receivables	6779.6	7164.3	221.8
Inventory (LIFO)	2533.4	2651.5	2604.8
Other	138.1	155.8	354.2
Current Assets	9676.1	10255.5	3330.2
Accts Payable	1134.3	1250.8	954.3
Debt Due	3557.1	3685.7	—
Other	1234.7	1324.1	715.8
Current Liab.	5926.1	6260.6	1670.1

ANNUAL RATES
of change (per sh)	Past 10 Yrs	Past 5 Yrs	Est '78-'80 to '83-85
Sales	8.5%	9.0%	12.5%
"Cash Flow"	6.0%	7.0%	11.0%
Earnings	5.5%	6.0%	11.5%
Dividends	7.0%	7.5%	6.0%
Book Value	7.5%	7.5%	7.0%

QUARTERLY SALES ($ mill.) (A) Full
Fiscal Year Begins	Apr. 30	July 31	Oct. 31	Jan. 31	Fiscal Year
1977	3607	4077	4545	4995	17224
1978	4072	4485	4458	4931	17946
1979	3627	4253	4528	5104	17514
1980	5471	6000	6462	7262	25195
1981	6102	6500	7000	7898	27500

EARNINGS PER SHARE (A) Full
Fiscal Year Begins	Apr. 30	July 31	Oct. 31	Jan. 31	Fiscal Year (B)
1977	.48	.65	.71	.78	2.62
1978	.48	.63	.73	1.02	2.86
1979	.47	.60	.67	.80	2.54
1980	.19	.42	.43	.88	1.92
1981	.30	.60	.60	1.10	2.60

QUARTERLY DIVIDENDS PAID ■ Full
Cal-endar	Mar. 31	June 30	Sept. 30	Dec. 31	c/Year
1977	.20	.375	.225	.24	1.04
1978	.24	.43	.28	.28	1.23
1979	.28	.32	.32	.32	1.24
1980	.32	.34	.34	.34	1.34
1981	.32	.34			

BUSINESS: Sears, Roebuck & Co., the world's largest retailer of general merchandise, sells through retail stores, catalog, telephone sales offices, and independent catalog merchants. Owns 40% of Simpson-Sears, a leading Canadian retailer. Credit sales over half of total. Also owns Allstate Insurance Company, a major underwriter. Equity in undistributed earnings of subsidiaries, principally Allstate Insurance, accounts for 70% of income. Has 390,000 employees. 350,000 stockholders. Payroll costs: est'd 23% of sales. Employee pension fund owns 23% of stock, insiders under 1%. Chrmn. & Pres.: E.R. Telling. Address: Sears Tower, Chicago, Illinois 60684.

Merchandise sales are looking much stronger. In contrast to the essentially flat sales comparisons for all of last year, Sears posted a 13.5% sales gain in the first quarter, the best showing since 1977. Good weather and a later Easter certainly helped. But we believe the principal stimulus was the absence of last year's credit controls.

Good, but less dramatic, gains are likely in the coming quarters. The credit controls were lifted last June, although they had a lingering effect. We think that business in the later months of the year will reflect some improvement in consumer spending, especially for hard goods, the largest component of Sears' sales. And we would also expect to see some results from the reorganization of the merchandising division.

Retailing profits may stage a sharp recovery this year. Promotional pricing might offset some, but not all, of the benefit of the higher sales we envision. And the greater volume should keep expense ratios in line. In this year's holiday season, a further help that we think likely will be lower short-term interest rates (compared with 1980). **But insurance profits may be little changed.** Inflation will probably continue to boost the cost of claims faster than rate increases are received. Accordingly, we expect the underwriting loss will be greater this year. But investment income, we think, will pick up the slack due to gains in premium volume and higher average yields.

Sears now has considerable investment interest. We believe Sears has the means to recover at least a portion of the share of retail trade that it lost in recent years, aided by its solid balance sheet and good image among consumers. The recent organizational changes may enable it to capitalize on these assets. On this basis, we are projecting a strong earning recovery through 1983-85, aided by gains in the areas of financial services and real estate development. Such progress might well be accompanied by a richer price-earnings multiple. In the year ahead, we expect the stock will keep pace with the market.   M.S./N.R.W.

Restated Revenues (and Net Profit Margins) by Business Line
	1978	1979	1980	1981
Merchandising	18979(2.3%)	18440(2.0%)	18612(0.7%)	20500(1.8%)
Allstate	5209(8.0%)	5750(7.0%)	6165(6.9%)	6500(6.5%)
Seraco	302(20.9%)	359(11.1%)	418(11.3%)	500(12.0%)
Company Total	24490(3.8%)	24549(3.3%)	25195(2.4%)	27500(3.0%)

(A) Fiscal yr. ends Jan. 31 of fol. cal. yr. Incl. previously unconsol. subs. from '80. (B) Based on avg. shs. outst'g. Next eps. rep't due late Aug. Est'd constant-dollar egs/sh.: '80, 70¢. (C) Next div'd meet'g about Aug. 4. Goes ex about Aug. 19. Div'd paym't dates: Jan. 3, Apr. 1, July 1, Oct. 1. ■ Div'd reinvest. plan av'ble. (D) Retail ops. only from '80. Incl. cap. leases from '77. (E) Incl.

Company's Financial Strength A+
Stock's Price Stability 85
Price Growth Persistence 15
Earnings Predictability 55

Figure 6.3   Sample Report from Value Line

Source: *The Value Line Investment Survey* (New York: Arnold Bernhard & Co.).
Reprinted by permission of the publisher. Copyright 1981 Arnold Bernhard & Co., Inc.

Brokerage Firm Reports

Many brokerage firms prepare reports on individual firms. In some cases, these are rather objective and only contain basic information, while some contain specific recommendations, usually regarding purchase.

Investment Magazines

Forbes   This magazine is published twice monthly and contains 12–14 articles on individual companies and industries. In addition, several regular columnists discuss the economy, the aggregate money and stock markets, and the commodity market.

Financial World   This is likewise published twice a month and generally contains about six articles on companies, industries, and the overall market, and a large number of regular features on taxes, options, and a section containing market data.

The Wall Street Transcript   This is a composite of sources of information other than market quotations and the like, that is published every Monday. It contains texts of speeches made at analysts' meetings, copies of brokerage house reports on companies and industries, and interviews with corporate officials. It also includes discussions of forthcoming new stock issues.

The Media General Financial Weekly   This is likewise published every Monday and contains a series of feature articles and columns. Of primary interest is a comprehensive set of financial and statistical information on 3,400 common stocks, including every common stock listed on the NYSE and ASE in addition to over 700 OTC issues. There are also charts on 60 major industry groups.

OTC Review   This is a monthly publication devoted to the analysis and discussion of stocks traded on the OTC market. It usually contains an analysis of an industry traded by numerous OTC companies and a discussion of three or four individual firms. In addition, extended earnings reports on OTC firms, name changes, stock exchange listings, and statistics on OTC trading (price and volume) are published in the review.

Pension and Investment Age   This newspaper of corporate and institutional investing is published every other Monday. It is intended for those who are involved in pension investing either as a corporate manager or as a money manager who manages pension funds assets. The emphasis is on stories and interviews related to pension fund management. There is substantial consideration of personnel changes.

Academic Journals

The material in academic journals differs from that in investment magazines in terms of timeliness and general orientation. Investment magazines are concerned with the *current* investment environment and with providing advice for current action. The articles in academic journals are longer and more theoretical in approach, and typically are not expected to be immediately useful. They deal with the long-run implications for investments.

Journal of Finance   This is a quarterly published by the American Finance Association. The articles are almost all by academicians and are rather theoretical and empirical. The typical issue will include 15 articles, notes and comments, and book reviews.

Journal of Financial and Quantitative Analysis   This is a quarterly published by the Western Finance Association and the University of Washington. It is very similar to the *Journal of Finance* in that almost all articles are by academicians. It differs in that it contains fewer articles in the area of monetary economics.

Journal of Financial Economics   This is a relatively new journal first published in May 1974 by North Holland Publishing Company in collaboration with the Graduate School of Management of the University of Rochester, New York. The intent of the quarterly is to publish academic research in the following areas: consumption and investment decisions under uncertainty, portfolio analysis, efficient markets, and the normative theory of financial management.

Financial Analysts Journal   This is published six times a year by the Financial Analysts Federation. An issue typically contains six or seven articles of interest to practicing financial analysts and/or portfolio managers, a regular feature on securities regulation, and book reviews.

Institutional Investor   This is published monthly by Institutional Investors Systems, and is aimed at professional investors and portfolio managers with emphasis on what is happening to the investment industry. It is written by a professional staff.

Journal of Portfolio Management   This is likewise published by Institutional Investors Systems. It is published quarterly with the avowed intent of being a vehicle for academic research of use to the practicing portfolio manager. Over half the articles are written by academicians, but written to be read by practitioners.

Financial Management   This is published quarterly by the Financial Management Association. It is intended for executives and academicians interested in the financial management of a firm, but also contains investment-related articles on such topics as stock splits, dividend policy, mergers, and stock listings.

The Financial Review   This journal is currently published three times a year by the Eastern Finance Association. It is a general finance journal directed at the academic community with about half the articles in a typical issue concerned with investments and portfolio management.

Journal of Financial Research   This is a joint publication of the Southern Finance Association and the Southwestern Finance Association. It is published three times a year and contains articles on financial management, investments, financial institutions, capital market theory, and portfolio theory.

The C.F.A. Digest   This is published quarterly by the Institute of Chartered Financial Analysts. Its purpose is to provide, as a service to members of the investment community, abstracts of published articles considered to be of interest to financial analysts and portfolio managers from a wide variety of academic and nonacademic journals.

Other General Business Journals

There are a number of general business and economics journals that include articles on finance and some specifically on investments. One of the foremost is the *Journal of Business,* published by the University of Chicago, which has contained some outstanding articles in the area of investments by members of the University's faculty. Other journals to consider include: *Quarterly Review of Economics and Business* (University of Illinois); *Review of Business and Economic Research* (University of New Orleans); *Journal of Business Research* (Elsevier North-Holland); *American Economic Review* (American Economic Association); *Journal of Political Economy* (University of Chicago); *Bell Journal of Economics and Management Science* (American Telephone and Telegraph).

Computerized Data Sources

In addition to the numerous published sources of data, some of the financial service firms have developed computerized data sources. Again, owing to space limitations, only the major sources will be discussed.

Compustat   This is a computerized databank of financial data developed by Standard & Poor's and currently handled by a subsidiary, Investors Management Services (P.O. Box 239, Denver, CO 80201). The Compustat tapes contain 20 years of data for approximately 2,220 listed industrial companies, 1,000 OTC companies, 175 utilities, 120 banks, and 500 Canadian firms. There are also quarterly tapes that contain 20 years of quarterly financial data for over 2,000 industrial firms, and 12 years of quarterly data for banks and utilities. The specific financial data on the annual tapes includes almost every possible item from a firm's balance sheet and income statement as well as stock market data (stock prices and trading volume).

Value Line Data Base   This contains historical annual and quarterly financial and market data for 1,600 industrial and finance companies. The annual data begins in 1954 and quarterly data starts in 1963. In addition to historical data, there is an estimate of dividend and earnings for the coming year.

University of Chicago Stock Price Tapes   The Center for Research in Security Prices (CRSP) at the University of Chicago (Graduate School of Business, Chicago, IL, 60637) has developed a set of monthly stock-price tapes and daily stock prices. The monthly tapes contain month-end prices from January 1926 to the present (updated annually) for every stock listed on the NYSE. Stock prices are adjusted for all stock splits, dividends, and any other capital changes. There is also a daily stock price tape that contains the daily high, low, and close since 1960 for every stock listed on the NYSE.

Media General Databank   This is provided by Media General Financial Services, Inc. (P.O. Box 26991, Richmond, VA 23261). The databank includes current price and volume data plus major corporate financial data on 2,000 major companies. In addition, extensive daily price and volume history on all NYSE- and ASE-listed stocks as well as a large number of major OTC stocks plus comparable data on the principal market indicator series are included.

ISL Daily Stock Price Tapes   These are prepared by Interactive Data Corporation (122 E. 42nd St., New York, NY 10017). The tapes are issued quarterly and contain the same information that is contained in the *Daily Stock Price Records* published by Standard & Poor's and discussed earlier in this chapter.

Summary

The intent of this chapter is to introduce the reader to the major sources of information on the economy, the aggregate securities markets, alternative industries, and individual firms. It should be recognized that this is *only a beginning*. It is virtually impossible to discuss all sources without writing a separate book. The reader is advised to use this as a starting point and attempt to spend time in a university library examining these and the many other sources available.

Questions

1. Assume that you want information on the Gross National Product for the past 10 years. Name at least *three* sources of such information.

2. Name two sources of information on rates of exchange with major foreign countries.

3. Assume you are interested in the steel and auto industry and want to compare production for these two industries to overall industrial production for the economy. How would you do it? What data would you use and where would you get the data? Be specific.

4. You are told that there is a relationship between growth in the money supply and stock price movements. Where would you go to get the data to verify this relationship?

5. You are an analyst for Hot Stock Investment Company, and the head of research tells you he just got a tip on the Baron Corporation, a stock that is traded on the OTC. He wants you to gather some data on the company's sales, earnings, and recent stock price movements. Where would you go for this information? Name several sources because the company may not be big enough to be included in some of them.

6. As an individual investor, discuss three publications you feel that you should subscribe to (besides *The Wall Street Journal*). In your discussion indicate what is contained in these publications and why it is appropriate for you as an individual investor.

7. As the director of the newly established research department of a bank, discuss the first three investment services that you will subscribe to and indicate why these are first.

8. Select one company from the NYSE, the ASE, and the OTC and look up the name and address of the financial officer you would write to obtain recent financial reports for each of the firms.

Sources of Investment Information

American Stock Exchange, 86 Trinity Place, New York, New York 10006.

Business Statistics may be obtained from Superintendent of Documents, U.S. Government Printing Office, Washington, D.C. 20402. Approximate price, $7.00.

Dow-Jones & Co., publishers of *The Wall Street Journal* and *Barron's*. Subscriptions office: 200 Burnett Rd., Chicopee, Massachusetts 01021.

Dow-Jones Handbooks. Each of the handbooks is published annually and can be obtained from Dow-Jones Books, P.O. Box 455, Chicopee, Massachusetts 01021. Approximate cost is $5.00 a book.

Economic Indicators. Available from the Superintendent of Documents (address as above). Approximate price, $12/year.

Economic Report of the President may be obtained from Superintendent of Documents, (address as above). Approximate price, $4.00.

Federal Reserve Bulletin may be obtained from the Division of Administrative Services, Board of Governors of the Federal Reserve System, Washington, D.C. 20551. Approximate cost, $20.00 a year.

Moody's Investor's Services, Inc., 99 Church Street, New York, New York 10007. (212) 267-8800.

New York Stock Exchange, 11 Wall Street, New York, New York 10005.

Quarterly Financial Report. Available from Superintendent of Documents (address as above). Approximate cost, $12.00 a year.

Standard & Poor's Corporation, 345 Hudson Street, New York, New York 10014.

Statistical Abstract of the United States may be obtained from the Superintendent of Documents. Approximate cost, $12.00 (cloth); $9.00 (paper).

Statistical Bulletin may be subscribed to through the Superintendent of Documents. Approximate cost, $20.00 a year.

Survey of Current Business may be obtained from Superintendent of Documents.

Value Line Services. These are published by Arnold Bernhard and Company, Inc., 5 East 44th Street, New York, New York 10017.

Valuation Principles
and Practices

PART·TWO

This section contains seven chapters dealing with the concepts of valuation and subsequently setting forth in detail how you can go about applying these principles to derive a value for the aggregate stock market, alternative industries, and specific companies.

We begin in Chapter 7 with the concept of efficient capital markets because of the important implications of this theory to the whole valuation process. Specifically, the efficient market hypothesis asserts that securities prices adjust very rapidly to all new information and, therefore, market prices at any point in time are a good estimate of the true value of the security. Following a review of the evidence that supports this theory (and some evidence that does not support it), we consider what this implies for those evaluating securities.

Chapter 8 contains a detailed discussion of basic valuation theory. Because a major part of the valuation process involves evaluating the performance of a given firm's management, Chapter 9 is concerned with financial statement analysis. The emphasis is on using financial ratios to evaluate the performance of management in a number of important areas. We also discuss how ratio analysis has been used in specific areas.

Chapters 10, 11, and 12 are the core of fundamental analysis. We begin with a discussion of why a three-step process is appropriate; this involves first analyzing the economy and the aggregate stock market, then alternative industries, and finally examining individual firms within desirable industries. Given this justification for the general approach to fundamental analysis, the chapters apply the basic valuation concepts derived in Chapter 8 to the analysis of the aggregate market, industries, and companies. In all instances, the goal is to derive an estimate of the future value of the entity involved and then use this future value to determine the expected return you will receive. Knowing the expected return and the risk involved, you can determine whether a given investment is appropriate for you.

In contrast to fundamental analysis, which is an attempt to estimate future values based upon intrinsic factors, many investors employ "technical" analysis which assumes that market prices generally move in trends that persist. Those who believe in these trends contend that past stock price movements provide information about future price movements; i.e., stock prices are their own best predictor. Technicians therefore attempt to derive trading rules to take advantage of these trends. Chapter 13 contains a discussion of the general philosophy of technical trading followed by a detailed discussion of a number of the best known and most popular trading rules.

You should finish this section with an understanding of what determines value and how you can make investment decisions using either fundamental analysis or technical analysis.

Eugene F. Fama

A major contributor to research in the area of efficient capital markets is Eugene F. Fama of the University of Chicago. Fama's dissertation, completed at the University of Chicago in 1964, was a detailed analysis of the behavior of stock prices. This study and some later articles confirmed research indicating that the distribution of stock price returns was generally not normal. He followed this with further work analyzing the nature of the distribution and what this implied for portfolio analysis: with Richard Roll, "Some Properties of Symmetric Stable Distributions," Journal of American Statistical Association (September 1968); and, also with Roll, "Parameter Estimates for Symmetric Stable Distributions," Journal of the American Statistical Association (June 1971); as well as "Portfolio Analysis in a Stable Paretian Market," Management Science (January 1965).

Fama is well known for a widely read study on stock splits coauthored with Lawrence Fisher, Michael Jensen, and Richard Roll (FFJR): "The Adjustment of Stock Prices to New Information," International Economic Review (February 1969). Probably the most widely quoted article in the efficient markets area is his review, "Efficient Capital Markets: A Review of Theory and Empirical Work," Journal of Finance (May 1970). In addition to his study on portfolio performance "Components of Investment Performance," Journal of Finance (June 1972), he has published several studies testing the Capital Asset Pricing Model (CAPM): "Risk, Return, and Equilibrium: Empirical Tests," coauthored with J. MacBeth, Journal of Political Economy (May-June 1973); "A

Note on the Market Model and the Two-Parameter Model," Journal of Finance *(December 1973); and "Tests of the Multiperiod Two-Parameter Model," also coauthored with MacBeth,* Journal of Financial Economics *(March 1974). More recently, he has published several studies on the important relationship between interest rates and inflation: "Short-Term Interest Rates as Predictors of Inflation,"* American Economic Review *(June 1975); "Forward Rates as Predictors of Future Spot Rates,"* Journal of Financial Economics *(October 1976);" Interest Rates and Inflation: The Message in the Entrails,"* American Economic Review *(June 1977); and with G. William Schwert, "Inflation, Interest and Relative Prices,"* Journal of Business *(April 1979), as well as other articles ranging*

along the full spectrum of finance, economics, and statistics. Fama is also the author of two books: The Theory of Finance *coauthored with Merton Miller (Holt, Rinehart and Winston, 1972), and* Foundations of Finance *(Basic Books, 1976).*

Professor Fama was born in 1939 in Boston, MA. He received a degree in Romance Languages with honors from Tufts University in 1960, and a Ph.D. from the University of Chicago in 1964. In 1968 Fama became a full professor at the University of Chicago. He is also an associate editor of the Journal of Finance *and an advisory editor of the* Journal of Financial Economics. *Currently he is the Theodore D. Yntema Professor of Finance at the University of Chicago.*

EFFICIENT CAPITAL MARKETS

⇒ 7 ⇐

One of the most important areas of academic research over the past ten years has been efficient capital markets. The subject is important because it has significant "real world" implications for investors and portfolio managers. In addition, it is one of the most controversial areas in finance with widely differing opinions on whether the capital markets are efficient. Therefore, it is important for you to understand the basic concept of efficient markets, the nature of the tests carried out, and the evidence supporting or contradicting the hypothesis. Finally, the reader should be aware of the implications for investment analysis and portfolio management.

We are considering efficient capital markets at this point in the book for two reasons. The first is that it follows from the previous chapters on the operation of the market. Now that we have an understanding of how the market functions, it seems natural to consider whether the market operates efficiently. Second, the overall evidence on the topic is best described as "mixed," meaning that some studies support the hypothesis and some do not. The implications are very important for the individual investor, the professional securities analyst, and the portfolio manager. A fairly large number of empirical studies of efficient markets will be mentioned in this chapter. Space limitations preclude dealing with them in depth. You are encouraged to consult the reference section at the end of this chapter and to become familiar with the literature.

There are four major sections in this chapter. The initial section contains a brief discussion of why capital markets *should* be efficient. In the second section we consider the alternative efficient market hypotheses. The specific tests used to examine the hypotheses are discussed in section three along with a consideration of the results for a number of studies. The final section deals with the implications of the results for technicians, fundamental securities analysts, and portfolio managers. We will also consider these results in the subsequent discussion on valuation analysis.

Rationale for the Efficient Capital Markets Theory

An efficient capital market can be defined as *a market in which security prices adjust rapidly to the infusion of new information, and current stock prices fully reflect all available information regarding the security.* While the definition of an efficient capital market is relatively straightforward, we often fail to consider *why* capital markets should be expected to be efficient. What conditions do we assume exist to have an efficient capital market?

An initial, and very important, premise of an efficient market is that *there are a large number of profit-maximizing participants concerned with the analysis and valuation of securities,* and operating independently of each other. A second assumption is that *new information regarding securities comes to the market in a random fashion,* and the announcements over time are generally independent of one another. The third assumption of an efficient market is especially crucial. *Investors adjust security prices rapidly to reflect the effect of new information.* While the price adjustment made is not always perfect, it is unbiased (i.e., sometimes there is an overadjustment, sometimes an underadjustment, but you don't know which it will be). It is contended that the attempt to adjust the security price takes place rapidly because the number of profit-maximizing investors is large. The combined effect of (1) information coming in a random, independent fashion, and (2) numerous investors who adjust stock prices rapidly to reflect this new information is that *price changes are independent and random.*

Finally, because security prices adjust to all new information and, therefore, supposedly reflect all public information at any point in time, *the security prices that prevail at any point in time should be an unbiased reflection of all currently available information.* The price of a security at any point in time is an unbiased estimate of the true intrinsic value of the security at that point in time given all the information available. Based upon the foregoing discussion, an efficient market is one in which security prices adjust rapidly to the infusion of new information, and current stock prices fully reflect all available information including the risk involved. Therefore, the returns implicit in the price reflect the risk involved, so *the expected return is consistent with risk.*

Alternative Efficient Market Hypotheses

A great deal of the early work in the area of efficient markets was done under the "random walk" hypothesis (i.e., that changes in stock prices occurred randomly) and contained extensive empirical analysis without much theory behind it. The first real attempt to synthesize the theory and organize the numerous empirical studies was made by Professor Eugene Fama in a 1970 *Journal of Finance* article,[1] which was the initial presentation of the efficient market theory in terms

---

[1] Eugene F. Fama, "Efficient Capital Markets: A Review of Theory and Empirical Work," *Journal of Finance* (1970): 383–417.

of the "fair game" model. Without going into the "fair game" presentation in detail, the basic conclusion is that in a "fair game" efficient market, investors can acquire securities at current prices and be confident that these prices "fully reflect" all available information and are consistent with the risk involved. In addition, Fama divided the overall hypothesis and empirical tests into three sub-hypotheses depending upon the information set involved. The following discussion is organized in terms of Fama's sub-hypotheses.

Weak Form Efficient Market Hypothesis

The weak form efficient market hypothesis assumes that current stock prices fully reflect all *stock market* information including the historical sequence of prices, price changes, volume information and any other information generated by the market itself such as odd-lot sales and specialist activity. Because current prices already reflect all past price changes and any other stock market information, this implies that there should be no relationship between past price changes and future price changes; i.e., price changes are independent and any trading rule that depends upon past price changes or any past market data to predict future price changes should be of little value.[2]

Semi-Strong Form Efficient Market Hypothesis

The semi-strong form efficient market hypothesis asserts that *security prices adjust rapidly to the release of all new public information;* i.e., stock prices "fully reflect" *all* public information. Obviously the semi-strong hypothesis encompasses the weak form hypothesis because all public information includes all market information (stock prices, trading volume, etc.), plus all nonmarket information such as earnings, stock splits, economic news, or political news. A direct implication of this hypothesis is that investors acting on important new information after it is public cannot derive above-average profits from the transaction, considering the cost of trading, because the security price already reflects the effect of the new information.

Strong Form Efficient Market Hypothesis

The strong form efficient market hypothesis contends that stock prices "fully reflect" *all* information (public and otherwise). Hence, it implies that no group of investors has monopolistic access to information relevant to the formation of prices. Therefore, *no group of investors should be able to consistently derive above-average profits*. The strong form hypothesis encompasses *both* the weak

[2]A trading rule is a set of prespecified conditions that will cause an investor to buy or sell stock. Examples of specific trading rules are briefly discussed in the section on test results and in the chapter on technical analysis (Chapter 13).

and semi-strong forms. Further, the strong form hypothesis requires not only efficient markets (where prices adjust rapidly to the release of new public information), but also requires *perfect* markets in which *all information is available to everyone at the same time*. This form of the EMH contends that, because all information is immediately available to everyone and is rapidly discounted by everyone, no group has monopolistic access to important new information and, therefore, *nobody* can derive above-average profits.

Tests of Alternative Efficient Market Hypotheses

Weak Form Hypothesis: Tests and Results

There have been two groups of tests of the weak form efficient market hypothesis. The first category involves statistical tests of the independence of stock price changes. The second group entails specific testing of trading rules which involve making investment decisions on the basis of past market information as opposed to a simple buy-and-hold policy (i.e., simply buying stock at the beginning of a test period and holding it to the end).

Statistical Tests of Independence   As discussed earlier, stock price changes over time should be independent because new information comes to the market in a random, independent fashion, and stock prices adjust rapidly to this new information. Therefore, in an efficient capital market, stock price changes should be independent and random.

Two major statistical tests have been employed to verify this. First were the autocorrelation tests which correlated price changes over time to see whether these changes were independent of each other; i.e., was there significant positive or negative correlation in price changes over time? Is the percent of price change on day t correlated with the percent of price change on day $t - 1$, $t - 2$, or $t - 3$?[3] Those who support the theory of efficient capital markets would expect such correlations to be insignificant.

The second statistical test of independence included "runs" tests. Given a series of price changes, each price change is designated a "plus" $(+)$ if it is an increase, or a "minus" $(-)$ if it is a decrease. The result is a set of pluses and minuses as follows: $+++-+--++--++$. A run occurs when there is no difference between two changes; two or three *consecutive* positive or consecutive negative price changes is one run. When the price change is to a different sign (e.g., a negative price change followed by a positive price change), the "run" is ended and a new run begins.[4] To test for independence, one calculates the number of runs for a given series and compares this with a table that provides the number of such runs that would occur in a random series.

---

[3]For a discussion of tests of independence see Ya-lun Chou, *Statistical Analysis*, 2d ed. (New York: Holt, Rinehart and Winston, 1975), pp. 540–542.

[4]For the details of a runs test see ibid., pp. 537–539.

Tests of Trading Rules   The second group of tests of the weak form hypothesis were prompted by the assertion of technical analysts that the statistical tests described above were too rigid to pinpoint the very intricate price patterns examined by technical analysts. Supposedly, technical analysts do not believe it is a mechanical number of positive or negative price changes that signal a move to a new equilibrium in the market, but that there is a general consistency in trend over time that might include both positive and negative changes. Technical analysts felt their trading rules were too sophisticated and complicated to be simulated using a rigid statistical test. Therefore, investigators attempted to specifically examine alternative technical trading rules through simulation. Advocates of an efficient market hypothesized that investors using any technical trading rule that asserted that stock prices moved in trends could not derive abnormal profits.[5] Further, any trading rule that depended solely on any past market information (e.g., price data, volume data, odd-lot sales, specialist activity) would likewise not enjoy above-average risk-adjusted profits after considering transactions costs.

Statistical Test Results

Analysis of the serial correlations among stock price changes has been done by various authors for several different intervals including one day, four days, nine days, and sixteen days.[6] The results consistently indicated *insignificant* correlation in stock price changes over time. The typical range of correlation coefficients was from +.10 to −.10, but the correlations were typically not statistically significant. Therefore, these serial correlation tests consistently indicated that *stock price changes over time are in general statistically independent*. These results imply that one *cannot* use past price changes alone to project future price changes.

Tests of stock price "runs" likewise indicated independence in stock price changes over time. While positive price changes were occasionally followed by positive price changes and vice versa, a number of such cases can be explained by a random model in which you would expect some positive and negative runs. The actual number of runs for stock price series consistently fell into the range expected for a random series. Therefore, these statistical tests likewise supported the notion that stock price changes over time are independent. These statistical tests of independence were repeated on the OTC market, and the results likewise supported the EMH.[7]

While the daily, weekly, and monthly data consistently supported the weak form EMH, the evidence from individual transaction price changes did not. In several studies, price changes for individual transactions on the NYSE were ex-

---

[5]Abnormal profits are defined as rates of return greater than the returns derived from a buy-and-hold policy, adjusting for differences in risk, i.e., above-average risk-adjusted returns.

[6]Eugene F. Fama, "The Behavior of Stock Market Prices," *Journal of Business* 38 (1965): 34–105.

[7]Robert L. Hagerman and Richard D. Richmond, "Random Walks, Martingales and the OTC," *Journal of Finance* 28 (1973): 897–909.

amined, and significant serial correlations were found which would imply that a transaction with a positive price change might be followed by a transaction that likewise had a positive price change. Notably, none of the authors of these studies attempted to show that the dependence of transaction price movements could be used to derive above average risk-adjusted returns. From the data it appears that the significant correlation among individual transactions is caused by the market-making activities of the specialist. However, it is highly unlikely that this small imperfection in the market could be used by an investor to derive excess profits after considering the substantial transactions costs that would be involved in following any trading rule.[8]

Trading Rule Simulation Results

In several studies there was an attempt to simulate the conditions under which a specific technical system was used to make investment decisions, and to compare the results derived from such a simulation, including commission costs, to the results from a simple buy-and-hold policy. The reader should be made aware of three major pitfalls that can negate the results of such studies: (1) The investigator should *only use data that is publicly available* in the decision rule; e.g., information regarding trading activity by the specialist may not be available until up to two weeks after the study period ends. Therefore, it is necessary to assume that you cannot act on the basis of this information until after the two-week period is over. (2) When determining the returns from a trading rule *all transactions costs* involved in implementing the trading strategy must be included. This is important because most trading rules involve many more transactions than a simple buy-and-hold policy does. (3) The *final results must be risk adjusted*. This is done because a trading rule may simply be of help in the selection of high-risk securities that would be expected to experience higher returns.

Two operational problems have been encountered in these tests. First, trading rules require a fair amount of personal interpretation. Therefore, it is often difficult, if not impossible, to mechanically simulate a trading rule. In many cases two technical analysts looking at the same set of data might differ in their projections. Therefore, *it is not possible to test some technical rules*. The second problem is that *there is an almost infinite number of potential trading rules* and, therefore, it is not possible to test all of them. As a result, only a number of the better-known technical trading rules that could be simulated have been tested.

It is also necessary to acknowledge that the tests may be somewhat biased because the studies have concentrated on the simple trading rules which many technicians contend are rather naive. In addition, the authors almost always employ readily available data from the NYSE. This means the sample is biased toward well-known, heavily traded stocks that *should* enjoy efficient markets. Specifically, our initial discussion pointed out that markets *should* be efficient if

---

[8]Victor Niederhoffer and M. F. Osborn, "Market-Making and Reversal on the Stock Exchange," *Journal of American Statistical Association* 61 (1966): 897–916; Kenneth Carey, "A Model of Individual Transactions Stock Prices" (Ph.D. dissertation, University of Kansas, 1971).

one assumes a large number of aggressive, profit-maximizing investors who attempt to adjust stock prices to reflect new information. This implies that efficiency is dependent on trading; i.e., the more trading in a security, the more efficient the market should be, up to a point. (Beyond some fairly high volume, it would probably be difficult to measure differences in efficiency.) Alternatively, in cases where there is very little trading activity, one could envision a lack of complete efficiency because there is not much interest in the security, and, therefore, there is not adequate trading activity to move the security to the new equilibrium price that reflects the new information. The most popular trading technique has been to use filter rules. (A filter is set for a given stock, which is traded when the price change exceeds the filter specified.) As an example, one might set up a 5 percent filter for a stock based upon past movements. When the stock has risen 5 percent from some base, it is hypothesized by the technical analyst that this movement indicates a "breakout" and that stock prices will continue to rise. Therefore, technical traders using this filter would acquire the stocks, expecting to take advantage of the continued rise. If the stock declines 5 percent from some peak price, technicians would identify this as a "breakout" on the downside and expect the price to continue to decline. Therefore, they would sell the stock acquired previously and possibly sell it short, based upon the expectation of a further price decline.

Studies of this trading rule have used a range of filters from very small (one-half percent) to very large (50 percent), and have generated consistent results which indicated that using *small* filters and *not* taking account of trading commission, one *can* derive above-average profits. Such results are consistent with the small correlation in price changes discussed earlier. However, the use of small filters resulted in numerous trades and substantial commissions. Therefore, when trading commissions were considered, all the trading *profits* turned to *losses*.

Trading techniques have been simulated using past market data other than stock prices. Trading rules have been devised that used odd-lot figures, advanced-decline ratios, and short sales or short positions. In a few cases there have been slight profits, but generally the simulations using these trading rules did *not* outperform a buy-and-hold policy on a risk-adjusted basis after taking account of commissions.[9] Therefore, it is probably safe to say that the great bulk of the evidence generated by simulating mechanical trading rules supports the weak form of the efficient market hypothesis.

Semi-Strong Form Hypothesis: Tests and Results

Recall that the semi-strong EMH asserts that security prices adjust rapidly to the release of *all new public information*; i.e., stock prices "fully reflect" all public information. Given the statement of the hypothesis and the direct implication,

[9]George Pinches, "The Random Walk Hypothesis and Technical Analysis," *Financial Analysts Journal* 26 (1970): 104–110.

studies of the semi-strong form of the EMH have involved one or both of the following:

(1) Examination of price movements around the time of an important announcement in an attempt to see when the expected price adjustment took place: did security prices adjust *before* the announcement was made; did prices adjust *during* the announcement period; or did prices appear to adjust *after* the announcement? The efficient market hypothesis would imply that prices adjust either *before* the announcement, because of news leaks or some such phenomenon, or *during* the period of announcement.

(2) Examination of the potential for above-average profit assuming an investor acted after the information became public. Specifically, one would assume an investor acquired the security after an announcement was made public and determine whether he enjoyed above-average risk-adjusted profits compared to those from a buy-and-hold policy after taking into account transactions costs.

Adjustment for Market Effects

Whether an analyst is going to use one or both tests of the semi-strong EMH, it is necessary to adjust the price movements, or the security returns, for aggregate price movements, or market returns, during the period considered. The point is, a 5 percent price change in a stock during the period surrounding an announcement is not meaningful until you know what the aggregate stock market did during the same period and how this stock "normally" acts under such conditions; e.g., if the market changed by 10 percent, the 5 percent change may be lower than expected. Authors have generally recognized the need to make such adjustments and typically assumed (pre-1970) that the individual stocks should experience returns or percentage price changes equal to those of the aggregate market. Therefore, the adjustment process simply entailed subtracting the market return from the actual return to derive "abnormal" returns as follows:

$$AR_{it} = R_{it} - R_{mt}$$

where:

AR_{it} = the abnormal rate of return on security i during period t

R_{it} = the rate of return on security i during period t

R_{mt} = the rate of return on a market index during period t.

Using the previous example in which the stock experienced a 5 percent price increase and the market increased 10 percent, the abnormal price change would be minus 5 percent.

In some studies the authors adjusted prices by an amount different from the average market rate of return because it was assumed that all stocks do *not* change by the same amount as the market; i.e., some stocks are more volatile than the market and some are less volatile. In these instances it is necessary to determine an expected rate of return for the stock based upon the market rate of return. As an example, if the stock is generally 20 percent more volatile than the market, and the market experiences a 10 percent rate of return, you would expect such a stock to experience a 12 percent rate of return. In such a case, you would determine the abnormal return by computing the difference between the stock's actual rate of return and its *expected* return. Continuing with the example, if this stock that was expected to have a 12 percent return only had a 5 percent return, its abnormal rate of return during the period would be a minus 7 percent. Over the normal long-run period, one would expect the abnormal returns to sum to zero (i.e., one period the returns will be above expectations, the next period they might be below expectations).

To summarize, various tests of the semi-strong EMH either examine abnormal price changes surrounding announcements of new information to see when the adjustment took place or they examine abnormal rates of return for the period immediately after an announcement to determine whether it is possible to derive above-average risk-adjusted rates of return. The numerous studies are best organized in terms of specific events: i.e., announcements of stock splits, exchange listings, accounting changes, etc.

Stock Split Studies One of the more popular kinds of information to examine is stock splits. There is a belief that the prices of stocks that split increase in value because the shares are priced lower, which will increase demand for them. In contrast, advocates of efficient markets would not expect a change in value because all the firm has done is issue additional stock and nothing fundamentally affecting value has occurred.

Numerous studies have examined the profit potential for investors who acquired stocks after a split. Although the results have not been unanimous, the bulk indicated that an investor who acquired the stock after it split would *not* experience above-average rates of return. In fact, in many instances in which a stock split and the company did not raise the dividend on the new shares, the stock declined relative to expectations. Investors generally expect the company to raise the dividend rate at the time of a split (which they do about 80 percent of the time).

In addition, several studies have examined the opportunities for profits if you bought the stock that was going to split right after the *announcement* of the split. Studies that used monthly and daily data generally agreed that it was not possible to generate abnormal profits after taking into account the costs of the transaction.

In summary, the results of numerous studies indicate that, unless you know about the proposed stock split *before* it is announced, it is not possible to experience above-average risk-adjusted returns on these stocks. These results clearly support the semi-strong EMH.[10]

---

[10]The classic study on this topic is, Eugene Fama, Lawrence Fisher, Michael Jensen, and Richard Roll, "The Adjustment of Stock Prices to New Information," *International Economic Review* 10 (1969): 1–20. A recent study that reviews the prior research is, Frank K. Reilly and Eugene F. Drzycimski, "Short-Run Profits From Stock Splits," *Financial Management* 10 (1981).

New Issues Studies   During the 1960s a number of closely-held companies decided to "go public" by selling some of their common stock. It is difficult to determine an appropriate price for such a stock, and there is risk involved in underwriting such issues. Hence, some authors expected underwriters to underprice the new issues, and investors, who acquired the new issues *at the offering price,* to receive abnormal profits. If the new issues are underpriced, it is possible to test the EMH by analyzing how long it takes for the market to adjust to the underpricing. The specific test examined the returns to an investor who acquires the new issues *in the after market* (purchases the stock after the initial offering) and holds it for various periods. Therefore, the studies considered two questions: (1) are new issues generally underpriced? and (2) how quickly does the market adjust the price to take account of the underpricing? The results of several studies that dealt with these questions were quite consistent.[11] *All* the studies indicated that, on average, new issues yield positive abnormal short-run returns assuming they were purchased *at the offering price.* Most authors attribute these excess returns to underpricing by the underwriters. The results also tended to support the semi-strong efficient market hypothesis because it appears that *the market adjusted the prices almost immediately.* There were no abnormal returns from acquiring the new issue shortly after the offering was made and holding it for various periods. The evidence for rapid adjustment is most evident in the Reilly study which indicates that prices adjust by the week following the offering.[12]

Exchange Listing   Another significant economic event is the decision by a firm to list its stock on a national exchange or, specifically, to be listed on the NYSE because it is the largest and most prestigious exchange. Such a listing is expected to increase the market liquidity of the stock and, possibly, add to the prestige of the firm. There are two questions of interest. First, does listing on a major exchange cause a permanent change in the value of the firm? Second, is it possible to derive abnormal returns from investing in the newly listed stock around the time of the listing? While there was some difference in the results of studies that dealt with these questions, the overall consensus was that listing on a national exchange did *not* cause a permanent change in the long-run value of a firm. Regarding whether it is possible to derive abnormal returns by investing in stocks; the results were mixed. All the studies agreed that the stocks moved up prior to any announcements, but stock prices generally *declined* after the listing. Observers generally agree that it is *not* possible to generate positive abnormal returns by purchasing a stock after the announcement of listing.

   In summary, the studies on the impact of an exchange listing indicated that there is no long-run benefit to the stockholders. On the question of profit opportunities, the results generally indicated that it is not possible to derive abnormal returns when the listing is announced.

---

[11]For a review of past studies in this area and confirmation of past results, see Frank K. Reilly, "New Issues Revisited," *Financial Management* 6 (1977): 28–42.

[12]Ibid.

Unexpected World Events   Almost all investors at one time or another receive some major information from TV or the newspaper and wonder whether they should call their broker in the morning with the intention of making a "quick killing." Prime examples might include President Nixon's announcement of Phase I price controls in 1977, President Eisenhower's heart attack in 1955, or Nixon's resignation from the presidency in 1974. Although such unexpected major world events do not occur very often, one may question whether they provide opportunities for abnormal profits. A study that examined a number of these events generally concluded that it was *not* possible to derive consistent returns by buying on good news and selling on bad news. The results consistently indicated that the major adjustment in stock prices took place during the time between the close of the market before the announcement and its opening after the announcement. The major stock price change occurred *before* the market re-opened. While some large stock price changes did occur after the market opened the direction of these changes was not consistent. On the question of whether investors could have made a profit from investing in stocks at the opening following the announcement, the results consistently indicated that this would *not* have been possible. Therefore, these tests generally supported the notion that the stock market was semi-strong efficient.

Announcements of Accounting Changes   Numerous studies have analyzed the impact of announcements of accounting changes on stock prices. These studies, which implicitly contend that the capital markets are relatively efficient, have implications for the semi-strong EMH. If markets are efficient, then they should react quickly to announcements of accounting changes. It is also possible to determine the effect investors expect the accounting change to have, if any. If the announcement is of a change in accounting technique that will affect the economic value of the firm, a rapid change in stock prices would be expected. If the accounting change only affects *reported* earnings but has no economic significance (e.g., a change in the technique used to compute depreciation for book-keeping purposes), an advocate of an efficient capital market would not expect the announcement to have an impact on stock prices.

A study of earnings reports indicated that the stock market reacted as one would expect to abnormally good or bad earnings reports, but the reaction occurred *during* the year—not when the final earnings numbers become available. This would indicate that the stock market reacted *before* the annual earnings report was issued and would be supportive of the EMH.

When a firm changes its depreciation accounting method for reporting purposes from accelerated to straight-line, it will experience an increase in reported earnings, but this change has no economic consequence. An analysis of stock price movements surrounding these changes in depreciation method generally supported the EMH because there was no indication of positive price changes, and there were some negative effects.

Because of the high rate of inflation during the late 1970s, many firms changed their inventory method from first-in-first-out (FIFO) to last-in-first-out (LIFO). Such a change causes a decline in reported earnings, but is of benefit to the firm because it reduces taxable earnings and, therefore, tax expenses. Advocates of efficient markets would expect positive price changes because of the tax savings. The results confirmed this; although earnings were lower than they would have been with FIFO, stock prices generally increased for firms that changed their inventory methods.

Stock prices and Quarterly Earnings Reports   A major area of study that does *not* support the semi-strong efficient market hypothesis relates to the usefulness of quarterly earnings reports. Some of the prior studies discussed indicated that stock prices react before the release of *annual* earnings reports. Other studies examined the potential for experiencing abnormal profits from investing on the basis of *quarterly* earnings reports. The basic approach has been to examine a group of quarterly earnings reports after they are made public and invest either in the stocks that had the lowest price-earnings ratio, or in the stocks with the largest difference between actual earnings and expected earnings. The results have consistently shown that if you purchased stocks on the basis of these criteria and held them for six months, you would have received a higher risk-adjusted return than you would from a market portfolio (i.e., a completely diversified portfolio of risky assets) of stocks. These results indicate that the information in quarterly income statements is of value. Apparently the market does not react to it as fast as the EMH would suggest, and, therefore, these results are not supportive of the semi-strong form.[13]

Differential Price-Earnings Ratios   Another area that does not generally provide support for the EMH involves differential price-earnings ratios. These ratios are typically computed as the ratio of the current price of a stock to the stock's earnings for the last 12 months. As an example, if a stock were selling for $60 a share and the earnings for the latest 12 months were $5.00 a share, the price-earnings ratio (p/e ratio) would be 12 times ($60/$5). As will be discussed in detail in the chapter on valuations, the p/e ratio is expected to reflect the risk and growth potential of the stock. Therefore, one should not expect a difference in the rate of return for stocks with high p/e ratios (e.g., over 20 times earnings) and that for stocks with low p/e ratios (e.g., less than 7 times). If there is a preference, most investors would probably expect the stocks with high p/e's to be more profitable because they are generally expected to have higher growth rates. In fact, the results of several studies of this topic have indicated that it is possible to derive abnormal positive risk-adjusted rates of return by investing in a portfolio of *low* p/e ratio stocks. In contrast, a portfolio of high p/e ratio stocks experienced rates of return that were below normal for the risk involved. The fact that these rates of

---

[13]An article that reviews a number of these studies is, O. Maurice Joy and Charles P. Jones, "Earnings Reports and Market Efficiencies: An Analysis of Contrary Evidence," *Journal of Financial Research* 2 (1979): 51–64.

return could be achieved on the basis of available information on prices and earnings would not be supportive of the semi-strong EMH.[14]

Conclusion Concerning Semi-Strong EMH   The great majority of the evidence has supported the semi-strong efficient market hypothesis because the results indicated that stock prices adjust rapidly to the announcement of new information and/or investors are typically not able to derive above-average returns from acting on important new information once it is available. The fact is, the support is *not* unanimous because the quarterly earnings results have consistently provided evidence against the hypothesis and the analysis of returns for low p/e stocks likewise did not support it. Therefore, while the *majority* of the evidence supports the hypothesis, more studies must be conducted to identify areas of inefficiency in the market and explain *why* the inefficiencies arise.

Strong Form Hypothesis: Tests and Results

The strong form efficient market hypothesis contends that stock prices "fully reflect" *all* information (public and private). Therefore, no group of investors possess information such that they could consistently generate above-average profits. As stated, this hypothesis is extremely rigid and requires not only that stock prices must adjust rapidly to new public information, but *also* that no group has monopoly access to specific information. This form of the hypothesis presupposes perfection in the information-adjusting process, and also in the information-*generating* process.

The tests of this hypothesis involve the analysis of returns over time for different identifiable investment groups to determine whether any group consistently received above-average returns on a risk-adjusted basis. If any group did consistently receive such returns, this would indicate either that they had monopolistic access to important information, or they had the ability to consistently act on public information before other investors could, so the market was not rapidly adjusting stock prices to *all* new information. There have been three major groups of investors examined in this regard. First, several studies have analyzed the returns of those possessing inside information by examining the returns obtained by *corporate insiders* from their stock trading. Another group of studies analyzed the returns available to *stock exchange specialists*. The third group of tests examined the overall performance of *professional money managers* with the emphasis on returns generated by mutual funds because data for these funds are readily available.

---

[14]The most widely quoted study in this area is, S. Basu, "Investment Performance of Common Stocks in Relation to Their Price-Earnings Ratios: A Test of the Efficient Market Hypothesis," *Journal of Finance* 32 (1977): 663–682.

Corporate Insider Trading   Insiders are typically defined as major corporate officers, members of the board of directors, and major stockholders of a given firm. Securities laws require that these individuals report their transactions (purchases or sales) in the stock of the firm for which they are insiders to the SEC each month. About six weeks after the reporting period, this insider trading information is made public by the SEC. It has consequently been possible to identify how corporate insiders traded over a period of time, and to determine whether their transactions were generally profitable; i.e., on balance, did they buy before abnormally good price movements and sell prior to poor market periods for their stock? The results of these studies have generally indicated that *corporate insiders consistently enjoyed significantly above-average profits.* Corporate insiders consistently had otherwise unavailable information which they were able to use to derive above-average returns on investments in their companies' stocks. These results would be considered evidence against the strong form EMH. In addition, there is evidence that public investors who consistently traded with the insiders based upon *announced* insider transactions would have enjoyed excess returns (after commissions). These results also constitute evidence against the semi-strong efficient market hypothesis because they imply that investors should be able to derive above-average returns simply by trading on the basis of available public information (insider transactions).

Stock Exchange Specialists   Several studies have examined the function of stock exchange specialists and determined that specialists have monopolistic access to certain very important information about unfilled limit orders. Therefore, one would expect specialists to derive above-average returns from this information, which is generally supported by the data. It appears that specialists generally make money on their transactions because they typically sell at prices above those of their purchases and are able to buy at lower prices. It has also been shown that they probably make money when they buy or sell following unexpected announcements, and that they even make money when they get involved in large block trades. The strongest evidence was provided by a study that examined the actual rate of return earned on capital by the specialist. The results indicated that the return on capital for specialists ranged from about 80 percent to 160 percent and averaged about *100 percent.* This is clearly an above-average rate of return and, therefore, would not support the strong-form EMH.

Performance of Professional Money Managers   The previous studies of the strong form EMH have been concerned with two small, unique groups of investors who have been able to consistently derive above-average returns *because they have monopolistic access to important information and take advantage of it.* The studies dealing with the third group, professional money managers, are more representative because these investors would not be expected to have monopolistic access to important new information on a consistent basis. These studies assume that money managers are highly trained professionals who work full time at investment management. Therefore, if any "normal" investors should be able to derive above-average profits without inside information, this group should. Also, if any noninsider should be able to obtain inside information, it should be someone from this group because professional money managers do extensive interviewing of corporate officers and the like.

While investigators would ideally like to examine the performance of a wide range of money managers, most of the studies have been limited to those managing mutual funds because data on these funds have been readily available. Only recently have data been available for bank trust departments, insurance companies, and investment advisers.

Several studies have examined the performance of a number of mutual funds over extended periods. The results indicated that the majority of the funds were *not* able to match the performance of a buy-and-hold policy. When a large sample of mutual funds was examined in terms of their risk-adjusted rates of return without considering commission costs, slightly more than half did better than the overall market. When commission costs, the costs of buying the fund, and management costs were considered, approximately two-thirds of the mutual funds generally did *not* match the performance of the overall market. In addition, it was found that funds were *not* consistent in their performance. A fund that did well one year could do well the next year, but it was just as likely to be a poor performer. A fund that did better than average two years in a row was no more likely to do well three years in a row than one would expect on the basis of random chance. It was concluded that it is clearly not possible to predict future performance for money managers based upon past performance.

Therefore, the performance of mutual fund managers supported the strong form efficient market hypothesis. The results indicated that most mutual fund managers, using publicly available information (and anything else available), could not consistently outperform a buy-and-hold policy.

Recently, some companies have been collecting performance figures for other institutional investors, and these have been quite consistent with the findings on mutual funds.

Conclusion Concerning the Strong Form Hypothesis   The tests of the strong form efficient market hypothesis generated mixed results, but the bulk of relevant evidence supported the strong form hypothesis. The results for two unique groups of investors (corporate insiders and stock exchange specialists) definitely did not support the hypothesis because both groups apparently have monopolistic access to important information, and they use it to derive above-average returns. Analysis of performance by professional money managers definitely *supported* the strong form hypothesis. Numerous studies have indicated that the investments of these highly trained, full-time investors could not consistently outperform a simple buy-and-hold policy on a risk-adjusted basis. Because this last group is similar to the bulk of investors who do not have consistent access to inside information, the results for money managers are considered more relevant to the hypothesis. Therefore, it is concluded that there is substantial support for the strong form hypothesis as applied to most investors.

Implications of Efficient Capital Markets

Overall, it is safe to conclude that the capital markets are generally efficient for the great majority of investors. Because of the substantial and consistent empirical results indicating an efficient market, anyone who assumes otherwise does so at great risk. This evidence supporting the existence of an efficient equity market makes it important to consider the implication of such a market for those most affected by this efficiency: investment analysts and portfolio managers.

Efficient Markets and Technical Analysis

It is widely recognized that a belief in technical analysis and the notion of efficient markets are directly opposed. A basic premise of technical analysis is that *stock prices move in trends that persist.*[15] This premise is based upon the belief that when new information comes to the market, it is *not* immediately available to everyone. Rather it is typically disseminated from the informed professional to the aggressive investing public, and then to the great bulk of investors. Also, it is felt that analysis of the information and subsequent action is *not* immediate but is spread over time. Therefore, it is hypothesized that the movement of stock prices to a new equilibrium following the release of new information does not occur rapidly, but takes place *over a period of time.* As a result, there are *trends in stock price movements that persist for a period of time.* Technical analysts feel that nimble traders can develop "systems" that help them to detect the beginning of a movement to a new equilibrium. Given some signal indicating the beginning of a movement to a new equilibrium (a "breakout"), the technical analyst attempts to buy or sell the stock immediately and thereby take advantage of the price adjustment yet to come.

The belief in such a pattern of events is in direct contrast to the efficient market hypothesis which contends that the information dissemination process is quite rapid and, therefore, most interested investors receive new information at about the same time. Advocates of an efficient market contend that the adjustment of security prices to the new information is *very rapid.* It is *not,* however, contended that the price adjustment is perfect. In some cases there will be an overadjustment and in some an underadjustment. Still, because there is nothing certain about whether the market will over or underadjust, it is not possible to consistently derive abnormal profits from the adjustment process.

If the capital market is efficient and prices "fully reflect" all relevant information, any technical trading system that depends only upon past trading data cannot be of any value because, by the time the information is public, the price adjustment has taken place. Therefore, a purchase or sale using a technical trading rule after information becomes public and after the rapid adjustment in stock prices takes place should not generate above-average returns after taking account of commissions.

[15]There is an extensive discussion of technical analysis and references listed in Chapter 13.

Efficient Markets and Fundamental Analysis

Advocates of fundamental analysis believe that, at any point in time, there is a basic intrinsic value for the aggregate stock market, and for alternative industries or individual securities, and that this value depends upon underlying economic values. The way to determine the intrinsic value at a point in time is to examine the variables that are supposed to determine value (i.e., current and future earnings and risk variables) and, based upon these variables, derive an estimate of intrinsic value for the aggregate stock market, an industry, or a company. If the prevailing market price differs substantially from the intrinsic value (enough to cover transaction costs), appropriate action should be taken; buy if the market price is substantially below the intrinsic value and vice versa. Advocates of fundamental analysis believe that there are instances in which the market price and intrinsic value differ, but they also believe that eventually the market will recognize the discrepancy and correct it. Therefore, if an analyst can do a superior job of *estimating* intrinsic value, he can consistently acquire undervalued securities and derive above-average returns. Fundamental analysis involves several levels of investigation beginning with overall or aggregate market analysis, and progressing through industry analysis, company analysis, and portfolio management. The efficient market hypothesis has important implications for all levels of fundamental analysis.

Aggregate Market Analysis   In Chapter 10, we make a strong case that intrinsic value analysis should begin with aggregate market analysis. Still, the efficient markets hypothesis implies that if analysis is limited to the examination of *past* economic events, it is unlikely that the analyst will be able to "beat" a buy-and-hold policy because the market adjusts very rapidly to known economic events. Alternatively, there is evidence that the market does experience long-run price movements, but to take advantage of these movements, the EMH would contend that it is necessary to *project* the relevant variables that cause these long-run movements.

Industry and Company Analysis   Given the wide distribution of returns from different industries and companies, industry and company analysis are clearly justified. Again, the EMH does not contradict the value of such analyses, but implies that it is necessary to understand the relevant variables that affect returns, and also recognize that movements in these valuation variables must be *projected*. Malkiel and Cragg developed a model that did an excellent job of explaining past stock price movements using historical company data.[16] However, when the authors attempted to employ this model to project further stock price changes, still using past company data, the results were consistently inferior to results that would be achieved with a buy-and-hold policy. This implies that, even with a

---

[16]Burton G. Malkiel and John G. Cragg, "Expectations and the Structure of Share Prices," *American Economic Review* 60 (1970): 601–617.

properly specified valuation model, it is *not* possible to select stocks using only *past* data. Another study showed that the crucial difference between the stocks that enjoyed the best price performance during a given year and the stocks that experienced the worst price performance was the relationship between *estimated* earnings and *actual* earnings; i.e., if actual earnings were substantially above estimated earnings, stock prices increased and *vice versa*. Thus, if an analyst can do a superior job of *projecting* earnings and also be *different* from the consensus, he will probably have a superior stock selection record.

Theory and evidence both indicate that it is *not* impossible to be a superior analyst, but it is *very difficult* to be consistently superior. An analyst must know which variables are relevant for changes in valuation and must be able to *consistently estimate future values* for these variables to be consistently superior. Because of the difficulties involved, analysts should be evaluated to determine if they are superior.

Evaluating Analysts   To determine who the superior analysts are, the following system is suggested. Examine the performance of numerous securities recommended by an analyst over time in relation to the performance of randomly selected stocks *of the same risk class,* to determine whether the analyst's selections consistently outperform a random selection. If the analyst produces results that are *consistently* better than those produced by random selection, he is a superior analyst. The consistency requirement is crucial because one would expect securities chosen by random selection to outperform the market about half the time.

Conclusion on Fundamental Analysis   A text on investments can indicate the relevant variables to analyze, explain why these variables are relevant, and point out the techniques used in attempting to project the variables, but the task of deriving the actual estimates is as much an art as it is a science. If estimating valuation variables were mechanical, it would be possible to program a computer to carry out the function and there would be no need for analysts. Therefore, the superior analyst must understand what is important and have the ability to *estimate* these variables.

Efficient Markets and Portfolio Analysis

Studies have indicated that the performance of professional money managers does not consistently improve upon a simple buy-and-hold policy on a risk-adjusted basis. One explanation of this is that there are no superior analysts and the cost of research produces these inferior results. Another explanation (favored by the author with no empirical support) is that institutions employ superior *and* inferior analysts. The average, or inferior, performance of the portfolio stems from the fact that the recommendations of the few superior analysts are offset by the costs and the recommendations of the inferior analysts.

Given this, the question comes down to this: how should a portfolio manager manage his portfolio, actively or passively? If you have superior analysts, you can manage it actively, attempting to find undervalued securities and trading accordingly. In contrast, if you do not have superior analysts, you should manage passively and simply assume that all securities are properly priced in an efficient market. In turn, this pricing is based on the risk of the security in relation to a "market portfolio" of risky assets.

Portfolio Management with Superior Analysts

If a portfolio manager has superior security analysts with unique insights and analytical ability, they should obviously by utilized. The system suggested above can be used to determine the truly superior analysts and updated to ensure that their performance continues to be superior. The portfolio manager would allow the superior analysts to make investment recommendations for a certain proportion of the portfolio, making sure that their recommendations are implemented in a way that would conform to the risk preferences of the client. In an article by Reilly it was suggested that the total market could be divided into three tiers as follows.[17]

1. Top Tier—companies large enough to accommodate *all* institutions wishing to establish a meaningful position in the market and yet retain liquidity. Assuming a required market value of $400 million or more to be in this tier, approximately 400 firms would meet this criterion.

2. Middle Tier—companies large enough to be acquired by most institutions and large investors, although probably *not* the largest 25–30 institutions. Assuming a required market value of $200 million, an additional 300 companies were estimated to be in this tier.

3. Bottom Tier—all remaining companies not large enough to be considered by institutions. The total number of public companies in this tier is at least 5,000 and could be over 8,000.

Based on these categories, the superior analysts should also be encouraged to *concentrate their efforts in the second tier of stocks,* because these stocks probably possess the required liquidity, but they do not receive the attention given the top-tier stocks, so the markets for them may not be as efficient. Recall that markets are expected to be efficient because many investors receive new information and analyze its effect on security values. If there is a difference in the number of analysts following a stock, one could conceive of differences in the efficiency of the markets. In the case of top-tier stocks, new information regarding the stock is well publicized and numerous analysts evaluate the effect. Therefore, one should expect the price to adjust rapidly and fully reflect the new information.

News about the middle-tier firms is not as well publicized and few analysts follow some of these firms. Therefore, prices may not adjust as rapidly to new

---

[17]Frank K. Reilly, "A Three Tier Stock Market and Corporate Finance," *Financial Management* 4 (1975): 7–15.

information, and it would be worthwhile to concentrate analytical skills on these stocks because the possibility of finding a temporarily undervalued security are greater. In fact, it seems that the attention paid to small firms is *decreasing* as the number of analysts on Wall Street declines. According to an article on Wall Street mergers and the layoff of analysts that resulted, the decrease in the number of analysts has affected the number of companies followed.[18] This basically involves small firms that are of limited interest to large, institutional customers.

The remainder of the portfolio (probably the majority) would be similar to the one created without superior analysts, which is discussed below. The resulting overall performance of the portfolio should be superior to the average market performance, assuming the superior analysts were not paid too much; i.e., their pay should not exceed the value of their recommendations.

Portfolio Management Without Superior Analysts

It will be remembered that risk is an important determinant of the return an investor expects from an asset—the greater the risk, the higher the expected return. It has been shown that the relevant measure of the risk of an individual asset is its systematic risk with the market portfolio (i.e., a hypothetical, completely diversified portfolio of risky assets). In other words, the relevant measure of risk for a given asset is the manner in which that asset's returns vary in relation to the returns of the market portfolio. This systematic risk (beta) for a portfolio of stocks is relatively stable over time. This was confirmed in a study by Sharpe and Cooper which also indicated that there was a relatively good relationship between the returns for a portfolio of stocks in period t and the systematic risk of that portfolio in the previous period.[19] The implication is that, given a specific risk preference, it is possible to build a portfolio of stocks using available historical information on risk from which an investor can expect to receive a rate of return that is fairly consistent with the risk level specified. The selection process involved does not appear to require extensive research efforts. Therefore, one can conceive of how the portfolio should be managed, without superior analysts, in a world with efficient capital markets to provide maximum risk-adjusted returns for the client.

Construction of a portfolio would, consequently, involve quantifying a client's risk preferences and deriving a given risk portfolio for these preferences by investing a certain proportion of the wealth available in risky assets and the rest into a risk-free asset. It is shown in Chapters 20 and 21 that this is the method that will place the investor on the highest utility curve, i.e., provide the greatest return for a given level of risk.

The risky asset portfolio must be *completely diversified* so that it moves consistently with the aggregate market. In this context, diversification means the

[18]Tom Herman, "For Highly Qualified, Wall Street Job Market is Increasingly Gloomy," *Wall Street Journal,* 20 April 1978, p. 1.

[19]William F. Sharpe and Guy M. Cooper, "Risk-Return Classes of New York Stock Exchange Common Stocks, 1931–1967." *Financial Analysts Journal* 28 (1972):46–54, 81.

elimination of all unsystematic (unique) variability that is not related to the aggregate market. There has been some discussion regarding how many securities there must be in a portfolio for *complete* diversification. Apparently, most of the benefits (over 90 percent) are derived with a total of about 15–20 securities, but it requires over 100 stocks to get *complete* diversification. How many securities are actually included is a matter of balancing the added benefits of diversification against the costs of research for the additional stocks in the portfolio.

If one assumes that the portfolio manager is not capable of predicting future market movements, then *the specified risk level must be maintained* instead of attempting to change the risk of the portfolio based upon market expectations. Because of changing market values, there will be some change in the weights for different stocks and, therefore, a change in the risk of a portfolio. As a result, it is necessary to occasionally trade to return the portfolio to the desired balance.

Finally, it is important to *minimize transactions costs*. Assuming that the portfolio is completely diversified, and that past relations between risk and return hold over the long-run, a major deterrent to the client receiving the expected return would be excessive transactions costs that do not generate added returns.

There are three factors involved in minimizing total transaction costs: One is *minimizing taxes* for the client. How this is accomplished will vary, but it should be given prime consideration when carrying out transactions. The second factor seems rather obvious, *reduce trading turnover to the level necessitated by liquidity needs and risk control* (i.e., trades necessary to maintain a given risk level). Finally, when trades are made, the portfolio manager should attempt to *minimize the liquidity costs of the trade*. There will typically be a number of stocks available that will accomplish the desired goal. The stocks used should be those that are relatively *liquid* so that the trade will have little effect on the price of the stock. To accomplish this, you should submit limit orders to buy or sell several stocks at prices that approximate the specialist's quote (i.e., put in limit orders to buy stock at the bid price or sell stock at the ask price). The stock that is bought or sold first is the one that meets the client's criteria and all other orders are withdrawn.

Index Funds

The discussion above indicates that, if one assumes that there are efficient capital markets and only a limited number of truly superior analysts, a large amount of money should be managed so that investment performance simply matches that achieved by the aggregate market and costs are minimized so as not to drop returns below the market. Following such reasoning, several institutions instigated "market funds," also referred to as "index funds." Index funds are security portfolios specially designed to duplicate the performance of the overall security market as represented by some selected market index series. Three major funds were started in the early 1970s: (1) American National Bank and Trust Company of Chicago; (2) Batterymarch Financial Management Corporation of Boston; and (3) Well Fargo Investment Advisors, a division of Wells Fargo Bank in San Francisco. In all cases, these equity portfolios were designed to match the performance of the S&P 500 Index.

Qtr./yr.	American National Bank	Battery-march Financial	Wells Fargo	S&P 500
1/74	− 2.80		− 2.92	− 2.81
2/74	− 7.43		− 7.90	− 7.54
3/74	−25.62		−25.11	−25.05
4/74	9.04		9.13	9.41
Year	−27.02		−26.93	−26.03
1/75	23.40	21.30	22.56	22.90
2/75	15.67	14.90	15.24	15.31
3/75	−11.12	−11.00	−10.95	−10.93
4/75	8.64	8.70	8.76	8.64
Year	37.65	34.80	36.36	36.92
1/76	14.89	14.80	14.82	14.96
2/76	2.67	2.80	2.53	2.44
3/76	2.06	1.80	1.71	1.89
4/76	2.11	2.20	3.24	3.18
Year	22.93	22.80	23.63	23.64
1/77	− 8.16	− 8.30	− 7.50	− 7.44
2/77	3.07	3.00	3.31	3.28
3/77	− 2.88	− 2.50	− 2.77	− 2.79
4/77	− 0.09	− 0.15	− 0.11	− 0.13
Year	− 8.15	− 8.05	− 7.19	− 7.19
1/78	− 4.98	− 5.50	− 4.99	− 4.95
2/78	8.62	8.00	8.42	8.52
3/78	8.88	8.10	8.70	8.66
4/78	− 5.16	− 4.20	− 4.97	− 4.95
Year	6.58	5.69	6.41	6.53
1/79	6.91	6.40	7.70	7.06
2/79	2.62	2.30	2.69	2.70
3/79	7.46	7.10	7.59	7.62
4/79	0.10	− 0.10	0.16	0.15
Year	17.92	16.46	18.49	18.24
1/80	− 4.05	− 3.30	− 4.00	− 4.11
2/80	13.40	12.50	13.38	13.43
3/80	11.03	10.00	11.13	11.19
4/80	9.46	9.50	9.54	9.54 (est)
Year	32.24	31.00	32.50	32.48 (est)

Table 7.1 Quarterly Returns for Index Funds and S&P 500: 1974–1980

Source: Individual Index Funds and Standard and Poor's. Reprinted with permission.

Initially the funds experienced slow growth and limited attention. However, as the result of a number of articles describing the reasoning behind index funds and the justification for their existence, client demand grew and a number of financial institutions established their own index funds. In fact, at present it is not a matter of institutions having index funds, but of their attempting to develop a "better" index fund.[20]

The ability of the three major index funds to match the market can be seen from the figures in Table 7.1. These quarterly figures for the period 1974–1980 for the major funds indicate that the correlation of quarterly rates of return for the index funds and the S&P 500 generally exceeded .98. Therefore, it appears that the funds generally are able to fulfill their stated goal of matching market performance.

Summary

It is necessary to consider efficient capital markets at this point because there are several very important implications of such markets that have a direct bearing on security analysis and portfolio management. Capital markets are expected to be efficient because there is a large number of rational, profit-maximizing investors who react quickly to the release of new information. Because investors adjust prices rapidly to reflect new information, stock prices at any point in time are unbiased estimates of the securities' true, intrinsic value, and, consequently, there is a consistent relationship between the return on an investment and the risk it involves.

Because of the voluminous research that has been done on the EMH, the overall hypothesis has been divided into three segments and each has been tested separately. The weak form EMH states that stock prices fully reflect all *market* information, so any trading rule that uses past market data to predict future returns should not be of value. The methods employed to test this hypothesis are pure statistical tests of independence (serial correlation tests and "runs" tests) and specific tests of various technical trading rules compared to buy-and-hold policies. The results consistently supported the weak form EMH.

The semi-strong EMH asserts that security prices adjust rapidly to the release of *all public* information, and, therefore, prevailing prices fully reflect all such information. The tests of this hypothesis involve detailed examination of abnormal price movements surrounding the announcement of important new information and an analysis of whether investors could derive above-average returns from trading on the basis of public information. Although the majority of the results supported the hypothesis, they were not unanimous.

The strong form efficient market hypothesis states that security prices reflect *all* information. No group of investors has monopolistic access to important information, and, therefore, no group should be able to consistently derive above-

[20]"Here Comes the 'Super' Indexers," *Institutional Investor* 7 (1978): 109–112.

average returns. The analysis of returns to corporate insiders and stock exchange specialists did not support the strong form hypothesis. In contrast, an analysis of results achieved by professional money managers supported the hypothesis because their performance was typically inferior to those achieved with buy-and-hold policies.

The implications for a number of major participants in the equity market, including technical analysts, fundamental analysts, and portfolio managers were discussed. The EMH indicates that technical analysis should be of no value. All forms of fundamental analysis are useful, but difficult to implement because they involve the ability to *estimate future values* for relevant economic variables. Note that it *is* possible to be a superior analyst, but it is *very difficult* because it requires the ability to consistently make projections that are superior to those made by other analysts.

Portfolio managers should constantly evaluate analysts to determine whether their performance is superior. If you do not have superior analysts, the portfolio should be run like an index fund. If you have superior analysts, allow them to make decisions for some part of the portfolio and concentrate on middle-tier firms where there is a higher probability of discovering misvalued stocks.

There is some good news and some bad news. The good news is that the practice of security analysis and portfolio management is not an art that has been lost to the great computer in the sky. These are still viable professions for those willing to extend the effort and able to accept the pressures.

The bad news is that, because of the existence of many bright, hardworking people with extensive resources, the game is not easy. In fact, the aforementioned competitors have created a very efficient capital market in which it is very difficult to be superior.

Questions

1. Discuss the rationale for expecting the existence of an efficient capital market.

2. Based upon the factors that contribute to an efficient market, what would you look for to differentiate the market for two alternative stocks; i.e., why should there be a difference between the markets for the stocks?

3. Define and discuss the weak form efficient market hypothesis (EMH).

4. Describe the two sets of tests used to examine the weak form efficient market hypothesis.

5. Define and discuss the semi-strong efficient market hypothesis.

6. Describe the two general tests used to examine the semi-strong EMH. Would you expect the results from the two different tests to be consistent? Why?

7. When testing the EMH using alternative trading rules versus a buy-and-hold policy, there are three common mistakes that can bias the results against the EMH. Discuss each individually and explain why it would cause a bias.

8. Describe the results of a study that supported the semi-strong EMH and specifically discuss why the results supported the hypothesis.

9. Describe the results of a study that did *not* support the semi-strong EMH and specifically discuss why the results did not support the hypothesis.

10. Define and discuss the strong form EMH. Why do some observers contend that the strong form hypothesis really requires a perfect market in addition to efficient markets? Be specific.

11. Discuss in general terms how one would go about testing the strong form EMH. Consider why these tests are relevant. Give a brief example.

12. Describe the results of a study that does *not* support the strong form EMH. Discuss specifically why these results do not support the hypothesis.

13. Describe the results of a study that indicates support for the strong form EMH. Discuss specifically why these results support the hypothesis.

14. What are the implications of the EMH for the use of technical analysis?

15. What are the implications of the EMH for fundamental analysis? Be specific and discuss what the EMH does imply and what it does not imply.

16. In a world with efficient capital markets, what is required to be a superior analyst? Be specific.

17. How would you determine whether an analyst is truly superior? Be very specific in discussing the test.

18. What are the implications of an efficient market for a portfolio manager without any superior analysts? Specifically, how should he run his portfolio?

19. Describe an "index" fund. What are its purposes and how is such a fund run?

20. You are told that the great majority of banks rejected the idea of index funds until forced into them by their clients. Does this surprise you? How would you explain this attitude?

21. It is contended by some observers that index funds are the ultimate answer in a world with efficient capital markets. Discuss the purpose of index funds and what they do that is correct in a world with ECMs.

22. At a social gathering you meet the portfolio manager for the trust department of a local bank. He confides to you that he has been following the recommendations of his six analysts for an extended period and has found that two are superior, two are average, and two are clearly inferior. What would you recommend that he do in terms of running his portfolio? Be specific.

23. Do you think the development of a tiered market has any implications for the discussion of efficient capital markets? If so, what are they?

References

Archibald, T. Ross, "Stock Market Reaction to the Depreciation Switch-Back." *Accounting Review* 47 (1972).

Ball, Ray, "Changes in Accounting Techniques and Stock Prices." *Empirical Research in Accounting* (Supplement to *Journal of Accounting Research,* Vol. 10, 1972).

Ball, Ray. "Risk, Return, and Disequilibrium—An Application to Changes in Accounting Techniques." *Journal of Finance* 27 (1972).

Ball, Ray. "Anomalies in Relationships Between Securities Yields and Yield-Surrogates," *Journal of Financial Economics* 6 (1978).

Basu, S. "Investment Performance of Common Stocks in Relation to Their Price-Earnings Ratios: A Test of the Efficient Market Hypothesis." *Journal of Finance* 32 (1977).

Black, Fisher. "Can Portfolio Managers Outrun the Random Walkers?" *Journal of Portfolio Management* 1 (1974).

Black, Fisher. "Implications of the Random Walk Hypothesis for Portfolio Management." *Financial Analysts Journal* 27 (1971).

Brown, Phillip, and Ball, Ray. "An Empirical Evaluation of Accounting Income Numbers." *Journal of Accounting Research* 6 (1963).

Brown, Stewart L. "Earnings Changes, Stock Prices, and Market Efficiency." *Journal of Finance* 33 (1978).

Carey, Kenneth. "A Model of Individual Transactions Stock Prices." Ph.D. dissertation, University of Kansas, 1971.

Charest, Guy. "Dividend Information, Stock Returns and Market Efficiency—II." *Journal of Financial Economics* 6 (1978).

Ehrbar, A. F. "Index Funds—An Idea Whose Timing is Coming." *Fortune,* June 1976.

Fama, Eugene F. "The Behavior of Stock Prices." *Journal of Business* 38 (1965).

Fama, Eugene F. "Efficient Capital Markets: A Review of Theory and Empirical Work." *Journal of Finance* 25 (1970).

Fama, Eugene F. "Random Walks in Stock Market Prices." *Financial Analysts Journal* 21 (1965).

Fama, Eugene F., and Blume, Marshall. "Filter Rules and Stock Market Trading Profits." *Journal of Business* 39, supplement (1966).

Fama, Eugene F.; Fisher, L.; Jensen, M.; and Roll, R. "The Adjustment of Stock Prices to New Information." *International Economic Review* 10 (1969).

Finnerty, Joseph E. "Insiders Activity and Inside Information: A Multivariate Analysis." *Journal of Financial and Quantitative Analysis* 11 (1976).

Finnerty, Joseph E. "Insiders and Market Efficiency." *Journal of Finance* 31 (1976).

Firth, Michael. "The Impact of Earnings Announcements on the Share Price Behavior of Similar Type Firms." *The Economic Journal,* June 1976.

Foster, G. "Stock Market Reactions to Estimates of Earnings Per Share by Company Officials." *Journal of Accounting Research* 11 (1973).

Furst, Richard W. "Does Listing Increase the Market Price of Common Stocks?" *Journal of Business* 43 (1970).

Goulet, Waldemar M. "Price Changes, Managerial Actions and Insider Trading at the Time of Listing." *Financial Management* 3 (1974).

Hagerman, Robert L., and Richmond, Richard D. "Random Walks, Martingales and the OTC." *Journal of Finance* 28 (1973).

Hausman, W. H.; West, R. R.; and Largay, J. A. "Stock Splits, Price Changes, and Trading Profits: A Synthesis." *Journal of Business* 44 (1971).

Hopewell, Michael H., and Schwartz, Arthur L., "Temporary Trading Suspensions in Individual NYSE Securities." *Journal of Finance* 33 (1978).

Ibbotson, Roger G. "Price Performance of Common Stock New Issues." *Journal of Financial Economics* 2 (1975).

Jaffe, Jeffrey. "Special Information and Insider Trading." *Journal of Business* 47 (1974).

Jensen, Michael. "The Performance of Mutual Funds in the Period 1945–64." *Journal of Finance* 23 (1968).

Jensen, Michael. "Some Anomalous Evidence Regarding Market Efficiency." *Journal of Financial Economics* 6 (1978).

Jones, C., and Litzenberger, R. "Quarterly Earnings Reports and Intermediate Stock Price Trends." *Journal of Finance* 25 (1970).

Jordan, Ronald J. "An Empirical Investigation of the Adjustment of Stock Prices to New Quarterly Earnings Information." *Journal of Financial and Quantitative Analysis* 8 (1973).

Joy, O. Maurice; Litzenberger, Robert H.; and McEnally, Richard W. "The Adjustment of Stock Prices to the Announcements of Unanticipated Changes in Quarterly Earnings." *Journal of Accounting Research* 15 (1977).

Joy, O. Maurice, and Jones, Charles P. "Earnings Reports and Market Efficiencies: An Analysis of Contrary Evidence." *Journal of Financial Research* 2 (1979).

Kaplan, Robert S., and Roll, Richard. "Investor Evaluation of Accounting Information: Some Empirical Evidence." *Journal of Business* 45 (1972).

Kiger, J. E. "An Empirical Investigation of NYSE Volume and Price Reactions to the Announcement of Quarterly Earnings." *Journal of Accounting Research* 10 (1972).

Langbein, John H., and Posner, Richard A. "Market Funds and Trust-Investment Law." *American Bar Foundation Research Journal,* Vol. 1976, No. 1.

Langbein, John H., and Posner, Richard A. "Market Funds and Trust-Investment Law II." *American Bar Foundation Research Journal,* Vol. 1977, No. 1.

Latané, H. A.; Joy, O. Maurice; and Jones, Charles P. "Quarterly Data Sort-Rank Routines, and Security Evaluation." *Journal of Business* 43 (1970).

Latané, H. A.; Tuttle, D. L.; and Jones, C. P. "Quarterly Data: E/P Ratios vs. Changes in Earnings in Forecasting Future Price Changes." *Financial Analysts Journal* 25 (1969).

Logue, Dennis E. "On the Pricing of Unseasoned New Issues, 1965–1969." *Journal of Financial and Quantitative Analysis* 8 (1973).

Lorie, James H., and Niederhoffer, Victor. "Predictive and Statistical Properties of Insider Trading." *Journal of Law and Economics* 11 (1968).

Neuberger, Brian M., and Hammond, Carl T. "A Study of Underwriters' Experience with Unseasoned New Issues." *Journal of Financial and Quantitative Analysis* 9 (1974).

Niederhoffer, Victor, and Osborne, M. F. M. "Market Making and Reversal on the Stock Exchange." *Journal of American Statistical Association* 61 (1966).

Pettit, R. Richardson. "Dividend Announcements, Security Performance, and Capital Market Efficiency." *Journal of Finance* 27 (1972).

Pinches, George. "The Random Walk Hypothesis and Technical Analysis." *Financial Analysts Journal* 26 (1970).

Pinches, George, and Singleton, J. Clay. "The Adjustment of Stock Prices to Bond Rating Changes." *Journal of Finance* 33 (1978).

Praetz, Peter D. "Testing for a Flat Spectrum on Efficient Market Price Data." *Journal of Finance* 34 (1979).

Pratt, Shannon P., and DeVere, Charles W. "Relationship Between Insider Trading and Rates of Return on NYSE Common Stocks, 1960–66." In *Modern Developments in Investment Management,* edited by James Lorie and Robert Brealey. New York: Praeger, 1972.

Reilly, Frank K. "Further Evidence on Short-Run Results for New Issue Investors." *Journal of Financial and Quantitative Analysis* 8 (1973).

Reilly, Frank K. "New Issues Revisited." *Financial Management* 6 (1977).

Reilly, Frank K., and Drzycimski, Eugene F. "Short-Run Profits From Stock Splits." *Financial Management* 10 (1981).

Reilly, Frank K., and Drzycimski, Eugene F. "Tests of Stock Market Efficiency Following Major World Events." *Journal of Business Research* 1 (1973).

Reilly, Frank K., and Hatfield, Kenneth. "Investor Experience with New Stock Issues." *Financial Analysts Journal* 25 (1969).

Ro, Byung T. "The Disclosure of Capitalized Lease Information and Stock Prices." *Journal of Accounting Research* 16 (1978).

Samuelson, Paul A. "Challenge to Judgment." *Journal of Portfolio Management* 1 (1974).

Samuelson, Paul A. "Proof That Properly Anticipated Prices Fluctuate Randomly." *Industrial Management Review* 6 (1965).

Sharpe, William F. "Mutual Fund Performance." *Journal of Business* 39, supplement (1966).

Stoll, Hans R., and Curley, Anthony J. "Small Business and the New Issues Market for Equities." *Journal of Financial and Quantitative Analysis* 5 (1970).

Sunder, Shyam. "Stock Price and Risk Related to Accounting Changes in Inventory Valuation." *The Accounting Review* 50 (1975).

Van Horne, James C. "New Listings and Their Price Behavior." *Journal of Finance* 25 (1970).

Verrechia, Robert E. "A Proof Concerning the Existence of Fama-Rubinstein Efficiency." *Journal of Finance* 34 (1979).

Watts, Ross L. "Systematic 'Abnormal' Returns After Quarterly Earning Announcements." *Journal of Financial Economics* 6 (1978).

Ying, L. K. W.; Lewellen, W. G.; Schlarbaum, G. G.; and Lease, R. C. "Stock Exchange Listings and Securities Returns." *Journal of Financial and Quantitative Analysis* 12 (1977).

John Burr Williams

When one considers modern valuation theory it is hard to believe that the initial exposition of valuation theory was set forth by John Burr Williams in 1938 in his classic book, The Theory of Investment Value *(Cambridge, MA: Harvard University Press, 1938).*

John Burr Williams was born in Hartford, CT, in 1900. He graduated from Harvard in 1923, and from the Harvard Business School in 1925. During the bull market of 1925–1929 and the bear market afterwards he worked for Hayden, Stone & Co., Charles E. Cotting, and the Lee, Higginson Trust Co. Returning to Harvard, he took a Ph.D. in economics and wrote The Theory of Investment Value, *asserting*

that common stocks are worth the present value of their future dividends. This theory has survived and proved applicable for over 40 years of change and progress in the investments field.

Dr. Williams subsequently published articles and books on international trade and speculative prices. He has been an economist for an investment counseling firm, a consultant to Lockheed Aircraft, and has lectured at numerous universities here and abroad. He currently resides in Wellesley Hills, Massachusetts, and continues to be active as indicated by his booklet titled, Fifty Years of Investment Analysis, *published in 1979. As of 1981, two additional books are in preparation.*

Merton H. Miller

Anybody who has ever taken a course in corporation finance knows about the classic article on cost of capital published by Modigliani and Miller in the American Economic Review in 1958. This article initiated controversy and research that still continues today. Miller and Modigliani subsequently wrote an article on "Dividend Policy, Growth, and the Valuation of Shares," (Journal of Business, 1961) that was meant as a treatise on the relevance of dividend policy, but was also an outstanding presentation of basic valuation theory that considered what is involved in true growth and what is involved in the valuation of true growth firms.

Aside from numerous articles written in response to published comments on these two works, Miller also coauthored with Daniel Orr two widely quoted articles on cash balances, "A Model of the Demand for Money by Firms," Quarterly Journal of Economics (August 1966); and "The Demand for Money by Firms: Extensions of Analytical Results," Journal of Finance (December 1968). He also coauthored with Myron Scholes a major study that tested the Capital Asset Pricing Model (CAPM): "Rates of Return in Relation to Risk: A

Reexamination of Some Recent Findings," published in Studies in the Theory of Capital Markets, edited by M. Jensen (New York: Praeger, 1972). In several recent studies Miller has examined the impact of taxes: "Debt and Taxes," Journal of Finance (May 1977); "Dividends and Taxes," with Myron Scholes, Journal of Financial Economics (December 1978); and also with Scholes "Executive Compensation, Taxes and Incentives." The latter was published in Financial Economics: Essays in Honor of Paul H. Gootner, edited by Kathryn Cootner and William Sharpe, (Prentice-Hall, 1981). He is also co-author with Eugene Fama, of The Theory of Finance (Holt, Rinehart and Winston, 1972).

Professor Miller was born in Boston, MA in 1923 and received his A.B. from Harvard and his Ph.D. from Johns Hopkins University in 1952. Besides his work in corporation finance and investments, he has written extensively in various areas of economics. He is a past president of the American Finance Association and currently is Leon Carroll Marshall Distinguished Service Professor at the University of Chicago.

INVESTMENT VALUATION

❧ 8 ❦

As noted previously, investments constitute the commitment of funds for a period of time to derive a rate of return that compensates the investor for the time during which the funds are invested and for the uncertainty involved. Obviously, before an individual makes an investment he must determine the required rate of return, and how much he should pay for a particular investment to get this required return. The determination of how much to pay for an investment is really a determination of the value of the asset. This chapter is involved with the basic background required to *value* alternative investments. The first section is an overview of the valuation process. The second section contains a consideration of the specific determinants of value; in the third section, these concepts are applied to the valuation of different assets, i.e., bonds, preferred stock, and common stock. In the final section, the determinants of the required rate of return and the expected growth rate of dividends are dealt with.

An Overview of the Valuation Process

The valuation process is much like the problem of the chicken and the egg. Do you first deal with individual securities and gradually build up to an analysis of the entire economy or vice versa? It is our contention that the discussion should first center on the analysis of the aggregate economy and the overall securities markets. Only after this is done can different industries be considered. Finally, following the industry analysis, one should consider the securities issued by various firms within the better industries. Therefore, the analysis should follow the three-step process schematized as follows:

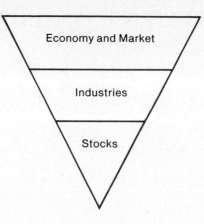

Why a Three-Step Process

General Economic Influences

It is well recognized that various agencies of the federal government have a major impact on the aggregate economy because they control monetary and fiscal *policy*. These basic economic forces exert an influence on *all* industries and *all* companies in the economy.

Fiscal policy can encourage spending (e.g., through investment credits) or discourage spending (e.g., through taxes on gasoline). Increases or decreases in spending on defense, unemployment, or highways also influence the general economic picture. All such changes have a major effect on those directly affected by the changes, but there is also a *multiplier* effect on those who supply goods and services to those directly affected.

The same overall impact can result from a significant change in monetary policy. A restrictive monetary policy that produces a decline in the growth rate of the money supply reduces the supply of funds available to all businesses for working capital and expansion, and funds available to individuals for acquiring goods and services. Monetary policy affects *all* segments of the economy.

Another overall economic variable that must be considered is *inflation* because it has a major impact on interest rates and on how consumers and corporations save and spend their money.

In addition to domestic monetary and fiscal actions, other occurrences such as war, political upheavals in foreign countries, or international monetary devaluations influence all segments of the aggregate economy. Therefore, it is difficult to conceive of any industry or company that will not be affected in some way by macroeconomic developments that affect the total economy.

Because events influencing the aggregate economy also have such a profound effect on all industries and all companies within these industries, *these macroeconomic factors must be considered before industries can be analyzed*. If the economic outlook indicates a recession that will have an impact on all industries and all companies, it must be expected that all security prices will also be affected.

Under such economic conditions, an analyst will probably be extremely apprehensive about recommending *any* industry or individual stock. The best recommendation would probably be high portfolio liquidity. In contrast, assume that the economic and stock market outlook is bullish. Under such conditions, the analyst would look for an outstanding industry. This industry search would be enhanced by economic analysis because, typically, the future performance of an industry depends upon the economic outlook and the particular industry's expected relationship to the economy.

Industry Influences

Because of the importance of the general economic outlook, one should only consider investing in alternative industries *after* it has been decided that the general outlook is favorable for investing in equities. Assuming that it is, the question then becomes one of deciding on the industry or industries to be considered. The industry outlook is determined by the general economic outlook and special industry factors that are generally national in scope, but have their greatest influence on one or several industries. Examples of industry influence are an industry-wide strike, import or export quotas or taxes, or government imposed regulations.

In addition, industries feel the influence of an economic change at different points in the business cycle. As an example, construction typically lags the business cycle, and, therefore, industries involved with this segment of the economy are only affected toward the end of a cycle. Finally, different industries respond differently to the business cycle. As an example, cyclical industries (e.g., steel, autos) typically do much better than the aggregate economy during expansions, but suffer more during contractions. Because of this differential performance it is important to analyze the industry *before* analyzing individual companies within the industry. It is unusual for a company to perform well in an industry experiencing poor performance. (Even the best company in a poor industry will suffer.)

Because of the significance and pervasiveness of industry influences, *an industry evaluation should be conducted before any individual firm is analyzed.* If the industry outlook is negative, an analyst should not spend a great deal of time on individual firms in the industry. If the industry outlook is good, the industry analysis will be useful because a major component of firm analysis is a comparison of relevant financial ratios for individual firms with those of the entire industry. In fact, many of the ratios employed in security analysis are only valid when viewed in terms of the entire industry.

Empirical Support for the Three-Step Process

While the foregoing discussion may appear logical, one may ask whether the implied importance of economic and industry analysis is empirically supported. Is there a relationship between the *earnings* of the aggregate economy, alternative industries, and individual firms? Is there a relationship among the *rates of return* for the aggregate stock market, the stocks in alternative industries, and individual stocks that would indicate that there is value in market and industry analysis?

Association of Corporate Earnings

A study by Philip Brown and Ray Ball examined the degree of association among the earnings of an individual firm, the earnings for the firm's industry, and the earnings of all firms in the economy, using six different measures of earnings for 316 firms over the 19-year period 1947–1965.[1] The results indicated that, on average, approximately 30–40 percent of the variability of a firm's annual earnings were associated with the variability of earnings averaged for all firms. Also on average, an additional 10–15 percent of the firm's earnings were associated with the earnings for the industry.

These results indicate that approximately 45–55 percent of a firm's total variability in annual earnings can be explained by the performance of the overall economy and firm's industry with the economy factor being of greater importance. The results also indicate that there was *variation among firms;* the earnings of large diversified firms are very highly correlated with the performance of the economy, while the earnings of some small firms are more independent than these averages imply.

Systematic Stock Price Fluctuations

To justify aggregate market analysis it is necessary to determine whether there is a cyclical pattern in stock prices. A detailed analysis of market movements by Julius Shiskin used the techniques employed by the National Bureau of Economic Research to break the stock price series down into several components: seasonal, irregular, and trend-cycle.[2] For short-run intervals of a day or week it appeared that the series were rather irregular. When Shiskin examined intervals of three months or longer, *the series showed a definite cyclical component.* A diffusion index which indicated the percent of 80 industries that experienced an increase at a point in time also showed a cyclical pattern when longer intervals were examined. Finally, Shiskin examined the relationship between the stock price series and a number of other economic series (employment, income, production). The results indicated that stock prices consistently conform to economic expansions and contractions, but *stock prices clearly lead the general economy.* Regarding prediction of these stock price fluctuations, some suggestions were made, but it was acknowledged that it would be difficult because the fluctuations vary in amplitude, pattern, and duration. Therefore, there *is* a cycle in stock prices, and it may be useful to predict the cycle if it can be shown to relate to individual stock price returns.

Market and Industry Effect

As noted, it is important to determine the impact of market and industry returns on the returns for individual stocks. Fortunately, several studies have examined

[1]Philip Brown and Ray Ball, "Some Preliminary Findings on the Association Between the Earnings of a Firm, Its Industry, and the Economy," *Empirical Research in Accounting, Selected Studies, 1967,* Supplement to Vol. 5, *Journal of Accounting Research,* pp. 55–77.

[2]Julius Shiskin, "Systematic Aspects of Stock Price Fluctuations," reprinted in *Modern Developments in Investment Management,* ed. James Lorie and Richard Brealey, 2d ed. (Hinsdale, Ill: Dryden Press, 1978), pp. 640–658.

these phenomena. A study by Benjamin King examined the relationship between market returns, industry returns, and the returns on individual stocks.[3] The object of the study was to determine how much of the total price movement over time for a given stock was attributable to overall market factors, how much was due to industry influences, and how much could be ascribed to a stock's "unique" component. To do this, King examined the price behavior of 63 securities listed on the New York Stock Exchange over a total period of 403 months from June 1927 through December 1960, and over four subperiods within this time frame. The variable examined was monthly percentages of change in price. The 63 securities were from the following six industries (number of companies in the industry shown in parentheses): tobacco products (11), petroleum products (11), metals (ferrous and nonferrous) (11), railroads (10), utilities (10), and retail stores (10).

Using factor analysis, King concluded that, for the overall period, *about half the variance in price movement for an individual stock (52 percent) was explained by variance in the aggregate stock market.*[4] An analysis of net price changes after the market effect was removed indicated that, on average for the total period, *an additional 10 percent of the total variation in the stock's price could be attributed to the industry influence.* Therefore, it appears that, for King's sample and time period, about 62 percent of the changes in a security's price could be explained by a combination of market and industry components. At the same time, King showed that the market impact tended to decline over time and there was also a clear difference in the importance of the market factor for different stocks.

A study by Meyers confirmed King's findings regarding market influence, but questioned some of his results regarding the importance of the industry factor.[5] Meyers selected a sample similar to King's and added a second sample of 5 stocks from each of 12 industries (a total of 60) that were less homogenous than those studied by King. He analyzed the samples for the same periods studied by King and for the seven-year period from January 1961 through December 1967. The results for both samples were consistent with those reported earlier by King. *The percent of variance explained by the market factor declined from more than 55 percent prior to 1944 to less than 35 percent for the period 1952–1967.* Meyers analyzed the importance of industry factors for the same 6 industries over the time period used by King and achieved similar results. However, the figures for the same industries for the period *after* 1952 indicated a weakening of the industry effect. Analysis of the 12 added industries confirmed the expectation that *industry clustering was less dominant for a sample that included less homogeneous and distinct industry groups.*

Therefore, these results confirm the earlier conclusions regarding the importance of market analysis even with the decline in explanatory power over time.

[3]Benjamin F. King, "Market and Industry Factors in Stock Price Behavior," *Journal of Business* 39 (1960): 139–190.

[4]Ibid., p. 251.

[5]Stephen L. Meyers, "A Re-Examination of Market and Industry Factors in Stock Price Behavior," *Journal of Finance* 28 (1973): 695–705.

Time Period	Number of Companies	Mean Beta	Coefficient of Determination (R²)
7/26–6/33	415	1.051	0.51
7/33–6/40	604	1.036	0.49
7/40–6/47	731	0.990	0.36
7/47–6/54	870	1.010	0.32
7/54–6/61	890	0.998	0.25
7/61–6/68	847	0.962	0.28

Table 8.1   Summary of Beta Results for Stocks on NYSE

Source: Adapted from Marshall E. Blume, "On the Assessment of Risk," *Journal of Finance,* 26 (1971): 1–10. Reprinted by permission.

They also confirm the importance of industry analysis, but indicate quite clearly that *the importance of the industry component varies across industries.*

A widely read study by Marshall Blume likewise contains evidence of the relative importance of the market factor.[6] Blume derived the beta coefficient (i.e., systematic risk) for all stocks on the NYSE for which there were adequate data for several subperiods from July 1926 through June 1968. The summary of these results contained in Table 8.1 documents the importance of the market factor because it indicates that, even after a decline, aggregate market behavior explains almost 30 percent of the variance for individual securities.

The discussion of empirical studies points toward the following generalizations:

1. The market factor was very important prior to 1940 and has declined so that it currently accounts for about 25–30 percent of individual stock price variance.

2. Even after the decline, the market still accounts for a significant part of the variance in individual securities so that market analysis is important.

3. The importance of the market factor in explaining individual price variance fluctuates among securities, ranging from over 50 percent to below 5 percent.

4. When using time intervals exceeding three months, there definitely are cycles in stock price movements which means it is feasible and practical to project market movements (i.e., over longer intervals the market does *not* move randomly). Therefore, market analysis is not only justified but also feasible because of the existence of cycles.

These generalizations confirm the statement made at the beginning—the most important decision is the first decision: *whether to be in common stocks at all!*

[6]Marshall E. Blume, "On the Assessment of Risk," *Journal of Finance* 26 (1971): 1–10.

An Alternative View

An article by Sharpe questioned the value of attempting to predict market movements and generally argues against the practice.[7] Sharpe pointed out that, if one assumes the existence of an efficient market, such information cannot be used to achieve superior returns. Likewise, one should not expect to be able to derive superior results from engaging in aggregate market predictions and investing in stocks during good market periods and T-bills during poor market periods. He pointed out that, because T-bills yield less than stocks do, if you miss a few turns of the market, you will be at a disadvantage and this loss, along with transactions costs, will yield a return below that from a buy-and-hold policy.

Sharpe analyzed results that could be produced by predicting market returns under three assumptions. First, the differential average annual capital growth from a buy-and-hold policy was compared to the growth derived from perfect foresight (timing) regarding annual peaks and troughs. Second, he assumed that, for each calendar year, a prediction is made as to whether the year will be a "good" market year (returns on stocks above the returns on cash equivalent T-bills) or a "bad" market year (return on cash equivalents above return on stocks). The returns from perfect foresight regarding good and bad market years and a buy-and-hold stock policy were compared in this context. It was assumed that, with perfect foresight, the investor will invest in T-bills during bad market years, and in stocks during good market years. Third, a comparison was made of returns from a buy-and-hold policy and returns with less than perfect timing. The first two comparisons were done for three time periods: 1929–1972; 1934–1972; and 1946–1972. The final analysis considered only 1934–1972.

The results assuming perfect timing of peaks and troughs indicated substantial returns would be obtained by an individual with the ability to project the absolute peaks and troughs in the market (about 4 percent for buy-and-hold versus 20 percent for perfect timing). While these results are not surprising, it is also clearly not realistic to expect such ability on a consistent basis. The analysis of results assuming the ability to predict "good" and "bad" years compared to a buy-and-hold policy or holding T-bills only, likewise indicated superior returns were achieved with the former. Even assuming 2 percent trading commissions were paid, the timing-ability portfolio had higher returns and lower risk (standard deviation of returns). The final analysis derived the returns from alternative decisions and examined these returns assuming the investor predicted correctly from 50 percent of the time (no real insight) to 100 percent of the time (perfect foresight). The returns were negative at 50 percent and improved and became positive at 74 percent. This implies that if you had predicted the behavior of the market correctly 74 percent of the time, you would derive superior returns compared to those for a buy-and-hold policy. Based upon these results, Sharpe concluded that, unless a portfolio manager is quite good at predicting where the market is going each year, he should not attempt to engage in market timing.

---

[7]William F. Sharpe, "Likely Gains from Market Timing," *Financial Analysts Journal* 31 (1975): 60–69.

One might question some of Sharpe's conclusions for several reasons. First his assumption of a 2 percent commission on T-bill shifts is unnecessary, and he does not consider the discounting on commissions since "May Day" (May 1, 1975). Also, because the study stopped in 1972 it missed several major swings that would have been very profitable to anyone with forecasting ability. Further, it seems that Sharpe underestimated the impact of small differences in returns on long-run wealth positions. However, his finding that an investor must be correct about seven times out of ten regarding market turns is important. Similar to other findings, it implies that it *is possible* to be a superior portfolio manager, but that it is *not easy*. Even so, it is worth the time and effort because as discussed previously, these market movements have a significant impact on the returns for individual stocks.

Determinants of Value

Given an understanding that the valuation process should proceed from the market to the individual stock, this section considers the specific factors that determine value. We will subsequently apply these valuation concepts to alternative types of investments (bonds, preferred stocks, and common stocks). In later chapters we will use the common stock valuation model to analyze the aggregate stock market, alternative industries, and individual common stocks.

The reader may recall from accounting, economics, or corporate finance courses that *the value of an asset is the present value of the expected returns from the asset during the holding period.* Specifically, an investment is expected to provide a stream of returns during the holding period and it is necessary to discount this stream of expected returns at the investor's required rate of return to determine the value of the asset. Therefore, to derive a value for an asset it is necessary to estimate: (1) the stream of expected returns; and (2) the required rate of return on the investment.

Streams of Returns

An estimate of the future returns expected from an investment encompasses the *size* of the returns, the *form* of the returns, the *time pattern* of returns, and the *uncertainty* of returns.

Form of Return   Returns from an investment can take many forms including earnings, dividends, interest payments, or capital gains based upon an increase in value during a period. A major question in valuation theory as applied to common stocks has been whether the appropriate form of returns to consider should be the *earnings* of the firm or the *dividends* of the firm. These can differ over time depending on whether a firm retains earnings for reinvestment. In such a case, the firm would have high earnings but would pay small dividends. Fortunately, it has been shown by Miller and Modigliani that this is an unnecessary controversy because, if one makes proper allowance for the investment decisions made by the issuing firm, the two are equivalent.[8] Later in this chapter we will set forth the dividend valuation model for common stocks because this model is quite intuitive and is very useful if one makes some simplifying assumptions. The point is, returns can come in many forms and it is necessary to consider all of them.

Time Pattern of Returns   In addition, it is important to estimate *when* the returns will be received because money has a time value (a dollar of income today is worth more than a dollar of income received a year from now). Therefore, it is necessary to know the time pattern of returns from an investment so that the stream can be properly valued relative to alternative investments.

Required Rate of Return

The reader will recall from the discussion in Chapter 1 that the required rate of return on an investment is determined by: (1) the economy's real risk-free rate of return plus (2) the expected rate of inflation during the holding period, plus (3) a risk premium. It was noted that *all* investments are affected by the risk-free rate and inflation (i.e., the nominal risk-free rate); the differentiating factor is the risk premium for alternative assets. In turn, this risk premium is a function of the uncertainty of returns on the assets.

The uncertainty of returns and what affects this can be considered in terms of the *internal* characteristics of the asset, or in terms of *market-determined* factors. Earlier we subdivided the internal characteristics into: business risk (BR), financial risk (FR), and liquidity risk (LR). Alternatively, developments in capital market theory indicate that the relevant risk measure is the systematic risk of the asset, i.e., that variability in an asset's returns that is due to variability in aggregate market returns (the asset's covariance with the market portfolio). When this systematic market risk is normalized relative to market variance, the result is a measure referred to as "beta."

Summary: Determinants of Value

To derive the value of an investment it is necessary to estimate the following:

1. The expected stream of returns. This includes the size of these returns and the form of the returns which can be either earnings, dividends, or interest.

2. The time pattern of expected returns. Because money has a time value it is necessary to consider alternative time streams and discount the streams to the present using an appropriate discount rate (i.e., the investor's required rate of return).

3. The required rate of return on the investment which is determined by the uncertainty of returns. Uncertainty can be examined in terms of internal charac-

---

[8]Merton H. Miller and Franco Modigliani, "Dividend Policy, Growth and the Valuation of Shares," *Journal of Business* 34 (1966): 411–433.

teristics or in terms of a market-determined measure of risk derived from capital asset pricing theory. A detailed discussion of the Capital Asset Pricing Model is contained in Chapter 21. One would expect these alternative approaches to the analysis of uncertainty to provide consistent results; assets that have high levels of internal risk should have large betas. This consistency between internal risk characteristics and market measures of risk has generally been supported by empirical studies.

Valuation of Alternative Investments

Valuation of Bonds

It is relatively easy to determine the value of bonds because the size and time pattern of the returns from the bond over its life are known. Specifically, a bond promises:

1. Interest payments every six months equal to one-half the coupon rate times the face value of the bond[9] and

2. The payment of the principal (also referred to as face value) at the maturity of the bond.

As an example, in 1982, a $10,000 bond due in 1997 with an 10 percent coupon will pay $500 every six months for the life of the bond (the next 15 years). In addition, there is a promise to pay the $10,000 principal at maturity in 1997. Therefore, assuming the borrower does not default, the investor knows *what* payments will be made and *when* they will be made.

Recalling the specification that the value of any asset is the present value of the returns from an asset, the value of the bond is the present value of the interest payments (i.e., an annuity of $500 every six months for 15 years), and the present value of the principal payment. The only unknown for this asset (assuming the borrower does not default) is the rate of return that should be used to discount the expected stream of payments. Assuming that the prevailing nominal risk-free rate is 9 percent and the investor requires a one percent risk premium on this bond (because there is some probability of default), the required rate of return would be 10 percent.

The present value of the interest payments is an annuity for 30 periods (15 years every six months) at one-half the required return (5 percent).

$$\$500 \times 15.375 = \$7,688 \text{ (present value of interest at 10 percent)}$$

[9]The coupon rate is the annual dollar interest payment which is expressed as a percentage of the bond's face value. In turn, the face value appears on the face of the bond and is the repayment due at the maturity of the bond. This face value is also referred to as the par value or principal of the bond.

The present value of the principal is likewise discounted at 5 percent for 30 periods[10]

$$\$10,000 \times .2312 = \$2,312$$

Present value of interest payments	$7,688
Present value of principal payment	2,312
Value of bond at 10 percent	$10,000

This is the amount that an investor should be willing to pay for this bond assuming that his required rate of return on a bond of this risk class was 10 percent. If the bond is selling for less than this in the market, this would clearly be acceptable. If the market price is above this value, an investor should not buy it because his promised yield to maturity will be less than his required rate of return.

Valuation of Preferred Stock

Preferred stock involves a promise to pay a stated dividend, usually each quarter, for an infinite period; i.e., there is no maturity. As was true with a bond, stated payments are to be made on specified dates. However, preferred stock does not entail the same *legal* obligation to pay as bonds do, and payments are made only *after* bond interest payments are met, so the uncertainty of payments is greater. This increased uncertainty implies that a higher rate of return should be required on a firm's preferred stock than is required on a firm's debentures. While this differential should exist in theory, it has not existed in practice for a number of years because of the tax treatment accorded dividends paid to corporations. As noted in Chapter 2, dividends received by corporations from other corporations are 85 percent tax-exempt, so the effective tax on dividends would be about 7.5 percent, assuming a corporate tax rate of 50 percent. As a result, there is a great demand for preferred stocks and the yield on them has generally been below that on AAA (the highest grade) corporate bonds.

Because preferred stock is a perpetuity, the value is simply the stated annual dividend divided by the required rate of return on the asset as follows:

$$V = \frac{\text{Dividend}}{i}$$

As an example, assume that a preferred stock has a $100 par value and a dividend of $8 a year. At the present time, assume that AAA corporate bonds are yielding 10 percent and, because of the uncertainty involved and the tax advantage of this preferred stock issue to you as a corporate investor, the required rate of return is 9 percent. Therefore, the value of this preferred stock to you is:

---

[10]If annual compounding were assumed, this would be .239 rather than .2312. Semiannual compounding is used because it is consistent with the interest payments and is also used in practice.

$$V = \frac{\$8}{.09}$$

$$= \$88.89$$

Also, given the price of preferred stock, it is possible to derive the promised yield on this investment

$$i = \frac{\text{Dividend}}{\text{Price}}$$

Valuation of Common Stocks

The valuation of common stocks is definitely more difficult than that of bonds or preferred stock because almost all the required inputs are unknown. Recall that in the case of a bond, the periodic payments are known as is the final payment at maturity. The only unknown is the discount rate which is calculated from the prevailing nominal RFR plus a risk premium that is dependent upon the uncertainty of the interest payment. Similarly, for preferred stock the only unknown is the required rate of return on the stock. In contrast, in the case of common stock, an investor is uncertain about the size of the returns, the time pattern of returns, *and* the required rate of return. In addition, as mentioned earlier, there is a question of what stream of returns should be discounted (earnings or dividends). Because it has been shown that the two approaches are equivalent if comparable assumptions are made, the approach used is a matter of choice. Some observers prefer to use earnings because they are the source of dividends. Alternatively, it is contended that investors discount that which they receive—dividends. In this discussion we will use the dividend model because it is intuitively appealing and because it has been used extensively by others so the reader may be familiar with the reduced form of the valuation model that will be derived later. Basically, the dividend model involves the assumption that the value of a share of common stock is the present value of all future dividends as follows:

$$V_j = \frac{D_1}{(1 + i)} + \frac{D_2}{(1 + i)^2} + \frac{D_3}{(1 + i)^3} + \cdots \frac{D_n}{(1 + i)^n}$$

where:

V_j = value of the common stock j

D_t = dividend during period t

i = required rate of return on stock j.

This model will be best understood if it is applied to several cases involving different holding periods ranging from short periods to longer intervals.

One-Year Holding Period

In this example, it is assumed that the investor wants to buy the stock, hold it for one year, and sell it at the end of the year. As noted, to determine the value of the stock (i.e., how much the investor should pay for it) the dividend to be received during the period, the expected price at the end of the holding period, and the required rate of return on this stock must be estimated.

The estimate of the dividend for the coming year will probably be based upon the current dividend and expectations regarding changes during the year. Assume that the company earned $2.50 a share last year and paid a dividend of $1.00 a share (a 40 percent payout which has been fairly consistent over time). Further, the firm is expected to earn about $2.75 during the coming year and to raise the dividend to $1.10 per share.

A crucial estimate is the expected price for the stock that will prevail a year from now. There are two alternative estimation procedures that can be employed. The one is to apply the expected earnings multiplier to the expected earnings figure.[11] The second is to estimate the expected dividend *yield* that will be prevailing a year from now and apply that to the expected dividend *rate*. The actual factors that go into making those estimates will be considered in more detail in subsequent chapters. For now, let us assume that you prefer the dividend yield approach and estimate that the dividend yield on this stock one year from now will be 5 percent. Applying this to the expected dividend of $1.10 generates an expected ending price of $22 ($1.10/.05).

Finally, it is necessary to determine the required rate of return on this stock investment. Naturally, this rate will be influenced by the fact that there are other potential investments entailing less risk, approximately equal risk, and more risk. Again, we will discuss the determination of this estimate for the aggregate market, industries, and companies in more detail in subsequent chapters. For the moment, assume that long-term AAA bonds are yielding 10 percent, and you feel that a 4 percent risk premium over the yield of these bonds is appropriate for the stock. Thus, you specify a required rate of return of 14 percent.

In summary, you have estimated the dividend at $1.10 (payable at year end), the ending price at $22, and the required rate of return at 14 percent. Given these inputs, the value of this asset to you is as follows:

$$
\begin{aligned}
V_i &= \frac{\$1.10}{(1 + .14)} + \frac{\$22.00}{(1 + .14)} \\
&= \frac{1.10}{1.14} + \frac{22.00}{1.14} \\
&= .96 + 19.30 \\
&= \$20.26
\end{aligned}
$$

Note that there has been no mention of the current price of the stock. This is be-

[11]The earnings multiplier approach will be discussed in detail in a later section of this chapter.

cause the current market price is *not* relevant to the investor until after he has derived an *independent* value based on *his* estimates of the relevant variables. *After* a value has been derived, it is necessary to consider the market price. The decision to acquire the stock is dependent upon whether the *computed* value is equal to or above the *market* price. Obviously, if the market price is above the derived value, you would not want to acquire the stock because, by definition, the stock will cost more than it is worth and you won't receive your required rate of return.

Multiple-Year Holding Period

In this instance it is assumed that you are considering acquiring the stock now and anticipate holding the stock for several years and then selling it. The decision to hold the stock for several years complicates the valuation procedure because it is necessary to estimate *several* future dividend payments and also to estimate the value of the stock for a number of years in the future.

The difficulty with estimating future dividend payments is that the future stream can have numerous forms. The exact estimate depends on your outlook for earnings growth, because earnings are the source of dividends and the firm's dividend policy (i.e., does it make a constant payout each year which implies a change in dividend each year or does the firm follow a step pattern). The easiest case to analyze is one in which the firm considered enjoys a constant rate of growth in earnings and also maintains a constant dividend payout. In this instance, the dividend stream will have a constant growth rate equal to the earnings growth rate. Alternatively, a firm could increase the dividend rate by a constant dollar amount each year, or change the rate by a given dollar amount every two or three years (i.e., a step pattern).

In the current example, assume the expected holding period is three years and you estimate the following dividend payments at the end of each year:

Year 1—$1.10/share

Year 2—$1.20/share

Year 3—$1.35/share

The next estimate to be made is the expected ending price for the stock three years in the future. Again, if we want to use the dividend yield approach, it is necessary to project the dividend yield on this stock three years from now. Assume that you think rates will be lower than your previous estimate for one year; i.e., you estimate a dividend yield of 4 percent. Given the $1.35 dividend payment, this implies an ending price of $33.75 ($1.35/.04).

The final estimate is the required rate of return on this stock during this period. Assuming that the 14 percent desired rate is still appropriate for this period, the value of this stock is as follows:

$$V_i = \frac{1.10}{(1 + .14)} + \frac{1.20}{(1 + .14)^2} + \frac{1.35}{(1 + .14)^3} + \frac{33.75}{(1 + .14)^3}$$

$$= \frac{1.10}{(1.14)} + \frac{1.20}{(1.30)} + \frac{1.35}{(1.4815)} + \frac{33.75}{(1.4815)}$$
$$= .96 + .92 + .91 + 22.78$$
$$= \$25.57$$

Again, at this point you would compare this derived value for the stock to its market price to determine whether you should buy the stock or not.

At this point the reader should recognize that the procedure of valuation being discussed is very similar to that followed in corporate finance when making investment decisions, but the cash flows we are concerned with are from dividends. Rather than estimating the scrap value or salvage value of a corporate asset, we are estimating the ending sales price for the stock. Finally, rather than cost of capital, we estimate our required rate of return for the individual investor. In both cases we are looking for excess present value which means the present value of expected cash inflows (i.e., the value of the asset) exceeds the present value of cash outflows (i.e., the cost of the asset).

Infinite Period Model

It would certainly be possible to extend the discussion of the multi-period model by considering longer holding periods (e.g., 5, 10, or 15 years). It is felt that the benefits to be derived from the extensions would be minimal and the boredom factor would quickly dominate. Therefore, at this point we will consider the very popular infinite period model.

This model assumes that investors estimate future dividend payments from the present to perpetuity. Needless to say, this is a formidable task! To allow mortal investors to carry out this valuation, it is necessary to make some simplifying assumptions about this future stream of dividends. The easiest assumption is that *the future dividend stream grows at a constant rate for the infinite period*. As we will discuss, this is a rather heroic assumption in many instances, but it allows us to derive a model that is very useful in valuing the aggregate market, alternative industries, and even some individual stocks. This model is specified as follows:

$$V_j = \frac{D_0(1 + g)}{(1 + i)} + \frac{D_0(1 + g)^2}{(1 + i)^2} + \cdots \cdot \frac{D_0(1 + g)^n}{(1 + i)^n}$$

where:

V_j = the value of stock j

D_0 = the dividend payment in the current period

g = the constant growth rate of dividends

i = the required rate of return on stock j

n = the number of periods, which is usually assumed to be perpetuity.

In the appendix to this chapter it is shown that this formulation can be simplified to the following expression:

$$V_j = \frac{D_1}{i - g}$$

The reader will probably recognize this formula as one that is widely used in corporate finance to derive the cost of equity capital for the firm. In many cases, rather than V_j, the expression is written:

$$P_j = \frac{D_1}{i - g}$$

Given this model, the major estimates to be made are: (1) the required rate of return (i), and (2) the expected growth rate of dividends (g). After estimating g, it is a simple matter to estimate D_1, because it is the current dividend (D_0) times $(1 + g)$.

Consider the example of a stock with a current dividend of $1.00 a share, which you expect to rise to $1.09 next year. Upon reflection you feel that, over the long run, this company's earnings and dividends will continue to grow at 9 percent; i.e., your estimate of g is .09.

Regarding the required rate of return, for the near term you felt 14 percent was appropriate due to a high current rate of inflation. For the long run, you expect the rate of inflation to decline and feel that your long-run required rate of return on this stock should be 13 percent; your estimate of i is .13. Therefore, the relevant variables are:

$$g = .09$$

$$i = .13$$

$$D_1 = 1.09 \ (\$1.00 \times 1.09)$$

$$P = \frac{1.09}{.13 - .09}$$

$$= \frac{1.09}{.04}$$

$$= \$27.25$$

A small change in any of the estimates will have a large impact, as can be shown by the following examples:

1. $g = .09; i = .14; D_1 = \$1.09$ (we assume an increase in i)

$$P = \frac{\$1.09}{.14 - .09}$$

$$= \frac{\$1.09}{.05}$$

$$= \$21.80$$

2. $g = .10; i = .13; D_1 = \$1.10$ *(we assume an increase in g)*

$$P = \frac{\$1.09}{.13 - .10}$$

$$= \frac{\$1.09}{.03}$$

$$= \$36.33$$

Obviously, a one-percent change in either g or i has a major impact on the computed price of the stock. The crucial relationship is the *spread between the required rate of return and the expected growth rate.* Anything that causes a *decline* in the spread will cause an *increase* in prices, while any change that results in an *increase* in the spread will cause a *decline* in stock prices.

Pragmatic Multiplier Approach

Rather than concentrate on dividends alone, many investors prefer to derive value based upon an earnings multiplier approach. The basic rationale for this approach is that assets are the capitalized value of future earnings, which implies that investors derive value by determining how many dollars they are willing to pay for a dollar of expected earnings (typically earnings during the next 12-month period). As an example, if investors are supposedly willing to pay 10 times expected earnings, a stock that is expected to earn \$2 a share will sell for \$20. This multiplier, also referred to as the price-earnings (P/E) ratio, is derived as follows:

$$\text{Earnings Multiplier} = \text{Price Earnings Ratio} = \frac{\text{Current Price}}{\text{Next 12 Mo. Earnings}}$$

The important question to consider is which factors influence the earnings multiplier (P/E ratio) over time? In the chapter on aggregate market valuation it is shown that the P/E ratio for the stock market has varied from about 6 times earnings to over 20 times earnings.[12] Again, we will see that the present-value-of-dividend model can be used to indicate the relevant variables. Specifically, the basic dividend valuation model is as follows:

$$P_i = \frac{D_1}{i - g}$$

If we divide both sides of the equation by E_1 (expected earnings during the next 12 months):

$$\frac{P_i}{E_1} = \frac{D_1/E_1}{i - g}$$

[12]When computing historical P/E ratios the practice is to use earnings for the *last* 12 months rather than expected earnings. Although this will influence the level, it should not affect the changes over time.

Thus, the P/E ratio is determined by:

1. the expected dividend payout ratio (dividends divided by earnings)
2. the required rate of return on the stock
3. the expected growth rate of dividends for the stock.

As an example, if we assume that a stock under consideration has an expected dividend payout of 50 percent (i.e., the firm generally pays out 50 percent of its earnings in dividends), a required rate of return of 13 percent, and an expected growth rate for dividends of 9 percent, we would have the following:

$$D/E = .50; i = .13; g = .09$$

$$P/E = \frac{.50}{.13 - .09}$$

$$= \frac{.50}{.04}$$

$$= 12.5$$

Again, a small change in either i or g will have a large impact on the multiplier, as shown in the following examples:

1.
$$D/E = .50; i = .14; g = .09 \text{ (we assume an increase in i)}$$

$$P/E = \frac{.50}{.14 - .09}$$

$$= \frac{.50}{.05}$$

$$= 10$$

2.
$$D/E = .50; i = .13; g = .10 \text{ (we assume an increase in g)}$$

$$P/E = \frac{.50}{.13 - .10}$$

$$= \frac{.50}{.03}$$

$$= 16.7$$

As before, the crucial factor is the spread between i and g. While the dividend payout ratio obviously has an impact, this ratio typically is a rather stable variable and so would not be very important in projecting year-to-year changes in security values.

Thus far, we have considered the estimates (future stream of flows and required rate of return) that are required and, given these estimates, how one determines the value of bonds, preferred stock, and common stock under several investment horizons. In the final section we will deal with the determinants of the required rate of return and the expected growth rate. In subsequent chapters we consider how an investor goes about estimating these determinants of value for the aggregate securities market, alternative industries, and individual firms.

Determinants of the Required Rate of Return and the Expected Growth Rate of Dividends

The Required Rate of Return

This discussion is basically a brief review of the presentation in Chapter 1 dealing with the determinants of the required rate of return on an investment. There are basically three major factors:

1. the economy's "real" risk-free rate (RFR)
2. the expected rate of inflation (I)
3. a risk premium (RP).

The Risk-Free Rate

This rate reflects the basic time value of money assuming no probability of default. It is a function of the underlying investment opportunities in the economy, which are determined by *the real growth rate of the economy*. In turn, the real growth rate for the economy is a function of: (a) the growth of the labor force; (b) the growth in number of hours worked per week; and (c) the growth in labor productivity.

As noted earlier, the average real growth rate for the U.S. economy has generally ranged from 2.5 percent to 3.5 percent a year, with the recent rate closer to 2.5 percent due to a decline in the growth of productivity during the late 1960s and the 1970s. It is also important to note that this basic determinant of the required rate of return is quite stable over any short-run or intermediate time period, i.e., one or two years. This stability is because the basic factors that influence the real growth in the economy are very slow to change.

The Expected Rate of Inflation

This rate is important because investors are interested in "real" rates of return that will allow them to increase their rate of consumption. Therefore, if investors expect a given rate of inflation, they will increase their "nominal" required rate of return to reflect this expectation as follows:

$$\text{Nominal RFR} = [1 + \text{RFR}][1 + \text{E(I)}] - 1$$

As an example, if the "real" RFR is 3 percent and the expected rate of inflation [E(I)] during the coming year is 8 percent, an investor should require a nominal rate of return of approximately 11 percent on a risk-free one-year security as follows:

$$(1 + .03)(1 + .08) = 1.1124 - 1 = .1124$$

The typical example of a risk-free security would be a one-year government bond. Given the basic stability of the "real" RFR, it is clear that changes in the expected rate of inflation have caused the *nominal* promised yield on government bonds (i.e., the nominal RFR) to fluctuate between 5 percent and 12 percent during the period 1974–1980.

Note that the two factors that determine the nominal RFR should affect *all* investments, from U.S. Government securities to highly speculative land deals. This is why the estimation of the expected rate of inflation is such a crucial part of the valuation process.

The Risk Premium

This causes a *difference* in required rates of return for alternative investments, e.g., for government bonds, corporate bonds, and common stocks. It also explains the difference in the expected return for various grades of corporate bonds (AAA vs. AA vs. A)[13] and different common stocks.

In Chapter 1 we discussed the notion that investors demand a risk premium because of the *uncertainty* of returns expected from an investment. Further, we pointed out that this uncertainty of returns was indicated by the *dispersion of expected returns*. In turn, this dispersion could be *measured* in terms of such factors as range, variance, standard deviation, or semivariance. Because the theoretical work in this area has generally used the variance or standard deviation, this is the one we will generally employ. Regardless of the method used to measure it, the important question is, *what factors influence this variability of expected returns?* It is possible to discuss the determinants of variability in terms of *internal* factors or a *market-determined* measure. The internal factors mentioned are: (1) business risk, (2) financial risk, and (3) liquidity risk.

Business risk (BR) is the uncertainty due to a firm's *sales volatility* which is generally related to the characteristics of the firm's industry. In addition, the variability of the firm's operating earnings is affected by the firm's production function (i.e., the mix of fixed and variable costs) which is indicated by its *operating leverage*.

Financial risk (FR) is the additional uncertainty (variability) caused by the method of financing an investment. This financial risk is typically an integral part of the investment, e.g., the stock of a firm that has fixed debt in its capital structure. Because as a stockholder, you are an owner of the firm, the fact that the firm has debt means that you implicitly share the risk. Therefore, the variability of returns on your stock is affected by the firm's financing decisions. Alternatively, it is possible for an investor to explicitly add financial risk to an investment by borrowing money on his own to finance the acquisition, such as by buying stock on margin or by borrowing money to buy real estate. In either case, the variability of expected returns increases and the investor's required rate of return should also increase.

---

[13]As will be discussed in detail in Chapter 14, corporate bonds are rated by investment services based upon their risk of default. In this regard AAA is very low risk and A would be higher risk.

Liquidity risk (LR) is uncertainty caused by the inability to buy or sell an asset quickly with little price change assuming no new information. This specification of liquidity has two components—the time involved and the price change. The lack of either a *quick* transaction or a *small* price change means that you are less certain of your ultimate return and you should be compensated for this added uncertainty.

Expected Growth Rate of Dividends

The growth rate of dividends is influenced by the basic growth rate of earnings and the proportion of earnings paid out in dividends (i.e., the payout ratio). For short-run periods, it is possible that dividends can grow faster or slower than earnings do if the economic unit changes its payout ratio. Specifically, if a firm's earnings are growing at 6 percent a year and the firm always pays out exactly 50 percent of earnings in dividends, then the firm's dividends will likewise grow at 6 percent a year. Alternatively, if the firm's earnings are growing at 6 percent a year, and, during a three-year period, the firm *increases* its payout from 50 percent of earnings to 65 percent of earnings, while the payout ratio is increasing, the dividends will increase by more than the earnings; the growth rate of dividends will be above 6 percent (e.g., 8 or 9 percent). In contrast, if the firm reduced its payout ratio, dividends would grow at a lower rate than earnings for a period of time. Clearly, there is a limit to how long this difference can continue because the payout cannot exceed 100 percent or be less than zero. We will also see that this payout ratio has an inverse relationship to the basic growth rate of earnings. Still, for long-run analysis, the typical assumption is that the dividend payout ratio is relatively stable. Thus, the analysis of what determines the growth rate of dividends is really an analysis of what factors determine the growth rate of equity earnings.

The internal growth rate of an economic unit, whether it is an industry or a company, is basically a function of what resources are retained and reinvested in the unit, and of the rate of return derived from these internal investments. Generally, a firm retains some proportion of current earnings and acquires additional assets (e.g., inventory, fixed plant, machinery). Assuming the firm is able to derive some positive rate of return on these additional assets, the total earnings of the firm will increase, simply because the firm has a larger asset base. Clearly, how much the earnings will increase depends upon: (1) how much is retained and reinvested in new assets and (2) the rate of return that is earned on these new assets. More specifically, it can be shown that the growth rate of equity earnings (i.e., earnings per share) without any external financing is equal to the proportion of net earnings retained (1 − payout ratio) times the rate of return on equity capital.

$$g = \text{(Retention Rate)} \times \text{(Return on Equity)}$$
$$= RR \times ROE$$

Therefore, a firm can increase its growth rate by increasing its rate of earnings-retention and continue to invest these added funds at the same rate as before. Alternatively, the firm can maintain the same rate of reinvestment but increase its rate of return on these investments. As an example, if a firm retains 50 percent of net earnings and reinvests these funds, consistently deriving a 10 percent rate of return on these investments, the net earnings for the firm will grow at the rate of 5 percent a year as follows:

$$g = RR \times ROE$$
$$= .50 \times .10$$
$$= .05$$

Alternatively, if the firm increases its retention rate to 75 percent and continues to invest these funds at 10 percent, the firm's growth rate will increase to 7.5 percent as follows:

$$g = .75 \times .10$$
$$= .075$$

Alternatively, if the firm continues to reinvest 50 percent of its earnings, but is able to derive a higher rate of return on these investments (e.g., 15 percent) the firm can likewise increase its growth rate as follows:

$$g = .50 \times .15$$
$$= .075$$

Breakdown of ROE

While the retention rate is basically a management decision, changes in the return on equity require basic changes in operating performance. As a means of seeing what is required in this respect, it is useful to break the ROE ratio into components. One alternative breakdown is as follows:

$$ROE = \frac{Net\ Income}{Equity} = \frac{Net\ Income}{Sales} \times \frac{Sales}{Equity}$$

$$\doteq (Profit\ Margin) \times (Equity\ Turnover)$$

This breakdown (which is really an identity) indicates that the return on equity depends upon how efficiently the firm operates in terms of generating sales from equity capital (equity turnover), but also depends upon how profitable these sales are, as indicated by the firm's profit margin. The point is, a firm can improve its ROE by increasing either of these components—generating additional sales per dollar of equity at a constant profit margin, or increasing the profit margin on the current level of sales. It is also possible to increase the equity turnover by changing the firm's financial structure. Specifically, if the firm increases its asset base by borrowing (i.e., issuing debt securities), sales will increase because the asset base is larger, but if equity was not used to finance the acquisition of assets, the equity turnover will increase. The effect of this change in financial structure can be examined using the following breakdown of ROE:

$$\text{ROE} = \frac{\text{Net Income}}{\text{Equity}} = \frac{\text{Net Income}}{\text{Sales}} \times \frac{\text{Sales}}{\text{Equity}}$$

$$= \frac{\text{Net Income}}{\text{Sales}} \times \frac{\text{Sales}}{\text{Total Assets}} \times \frac{\text{Total Assets}}{\text{Equity}}$$

$$= (\text{Profit Margin}) \times (\text{Total Asset Turnover}) \times (\text{Leverage})$$

The ratio of total assets to equity is a measure of leverage because it indicates the relationship of total assets to equity. The higher this ratio, the more total assets are financed with nonequity capital (i.e., debt). As an example, if this ratio is two, it means that 50 percent of the firm's assets are financed with equity and 50 percent with debt. Alternatively, a ratio of three means that only 33 percent is financed with equity and two-thirds is debt. Over time, what you would look for is a change in this ratio that would signal a change in the firm's capital structure and, therefore, its financial risk.

By breaking down the equity turnover into total asset turnover and a measure of leverage (total assets/equity) it is possible to determine whether a firm is really operating efficiently (total asset turnover) or whether a change in financial structure (leverage) caused the change in equity turnover. The point is, if total assets increase by a larger proportion than equity, it means that more of these assets are being financed by debt securities. This does not mean that it is wrong to increase ROE by increasing financial leverage. Rather, it is important to recognize that the increase in ROE is not due to an increase in profitability or higher operating efficiency, but was caused by a change in the firm's capital structure.

Summary

This chapter had three major parts. The first part contained an overview of the valuation process including the overall procedure that should be followed. Specifically, it is contended that market analysis and industry analysis should be considered prior to company and stock analysis. Besides having intuitive appeal (the economy affects all industries and industry performance influences all firms in the industry), there is substantial empirical support for this "three-step" process. It is acknowledged that when markets are efficient, it is not easy to be a superior market analyst, but the potential rewards from correct estimates make the attempt worthwhile.

The second part of the chapter was a discussion of the basic concept of value as the present value of future expected returns and considerations of the variables that must be estimated in the valuation process. Assuming knowledge of these variables, we discussed the specific valuation of bonds, preferred stock, and common stock under several different holding-periods, from one year to perpetuity. It was shown that, with the constant growth model, the crucial factor determining the value of common stock and *changes* in common stock value is the spread between the required rate of return and the expected rate of growth.

The final part of the chapter dealt with the specific factors that determine these two major elements of value: the required rate of return and the expected rate of growth. The discussion of the required rate of return was basically a review of the presentation in Chapter 1. The elements of expected growth can be summarized as follows:

A. Rate of Earnings Retention (RR)

B. Rate of Return on Equity (ROE)
   —Profit Margin
   —Equity Turnover
      or
   —Profit Margin
   —Total Asset Turnover
   —Leverage.

Given this background on the procedure and determinants of value, in the following chapters we will apply these concepts to the valuation of the aggregate stock market, alternative industries, and finally individual firms within industries.

Questions

1.   Discuss why it is contended that market analysis and industry analysis should come before individual security analysis.

2.   Discuss briefly the empirical evidence given by King that supports the above contention.

3.   Would you expect all industries to have a similar relationship to the economy? Why or why not? Give an example.

4.   Would you expect all individual stocks to have a similar relation to the aggregate stock market? What factors would contribute to any differences?

5.   What "batting average" is required to be superior in terms of predicting market turns? Does it seem to be worthwhile to spend time attempting to predict aggregate market turns? Why or why not?

6.   Given an efficient stock market, what do you feel is necessary to make such predictions? Of what value is past information regarding market performance? Discuss.

7.   What is the value to you of a 12 percent coupon bond with a par value of $10,000 that matures in 12 years if you want a 10 percent return on the bond? Use semiannual compounding.

8.   What would the value of the bond in Question 7 have to be if you wanted a 14 percent rate of return on this bond?

9.   The preferred stock of the Raymond Engineering Company has a par value of $100 and an $11 coupon. You feel that you would require a 9 percent yield on this stock. What is the maximum price you would pay for it?

10. The Bourke Basketball Company (BBC) earned $5 a share last year and paid a dividend of $3 a share. Next year you expect the company to earn $5.50 and continue their payout ratio. Assuming you expect a 5 percent dividend yield a year from now when you anticipate selling the stock, if you require 12 percent on this stock, how much would you be willing to pay for it?

11. Given the expected earnings and dividend payments in Question 10, if you expected a 4 percent dividend yield, but decided you wanted a 14 percent return on this investment, what would you pay for the BBC stock?

12. Over the very long run you expect dividends for BBC to grow at a 10 percent rate and you require 14 percent on the stock. Using the dividend model that assumes a perpetuity, how much would you pay for this stock?

13. Based upon new information regarding the popularity of basketball, you revise your growth estimate to 9 percent. What is the maximum P/E ratio you will apply to BBC and what is the price you will pay for the stock?

14. The Baron Dogfood Company (BDC) has consistently paid out 30 percent of its earnings in dividends. The company's return on equity is 15 percent. What would you estimate as its growth rate of dividends?

15. Given the low risk in dog food, your required rate of return on BDC is 12 percent. What P/E ratio would you apply to the firm's earnings?

16. What P/E ratio would you apply if you understood that Baron had decided to increase its payout to 40 percent?

17. Discuss three ways a firm can increase its ROE. Make up an example to illustrate your discussion.

18. It is widely known that grocery chains have very low profit margins (e.g., about 1 percent). How would you explain the fact that their ROE is about 12 percent. Does this seem logical?

References

Ahearn, Daniel S. "Investment Management and Economic Research." *Financial Analysts Journal* 20 (1964).

Brown, Philip, and Ball, Ray. "Some Preliminary Findings on the Association Between the Earnings of a Firm, Its Industry, and the Economy." *Empirical Research in Accounting: Selected Studies 1967,* supplement to Vol. 5, *Journal of Accounting Research.*

Farretti, Andrew P. "The Economist Role in the Stock Market." *Business Economics* 4 (1969).

Keran, Michael W. "Monetary and Fiscal Influences on Economic Activity—The Historical Evidence." Federal Reserve Bank of St. Louis, *Review* 51 (1969).

King, Benjamin F. "Market and Industry Factors in Stock Price Behavior." *Journal of Business* 39 (1966).

Mennis, Edmund A. "Economics and Investment Management." *Financial Analysts Journal* 22 (1966).

Meyers, Stephen L. "A Re-Examination of Market and Industry Factors in Stock Price Behavior." *Journal of Finance* 28 (1973).

Appendix A to Chapter 8
Derivation of Constant Growth
Dividend Model

The basic model is:

$$P_0 = \frac{D_1}{(1 + i_j)^1} + \frac{D_2}{(1 + i_j)^2} + \frac{D_3}{(1 + i_j)^3} + \cdots \frac{D_n}{(1 + i_j)^n}$$

where:

P_0 = current price

D_i = expected dividend in period i

i_j = required rate of return on asset j.

If growth rate (g) is constant:

$$P_0 = \frac{D_0(1 + g)^1}{(1 + i)^1} + \frac{D_0(1 + g)^2}{(1 + i)^2} + \cdots \frac{D_0(1 + g)^n}{(1 + i)^n}$$

This can be written:

$$P_0 = D_0\left[\frac{(1 + g)}{(1 + i)} + \frac{(1 + g)^2}{(1 + i)^2} + \frac{(1 + g)^3}{(1 + i)^3} + \cdots \frac{(1 + g)^n}{(1 + i)^n}\right] \qquad (8A.1)$$

Multiply both sides of Equation (8A.1) by $\dfrac{1 + i}{1 + g}$:

$$\left[\frac{(1 + i)}{(1 + g)}\right]P_0 = D_0\left[1 + \frac{(1 + g)}{(1 + i)} + \frac{(1 + g)^2}{(1 + i)^2} + \cdots \frac{(1 + g)^{n-1}}{(1 + i)^{n-1}}\right] \qquad (8A.2)$$

Subtract Equation (8A.1) from Equation (8A.2):

$$\left[\frac{(1 + i)}{(1 + g)} - 1\right]P_0 = D_0\left[1 - \frac{(1 + g)^n}{(1 + i)^n}\right]$$

$$\left[\frac{(1 + i) - (1 + g)}{(1 + g)}\right]P_0 = D_0\left[1 - \frac{(1 + g)^n}{(1 + i)^n}\right]$$

Assuming i > g, as N → ∞ the terms in brackets on the right side of the equation goes to 1 leaving

$$\left[\frac{(1 + i) - (1 + g)}{(1 + g)}\right]P_0 = D_0$$

This simplifies to:

$$\left[\frac{1 + i - 1 - g}{(1 + g)}\right] P_0 = D_0$$

which equals:

$$\left[\frac{i - g}{(1 + g)}\right] P_0 = D_0$$

This equals:

$$(i - g)P_0 = D_0(1 + g) \text{ but } D_0(1 + g) = D_1$$

so:

$$(i - g)P_0 = D_1$$

$$P_0 = \frac{D_1}{i - g}$$

Remember this model assumes:

a constant growth rate, an infinite time period, and that the required return on the investment (i) is greater than the expected growth rate (g).

ANALYSIS OF
FINANCIAL STATEMENTS

❧ 9 ❧

The main source of information on which major business decisions are made is the financial statements of individual firms. The kinds of decisions involved include whether to lend money to a firm, whether to invest in the preferred or the common stock of a firm, and whether to acquire a firm. To properly make such decisions, it is necessary to understand what financial statements are available, what information is included in the different types of statements, and how to analyze this financial information to arrive at a rational decision. The purpose of this chapter is to briefly discuss the three major types of financial statements, and then consider in some detail the major financial ratios used to analyze various characteristics of firms, how they are calculated, and how they are used.

Major Financial Statements

The underlying purpose of financial statements is to provide information to interested parties on the resources available to management, how these resources were financed, and what was accomplished with these resources. This information is contained in three financial statements: the balance sheet, the income statement, and the sources and uses statement which reconciles data in the first two financial reports.

The Balance Sheet

This financial report indicates what resources (assets) are controlled by the firm and how these assets have been financed. Specifically, it indicates *at a point in time* (usually the end of the fiscal year or the end of a quarter) the current and fixed assets available to the firm. Typically, these assets are owned by the firm, but with recent changes in accounting procedures, some of these assets may be leased to the firm on a long-term basis.

Beyond knowing what resources are available, it is important to know how these assets were acquired, i.e., how they were financed. This information is likewise indicated in the balance sheet in terms of current liabilities (typically used to finance current assets such as inventory); long-term liabilities (fixed debt); and owners' equity which includes preferred stock, common stock, and retained earnings.

An example of a balance sheet for a manufacturing firm is contained in Table 9.1. It is important to recognize that the information on the balance sheet represents the *stock* of assets and financing alternatives for the firm at a point in time; in the example, it is as of December 31, 1980 and 1981.

The Income Statement

This statement contains information on the efficiency, control, and profitability of management during some specified period of time (a quarter or a year). Specifically, efficiency is indicated by the sales generated during the period, expenses indicate control, and the earnings derived from these sales indicate the profitability. In contrast to the stock concept in the balance sheet, the income statement indicates the *flow* of sales, expenses, and earnings during a period of time. The income statement for the Baron Manufacturing Company for the years 1980 and 1981 is contained in Table 9.2.

The Sources and Uses Statement

This financial statement is especially useful because it integrates the information contained in the two statements just discussed. Specifically, for a given period the sources and uses statement indicates how alternative items on the balance sheet changed, by giving the beginning and ending balance sheet totals, and, likewise, shows the impact of relevant items from the income statement. This statement is extremely helpful in determining where funds for expansion and other activities such as stock acquisition or debt retirement are generated.[1]

Purpose of Financial Statement Analysis

The underlying purpose of financial statement analysis is to aid in the evaluation of management performance. Specifically, the analysis is intended to help evaluate past management performance in terms of *profitability, efficiency,* and *risk.* More important than the historical analysis is a projection of future management performance based upon the analysis of the historical results. The expected future

---

[1]A complete discussion of this statement and its preparation is contained in Erich Helfert, *Techniques of Financial Analysis,* 4th ed. (Homewood, IL: Richard D. Irwin, 1976).

Assets	1981	1980
Current Assets		
Cash and Marketable Securities	$1,400,000	$1,260,000
Accounts Receivable (less allowance for bad debts: 1981, $100,000; 1980, $95,000)	2,200,000	2,100,000
Inventories	3,200,000	3,000,000
Total Current Assets	$6,800,000	$6,360,000
Fixed Assets		
Land	$1,550,000	$1,550,000
Building	4,000,000	3,900,000
Machinery	3,700,000	3,500,000
Office Equipment	125,000	105,000
Gross Fixed Assets	$9,375,000	$9,055,000
Less Accumulated Depreciation	1,700,000	1,500,000
Net Fixed Assets	$7,675,000	$7,555,000
Prepayments and Deferred Charges	125,000	110,000
Intangible (goodwill, patents)	150,000	150,000
Total Assets	$14,750,000	$14,175,000

Liabilities	1981	1980
Current Liabilities		
Accounts Payable	$1,300,000	$1,050,000
Notes Payable	1,100,000	1,400,000
Accrued Expenses Payable	400,000	350,000
Taxes Payable (Federal and State)	300,000	275,000
Total Current Liabilities	$3,100,000	$3,075,000
Long-Term Liabilities		
First Mortgage Bonds (10% coupon; due 1996)	$4,000,000	$4,000,000
Stockholder's Equity		
Capital Stock		
Preferred Stock, 8% cumulative, (10,000 shares, $100 par)	1,000,000	1,000,000
Common Stock, $2 par, one million shares outstanding	2,000,000	2,000,000
Capital Surplus	950,000	950,000
Accumulated Retained Earnings	3,700,000	3,150,000
Total Stockholder's Equity	7,650,000	7,100,000
Total Liabilities and Stockholder's Equity	$14,750,000	$14,175,000

Table 9.1   Baron Manufacturing Company Consolidated Balance Sheet
(Year Ended December 31)

	1981	1980
Net Sales	$20,750,000	$19,600,000
Cost of Goods Sold (Includes Depreciation: 1981, $200,000; 1980, $175,000)	15,773,000	14,842,000
Gross Profit	4,977,000	4,758,000
Selling, General & Administrative Expenses	2,740,000	2,650,000
Operating Profit	2,237,000	2,108,000
Other Income (Expense)	(82,000)	(53,000)
Earnings Before Interest and Taxes	$2,155,000	$2,055,000
Interest on Bonds	400,000	400,000
Earnings Before Taxes	$1,755,000	$1,655,000
Income Taxes	825,000	790,000
Net Income	$ 930,000	$ 865,000
Common Shares Outstanding	1,000,000	1,000,000
Net Income per Share	$ 0.93	$ 0.86
Preferred Dividends (8%)	80,000	80,000
Common Dividends (1981, $0.30/share; 1980, $0.25/share)	300,000	250,000

Table 9.2   Baron Manufacturing Company Consolidated Income Statement

performance will influence decisions regarding whether to lend money to or invest in the firm. The principal technique employed is the analysis of various sets of financial ratios that should indicate how management has performed in various areas. In this regard, the following section discusses why you should use ratios for this purpose, how you should analyze the ratios, sets forth the specific ratios that should be considered, and shows how to compute them.

Analysis of Financial Ratios

Why Ratios?

Analysts employ financial ratios simply because *numbers in isolation are typically of little value.* For example, what does it mean if the net income for a firm was $100,000? Obviously, an analyst would want to know the sales figure that generated this income ($1 million or $10 million) and the assets or capital employed in generating these sales or this income. Therefore, *ratios are used to provide meaningful relationships between individual values in the financial statements.*[2] Because there are numerous individual items in the major financial state-

---

[2]For a discussion of the history of ratio analysis, see James O. Horrigan, "A Short History of Financial Ratio Analysis," *Accounting Review* 43 (1968): 284–294.

ments, the number of potential combinations of these items is also quite large. An important task of the analyst is to limit the examination to the *relevant* ratios and categorize the ratios in groups that provide information on different economic aspects of the firm's operation. In addition, these ratios must be related to other relevant ratios or figures.

Why Relative Ratios?

Only relative financial ratios are relevant! Just as a single number from a financial statement is not of value, an individual financial ratio is of little value until it is placed in the perspective of other ratios. The important comparisons are made *relative* to:

the aggregate economy

the company's industry or industries

the firm's major competitors within the industry

the firm's own past performance.

The comparison to the aggregate economy is important because the economy has consistently experienced business cycles and almost all firms are influenced by the phase of the business cycle (an expansion or a contraction). As an example, it is not reasonable to expect an increase in the profit margin for a firm during a contraction (recession). Alternatively, a small increase in a firm's margin during a major business expansion may be considered a sign of weakness. Such an analysis will also help you understand how a firm reacts to the business cycle which indicates the firm's relative business risk (discussed more fully below) and helps in the projection of the firm's performance during subsequent business cycles.

Probably the most popular comparison is of a firm's performance relative to its industry.[3] This is considered important because the performance of a given industry has a great effect on the firms within that industry. This influence will vary by industry and is strongest within industries that involve a single product, e.g., steel, rubber, glass, wood products. In such instances, there is typically a common demand for the product and all firms within the industry will experience relatively homogeneous shifts in demand. In addition, the technology and production process within these industries are fairly similar. Consequently, analyzing an individual firm within an industry without considering the overall industry trend or cycle is meaningless because of the strong industry effect; even the best-managed steel firm is going to experience a decline in profit margins during a recession. In line with prior discussion, it is generally useful to examine an indus-

[3]An excellent source of comparative ratios for different industries is *"Key Business Ratios* published by Dun and Bradstreet, Inc., 99 Church Street, New York, NY 10007. Robert Morris Associates, Philadelphia National Bank Building, Philadelphia, PA. also provides comparative ratios by industry.

try's performance relative to the economy to understand the relative cyclical behavior of the industry; i.e., how does this industry respond to the business cycle?

A major problem with comparing a firm to its industry is that you may not feel comfortable with the measure of central tendency used for the industry. Specifically, you may feel that the average (mean) value is not a very useful measure because of the wide dispersion of values for the individual firms within the industry. Alternatively, you might feel that the firm being analyzed is not "typical," that it has a strong "unique" component. In either case, it might be preferable to compare the firm to one or several other individual firms within the industry that are considered comparable to the firm being analyzed in terms of size or clientele. As an example, within the computer industry it might be optimal to compare IBM to certain individual firms within the industry (e.g., Burroughs, Control Data) rather than to some total industry data that might include numerous small firms that serve unique components of the industry. Another example might be found in the utility industry. You would probably want to limit the industry comparison to comparable utilities, e.g., compare an electric utility to other electric utilities and not to gas and water utilities. Even within the electric utility segment you would probably consider electric utility firms from the same geographical area (South, Midwest) and also those with a comparable mix of residential, commercial, and industrial customers.

Finally, it is important to examine a firm's performance over time to determine whether the firm is progressing or regressing; what is happening to its profit margins or return on equity compared to those for past periods? This time-series analysis is especially crucial if you are attempting to estimate *future* performance. Too often we tend to consider an average for five- or ten-year periods without considering the trend. It is possible to derive an average rate of return of 10 percent based upon rates of return going from 5 percent to 15 percent over time, or based upon a series that begins at 15 percent and declines to 5 percent. Obviously the difference in the time-series trend would have a major impact on what you would estimate for the future.

In summary, financial ratios can be a very valuable tool in the analysis of financial statements, but in order to derive maximum benefit it is important to remember that *only relative financial ratios are relevant.*

Computation of Financial Ratios

The ratios that may be considered in this context can be divided into five major categories based upon different economic aspects of a firm:

1. Internal liquidity (solvency)
2. Operating performance
3. Risk analysis
4. Growth analysis
5. External liquidity (marketability).

Internal Liquidity Ratios

These solvency ratios are intended to indicate the ability of the firm to meet future short-term financial obligations. The idea is to match the potential near-term obligations, such as accounts payable, with current assets that are available on short notice to meet these obligations.

Current Ratio

Clearly the best-known liquidity measure is the current ratio which is the relationship between current assets and current liabilities:

$$\text{Current Ratio} = \frac{\text{Current Assets}}{\text{Current Liabilities}}$$

For the Baron Manufacturing Company (BMC), the current ratios were:

$$1981 \quad \frac{\$6,800,000}{\$3,100,000} = 2.19$$

$$1980 \quad \frac{\$6,360,000}{\$3,075,000} = 2.07$$

While both ratios appear quite adequate, you would want to compare these values to comparable figures for the firm's total industry and its major competitors to determine their significance. Also, it is recognized that the ratio can be manipulated.[4]

Quick Ratio

Some observers feel that *total* current assets are not a very conservative estimate of available assets because inventories are generally not a very liquid asset. Instead, they prefer to use the quick ratio which relates current liabilities to the most liquid current assets as follows:

$$\text{Quick Ratio} = \frac{\text{Cash plus Receivables}}{\text{Current Liabilities}}$$

This ratio is intended to indicate the amount of very liquid assets available to pay near-term liabilities. For BMC, the quick ratios were:

$$1981 \quad \frac{\$3,600,000}{\$3,100,000} = 1.16$$

$$1980 \quad \frac{\$3,360,000}{\$3,075,000} = 1.09$$

---

[4]In this regard, see Kenneth Lemke, "The Evaluation of Liquidity: An Analytical Study," *Journal of Accounting Research,* 8 (1970): 47–77.

Receivables Turnover

In addition to looking at supposedly liquid assets relative to near-term liabilities, some analysts attempt to analyze the quality of the receivables by examining how often they turn over, which can be used to determine the average collection period. Put another way, the intent is to find out how liquid these current assets are. The receivables turnover is computed as follows:

$$\text{Receivables Turnover} = \frac{\text{Net Annual Sales}}{\text{Average Receivables}}$$

The average receivables is typically the beginning figure plus the ending value divided by two. BMC's receivables turnover for 1981 was:

$$\frac{\$20,750,000}{(\$2,200,000 + \$2,100,000)/2} = \frac{\$20,750,000}{\$2,150,000} = 9.65$$

It is not possible to compute a turnover value for 1980 because there is no beginning receivables figure (i.e., the ending figure for 1979) for that year.

One can compute an average collection period as follows:

$$\text{Average Collection Period} = \frac{365}{9.65} = 37.8 \text{ days}$$

This indicates that receivables are generally collected in about 38 days. To determine whether this is good or bad it should be related to the firm's credit policy and to a comparable estimate for other firms in the industry.

Some analysts also compute an inventory turnover figure to derive some insight into the liquidity of the firm's inventory. For our purposes, this ratio is considered in the "operating performance" category.

Operating Performance

The ratios in this category indicate how well the management is operating the business and are typically broken down into subcategories: (1) efficiency ratios, and (2) profitability ratios. The efficiency ratios indicate how management uses the assets and capital at its disposal, mainly in terms of the dollar sales generated by various asset categories or capital categories.

Total Asset Turnover

This ratio is intended to indicate the use of the firm's total asset base (net assets equal gross assets minus depreciation on fixed assets). It is computed as follows:

$$\text{Total Asset Turnover} = \frac{\text{Net Sales}}{\text{Average Total Net Assets}}$$

The asset turnover value for BMC during 1981 was:

$$\frac{\$20,750,000}{(\$14,750,000 + \$14,175,000)/2} = \frac{\$20,750,000}{\$14,462,500} = 1.43$$

As with all ratios that use an average balance sheet figure, it is not possible to compute a ratio for 1980 because we don't have a year-end figure for 1979. This ratio should be compared to that for other firms in the same industry because it varies substantially between industries. As an example, it will range from about one for large capital firms (e.g., steel companies), to over ten for many retailing operations. It is also affected by the use of leased facilities which may not be reported on the balance sheet. One should also consider a *range* of values because, in many instances, it is poor management to have too few assets for the potential business (sales), just as it indicates poor judgment to have excess assets.

Beyond the analysis of the total asset base, insight can be gained from examining the utilization of some specific assets such as inventories and fixed assets.

Inventory Turnover
This ratio should indicate the utilization of inventory by management. It is computed as follows:

$$\text{Inventory Turnover} = \frac{\text{Net Sales}}{\text{Average Inventory}}$$

or

$$= \frac{\text{Cost of Sales}}{\text{Average Inventory}}$$

It is probably preferable to use the cost-of-sales figure because inventory is at cost. However, the cost of sales figure is not generally available in a published statement, so the net sales figure is typically used. The inventory turnover ratio for BMC during 1981, using sales, was:

$$\frac{\$20,750,000}{(\$3,200,000 + \$3,000,000)/2} = \frac{\$20,750,000}{\$3,100,000} = 6.69$$

Again, it is crucial that the emphasis be on the firm's performance *relative* to that of the firm's industry because the appropriate values vary widely. It is also important to consider a range because a value that is too low *or* too high is not good. Too low a turnover means excess inventory and possibly obsolescence. In contrast, while a high turnover may indicate efficiency, if it is too high it can indicate inadequate inventory that can lead to shortages and eventually to a loss of sales.

Net Fixed Asset Turnover

This ratio provides information on the firm's utilization of fixed assets. It is computed as follows:

$$\text{Fixed Asset Turnover} = \frac{\text{Net Sales}}{\text{Average Net Fixed Assets}}$$

The fixed asset turnover ratio for BMC during 1981 was:

$$\frac{\$20,750,000}{(\$7,675,000 + 7,555,000)/2} = \frac{\$20,750,000}{\$7,671,000} = 2.72$$

It is important to examine this turnover relative to that of comparable firms in the same industry and take into account the impact of leased assets. Also remember that a very high ratio can be due to the use of old, fully depreciated equipment that may be obsolete.

Equity Turnover

In addition to specific asset turnover ratios, it is useful to examine the turnover for different capital components. One of the most important in this regard is equity turnover, which is computed as follows:

$$\text{Equity Turnover} = \frac{\text{Net Sales}}{\text{Average Equity}}$$

Equity includes common stock, paid-in capital, and total retained earnings. The purpose of the ratio is to determine the dollar of sales generated per dollar of equity capital. The difference between this ratio and the total asset turnover is the capital provided from current liabilities, long-term debt, and preferred stock. Therefore, it is important when examining the trend for this series, to be aware of the capital ratios for the firm because it is possible to show improvements in this ratio by increasing the firm's proportion of debt capital (i.e., its debt-equity ratio). The equity turnover ratios for BMC during 1981 was:

$$\frac{\$20,750,000}{(\$6,650,000 + \$6,100,000)/2} = \frac{\$20,750,000}{\$6,375,000} = 3.25$$

Now that we have some idea of the firm's relative ability to generate sales from

---

[5]The reader will note that the equity figure used does *not* include the preferred stock, which is considered equity by accountants. This author's preference is to consider only owner's equity which would not include preferred stock.

the assets and capital at its disposal, the next step is to determine the profitability of the sales.

Analysis of Profitability

The ratios in this category are intended to indicate the rate of profit on sales and ultimately the profit on the capital employed.

Gross Profit Margin Gross profit is equal to net sales minus the cost of goods sold. It is computed as:

$$\text{Gross Profit Margin} = \frac{\text{Gross Profit}}{\text{Net Sales}}$$

The gross profit margins for BMC were:

$$1981 \quad \frac{\$4,977,000}{\$20,750,000} = 23.99$$

$$1980 \quad \frac{\$4,758,000}{\$19,600,000} = 24.28$$

This ratio should indicate the basic cost structure of the firm. An analysis of this margin over time relative to the industry figure is a prime indicator of the cost-price position of the firm.

Operating Profit Margin Operating profit is gross profit minus sales, general, and administrative expenses (SG+A). The margin is equal to:

$$\text{Operating Profit Margin} = \frac{\text{Operating Profit}}{\text{Net Sales}}$$

For BMC, the margins were:

$$1981 \quad \frac{\$2,237,000}{\$20,750,000} = 10.78$$

$$1980 \quad \frac{\$2,108,000}{\$19,600,000} = 10.76$$

The variability of this margin over time is a prime indicator of the business risk of a firm. If the firm has other income or expenses, these are considered before arriving at the earnings before interest and taxes. In the case of BMC, the other income (expense) figure is rather small, so the margins would be quite similar.

In some instances analysts will add back depreciation and compute a margin that is earnings before depreciation, interest, and taxes as a percentage of sales. This is considered an alternative operating profit margin ratio that reflects all "controllable" expenses.

	1981		1980	
	Dollar	Percent	Dollar	Percent
Net Sales	20,750,000	100.00	19,600,000	100.00
Cost of Goods Sold	15,773,000	76.01	14,842,000	75.72
Gross Profit	4,977,000	23.99	4,758,000	24.28
S.G. & A. Expense	2,740,000	13.20	2,650,000	13.52
Operating Profit	2,237,000	10.79	2,108,000	10.76
Other Income	(82,000)	0.40	(53,000)	0.27
Earnings before Interest and Taxes	2,155,000	10.39	2,055,000	10.48
Interest on Bonds	400,000	1.93	400,000	2.04
Earnings before Taxes	1,755,000	8.46	1,655,000	8.44
Income Taxes	825,000	3.98	790,000	4.03
Net Income	930,000	4.48	865,000	4.41

Table 9.3   Baron Manufacturing Company Common Size Income Statement

Net Profit Margin   Net income is earnings after taxes but before dividends on preferred and common stock. It is equal to:

$$\text{Net Profit Margin} = \frac{\text{Net Income}}{\text{Net Sales}}$$

For BMC the net profit margins were:

$$1981 \quad \frac{\$930,000}{\$20,750,000} = 4.48$$

$$1980 \quad \frac{\$865,000}{\$19,600,000} = 4.41$$

Common Size Income Statement

Beyond the analysis of these ratios that involve various income figures, an additional "common size" income statement may be prepared which includes all expenses and income items as a percentage of sales. The analysis of such a statement for several years (five at least) indicates the trend in cost figures and profit margins. A common size statement for the Baron Manufacturing Company for the two available years is contained in Table 9.3. As noted, the greatest value comes from a detailed analysis of various cost and margin figures over time relative to comparable figures for other firms in the industry.

Beyond the analysis of earnings on sales, the ultimate determination of the success of management is the rate of return earned on the assets of the firm or the capital committed to the enterprise.

Return on Total Capital

The purpose of this calculation is to determine the earnings available for all the capital involved in the enterprise (debt, preferred stock, and common stock). Therefore, the earnings figure used is net income (before any dividends) plus interest paid on debt.

$$\text{Return on Total Capital} = \frac{\text{Net Income plus Interest}}{\text{Average Total Capital}}$$

For BMC, it is assumed that the only interest is for long-term debt. Thus, the rate of return on total capital for 1981 was:

$$\frac{\$930,000 + \$400,000}{\$14,462,500} = 9.19$$

Again, it is not possible to compute a comparable rate of return for 1980 because we cannot derive an average total capital figure. This ratio indicates the overall return earned on all capital employed by the firm and should be compared to that for other firms in the industry and for the overall economy. Obviously, if this rate of return is not commensurate with the perceived risk of the firm, one should question whether the entity should continue to exist because the capital supposedly could be used more productively elsewhere in the economy.

Return on Owners' Equity   Again, this ratio is extremely important to the owner of the enterprise (the common stockholder) because it indicates the rate of return the manager is earning on the capital provided by the owner after taking into account payments to all other capital suppliers. If one were to consider *all* equity (including preferred stock), this would be equal to:

$$\text{Return on Total Equity} = \frac{\text{Net Income}}{\text{Average Total Equity}}$$

For BMC, in 1981 this would be:

$$\frac{\$930,000}{(\$7,650,000 + \$7,100,000)/2} = 12.61\%$$

If one is only concerned with owners' equity (i.e., common equity), the ratio would be:

$$\text{Return on Common Equity} = \frac{\text{Net Income minus Preferred Dividend}}{\text{Average Common Equity}}$$

For BMC, in 1981 this would be:

$$\frac{\$930,000 - \$80,000}{(\$6,650,000 + \$6,100,000)/2} = 13.33\%$$

This ratio reflects the rate of return on the equity capital provided by the owners. As such it should reflect not only the overall business risk involved, but also the additional *financial* risk assumed by the common stockholder because of the previous claims on the firm's debt. Notably, this return on equity ratio can be broken down into two of the ratios discussed:

$$\frac{\text{Sales}}{\text{Equity}} \times \frac{\text{Net Income}}{\text{Sales}} = \frac{\text{Net Income}}{\text{Equity}}$$

Equity Turnover $\times$ Net Profit Margin = Return on Equity

Therefore, a firm's return on equity can be improved by either using the equity more efficiently (i.e., increasing the firm's equity turnover) *or* by increasing the firm's net profit margin. It is possible to increase the equity turnover by employing more debt capital. While such a change in capital structure (i.e., an increase in the proportion of debt capital) will increase the equity turnover, it will also increase the financial risk of the firm which, in turn, should increase the required rate of return on equity.

Risk Analysis

The purpose of risk analysis is to determine the uncertainty of income flows for the total firm and for individual capital sources (i.e., debt, preferred stock, and common stock). Specifically, one can derive an estimate of the uncertainty of flows to the various sources of capital by examining the uncertainty of flows to the firm. In turn, the typical approach is to consider the major factors that cause uncertain flows to the firm, with uncertainty being measured in terms of the variability of returns over time; i.e., the more variable the income flows, the greater the uncertainty or risk to the investor. In this regard, the total risk of the firm is generally divided into: (1) business risk and (2) financial risk.

Business Risk[6]

Business risk is the uncertainty of income that is due to the firm's industry (i.e., its products and customers) and the way it produces its products (i.e., its production function). A firm's earnings vary over time because its sales vary and because its production costs vary. As an example, one would expect the earnings for a steel firm to vary more than those of a grocery chain would because steel sales are more volatile than grocery sales over a business cycle. Also, because the steel firm has more fixed production costs, its earnings vary more than its sales. Business risk is generally measured by *the variability of the firm's operating income over time*. It is reasoned that a more volatile earnings series means that an investor/lender will be more uncertain regarding future earnings; i.e., a more volatile earn-

---

[6]For a more detailed discussion of this topic see Stephen H. Archer, G. Marc Choate, and George Racette, *Financial Management: An Introduction* (New York: John Wiley & Sons, 1979); pp. 46–56.

ings series indicates greater business risk. In turn, earnings volatility is generally computed in terms of the standard deviation of the historical earnings series. Further, because the standard deviation of a series is influenced by the magnitude of the numbers, analysts have attempted to normalize this measure by dividing the standard deviation by the mean value for the series. The resulting ratio of the standard deviation of operating earnings divided by the average operating earnings is the coefficient of variation (CV). Thus:

$$\text{Business Risk} = f(\text{Coefficient of Variation of Operating Earnings})$$

$$= \frac{\text{Standard Deviation of Operating Earnings}}{\text{Mean Operating Earnings}}$$

$$= \frac{\sqrt{\dfrac{\displaystyle\sum_{i=1}^{n} (OE_t - \overline{OE})^2}{N}}}{\dfrac{\displaystyle\sum_{i=1}^{n} OE_t}{N}}.$$

An advantage of using the coefficient of variation of operating earnings is that one can compare these normalized measures for firms of different size; e.g., DuPont can be compared to a smaller chemical firm. The computation of the CV of operating earnings generally covers from a minimum of five years up to about ten years. A calculation for fewer than five years is not very meaningful, while data for much more than ten years can be out of date for current purposes. It is not possible to compute the CV for BMC because we only have data for two years.

In addition to an overall measure of business risk, one should attempt to determine the components that contribute to this variability; i.e., what causes the variability of operating earnings. In general, there are two components: (1) sales volatility and (2) operating leverage.

Sales Volatility   This is the prime determinant of earnings volatility because *operating earnings volatility cannot be lower than sales volatility;* i.e., operating leverage can only increase earnings volatility above the level derived from sales volatility. To understand this, conceive of a case in which all costs for the firm were variable costs. In this instance, the sales volatility and the earnings volatility for the firm would be equal. Also, note that the sales volatility is *basically outside of the control of management;* i.e., the sales volatility for a firm is a function of the aggregate economic environment and the particular industry involved. As an example, a firm in a cyclical industry (automobiles) will have a very volatile sales pattern over the business cycle compared to a firm in a noncyclical industry such as hospital supplies. The sales volatility is typically measured by the coefficient of variation of sales during some specified time period (5 to 10 years). Recall that the coefficient of variation (CV) is equal to the standard deviation of sales divided by mean sales for the period.

$$\text{Sales Volatility} = \text{Coefficient of Variation of Sales}$$

$$= \frac{\text{Standard Deviation of Sales}}{\text{Mean Sales}}$$

$$= \frac{\sqrt{\dfrac{\displaystyle\sum_{i=1}^{n} (S_i - \bar{S})^2}{N}}}{\dfrac{\displaystyle\sum_{i=1}^{n} S_i}{N}}.$$

Operating Leverage   In addition to the effect of sales volatility, the variability of a firm's operating earnings is also affected by the production function of the firm; i.e., what mixture of costs are involved in producing the goods and services sold? As mentioned, if a firm does not have any fixed production costs, then *total production costs vary directly with sales and operating profits would be a constant proportion of sales* (i.e., the operating profit margin would be constant). Under these conditions, the operating profit series would have the same relative volatility as sales have. Realistically, firms almost always have some fixed production costs (e.g., buildings, machinery), or they employ some relatively permanent personnel (supervisors, foremen, etc.). The existence of fixed production costs means that *operating profits will vary more than sales vary over the business cycle.* During slow periods profits will decline by more than sales decline, while during periods of economic expansion profits will increase by more than sales increase. These fixed production costs are referred to as *operating leverage.* Clearly, *the greater the firm's operating leverage, the more volatile the operating earnings series will be relative to the sales series.*[7] Given this basic relationship between operating profit and sales, operating leverage is measured as the percentage of change in operating earnings relative to a percentage of change in sales as follows:

$$\text{Operating Leverage} = \Sigma \left| \frac{\%\Delta\,\text{OE}}{\%\Delta S} \right|$$

The absolute value of the changes are considered because it is possible for the two series to move in opposite directions. The direction is not important, but the relative size of the change is. The more volatile the operating earnings compared to sales, the greater the operating leverage.

[7]For a further treatment of this area, see James C. Van Horne, *Financial Management and Policy,* 5th ed. (Englewood Cliffs, NJ: Prentice-Hall, 1980), chap. 27.

In summary, business risk is measured by the relative variability of operating earnings for a firm over time. In turn, the variability of operating earnings is caused by sales volatility and the amount of operating leverage employed by the firm.

Financial Risk

Financial risk is the additional uncertainty of returns faced by equity holders because a firm uses fixed-obligation debt securities. Note that this financial uncertainty is *in addition* to the business risk discussed above. Specifically, if the firm did not derive any of its capital from debt obligations (i.e., it was an all-equity firm), the only uncertainty for the owner would be that due to sales volatility and operating leverage (i.e., business risk). With only business risk, the earnings available to the common stockholder would have the same volatility as the operating earnings. The point is, when a firm derives some of its capital from debt securities, the payments on this capital take priority over the common stock earnings and are a *fixed* obligation. Therefore, as was true with operating leverage, during good times, the earnings on equity will *increase more* than operating earnings, while during a period of adverse business behavior, the earnings available to equity holders will *decline more* than operating earnings do. Put another way, because of the use of fixed-debt obligations, the volatility of earnings available for equity is greater than the volatility of operating earnings.[8] There are two sets of ratios used to measure financial risk. The first set is intended to indicate the proportion of capital derived from debt securities. The second set involves the coverage of earnings available to pay the fixed obligations.

Proportion of Debt Ratios   These ratios indicate the proportion of a firm's capital that is derived from long-term debt in comparison to other sources of capital such as preferred stock and common equity. Clearly, the higher the proportion of debt compared to other sources of capital, the more volatile the earnings available to common stock and the higher the probability of the firm defaulting on the bonds. Therefore, *higher debt ratios indicate greater financial risk*. Also, the acceptable level of financial risk depends upon the firm's business risk. If the firm has lower business risk, investors are willing to accept higher financial risk.

Debt-Equity Ratio   This ratio is equal to:

$$\text{Debt-Equity Ratio} = \frac{\text{Total Long-Term Debt}}{\text{Total Equity}}$$

Debt includes all long-term fixed obligations including subordinated convertible bonds. (Subordinated bonds are junior to debentures and mortgage debt in terms

---

[8]This relationship is referred to as financial leverage and is discussed in Van Horne, *Financial Management,* chap. 27, and also in Sol S. Shalit, "On the Mathematics of Financial Leverage," *Financial Management* 4 (1975): 57–66.

of interest payments and in case of liquidation.) Equity is typically expressed as the book value and includes preferred stock, common stock, and retained earnings. In some cases you may want to exclude preferred stock and only consider common equity. Considering total equity is probably preferable if some firms have preferred stock and some do not. Alternatively, if the preferred stock dividend is considered as akin to an interest payment, a ratio of debt plus preferred stock relative to common equity could be derived.

The debt-total equity ratios for BMC were:

$$1981 \quad \frac{\$4,000,000}{\$7,650,000} = 0.52$$

$$1980 \quad \frac{\$4,000,000}{\$7,100,000} = 0.56$$

Alternatively, the debt plus preferred stock to common equity ratios for BMC were:

$$1981 \quad \frac{\$5,000,000}{\$6,650,000} = 0.75$$

$$1980 \quad \frac{\$5,000,000}{\$6,100,000} = 0.82$$

Debt-Total Capital Ratio   This ratio indicates what proportion of long-term capital is derived from debt capital. It is computed as:

$$\text{Debt to Capital Ratio} = \frac{\text{Total Long-Term Debt}}{\text{Total Long-Term Capital}}$$

The long-term capital would include all debt, any preferred stock, and total equity. While this ratio is completely consistent with the debt-equity ratio, it is somewhat more intuitive. In some cases it might also be preferable to examine *total* debt (current liabilities plus long-term debt) to total capital if a firm derives substantial funds from short-term borrowing.

The long-term debt to total long-term capital ratios for BMC were:

$$1981 \quad \frac{4,000,000}{11,650,000} = 0.34$$

$$1980 \quad \frac{4,000,000}{11,100,000} = 0.36$$

Coverage Ratios   In addition to the balance-sheet ratios that indicate the *stock* of debt, analysts prefer to employ ratios that reflect the *flow* of funds from earnings that are available to meet fixed-payment debt obligations. In this case, the *higher* the value (i.e., the greater the coverage) the *lower* the financial risk.

Interest Coverage   This is computed as follows:

$$\text{Interest Coverage} = \frac{\text{Income before Interest and Taxes}}{\text{Debt Interest Charges}}$$

This ratio indicates how many times the fixed interest charges are earned based upon the earnings available to pay these charges. Alternatively, one minus the reciprocal of the coverage ratio indicates how much earnings could decline before it would not be possible to pay these fixed financial charges. For example, a coverage ratio of five means that earnings could decline by 80 percent (1 minus 1/5) and the firm could still pay the fixed financial charges. The interest coverage ratios for BMC were:

$$1981 \; \frac{\$2,155,000}{\$400,000} = 5.39$$

$$1980 \; \frac{\$2,055,000}{\$400,000} = 5.14$$

Total Fixed Charge Coverages   On the other hand, an analyst might want to determine the coverage for fixed financial charges including preferred dividends. This necessitates consideration of the fact that preferred dividends are paid out of earnings *after* taxes. It is therefore necessary to determine the pretax earnings required for these payments, which is done as follows:

$$\text{Fixed Charge Coverage} = \frac{\text{Income Before Interest and Taxes}}{\text{Debt Interest} + \dfrac{\text{Preferred Dividend}}{(1 - \text{Tax Rate})}}$$

For BMC these would be:

$$1981 \; \frac{\$2,155,000}{\$400,000 + \dfrac{(80,000)}{(.53)}} = \frac{2,155,000}{551,000} = 3.91$$

$$1980 \; \frac{\$2,055,000}{\$400,000 + \dfrac{(80,000)}{(.53)}} = \frac{2,055,000}{551,000} = 3.73$$

Growth Analysis

Growth analysis involves the examination of specific ratios that indicate how fast a firm should grow. Such analysis is important for both lenders and owners. The rationale for owners analyzing growth potential is obvious because the future value of the firm is heavily dependent on future growth in earnings and dividends. You will recall the standard dividend valuation model discussed in Chapter 8, which showed that the value of a firm is a function of dividends in period one, the required rate of return for the stock (i_i), and the expected growth rate of dividends for the firm (g_i). Therefore, an estimation of expected growth of earnings and dividends on the basis of the variables that influence growth is obviously crucial. An analysis of past values for these growth determinants should be helpful in the estimation process.

A firm's growth potential is also important to creditors because the major determinant of the firm's ability to pay an obligation is the firm's future success which, in turn, is influenced by its growth. Many financial ratios employed in credit analysis consider the amount of assets covering financial obligations. Using these ratios implies that it is possible to liquidate these assets to pay off the loan in case of a default. The fact is, the ability to use these assets for such a purpose is extremely questionable because the usual payoff on assets sold in a forced liquidation is about 10–15 cents on the dollar. Clearly, the more relevant analysis is the ability of the firm as an *ongoing* enterprise to pay off the obligations. In this regard, the analysis of growth potential indicates the future status of the firm.

Determinants of Growth

The growth of a business firm is similar to the growth of any economic entity, including the aggregate economy. Specifically, the rate of growth depends on:

1. *the amount of resources retained and reinvested in the entity;* and
2. *the rate of return that is earned on the resources retained.*

Obviously, the more a firm reinvests, the faster it will grow. Alternatively, for a given level of reinvestment, a firm will grow faster if it is able to earn a higher rate of return on the resources reinvested.

For both lenders and owners, the growth of *net earnings available to the owners* is of prime importance. While the importance of this variable to equity holders is obvious, it is also important to the lender because this growing stream of earnings protects the debt holder and determines the overall health of the enterprise. Having established this fact, and given the book's focus, we will concentrate on the growth of equity earnings. This growth rate is a function of two variables: (1) the percentage of net earnings retained and (2) the rate of return on the firm's equity capital. These ratios logically follow directly from the above discussion. The retention rate (1 minus the percentage of payout) indicates the proportion of earnings that are retained for reinvestment. The return on equity indicates the rate of return on these retained earnings because, when earnings are retained, they become equity. Specifically.

$$g = \text{(percentage of earnings retained)} \times \text{(return on equity)}$$
$$= \text{RR} \times \text{ROE}$$

The retention rate is decided upon by a firm's board of directors based on the investment opportunities available to the firm. Theory would indicate that the firm should retain earnings and reinvest them as long as the expected rate of return on the investment exceeds the firm's cost of capital.

As discussed in the profitability section, it is possible to examine the firm's ROE in terms of two components:

$$\text{ROE} = \frac{\text{Sales}}{\text{Equity}} \times \frac{\text{Income}}{\text{Sales}} = (\text{Equity Turnover}) \times (\text{Net Profit Margin})$$

Therefore, it is possible for a firm to improve its ROE either by becoming more efficient in the use of its equity capital (increase its turnover) *or* by increasing its profit margin on sales. When examining equity turnover you should examine the debt/equity ratio to ensure that an increase in the equity turnover is not attributable to a change in the capital structure. An increase in equity turnover accompanied by an increase in the debt/equity ratio would cause a faster rate of growth in equity earnings, *but* would also cause an increase in financial risk which means equity holders would increase their required rate of return on the stock.

It is possible to derive a more specific idea of any change in financial leverage by breaking the equity turnover into two components as follows.

$$\frac{\text{Sales}}{\text{Equity}} = \frac{\text{Sales}}{\text{Total Assets}} \times \frac{\text{Total Assets}}{\text{Equity}}$$

This specification shows that equity turnover can be changed either by changing total asset turnover or by changing the proportion of total assets financed by equity (i.e., changing capital structure). The higher the ratio of: total assets/equity, the greater the financial leverage because total assets are financed either by debt or equity, and if a firm has a lot of assets relative to its equity, it must have used a lot of debt to finance the assets.

Substituting this into the previous equation, we derive the following relationship:

$$\text{ROE} = \frac{\text{Sales}}{\text{Total Assets}} \times \frac{\text{Total Assets}}{\text{Equity}} \times \frac{\text{Income}}{\text{Sales}}$$

$$= (\text{Total Asset Turnover}) \times (\text{Financial Leverage}) \times (\text{Net Profit Margin})$$

This now shows very clearly that the ROE can be increased by greater asset efficiency (total asset turnover), by changing capital structure (increasing financial leverage), or by increasing profitability (raising the profit margin).

The retention rates for BMC (after preferred dividends) were:

$$1981 \frac{\$850,000 - 300,000}{\$850,000} = 0.65$$

$$1980 \frac{\$785,000 - 250,000}{\$785,000} = 0.68$$

The firm's returns on year-end common equity were:

$$1981 \ \frac{\$850,000}{\$6,650,000} = 12.78$$

$$1980 \ \frac{\$785,000}{\$6,100,000} = 12.87$$

This would imply growth rates for BMC of:

$$1981 \quad 0.65 \times 12.78 = 8.31$$
$$1980 \quad 0.68 \times 12.87 = 8.75$$

Over a long period of time, an analyst would want to examine the breakdown of ROE to determine the causes of the return, and compare it to the return for other firms in the same industry.

External Market Liquidity

Market liquidity is the ability to buy or sell an asset quickly with little change in price from that involved in a prior transaction, assuming no new information has been obtained. To determine how liquid an asset is, one should ask two questions: (1) how long will it take to sell the asset; and (2) what will the selling price be compared to recent selling prices? In the case of a liquid asset, you should be able to sell it very quickly (in less than an hour), at a price close to the prior transaction price (e.g., if the last sale for a stock was at $30 a share, you should be able to sell your share at $29⅞ or even $30). Examples of very liquid common stocks would be AT&T and IBM because large amounts of these stocks can be sold very quickly with very little price change. In contrast, in the case of an illiquid stock you might be able to sell it quickly, but the price would be significantly different from the previous price (e.g., receiving $28 for a stock that sold recently for $30). Alternatively, the broker might be able to get $30 a share, but it could take several days.

Determinants of Market Liquidity

Investors should be aware of the liquidity of the securities they hold because it affects their ability to change the composition of their portfolios. While the major factors indicating market liquidity are derived from market trading data, there are several internal corporate variables that are good proxies for these market variables. The most important indicators of external market liquidity are the number of shares traded in the security and/or the dollar value of shares traded. These indicators are significant because, when there is more trading activity, there is a greater probability of being able to buy or sell a given stock. Another variable that has been widely used as an indicator of market liquidity is the bid-ask spread, i.e., the difference between the market-maker's bid price and his asking price on a security. Fortunately, some internal corporate variables are typically highly correlated with these trading variables.

1. total market value of outstanding securities
2. number of security owners.

Numerous studies have shown that the main determinant of the market spread (besides price) is the dollar value of trading. In turn, the value of trading is highly correlated with the market value of the outstanding securities, and with the number of security holders. The intuitive explanation for this relationship is that with more shares outstanding, there will be more stockholders, and, at any point in time, some of these security holders will be buying or selling for a variety of purposes. It is this availability of buyers and sellers that provides liquidity.

Uses of Financial Ratios

We have discussed some general uses of financial ratios as related to credit analysis and security valuation. Beyond this, specific ratios have been employed in several studies, principally for three types of financial analysis: (1) stock valuation, (2) assigning quality ratings to bonds, and (3) predicting insolvency of firms.

Stock Valuation Models

Most valuation models attempt to derive an appropriate price-earnings ratio for a stock, i.e., an earnings multiple as discussed in Chapter 8. You will recall that the earnings multiple should be influenced by the expected growth rate of dividends and the required rate of return on the stock. Financial ratios can be used in generating both estimates. A growth rate estimate involves the ratios discussed in the section on growth analysis (i.e., the retention rate and the return on equity). In turn the components of ROE are used to determine whether the current ROE can be sustained.

In addition, when attempting to determine an appropriate required rate of return (i_j), it was noted that the required rate depends on the risk premium for the security, which is a function of business risk, financial risk and liquidity risk. Again, in this chapter we have discussed all of these risks. Business risk is typically measured in terms of earnings variability, financial risk is determined using either the debt-equity ratio or the fixed charge coverage ratio and liquidity risk is related to the value of shares outstanding or number of shareholders.

Bond Ratings

As will be discussed in Chapter 14, there are four financial services that assign quality ratings to bonds on the basis of the ability of the issuer to meet all the obligations of the bond. A triple-A rating (AAA) indicates very high quality and almost no chance of default, while a C rating indicates the bond is already in default. Because it is important to understand the variables used by these rating services, several studies have attempted to build models that use financial ratios to predict the rating that will be assigned to a given bond. The major ratios used have been those concerned with internal liquidity and financial risk as follows:

1. Current ratio
2. Debt-equity ratio
3. Interest coverage ratio
4. Value of outstanding bonds.

In addition to these ratios, which we discussed earlier, the size of the issuing firm and the subordination of a given issue have also been used in these analyses.

Predicting Insolvency

There is obvious interest in determining which financial ratios can best be used to detect a forthcoming case of insolvency (bankruptcy). Based upon several studies of this topic, the following ratios were found to be most consistent in this regard:

1. Current ratio
2. Debt-equity ratio
3. Cash flow/total debt
4. Total asset turnover
5. Return on capital.

The only ratio not specifically covered in our discussion is cash flow/total debt which combines cash flow from the income statement to the total debt value from the balance sheet.

Summary

In this chapter we were concerned with different types of financial statement analysis and the uses to which they are put. Given that the overall purpose is to help you make decisions concerning investing in the bonds or stocks of a given firm, we initially considered why ratios are important and how these ratios should be examined (i.e., relative to the economy, the industry, and past ratios).

The specific ratios considered were divided into five categories (i.e., internal liquidity, operating performance, risk analysis, growth analysis, and external market liquidity) depending upon the purpose of the analysis. You should realize that the discussion of ratios presented is not exhaustive, but involved the most widely used ratios for the purposes specified. We concluded the chapter with a discussion of three major uses of financial ratios. This presentation indicated the broad uses and the specific ratios that are most important for these purposes.

A final caveat: it is clearly possible to envision a very large number of potential ratios that will examine almost every possible relationship. The trick is not to come up with more ratios, but to attempt to *limit* the number of ratios and *examine them in a meaningful way*. This entails an analysis of their time-series properties *relative* to the economy, the industry, or the past. Any additional effort should be spent on deriving good comparisons for a limited number of ratios.

Questions

1. What is the overall purpose of financial statements?

2. Briefly discuss some of the decisions that require the analysis of financial statements.

3. Why do analysts employ financial ratios rather than analyzing absolute numbers?

4. You are told that the Geno Company, producers of Polish sausage, earned 12 percent on equity last year. What does this indicate to you about the management of Geno's? Is there any other information you want? What is it and why do you want it?

5. Besides comparing a company's performance to that of its total industry, what other comparisons should be considered *within* the industry? What is the justification for this comparison?

6. What is the purpose of the internal liquidity ratios; i.e., what information are they intended to provide? Who would be most interested in this information?

7. What are the components of operating performance? Discuss each of them and the ratios that would be involved in assessing company performance.

8. In terms of asset turnover and profit margin, how do a jewelry store and a grocery store differ? Would you expect their returns on equity to differ assuming equal risk? Discuss.

9. Discuss the components of business risk and how the components affect the variability of operating earnings.

10. Would you expect a steel firm or a utility to have greater business risk? Discuss your reasoning in terms of the components of business risk.

11. When examining a firm's financial structure, would you be concerned with the firm's business risk? Why or why not?

12. How does the fixed-charge coverage ratio differ from the debt-equity ratio? Which would you prefer to use and why?

13. Why is growth analysis important to the common stockholder? Why is it important to the debt holder?

14. In a general sense, what are the factors that determine the rate of growth of *any* economic unit? Discuss each of the factors.

15. IBM pays out about 40 percent of its earnings in dividends and earns about 18 percent on equity. What is its expected growth rate under these conditions?

16. If a firm is earning 20 percent on equity, would you expect it to have a high or low retention rate? Why?

17. Assume you are told that the ND Company earned 18 percent on equity while the MSU Company only earned 14 percent on equity. Does this mean that ND is better than MSU? What else do you want to consider?

18. Briefly discuss the two components of external market liquidity.

19. Given the components of market liquidity, why do people consider real estate to be a relatively illiquid asset? Be specific.

20. What internal factors about a company would indicate probable market liquidity? Discuss why these factors are potentially useful for this purpose.

References

Bernstein, Leopold A. *Financial Statement Analysis: Theory, Application, and Interpretation.* rev. ed. Homewood, IL: Richard D. Irwin, 1978.

Foster, George. *Financial Statement Analysis.* Englewood Cliffs, NJ: Prentice-Hall, 1978.

Foulke, R. A. *Practical Financial Statement Analysis.* 6th ed. Highstown, NJ: McGraw-Hill, 1968.

Helfert, Erich A. *Techniques of Financial Analysis.* 4th ed. Homewood, IL: Richard D. Irwin, 1977.

Horrigan, James D. "A Short History of Financial Ratio Analysis." *Accounting Review* 43 (1968).

Jaedicke, Robert K., and Sprouse, Robert T. *Accounting Flows: Income, Funds, and Cash.* Englewood Cliffs, NJ: Prentice-Hall, 1965.

Lev, Baruch. *Financial Statement Analysis: A New Approach.* Englewood Cliffs, NJ: Prentice-Hall, 1974.

Seitz, Neil. *Financial Analysis: A Programmed Approach.* Reston Publishing Company, 1976.

Sprouse, R. T., and Swieringa, R. J. *Essentials of Financial Statement Analysis.* Reading, MA: Addison-Wesley, 1972.

Viscione, Jerry A. *Financial Analysis: Principles and Procedures.* Boston: Houghton, Mifflin, 1977.

AGGREGATE STOCK MARKET ANALYSIS

≫ 10 ≪

In Chapter 8 we discussed the importance of attempting to estimate future aggregate stock market values which, in turn, indicate future return from investing in common stocks. It was pointed out that such an analysis should be done before an industry analysis or a company analysis is attempted. Consequently, investors should become familiar with the major techniques available for estimating future market values or changes in market values. There are basically three techniques employed in this regard. The first is a *macroeconomic* approach which is based upon the underlying relationship between the aggregate economy and the securities markets. The second technique is the *present value of dividends* approach which follows directly from the valuation theory discussed in Chapter 8. Specifically, the idea is to apply the basic dividend valuation model to the aggregate stock market. The third is the *technical analysis* approach which assumes that the best way to determine *future* changes in stock market values is to examine *past* movements in security prices and other market variables.

In this chapter we consider the macroeconomic approach and the present value of dividends approach. The technical analysis approach is discussed in Chapter 13.

The Stock Market and the Economy

It is widely accepted that there is a strong relationship between the aggregate economy and the stock market. This is not surprising if you consider that the price of a given stock reflects investor expectations as to how the issuing firm will perform, and that performance is, in turn, affected by the overall performance of the economy. There is substantial empirical support for the existence of this relationship, most of it derived by the National Bureau of Economic Research (NBER) in connection with the Bureau's work on business cycles. Based on the

237

relationship of alternative economic series to the behavior of the entire economy, the NBER has classified numerous economic series into three groups: leading, coincident, and lagging. Based upon extensive analysis, it has been shown that stock prices are one of the "better" leading series in terms of consistency and stability.

The evidence clearly indicates not only a relationship between stock prices and the economy, but also indicates that stock prices consistently turn *before* the economy does; i.e., stock prices turn down prior to a peak in the economy and start rising before the economy begins its recovery from a recession. There are two possible reasons for this phenomenon. One is that stock prices reflect *expectations* of earnings and dividends and thus they react to investor perceptions of *future* earnings and dividends. Hence, because investors attempt to estimate *future* earnings, stock prices are based upon *future* economic activity, not on current activity. A second possible reason is that the stock market reacts to various economic series, but the series considered most important by equity investors are *leading indicator* series of the economy. In this regard, the economic series mentioned most often as important to stock prices are corporate earnings, corporate profit margins, and changes in the growth rate of the money supply. Therefore, because analysts and portfolio managers analyze economic series that lead the economy, and adjust stock prices rapidly to changes in these relevant economic series, stock prices become a leading series.

Given that stock prices lead the aggregate economy, our macroeconomic approach to market analysis will concentrate on economic series that likewise lead the economy—hopefully by more than stock prices do. The initial discussion considers the cyclical indicator approach of the National Bureau of Economic Research (NBER) with specific reference to leading economic indicators and their relationship to stock prices. The subsequent discussion considers a very popular leading series, the money supply, and how growth in the money supply relates to stock prices.

Cyclical Indicator Approach

The cyclical indicator approach to economic forecasting is based on the belief that the economy experiences discernible periods of expansion and contraction. This view has been investigated by the National Bureau of Economic Research (NBER), a nonprofit organization that attempts to ascertain and to present important economic facts and interpret them in a scientific and impartial manner. The NBER explains the business cycle as follows:

The "business cycle" concept has been developed from the sequence of events discerned in the historical study of the movements of economic activity. Though there are many cross-currents and variations in the pace of business activity, periods of business expansion appear to cumulate to peaks. As they cumulate, contrary forces tend to gain strength bringing about a reversal in business activity and the onset of a recession. As a recession continues, forces making for expansion gradually emerge until they become dominant and a recovery begins. . . .[1]

This explanation emphasizes the *cumulative* aspects of the process and indicates that there are certain events that regularly take place during the various phases of the business cycle.

Based upon an examination of the behavior of hundreds of economic time series in relation to past business cycles, the NBER grouped various economic series into three major categories in terms of this relationship. The initial list was compiled in 1938 and it has undergone numerous revisions over the years. The most recent revision was completed in May and November of 1975 by Zarnowitz and Boschan.[2]

Indicator Categories

The first category is the *leading indicators* and includes those economic time series that have usually reached peaks or troughs before the corresponding points in aggregate economic activity were reached. The group currently includes the 12 series shown in Table 10.1. The table indicates the median lead or lag for each economic series relative to business cycle peaks or troughs. The bureau also graded each economic series in terms of several characteristics considered important, and these scores are also included. One of the 12 leading series is common stock prices which has a median lead of 9 months at peaks and 4 months at troughs. Another leading series is the money supply in constant dollars which has a median lead of 10 months at peaks and 8 months at troughs.

The second category is *coincident indicators* which consist of those economic time series in which the peaks and troughs of the series roughly coincide with the peaks and troughs in the business cycle. Many of the economic time series in this category are employed by the Bureau to help define the different phases of the cycle.

The third category is *lagging indicators,* which includes series that have experienced their peaks and troughs after peaks and troughs occur in the aggregate economy. Timing and scores for the coincident and lagging series are contained in Table 10.2.

A final category is titled "other selected series," and include series that are expected to influence aggregate economic activity, but that cannot be neatly categorized in one of the three main groups. This includes such series as U.S. balance of payments, federal surplus or deficit, and military contract awards.

---

[1]Julius Shiskin, "Business Cycle Indicators: The Known and the Unknown," *Review of the International Statistical Institute* 31 (1963): 361–383.

[2]Victor Zarnowitz and Charlotte Boschan, "Cyclical Indicators: An Evaluation and New Leading Index," *Business Conditions Digest,* May 1975, pp. 5–22; and idem, "New Composite Indexes of Coincident and Lagging Indicators," *Business Conditions Digest,* November 1975, pp. 5–24.

Series	Median Lead (−) or Lag (+) in months			Scores						
	Peaks	Troughs	All Turns	Economic Significance	Statistical Adequacy	Timing	Conformity	Smoothness	Currency	Total
1. Average work week of prod. worker–mfg.	−12	−2	−5	70	80	81	60	60	80	73
2. Index of new business formations	−11	−2	−3	80	61	78	59	80	80	73
3. Index of stock prices: 500 common stocks	−9	−4	−5½	80	85	89	51	80	100	80
4. Index of new building permits	−13	−8	−9½	90	70	80	55	80	80	76
5. Layoff rate–manufacturing	−11	−1	−6½	70	80	79	80	60	80	76
6. New orders–consumer goods (1967 dollars)	−6	−1	−4½	80	75	76	70	60	80	74
7. Contracts & orders for plant & equipment (1967 dollars)	−9	−2	−5½	90	50	87	72	40	80	72
8. Net change in inventory (1967 dollars)	−5	−4	−4½	90	53	83	60	80	40	71
9. Net change in sensitive prices	−15	−5	−5½	70	80	82	60	60	66	72
10. Vendor performance	−6	−5	−6	70	75	79	46	60	80	69
11. Money balance (MI)–1967	−10	−8	−9	90	85	80	41	100	80	79
12. Percent change in total liquid assets	−6½	−6	−6	90	81	84	41	80	66	75

Table 10.1 Economic Series in NBER Leading Indicator Group

Source: Victor Zarnowitz and Charlotte Boschan, "Cyclical Indicators: An Evaluation and New Leading Indexes," *Business Conditions Digest*, May 1975, pp. 5–22.

| Series | Median Lead (−) or Lag (+) in months | | | Scores | | | | | | |
	Peaks	Troughs	All Turns	Economic Significance	Statistical Adequacy	Timing	Conformity	Smoothness	Currency	Total
Coincident										
1. Number of employees on nonagricultural payrolls	−2	0	0	100	78	89	80	100	80	88
2. Index of industrial production	−3	0	−½	90	72	90	85	100	80	86
3. Personal income, less transfers (deflated by PEE)	0	−1	−½	90	70	74	64	100	80	78
4. Manufacturing & trade sales, deflated	−3	0	−½	90	65	90	75	80	53	78
Lagging										
1. Average duration of employment	+1	+8	+3½	90	78	89	95	80	80	86
2. Manufacturing & trade inventories (1967 dollars)	+2½	+3	+3	90	70	89	64	100	53	80
3. Labor cost per unit output, manufacturing	+8½	+11	+10	80	55	87	51	80	80	73
4. Commercial & industrial loans outstanding, weekly rep. banks	+1½	+5	+3½	80	60	86	81	100	100	83
5. Ratio of consumer installment debt to personal income	+6½	+7	+7	80	70	87	44	100	53	74
6. Average prime rate charged by banks	+3½	+14	+4	90	95	85	62	100	100	87

Table 10.2   Economic Series in NBER Coincident and Lagging Indicator Group

Source: Victor Zarnowitz and Charlotte Boschan, "New Composite Indexes of Coincident and Lagging Indicators," *Business Conditions Digest*, November 1975, pp. 5–24.

Analytical Measures

When examining a given economic series for predictive purposes, it is important to consider more than simply the behavior of the series overall. The NBER has devised certain analytical measures for examining behavior within a series.

Diffusion Indexes   As the name implies, these indexes indicate how pervasive a given movement is in a series. They are used to specify *the percent of reporting units in a series indicating a given result.* If there are 100 companies that constitute the sample reporting new orders for equipment, the diffusion index for this series would indicate what proportion of the 100 companies was reporting higher orders during an expansion. In addition to knowing that aggregate new orders are increasing, it is helpful to know whether 55 percent of the companies in the sample are reporting higher orders or whether 95 percent are. Such information helps the analyst project the future length and strength of an expansion. It is also helpful to know past diffusion index values to determine whether a trend exists. The existence of a trend is important because it has been shown that *the diffusion indexes for a series almost always reach their peak or trough before the peak or trough in the corresponding aggregate series.* Therefore, it is possible to use the diffusion index of a series to predict the behavior of the series itself. As an example, assume that you are interested in the leading series, "New Orders—Consumer Goods." It is possible to derive an early indication of weakening in this series by observing the diffusion index. If the diffusion index goes from 85 percent to 75 percent and then to 70 percent, it indicates widespread receipt of new orders, but also indicates *weakening* in terms of the breadth of the increase and possibly an impending decline in the series itself.

Besides creating diffusion indexes for individual series, the bureau has derived such indexes for the 12 leading indicators that show the percentage of the indicators that are rising or falling during a given period.

Rates of Change   Somewhat similar to the diffusion index is the rate of change measure for the series. It is one thing to know that there has been an increase in a series, but quite another to know that it is a 10 percent increase as compared to a 7 percent increase the previous month. Like the diffusion index, the rate of change values for a series reach a peak or trough prior to the peak or trough in the aggregate series.

Direction of Change   These tables show at a glance which series went up or down (plus or minus) during the period and how long the movement in this direction has persisted.

Comparison with Previous Cycles   These tables show the movements of individual series over previous business cycles. Current movements are then compared to previous cycles for the same economic series. This comparison indicates how this series is acting in the current expansion or contraction: is it slower or faster, stronger or weaker than it was during the last cycle? This information can be useful because, typically, movements in the *initial* months of an expansion or contraction indicate the *ultimate* length and strength of the expansion or contraction.[3]

Limitations of the Indicator Approach

The NBER has consistently attempted to improve the usefulness of the indicator approach while acknowledging some very definite limitations. The most obvious limitation is "false signals"; i.e., past patterns suggest that the indicators are currently signaling a contraction, but they turn up again and nullify previous signals.

A similar problem occurs when the indicators do not point toward a definite change in direction, but experience a period of hesitancy which is difficult to interpret. These problems are likewise caused by another limitation, the *variability* of the leads and lags. While a given economic series may *on the average* lead the peak or trough in the business cycle by five or six months, the range of leads over the years may have varied from one to ten months. This variability means that the analyst is not able to act with complete confidence based upon short-run signals.

There are also problems both gathering the data (getting the original data as soon as possible) and revising it. Also, many of the series are seasonally adjusted, and there may be subsequent adjustments to the seasonal adjustment factors. Finally, the NBER points out that there are numerous political or international developments which significantly influence the economy, but which cannot be encompassed in a statistical system.

Leading Indicators and Stock Prices

Because of the relationship between leading indicators and the economy, some authors have suggested that one might be able to use leading indicators to predict stock prices. A study by Heathcotte and Apilado examined this relationship using the "1966 short list" of leading economic series and a stock price series (the S&P 500).[4] The authors derived a three-month moving average of the diffusion index and used the moving average of these diffusion indexes with different filter rules to construct an investment policy. That is, if the index increased by some specified percentage, they would buy and hold until the index declined by some percentage. The authors compared their investment results to those for a buy-and-hold policy and found that, as long as they had perfect foresight regarding the correct filters to use, they "beat" buy-and-hold. When the authors used the trading rule without foresight as to the best filter (they merely used the previous best filter), the results were very mixed.

From this, it appears that several of the leading series do lead stock prices

---

[3]All the series and analytical measures are given monthly in U.S. Department of Commerce, *Business Conditions Digest* (Washington, D.C.: U.S. Government Printing Office).

[4]Bryan Heathcotte and Vincent P. Apilado, "The Predictive Content of Some Leading Economic Indicators for Future Stock Prices," *Journal of Financial and Quantitative Analysis* 9 (1974). 247–258.

and that a diffusion index of these series could be useful if one could determine an appropriate filter. Without such foresight these series do not appear to be able to beat a buy-and-hold policy when one takes commissions into account.

Monetary Variables and Stock Prices

One of the economic factors assumed to be most closely related to stock prices is monetary policy. The best-known monetary variable in this regard is the money supply. In actuality, the influence of the money supply on stock prices is an off-shoot of its influence on the aggregate economy. Milton Friedman and Anna J. Schwartz have thoroughly documented the historical record of the empirical relationship that exists between changes in the growth rate of the stock of money and subsequent changes in aggregate economic activity.[5] Their research indicated that, during the period 1867–1960, declines in the rate of growth of the money supply preceded business contraction by an average of 20 months.[6] Expansions in the growth rate of the money supply, on average, preceded expansions in the business activity by about 8 months. The timing of the relationship was highly variable but its existence was consistent; every major contraction or expansion during the period 1867–1960 was preceded by a contraction or expansion in the growth rate of the money supply. In addition, Friedman specified the transmission mechanism through which changes in the growth rate of the money supply affect the aggregate economy, and this work led several authors to specifically examine the relationship between alternative monetary variables (typically the MI money supply) and stock prices. According to the hypothesis, when the Federal Reserve buys or sells bonds to adjust bank reserves and, eventually, the money supply, the initial impact is on the government bond market, then on corporate bonds, then on common stocks, and subsequently on the real goods market.[7] This means that the initial effect is on financial markets and only subsequently on the aggregate economy. In terms of the securities market, this would indicate that there should be a relationship between changes in the growth rate of the money supply and changes in stock prices; i.e., changes in the growth rate of the money supply should *precede* changes in the level of stock prices.

Several studies have examined the empirical evidence supporting this hypothesized relationship. Some of the earliest and most widely read research on this topic was carried out by Sprinkel who examined a six-month moving average of

[5]Milton Friedman and Anna J. Schwartz, "Money and Business Cycles," *Review of Economics and Statistics* 45 (1963): 32–78; reprinted in Milton Friedman, *The Optimum Quantity of Money and Other Essays* (Chicago: Aldine Publishing, 1969), pp. 189–235.

[6]In the Friedman-Schwartz study money supply was defined as bank demand deposits and time deposits plus currency in the hands of the public (M2). Business cycle expansions and contractions were as defined by the National Bureau of Economic Research.

[7]Leonall C. Anderson and Jerry L. Jordan, "Money in a Modern Quantity Theory Framework," Federal Reserve Bank of St. Louis, *Review* 49 (1967): 4–5.

the growth rate of the money supply and the S&P 425 stock price series for the period 1918–1963 and, subsequently, 1970.[8] Based upon a visual analysis of the two series, Sprinkel generally concluded that there was a relationship between them, but that the timing was not always consistent and the lead appeared to be getting shorter. A subsequent study by Palmer examined the relationship between the growth rate of the money supply and a moving average of percentage changes in stock prices for the period 1959–1969.[9] The author concluded that there was a consistent relationship between the two series and that changes in the money supply generally led stock price changes. Keran developed a model intended to explain the level of stock prices that included money supply growth as one of the affecting factors.[10] While the overall results were quite good and the money supply variable was statistically significant, the impact of the money supply appeared to be slight. Homa and Jaffee (H-J) employed a regression model that used the level of money supply and the rate of growth of the money supply to predict the level of stock prices.[11] The results were supportive of the hypothesis because an investment policy assuming perfect foresight regarding the money supply outperformed buy-and-hold. The investment results without foresight were mixed. Hamburger and Kochin tested the hypothesis that the money supply had a direct effect on the stock market and also considered the impact of the money supply on common stock risk.[12] They concluded that changes in the money supply have a direct effect on the level of stock prices, and that the volatility of the money supply had an impact on common stock risk.

Note that all of these studies indicated a strong relationship between money supply changes and stock prices. Beyond this, some of the studies indicated that money supply changes *preceded* stock price changes which would indicate that the money supply could be used as an indicator of stock price changes.

In contrast, there have been studies that questioned these findings in terms of the statistical techniques used and the conclusions reached. Merton Miller questioned the Keran and the Hamburger-Kochin studies on statistical grounds.[13] Pesando, likewise, discussed some potential empirical problems in the Keran, Hamburger-Kochin, and Homa-Jaffee studies.[14] After re-estimating the models

---

[8]The original work is contained in Beryl W. Sprinkel, *Money and Stock Prices* (Homewood, IL: Richard D. Irwin, 1964). An update is contained in ibid., *Money and Markets: A Monetarist View* (Homewood, IL: Richard D. Irwin, 1971).

[9]Michael Palmer, "Money Supply, Portfolio Adjustments and Stock Prices," *Financial Analysts Journal* 26 (1970): 19–22.

[10]Michael W. Keran, "Expectations, Money and the Stock Market," Federal Reserve Bank of St. Louis, *Review* 53 (1971): 16–31.

[11]Kenneth E. Homa and Dwight M. Jaffee, "The Study of Money and Common Stock Prices," *Journal of Finance* 26 (1971): 1045–1066.

[12]Michael J. Hamburger and Levis A. Kochin, "Money and Stock Prices: The Channels of Influence," *Journal of Finance* 27 (1972): 231–249.

[13]Merton H. Miller, "Discussion of Hamburger and Kochin, 'Money and Stock Prices'..," *Journal of Finance* 27 (1972): 294–298.

[14]James E. Pesando, "The Supply of Money and Common Stock Prices: Further Observations on the Econometric Evidence," *Journal of Finance* 29 (1974): 909–921.

and running them with Canadian data, Pesando concluded that, "one should not place undue confidence in the quantitative estimates of the impact of fluctuations in the money supply on common stock prices."[15]

Richard Cooper examined the relationship between money supply and stock prices in terms of the efficient market hypothesis.[16] He discussed the simple quantity theory of money concept (SQ) and the efficient market hypothesis (EM) that contends one should not be able to use past data to forecast price changes. His combined theory (SQ-EM) states that money supply may influence the market rate of return, but that because of the existence of aggressive investors who attempt to forecast important variables, market returns may actually *lead* money changes. Test results indicated a definite relationship between the money supply and stock prices, but the analysis of the lead-lag relationship indicated that the money supply appeared to *lag* stock returns by about one to three months on a relatively consistent basis. Based upon further tests, Cooper concluded that money supply changes appear to have an important effect on stock returns, but the evidence indicated that stock returns *lead* money supply changes.

A study by Auerbach likewise questioned the Keran and Homa-Jaffee findings for statistical reasons.[17] He noted that it is necessary to take account of common long-run trends and cycles in variables that are related, and demonstrated that this could have been a problem with previous studies. Auerbach removed the trend and cyclical components of the money and stock prices series and correlated the adjusted series. The results indicated that past changes in the M1 money supply were *not* related to future stock price changes, but that stock returns *were* related to current and *future* changes in the M1 money supply series, although the relationship was weak. He concluded that his results are consistent with the efficient market hypothesis which contends that historical information is not of value in predicting future stock prices.

Two studies by Rozeff also raised doubts about the usefulness of the money supply in predicting stock price changes.[18] The author re-examined the returns achieved using the trading rule reported in Sprinkel's first book, and using more realistic assumptions, derived returns below those from a buy-and-hold policy. Using regression analysis, Rozeff, found a very weak relationship when money supply led stock prices. There was an increase in explanatory power when contemporaneous money supply changes were taken into account, and there was a significant increase in the correlation when *future* money supply changes were included. These regression results were confirmed with trading-rule tests. It was

[15]Ibid., p. 921.

[16]Richard V. L. Cooper, "Efficient Capital Markets and the Quantity Theory of Money," *Journal of Finance* 29 (1974): 887–908.

[17]Robert D. Auerbach, "Money and Stock Prices," *Monthly Review,* Federal Reserve Bank of Kansas City, September-October 1976, pp. 3–11.

[18]M. S. Rozeff, "Money and Stock Prices: Market Efficiency and the Lag Effect of Monetary Policy," *Journal of Financial Economics* 1 (1974): 245–302; idem, "The Money Supply and the Stock Market," *Financial Analysts Journal* 31 (1975): pp. 18–26.

concluded that money supply changes are important, but the timing relationship indicates that stock prices *lead* the money supply.

Summary of Money Supply Studies

The early work done by Sprinkel indicated that, on average, there was a lead of money over stock prices, but the relationship was variable and the lead declined during the 1960s. This was generally confirmed in studies by Palmer, Keran, Homa-Jaffee, and Hamburger-Kochin, although Miller and Pesando questioned some of the methodology.

Studies by Cooper, Rozeff, and Auerbach contended that, with efficient capital markets, one should not expect changes in monetary growth to precede stock price changes. The recent empirical results have generally supported the efficient market hypothesis. All of these studies have basically concluded that, although there *is* a relationship between money supply growth and stock prices, it is not possible to use the relationship to derive above-average returns because the stock market *anticipates* changes in monetary growth.

Summary of Macroeconomic Analysis

This discussion of aggregate market analysis using macroeconomic variables indicates ample evidence of a strong and consistent relationship between activity in the overall economy and in the stock market. At the same time, it has been shown that stock prices consistently turn from four to nine months *before* the economy does. This means it is necessary to either forecast economic activity twelve months ahead or examine indicator series that lead the economy by more than stock prices do. The subsequent discussion examined two sets of series that possibly lead the economy by more than stock prices do, the NBER leading indicator series and money supply.

Following a description of the leading indicator approach and the specific series available, there was a discussion of a study that attempted to use the leading indicators to time investment decisions. The results indicated that, if the investigator had *perfect foresight* regarding the appropriate filter to use with a diffusion index of leading series, the investment results would clearly be superior to those achieved with a buy-and-hold policy. If the investor attempted to invest using *past* filters as a guide, the results were mixed.

There was an extensive discussion of the expected relationship between the money supply and stock prices which is an outgrowth of the quantity theory of money. Interestingly, the empirical results have changed over time. The early work indicated that money supply was important and that it could be used in making investment decisions, while contrary evidence began to appear in 1974. However, all of the studies acknowledge that *there is a significant relationship between money supply and stock prices*. Unfortunately for those looking for a mechanical trading device, recent rigorous research indicates that *monetary growth and stock prices generally turn at about the same point in time or that stock prices turn before the money supply does.* Therefore, it is *not* possible to use the monetary series to develop a mechanical trading rule that will outperform a buy-and-hold policy because the market reacts very quickly to relevant information.

Micro Analysis of The Stock Market

The determination of the future value of the aggregate stock market employing microeconomic techniques is simply the application of basic valuation theory to the aggregate stock market. Therefore, our initial discussion recalls what is involved in the derivation of a valuation model for common stocks. Given the model, it will be shown that the valuation process can be divided into two main parts. Subsequently, we will discuss how this valuation process is applied to an aggregate stock market series.

Determinants of Value

The reader will remember that in Chapter 8 we discussed the basic determinants of value for any earning asset (e.g., bonds, stock, real estate, etc.). Valuation required the analyst to estimate the following:

1. the stream of expected returns
2. the time pattern of expected returns, and
3. the required rate of return on the investment.

Given this background, we considered the application of these concepts to the valuation of bonds, preferred stock, and common stock under several different assumptions regarding the holding period and the stream of future dividends. Specifically, we assumed a one-year holding period, a multiple-year holding period, and finally an infinite holding period. In the case of the infinite holding period model, we also assumed a constant growth rate. The specific model derived from this set of assumptions was as follows:

$$V_j = \frac{D_0(1 + g)}{(1 + i)} + \frac{D_0(1 + g)^2}{(1 + i)^2} + \cdots \cdots \frac{D_0(1 + g)^n}{(1 + i)^n}$$

where:

V_j = the value of stock j

D_0 = the dividend payment in the current period

g = the constant growth rate of dividends

i = the required rate of return on stock j

n = the number of periods, which is assumed to be a perpetuity.

It was shown in the appendix to Chapter 8 that this information could be simplified to the following expression:

$$V_j = \frac{D_1}{i - g} \text{ or } P_j = \frac{D_1}{i - g}$$

where:

$$P_j = \text{the price of stock j.}$$

Given this model, the parameters to be estimated are: (1) the required rate of return (i), and (2) the expected growth rate of dividends (g). After estimating g, it is a simple matter to estimate D_1, because it is the current dividend (D_0) times $(1 + g)$.

After deriving the basic valuation model it was shown that it is possible to transform this into a pragmatic earnings multiplier model as follows:

$$\frac{P_j}{E_1} = \frac{\dfrac{D_1}{E_1}}{i - g}.$$

Thus, the P/E ratio (the earnings multiplier) is determined by:

1. the expected dividend payout ratio (D_1/E_1),
2. the required rate of return on the stock (i), and
3. the expected growth rate of dividends for the stock (g).

It was shown that the difficult parameters to estimate are i and g, or more specifically, the *spread* between i and g. It was demonstrated that very small changes in either of these can affect the spread and change the value substantially.

Two-Part Valuation Procedure

We will be using the earnings multiplier version of the model to generate an estimate of the future value for the stock market for several reasons: it is more commonly used in practice; it is the more extensive model; and once the earnings multiplier model is grasped, understanding the dividend model becomes rather straightforward. Finally, before a future dividend figure or dividend growth estimate can be derived, it is necessary to determine the growth of earnings.

The ultimate objective is to estimate the future market value for some major

Year	Earnings per Share	Percent of Change	Year-End Earnings Multiple	Percent of Change	Year-End Stock Prices	Percent of Change
1960	3.40	—	18.09	—	61.49	—
1961	3.37	− 0.9	22.49	24.4	75.72	23.11
1962	3.83	13.6	17.23	−23.4	66.0	−12.8
1963	4.24	10.7	18.69	8.5	79.25	20.1
1964	4.85	14.4	18.48	− 1.1	89.62	13.1
1965	5.50	13.4	17.90	− 3.1	98.47	9.9
1966	5.87	6.7	14.52	−18.9	85.24	−13.4
1967	5.62	− 4.3	18.70	28.8	105.11	23.3
1968	6.16	9.6	18.35	− 1.9	113.02	7.5
1969	6.13	− 0.5	16.56	− 9.8	101.49	−10.2
1970	5.41	−11.7	18.65	12.6	100.90	− 0.6
1971	5.97	10.4	18.88	1.2	112.72	11.7
1972	6.83	13.9	19.31	2.3	131.87	17.0
1973	8.89	30.9	12.28	−36.4	109.14	−17.2
1974	9.61	8.9	7.96	−35.2	76.47	−29.9
1975	8.58	−10.7	11.62	46.0	100.88	31.9
1976	10.69	24.0	11.17	− 3.9	119.46	18.4
1977	11.54	8.0	9.07	−18.8	104.71	−12.4
1978	13.08	13.3	8.20	− 9.6	107.21	2.4
1979	16.27	24.4	7.44	− 9.3	121.02	12.9
Mean	—	9.16	—	− 2.51	—	4.99
Standard Deviation	—	11.17	—	20.80	—	16.80
Coefficient of Variability	—	1.22	—	− 8.30	—	3.37

Table 10.3   Annual Changes in Corporate Earnings, the Earnings Multiplier, and Stock Prices: The S&P 400, 1960–1979

Source: *Analysts Handbook* (New York: Standard & Poor's , various issues).

stock market series, such as the DJIA or the S&P 400. This estimation process is a two-step procedure:

1. estimating the future earnings value, and
2. estimating a future earnings multiplier for the series.[19]

---

[19]In line with the efficient market hypothesis, our emphasis will be on *estimating future* values. The intent is to show the relevant variables and provide a procedural framework. The final estimate depends upon the ability of the analyst.

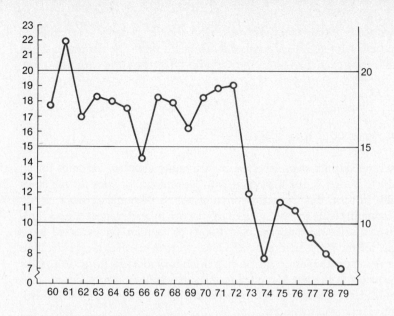

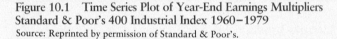

Figure 10.1   Time Series Plot of Year-End Earnings Multipliers
Standard & Poor's 400 Industrial Index 1960–1979
Source: Reprinted by permission of Standard & Poor's.

Some studies have tended to concentrate on estimating earnings for these series, but have generally ignored changes in the earnings multiplier. The implicit assumption is that the earnings multiplier is relatively constant over time, so that stock prices would generally move in line with earnings. The fallacy of such an assumption and the incomplete procedure it implies is obvious when one examines what transpired during the period since 1960, as shown in Table 10.3.

Examples would include figures for 1973 when aggregate profits *rose* by about 30 percent, while stock prices *declined* steadily by about 17 percent. Again, in 1974, earnings *increased* by about 9 percent and stock prices *dropped* by almost 30 percent. The earnings multiplier was not stable but declined drastically. The reverse occurred in 1975 when earnings *declined* by 10 percent and stock prices *rose* by over 30 percent. Clearly stock prices were mainly affected by the 46 percent increase in the multiplier.

The consistency of large changes in the multiplier can be seen from the summary figures at the bottom of Table 10.3 and from the time series plot in Figure 10.1. The mean percentage of change for the multiplier is much larger than the mean change in earnings. Therefore, we will initially consider the procedure for estimating aggregate earnings and then discuss the procedure for estimating the aggregate earnings multiplier.

We will initially attempt to derive an estimate of expected earnings for the market series for the coming year based upon the outlook for the aggregate economy and for the corporate sector. The second major step is deriving an expected earnings multiplier for the stock market series based upon the current earnings multiplier and projected changes in the variables that affect the earnings multiplier.

Estimate of Expected Earnings

There are several distinct steps involved in estimating expected earnings for an aggregate stock market series, beginning with an estimate of sales for the stock market series. In turn, this involves estimating Gross National Product (GNP) and then relating the sales for the stock market series to aggregate economic production. Given a sales estimate, the next step is to estimate the expected gross profit margin for the stock market series. This estimate involves a consideration of a number of factors that affect the profit margin for industrial firms. When this estimated gross profit margin is applied to the sales estimate it provides the estimate of gross earnings per share for the upcoming year. We conclude with an estimate of depreciation and a tax rate.

Estimating Gross National Product

Because GNP is a basic measure of aggregate economic sales, one would expect aggregate *corporate* sales to be related to GNP. Hence, an earnings projection begins with an estimate of nominal GNP which can often be obtained from one of several banks or financial services that regularly publish such estimates for public distribution.[20]

After the analyst has derived a reasonable estimate of nominal GNP from one of several public sources, the next step is to estimate corporate sales relative to aggregate economic sales (GNP).[21]

Corporate Sales Relative to GNP

To derive an estimate of earnings for an aggregate stock market series, it is best to use sales figures for such a series if they are available. Fortunately, there is a sales figure available for the S&P 400 Industrial series on a per share basis.[22] Figure 10.2 contains a scatter plot for annual GNP and S&P 400 sales for the

---

[20]This would include, "Business and Money," Harris Trust and Savings Bank, 111 West Monroe Street, Chicago, Illinois 60690, and projections by Standard & Poor's appearing late in the year in *The Outlook*.

[21]For an extended discussion of the GNP and its components, the reader is referred to any one of several macroeconomics texts.

[22]The figures are available back to 1945 in Standard & Poor's *Analysts Handbook* (New York: Standard & Poor's Corporation). The book is updated annually and some series are updated quarterly in a monthly supplement.

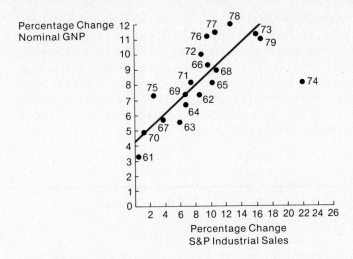

Figure 10.2   Scatter Plot of Annual Percentage
Changes in Nominal GNP and S&P Industrial Sales 1960–1979
Source: Reprinted by permission of Standard & Poor's.

period 1960–1979. The plot indicates a very close relationship between the two series, with only a few years (most notably 1974) in which the difference in percentage changes is more than 2 percent. This indicates that a large proportion of the percentage changes in S&P 400 sales can be explained by percentage changes in nominal GNP. Therefore, it is possible to derive a fairly good estimate of the percentage change in S&P 400 sales from the estimate of the percentage change in GNP. The approximate slope of the line in Figure 10.2 is 1.30 which means that, if the estimate of GNP indicates a 10 percent increase, one would expect S&P 400 sales per share to increase by approximately 13 percent.

Estimating the Gross Profit Margin

Once sales per share for the market series have been estimated, after-tax profit as a percent of sales, i.e., the net profit margin, for industrial corporations, must be estimated, which is difficult. Obviously, multiplying the sales per share figure by the net profit margin will yield an earnings-per-share estimate for the market series. While a direct estimate of the net profit margin appears easiest, it is not considered the best procedure because *the net profit margin is the most volatile of the margins.* The preferable procedure is to estimate the *gross* profit margin (i.e., income before taxes and depreciation as a percentage of sales), and then carry out a separate estimate of depreciation and the tax rate to arrive at the net income estimate.

In the next section, we will discuss the factors influencing the gross profit margin. For the time being, once you have derived an estimate of this gross profit margin, you will multiply this by the estimate of sales to derive *a dollar value of earnings before depreciation and taxes (EBDT)*. The second step is to derive a separate estimate of *aggregate depreciation* for the year. This depreciation estimate is then subtracted from the EBDT figure to arrive at earnings before taxes (EBT). Finally, you should separately estimate the expected tax rate based upon the recent trend and current government policy. The estimated tax rate applied to the earnings before tax (EBT) figure indicates the estimated taxes. Subtracting estimated taxes from the EBT figure gives the net income estimate for the coming year.

Determinants of Aggregate Gross Profit Margin

A study by Finkel and Tuttle suggested and tested the following variables as factors influencing the gross profit margin:

1. utilization rate of existing industrial capacity (proportions of capacity being used)

2. unit labor costs of production

3. the rate of inflation

4. the level of foreign competition.[23]

Utilization Rate   The relationship between the utilization rate and the profit margin is quite straightforward. If production increases as a proportion of total capacity, there is a decrease in the fixed production costs per unit of output because more units are being produced in the given plant. In addition, fixed *financial* costs per unit decline. Therefore, one should expect a *positive* relationship between the aggregate utilization rate and the aggregate profit margin. The figures in Table 10.4 indicate that capacity utilization ranged from a peak of over 91 percent in 1966 to less than 73 percent during the recession of 1975.

Unit Labor Cost   The change in unit labor costs is really a compound effect of two individual factors: (1) changes in wages per hour, and (2) changes in worker productivity (referred to as Output/Work Hours). Wage costs per hour typically increase every year by varying amounts depending upon the economic environment. The figures in Table 10.4 indicate that the annual percent of increase in wages varied from 3.4 percent to about 9.6 percent. If workers did not become more productive, this increase in per hour wage costs would be the increase in per unit labor cost. Fortunately, because of advances in technology and greater mechanization, the units of output produced by the individual laborer per hour

[23]Sidney R. Finkel and Donald L. Tuttle, "Determinants of the Aggregate Profits Margin," *Journal of Finance* 26 (1971): 1067–1075.

Year	Utilization Rate	Compensation/Work Hours[a]		Output/Work Hours[a]		Unit Labor Cost[a]	
		Index	Percentage Change	Index	Percentage Change	Index	Percentage Change
1960	80.2	74.4	4.3	81.2	2.4	91.6	1.8
1961	77.4	76.8	3.2	83.6	3.0	91.8	0.2
1962	81.6	79.9	4.0	86.6	3.6	92.2	0.4
1963	83.5	82.6	3.4	89.4	3.2	92.4	0.1
1964	85.6	86.4	4.6	92.9	3.9	93.0	0.2
1965	89.6	89.3	3.4	95.8	3.1	93.2	0.2
1966	91.1	94.7	6.0	98.2	2.5	96.5	3.5
1967	86.9	100.0	5.6	100.0	1.8	100.0	3.6
1968	87.1	107.4	7.4	103.3	3.3	103.9	3.9
1969	86.2	114.4	6.5	103.0	−0.3	111.1	6.9
1970	79.3	122.4	7.0	103.3	0.3	118.4	6.6
1971	78.4	130.4	6.5	106.8	3.4	122.1	3.1
1972	83.5	139.1	6.7	110.8	3.7	125.6	2.9
1973	87.6	149.6	7.5	113.6	2.5	131.7	4.9
1974	83.8	163.7	9.4	110.9	−2.4	147.6	12.1
1975	72.9	179.4	9.6	113.2	2.1	158.5	7.4
1976	79.5	194.0	8.1	116.9	3.3	166.0	4.7
1977	81.9	208.7	7.6	119.1	1.9	175.2	5.5
1978	84.4	226.4	8.5	118.9	−0.2	190.4	8.7
1979	85.7	248.0	9.5	117.9	−0.8	210.2	10.4

Table 10.4   Variables that Affect the Aggregate Profit Margin: Utilization Rate, Compensation, Productivity, and Unit Labor Cost: 1960–1979

Source: Federal Reserve Board Series, "Total Manufacturing," contained in *Economic Report of the President,* 1981 (Washington, D.C.: U.S. Government Printing Office).

[a]Private nonfarm business, 1967 = 100: Source: Department of Labor, Bureau of Labor Statistics.

have increased over time; the laborer has become *more productive.* If wages per hour increase by 5 percent and labor productivity increases by 5 percent, there would be *no* increase in unit labor costs because the workers would *offset* the wage increase by producing more. Therefore, the increase in *per unit labor cost* is a function of the percentage of change in hourly wages minus the increase in productivity during the period. The actual relationship is typically not this exact because of measurement problems, but it is quite close as indicated by the figures in Table 10.4. As shown, there is only one instance (1962) in which productivity increased by more than the hourly compensation did, and the result was a decline in unit labor cost. In sharp contrast, during 1974 wage rates increased by 9.4 percent, productivity actually *declined* by 2.9 percent because of the recession and, therefore, unit labor costs increased by over 12 percent. Because unit labor is the major variable cost of a firm, one would expect a *negative* relationship between the aggregate profit margin and percentage changes in unit labor cost.

Inflation   The precise effect of inflation on the aggregate profit margin is unresolved. Some observers hypothesize that there is a positive relationship between inflation and the aggregate profit margin because an increase in the level of inflation increases the ability of firms to pass increasing service costs on to the consumer and thereby increase their profit margins. In addition, if the inflation were the classical demand-pull type where excess demand causes the inflation, the increase would indicate an increase in general economic activity that would cause an increase in margins. Finally, an increase in the rate of inflation might stimulate consumption as individuals attempt to shift their holdings from financial assets to real assets.

In contrast, other observers doubt the ability of businesses to consistently raise prices in line with costs. Typically, costs increase in line with inflation, but firms are not able to pass all of them along.[24] Note that *only* if the firm can increase its prices by *more* than the inflation rate will it enjoy a higher margin. This would suggest stability or a decline in the profit margin during inflation.

In summary, the specific impact of inflation on corporate profit margins is unresolved and may depend on the *type* of inflation, i.e., demand-pull or cost-push. Also, the effect may change over time during a period of inflation such as we have experienced since 1965; during some years there will be a positive effect, but subsequently it will become negative.

Foreign Competition   The impact of foreign competition is also a topic of controversy. Some contend that foreign sales are made at lower margins, so that a reduction in export sales would cause an increase in profit margins. Others contend that it is also necessary to consider the proportion of export sales. Import sales could have a negative effect because imported goods compete with domestic goods.

Empirical Evidence on Determinants

The empirical evidence is generally consistent with the statement of expectations. There has been consistent strong support for a positive relationship between profit margins and the utilization rate, and a negative relationship between the profit margin and changes in unit labor cost. Alternatively, the results for inflation and foreign competiton have been mixed and the relationships are best described as unresolved.

---

[24]An extreme example of this inability is regulated industries that may not be able to raise prices at all until after a lengthy hearing before a regulatory agency, and even then the increase may still not match the cost increases.

Estimating Changes in Gross Profit Margin

The foregoing results indicate that the major factors to consider when attempting to determine changes in the aggregate profit margin are changes in capacity utilization and percentage changes in unit labor cost. As an obvious example, if the economy is recovering from a recession you would expect large increases in capacity utilization and likewise small increases in unit labor cost because productivity generally increases rapidly during the early stages of a recovery. Under such conditions you would estimate a major increase in the gross profit margin similar to those that occurred during previous economic recoveries. In contrast, if you were near the peak of an economic cycle, you would not expect capacity utilization to increase, and it might decline in the near future. Productivity increases would also be minimal and likewise might actually decline at the peak or slightly afterward, so unit labor cost would experience large increases. The result under these assumptions would be a definite decline in the estimated gross profit margin.

You should also be aware of changes in the rate of inflation and the foreign trade environment, but these variables should receive less emphasis because of the mixed empirical evidence concerning their effect. After estimating the gross profit margin, you can derive the dollar value of earnings before depreciation and taxes (EBDT) by applying this gross profit margin estimate to the previously estimated sales figure. The next step is to estimate aggregate depreciation.

Estimating Depreciation

As shown in Table 10.5, the depreciation series has not experienced a decline since 1960 (actually it has not declined since 1946). This is not too surprising because depreciation expense is, by definition, a fixed cost related to the total amount of fixed assets in the economy, and these fixed assets have consistently increased over time. Therefore, the relevant question for you when estimating aggregate depreciation is *not* whether it will increase or decrease, but by *how much will depreciation expense increase?* The data in Table 10.5 indicate that the average percentage of increase in depreciation expense has been about 7 percent, with most years falling in the 5 to 9 percent range. To continue with our calculations, the estimated depreciation figure is subtracted from the gross profit estimate. The result is an earnings before taxes (EBT) estimate.

Expected Tax Rate

The annual tax rates are contained in Table 10.5. The tax-rate series was steady during the initial years, declined during 1964–1967, and then returned to the 45–46 percent range in the early 1970's. In 1974, the rate increased sharply to over 50 percent and subsequently remained at that level until 1978 and 1979 when it declined again.

Estimating the future tax rate is difficult because it is heavily influenced by political action. Therefore, it is necessary to consider the current tax rate, but also to evaluate recent tax legislation affecting business firms (e.g., tax credits, etc.).

Year	Depreciation	Percentage Change	NBT[a]	Income Taxes	Tax Rate
1960	2.56	—	6.27	2.87	45.8
1961	2.66	3.9	6.17	2.80	45.4
1962	2.89	8.6	6.99	3.16	45.2
1963	3.04	5.2	7.75	3.51	45.3
1964	3.24	6.6	8.55	3.70	43.3
1965	3.52	8.6	9.64	4.14	42.9
1966	3.87	9.9	10.22	4.35	42.6
1967	4.25	9.8	9.73	4.11	42.2
1968	4.56	7.3	11.30	5.14	45.5
1969	4.87	6.8	11.27	5.14	45.6
1970	5.17	6.2	9.64	4.23	43.9
1971	5.45	5.4	10.95	4.98	45.5
1972	5.76	5.7	12.71	5.90	46.4
1973	6.25	8.5	16.48	7.59	46.1
1974	6.86	9.8	19.83	10.22	51.5
1975	7.36	7.3	17.98	9.40	52.1
1976	7.58	3.0	20.90	10.21	51.0
1977	8.52	12.4	22.69	11.15	49.1
1978	9.64	13.1	25.24	12.16	48.2
1979	10.77	11.7	30.22	13.95	46.2
Average	—	7.9	—	—	46.2

Table 10.5   Percentage Changes in Depreciation and Tax Rate for S&P Industrial Index, 1960–1979

[a]NBT = net before tax

Source: Reprinted by permission of Standard & Poor's.

Once an estimate of the tax rate is derived, we multiply the net before-tax earnings estimate by one minus the tax rate to derive the estimated net income for industrial corporations. This estimate of net income is subsequently used with an earnings multiplier to arrive at an estimate of the future value for the aggregate market.

Summary of Earnings Estimate
The major steps in the process are as follows:

1. Estimate the Nominal GNP for the coming year.

2. Estimate sales per share for the S&P 400 based upon the estimated percentage change in nominal GNP and the relationship between percentage changes in GNP and percentage changes in S&P 400 sales.

3. Estimate the gross profit margin for the S&P series, i.e., the profit margin before taxes and depreciation. This estimate would be based upon expected changes in the gross profit margin caused by changes in the basic determinants of the gross margin:

   a. changes in the capacity utilization rate during the next year

   b. percentage change in unit labor cost, which is a function of changes in hourly wages and changes in productivity

   c. changes in the rate of inflation

   d. changes in foreign trade as a percentage of GNP.

   Note: By multiplying the estimated gross profit margin by the sales per share estimate you derive the earnings before depreciation and tax (EBDT) per share.

4. Estimate the increase in aggregate depreciation expenses for the coming year based upon recent changes in capital expenditures. Subtract this estimated depreciation from the gross profit derived in step 3. The result is earnings before tax (EBT) per share.

5. Estimate the average corporate tax rate for the coming year based upon the recent tax rate and any new tax legislation. The earnings before tax per share, derived from step 4, times $(1 - T)$, where T is the estimated tax rate, indicate the earnings per share (EPS) for the S&P 400 market series.

Example of Earnings Estimate

Assume that as of November of a given year you are attempting to determine the outlook for the stock market for the coming year and need to estimate the earnings per share for a representative market series. At this point let us walk through the estimation process using hypothetical numbers.

   Based upon reading several letters from banks or business magazines (e.g., *Business Week, Fortune*) you determine that the consensus of most economists is that nominal *GNP for next year will increase about 10 percent.* You recall that the typical relationship between corporate sales and GNP is about 1.3 to 1.0 (i.e., corporate sales experience a larger percentage change than GNP does). Therefore, you estimate that *sales per share for your market series will increase by about 13 percent next year.* Based upon the results for the first nine months of this year, it looks as though sales per share for *this* year will be $300. Thus, you estimate that *sales per share for next year will be $339* (300 × 1.13).

   The gross profit margin for your market series (EBDT/Net Sales) is expected to be 14 percent *this* year on the basis of results for the first three quarters. You know that the economy is currently in the second year of a business recovery, and the general consensus is that the recovery will extend through next year. Based upon this economic outlook, you anticipate an increase in capacity utilization and further gains in worker productivity. At the same time, the rate of inflation is relatively constant and expected to remain stable. Finally, foreign trade is likewise stable. On the basis of these factors you expect a small increase in the gross profit margin for next year to *14.2 percent.* Therefore, you estimate *gross profit (EBDT) per share of $48.14* (.142 × $339).

Regarding depreciation, you expect the increase to be fairly normal, in line with prior capital expenditures; i.e., you expect an increase of 7 percent over the estimate for this year, which is $12.00 per share. Thus, you expect *depreciation per share for next year of $12.84* ($12.00 × 1.07). This indicates estimated *earnings before taxes (EBT) of $35.30* ($48.14 − $12.84).

An estimate of the expected tax rate will likewise depend upon the current figure and expectations regarding forthcoming changes. If you assume a current tax rate of 46 percent and a tendency for further cuts by the government, you might estimate that *next year's tax rate will be 45.5 percent.* This implies net *earnings per share of $19.24* ($35.30 × .545). This is the earnings figure that will subsequently be used with the earnings multiplier estimate to derive an estimate of the market value for next year.

This completes the first step in the micro estimate of the aggregate stock market value. We now turn to the second part of the process, which is estimating the earnings multiplier that is expected to prevail at the end of the period.

Estimating the Earnings Multiplier for the Aggregate Stock Market

Many analysts, when attempting to estimate the future value of the aggregate stock market, concentrate their efforts on the earnings estimate, thereby implicitly assuming that the value of the market will move with the earnings changes (i.e., that the aggregate earnings multiplier is constant over time). Reilly and Drzycimski contended that it is incorrect to assume that the multiplier is stable because there has been *more volatility* in the *earnings multiplier series* over time than in the earnings series.[25] The evidence also indicates that the multiple series turned *before* the earnings series did. Therefore, it is obviously important to consider the variables that influence the earnings multiplier and attempt to project them.

Determinants of the Market Earnings Multiplier

The factors that influence the earnings multiplier depend upon the earnings figure used. If the earnings multiplier is being applied to the true *expected* earnings figure that takes into account *all future earnings growth,* then the earnings multiplier is only a function of the required rate of return on the investment. In the more typical real-world situation, investors apply an earnings multiplier to near-

[25]Frank K. Reilly and Eugene F. Drzycimski, "Aggregate Market Earnings Multiples Over Stock Market Cycles and Business Cycles," *Mississippi Valley Journal of Business and Economics* 10 (1974–75): 14–36.

term future earnings (earnings for the following year), which means that it is necessary to adjust the earnings multiplier to take into account long-run future growth expectations. How this is done is discussed below.

Multiplier Determinants Without Growth

Assume that no growth opportunities exist or that all future growth expectations have been included in the expected earnings figure. Under these assumptions the earnings multiplier, given an infinite time horizon, becomes 1/i, where i is the total required return on the investment. The multiplier is inversely related to the required rate of return; the higher the required rate of return an investor wants, the less he will pay for current and future earnings. On several previous occasions (in Chapters 1 and 8) we discussed the factors that determine the required rate of return on an investment: (1) the economy's risk-free rate (RFR); (2) the expected rate of inflation during the period of investment (I); and (3) the risk premium (RP) for the specific investment being considered. The reader will recall that we combined the first two factors (the RFR and I) into a *nominal risk-free rate* which affects *all* investments. In turn the "real" RFR rate is influenced, for short periods, by liquidity in the capital market, but is determined in the long-run by the real growth rate of the economy.

Obviously the major factor that has caused and will continue to cause changes in the nominal RFR is changes in the rate of inflation. Because investors forgo current consumption to increase future consumption by some rate (i.e., the "real" RFR), they are looking for increases in *real* goods. Therefore, if there is a change in the rate of inflation, investors should increase their nominal rate of return by the same amount. Actually, the nominal RFR should equal:

$$\text{Nominal RFR} = (1 + \text{``Real'' RFR})(1 + I) - 1$$

As an example, if the real RFR were 3 percent and you expected the rate of inflation during your period of investment to be 8 percent, your nominal rate of return would be 11.24 percent $[(1.03)(1.08)] - 1$.[26] A good proxy for the nominal risk-free rate is the current promised yield to maturity of a government bond that has a maturity equal to your investment horizon. For example, if you had a short horizon you could use the rate on treasury bills, while you would use the long-term government bond rate if your horizon extended over several years.

The major factor causing differences in required return for alternative investments is the risk premium. In the valuation of common stocks, it is necessary to consider the "normal" risk premium for stocks and then determine whether current conditions are such that the "normal" premium should prevail. This analysis should indicate the current risk premium. Given this current premium, it is neces-

---

[26]The specific effects of inflation on stock prices have been discussed and empirically tested in Keran, "Expectations, Money and the Stock Market"; and in Daniel Seligman, "A Bad New Era for Common Stocks," *Fortune,* October 1971, 73–79. Specific tests of returns to common stockholders during periods of significant inflation are discussed in detail in Frank K. Reilly, "Companies and Common Stocks as Inflation Hedges," New York University Graduate School of Business Administration, Center for the Study of Financial Institutions, *Bulletin,* 1975–2 (April, 1975), 39–44.

sary to determine whether the risk premium will change during the subsequent period.

Regarding the "normal" risk premium for common stocks, a study by Ibbotson and Sinquefield estimated the equity risk premium as the difference in annual rates of return from common stocks and treasury bills.[27] They found that the geometric mean of this risk premium for the period 1926–1978 was 6.2 percent. Given this long-run historical estimate, it is possible to determine what the normal expected return should be by combining this premium with the nominal RFR. As an example, assume that the current yield on government bonds with the appropriate maturity is 10 percent. If you consider the current equity-market environment normal, you would estimate the current required return on common stock to be about 16 percent. Obviously, the important question is whether the expected rate of inflation or the risk premium on common stock will change during the investment horizon so as to change the required returns.

You will recall that in Chapter 1 and 8 we discussed the factors that influence the risk premium on investments from a fundamental point of view and also considered a market derived risk variable. Specifically, the intrinsic determinants of the risk premium were business risk (BR), financial risk (FR), and liquidity risk (LR). Alternatively, one can derive a market measure of risk that was shown to be the covariance of an asset with the market portfolio of risky assets. Because a stock market index is typically used as the market portfolio, *the relevant measure of market risk is the variance of returns for stocks*. Therefore, when there is a change in the variability of stock prices, one would expect a change in the risk premiums on stocks.

The required return on common stocks can therefore be stated as:

$$i_{cs} = f(RFR, I, BR, FR, LR)$$

or

$$i_{cs} = f(RFR, I, \sigma_m^2)$$

where:

i_{cs} = the required return on common stocks

RFR = the economy's risk-free rate of return

I = the expected rate of inflation

BR = aggregate corporate business risk

FR = aggregate corporate financial risk

LR = aggregate stock market liquidity risk

σ_m^2 = market risk for common stocks measured as the variance of returns.

[27]Roger G. Ibbotson and Rex A. Sinquefield, *Stocks, Bonds, Bills, and Inflation: Historical Return (1976–1978)* (Charlottesville, VA.: Financial Analysts Research Foundation 1979).

Multiple Determinants With Growth

In the more realistic situation in which the earning and dividend streams are growing, and/or investors do not fully adjust the expected earnings figure for all future growth, the earnings multiple must take into account the expected growth rate (g) for the common stock earnings stream.[28] There is a positive relationship between the earnings multiplier and the rate of growth, i.e, the higher the expected growth rate, the higher the multiple. It is important, when attempting to estimate an earnings multiplier for the aggregate market, to consider the expected rate of growth during the investment horizon period and estimate any *changes* in the rate. Such changes will indicate a change in the relationship between i and g and have a profound effect on market value.

A firm's growth rate has been shown to be a function of: (1) the proportion of earnings retained and reinvested by the firm, and (2) the rate of return earned on investments.[29] In fact, assuming an all-equity firm, it can be shown that the expected growth rate (g) is equal to the product of the retention rate expressed as a percentage (b), times the rate of return on investments (r). The multiplier should be positively related to both of these variables because an increase in either or both of them causes an increase in the growth rate and an increase in the multiplier. Therefore, the growth rate can be stated as:

$$g = f(b, r)$$

where:

g = expected growth rate

b = the expected retention rate equal to $1 - \dfrac{D}{E}$

r = the expected return on equity investments.

Because the multiplier (M) is a function of i and g, this can be summarized as:

$$M = f(RFR, I, BR, FR, LR, b, r)$$

or

$$M = f(RFR, I, \sigma_m^2, b, r)$$

---

[28]The reader will recognize that the g in the valuation model is the expected growth rate for dividends. In most of the present discussion it is assumed that there is a relatively constant dividend payout ratio (dividend/earnings), so the growth of dividends is dependent on the growth in earnings and the growth rates are approximately equal.

[29]For an excellent discussion of alternative growth models, see Ezra Solomon, *The Theory of Financial Management* (New York: Columbia University Press, 1963), pp. 55–68. A further discussion of growth models, with consideration of outside financing, is contained in Merton Miller and Franco Modigliani, "Dividend Policy, Growth, and the Valuation of Shares," *Journal of Business* 34 (1966): 411–433.

Year	Dividend per Share	Percentage Change	Retention Rate	Equity Turnover	Net Profit Margin	Return on Equity
1960	2.00	—	41.2	1.76	5.72	10.08
1961	2.07	3.5	38.6	1.71	5.66	9.67
1962	2.20	6.2	42.6	1.78	5.93	10.53
1963	2.36	7.2	44.3	1.79	6.19	11.11
1964	2.58	9.3	46.8	1.82	6.63	12.06
1965	2.82	9.3	48.7	1.85	6.82	12.64
1966	2.95	4.6	49.7	1.94	6.64	12.88
1967	2.97	0.7	47.1	1.92	6.12	11.76
1968	3.16	6.4	48.7	2.02	6.07	12.27
1969	3.25	2.8	47.0	2.10	5.65	11.86
1970	3.20	−1.5	41.8	2.09	4.92	10.28
1971	3.16	−1.2	47.1	2.14	5.04	10.80
1972	3.22	1.9	52.9	2.21	5.30	11.71
1973	3.46	7.5	61.1	2.37	5.96	14.15
1974	3.71	7.2	61.4	2.69	5.28	14.17
1975	3.72	0.1	56.6	2.61	4.63	12.11
1976	4.22	13.4	60.5	2.66	5.27	14.02
1977	4.95	17.3	57.1	2.72	5.15	14.04
1978	5.38	8.7	58.9	2.82	5.19	14.64
1979	6.02	11.9	63.0	2.96	5.57	16.48
Average:—		6.1	50.8	2.20	5.69	12.36

Table 10.6   Factors Influencing The Aggregate Growth Rate of Corporate Earnings Per Share Standard & Poor's 400 Index 1960–1979

Source: Reprinted by permission of Standard & Poor's.

Estimating Changes in the Growth Rate

When attempting to estimate changes in the growth rate, it is necessary to examine the basic factors that determine this rate. Recall that the growth rate (g) was a function of the retention rate (b), and the return on equity (r): $g = f(b,r)$. Therefore, you must first estimate changes in the aggregate retention rate. The figures in Table 10.6 indicate that this series was relatively constant in the 45–50 percent range prior to an increase in 1972–1974 that accompanied large earnings increases.

Because the valuation model is a long-run model, it is important to consider only changes that are relatively permanent, although short-run changes can affect expectations.

The second variable of interest is changes in the return on equity (r) defined as:

$$r = \frac{\text{Net Income}}{\text{Equity}}$$

This return can be broken down into components as follows:

$$\frac{\text{Net Income}}{\text{Equity}} = \frac{\text{Sales}}{\text{Equity}} \times \frac{\text{Net Income}}{\text{Sales}} = \left(\frac{\text{Equity}}{\text{Turnover}} \right) \times \left(\frac{\text{Net Profit}}{\text{Margin}} \right)$$

This identity indicates that the two factors affecting the return on equity are the *equity turnover* and the *net profit margin* on sales. A firm, or the aggregate economy, can improve its return on equity and, thereby, its growth rate by *either* increasing its equity turnover or increasing its net profit margin. The figures in Table 10.6 indicate that the aggregate return on equity for the S&P 400 Index has increased from about 10 percent to the 12–14 percent range. The increase is *completely* attributable to the increase in the equity turnover from about 1.7 to over 2.6, which more than offset the overall *decline* in the net profit margin during this period. One must ask what caused the increases in equity turnover and whether the increases can continue. To derive some understanding in this regard, it is useful to break the equity turnover into its components as follows:

$$\frac{\text{Sales}}{\text{Equity}} = \frac{\text{Sales}}{\text{Total Assets}} \times \frac{\text{Total Assets}}{\text{Equity}} = (\text{Total Asset Turnover}) \times (\text{Financial Leverage})$$

Again, this is an identity and indicates that one can increase the equity turnover by increasing the total asset turnover and/or by increasing financial leverage. The point is, it is entirely possible to have no increase in operating efficiency as shown by an increase in total asset turnover but experience an increase in equity turnover simply by increasing the proportion of total assets financed with debt. In other words, because assets must be financed by either debt or equity, if the ratio of total assets to equity increases, the proportion financed with debt must have increased.

During a period of inflation, it is possible that both of the components increase and contribute to the higher equity turnover. Total asset turnover has an upward bias, because sales will be influenced more by inflation than the book value of total assets will. Unfortunately, the data provided on the S&P 400 series does not include information on total assets so it is not possible to examine this breakdown between total asset turnover and financial leverage, but other sources indicate a secular increase in financial leverage since the 1960s.

A noteworthy point in this context is that return on equity has increased due to an increase in equity turnover. Therefore, it is important to understand the factors contributing to that increase and consequent growth.

Summary of Multiple Estimate

Such an estimate is begun with the current multiple and the direction and extent of the change is estimated based on expectations for the variables that influence the aggregate i and g. The *direction* of the change is probably more important than the extent of the change is. The overall estimate requires that an estimate be derived for each of the following component variables:

1. dividend-payout ratio defined as dividend/earnings
2. real RFR
3. expected rate of inflation
4. risk premium for common stock
5. retention rate
6. return on equity:
   a. net profit margin
   b. equity turnover.

As noted, in addition to estimating the level for each of these variables, the important thing to forecast is what *changes* will occur during the investment period. As stated previously, the crucial change is in *the size of the spread between i and g*. Note that it is possible to derive an estimate of the size of the spread as follows:

$$P = \frac{D_1}{i - g}$$

$$\frac{P}{D_1} = \frac{1}{i - g}$$

$$\frac{D_1}{P} = i - g$$

Therefore, the prevailing dividend yield (using an estimate of the dividend for next year) is an estimate of the spread. Note that this does not indicate the two factors that determine the spread (i.e., the actual value of i and g), but it tells you the approximate difference between them.

Examples of Earnings Multiple Estimates

To derive a feel for how the derivation of a market earnings multiplier works, consider the following examples. To begin, let us consider the "typical" long-run situation. The average values for the three variables (adjusted for inflation) have been as follows:

Dividends/Earnings = .55; i = .08; g = .04

Thus:

$$P/E = \frac{.55}{.08 - .04} = 13.75$$

Now let us consider the impact of inflation. During a period of inflation firms tend to *reduce* their dividend payout for several reasons. First, they recognize that their earnings are overstated owing to inventory profits, and that depreciation, which is based on historical cost, is understated. Second, firms recognize that they will need additional funds to replace assets at prices that are inflated relative to the depreciation allowance. We have already discussed at length the direct impact of inflation on the required rate of return (i). Finally, an important question is, what is the impact of inflation on the growth rate of earnings and dividends? While it is possible to show how earnings growth *could* change in line with inflation, the empirical evidence is quite convincing that U.S. business firms have *not* been able to increase the growth rate of earnings and dividends in line with higher rates of inflation. As an example, the long-run growth rate of real earnings during periods of very low inflation has been approximately 4 percent. During the 1970s, when the average rate of inflation was about 7 percent, the growth rate of earnings was only about 9 percent, not 11 percent as some might expect.

As a second example, assume a 4 percent rate of inflation which causes a decline in the dividend payout ratio. Further, as stated, an increase in i from 8 percent to 12 percent is expected.[30] Finally, assume that the growth rate of earnings and dividends increases, but only by 3 percent. Therefore:

$$\text{Dividends/Earnings} = .50; \text{ i} = .12; \text{ g} = .07$$

Thus:

$$\text{P/E} = \frac{.50}{.12 - .07} = 10.0$$

Clearly, the inflation has caused a fairly substantial decline in the earnings multiplier because investors recognize that firms are typically not able to increase the growth rate of earnings and dividends in line with increases in the rate of inflation.

Next, assume a higher rate of inflation of 10 percent. Given this rate, one might expect a further decline in the payout rate to 45 percent, and an increase in the required return to 18 percent. Again, you would probably expect an increase in the growth rate to 12 percent (i.e., the inflation rate rose by 6 percent and the growth rate by 5 percent). Thus:

$$\text{Dividend/Earnings} = .45; \text{ i} = .18; \text{ g} = .12$$

$$\text{P/E} = \frac{.45}{.18 - .12} = 7.5$$

Again, the higher rate of inflation has resulted in a further decline in the earnings multiplier. The good news is that once the multiplier has declined to this low level

---

[30]Actually the new rate would theoretically be slightly higher than this due to the multiplication of (1.08) and (1.04). For our purposes the simple addition will suffice.

due to inflation, it can experience a comparable increase when the rate of inflation declines.

Estimating The Market Value

At this point we have derived a hypothetical earnings estimate for the market ($19.24), discussed the factors that influence the earnings multiplier, and dealt with how to combine these factors to derive an actual estimate. It is now possible to combine these two estimates and compute an estimate of the future market value.

Regarding the appropriate market earnings multiplier to use, let us assume that we expect a rate of inflation of 6 percent which implies a required i of about 14 percent (i.e., an 8 percent historical real return on stocks plus the 6 percent inflation). Further, we expect the growth rate of earnings and dividends to be about 9 percent (i.e., 4 percent real growth plus a 5 percent increase due to inflation). Finally, we expect a 50 percent dividend payout. Thus:

$$\text{Dividend/Earnings} = .50; \, i = .14; \, g = .09$$

$$P/E = \frac{.50}{.14 - .09} = 10.0$$

Therefore, the expected future market value is:

Expected Earnings per Share = $19.24

Expected Earnings Multiplier =   10.0

Expected Market Value   =   192.40.

Estimating Expected Returns

Given the estimate of the future value for the market, it is possible to derive an estimate of the return you will receive from investing in stocks during the coming year. You will recall that the rate of return is defined as follows:

$$R_t = \frac{P_{t+1} - P_t + Div_t}{P_t}$$

where:

R_t = rate of return during period t

P_t = price at beginning of period t

P_{t+1} = price at end of period t

Div_t = dividend payments during period t.

If we assume that the current value of the market series is 175.00 and the expected dividend for the period is 9.50, the expected rate of return is:

$$R_t = \frac{192.40 - 175.00 + 9.50}{175.00}$$

$$= \frac{17.40 + 9.50}{175.00} = \frac{26.90}{175.00}$$

$$= .1537 = \underline{15.37\%}$$

Having derived an expected return from investing in stocks, it is necessary to determine whether this rate of return is consistent with other investment alternatives available in terms of expected return and risk. In addition, it is important to recognize that this is a single point estimate, and you may want to consider other scenarios that would provide higher and lower values and estimate the probabilities attached to each of these.

Summary

In the earlier chapters we emphasized the importance of analyzing the aggregate stock market before an industry or a company analysis. The point was made that it is very important to determine whether the market outlook justifies investing in stock at all before you consider the best industry or company. The purpose of this chapter was to present techniques that will assist you in making that decision. The techniques can be described as either macro techniques that are based upon the strong relationship between the aggregate economy and the stock market, or micro techniques that attempt to determine future market values by applying basic valuation models to the aggregate stock market.

The discussion indicated that there is a strong, consistent relationship between the behavior of the aggregate economy and that of the stock market, but also noted that the stock market generally turned before the economy did. Therefore, the macro techniques emphasized using series that likewise led the economy and possibly the stock market. We discussed the NBER leading indicator series (which includes stock prices) and a study that specifically used a composite of the leading series to predict stock prices. It was shown that the NBER Leading Indicator series could be useful if the analyst could choose an appropriate filter. Unfortunately, without this ability, the investment results were similar to those from a buy-and-hold policy.

The second macro technique considered was using the money supply to predict aggregate market behavior because extensive research has indicated that changes in the growth rate of the money supply lead the economy by several months, and the average lead appeared to be even longer than the lead of stock prices relative to the economy. In addition, theoretically, monetary changes should have an impact on financial markets. A review of the numerous empirical studies in this area indicated that these assumptions may be in error. Specifically, the earlier studies indicated a strong relationship between money supply and stock prices and indicated that money supply changes generally *led* stock prices. In contrast, more recent studies confirmed the link between money supply and stock prices, but have generally indicated that stock prices turned coincidentally with or before money supply changes, as one might expect in a world with efficient capital markets. These later results imply that money supply changes have an important impact on stock prices, but it is not possible to use the money supply in a mechanical way to predict stock price changes.

The micro technique presented involved applying the basic dividend valuation model discussed in Chapter 8 to the aggregate stock market. We discussed how to derive an estimate of earnings per share for a market series and of an earnings multiplier. Given these two components, it is possible to compute an estimate of the future value for the market and derive an expected return for common stocks during the period. It is important to recognize that the procedure generated only a "best estimate", and it is appropriate to make several estimates that reflect various possible conditions.

Following this aggregate market analysis, you are ready to make a decision as to whether to commit part of your portfolio to stocks during the forthcoming investment period. If the answer is affirmative, the next step in the analysis procedure is industry analysis, which is considered in the following chapter.

Questions

1. Why would you expect there to be a relationship between economic activity and stock price movements?

2. While at a social gathering you discuss the reason for the relationship between the economy and the stock market, but one of the listeners points out that stock prices typically turn *before* the economy does. How would you explain this phenomenon?

3. Define leading, lagging, and coincident indicators. Give an example of each and discuss why you think it is classified as such, i.e., the economic reasons for a relationship between this series and the economy.

4. Discuss a diffusion index of leading series and why you might expect it to be useful in predicting stock market movements.

5. Assuming that changes in monetary growth *should* effect stock price movements, what argument would an advocate of the efficient market hypothesis set forth regarding use of the monetary series to predict stock price changes?

6. Is it a contradiction to say that there is a strong, consistent relationship between money supply changes and stock prices and yet also say that money supply changes cannot be used to predict price movements?

7. At a social gathering you are talking to another investor who contends that the stock market will experience a substantial increase next year because it is esti-

mated that corporate earnings are going to rise by at least 12 percent. Would you agree or disagree with the investor? Why or why not?

8.   Go to the library and find at least *three sources* of *historical* information on nominal and real GNP. Attempt to find two sources that provide an *estimate* of nominal GNP for the coming year or that gave one for the previous year.

9.   Prepare a table for the last ten years showing the percentage changes each year in: (a) consumer price index (all items); (b) nominal GNP; (c) real GNP (in constant dollars); (d) the GNP deflator. Discuss what proportion of nominal growth was due to "real" growth and what part to inflation. Is the outlook for the coming year any different from that for last year? Discuss.

10. Assuming you are told that nominal GNP will increase by about 8 percent next year; using Figure 2, what would you estimate to be the "most likely" increase in corporate sales? What would be your most optimistic estimate? Most pessimistic estimate?

11. Given that you eventually want to arrive an an estimate of the *net profit margin,* why do you spend time estimating the gross margin and working down?

12. You are convinced that capacity utilization next year will decline from 91 percent to about 89 percent. What would you expect the effect of this to be on the gross profit margin? Explain your reasoning.

13. There are contrary arguments regarding the expected relationship between inflation and the aggregate profit margin. Brieflly discuss the alternative arguments.

14. There are well-regarded estimates that hourly wage rates will increase by about 6 percent next year. How does this affect your estimate of the aggregate profit margin? Is there any other information you need to use this information? What is it and why do you need it?

15. It is estimated that hourly wage rates will increase by 7 percent, and that productivity will increase by 5 percent. Approximately what would you expect to happen to unit labor cost? How would this estimate influence your estimate of the aggregate profit margin? Discuss.

16. There has generally been a strong cyclical pattern to productivity changes. Specifically, following a cyclical trough the gains in productivity are substantial, while immediately following a peak the productivity gains are very slight or in some instances productivity declines. Discuss this phenomenon and why it occurs.

17. It is stated that, "The factors that influence the earnings multiplier depends upon the earnings figure used." What is meant by this statement?

18. Assuming no growth in earnings or that the earnings figure used is long-run expected earnings, what factors influence the earnings multiplier? Discuss each of the variables and indicate *how* and *why* they influence the multiplier.

19. Assume a growing earnings stream; what additional variables besides those concerned with required return must be considered to determine changes in the earnings multiplier? Discuss each of them.

20. Assume that each of the following changes are independent and, except for

this change, all other factors remain unchanged. In each case, indicate *what* will happen to the earnings multiplier and discuss *why* it should happen.

    a. there is an increase in the return on equity

    b. there is an increase in stock price volatility

    c. the aggregate debt-equity ratio increases

    d. the overall productivity of capital increases.

21. Currently, the dividend payout (D/E) for the aggregate market is 55 percent, the required return (i) is 14 percent, and the expected growth rate for dividends (g) is 9 percent:

    a. Compute the current earnings multiplier.

    b. Assume you expect the D/E ratio to decline to 45 percent, but no other changes. What will be the P/E?

    c. Starting with the initial conditions, you expect the dividend payout to be constant, but expect the rate of inflation to increase by 3 percent while growth will increase by 2 percent. Compute the expected P/E.

    d. Starting with the initial conditions, you expect the dividend payout to be constant, but expect the rate of inflation to decline by 3 percent while growth will decline by 2 percent. Compute the expected P/E.

References

Arditti, Fred D. "Risk and the Required Return on Equity." *Journal of Finance* 22 (1967).

Auerbach, Robert D. "Money and Stock Prices." *Monthly Review,* Federal Reserve Bank of Kansas City, September–October 1976.

Bolton, A. H. *Money and Investment Profits.* Homewood, IL.: Dow Jones-Irwin, 1967.

Cooper, Richard V. L. "Efficient Capital Markets and the Quantity Theory of Money." *Journal of Finance* 29 (1974).

Finkel, Sidney R., and Tuttle, Donald L. "Determinants of the Aggregate Profit Margin." *Journal of Finance* 26 (1971).

Fisher, Lawrence. "Determinants of Risk Premiums on Corporate Bonds." *Journal of Political Economy* 67 (1959).

Fouse, William L. "Risk and Liquidity: The Keys to Stock Price Behavior." *Financial Analysts Journal* 32 (1976).

Friedman, Milton, and Schwartz Anna J. "Money and Business Cycles." *Review of Economics and Statistics* 45 (1963), supplement.

Gray, H. Peter. "Determinants of the Aggregate Profit Margin: Comment." *Journal of Finance* 31 (1976).

Hamburger, Michael J., and Kochin, Levis A. "Money and Stock Prices: The Channels of Influence." *Journal of Finance* 27 (1972).

Heathcotte, Bryan, and Apilado, Vincent P. "The Predictive Content of Some Leading Economic Indicators for Future Stock Prices." *Journal of Financial and Quantitative Analysis* 9 (1974).

Hirsch, Michael D. "Liquidity Filters: Tools for Better Performance." *Journal of Portfolio Management* 2 (1975).

Homa, Kenneth E., and Jaffee, Dwight M. "The Supply of Money and Common Stock Prices." *Journal of Finance* 26 (1971).

Keran, Michael W. "Expectations, Money and the Stock Market." Federal Reserve Bank of St. Louis, *Review* 53 (1971).

Malkiel, Burton G., and Cragg, John G. "Expectations and the Structure of Share Prices." *American Economic Review* 60 (1970).

Miller, Merton H. "Money and Stock Prices: The Channels of Influence, Discussion." *Journal of Finance* 27 (1972).

Miller, Merton, and Modigliani, Franco. "Dividend Policy, Growth, and the Valuation of Shares." *Journal of Finance* 34 (1966).

Palmer, M. "Money Supply, Portfolio Adjustments and Stock Prices." *Financial Analysts Journal* 26 (1970).

Pesando, James E. "The Supply of Money and Common Stock Prices: Further Observations on the Econometric Evidence." *Journal of Finance* 29 (1974).

Reilly, Frank K. "Companies and Common Stocks as Inflation Hedges." New York University Graduate School of Business Center for the Study of Financial Institutions, *Bulletin,* 1975-April 1975.

Rozeff, M. S. "Money and Stock Prices: Market Efficiency and the Lag Effect of Monetary Policy." *Journal of Financial Economics* 1 (1974).

Rozeff, M. S. "The Money Supply and the Stock Market." *Financial Analysts Journal* 31 (1975).

Seligman, Daniel. "A Bad New Era for Common Stocks." *Fortune,* October 1971.

Sprinkel, Beryl W. *Money and Stock Prices.* Homewood, IL.: Richard D. Irwin, 1964.

Sprinkel, Beryl W. *Money and Markets: A Monetarist View.* Homewood, IL.: Richard D. Irwin, 1971.

Zarnowitz, Victor, and Boschan, Charlotte. "Cyclical Indicators: An Evaluation and New Leading Index." *Business Conditions Digest,* May 1975.

Zarnowitz, Victor and Boschan, Charlotte. "New Composite Indexes of Coincident and Lagging Indicators." *Business Conditions Digest,* November 1975.

INDUSTRY ANALYSIS

⇉ 11 ⇇

In Chapter 8 we discussed the justification for the three-step approach to investment decision making and set forth the valuation procedure. In Chapter 10 we considered alternative techniques for estimating future values for the aggregate stock market which generated an expected rate of return for investing in equities. At this point, we assume that, based upon the earlier analysis you have decided to invest in equities. The question facing you now is: in which stocks do I invest? As noted, there are intuitive reasons for beginning this search process with industry analysis so that the most desirable industries for investment can be identified. Logically, you would then attempt to select the best companies in the most desirable industries.

In addition to the empirical evidence discussed in Chapter 8 regarding the relationship of company returns to industry returns, there have been other studies that have specifically examined the performance of different industries at a point in time or over time, and that have also examined industry risk measures. The results of these studies provide further support for the value of industry analysis and also indicate which factors should be emphasized when analyzing an industry. We will begin our discussion by considering these studies, and then discuss the factors that should be considered in industry analysis and how industries should be analyzed. That is, we will describe the procedure for determining the future return and risk for specific industries.

Previous Studies of Industry Analysis

Cross-Sectional Return Performance

Several studies have examined the performance of different industries during specific periods of time; e.g., how did different industries perform during 1982? Such studies have major implications for industry analysis because, if there is complete consistency over time for different industries, it would indicate that industry analysis is not necessary once market analysis has been completed. Assume that, during 1982, the aggregate market rose by 10 percent, and *all* industry returns were bunched between 9 and 11 percent. Under these conditions, one might ask how much it would be worth to find an industry that will return 11 percent when random selection would provide about 10 percent (the average return). In contrast, assume you were told that the distribution of returns was normal and the range was from minus 15 percent to plus 30 percent. Under these conditions, most investors would probably agree that it is worth a great deal to engage in industry analysis to identify the very successful industries. Therefore, it is important to determine whether the cross-sectional studies indicated a tight or wide distribution of returns for alternative industries.

A study of industry performance by Latané and Tuttle examined the long-run price performance of 59 industries for the years 1950 and 1958 and for the month of October, 1967.[1] The results indicated that, between 1950 and 1967, the aggregate market had increased by a factor of more than five, but that *the difference between alternative industries was substantial,* ranging from a decline for one industry (brewing) to an increase of almost 40 times (office and business equipment). They also found that the wide dispersion between industries did not decline over time even with the growth of conglomerates.

These findings were confirmed in a study done by Brigham and Pappas of rates of return for 658 industrial and utility firms during the period 1946–1965.[2] After examining the difference between industries they concluded that "an aggregate rate of return is by no means representative of all industries in the sample."[3]

Reilly and Drzycimski examined the performance of the 30 *Barron's* Industry Averages for the total period 1958–1970 and during selected subperiods.[4] The *Barron's* Industry Averages typically include from eight to ten companies within an industry and are computed in the same way as the Dow-Jones Averages. The authors concluded that there was substantial divergence in relative performance among industries during any given time period.

There is consistent empirical evidence that industries do *not* perform in the same way over a long time period or over selected shorter subperiods.[5] This would imply that *industry analysis is a very necessary part of the valuation and portfolio management process.* It is clearly worthwhile to attempt to determine the differences in performance that can be expected for various industries.

[1]Henry A. Latané and Donald L. Tuttle, "Framework for Forming Probability Beliefs," *Financial Analysts Journal* 24 (1968): 51–61.

[2]Eugene F. Brigham and James L. Pappas, "Rates of Return on Common Stock," *Journal of Business* 42 (1969): 302–316.

[3]Ibid., p. 311.

[4]Frank K. Reilly and Eugene Drzycimski, "Alternative Industry Performance and Risk," *Journal of Financial and Quantitative Analysis* 9 (1974): 423–446.

[5]Various financial services provide graphs of *annual* rates of return for alternative industries. Again, these indicate a substantial variance between industries.

Time Series Return Performance

This discussion naturally leads to our next question, whether the performance of individual industries is consistent over time. Do industries that perform well in one time period continue to perform well or at least continue to outperform the aggregate market in subsequent periods? Latané and Tuttle examined the performance of individual industries and found *almost no association in industry performance over time.*[6] These results are confirmed in the Reilly-Drzycimski study that analyzed the relative performance of alternative industries for different types of market periods and concluded that there was a *very low correlation* in industry performance over sequential rising or falling markets, or over sequential periods irrespective of market behavior.[7] Tysseland examined the performance of 40 major industries over the period 1949–1966, inclusive.[8] He found significant and positive results for short-run periods, but negative results (with few exceptions) for longer periods of time.

These studies imply that it is *not* possible to use past performance to project the future performance of an industry. Although this conclusion is consistent with the weak form efficient market hypothesis, it does *not* negate the usefulness of industry analysis. Such findings mean that it is not possible to simply extrapolate past performance, and, therefore, it is necessary to *project* future industry performance on the basis of *future estimates of* the relevant variables.

Performance Within Industries.

The final relevant question with regard to industry performance is whether there is consistency *within* an industry. Do the firms within an industry experience similar performance during a specified time period? If the distribution of returns were consistent within an industry, it would reduce the need for company analysis because, once the industry analysis was complete, one could expect all the firms in the industry to perform similarly.

A detailed discussion of 14 firms in the paper industry, done by Brigham and Pappas, indicated that there was *a wide range of returns* for alternative firms, leading the authors to state: "A further examination of the data revealed that the volatility found in the paper industry is not atypical."[9]

Tysseland also contended that there is variability *within* industries.[10] A study by Cheney examined percent of price changes for a sample of eight industries and

---

[6]Latané and Tuttle, "Framework for Forming Probability Beliefs."

[7]Reilly and Drzycimski, "Alternative Industry Performance."

[8]Milford S. Tysseland, "Further Tests of the Validity of the Industry Approach to Investment Analysis," *Journal of Financial and Quantitative Analysis* 6 (1971): 835–847.

[9]Brigham and Pappas, "Rates of Return," p. 311.

[10]Tysseland, "Further Tests," p. 840.

227 stocks.[11] He examined both growth and nongrowth industries to determine the amount of cohesion within these two types of industry. Cheney found a definite central tendency for the food industry; "some" central tendency for the building, paper, and steel industries; and no central tendency for the growth industries.

Several other studies have implicitly considered the relationship between a company and its industry by examining the relationship of returns over time for a group of stocks relative to the aggregate market and other stocks. The study by King discussed in Chapter 8 found, on average, about 52 percent of the variance of individual stocks was attributable to the market and an additional 10 percent was related to the industry component.[12] King clearly felt that there was an industry influence after taking account of the market. Gaumnitz attempted to detect the impact of the industry component on stock price movements.[13] He concluded that there was a clustering of *some* stocks along industry lines, but for the majority of stocks the clusters had little correspondence to the initial industrial classifications. Meyers looked at an expanded sample of industries over a longer period and came to conclusions similar to those reached by Gaumnitz.[14]

The studies done by Gaumnitz and Meyers indicate that there is a strong comovement for companies within some industries, but the pattern is clearly not universal. For most industries, there is not a strong relationship between returns for different companies within a given industry.

Livingston analyzed the industry effect after removing the market effect and found strong evidence of positive within-industry comovement after the market effect is removed.[15] Also, while the *average* within-industry correlation was significant, it was definitely *not* universal for all industries. Livingston suggested that *each industry be examined to determine the importance of residual industry comovement.* However, it was concluded that the results supported the concept of industry analysis and also implied that different industries should be considered when diversifying one's portfolio.

Implications of Intra-industry Dispersion

Some observers have mistakenly contended that, because there is dispersion within some industries, industry analysis is useless. However, even for the nonhomogeneous industries, industry analysis is valuable because it is much easier to select a superior company from a good industry than to find a good company in an in-

[11]Harlan L. Cheney, "The Value of Industry Forecasting as an Aid to Portfolio Management," *Appalachian Financial Review* 1 (1970): 331–339.

[12]Benjamin F. King, "Market and Industry Factors in Stock Price Behavior," *Journal of Business* 39 (1966): 139–190.

[13]Jack E. Gaumnitz, "The Influence of Industry Factors in Stock Price Movements" (Paper presented at Southern Finance Association Meeting, October, 1970). Subsequently released as University of Kansas, School of Business Working Paper no. 42 (June 1971).

[14]Stephen L. Meyers, "A Re-Examination of Market and Industry Factors in Stock Price Behavior," *Journal of Finance* (1973): 695–705.

[15]Miles Livingston, "Industry Movements of Common Stocks," *Journal of Finance* 32 (1977): 861–874.

dustry expected to experience inferior performance. It seems likely that one of the *worst* companies in a *good* industry will outperform the *better* companies in one of the *poor* industries. Therefore, after completing the industry analysis, you have a *substantially higher probability* of selecting a high-return stock. Once you have selected the best stock or stocks in an industry with good expectations, the chances are *substantially lessened* that your good company performance will be negated by poor industry performance. In addition, given the dispersion indicated by these studies, this implies that industry analysis alone will not suffice. Company analysis *is* necessary.

Analysis of Differential Industry Risk

In contrast to numerous studies on industry return performance, there have been few done on industry *risk* measures. The Reilly-Drzycimski study (R&D) referred to earlier contained an analysis of industry risk in terms of the beta coefficient.[16] The study involved two questions of interest: (1) what was the difference in risk for alternative industries during a given time period; and (2) how stable was the industry risk measure over time?

The analysis of the beta coefficients during specified time periods indicated *a wide range of systematic risk.* The systematic risk for the total period ranged from 1.426 (air transportation) to −0.002 for gold mining. The range between industries typically increased with successive rising and falling markets. An analysis of the risk measures for various subperiods indicated a *reasonably stable relationship* between them. These results agree substantially with those obtained by Blume and Levy for portfolios of stocks, which is what an industry can be considered.[17]

Therefore, regarding industry risk, there is some bad news and some good news. The bad news is that there is a substantial amount of dispersion in the risk for alternative industries, which means that this risk must be considered in analyzing industries. The good news is that there is a fair amount of stability in the risk measure over time, which means that the past risk analysis for an industry can be of some benefit in analyzing future risk.

Summary and Implications
In summary, certain conclusions and implications related to industry analysis can be drawn from the studies discussed.

1. There is fairly wide dispersion in the performance of various industries during specified time periods. This implies that it is worthwhile to engage in industry analysis to identify the good industries and the poor industries.

[16]Reilly and Drzycimski, "Alternative Industry Performance."

[17]Marshall E. Blume, "On the Assessment of Risk," *Journal of Finance* 26 (1971): 1–10; Robert A. Levy, "On the Short-Term Stationarity of Beta Coefficients," *Financial Analysts Journal* 27 (1971): 55–62.

2. There is very little consistency in absolute or relative industry performance over time. This means that it is *not* possible to simply extrapolate future behavior from past performance. Therefore, when carrying out industry analysis it is necessary to determine future performance on the basis of future expectations of earnings and the earnings multiplier.

3. There is dispersion in the performance of various companies within industries. This finding does *not* negate the value of industry analysis, but means that after you have engaged in industry analysis to determine the industries expected to enjoy above-average performance, it is necessary for you to carry out company analysis to find the better companies within the desirable industries.

4. The analysis of risk measures for alternative industries indicated that there was dispersion between industries at a given point in time, but the risk measures for individual industries were reasonably consistent over time. This implies that it is necessary to examine the risk for alternative industries to determine those that are high risk or low risk. At the same time, the consistency over time means that, once you have determined that an industry is in a specified risk class, it will probably not change dramatically on a year-to-year basis.

What Industries to Analyze?

Given that the decision has been made to carry out industry analysis, one may ask what industries should be considered? Before answering this specific question, it is important to remember that the overall goal is to find industries that promise expected returns that are equal to or exceed the required returns based upon the risk involved. As an example, an industry with risk that would require a rate of return of 14 percent, but that, based upon your analysis (to be discussed in the following sections), has an *expected* rate of return of 18 percent, is temporarily undervalued because the expected return exceeds the required return. Having found such an industry you would begin to analyze specific companies to determine the best investments within the industry. In contrast, if the industry risk indicated that you should require 15 percent, and your analysis indicated that the likely return during the period would only be 10 percent, you would conclude that this is apparently an overvalued industry and you would not become involved in analyzing companies within this industry.

Given this background regarding our overall objective, you may still be wondering how you initially determine which industries to select for analysis. Unfortunately, there is no obvious answer to this question because it depends upon the style of the investor. For example, a broad-based trust department would not preselect industries, but would simply examine *all* the major industries. Some investors attempt to uncover emerging new industries so they can evaluate the industry before the general market does. In this instance, the investor might prescreen industries on the basis of sales growth, profit margin, and return on equity. In contrast, other investors attempt to invest in industries that are currently out of favor with the intent of buying into the industry at bargain prices that over compensate for adverse behavior. In this instance the prescreening would be on the basis of low earnings multipliers relative to the overall market and/or relative to the industry's historical multiplier.

Irrespective of how one selects the industries to examine, the important task is to arrive at a valid future value and expected return for the industry relative to the industry's risk. The investor who does the best job of estimating the expected return and can relate this to the industry's risk will be in the best position to select undervalued industries. How this is done is the subject of the following section.

Estimating Industry Returns

The Overall Procedure

The procedure for estimating the expected returns for alternative industries is similar to that employed in aggregate market analysis. It is a two-step process in which the initial phase involves estimating the expected earnings per share for an industry. This is followed by an estimate of the future industry earnings multiplier.

Estimating Earnings Per Share

This involves several phases, the first of which is deriving an estimate of sales per share based upon an analysis of the relationship between sales for the given industry and aggregate sales for some relevant economic series; e.g., automobile sales are influenced by aggregate GNP or national income, but are typically more closely related to disposable personal income. Having derived a relationship of industry sales to some economic variables, the next step is to estimate the future performance of these independent variables for the next year and thereby derive an estimate of sales per share for the industry.

If this analysis is meant to generate a long-run estimate of the sales outlook rather than a one-year projection, input-output analysis should be used to indicate the long-run relationship between industries. Such an analysis indicates which other industries supply the input for the industry of interest and who gets the output. Knowing this, you can determine the long-run outlook for both suppliers and major customers. For an explanation of input-output analysis, you should read an article by Hodes.[18]

The second step is deriving an estimate of the profit margin for the industry. As before, you can consider the gross margin (EBDT, earnings before taxes and depreciation), the earnings before-tax margin (EBT), or the net margin. The gross

---

[18]D. A. Hodes, "Input-Output Analysis: An Illustrative Example," *Business Economics* 1 (1965): 35–37.

margin is preferred because it should be relatively less volatile. The depreciation and tax rate figures must then be estimated to derive a net income estimate.

An Industry Example

To demonstrate the analysis procedure, we will use the information in Standard & Poor's Composite Retail Store Index. This composite index contains information for four subindustries: (1) department stores, (2) retail stores (drugs), (3) food chains, and (4) general merchandise chains. The reader is probably familiar with a number of the companies included in these categories. The department store group includes eight companies:

Allied Stores	Associated Dry Goods
Carter Howley Hales Stores	Dayton Hudson
Federated Department Stores	R. H. Macy
Marshall Field & Co.	May Department Stores

The retail drug stores index was started in 1970 and includes:

Eckerd (Jack)

Rite Aid

Revco D. S. Incorporated

The retail food chain group includes:

American Stores	Kroger Company
Food Fair Stores	Lucky Stores
Great Atlantic and Pacific	Safeway Stores
Jewel Company	Winn-Dixie Stores

Finally, the general merchandise chains index was started in 1970 and includes;

S. S. Kresge Company	Sears, Roebuck & Company
J. C. Penney Company	F. W. Woolworth Company

Given the companies involved and the wide spectrum of stores, this industry group involves a fairly diversified portfolio.

Industry Sales Forecast

The sales forecast for the retail store industry involves an analysis of the relationship between sales for the industry and some aggregate economic series that is related to the goods and services produced by the industry. The products of the retail store industry range from a basic necessity (food) to general merchandise such as that sold by Sears, Roebuck, to an equally varied range of products sold in department stores like R. H. Macy. Therefore, the economic series should be fairly broad to reflect the demand for these products. The primary economic series considered are disposable personal income (DPI) and personal consumption expenditures (PCE). Table 11.1 contains the aggregate and the per capita values for the two series.

The scatter plot of retail sales versus the two economic series contained in Figure 11.1 indicates *a strong linear relationship between retail sales per share and these economic series*. Retail sales appear to be strongly related to either disposable personal income or personal consumption expenditures. Therefore, if one can do a good job of estimating changes in either of these series, one should derive a good estimate of expected changes in sales per share for a composite of retail stores. This close relationship with an aggregate economic series is not too surprising given the number of retail stores involved and the diverse nature of these stores, which means they would be a good reflection of aggregate retail sales. If the intent is to project sales for one of the component groups, such as food chains, it would be preferable to consider a subset of consumer expenditures, such as expenditures for nondurables. *As the industry becomes more specialized and unique, it is necessary to find a more unique economic series that reflects the demand for the industry's product.*

One might also consider *per capita* disposable personal income. Although aggregate DPI increases each year, there is also an increase in the aggregate population, so the increase in the DPI per capita (the average DPI for each adult and child) will typically be less than the increase in the aggregate series. During 1980 aggregate DPI increased about 11 percent, but per capita DPI only increased 9.9 percent. Because the per capita series may have a closer relationship to the retail sales series in some instances it should be considered. Finally, it is often useful to analyze the relationship between *changes* in the economic variable and changes in industry sales. Such an analysis will indicate how the two series move together, but will also highlight any changes in the relationship. An analysis of the past relationship between percentage changes in retail sales and in personal consumption expenditures indicates that the retail sales series has only been about 70 percent as volatile; i.e., when personal consumption expenditures increase by 10 percent, retail sales generally rise about 7 percent.

Therefore, after deriving an estimate of DPI or PCE, one can use a scatter plot similar to Figure 11.1 or apply a factor to the estimated percentage change to arrive at a sales per share estimate for the industry.

Industry Profit Margin Forecast

The next step is to estimate the industry profit margin. As before, it is best to initially consider the *gross* profit margin (earnings before taxes and depreciation), and subsequently estimate depreciation and the industry tax rate to arrive at a

Year	Composite Retail Stores (Dollars per share)	Disposable Personal Income (Billions of Dollars)	Personal Consumption Expenditures (Billions of Dollars)	Per Capita	
				Disposable Personal Income (Dollars)	Personal Consumption Expenditures (Dollars)
1960	122.65	352.0	324.9	1,947	797
1961	127.04	365.8	335.0	1,991	1,823
1962	134.34	386.8	355.2	2,073	1,904
1963	140.75	405.9	374.6	2,144	1,979
1964	147.58	440.6	400.5	2,296	2,087
1965	156.75	475.8	430.4	2,448	2,214
1966	169.68	513.7	465.1	2,613	2,366
1967	179.15	547.9	490.3	2,757	2,467
1968	198.39	593.4	536.9	2,956	2,674
1969	214.75	638.9	581.8	3,152	2,870
1970	224.38	695.3	621.7	3,393	3,034
1971	239.11	751.8	672.2	3,630	3,246
1972	263.04	810.3	737.1	3,880	3,529
1973	284.72	914.5	812.0	4,346	3,858
1974	311.56	998.3	888.1	4,710	4,190
1975	315.80	1,096.1	976.4	5,132	4,572
1976	342.01	1,194.4	1,084.3	5,550	5,038
1977	374.41	1,311.5	1,205.5	6,046	5,557
1978	397.76	1,462.9	1,348.7	6,688	6,166
1979	418.52	1,641.7	1,510.9	7,441	6,848
1980(p)[a]	452.34	1,821.7	1,670.1	8,176	7,496

Table 11.1   S&P Composite Retail Store Sales and Various Economic Series 1960–1980

[a](p) preliminary

Source: *Analysts Handbook* (New York: Standard & Poor's Corp., 1980). *Economic Report of the President* (Washington, D.C.: U.S. Government Printing Office, 1981). Reprinted by permission of Standard & Poor's.

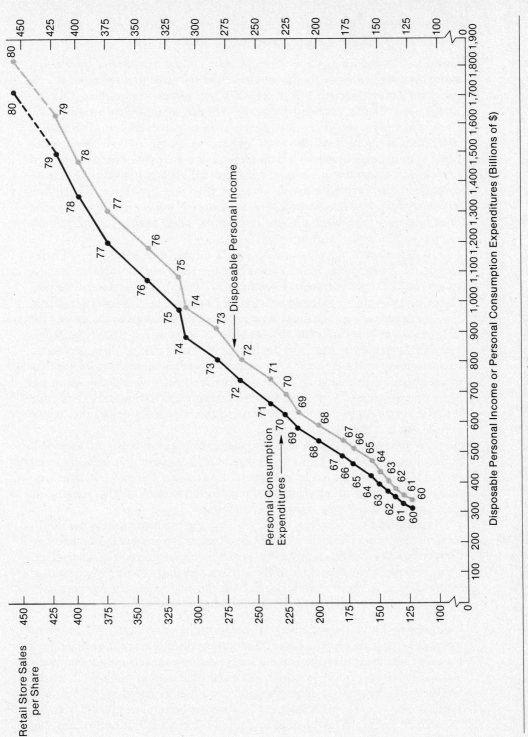

Figure 11.1   Scatter Plot of Retail Store Sales and Disposable Personal Income
and Retail Store Sales and Personal Consumption Expenditures 1960–1980

projection of net earnings per share for the industry. Therefore, the initial step involves an estimate of the gross profit margin for the industry.

Estimating the Industry's Gross Profit Margin   In the market analysis we considered specific factors that influence changes in the gross profit margin, i.e., capacity utilization, unit labor cost, inflation, and foreign competition. Unfortunately, none of these variables is typically available for individual industries. An alternative is to assume that movements in these industry variables are related to movements in similar variables for the aggregate economy. As an example, when there is an increase in capacity utilization for the aggregate economy, there is probably a comparable increase in utilization for various industries. The same could be true for unit labor cost and exports. *If there is some generally stable relationship between these variables for the industry and for the economy, one should expect a relationship to exist between the profit margin for the industry and the profit margin for the economy.*

To demonstrate, the gross profit margins for the S&P 400 Industrial Index and the S&P Composite Retail Store Index are contained in Table 11.2 and a scatter plot of the profit margins is contained in Figure 11.2. As shown in the plot, except for 1974, the relationship between the profit margins was quite consistent.

One might also consider analyzing *percentages of change* in the profit margins for each year to determine how sensitive the industry margin is to change in the aggregate profit margin. An analysis of a scatter plot of these percentage changes indicates that the retail store industry's profit margin is less volatile than the aggregate profit margin. It does not increase or decrease as much as the aggregate margin does. The plot has a slope of about .45, which would indicate that if the aggregate margin declined 10 percent, the margin for retail stores would only decline by about 4.5 percent.

Therefore, given an estimate for the aggregate gross profit margin, an analyst can use a scatter plot similar to that in Figure 11.2 to estimate an industry profit margin. Alternatively, given an estimate of a percentage change in the aggregate profit margin, he might estimate the change in the industry margin using some ratio similar to that for the historical relationship.

This analysis can be a very useful tool, but the technique should not be applied mechanically. The analyst should be aware of any unique factors affecting the specific industry, such as price wars, contract negotiations, or building plans. These "unique" events should be considered as adjustment factors when estimating the final gross profit margin, or used in estimating a range of profit margins (optimistic, pessimistic, most likely) for the industry.

Estimating Industry Depreciation   After estimating the industry's gross profit margin, the next step is to estimate the industry's depreciation. Depreciation is typically easier to estimate than other variables because the series is almost always increasing; the only question is by how much. As shown in Table 11.2, except for 1969, the depreciation series for retail stores has increased every year since 1960. During recent years, the typical increase has been rather volatile, between .10 and .20 per share. The figures in Table 11.2 indicate a strong relationship

Year	Gross Profit Margin[a]		Depreciation		NBT Margin		Tax Rate		Net Profit Margin	
	S&P 400	Composite Retail Store	S&P 400	Composite Retail Store	S&P 400	Composite Retail Store	S&P 400	Composite Retail Store	S&P 400	Composite Retail Store
1960	14.85	5.52	2.56	1.30	10.54	4.46	45.8	49.9	5.72	2.23
1961	14.84	5.57	2.66	1.38	10.37	4.48	45.4	49.4	5.66	2.27
1962	15.29	5.52	2.89	1.51	10.82	4.40	45.2	49.4	5.93	2.23
1963	15.75	5.43	3.04	1.61	11.31	4.28	45.3	47.4	6.19	2.25
1964	16.11	5.85	3.24	1.71	11.68	4.69	43.3	45.5	6.63	2.55
1965	16.31	5.96	3.52	1.83	11.95	4.79	42.9	44.6	6.82	2.65
1966	15.93	5.76	3.87	2.04	11.55	4.56	42.6	44.4	6.64	2.53
1967	15.22	5.75	4.25	2.21	10.59	4.52	42.2	44.3	6.12	2.52
1968	15.63	6.15	4.56	2.57	11.13	4.85	45.5	49.1	6.07	2.47
1969	14.87	5.92	4.87	2.52	10.38	4.75	45.6	49.1	5.65	2.42
1970	13.48	5.58	5.17	2.62	8.78	4.41	43.9	47.0	4.92	2.34
1971	13.87	5.60	5.45	2.82	9.26	4.42	45.5	45.1	5.04	2.43
1972	14.34	5.25	5.76	3.05	9.87	4.09	46.4	43.2	5.30	2.32
1973	15.23	5.43	6.25	3.24	11.04	4.30	46.1	44.0	5.96	2.41
1974	14.66	3.89	6.86	3.58	10.89	2.74	51.5	47.6	5.28	1.43
1975	13.69	5.35	7.36	3.71	9.71	4.18	52.3	46.5	4.63	2.24
1976	14.05	5.31	7.58	3.79	10.31	4.20	48.9	43.8	5.27	2.37
1977	13.94	5.48	8.52	4.38	10.13	4.31	49.1	42.5	5.15	2.48
1978	13.85	5.64	9.64	5.23	10.02	4.33	48.2	41.9	5.19	2.51
1979	14.03	5.36	10.77	5.68	10.34	4.01	46.2	38.8	5.57	2.46

Table 11.2   Profit Margins for S&P 400 Industrial Index and S&P Composite Retail Store Index 1960–1979 (in percents)

[a]Gross profit margin = Net before tax and depreciation/sales.

Source: *Analysts Handbook* (New York: Standard & Poor's Corp., 1980). Reprinted by permission of Standard & Poor's.

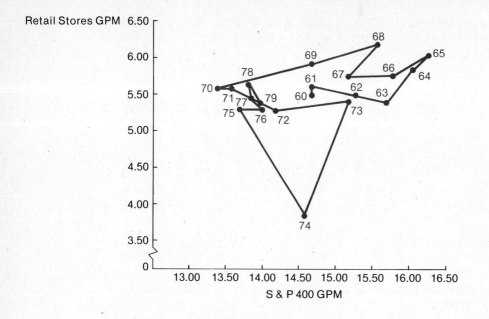

Figure 11.2   Scatter Plot of Gross Profit Margin (GPM) for S&P 400 and S&P Composite Retail Stores

Source: Reprinted by permission of Standard & Poor's.

between levels for the industry and the S&P 400, with the retail store depreciation consistently at least 50 percent of that for the aggregate stock market. This relationship holds true for the total period and for most individual years.

When the estimated depreciation is subtracted from the gross profit figure, the result is an earnings-before tax (EBT) figure. Given this figure, the final step in our analysis is estimating the tax rate for the industry and, therefore, the net income profit margin for the industry.

Estimating the Industry Tax Rate   Although different industries have different tax factors to contend with, one would generally assume that most tax changes influence all industries in a comparable manner. Therefore, one would expect a relationship to exist between changes in the aggregate tax rate and changes in the tax rate for various industries.

The composite retail store industry's tax rate has generally moved with the economy's tax rate. However, because of a few unique years, the relationship between the tax rate for the industry and that of the economy has changed. During the early years of the period in question, the industry tax rate was *above* the economy's rate and the tax rates almost always moved in the same direction. In 1971 and 1972, the economy's tax rate increased and the industry tax rate declined to *below* the economy's. The percentage of change results indicated that the industry tax rate has not been as volatile as the market rate has been. Again, given some estimate of a change in the market tax rate, you should be able to estimate a tax rate for the retail store industry.

Summary of Earnings Estimate

1. Estimate sales per share for the industry based upon the estimated change for some aggregate economic series that is related to the industry (e.g., GNP, DPI, PCE). The important task is finding an appropriate economic series.

2. Estimate the gross profit margin (GPM) for the industry based upon expected changes in the aggregate GPM for the next year. This assumes a relatively stable relationship between the profit margins for the industry and the aggregate series. This GPM multiplied by the sales per share estimate indicates the gross profit per share for the industry.

3. Estimate depreciation per share for the industry based upon the estimate of aggregate depreciation and the industry's relationship to the aggregate market's depreciation. You can determine the relationship on the basis of absolute levels or percentage changes. The gross profit figure minus this estimate of depreciation expense indicates net income before taxes.

4. Estimate the industry tax rate based upon the estimate of the aggregate market tax rate and its relationship to your industry's tax rate. Analysis of historical data should indicate the form of the relationship. The net income before tax estimate multiplied by one minus the estimated tax rate provides an estimate of the net income per share for this industry.

An important point related to all of these estimates is that they are generally based upon a historical relationship *that may require adjustment for near-term changes or events*. It is crucial that you make these adjustments. Put another way, the accuracy of your estimate will probably depend upon how good the adjustments are. The superior investor is the one who makes the best adjustments reflecting the unique events in the forthcoming period.

At this point, you have derived an estimate of the industry's net income per share. The next step is to estimate the earnings multiplier for this industry in the period ahead.

Industry Earnings Multiplier

There are two approaches to estimating a multiplier for an industry. One is similar to the technique used for estimating the market multiplier, i.e., examining the specific variables that influence the earnings multiplier—the dividend payout ratio, the required rate of return (i), and the expected growth rate of earnings and dividends (g). This technique will be referred to as the *micro* approach. On the other hand, one can conceive of a *macro* approach in which the relationship between the industry multiplier and the aggregate market multiplier is analyzed.

Macro Analysis of Industry Multiples

The macro approach is based on the assumption that several of the major variables influencing the industry multiple are related to similar variables for the aggregate market. It is hypothesized that there is a relationship between changes in i and g for specific industries and comparable changes in i and g for the aggregate market. If these relevant variables are related in their movements (even though they are not the same values), then there will be a relationship between *changes* in the industry multiple and *changes* in the market multiple.

A study by Reilly and Zeller contained an extensive analysis of the relationship between the P/E ratios for 71 Standard & Poor's industries and the P/E for the S&P 400 Index during the period 1946–1971.[19] The study examined both levels and percentages of change. The results indicated that there was a significant positive relationship for the majority of the industries. At the same time, the results were not universal which led the authors to state that it is necessary to examine the quality of the relationship between the industry multiplier and the market multiplier before using this technique to estimate the industry multiplier.

The multiplier figures for the Composite Retail Store industry and the market are contained in Table 11.3. An analysis of the figures over time indicates a reasonably close relationship, but the form of the relationship appears to change somewhat over time. Therefore, you would probably consider using this technique but recognize that it would be necessary to consider the micro approach and analyze the multiplier on the basis of the variables that determine it.

Micro Analysis of Industry Multiplier

The micro analysis involves the three major variables affecting the earnings multiplier and compares the industry values to the comparable market values to determine how the industry multiplier should relate to the market multiplier—should it be above, below, or about equal to the market's multiplier during the next period. Initially, one should examine the long-run relationship between the industry and market multipliers and then look for factors that would cause differences over time.

Industry vs. Market Multiplier

The mean of the high and low multiplier for the aggregate market and for the composite retail store industry is contained in Table 11.3. The figures indicate that the multiple for retail stores has almost always been above the aggregate market multiplier. The only exceptions were during 1960, 1967, and 1971. This observation is also supported by the average multipliers for the period (15.02 for the market compared to 16.99 for the composite store index). *Why do the multipliers differ over time?* Why are investors consistently willing to pay more for a

---

[19]Frank K. Reilly and Thomas Zeller, "An Analysis of Relative Industry Price-Earnings Ratios," *The Financial Review* 1974, pp. 17–33.

Year	Mean Earnings Multiplier		Retention Rate		Return on Equity		Equity Turnover		Net Profit Margin	
	S&P 400	Composite Retail Store	S&P 400	Composite Retail Store	S&P 400	Composite Retail Store	S&P 400	Composite Retail Store	S&P 400	Composite Retail Store
1960	17.70	17.47	41.2	41.2	10.08	9.18	1.76	4.11	5.72	2.23
1961	20.41	21.21	38.6	43.1	9.67	9.46	1.71	4.17	5.66	2.27
1962	16.98	19.82	42.6	40.8	10.53	9.55	1.78	4.29	5.93	2.23
1963	17.07	19.67	44.3	43.2	11.11	9.45	1.79	4.20	6.19	2.25
1964	17.63	20.89	46.8	49.3	12.06	11.18	1.82	4.38	6.63	2.55
1965	16.82	22.05	48.7	50.0	12.64	11.74	1.85	4.42	6.82	2.65
1966	15.20	17.37	49.7	48.6	12.88	11.66	1.94	4.60	6.64	2.53
1967	17.04	16.21	47.1	50.1	11.76	11.13	1.92	4.42	6.12	2.52
1968	17.30	18.66	48.7	51.8	12.27	10.98	2.02	4.44	6.07	2.47
1969	17.46	19.23	47.0	52.8	11.86	11.96	2.10	4.95	5.65	2.42
1970	16.49	17.72	41.8	52.6	10.28	11.33	2.09	4.84	4.92	2.34
1971	18.02	16.66	47.1	54.8	10.80	11.61	2.14	4.79	5.04	2.43
1972	17.95	24.11	52.9	57.3	11.71	11.39	2.21	4.90	5.30	2.32
1973	13.38	19.24	61.1	61.2	14.15	12.11	2.37	5.03	5.96	2.41
1974	9.43	20.63	61.4	38.3	14.17	7.75	2.69	5.40	5.28	1.43
1975	10.79	12.83	56.6	62.0	12.11	11.72	2.61	5.24	4.63	2.24
1976	10.41	13.38	60.5	66.3	14.02	12.45	2.66	5.25	5.27	2.37
1977	9.49	10.50	57.1	63.8	14.04	13.06	2.72	5.28	5.15	2.48
1978	8.19	8.21	58.9	61.4	14.64	13.18	2.82	5.24	5.19	2.51
1979	7.12	7.49	63.0	60.0	16.48	12.84	2.96	5.23	5.57	2.46
Mean[a]	15.02	16.99	50.2	53.2	12.27	11.37	2.17	4.72	5.71	2.40

Table 11.3   Earnings Multiplier for the S&P 400 Index and the Composite Retail Store Index with Variables that Influence the Earnings Multiplier 1960–1979

[a]1974 not included

Source: Reprinted by permission of Standard & Poor's.

dollar of earnings from retail stores than they are for a dollar of earnings from the aggregate market? An analysis of the factors that determine the earnings multiplier should indicate the cause for this difference.

Dividend Payout   As shown in Table 11.3, the retention rates have typically been quite similar, usually within 2 percentage points of each other. On balance, the payout for the S&P 400 has been slightly higher, 49.8 percent for the aggregate market and 46.8 percent for the composite retail store index. This small differential would not be a major factor in explaining the difference in the multiplier. Still, the difference that does exist would indicate a higher multiplier for the S&P 400 series.

Required Return   The required rate of return on *all* investments is influenced by the risk-free rate and the inflation rate, so the *differentiating factor is the risk premium*. The difference in the required return on the aggregate stock market, and the required return for composite retail stores is caused by a difference in the risk premium for the two indexes. The risk premium can be considered a function of business risk (BR), financial risk (FR), and liquidity risk (LR). Alternatively, according to the Capital Asset Pricing Model (which we will discuss in detail in Chapter 21), the risk premium is a function of the systematic risk of the asset, i.e., its covariance with the market portfolio of risky assets. Therefore, you could either measure the BR, FR, and LR for the industry and compare these directly to comparable variables for the aggregate market, or compute the systematic risk for the industry and determine whether it is above or below unity.

The business risk for the retail store industry is clearly below average. Business risk is typically considered to be a function of relative sales volatility and operating leverage. Analysis of the percentage of change in retail sales compared to aggregate sales indicated that industry sales were only about 70 percent as volatile as overall economy sales were. Analysis of the gross profit margin likewise indicated that the GPM for retail stores was also much less volatile than the aggregate market GPM was. Therefore, because both sales and the GPM were less volatile, operating profits can also be assumed to be substantially less volatile and *business risk for the retail store industry is below average*. The financial risk for this industry is fairly high because leases on buildings are extensive. If one considers the capitalized leases, the firms in this industry generally have *average financial risk*.

Based upon an analysis of liquidity ratios for a number of companies in the retail store industry, there is substantial variation among the firms. Specifically, they range from Safeway and Sears, Roebuck, which are *very* liquid, to American Stores, quite illiquid.[20] Generally, most of the stocks are slightly below average in liquidity. Therefore, retail stores probably have *slightly above-average liquidity risk*.

[20]Amivest Corporation, *The Liquidity Report* 10 (1980).

In summary, business risk is definitely below average, financial risk is average, and liquidity risk is slightly above average for retail stores. Assuming that business risk is the most significant variable, the consensus is that the *overall risk for retail stores is slightly below average* on the basis of internal characteristics.

The systematic risk for the composite retail store industry is computed using the market model which relates monthly rates of return for the industry index to the rates of return for a composite stock market series (i.e., the S&P 500 Index). To derive an estimate in the current case, this model was run with monthly data for the five-year period 1976–1980. The results likewise indicated that the systematic risk (beta) for the retail stores industry was below average (i.e., equal to 0.97).

These results are consistent with the micro analysis of business risk, financial risk, and liquidity risk. However, results using the two methods are not always consistent, which means that you must decide which estimate to employ, the fundamental estimate or the market estimate. The author prefers the fundamental estimate which is based upon intrinsic factors, especially if the internal risk factors are consistent. In the current instance, both estimates indicate below-average risk which would suggest that the required rate of return for the retail store industry should be below the market rate of return. All else remaining the same, this would imply an earnings multiplier for this industry that is *above* the market earnings multiplier.

Following this analysis of the risk characteristics of the industry, the next step is estimating the expected growth rate of earnings and dividends (i.e., estimating g). As before, although g is theoretically the expected growth rate of dividends, we typically assume that the payout ratio is relatively stable, and so we concentrate on estimating the growth rate of earnings and assume that earnings and dividends grow at approximately the same rate.

Expected Growth

The prime determinants of earnings growth are the retention rate and the return on equity investments; i.e., how much is put back into investments and what is the return on these investments:

$$g = f(\text{retention rate; return on equity})$$

Return on equity can be broken down into equity turnover and net profit margin as follows:

$$\text{Net Income/Equity} = \frac{\text{Sales}}{\text{Equity}} \times \frac{\text{Net Income}}{\text{Sales}}$$

Therefore, it is necessary to examine each of these variables to determine whether there is any factor that would imply a difference in expected growth for the composite retail trade as compared to expected growth for the aggregate market. The data for the series involved are contained in Table 11.3.

Retention Rate   The retention rate is simply one minus the payout rate discussed earlier. The two series were quite similar, with the S&P 400 series having a slightly higher payout rate, which means that the composite retail store industry has a slightly higher retention rate (53.2 percent versus 50.2 percent). The small difference indicates a higher growth rate for the composite retail store industry.

Return on Equity   Because return on equity is a function of the equity turnover and the profit margin, these two variables are examined individually.

A comparison of the equity turnover indicates that both series experienced a substantial increase over time and that the Retail Store series has consistently been higher. The S&P 400 series turnover increased from 1.76 in 1960 to 2.96 in 1979, a 68 percent increase. Concurrently, the Retail industry turnover went from 4.11 to 5.23, a 27 percent increase. The average for the period was 2.17 for the S&P 400 versus 4.72 for the composite Retail Store series. Therefore, *the average equity turnover for the Retail industry was more than double that for the aggregate market.*

A comparison of the net profit margin tells a different story. *The profit margin for the S&P 400 was consistently higher than the margin for the CRS industry, typically more than double.* Both series were relatively stable during the total period; the S&P 400 series declined a little, while the composite Retail series increased slightly. The higher profit margin for the market offset the higher turnover in the Retail industry. This is a prime example of what can be done to generate high returns on investment. One can either have a low turnover but a high profit margin, or accept a lower profit margin but have rapid turnover of equity.

Combining the two factors, the return on equity for the two groups is reasonably close, with the S&P 400 being higher for almost every individual year and on average (12.27 percent versus 11.37 percent). These average percentages are quite consistent with what would be derived from multiplying the components as follows:

$$\text{Equity Turnover} \times \text{Profit Margin} = \text{Return on Equity}$$
$$\text{S\&P 400: } 2.17 \times 5.71 = 12.39$$
$$\text{Composite Retail Stores: } 4.72 \times 2.40 = 11.33$$

Estimating Growth   The growth rate is a function of the retention rate times the return on equity. The Retail industry has a slightly higher retention rate (53.2 vs. 50.2), while the S&P 400 has a slightly higher return on equity (12.27 vs. 11.37). When these are combined, the estimated long-run growth rate is as follows:

$$\text{S\&P 400: } 50.2 \times 12.27 = 6.16 \text{ percent}$$
$$\text{CRS: } 53.2 \times 11.37 = 6.05 \text{ percent}$$

Clearly, *the expected growth rates for the two series based upon the historical values are almost identical.* Therefore, the difference in past earnings multipliers probably cannot be explained on the basis of a difference in the growth rates.

Why the Difference?

Based upon the dividend growth model, it was noted that the earnings multiplier was a function of (1) the dividend payout ratio, (2) the required rate of return, and (3) the expected growth rate. Any differences in earning multipliers should likewise be explained in terms of differences in one or several of these variables.

Our initial analysis indicated that the earnings multiplier for the combined retail store industry was consistently higher than the multiplier for the S&P 400. The question then became: why should the CRS industry have this premium in terms of its multiplier? There was almost no difference in the payout ratio for the two series. The analysis of risk in terms of internal characteristics and a market measure of risk concluded that the best estimate was that the industry risk was slightly lower than the market risk.

Finally, an analysis of the growth characteristics of the two series indicated very significant differences in equity turnover and profit margin, but relatively similar return on equity figures. When the return on equity figures were combined with offsetting retention rates, the implied growth rates were almost identical.

In summary, the historical record indicated that the multiplier for the retail store industry was above the market multiplier. The analysis of the individual determinants of the multiplier indicated that the payout and growth rates have been almost identical, while the retail industry risk is slightly lower. Therefore, it appears that the risk differential explains the difference in the multiplier.

Estimating the Future

The purpose of our discussion up to this point was to demonstrate a technique and to indicate the relationships that should exist between an industry and the market so that you will be aware of the variables that are important to the analysis. At the same time, it should never be forgotten that *the past alone is of little value in projecting the future* because past relationships may not hold in the future, *especially in the short-run.* When you are attempting to *project* the earnings multiplier for an industry, it is necessary to have an estimate of the market multiplier and then to determine whether the industry multiplier will be above or below the market multiplier based upon estimates of the expected relevant variables. Our previous discussion indicated the relevant variables to consider and how these variables are related to each other and to the multiplier. You must determine the future values for these relevant variables based upon your unique knowledge of the industry. The investor who does a better job of estimating the payout, risk, and growth for the industry will derive a better estimate of the industry earnings multiplier relative to the market multiplier and a better estimate of returns for the industry.

Summary of Industry Multiplier Estimate

This said, let us briefly review the steps involved in estimating the industry multiplier.

1. Examine the historical relationship between the industry earnings multiplier and the aggregate stock market multiplier. Your analysis should consider the relationship between the level of the multiplier and also percentage changes in the multiplier over time. Important questions include whether the industry multiplier is above or below the market multiplier and whether the relationship between changes is stable.

2. Examine the components of the multiplier (i.e., dividend payout, risk, and growth rate). In each instance compare the industry figure to the aggregate market figure. Risk should be analyzed in terms of internal characteristics and also on the basis of market-determined risk (i.e., beta). Ideally, your analysis of the components of the industry multiplier relative to the market multiplier will be consistent and explain the historical difference in the multiplier.

3. Based upon the previous estimate of the aggregate market multiplier and your estimate of any changes in the industry components, you should be able to estimate the industry multiplier.

The Total Estimate

Assume that you have derived an estimate of the earnings per share for the industry. The earnings estimate combined with this earnings multiplier estimate provides an estimate of the future value for the industry index. Deriving an expected return for this industry during the investment period is simply a matter of combining the expected price change (i.e., the future value minus the current value) and the estimated dividend over the current price as follows:

$$E(R_{i,t}) = \frac{P_{i,t+1} - P_{i,t} + Div_{i,t}}{P_{i,t}}$$

where:

$E(R_{i,t})$ = expected return for industry i during period t

$P_{i,t+1}$ = expected price of the industry i index at the end of the investment horizon

$P_{i,t}$ = current price of the industry i index

$Div_{i,t}$ = expected dividend for industry i during the investment horizon period t.

As an example, assume that currently the index value for your industry is 110. Based upon your analysis, you derive an expected earnings value of $13.00

and an expected earnings multiplier of 9.5. This implies a future index value of 123.50. In addition, if you expect a dividend of $6.00 per share, your expected return would be

$$E(R_{i,t}) = \frac{123.50 - 110.00 + 6.00}{110.00}$$

$$= \frac{13.50 + 6.00}{110.00}$$

$$= \frac{19.50}{110.00}$$

$$= 17.72\%$$

Finally, it is necessary to determine whether this expected return is consistent with the risk involved.

Summary

This chapter had two major parts. In the first, a number of studies dealing with cross-sectional industry performance and risk and time series measures of industry performance were discussed. The studies generally showed that there was a wide dispersion in the performance of alternative industries during specified time periods which implies that industry analysis would be of value. It was also shown that the performance of specific industries over time was *not* consistent, which means past performance is not of value in projecting future performance. In addition, performance within industries is not very consistent for many industries, which means that individual companies must be analyzed after an industry analysis is done. The analysis of industry *risk* indicated wide dispersion between industries, but a fair amount of consistency over time for individual industries. This implies that risk analysis is important, but also that past values may be of some use.

The second section discussed the procedure for analyzing an industry using the dividend growth model. This procedure involves estimating sales based upon the relationship of the industry to some economic variables. Then the net profit margin was derived based upon an estimate of the gross profit margin, depreciation, and the industry tax rate. The second half of the procedure involves estimating the earnings multiplier for the industry using either a macro or micro approach.

Because of the dispersion of industry performance and its volatility over time, it seems clear that industry analysis is both necessary and can be very lucrative. The point is, an investor must estimate the relevant variables. As always, the superior investor will be the one who does the best job of *estimating* based upon knowledge of the industry and insights regarding relevant information.

Questions

1. Several studies have examined differences in the performance of alternative industries over specific time periods. Briefly describe the results of these studies and discuss their implications for industry analysis.

2. A number of studies have considered the time series of industry performance. Briefly describe the empirical results of these studies and discuss their implications for those who are involved in industry analysis. Do they make industry analysis easier or harder?

3. Assuming you are told that all the firms in a particular industry have consistently experienced rates of return *very similar* to the results for the aggregate industry, what does this imply regarding the importance of industry analysis for this industry? What does it imply regarding the importance of individual company analysis for this industry? Discuss.

4. Some authors contend that, because there is a great deal of dispersion in the performance of different firms in an industry, industry analysis is of little value. Would you agree or disagree with this contention? Why?

5. Would you expect there to be a difference in the industry influence for companies in different industries? What is the empirical evidence on this question? Describe it briefly.

6. There has been an analysis of the difference in the risk for alternative industries during a specified time period. Describe the results of this analysis briefly and discuss their implications for the practice of industry analysis.

7. Select three industries from the S&P *Analyst's Handbook* with different characteristics in terms of demand and indicate what economic time series you would use in the analysis of the sales growth for each industry. What is the source of the economic time series? *Why* is this economic series relevant for this industry?

8. Do a scatter plot of industry sales and economic values over the last ten years using information available in the *Analyst's Handbook* for one of the three industries selected in Question 7. Discuss the results of the scatter plot; do you think the economic series was very closely related to industry sales?

9. Why is it contended that one should expect a relationship between the profit margin for a given industry and the aggregate profit margin?

10. Prepare a scatter plot of the profit margin for a selected industry and the profit margin for the S&P 400 Index for the most recent ten years. How close is the relationship? What factors would make this industry's margin different?

11. Prepare a time series plot of the annual mean price-earnings ratio (highest ratio + lowest ratio/2) for your industry and the S&P 400 for the most recent ten years available. Has the relationship between the two series been consistent over time?

12. Prepare a table that contains the relevant variables that influence the earnings multiplier for your industry and the S&P 400 series for the most recent ten years.

a. Does the average payout differ and how should this influence the difference between the multipliers?

b. Would you expect the systematic risk for this industry to differ from that for the market? In what direction and why? What effect will this have on the industry multiplier relative to the market multiplier?

c. Analyze the different components of growth (retention rate, equity turnover, and profit margin) for your industry and the S&P 400 during the most recent ten years and discuss each of the components. On the basis of this discussion, would you expect the growth rate for your industry to be above or below the growth rate for the S&P 400? How would this difference affect the difference between the multipliers?

d. Given the conclusions reached in a, b, and c above, is the difference in the industry multiplier found in Question 11 logical and justified?

References

Brigham, Eugene F., and Pappas, James L. "Rates of Return on Common Stock." *Journal of Business* 42 (1969).

Cheney, Harlan L. "The Value of Industry Forecasting as an Aid to Portfolio Management." *Appalachian Financial Review* 1 (1970).

Gaumnitz, Jack E. "The Influence of Industry Factors in Stock Price Movements." Paper presented at Southern Finance Association Meeting, October 1970. Subsequently released as University of Kansas, School of Business Working Paper, no. 42. June 1971.

King, Benjamin F. "Market and Industry Factors in Stock Price Behavior." *Journal of Business* 39 (1966).

Latané, Henry A., and Tuttle, Donald L. "Framework for Forming Probability Beliefs." *Financial Analysts Journal* 24 (1968).

Livingston, Miles, "Industry Movements of Common Stocks," *Journal of Finance* 32 (1977).

Meyers, Stephen L. "A Re-Examination of Market and Industry Factors in Stock Price Behavior," *Journal of Finance* 28 (1973).

Reilly, Frank K., and Drzycimski, Eugene. "Alternative Industry Performance and Risk." *Journal of Financial and Quantitative Analysis* 9 (1974).

Reilly, Frank K., and Zeller, Thomas. "An Analysis of Relative Industry Price-Earnings Ratios." *The Financial Review,* (1974).

Tysseland, Milford S. "Further Tests of the Validity of the Industry Approach to Investment Analysis." *Journal of Financial and Quantitative Analysis* 6 (1971).

Jerome Wenger

When most investors contemplate investing in stocks they probably think about stocks like McDonald's, IBM, Polaroid, and Xerox. Given the current status of these stocks, it is hard to realize that at one time these stocks sold for just a few dollars a share and were even somewhat speculative. We all dream about buying a stock like IBM or Xerox for a few dollars a share and selling it several years later for much more after it has split several times. The returns for such an investment are enormous. A lot of investors are interested in learning about low-priced stocks that might have the potential of an IBM or Xerox. The problem is that typically very little information is available on such stocks. Jerome Wenger was intrigued by this problem and initiated a publication, The Penny Stock Newsletter, to help alleviate this obstacle.

Wenger, who is 35 years old, has been a stock enthusiast since he was in his teens and bought large blue-chip stocks. More recently he acquired a low-priced stock which did very poorly; when he attempted to find out why, he discovered he could not get any information on the stock or the company. At that point he realized there was a need for a publication that would concentrate on such stocks, and he founded The Penny Stock Newsletter (PSN). Jerry produced the first issue single handedly from the basement of his home. A few issues later he hired his first employee. By the first anniversary of the publication in July 1981, a staff of ten published the 32-page tabloid in Columbia, Maryland, and the newsletter was being read by 75,000 nationwide.

The bi-weekly publication contains several general columns on the economy and the stock market, but the clear emphasis is on discussions of stocks currently selling for under $5 a share. A feature called "Penny

Stocks of Yesterday" describes what has happened to successful low-priced stocks. One example highlighted was MGIC Investment Corp. which is currently listed on the NYSE. It sold for $1.70 a share in 1966 and subsequently split in 1968, 1971, and 1972. As of August 1981, the 100 shares that had cost $170 in 1966 were 1800 shares worth $66,600. Similarly, Automatic Data Processing, Inc. is currently listed on the NYSE. It sold for 40¢ a share in 1965 and subsequently had stock splits in 1966, 1970, 1976, and 1981. The 100 shares that had cost $40 in 1965 were 3,600 shares as of July 1981 and were worth $108,000. (The newsletter points out that not all penny stocks become success stories.) Besides columns, the newsletter also includes extensive advertising by brokers that serve this low-priced stock market and by companies that want to reach interested investors. Finally the publication has a calendar of new stock issues forthcoming and a presentation or recap of the aftermarket for previous new stock issues.

The Penny Stock Newsletter is Wenger's first publishing endeavor, but its success is representative of his marketing experience. He was a senior sales executive with Polaroid Corporation for seven years. Before that he was a sales representative for James H. Mathews Co., where he helped develop the universal product code. Wenger, who holds a B.S. in business administration from the University of Alabama, was also assistant controller for the Container Corporation. In addition to his publishing duties, he writes a weekly column on penny stocks for Hearst Publications, hosts a radio program, and has contributed to several books on the stock market.

COMPANY ANALYSIS

≫ 12 ≪

At this point it is assumed that you have made two decisions. First, after an extensive analysis of the economy and aggregate stock market, you have decided that some portion of your portfolio should be in common stocks. Second, after an extensive analysis of a number of industries, you determined that certain industries will experience above-average risk-adjusted performance over the relevant investment horizon. The question you now face is, *which companies within these desirable industries are best?* In this chapter we will discuss the procedure for analyzing all the companies in an industry. Although in the discussion we will only consider one firm, *the same procedure should be applied for all firms in the industry to derive a ranking of firms.* Our ultimate objective is to select the best firms in the better industries and invest in them. But before we discuss company analysis, we must consider the differences between companies and types of stocks.

Types of Companies and Types of Stock[1]

The designation (e.g., growth company, speculative company, etc.) given a company is principally determined *internally* by the investment decisions of the firm (what assets they own) and by the operating and financial philosophy of the firm's management. When a company invests in assets (whether human or physical), it thereby determines its characteristics and accepts the accompanying risks and opportunities. At the same time, two different sets of management personnel can obtain substantially different results with the same set of assets. Management's operating and financial decisions can influence not only the expected flow of

[1]The discussion of this section draws heavily on Frank K. Reilly, "A Differentiation Between Types of Companies and Types of Stock," *Mississippi Valley Journal of Business and Economics* 7 (1971): 35–43.

earnings, but also the *risk* inherent in it. Therefore, it is necessary to consider the assets of the firm, what the corporate management is capable of doing with these assets, and what they intend to do with them. Finally, these company factors should be compared to similar factors for all other companies to determine the firm's *relative* position in the universe of all companies.

However, the stock of the company does not necessarily have the same characteristics as the company. The type of stock is determined *externally,* by how investors perceive the expected performance of the firm and how they adjust stock prices to account for these perceptions. Therefore, the type of stock is determined by comparing the expected return and the uncertainty of the returns for a particular stock to these same measures for all other available stocks. Consequently, there can be differences between the designation given a particular company and the designation given the stock that company issued, as we will demonstrate below.

Examples of Companies Versus Stocks

Growth Companies and Growth Stocks

One of the best examples of potential differences between the type of company and the stock involved is the case of growth companies and growth stocks. Generally, growth companies are firms that experience above-average growth in sales and earnings. This is a historical designation. A better specification, which indicates the *source* of the growth, is that *a true growth company is a firm with the management ability and the opportunities to invest in projects that yield returns greater than the firm's required rate of return (i.e., its average cost of capital).*[2] In other words, a growth company would be one that has the ability to acquire capital at an average cost of, say, 10 percent and yet has the management ability and the opportunity to invest those funds (whether internally generated or externally acquired) at rates of return in excess of 10 percent. As a result, the firm enjoys profits and earnings growth greater than that experienced by other firms in a similar risk category. Obvious examples of growth *companies* would be firms like IBM, Eastman Kodak, Avon, Johnson & Johnson, McDonald's, and Wendy's.

A growth stock is a stock possessing superior return capabilities when compared to other stocks in the market with similar risk characteristics. This superior return potential is due to the fact that the stock is undervalued at a given point in time relative to other stocks in the market. If the stock is undervalued, its price should increase to reflect its true intrinsic value when the correct information becomes available. During the period in which the stock changes from an under-

[2]Ezra Solomon, *The Theory of Financial Management* (New York: Columbia University Press, 1963), pp. 55–68; Merton Miller and Franco Modigliani, "Dividend Policy, Growth, and the Valuation of Shares," *Journal of Business* 34 (1966): 411–433.

valued security to a properly valued security, returns will exceed the market average, and the stock will be considered a growth stock.

A future growth stock is basically a currently undervalued stock that has a high probability of being properly valued in the near term. This means that *growth stocks are not necessarily limited to growth companies*. If investors recognize a growth firm and discount the future earnings stream properly, the current market price will reflect the future growing earnings stream. The investor who acquires the stock at this "correct" market price will receive only the market rate of return, even when superior earnings growth is attained. If investors *overprice* the stock of a growth company and an investor pays the inflated price, his returns will be below the risk-adjusted normal return. A future growth stock can be issued by any type of company; it is only necessary that the stock has not been properly valued by the market at a given point in time.

Cyclical Companies/Cyclical Stocks

A *cyclical company is one with future earnings that will be heavily influenced by aggregate business activity*. In turn, this volatile net earnings pattern is a function of the firm's business risk and financial risk.

A *cyclical stock is expected to experience changes in rates of return as great, or greater than changes in overall market rates of return*. As was true of the growth company—growth stock relationship, the stock of a cyclical company is not necessarily cyclical. If investors recognize that a company is cyclical and discount future earnings accordingly, it is possible that the rates of return on the stock of a cyclical company may hold up substantially better than aggregate market rates of return during a market decline.

Speculative Companies/Speculative Stocks

A *speculative company is one whose assets involve great risk; it offers a relatively large chance for a loss and a small chance for a large gain*. The returns from the assets of a speculative firm have a great risk connected with them. There is a high probability that the returns to the firm will be either very low, nonexistent, or negative. Typically, there is also a small probability of very substantial returns. A good example of a speculative firm is one involved in oil exploration.

A *speculative stock is one that possesses a high probability of low or negative rates of return during a given period, and a low probability of normal or high rates of return*. There are two types of speculative stocks. The first has characteristics closely akin to those of the speculative company and is typified by penny mining stocks. There is a high probability that there will be no return on the stock during a given period and eventually a complete loss. At the same time, there is some small probability of very substantial gains.

The second type of speculative stock is one that is overpriced; therefore, there is a high probability that, in the future, when the market adjusts the stock price to its true value, there will be either very low or possibly negative rates of return on it. This might be the case for an excellent growth company whose stock is selling at an extremely high price-earnings ratio reflecting a belief that outstanding growth will continue for a substantial period in the future.[3] If there is any reduction in the growth pattern, or any disruption in growth, this price-earnings ratio can drop rapidly and substantially. Therefore, there is a very strong likelihood of a substantial decline if everything does not conform to the most optimistic expectations; an overpriced stock is considered speculative.

In summary, analyzing an individual firm involves examining the internal characteristics of the firm and its relationship to its industry and to the economy. Based upon such an examination, an analyst should have some very strong opinions on the time pattern of the firm's earnings stream and its financial characteristics. Specifically, the analyst should have an opinion about the *type of company* he is dealing with—is it a cyclical company, a speculative company, or a growth company? After analyzing the company, it is necessary to consider the characteristics of the firm's common stock. *The type of company and the type of stock may not necessarily be the same!*

Company Analysis

It is assumed that you have decided to invest in equities and also that you predict that the retail food chain industry should experience above-average performance during the relevant investment horizon. Therefore, your company analysis involves examining all of the firms in the retail food chain industry to determine which stocks should experience the best performance within the industry. The objective is to estimate the expected return and risk for each individual firm over the investment horizon. These values are then used to select desirable stocks.

To demonstrate the procedure, we will analyze Safeway Stores, one of the firms in the retail food chain industry. For purposes of comparison with the industry analysis, using a firm within the composite retail store group seemed appropriate. Unfortunately, it was not possible to examine any companies in the retail drug or the general merchandise group because the industry indexes for both of these were only started in 1970 and we wanted specific industry data available since 1960 to allow reasonable historical analysis.

Safeway Stores is the largest grocery store chain in the United States. As of January, 1981, the firm operated over 2,400 stores: about 2,100 in the U.S., the remainder in Canada, the United Kingdom, Australia, and West Germany. Of the stores in the U.S., the vast majority (about 90 percent) are located west of the Mississippi River.

---

[3]For a method of measuring the implied period of growth see Charles C. Holt, "The Influence of Growth Duration on Share Prices," *Journal of Finance* 17 (1962): 465–475.

Year	Safeway Stores (Millions of $)	Retail Stores Food Industry (Sales per Share)	Personal Consumption Expenditures (PCE) (Billions of $)	PCE per Capita ($)	PCE–Food (Billions of $)	PCE: Food/Total %
1960	2,469.0	293.76	324.9	1,797	81.1	25.0
1961	2,538.0	302.82	335.0	1,823	83.2	24.8
1962	2,509.6	311.17	355.2	1,904	85.5	24.1
1963	2,649.7	318.81	374.6	1,979	87.8	23.4
1964	2,817.6	331.89	400.5	2,087	92.7	23.2
1965	2,939.0	339.20	430.4	2,214	98.9	23.0
1966	3,345.2	367.21	465.1	2,366	106.6	22.9
1967	3,360.9	377.07	490.3	2,467	109.6	22.3
1968	3,685.7	399.19	536.9	2,674	118.7	22.1
1969	4,099.6	439.97	581.8	2,870	127.5	21.9
1970	4,860.2	464.40	621.7	3,034	138.9	22.3
1971	5,358.8	482.38	672.2	3,246	144.2	21.5
1972	6,057.6	526.29	737.1	3,529	154.9	21.0
1973	6,773.7	563.16	812.0	3,858	172.1	21.2
1974	8,185.2	588.26	888.1	4,190	193.7	21.8
1975	9,716.9	637.67	976.4	4,572	213.6	21.9
1976	10,442.5	619.07	1,084.3	5,038	230.6	21.3
1977	11,249.4	667.55	1,205.5	5,557	250.3	20.8
1978	12,550.6	691.43	1,348.7	6,166	276.4	20.5
1979	13,717.9	714.75	1,510.9	6,848	312.1	20.7
1980(p)[a]	15,100.0	764.78	1,670.1	7,496	345.0	20.7

Table 12.1   Sales for Safeway Stores, the Retail Food Store Industry, and Various Economic Series, 1960–1980

[a](p) — preliminary

Source: Reprinted by permission of Standard & Poor's and Safeway Stores, Incorporated

Estimating Expected Return

The analyst estimates the expected return for the investment by estimating the future value of the security which indicates the expected capital gain or loss and, when combined with the expected dividend yield, indicates the expected return. The future value of the security is estimated based upon the expected earnings and the expected earnings multiplier for the stock. In turn, expected earnings is a function of the sales forecast and the estimated profit margin for the firm.

Sales Forecast

The sales forecast includes an analysis of the relationship of company sales to various economic series that should influence the demand for the firm's products, and a comparison of the firm's sales to the sales for the company's industry. Such an analysis is supported by the sales forecast derived in the industry analysis. This company-industry analysis indicates how the company is performing in relation to its most immediate competition.

Table 12.1 contains data on sales for Safeway Stores, sales per share for the retail food store industry, and several personal consumption expenditure (PCE) series. The most relevant is the personal consumption expenditure for food (PCE−Food), which has comprised between 20 and 25 percent of total PCE. The scatter plot of Safeway sales and the PCE−Food expenditures in Figure 12.1 indicates a good linear relationship, and also indicates that Safeway sales have been growing at a faster rate than the PCE for food has. During the period 1960−1980 Safeway sales increased by about 356 percent, compared to an increase in PCE−Food of 204 percent. In addition, Safeway sales grew from about 3.0 percent of the total PCE for food to over 4.6 percent. Therefore, Safeway derived an increasing share of these expenditures.

The figures in the last column of Table 12.1 indicate that, during this period, the proportion of PCE allocated to food declined from 25 percent in 1960 to only 20.7 percent in 1980. The declining proportion of PCE spent on food, especially at retail food chains, apparently is a function of the changing life style of consumers. An increasing proportion of meals is consumed outside the home, so a larger percentage of income is spent at restaurants and fast-food outlets.

Regarding the relationship between Safeway sales and the total PCE, Safeway grew faster than the total, 512 percent for Safeway versus 414 percent for total PCE. Most of Safeway's growth has been internal; the number of common shares outstanding during this period has only gone from 24,866,580 (adjusted for a split) in 1960 to 26,115,917 at the end of 1980. In turn, internal growth has been a function of a small increase in the number of stores, from 2,207 in 1960 to 2,416 in 1980. *The more important change has been a major increase in the annual sales per store because of the upgrading of stores.* The net number of stores has increased by about 200, which includes the construction of a number of new, large stores and the closing of many smaller stores in declining areas. This change is supported by the figures in Table 12.2.

The relationship between sales for Safeway Stores and sales per share for the

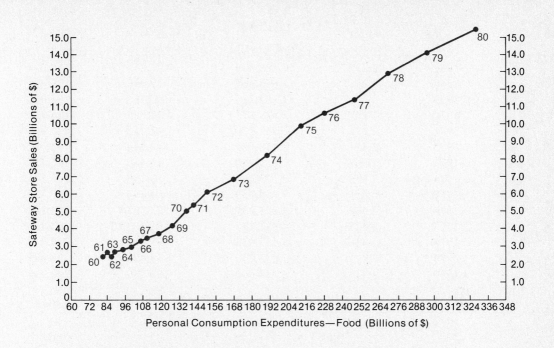

Figure 12.1   Scatter Plot of Safeway Sales and Personal Consumption
Expenditures for Food: 1960–1980 (Billions of $)

retail food store industry is not as consistent as the relationship just described, but is even more impressive in terms of the performance by Safeway. Again, for the total period, Safeway sales increased by 512 percent compared to an increase for the industry of only 160 percent. Because industry figures are sales per share, this could make some difference, but would have little effect on Safeway because total outstanding shares have only increased by about 5 percent during the 20 years being considered.

This performance by Safeway is not very surprising given the previous analysis. Safeway sales grew faster than the total PCE, and the total PCE has grown faster than the PCE for food. Finally, the sales growth for the retail food store index has been smaller than the growth in the PCE for food. The industry index grew 160 percent during the period 1960–1980 as compared to PCE–Food growth of 325 percent.

Estimating Company Sales

Based on the foregoing discussion, an analyst would probably concentrate on the relationship between Safeway sales and the PCE–Food. To estimate PCE–Food

Year	Number of Stores	Sales Per Store	Store Area (1,000 sq. ft)	Sales Per 1,000 sq. ft.
1967	2,237	$1,502,405	37,850	$ 88,795
1968	2,241	1,644,663	39,033	94,425
1969	2,260	1,784,783	40,169	102,060
1970	2,297	2,115,876	41,769	116,358
1971	2,283	2,347,279	42,752	125,347
1972	2,331	2,258,727	44,844	135,082
1973	2,364	2,865,350	46,480	145,733
1974	2,426	3,373,945	50,159	163,185
1975	2,451	3,964,459	51,854	187,398
1976	2,438	4,283,237	53,223	196,203
1977	2,428	4,633,195	55,184	203,853
1978	2,436	5,152,122	57,461	218,419
1979	2,425	5,656,850	59,470	230,669
1980	2,416	6,250,000	62,080	243,235

Table 12.2   Data on Number of Stores, Store Area and Sales for Safeway: 1967–1980.

for the forthcoming investment period, it would be preferable to initially estimate total PCE and then estimate the food component. Specifically, the analyst would derive an estimate of the expected percentage change in PCE based on his own analysis or the estimate of an economist. Given this estimate of the change in PCE, it is necessary to project how much of this will be spent on food. An obvious assumption is that a constant proportion will be spent on food, which implies that the PCE–Food will increase by the same percent as PCE. Alternatively, because the data in Table 12.1 indicate that the percentage spent on food has declined steadily, one would probably expect a further small decline, so the percentage increase for PCE–Food would be less than the increase in total PCE.

Armed with this estimate of PCE–Food, you could use the scatter plot in Figure 12.1 to derive an estimate of Safeway Sales. Another option is to use the percentage change estimate for PCE–Food and estimate a larger percentage change for Safeway that is consistent with the recent results. Specifically, the data indicate that Safeway sales have been increasing about 1.4 times faster than the PCE–Food is. Therefore, as an example, if the PCE–Food estimate indicated an increase of 8 percent for the next year, you would expect Safeway sales to increase by approximately 11.2 percent (1.4 × .08).

The analyst can also derive an estimate using company data on stores, square footage, sales per store, and sales per square foot. The figures are contained in Table 12.2. The data confirm the earlier discussion in which it was noted that Safeway had experienced substantial increases in sales with a relatively small increase in the net number of stores. In general, the company has closed smaller stores and built a number of very large stores that sell a variety of higher priced items. The result has been a consistent increase in total store area *and* an increase in sales per 1,000 square feet.

The estimate would be a two-step process. First, it would be necessary to estimate the increase in square feet for the coming year based upon capital expenditure estimates and conversations with management. Current square footage plus the increase equals the expected size of all stores. The second estimate is the dollars of sales per square foot. As noted, this has likewise experienced strong growth. Assuming this increase in sales per 1000 square feet would continue, you could estimate by how much, and then, multiplying the estimated square footage by the estimated sales per square foot, derive an alternative estimate of total sales.

Note that we have suggested three alternative techniques for estimating sales. The idea is *not* to choose between the alternatives, but to *employ all three* to provide a *range* of estimates, and, hopefully, confirmation of your estimate.

The next step is to derive an estimate of the profit margin for the firm.

Estimating the Profit Margin

Analysis of the firm's profit margin should involve consideration of two general areas: the firm's internal performance, including any changes that have occurred; and the firm's relationship to its industry. The initial analysis should indicate general trends for the firm and point out areas of concern. When company performance is related to the industry, the analysis should indicate whether the company's performance (good or bad) is attributable to the industry or is unique to the firm. Profit margin figures for Safeway and the retail food industry are given in Table 12.3. The figures on the net before-tax margin for Safeway and the retail food industry indicate a relatively steady decline for both series. This indicates that Safeway experienced a decline in its profit margin over the past 18 years, and that part of this decline is related to a similar phenomenon in the total industry. Moreover, the change in the margin for Safeway during 1976 was inferior to that for the industry because Safeway declined during 1976 while the industry was constant after a recovery in 1975. At this point, we should attempt to understand the reason for the industry decline, and also what added factors contributed to Safeway's performance.

Industry Factors
The major factors influencing the decline in industry profit margins over the past two decades have been the increased cost of advertising and other promotional devices, and, more important, a number of price wars among the large chains.[4]

---

[4]For a more complete discussion see *Standard & Poor's Industry Surveys: Retailing-Food* (New York: Standard & Poor's, 1981).

	Safeway Stores						Retail Food Store Index[b]		
Year	Earnings After Costs & Expenses[a] (Millions of $)	Percentage Sales	Income Before Taxes (Millions of $)	Percentage Sales	Net Income (Millions of $)	Percentage Sales	Operating Profit Margin	NBT Margin	Net Profit Margin
1960	76.9	3.11	75.2	3.05	34.8	1.41	3.61	2.70	1.29
1961	81.1	3.20	78.6	3.10	36.6	1.44	3.54	2.59	1.25
1962	85.7	3.41	83.3	3.32	39.3	1.57	3.58	2.56	1.23
1963	95.9	3.62	94.7	3.57	44.8	1.69	3.41	2.40	1.19
1964	101.9	3.62	97.9	3.47	50.0	1.77	3.45	2.39	1.24
1965	99.1	3.37	95.1	3.24	48.2	1.64	3.33	2.28	.123
1966	121.2	3.62	117.8	3.52	59.7	1.78	3.28	2.22	1.20
1967	103.4	3.08	100.2	2.98	50.9	1.51	3.08	2.07	1.10
1968	118.5	3.21	115.5	3.13	55.1	1.49	3.19	2.11	1.07
1969	112.9	2.75	108.9	2.66	51.3	1.25	3.18	2.13	1.07
1970	146.1	3.01	140.7	2.89	68.9	1.41	3.19	2.14	1.10
1971	158.4	2.96	155.3	2.90	80.2	1.50	2.77	1.69	0.92
1972	176.3	2.91	168.6	2.78	91.1	1.50	1.90	0.86	0.53
1973	166.6	2.46	157.5	2.33	86.3	1.27	2.48	1.35	0.78
1974	156.2	1.91	140.8	1.72	79.2	0.97	2.58	0.85	0.27
1975	287.9	2.96	275.3	2.83	148.6	1.53	2.53	1.59	0.90
1976	196.9	1.89	191.3	1.83	105.6	1.01	2.53	1.57	0.87
1977	250.4	2.22	184.2	1.64	102.3	0.91	2.76	1.47	0.82
1978	349.5	2.79	276.7	2.20	146.1	1.16	3.25	1.79	0.93
1979	303.6	2.21	224.8	1.64	143.3	1.04	3.22	1.78	1.05

Table 12.3   Profit Margins for Safeway Stores and the Retail Food Industry 1960–1979

[a]Costs and expenses include "costs of sales" and selling, general, and administrative expenses.
[b]Source: Standard & Poor's, *Analysts Handbook* (New York: Standard & Poor's Corp., 1980). Reprinted by permission.

Because of some overbuilding of stores during the 1950s, the food chains engaged in heavy promotion and advertising during the 1960s in an attempt to hold their share of the market or even to increase it. In the early 1970s there were numerous price wars as A&P (The Great Atlantic and Pacific Tea Company), experiencing a decline in volume, introduced price cuts to become competitive. These price wars continued sporadically for several years and seriously affected profit margins for several of the chains. The outlook is for generally more stable prices and some improvement in the industry margins.

Company Factors

The major factor that affected Safeway's profit margin over the last several years has been the sporadic outbreak of price wars. The effect on Safeway was more intense because the conflict was especially heavy in California where Safeway is highly concentrated. The long-run outlook for profit margins is good because of Safeway's continued building of larger stores that contain more nonfood items and high-margin facilities like delicatessens. There is one factor that causes problems in predicting the firm's profit margin. This is ascertaining foreign gains and losses because the firm has heavy exposure in the overseas market. As of 1981, there were 283 stores in Canada, and 186 in the United Kingdom, Australia, and Germany. Consequently, either positive or negative foreign exchange adjustments in excess of 10 cents a share are involved.

Specific estimates of Safeway's profit margin should probably begin with an analysis of the relationship between the firm's margin and the food chain industry margin. Analysis indicated a reasonably good historical relationship between the firm and the industry such that you could use a scatter plot to estimate the company profit margin after an industry margin is derived. As always, you should consider any unique factors that would cause this long-run relationship to deviate from expectations in the coming year, e.g., foreign exchange charges; an abnormal number of store openings; any expectations regarding price wars that would affect Safeway more or less than they would other food chains.

You also might want to consider the relationship between percentages of change in the profit margin for Safeway and for the industry. An analysis of this relationship indicates that there has been a fairly good relationship and that the Safeway margin is generally less variable than the industry profit margin is; the Safeway profit margin does not fluctuate as much as the industry margin does. Again, as a result of your industry analysis, you already have an estimate of the percentage of change in the industry profit margin. Based upon the long-run relationship between the Safeway margin and the industry margin you could derive another estimate for the Safeway profit margin that could be adjusted for any unique expectations.

In addition, you should analyze the firm's income statement for several years on the basis of a 100 percent breakdown (also referred to as a common size statement). The extent of the income statement breakdown depends upon the con-

	1980		1979		1978	
	('000)	%	('000)	%	('000)	%
Sales	$15,102,673	100.0	$13,717,861	100.0	$12,550,569	100.0
Cost of Sales	11,817,141	76.02	10,793,874	78.7	9,829,071	78.3
Gross Profit	3,285,532	21.8	2,923,987	21.3	2,721,498	21.7
Operating & Administrative Expense	3,000,627	19.9	2,620,415	19.1	2,371,949	18.9
Interest Expense	99,614	0.7	91,276	0.7	74,110	0.6
Other Income—Net	(8,621)	0.1	(12,483)	0.1	(1,279)	0.0
Net Before Taxes	193,912	1.3	224,779	1.6	276,718	2.2
Income Taxes	74,544	0.5	81,456	0.6	130,600	1.0
Net Income	119,368	0.8	143,323	1.0	146,118	1.2
Tax Rate	38.4%		36.2%		47.2%	

Table 12.4   Common Size Income Statement for Safeway Stores: 1978–1980

Source: Safeway *Annual Report,* 1980, Safeway Stores, Inc. Reprinted by permission.

sistent detail provided by the firm. As an example, Table 12.4 contains a common size statement for Safeway for the period 1978–1980. In this example we have only considered three years. In actual practice you would probably want to examine between five and ten years to gain a perspective on relevant trends.

Analysis of the cost of sales percentage indicates there was some decline in gross profit for 1980 and 1979, as compared to 1978, so this must be watched. However, you would also want to see how competitive food chains have fared during this period. Of more concern is the "operating and administrative expense" item. This expense as a percentage of sales has been increasing steadily since 1974 when it was only 16.4 percent. A constant increase in this percentage when sales have been increasing consistently is rather discouraging regarding control by management. Interest expense has also grown in absolute amount and as a percentage which can be partially explained by the higher level of market interest rates. The decline in the net before-tax margin is simply a combination of the increases in cost of sales and operating and administrative expenses. The net profit margin did not decline as much as NBT did because of the lowered tax rate. In summary, your main concern would be the small decline in gross margin and the constant increase in operating and administrative expense. A major question you need to answer is what management is doing to bring these expenses under control. The obvious good news is that, if these trends can be reversed, the impact on net earnings could be substantial based upon the very fine growth rate of sales.

Summary of Net Margin Estimate

We began by assuming that you have already derived an estimate of the net profit margin for the industry, which implies an estimate of how next year's industry margin will change from this year's margin. Given this industry margin, you can derive one estimate for the firm by examining the historical relationship between the company's profit margin and the industry margin and project what this implies for next year, taking into account any unique circumstances for the particular company concerned.

You can derive a second estimate on the basis of the expected *percentage of change* in the industry profit margin and determine what this implies for Safeway based upon the historical relationship. As an example, assuming you expect the industry margin to increase by 10 percent, you might estimate that the company's profit margin will rise by 8 percent, if the historical relationship shows that the company's profit margin generally changes by about 80 percent of the industry change (i.e., the company's profit margin goes up *and* down by less than the industry margin does). Again, it is necessary to consider any unique events that could affect this estimate.

Finally, you can derive an estimate based upon a specific analysis of the major items in the income statement, working from the common size statement. Some expense items will be estimated on the basis of percentages (cost of sales), while, in other cases, you would estimate absolute dollar amounts (operating and administrative expense; interest expense).

Again, the idea is *not* to choose between the different estimating procedures, but to *do all three* and reconcile any differences. This profit margin multiplied by the sales estimate calculated in the previous section will produce an earnings estimate. Net earnings divided by the expected shares outstanding is the earnings per share estimate. The next step is to project the earnings multiplier for the firm.

Estimating the Earnings Multiplier

As was true of the procedure for estimating the industry multiplier, this analysis involves examining the macro relationships between the company multiplier and the industry and market multipliers, and/or a micro analysis of the individual variables that affect a firm's multiple.

Macro Analysis of Earnings Multiplier

Table 12.5 contains the mean earnings multiplier for the company, the retail food store industry, and the aggregate market for each year from 1960 to 1979. In general, the earnings multiplier for Safeway has been lower than the multiplier for either the retail food industry or the aggregate market. This is true for almost all the individual years and on average. Further, an analysis of annual percentage changes for the company multiplier compared to percentage changes for the industry and market multiplier indicates that Safeway's earnings multiplier is less

Year	Safeway Price-Earnings Ratio			Retail Food Stores Price-Earnings Ratio			S&P 400 Price-Earnings Ratio		
	High[a]	Low[b]	Mean[c]	High[a]	Low[b]	Mean[c]	High[a]	Low[b]	Mean[c]
1960	14.89	11.95	13.42	15.75	13.58	14.67	19.12	16.28	17.70
1961	22.44	12.91	17.68	23.90	15.30	19.60	22.76	18.06	20.41
1962	19.73	11.84	15.79	21.88	13.28	17.58	19.64	14.31	16.98
1963	18.50	12.96	15.73	18.75	15.40	17.08	18.69	15.44	17.07
1964	19.46	14.43	16.95	18.55	14.77	16.66	18.82	16.44	17.63
1965	22.35	15.94	19.15	19.55	15.79	17.67	17.92	15.71	16.82
1966	13.40	10.07	11.65	15.74	11.28	13.51	17.14	13.27	15.20
1967	14.06	10.69	12.38	14.02	11.86	12.94	18.89	15.18	17.04
1968	14.47	10.76	12.62	16.41	12.26	14.34	19.16	15.43	17.30
1969	15.05	11.69	13.37	14.26	11.97	13.12	18.96	15.95	17.46
1970	12.73	8.19	10.46	13.24	10.14	11.69	19.01	13.97	16.49
1971	12.78	10.20	11.49	17.87	13.29	15.58	19.40	16.64	18.02
1972	12.46	9.58	11.02	24.61	19.41	22.01	19.47	16.43	17.95
1973	13.21	8.16	10.69	14.50	9.97	12.74	15.13	11.63	13.38
1974	14.34	9.68	12.01	37.48	24.85	31.17	11.62	7.24	9.43
1975	9.18	5.95	7.57	10.58	7.69	9.14	12.52	9.06	10.79
1976	12.38	9.67	11.02	11.62	9.60	10.61	11.31	9.51	10.45
1977	12.85	9.92	11.39	11.35	9.46	10.41	10.31	8.66	9.49
1978	8.21	6.34	7.28	9.70	7.68	8.69	9.08	7.30	8.19
1979	8.01	6.15	7.08	8.49	7.27	7.88	7.65	6.58	7.12

Table 12.5   Average Earnings Multiplier for Safeway, the Retail Food Store Industry, and the S&P 400: 1960–1979

[a]High price for the year divided by earnings per share for the year.

[b]Low price for year divided by earnings per share for the year.

[c]High price-earnings ratio plus low price-earnings ratio divided by two.

Source: Reprinted by permission of Standard & Poor's.

volatile than the industry multiplier, and about equal in volatility to the market multiplier. Actually, it appears that changes in the Safeway multiplier were more closely related to changes in the market multiplier than to changes in the industry multiplier. The point is, given your previous estimates of the expected change in the market multiplier and the industry multiplier, you could derive alternative estimates of changes in Safeway's multiplier.

Micro Analysis of Earnings Multiplier

The variables that should influence the multiplier are the dividend payout ratio, the risk for the security, and the expected growth rate for the firm. In turn, the growth rate is a function of the retention rate and the return on equity. The historical data for these series are contained in Table 12.6. The relevant questions are: why has the Safeway multiplier been consistently below the market multiplier, and would we expect this relationship to persist based upon the relationship of the relevant variables?

Dividend Payout   The dividend payout ratio for Safeway compared to its industry indicates that the payout for Safeway has usually been lower than that of its industry, and this is reflected in the average for the period (47.28 vs. 52.70). Likewise Safeway has a slightly lower payout than the market in most instances. Taken by themselves, these results would indicate that the Safeway multiplier should be *below* the multiplier for the industry or the aggregate market.

Required Rate of Return (i)   This analysis should involve the firm's internal risk characteristics (BR, FR, LR), and the stocks's systematic market risk (beta). One would expect Safeway to have relatively low business risk because of its sales growth, which has been more stable than that of both its industry and the aggregate economy (in terms of food expenditure). Unfortunately, over the long-run the firm has experienced a relatively high level of operating leverage because of the price wars discussed earlier. As a result, the operating profit figures for Safeway have been quite volatile. An analysis of the operating earnings compared to the industry and the market confirms the higher level of variability. This would indicate that during this period, Safeway experienced *higher business risk* than the industry or the aggregate stock market did.

Assuming the capitalization of financial leases, the financial risk for Safeway is about equal to that of the retail store industry and above the aggregate market's risk. Specifically, the firm's interest coverage ratio is about the same as the industry ratio and lower than the value for the aggregate market. The debt to total capital ratio is likewise approximately equal to the industry ratio and above the market's in general. Therefore, one would conclude that Safeway's *financial risk is somewhat above average.*

The firm's external market *liquidity risk* is quite low compared to that for its industry and substantially below the figure for the average firm in the aggregate. The factors generally indicating market liquidity are: (1) the number of stockholders; (2) the number of shares outstanding; (3) the number of shares traded; and (4) institutional interest in the stock as indicated by the number of institutions that own the stock and the proportion of stock owned by institutions. Based on any or all of these factors, Safeway's stock is very liquid. Specifically, the company has numerous stockholders with a large number of shares outstanding that are heavily traded. Finally, there is a large number of institutions that own major positions in the stock. Therefore, it is clear that Safeway's common stock has much lower liquidity risk than the average stock.

In summary, it appears that Safeway has above-average business risk and financial risk, but very low liquidity risk. On balance this would imply overall risk slightly above average.

The systematic risk for Safeway is derived by relating rates of return for Safeway to comparable rates of return for the S&P 500 series. According to a 1981 *Value Line* report on Safeway, the firm's historical beta was .75, which would indicate a below-average market risk.

Year	Safeway				Retail Food Chains				S&P 400			
	Div./Earn	Equity Turnover	Profit Margin	ROE	Div./Earn	Equity Turnover	Profit Margin	ROE	Div./Earn	Equity Turnover	Profit Margin	ROE
1960	50.77	10.63	1.41	15.00	48.94	10.02	1.29	12.89	58.82	1.76	5.72	10.08
1961	52.03	10.11	1.44	14.58	52.12	9.67	1.25	12.07	61.42	1.71	5.66	9.67
1962	51.06	9.29	1.57	14.54	59.27	9.45	1.23	11.63	57.44	1.78	5.93	10.53
1963	46.24	9.00	1.69	15.22	59.37	9.30	1.19	11.06	55.66	1.79	6.19	11.11
1964	46.75	8.74	1.77	15.51	57.14	9.15	1.24	11.39	53.20	1.82	6.63	12.06
1965	52.66	8.49	1.64	13.92	58.89	9.06	1.23	11.11	51.27	1.85	6.82	12.64
1966	43.58	8.74	1.78	15.60	57.63	9.28	1.20	11.10	50.26	1.94	6.64	12.88
1967	54.97	8.34	1.51	12.63	63.20	9.18	1.10	10.05	52.85	1.92	6.12	11.76
1968	50.92	8.58	1.49	12.82	58.04	9.27	1.07	9.96	51.30	2.02	6.07	12.27
1969	54.65	8.99	1.25	11.25	54.04	9.54	1.07	10.19	53.02	2.10	5.65	11.86
1970	42.55	9.78	1.41	13.86	50.29	9.67	1.10	10.60	59.15	2.09	4.92	10.28
1971	41.41	9.79	1.50	14.64	59.91	9.63	0.92	8.86	52.93	2.14	5.04	10.80
1972	38.04	9.94	1.50	14.94	75.36	10.44	0.53	5.55	47.14	2.21	5.30	11.71
1973	44.79	10.25	1.27	13.06	41.88	10.75	0.78	8.34	38.92	2.37	5.96	14.15
1974	55.46	11.75	0.97	11.37	133.54	12.27	0.27	3.36	38.61	2.69	5.28	14.17
1975	33.14	12.28	1.53	18.78	36.43	12.60	0.90	11.28	43.36	2.63	4.63	12.11
1976	50.37	12.30	1.01	12.43	41.22	12.87	0.87	11.25	39.47	2.66	5.27	14.02
1977	55.98	13.26	0.91	12.06	45.36	13.30	0.82	10.94	42.89	2.72	5.15	14.04
1978	41.07	13.40	1.16	15.60	41.74	13.63	0.93	12.66	41.13	2.82	5.19	14.64
1979	47.36	13.55	1.04	14.15	40.56	13.76	1.05	14.38	37.00	2.96	5.57	16.48
Mean[a]	47.28	10.29	1.41	14.24	52.70	10.56	1.04	10.81	49.85	2.17	5.71	12.27

Table 12.6 Variables That Influence the Earnings Multiplier for Safeway, Retail Food Chains, and the S&P 400, 1960–1979

[a]Excluding 1974.

Source: Reprinted by permission of Standard & Poor's.

The overall consensus probably indicates risk about equal to that of the aggregate market or slightly above-average risk. This would suggest a multiplier equal to or slightly below the market multiplier.

Expected Growth Rate (g)   The expected growth rate of dividends is dependent on the expected growth rate of earnings, which is a function of the retention rate and the return on equity (ROE). Based upon our discussion of the dividend payout, we know that, generally, Safeway has had a lower payout than either the industry or the aggregate market had, which implies a slightly higher retention rate.

We know that the firm's ROE is a function of equity turnover and the profit margin. The figures in Table 12.6 indicate that the equity turnover for Safeway has been consistently *lower* than it has been for the overall industry, although *the difference is not very large as* shown by the average values (10.29 vs. 1056). The average turnover for Safeway is substantially larger than that for the aggregate market, as one would expect given the nature of the retail food industry. This comparison indicates that the industry should grow at a higher rate than Safeway will.

The profit margin results indicate that Safeway has traditionally done better than the industry overall. The profit margin for Safeway has always been larger than that for the industry until 1979 when it was about equal. The average margin for Safeway is about 35 percent larger than the industry margin (1.41 vs. 1.04). Again, as expected, the Safeway margin is always lower than the profit margin for the aggregate stock market.

An important point here is that the differential in profit margin has declined substantially over the last four years (since 1976), to the point where there currently is *no difference* between the company and the industry. Therefore, in terms of projecting the future, you may want to give these recent years more weight. For consistency, the subsequent discussion will continue to use the long-run historical averages.

The combined effect of equity turnover and profit margin indicates an ROE for Safeway that is higher than the industry figure (14.24 vs. 10.81) and also higher than the aggregate market figure (14.24 vs 12.27). The computed ROE figures implied by the turnovers and margin figures are very close to the long-run average figures, as one would expect:

	Equity Turnover	Profit Margin	Expected ROE	Average ROE
Safeway	10.29	1.41	14.51	14.24
Industry	10.56	1.04	10.98	10.81
S&P 400	2.17	5.71	12.39	12.27

These results for ROE combined with the results for the retention rate imply a much higher growth rate for Safeway than for the industry or the economy:

	Retention Rate	ROE	Expected Growth Rate
Safeway	.527	14.24	7.50
Retail Food Chain Industry	.473	10.81	5.11
S&P 400	.501	12.27	6.15

Source: Reprinted by permission of Standard & Poor's.

This also suggests, other things being equal, a higher multiplier for Safeway. Again, it is important to remember that the ROE and hence the growth rate are heavily influenced by the profit margin. As noted, the profit margin for Safeway has decreased during the last several years relative to the industry and aggregate market margins.

The Combined Effect   Overall, the three variables considered indicate that the earnings multiplier for Safeway should be about equal to, or slightly below that for its industry and the market. The payout indicates a lower multiplier for Safeway as does the risk. In contrast, the growth rate for Safeway has been above that of the industry and the market, but it is necessary to discount this historical growth because of the recent weakness in the profit margin.

Summary of the Multiplier Estimate

The macro analysis involves comparing the company's earnings multiplier to the industry multiplier and the aggregate market multiplier. The relationship between annual percentage changes in these multipliers, should also be examined. Using the previous estimates of the industry and market multiplier, a likely earnings multiplier for the company of interest can be projected. Alternatively, a percentage change for the company multiplier can be based on expected percentage changes in the earnings multiplier for the industry and the market.

The micro analysis involves examination of each of the components of the earnings multiplier (the dividend payout ratio, the required rate of return for the stock, and the expected growth rate of dividends) for the company and similar variables for the industry and the market. This analysis should indicate how the company's multiplier will compare to the industry and market multipliers, i.e., whether the company's multiplier will be higher, lower, or about equal.

Price Estimate

The price estimate necessitates combining the earlier earnings per share estimate and the earnings multiplier estimate to derive a stock price estimate for the future period. It is important for you to recognize the importance of both components. There are numerous examples of companies experiencing increases in earnings, but stock prices declined because the earnings multiplier declined. It may be that the earnings multiplier did *not* decline because of any change in the company, but the decline was caused by a macroeconomic change that affected the company's industry or *all* stocks; e.g., an increase in the rate of inflation with no comparable increase in the expected growth rate of dividends.

As a sample price estimate, assume that, based upon your analysis, you estimated earnings during the investment period to be $6.50 a share. Further, your analysis of the market multiplier, the industry multiplier and the relationship of these to the company multiplier indicated that the company's multiplier should be about nine times earnings. This would imply a price estimate of $58.50 (9 × $6.50).

Return Estimate

The estimate of the rate of return during the investment period involves comparing the future estimated price and dividend to the current price as follows:

$$E(R_{i,t}) = \frac{P_{i,t+1} - P_{i,t} + D_{i,t}}{P_{i,t}}$$

where:

$E(R_{i,t})$ = the expected rate of return on stock i during period t

$P_{i,t+1}$ = the expected price for stock i at the end of the investment period

$P_{i,t}$ = the current price of stock i

$D_{i,t}$ = the expected dividend on stock i during period t.

This return estimate, along with the risk estimate, will determine whether you want to invest in this stock during the forthcoming investment period.

As an example, if the current price of the stock were $53.50 and you expected the firm to pay dividends during the period of $3.25 a share (about a 50 percent payout), the expected return would be:

$$E(R_{i,t}) = \frac{58.50 - 53.50 + 3.25}{53.50}$$

$$= \frac{5.00 + 3.25}{53.50} \qquad \text{(continued)}$$

$$= \frac{8.25}{53.50}$$

$$= 15.42\%$$

This expected return is then compared to the required return for securities of comparable risk.

Summary

This chapter dealt with the procedure for evaluating individual common stocks using the dividend growth model. It was initially pointed out that you should be aware that there are several different types of companies and types of common stocks, and that there is a high probability that the two are not the same; e.g., the stock of a growth company may not be a growth stock.

The analysis procedure was demonstrated using Safeway Stores as an example. The earnings estimate was derived based upon an analysis of the sales performance of Safeway in relation to the performance of its industry and of an aggregate economic series. The profit margin estimate involved the firm's relationship to its industry and any unique features.

The comparison of the earnings multiplier for Safeway to the figure for its industry and the market indicated that the Safeway multiplier was consistently below the others. Each of the components that influence the multiplier was analyzed indicating that, on balance, the Safeway multiplier should have been about equal to or slightly below that for the industry or the market. We concluded with a consideration of the price estimate using the earnings estimate and the earnings multiplier. Finally we dealt with the expected return estimate using the expected price and the dividend estimate.

Questions

1.   Give an example of a growth *company* and discuss why you would expect it to be considered a growth company. Be specific.

2.   Do you think the common stock of the company in Question 1 is a growth stock? Why or why not? Be specific.

3.   Give an example of a cyclical *stock* and discuss why you have designated it as such a stock. Is it issued by a cyclical company?

4.   Select a company outside the retail store industry and indicate which economic series you would use to make a sales projection. Discuss why this is a relevant series.

5.   Select a company outside the retail store industry and indicate the *industry* series you would use in an industry analysis (try to use one of the industry groups

designated by Standard & Poor's). Discuss why this is the most appropriate series and whether there were several possible alternatives.

6. Taking the company and industry selected in Question 5, examine the operating profit margin for the company as it relates to the operating margin for the industry. Discuss the annual results in terms of levels and changes and the long-run averages for the latest ten-year period.

7. Compute the average earnings multiplier for a company for each of the last ten years and relate this to a comparable multiplier for the market (consider using the High + Low/2, in which case the market figures are included in Table 12.5). Discuss the short-run and long-run differences.

8. Compare your average company multiplier to a similar industry multiplier for the last ten years. Discuss the short-run differences.

9. Assume that there is some difference between the earnings multiplier for your company and its industry. What are the three major variables that could account for this difference? Discuss each individually and indicate what difference in each (holding everything else constant) would explain it; e.g., the company multiplier is higher because variable A is lower and this influences the multiplier in the following way.

10. *Case Project*—Collect the data for your company and your industry and analyze all the variables that should affect the multiplier to determine whether the historical differences are consistent with the historical relationship between the multipliers; i.e, can you explain why the average company multiplier is higher or lower than the industry multiplier?

References

Arditti, Fred D. "Risk and the Required Return on Equity." *Journal of Finance* 22 (1967).

Benishay, Haskell. "Variability in Earnings-Price Ratios of Corporate Equities." *American Economic Review* 51 (1961).

Bernstein, Peter L. "Growth Companies vs Growth Stocks." *Harvard Business Review* 34 (1956).

Bower, Richard S., and Bower, D. H. "Risk and the Valuation of Common Stock." *Journal of Political Economy* 77 (1969).

Brigham, Eugene F., and Pappas, James L. "Duration of Growth, Change in Growth Rates, and Corporate Share Prices." *Financial Analysts Journal* 22 (1966).

Cragg, John G., and Malkiel, Burton G. "The Consensus and Accuracy of Some Predictions of the Growth of Corporate Earnings." *Journal of Finance* 23 (1968).

Durand, David. "Growth Stocks and the Petersburg Paradox." *Journal of Finance* 12 (1957).

Friend, Irwin, and Puckett, M. "Dividends and Stock Prices." *American Economic Review* 54 (1964).

Gordon, Myron J. *The Investment, Financing, and Valuation of the Corporation.* Homewood, IL: Richard D. Irwin, 1962.

Graham, Benjamin; Dodd, D. L.; and Cottle, S. *Security Analysis, Principles and Techniques.* 4th ed. New York: McGraw-Hill, 1962.

Holt, Charles C. "The Influence of Growth Duration on Share Prices." *Journal of Finance* 17 (1962).

Lintner, John. "The Valuation of Risk Assets and the Selection of Risky Investments in Stock Portfolios and Capital Budgets." *Review of Economics and Statistics* 47 (1965).

Lintner, John, and Glauber, Robert. "Higgledy Piggledy Growth in America." In *Modern Developments in Investment Management,* edited by James Lorie and Richard Brealey. New York: Praeger Publishers, 1972.

Malkiel, Burton. "Equity Yields, Growth, and the Structure of Share Prices." *American Economic Review* 53 (1963).

Malkiel, Burton G., and Cragg, John G. "Expectations and the Structure of Share Prices." *American Economic Review* 60 (1970).

Mao, James C. T. "The Valuation of Growth Stocks: The Investments Opportunity Approach." *Journal of Finance* 21 (1966).

Miller, Merton, and Modigliani, Franco. "Dividend Policy, Growth, and the Valuation of Shares." *Journal of Business* 34 (1966).

Molodovsky, Nicholas; May, C.; and Chottiner, S. "Common Stock Valuation: Theory and Tables." *Financial Analysts Journal* 20 (1965).

Nerlove, Marc. "Factors Affecting Differences Among Rates of Return on Investments in Individual Common Stocks." *Review of Economics and Statistics* 50 (1968).

Niederhoffer, Victor, and Regan, Patrick J. "Earnings Changes, Analysts Forecasts, and Stock Prices." *Financial Analysts Journal* 28 (1972).

Reilly, Frank K. "A Differentiation Between Types of Companies and Types of Stocks." *Mississippi Valley Journal of Business and Economics* 7 (1971).

Soldofsky Robert J., and Murphy, James T. *Growth Yield on Common Stocks: Theory and Tables.* rev. ed. Iowa City: State University of Iowa, Bureau of Business and Economics Research, 1964.

Wendt, Paul F. "Current Growth Stock Valuation Methods." *Financial Analysts Journal* 21 (1965).

Whitbeck, V., and Kisor, M. "A New Tool in Investment Decision Making." *Financial Analysts Journal* 19 (1963).

Joseph E. Granville

In the area of technical analysis, few if any have written more extensively than Joseph Granville, and probably nobody is better known. He has the ability to make predictions that are typically extreme and always flamboyant (whether they are always correct is a matter of interpretation and depends upon whom you ask). An example of the power of his service (the Granville Market Letter) occurred in 1981 when the DJIA declined by 23.80 points (on a record volume of 92,890,000 shares) following Granville's recommendation to his subscribers the preceding night that they should sell everything.

Granville has authored 12 books including: A Strategy of Daily Stock Market Timing for Maximum Profit, Prentice-Hall, 1960 (Japanese edition published in 1962); Granville's New Key to Stock Market Profits, Prentice-Hall, 1963; Granville's New Strategy of Daily Stock Market Timing for Maximum Profit, Prentice-Hall, 1976; and How to Win at Bingo: An Adventure in Probability, Parker Publishing, 1977; as well as the Granville Market Letter, first published in 1963.

Throughout the years he has been featured in Colliers, Omnibook, Barron's, The Wall Street Journal, Financial World, and a number of other journals and magazines.

Granville introduced the concept of technical indicators while working at E. F. Hutton from 1957–1963. From these, several stock market indices, including a 200-day moving average, were generated.

Granville's attack on the fundamentalist analysis approach is total. According to him, the application of fundamental techniques immediately lowers chances for market success. He expresses delight in the fact that very few investors actually follow his techniques and advice. This has inspired his next book, The Bagholders, which is intended to explain why people habitually lose money in the market and, at the same time, how his methods will make money.

Joseph Granville was born August 20, 1923 in Yonkers, New York. He received a B.A. from Duke University in 1948. He worked as a statistician prior to graduation, then formed his own stamp corporation and wrote the Philatelic Investment Letter prior to joining E. F. Hutton in 1957. He left E. F. Hutton in 1963 to start the publication of the Granville Market Letter as a private service.

His credo is: "The stock market talks a language of its own, and it's always been honest to those who are willing to do their homework!"

TECHNICAL ANALYSIS

❧ 13 ❧

"The market reacted yesterday to the report of a large increase in the short interest on the NYSE."

"Although the market declined today it was not considered bearish because there was very light volume."

"The market declined today after three days of increases due to profit taking by investors."

These and similar statements appear almost daily in the financial news as commentators attempt to explain stock market changes. All of these statements have as their rationale one of numerous technical trading rules. The purpose of this chapter is to explain the reasoning behind technical analysis and discuss many of the trading rules.

Prior to the development of the efficient market theory, investors were generally divided into two groups—"fundamentalists" and "technicians." Fundamental analysts contend that the price of a security is determined by basic underlying economic factors such as expected return and risk considerations. To arrive at estimates of these return and risk expectations for a security, an investor should examine the underlying factors in the economy, the industry, and then in the company. After extensive analysis, the investor would derive an estimate of the "intrinsic value" of the security, which is then compared to its market price. If the "value" exceeds the market price, the security should be acquired and vice versa. A fundamentalist attempts to derive value and compare it to market price, acting on the implicit assumption that the market price for the security should approach the "intrinsic value" in the future.

Technicians contend that it is *not* necessary to study economic fundamentals to know where the price of a security is going because past price movements will indicate future price movements. In the first section of this chapter, we will examine the basic philosophy underlying these technical approaches to market analysis and the assumptions these approaches involve. The next section contains a discussion of the supposed advantages of the technical approach and some problems involved in technical analysis. The remaining sections discuss alternative technical trading rules.

Basic Philosophy and Assumptions of Technical Analysis

The basic philosophy and assumptions of technical analysis are well summarized in an article by Robert A. Levy:

1. Market value is determined solely by the interaction of supply and demand.

2. Supply and demand are governed by numerous factors, both rational and irrational. Included in these factors are those relied upon by the fundamentalist, as well as opinions, moods, guesses, and blind necessities. The market weighs all of these factors continually and automatically.

3. Disregarding minor fluctuations in the market, *stock prices tend to move in trends which persist for an appreciable length of time.* (Emphasis added.)

4. Changes in trend are caused by the shifts in supply and demand relationships. These shifts, no matter why they occur, *can be detected sooner or later in the action of the market itself.*[1] (Emphasis added.)

The emphasis is added to highlight those aspects of the technical approach that differ from the belief of fundamentalists and advocates of an efficient market. The two initial statements are almost universally accepted by technicians and nontechnicians alike. Almost anyone who has had a basic course in economics would agree that, at any point in time, the price of a security (or any goods or service) should be determined by the interaction of supply and demand. In addition, most observers would acknowledge that supply and demand are governed by a multitude of variables. The only difference might be that some observers would expect the irrational factors to be rather transitory and that, therefore, the rational factors would prevail in the long run. Finally, everyone would expect the market to weigh and evaluate these factors continuously.

A difference of opinion begins to become apparent in the third statement because it implies something about the *speed of adjustment* of stock prices to changes in supply and demand factors. *Technicians expect stock prices to move in trends which persist for long periods.* This is based upon a belief that new information causing a change in the relationship between supply and demand does *not* come to the market at one point in time, but comes over a period of time because there are alternative sources of information or because certain investors receive the information earlier than others and analyze the effect before others do. As various groups ("insiders," well-informed professionals, the "average" investor) receive the information and invest or disinvest accordingly, the price is *partially* adjusted toward the new equilibrium. Therefore, technicians believe that

[1]Robert A. Levy, "Conceptual Foundations of Technical Analysis," *Financial Analysts Journal* 22 (1966): 83.

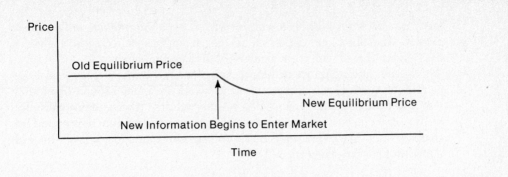

Figure 13.1   Technicians' View of Price Adjustment to New Information

the price adjustment is *not* abrupt because there is a *gradual* flow of information from insiders, to high-powered analysts, and eventually to the mass of investors. As a result, the pattern of price adjustment involves a *gradual* movement to the new equilibrium price. The graph in Figure 13.1 shows what technicians contend happens when new information causing a decrease in the equilibrium price for a security begins to enter the market.

The price adjusts, but the implied adjustment is not very rapid. Therefore, *during the adjustment period,* prices tend to move in one direction (i.e., in a trend) that persists until the stock reaches its new equilibrium. Given this *gradual* adjustment in price, the point made in the fourth statement follows: *when the change occurs, the shift to a new equilibrium can be detected in the market itself.* Therefore, the task of the technical analyst is to derive a system that allows him to detect the *beginning* of a movement from one equilibrium value to a higher or lower equilibrium value in a stock (or in the aggregate market). Technical analysts are *not* concerned with why the change in equilibrium value occurred, but only with the fact that there is a definite movement and that they can take advantage of this change in equilibrium value to derive above-average returns. Technicians emphasize *detecting the start of a change* in the supply-demand relationship. You must get on the bandwagon early and benefit from the ride to a new equilibrium. If the adjustment process were rapid, the ride would be very short and not worth the effort; i.e., it would be over before you could get on the bandwagon.

Advantages of Technical Analysis

Most technical analysts would probably admit that a fundamental analyst with good information and good analytical ability should be able to do better than a technician, but that is a qualified statement. *If* the analyst can get the new information before other investors can, and *if* he has the ability to process it correctly and quickly, *then* he should be able to derive returns above those a technical analyst can expect, because the technician must wait until the movement is underway, and so misses part of the potential return. However, *technical analysts do not believe that it is possible to consistently get good information and process it quickly.* Therefore, our discussion of the advantages of technical analysis is basically concerned with the limitations of fundamental analysis.

A major advantage claimed for technical analysis is that it is not heavily dependent on financial accounting statements, which are a major source of information about the past performance of a firm or industry. The fundamentalist uses them to evaluate past performance and thereby to project future returns and risk characteristics. The technician is quick to point out several major problems with published financial statements.

1. They do not contain a great deal of the information that is desired by analysts, such as details on sales and general expenses, or sales and earnings by product line and customers.

2. There are several ways of reporting expenses, assets, or liabilities that can give vastly different results and, typically, several of these alternatives are equally acceptable for accounting purposes. As a result, it is difficult to compare the statements of two firms in the same industry, much less firms in different industries.

3. Many psychological factors and other nonquantitative variables are not included in financial statements. Examples would include employee training and loyalty, customer goodwill, and general investor attitude toward an industry (e.g., tobacco companies).

Technicians are somewhat suspicious of financial statements and consider it an advantage that they generally are not dependent upon them. As our later discussion will show, most of the data used by technicians is derived from the stock market itself.

Once a fundamental analyst has some new information, it is necessary to process this data *correctly* and *very quickly* to derive a new value before the competition can. The technician asks how many analysts can do this consistently and remain ahead of the competition. Technicians contend that they do not have to be the first to see the impact, but only be quick to recognize a movement to a new equilibrium value *for whatever reason.*

Finally, assume an analyst has determined that a given security is under or overvalued a long time before the competition has. This can present the problem of determining *when* to make the purchase or sale. Ideally, an investor would like to buy or sell a stock just before the change in market value occurs. Because a technician doesn't invest until the move to the new equilibrium is under way, he is not likely to purchase a stock that must be held for a long period of time before it is revalued.

Disadvantages of Technical Analysis

The major problem with technical analysis stems from the efficient market hypothesis. The problems considered here are in addition to this.

An obvious problem is that the past price patterns may not be repeated in the future. As a result, there will be instances in which a technique that worked for some period of time misses later market turns. It is because of this attribute that almost all technicians follow several trading rules and attempt to arrive at a consensus. In addition, many price patterns may become self-fulfilling prophecies because everyone believes in them. Assume that a stock is selling at $40 a share and it is widely recognized that, if it "breaks out" of a trading channel at $45, it will be expected to go to $50 or more. If it does get to $45, a number of technicians will buy and the price will probably go to $50, which is exactly what was predicted. In fact, some technicians may place a stop-buy order at such a "break-out" point. Under such conditions, the increase will probably only be temporary and the price will return to its true equilibrium.

Also, the success of a trading rule will encourage competition which will eventually neutralize the value of the technique. If a large number of investors are using a given rule, some of them will eventually attempt to anticipate what will happen and either ruin the "expected" price pattern or take the profits away from most users of the rule. As an example, assume it becomes known that technicians who have been investing on the basis of odd-lot data have been enjoying very high rates of return. You would expect that other technicians will start using these data and affect the stock price pattern following odd-lot changes so that the rule that worked previously may no longer work, or will only work for the first few investors who react.

Finally, as will be discussed later, all of the rules or techniques imply a great deal of subjective judgment. In some cases, two technical analysts looking at the same price pattern will arrive at widely different interpretations and investment decisions. This implies that the use of various techniques is neither completely mechanical nor easy. Also, as will be discussed in connection with several trading rules, the standard values that signal investment action can change over time. Therefore, it is necessary to change the trading rule over time to conform to the new environment.

Technical Trading Rules

There are numerous technical rules and a large number of interpretations for each of them. Almost all technical analysts use more than one rule and some watch many alternatives. This section contains a discussion of most of the well-known techniques, but certainly does not attempt to be all-inclusive.

Contrary Opinion Rules

One set of technical trading rules contends that the majority of investors are wrong most of the time, or at least they are wrong at peaks and troughs. Therefore, the idea is to determine when the majority is either very bullish or very bearish and trade in the opposite direction.

The Odd-Lot Theory   This contends that, although the small investor is generally correct, he or she is almost always wrong at the peaks and troughs. To determine what the small investor is doing, you should watch the odd-lot transactions (i.e., transactions involving less than a round lot, which is usually 100 shares of stock) reported daily in the financial press. In contrast to other trading reports, the figures on odd lots indicate how many shares were purchased and how many were sold, and the two figures obviously do not have to match. Using these figures, technicians develop a ratio of purchases to sales and examine the trend of this ratio, trading when it becomes very bullish or bearish. Historically, the purchase to sales ratio has fluctuated between .60 (very strong sales ratio) to about 1.35 (high proportion of purchases). Therefore, when the ratio approaches the low end of this range (e.g., below .65 or .70) the contrary technician would contend that the odd lotter is very bearish and it is time for a market trough and subsequent rally. In contrast, when the ratio approached the upper end of the range (e.g., above 1.25), this would indicate that the small investor was extremely bullish, and the follower of this ratio would expect the market to peak in the very near future. A major problem with this ratio is that individual investors have been net sellers of common stocks (i.e., selling more than they buy) since the later 1960s, so the ratio is biased downward by this trend. This makes the range of values change over time and, therefore, the purchase/sales ratio values that are considered extreme must be adjusted. The required data for this technique is contained in the *Wall Street Journal* daily and in *Barron's* on a weekly basis.[2]

The Odd-Lot Short-Sales Theory   This is an extension of the general odd-lot theory. The use of short sales is generally considered bearish because it is based upon an expectation of declining stock prices. It is also considered to be a fairly high-risk form of investing. Most small investors are optimists and would consider short selling too risky. Therefore, they do not get involved in it except when they feel especially bearish. Therefore, the technical rule contends that a relatively high rate (3 percent or more) of odd-lot short sales as a percentage of total odd-lot sales is an indication of a very bearish attitude by small investors. Contrary opinion would consider this bearish attitude by small investors an indicator of a near-term trough and technicians following this rule would become bullish. Alternatively, when the ratio declines to below 1 percent, it would indicate that small investors are very bullish, and would cause the contrarian to become bearish.

Mutual Fund Cash Positions   This is considered a contrary tool by some technical analysts. Mutual funds report the ratio of cash as a percentage of total assets in their portfolios over time and this ratio typically varies from a low point of less than 5 percent to a high point in excess of 15 percent. The contrary opin-

---

[2]*Barron's* is a prime source for numerous technical indicators. For a readable discussion of this data and its use, see Martin E. Zweig, *Understanding Technical Forecasting* (New York: Dow-Jones & Co. 1978). Complimentary copies are available from Dow-Jones & Co. A test of this technique is contained in Stanley Kaish, "Odd-Lot Profit and Loss Performance," *Financial Analysts Journal* 25 (1969): 83–89.

ion technicians consider the mutual funds the odd lotters of the institutional investor group and contend that mutual funds are usually wrong at the peaks and troughs. They expect mutual funds to have heavy cash positions (a high ratio of cash) near the trough of a market cycle. This would indicate that the mutual funds are very bearish exactly at the time that they should be fully invested to take advantage of the impending market rise. At the peak, the technicians expect mutual funds to be almost fully invested (a low ratio of cash), indicating a bullish outlook at a point where the funds should have liquidated part of their portfolios. Therefore, these technicians watch for the mutual fund cash position to be at one of the extremes and act contrary to mutual funds behavior; i.e., they would invest when the cash ratio exceeds 12–13 percent and sell when the cash ratio approaches 5 percent.

Heavy mutual fund cash positions are also considered bullish because they are potential buying power. Whether the cash balances have built up because of the previous sale of stocks in the portfolio, or because of purchases of the fund by investors, technicians feel these funds will eventually be invested and cause an increase in stock prices. Obviously, a low cash ratio would indicate a low level of potential buying power.

Credit Balances   These result when investors sell stocks and leave the proceeds with their brokers because they expect to reinvest them shortly. These credit balances are reported by the SEC and the NYSE and are contained in *Barron's*. A declining level of credit balances is subject to two interpretations. One is that these funds are considered to be a pool of potential purchasing power, so a decline in this pool would be considered bearish, i.e., the market is approaching a peak. The other interpretation of some contrary opinion technicians is that these balances are maintained by small investors and they are drawn down just before peaks because of the enthusiasm of this group, which is typically wrong.[3]

Notably, the decision rule is stated in terms of a rising or declining series rather than relative to some other base series. This assumption of an absolute trend could make interpretation difficult as market levels change.

Investment Advisory Opinions   These are another contrary opinion technique. The idea is that when a large proportion of investment advisory services become bearish, this signals the approach of a market trough and it is time to become bullish. The specific ratio examined is the number of advisory services that are bearish as a ratio of the number of services expressing an opinion. When this "Bearish Sentiment Index" reaches 60 percent, it indicates a pervasive bearish attitude and is considered bullish for those who are contrarians. In contrast, when this Bearish Sentiment Index ratio declines to 10 percent, this indicates a pervasive optimistic attitude by investment services and the followers of this index would

---

[3]A discussion of this series for this purpose is contained in Martin E. Zweig, "New Sell Signal?" *Barron's*, 13 October 1975, p. 4.

become bearish. An analysis of this index made by *Investors Intelligence* indicated that it has been a useful series.[4]

Follow the Smart Money

An alternative set of rules for technical analysts involves determining what smart, sophisticated investors are doing and following them.

The Confidence Index   This is published by *Barron's* and is the ratio of *Barron's* average yield on 10 top-grade corporate bonds to the yield on the Dow-Jones average of 40 bonds, indicating the difference in yield spread between high-grade bonds and a large sample of bonds.[5] (The differences in grades of bonds will be dealt with fully in the next chapter.) One would expect the yield on high-grade bonds to be lower than that on a large cross section of bonds, so the ratio should never exceed 100.

The theory behind the ratio is that, during periods of high confidence, investors invest more in lower quality bonds for the added yield. This increased demand for lower quality bonds should cause a decrease in the yield on a large cross section of bonds relative to the yield on high-grade bonds. Therefore, the ratio of yields will increase (the Confidence Index increases). When investors are pessimistic, they avoid the low-quality bonds and increase their investments in high-grade bonds, which increases the yield differential between the two groups and the Confidence Index declines.

A major problem with the concept has been that it is basically demand oriented. It assumes that changes in the yield spread are almost wholly caused by changes in investor demand for different quality bonds. There have been several instances in which the yield differences have changed because of an increased *supply* of bonds in one of the groups or in a related group (e.g., government bonds). A large issue of high-grade AT&T bonds could cause a temporary increase in yields on all high-grade bonds which would cause an increase in the Confidence Index although investors' attitudes did not change. In other words, the change was supply oriented. Under such conditions, the series gives a false signal of a change in confidence. Advocates of the index feel that it can be used as an indicator of future stock-price movements, although one may ask why investors in bonds would change their attitude before equity investors do. Several studies that have examined its usefulness for predicting stock-price movements have not been very supportive regarding the predictive ability of the series, as related to common stock.

Short Sales by Specialists   These are regularly reported by the NYSE and the SEC. It will come as no surprise that technicians who want to follow the smart

---

[4]A. W. Cohen, "A Contrary Opinion Indicator," *Investors Intelligence, 23 October 1975, p. 1.*

[5]Historical data for this series is contained in Maurice L. Farrell, ed., *The Dow-Jones Investor's Handbook* (Princeton, NJ: Dow-Jones Books, annual).

money attempt to determine what the specialist is doing and act accordingly. Specialists regularly engage in short-selling as a part of their market-making function, but they also have some discretion when they feel strongly about market changes. The "normal" ratio of specialists' short sales to the total amount of short sales on the exchange has been about 55 percent. When this ratio declines much *below 40 percent* it is considered a sign that specialists are generally *bullish* and are attempting to avoid short-selling. When the ratio *exceeds 65 percent,* it is contended that specialists are generally *bearish* and are attempting to do as much short-selling as possible. Two points should be noted regarding this ratio. First, you should not expect it to be a long-run indicator; given the nature of the specialists' portfolio, it will probably serve only in the short run. Second, there is a two-week lag in the reporting of this data; e.g., the data for a week ending April 14 would be contained in *Barron's* dated May 1. Even with the lags, an analysis of the graph for the ratio indicates some instances in which an investor could have made timely purchase decisions on the basis of the extreme values.[6]

Debit Balances in Brokerage Accounts   These are considered indicative of the attitude of a sophisticated group of investors because debit balances represent borrowing by knowledgeable investors from their brokers, i.e., margin purchases. Therefore, an increase in these balances indicates an increase in purchasing by this astute group and would be a bullish sign. There can be problems in using this series because it does not include borrowing from other sources (banks, etc.). In addition, an increase in debit balances is considered bullish because it is a source of increased demand for stocks. In contrast, a decline in debit balances would indicate an increase in the supply of stocks as these investors liquidate their positions.

Other Techniques

Breadth of Market   This is a measure of the number of issues that have increased each day and the number of issues that have declined. Everyone is aware of the direction of change in a composite market indicator series like the DJIA or the S&P 400 Index, but they may not be aware of what caused the change. Most of the popular stock market indicator series are either confined to large, well-known stocks or are heavily influenced by the stocks of large firms because most indicator series are value weighted. On occasion composite market indicator series may go up, but the majority of individual issues are not increasing, which is cause for concern. Such a situation can be detected by examining the advance-decline figures along with the composite series.

The advance-decline series is a cumulative series of net advances or net declines. Each day major newspapers publish figures on the number of issues on the

---

[6]A recent study of the ratio is Frank K. Reilly and David T. Whitford, "The Specialists Short Sale Ratio as an Investment Tool," *Journal of Portfolio Management,* forthcoming.

NYSE that advanced, the number of issues that declined, and the number that were unchanged. The figures for a five-day sample, as reported in *Barron's,* were as follows:

Day	1	2	3	4	5
Issues Traded	1,908	1,941	1,959	1,951	1,912
Advances	1,110	1,050	708	1,061	1,125
Declines	409	450	749	433	394
Unchanged	389	441	502	457	393
Net Advances (Advances minus declines)	+701	+600	−41	+628	+731
Cumulative Net Advances	+701	+1,301	+1,260	+1,888	+2,619
Changes in DJIA	+10.47	+3.99	−5.15	+4.16	+5.56

Table 13.1   Daily Advances and Declines on NYSE
Source: Reprinted by permission of the New York Stock Exchange.

These figures, along with the market indicator figures at the bottom of the table, indicate a strong market advance. Not only was the DJIA increasing, but there was a strong net advance figure which indicates that the increase was broadly based; i.e., most individual stocks were increasing. Even the results on Day 3, when the market declined 5 points, were somewhat encouraging because there was a very small net decline figure of 41. The market average was down, but individual stocks were split just about 50-50.

The usefulness of the advance-decline series is supposedly greatest at market peaks and troughs because, at such times, the composite value-weighted market series might be moving either up or down, but the advance or decline would *not* be broadly based and the majority of individual stocks might be moving in the opposite direction. Near a peak, the DJIA would be increasing, but the net advance-decline ratio for individual days would become negative and the cumulative series would begin to decline. The *divergence* between the aggregate market indicator series and the cumulative advance-decline series is a signal for a market peak. At the trough, the composite series would be declining, but the advance-decline ratio would become positive and the cumulative series would turn up before the aggregate market series did.

The principle behind the advance-decline ratio is somewhat akin to the notion of the diffusion index used by the National Bureau of Economic Research. A diffusion index for a given economic series, such as new orders for durable goods, indicates how many of the reporting units show an increase in new orders; i.e, a diffusion index of 60 means 60 percent of the sample report an increase in new orders. During a period of rapid expansion, the diffusion index would be high and the composite series would be increasing rapidly. Near the peak of an economic expansion, the diffusion index would turn down (e.g., from 90 to 70), but the composite would continue to increase. Therefore, the diffusion index turns *before* the composite series does. Similarly, a technician would expect the net advance-decline series and the cumulative advance-decline series to turn before the composite market series.

Short Interest   This is the ratio between the number of shares sold short and not covered, and the average daily volume on the exchange. The interpretation of this ratio by technicians is probably contrary to your initial intuition. Because short sales are made by investors who expect stock prices to decline, one would expect an increase in the short-interest ratio to be bearish. On the contrary, technicians consider a high short-interest ratio *bullish* because it indicates *potential demand* for stock by those who sold short. It is reasoned that they will have to buy the stock in the future to cover their outstanding short position. The ratio has generally fluctuated between 1.00 and 1.75 (i.e., a ratio of 1.00 means that the outstanding short interest on the NYSE is equal to about one day's trading volume). The short interest position is calculated as of the twentieth of each month and reported about two days later in the *Wall Street Journal.* As the short-interest ratio approaches 1.75 it would be considered very bullish, while a decline toward 1.00 would be bearish.

The results of a number of studies on the usefulness of the short-interest series as a predictor of stock-price movements have been extremely mixed. For every study that supported the technique, another indicated that it should be rejected.[7]

Stock Price and Volume Techniques

Most technicians also use trading rules for the market and individual stocks that are based upon stock price and volume movements. Technicians believe that prices move in trends that persist so they contend that it is therefore possible to determine future price trends from an astute analysis of past price and volume trends. Technicians contend that *price alone is somewhat inadequate* and investors should also examine the volume of trading that accompanies price changes.

The Dow Theory   Any discussion of technical analysis using price and volume must begin with a consideration of the Dow Theory developed by Charles Dow, publisher of the *Wall Street Journal,* during the late 1800s.[8] Dow contended that

---

[7]Barton M. Biggs, "The Short Interest—A False Proverb," *Financial Analysts Journal* 22 (1966): 111–116. Joseph J. Seneca, "Short Interest: Bearish or Bullish?" *Journal of Finance* 22 (1967): 67–70. Thomas H. Mayor, "Short Trading Activities and the Price of Equities: Some Simulation and Regression Results," *Journal of Financial and Quantitative Analysis* 3 (1968): 283–298. Randall Smith, "Short Interest and Stock Market Prices," *Financial Analysts Journal* 24 (1968): 151–154. Thomas J. Kerrigan, "The Short Interest Ratio and Its Component Parts," *Financial Analysts Journal* 32 (1974): 45–49. William Goff, "Letter to the Editor," *Financial Analysts Journal* 31 (1975): 8–10.

[8]An extensive discussion of the Dow Theory is contained in George W. Bishop, Jr. "Evolution of the Dow Theory," *Financial Analysts Journal* 17 (1961): 23–36.

stock prices moved in trends that were analogous to the movement of water. There were three types of price movements that should be analyzed over time: (1) major trends that are like tides in the ocean; (2) intermediate trends that are similar to waves; and (3) short-run movements that are like ripples. The idea is to detect which way the major price trend (tide) is going, recognizing that there will be intermediate movements (waves) in the opposite direction. A major market advance does not go straight up, but is accompanied by small price declines as some investors decide to take profits. The typical bullish pattern will be as follows:

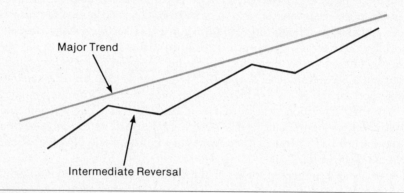

Figure 13.2　An Example of a Bullish Price Pattern

The technician would look for every recovery to reach a high point above the prior peak with heavy trading volume, while each reversal should have a trough above the prior trough and volume should be relatively light during the reversals. When this no longer happens, the major trend (tide) may be ready for a permanent reversal.

Support and Resistance Levels　A *support level* is the price range at which the analyst would expect a considerable increase in the demand for a stock. Generally, a support level will develop after the price has increased and the stock has begun to experience a reversal because of profit taking. At some price there are other investors who did not buy during the first rally and have been waiting for a small reversal to "get into" the stock. When the price reaches the point at which they want to buy, there is an increase in demand and the price begins to increase again.

　A *resistance level* is the price range at which the analyst would expect the supply of stock to increase substantially and any price rise to be abruptly reversed. A resistance level tends to develop after a stock has experienced a steady decline from a higher price level. Because of the decline, investors who acquired the stock at a higher price are waiting for an opportunity to sell it and get out at about the break-even point. Therefore, this supply of stock is overhanging the market and, when the price rebounds to the target price set by these investors, the supply increases dramatically and the price increase is reversed.

Importance of Volume   Technicians are clearly not only concerned with price movements, but also watch volume changes as an indicator of changes in supply and demand for a stock or for stocks in general. A price movement in one direction indicates that the *net* effect is in that direction, but does not say anything about how *widespread* the excess demand or supply is at that time. A price increase of a half point on volume of 1,000 shares indicates excess demand, but not much overall interest. In contrast, a one-point increase on volume of 20,000 shares indicates a large demand. Therefore, it is not only a price increase, but also heavy volume relative to the stock's normal trading volume that interests the technician. Following the same line of reasoning, a price decline with heavy volume is very bearish because it means strong and widespread desire to sell the stock. A generally bullish pattern is a price increase on heavy volume and a price reversal with light trading volume indicating only limited desire to sell and take profits.

Moving-Average Line   Technicians are constantly looking for ways of detecting changes in major price trends for an individual stock or for the aggregate market. One relatively popular tool is constructing a moving average of past stock prices as an indicator of the long-run trend and examining current prices in terms of this trend to see whether the relationship between current prices and the long-term trend signals a change. The number of days used in computing the moving average is a matter of judgment but a *200-day moving average* is a relatively popular measure for the aggregate market. If the overall trend has been down, the moving-average line would generally be above the current individual prices. If prices reverse and *break through the moving-average line from below on heavy volume,* a technician might speculate that the declining trend has been reversed. In contrast, given a rising trend, the moving-average line would be rising and would be below the current prices. If current prices broke through the moving-average line from above on heavy volume, this would be a bearish indication of a reversal of the long-run rising trend.[9]

Relative Strength   Technicians believe that, once a trend is initiated, it will continue until some major event causes a change in direction. This is also true of *relative* performance. If a stock is outperforming the market, technicians believe it will continue to outperform the market. To detect this relative performance, technicians compute relative-strength ratios for individual stocks in terms of some aggregate market series on a weekly or monthly basis. This is simply a ratio of the stock price to the value for some market series like the DJIA or the S&P 400. If the ratio increases over time, the stock is outperforming the market and it

[9]A test of this technique is contained in F. E. James, Jr., "Monthly Moving Averages—An Effective Investment Tool?" *Journal of Financial and Quantitative Analysis* 3 (1968): 315–326; and in I. C. Van Horne and G. C. Parker, "The Random Walk Theory: An Empirical Test," *Financial Analysts Journal* 23 (1967): 57–64.

is believed that this superior performance will continue for a time. The relative-strength ratios work during declining and rising markets (i.e., if the stock does not decline as much as the market does, the relative-strength ratio will continue to rise). It is felt that, if the ratio holds up or increases during a bear market, the stock should do very well during the ensuing bull market. These ratios are used for industry analysis as well as for company analysis.[10]

Bar Charting   The basic chart used in technical analysis is one on which the time series of prices for specified time intervals (daily, weekly, monthly) are plotted. For a given interval, the technical analyst will plot the high and low price and connect the two points to form a bar. Typically, he will also draw a small horizontal line across it to indicate the closing price. Finally, almost all bar charts also include the volume of trading at the bottom of the chart so that the analyst can relate the price and volume movements. An example is given in Figure 13.3 which is the bar chart for the DJIA from *The Wall Street Journal* along with the volume figures for the NYSE.

The technical analyst might also include a 200-day moving average for the series and possible resistance and support levels based upon past patterns. Finally, if it is a bar chart for an individual stock, it could contain a relative-strength line. Most technicians include as many price and volume series as is reasonable on one chart and attempt to arrive at a consensus concerning future movement for the stock based upon the performance of several technical indicators.

Point-and-Figure Charts   Another popular device used by technicians is called point-and-figure charting.[11] As is true of all other technical tools, its purpose is to detect changes in the supply and demand for a particular security. In contrast to the bar chart that typically includes all ending prices and volume for purposes of detecting a trend, the point-and-figure chart only includes "significant" price changes irrespective of the time interval involved. The analyst determines which significant price changes will be recorded (1 point, 2 points, etc.) and when a price reversal will be recorded. The following example should make this clear. Assume that you want to chart a stock that is currently selling for $40 a share and is quite volatile (beta of 1.60). Because of its volatility, you feel that anything less than a two-point price change is not relevant. Also, you feel that anything less than a four-point reversal is quite minor. Therefore, you would set up a chart similar to the one in Figure 13.4 that starts at 40 and progresses in two-point increments. If the stock moves to 42, you place an X in the box above 40 and do nothing else until the stock rises to 44 or drops to 38 (a four-point reversal from its high

[10]For further discussion of this technique by a leading advocate, see Robert A. Levy, "Relative Strength as a Criterion for Investment Selection," *Journal of Finance* 22 (1967): 595–610; Robert A. Levy and Spero L. Kripotos "Sources of Relative Price Strength," *Financial Analysts Journal,* 25 (1969): 60 et seg.; Robert A. Levy, *The Relative Strength Concept of Common Stock Price Forecasting* (Larchmont, NY: Investors Intelligence, 1968). A more recent study is Charles A. Akemann and Werner E. Keller, "Relative Strength Does Persist!" *Journal of Portfolio Management* 4 (1977): 38–45.

[11]Daniel Seligman, "The Mystique of Point-and-Figure," *Fortune,* March 1962, pp. 113–115.

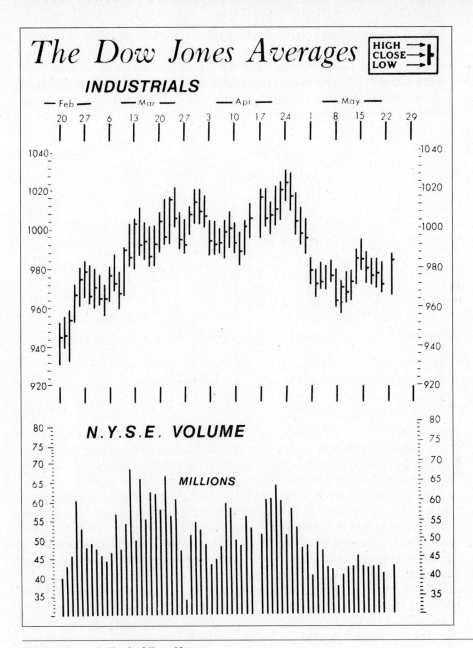

Figure 13.3   A Typical Bar Chart

of 42). If it drops to 38, you move over a column to the right begin again at 38 (fill in boxes at 42 and 40). Assuming the stock price drops to 34, you would enter an X at 36 and another at 34. If the stock then rises to 38 (another four-point reversal), you move to the next column and begin at 38 going up (fill in 34 and 36). Assuming the stock then goes to 46, you would fill in as shown and wait for further increases or a reversal.

```
50 │     │     │     │     │     │     │
48 │     │     │     │     │     │     │
46 │     │   X │     │     │     │     │
44 │     │   X │     │     │     │     │
42 │ X │ X │ X │     │     │     │     │
40 │ X │ X │ X │     │     │     │     │
38 │   │ X │ X │     │     │     │     │
36 │   │ X │ X │     │     │     │     │
34 │   │ X │ X │     │     │     │     │
32 │     │     │     │     │     │     │
30 │     │     │     │     │     │     │
```

Figure 13.4   Example of a Point-and-Figure Chart

Depending upon how fast the prices rise and fall, this process may have taken anywhere from two to six months. Given these figures, the analyst would attempt to determine trends in the same manner as he did with the bar chart.

As always, you are looking for "breakouts" to either higher or lower price levels.[12] A long sideways movement in which there are many reversals but no major shifts in any direction would be considered a period of "consolidation" as the stock is moving from one group to another with no strong consensus of direction. Once the stock "breaks out" and moves up or down after a period of consolidation, it is assumed that this is a major move because of the previous trading that set the stage for it. The difference between point-and-figure and bar charts is that with the former you have a compact record of movements because only those price changes considered relevant for the particular stock analyzed are recorded. Therefore, it is easier to work with and to use in visualizing movements.

[12]A study that examined the usefulness of various price patterns is Robert A. Levy, "The Predictive Significance of Five Point Chart Patterns," *Journal of Business* 44 (1971): 316–323. The results were not encouraging for the technician.

Summary

The purpose of this chapter was to introduce the reader to *what* technical analysts do, *why* they do it, and *how* they do it. Our initial discussion considered the basic rationale behind technical analysis and how it differed from the practices of those who believe in an efficient stock market. The main differences relate to the information dissemination process (does everybody get the information at about the same time?) and to how quickly investors adjust stock prices to reflect this new information. Because technical analysts believe that the information dissemination process is not the same for everyone, and that price adjustment is not instantaneous, they contend that *stock prices move in trends that persist* and, therefore, that you can use past price trends to determine future price trends.

Subsequently we discussed the advantages and disadvantages of technical analysis. The rest of the chapter discussed specific technical trading rules under four general categories: contrary opinion rules, follow the smart money, other trading rules, and stock price and volume techniques. It was noted that most technicians use several rules at any one point in time and attempt to derive a consensus decision which can be buy, sell, or do nothing. According to many technicians, their conclusion on many occasions is to do nothing.

Questions

1. The basic belief of technical analysts is that it is possible to use past price changes to predict future price changes. What is the principal contention that makes this basic belief possible?

2. Technicians contend that stock prices move in trends that persist for a long time. What is there about the real world that causes those trends? Put another way, what do technicians believe happens in the real world that would cause stock prices to move in trends?

3. Briefly discuss the problems involved with fundamental analysis that are considered to be advantages for technical analysis.

4. What are some of the disadvantages of technical analysis?

5. The odd-lot purchase/sales ratio reaches 1.40. What would this indicate to a contrary opinion technician? What is the reasoning behind this?

6. The mutual fund cash position increases to 13 percent; is this bullish or bearish? Why? Give two reasons for your position.

7. There is a strong decline in credit balances at brokerage firms. Give two reasons why this is considered bearish.

8. The Bearish Sentiment Index of advisory service opinions increases to 61 percent; is this bullish or bearish? Discuss the concept and indicate why this figure is bullish or bearish.

9. Define the Confidence Index and describe the reasoning behind it. Discuss why the fact that the Confidence Index is demand oriented is a problem.

10. The ratio of specialists' short sales to total short sales increases to 70 percent. As a technician would you consider this bullish or bearish and why? How would you feel if there were an increase in odd-lot short sales? Why?

11. Why is an increase in debit balances considered bullish? What problems are involved with using this series as a technical tool?

12. Describe the Dow Theory and its three components. Which component is most important?

13. Why is volume important to a technician? Describe a bearish price and volume pattern and discuss why it is bearish.

14. Describe the computation of the breadth of market index and discuss how it is used to confirm an important peak in stock prices.

15. Describe a support and a resistance level and explain why they are expected to occur.

16. What is the purpose of computing a moving-average line for a stock? Describe a bullish pattern using a moving-average line and discuss why it is considered bullish.

17. How would you construct a relative-strength series for a stock? What do you mean when you say a stock had good relative strength during a bear market?

18. Select a stock on the NYSE and construct a daily high, low, close bar chart for the stock that includes volume for ten trading days.

19. Compute the relative-strength ratio for the stock in Question 18 relative to the S&P 500 Index and prepare a table that includes all the data and indicates the computations as follows:

Day	Closing Price		Stock Price/S&P 500
	Stock	S&P 500	

20. Plot the relative-strength ratio computed in Question 19 on your bar chart and discuss whether the stock's relative strength is bullish or bearish.

21. Construct a one-point interval point-and-figure chart and use a two-point reversal rule for a stock selling at $25 a share. Fill in the chart for the following closing prices: 24, 22, 21, 24, 26, 28, 29, 27, 24, 22, 20, 19.

22. Most technicians follow several technical rules and attempt to derive a consensus. What is the reason for this?

References

Akemann, Charles A., and Keller, Werner E. "Relative Strength Does Persist!" *Journal of Portfolio Management* 4 (1977).

Arnott, Robert D. "Relative Strength Revisited." *Journal of Portfolio Management* 5 (1979).

Biggs, Barton M. "The Short Interest—A False Proverb." *Financial Analysts Journal* 22 (1966).

Bishop, George W., Jr. "Evolution of the Dow Theory." *Financial Analysts Journal 17 (1961).*

Bishop, George W., Jr. *Charles H. Dow and the Dow Theory.* New York: Appleton-Century-Crofts, 1960.

Branch, Ben. "The Predictive Power of Stock Market Indicators." *Journal of Financial and Quantitative Analysis* 11 (1976).

Crouch, Robert L. "Market Volume and Price Changes." *Financial Analysts Journal* 26 (1970).

Dines, James. *How the Average Investor Can Use Technical Analysis for Stock Profits.* New York: Dines Chart Corporation, 1974.

Drew, Garfield A. *New Methods for Profit in the Stock Market.* 4th ed. Wells, T.: Fraser Publishing, 1966.

Drew, Garfield A. *"A Clarification of the Odd Lot Theory."* Financial Analysts Journal 23 (1967).

Edwards, R. D., and Magee, John, Jr. *Technical Analysis of Stock Trends.* Springfield, MA.: Stock Trend Service, 1966.

Ehrbar, A. F. "Technical Analysts Refuse to Die." *Fortune,* August 1975.

Encyclopedia of Stock Market Techniques. Larchmont, NY: Investor's Intelligence, 1971.

Garbisch, Michael W., and Alexander, Gordon J. "Is Standard and Poor's Master List Worthless?" *Journal of Portfolio Management* 4 (1977).

Gould, Alex, and Buchsbaum, Maurice. "A Filter Approach to Stock Selection." *Financial Analysts Journal* 25 (1969).

Grant, Dwight. "Market Timing: Strategies to Consider." *Journal of Portfolio Management* 5 (1979)

Hardy, C. Colburn. *Investor's Guide to Technical Analysis.* New York: McGraw-Hill, 1978.

James, F. E., Jr. "Monthly Moving Averages—An Effective Investment Tool?" *Journal of Financial and Quantitative Analysis* 3 (1968).

Jiler, William L. *How Charts Can Help You in the Stock Market.* New York: Commodity Research Publications Corp., 1967.

Kaish, Stanley. "Odd Lot Profit and Loss Performance." *Financial Analysts Journal* 25 (1969).

Kaish, Stanley. "Odd Lotter Trading of High and Low Quality Stocks." *Financial Analysts Journal* 25 (1969).

Kerr, H. S. "The Battle of Insider Trading vs Market Efficiency," *Journal of Portfolio Management* 6 (1980).

Kerrigan, Thomas J. "The Short Interest Ratio and Its Component Parts." *Financial Analysts Journal* 32 (1974).

Levy, Robert A. "Conceptual Foundations of Technical Analysis." *Financial Analysts Journal* 22 (1966).

Levy, Robert A. "The Predictive Significance of Five Point Chart Patterns." *Journal of Business* 44 (1971).

Levy, Robert A. *The Relative Strength Concept of Common Stock Price Forecasting.* Larchmont, NY: Investors Intelligence, 1968.

Levy, Robert A. "Random Walks: Reality or Myth." *Financial Analysts Journal* 23 (1967).

Levy, Robert A. "Relative Strength as a Criterion for Investment Selection." *Journal of Finance* 22 (1967).

Levy, Robert A., and Kripotos, Spero L. "Sources of Relative Price Strength." *Financial Analysts Journal* 25 (1969).

Massey, Paul F. "The Mutual Fund Liquidity Ratio: A Trap for the Unwary." *Journal of Portfolio Management* 5 (1979).

Pinches, George E. "The Random Walk Hypothesis and Technical Analysis." *Financial Analysts Journal* 26 (1970).

Reilly, Frank K. and Whitford, David T. "The Specialists Short Sale Ratio as an Investment Tool," *Journal of Portfolio Management,* forthcoming.

Seligman, Daniel. "The Mystique of Point-and-Figure." *Fortune,* March 1962.

Seneca, Joseph J. "Short Interest: Bearish or Bullish?" *Journal of Finance* 22 (1967).

Shaw, Alan R. "Technical Analysis." In *Financial Analysts Handbook* edited by Sumner N. Levine. Vol. 1. Homewood, IL: Dow-Jones Irwin, 1975.

Smith, Randall, "Short Interest and Stock Market Prices" *Financial Analysts Journal* 24 (1968)

Tabell, Edmund W., and Tabell, Anthony W. "The Case for Technical Analysis." *Financial Analysts Journal* 20 (1964).

Van Horne, James C., and Parker, G. C. "The Random Walk Theory: An Empirical Test," *Financial Analysts Journal* 23 (1967).

Ying, Charles C. "Stock Market Prices and Volume of Sales." *Econometrica* 34 (1966).

Zweig, Martin E. "New Sell Signal?" *Barron's,* 13 October 1975.

Zweig, Martin E. *Understanding Technical Forecasting.* New York: Dow-Jones & Co., 1978.

ANALYSIS AND MANAGEMENT
OF BONDS

PART·THREE

As an investment vehicle, bonds have undergone a cycle of popularity during the twentieth century. In the early decades, bonds were the major investment instrument. This changed during the "Roaring 20s" when the stock market became the favorite of investors who thought they could become wealthy overnight by investing in common stock purchased on large margins. This dream ended with the stock market crash in 1929. In reaction to the crash there was increased interest in bonds because of the safety involved. During the "Flying Fifties" and "Soaring Sixties" the pendulum again swung in favor of common stocks, and it was generally felt that the only investors interested in bonds were those on pensions or those who did not recognize the excitement and advantages of common stock. Toward the end of this period (about 1965), even the large financial institutions drastically changed their portfolio mix toward common stocks. Starting in about 1966 the U.S. economy experienced an extended period of significant inflation. In contrast to previous belief, this long period of inflation made investors recognize that common stocks have not been a good hedge against significant inflation. After about a decade of poor performance by common stocks and reasonably good returns from bonds, beginning in 1975, the pendulum began swinging back toward a renewed interest in bonds. There were signs of a reversal in 1980 because of the very large and rapid changes in interest rates during the year. Specifically, during 1980, short-term rates reached a high point of about 18 percent in March and then declined to a low of less than 7 percent in August before rising again to over 16 percent in December. During the same period, long-term rates of interest went from 14 percent to 9 percent and back to about 14 percent. As a result of these interest rate movements, the holding-period returns for the investor who owned bonds during this time period were very volatile.[1] The net result has been that investors have a more realistic attitude towards bonds: they recognize the profit opportunities, but also the added risk of investing in bonds because of interest rate volatility. There is a growing awareness that it is neither necessary nor desirable to invest only in bonds or stocks. The fact is, both of these financial instruments should be part of a properly diversified portfolio.

The purpose of Chapter 14 is to provide you with a thorough background in the overall makeup of the bond market, attributes of major fixed-income instruments, and sources of information regarding bonds. Chapter 15 is concerned with the valuation of bonds and considers the several factors that influence bond values and bond price movements. There is also a consideration of alternative bond portfolio strategies and how they are implemented.

---

[1]In this regard, see Daniel Hertzberg, "Bond Market Becomes Increasingly Volatile, With Some Big Losses," *Wall Street Journal,* 21 February 1980, p. 1; and idem, "Bond Trading Has Been Basically Changed by Inflation, Price Volatility, Experts Say," *Wall Street Journal* 7 November 1980, p. 46.

Burton G. Malkiel

Very few individuals can carry on highly respected academic research and can also write for the popular audience. A person that has clearly accomplished both is Burton Malkiel. He has written a number of outstanding articles in investments and economics and several significant academic books. At the same time, he has managed to author two very readable and very successful books for the popular market.

His academic research has been heavily involved with an analysis of the impact of expectations on bond prices, the term structure of interest rates, and equity prices. His articles include: "Expectations' Bond Prices, and the Term Structure of Interest Rates," Quarterly Journal of Economics *(May 1962); "Equity Yields, Growth, and Structure of Share Prices," "American Economic Review (December 1963); "The Term Structure of Interest Rates,"*

American Economic Review *(May 1964);* "The Consensus and Accuracy of Some Predictions of the Growth of Corporate Earnings," *(with John Cragg),* Journal of Finance *(March 1968); "Expectations and the Structure of Share Prices," (with John Cragg),* American Economic Review *(September 1970); "Financial Analysis in an Inflationary Environment," (with George Von Furstenberg),* Journal of Finance *(May 1977); "A Winning Strategy for an Efficient Market, (with Paul Firstenberg),* Journal of Portfolio Management *(Summer 1978), and* "The Valuation of Closed-End Investment Company Shares," *Journal of Finance (June 1977). He is also the co-author (with Richard E. Quandt of* Strategies and Rational Decisions in the Securities Options Market *(Cambridge: MIT Press, 1969). This book had a major impact on the establishment of* the Chicago Board Options Exchange (CBOE).

Besides these several significant academic contributions, Dr. Malkiel is the author of A Random Walk Down Wall Street (New York: W. W. Norton & Co., 1981). This book was originally published in 1973 and became a bestseller because of its easy-to-read discussion of the efficient markets hypothesis and the implications of this theory to the typical investor. The 1981 edition updated the initial analysis and discusses the implications for the 1980s. He also published another widely read book, The Inflation-Beater's Investment Guide (New York: W. W. Norton & Co., New York, 1980), which specifically analyzes the recent inflationary period and explains how investors can cope with this economic environment.

Burton G. Malkiel was born August 28, 1932, in Boston. He received his B.A. degree from Harvard in 1953 and an MBA from the Harvard Graduate School of Business in 1955. After three years in the army and two years as an analyst for Smith Barney & Co., he returned to Princeton University and received his Ph.D. in 1964. He was hired as an assistant professor of economics at Princeton in 1964, became an associate professor in 1966, and professor in 1968. He was named the Gordon S. Rentschler Memorial Professor in 1969 and chairman of the economics department in 1974. He was also appointed the director of the Financial Research Center at Princeton in 1966 and is a past president of the American Finance Association. In 1981 he became dean of the Yale School of Organization and Management.

BOND FUNDAMENTALS

⇒ 14 ⇐

The market for fixed-income securities is large and diverse, and represents an exciting and profitable outlet for investment. This chapter is primarily concerned with publicly-issued, long-term, nonconvertible, straight-debt obligations of both public and private issuers. In later chapters, we consider other fixed-income securities, such as preferred stock and convertible bonds. An understanding of bonds is helpful in an efficient market because bonds and other forms of fixed-income securities increase the universe of investment options necessary for diversification.[1]

In this chapter we will discuss bond fundamentals, reviewing some basic features of bonds, extensively examining the fixed-income securities market structure, and looking at alternative fixed-income investment vehicles. The chapter ends with a brief review of the data requirements of bond investors and the sources of such information.

Basic Features of a Bond

Essentially, bonds are an issuer's long-term, public debt which is marketed in a convenient and affordable denomination. They differ from other forms of debt, such as mortgages and privately placed obligations, because they have been placed in the hands of numerous public investors, rather than channeled directly to a single lender. Bond issues are considered fixed-income securities because the debt-service obligations of the issuer are fixed. Specifically, the issuer agrees to:

1. pay a fixed amount of periodic *interest* to the holder of record, and
2. repay a fixed amount of *principal* at the date of maturity.

---

[1]William F. Sharpe, "Bonds Versus Stocks: Some Lessons from Capital Market Theory," *Financial Analysts Journal* 29 (1973): 73–79.

Normally, interest on bonds is paid every six months. Occasionally, however, a bond issue may carry provisions to pay interest in intervals as short as a month or as long as a year. The principal is due at maturity; this is the *par value* of the issue. The par value of most debt issues is fairly substantial, very rarely less than $1,000 and often more.

Another important dimension of bonds is their term to maturity, or the life of issue. The public debt market is often divided into three time segments, defined in terms of an issue's original maturity as follows:

1. Short-Term—instruments with maturities of one year or less. This segment is commonly known as the "money market."

2. Intermediate—involves issues with maturities in excess of one year, but less than seven to ten years. These are known as "notes."

3. Long-Term—includes obligations with maturities in excess of seven to ten years. These are referred to as "bonds."

The lives of debt obligations, however, are constantly changing as the issues progress toward maturity. Thus, "seasoned" issues (i.e., those that have been outstanding in the secondary market for any period of time) move from one maturity segment to shorter segments. As an example, a bond issued in 1980 with a maturity in 2005 will originally be a long-term bond but eventually will become an intermediate-term security when it has less than ten years to maturity, and finally will be a short-term security when there is less than a year to maturity. This movement is important because the price volatility of a debt obligation is affected by, among other things, the prevailing maturity of the issue. Thus, a 3-year obligation, other things being equal, will have less price volatility than, say, a 25-year obligation has. The fact that the 3-year bond was originally a 25-year bond would have absolutely no effect on its *current* price behavior.

Bond Characteristics

One can characterize a bond in many different ways: each bond has intrinsic features that relate to the issue itself; there are different types of bonds; and there are various indenture provisions that can affect the yield and/or price behavior.

Intrinsic Characteristics

There are several intrinsic features that are important: coupon, maturity, the principal value of the issue, and finally, the type of bond ownership. The coupon indicates the income that the bond investor will receive over the life (or holding period) of the issue, and is known as interest income, coupon income, or nominal yield.

The maturity of an issue specifies the date at which the bond will mature (or expire), and is referred to as term to maturity. Two important types of bonds can be distinguished on the basis of maturity, a term bond and a serial issue. A *term bond* has a single maturity date specified in the issue and is the most common type of corporate or government bond. A *serial obligation* actually involves a series of maturity dates. Thus, a single 25-year issue, for example, may possess 20 or 25 different maturity dates. Each maturity, though a subset of the total issue, is really a small bond issue in itself with a different maturity and, generally, a different coupon. Municipalities are the biggest issuers of serial bonds.

The principal, or par value, of the issue represents the original principal value of the obligation and is generally stated in thousand-dollar increments. While $1,000 is a popular principal value, there are many issues with denominations that go much higher, to $25,000 or more. Principal value is *not* necessarily the same as market value. It is not uncommon to find issues traded at market values that are substantially above or below their original principal value. Such price behavior is the result of a difference between the coupon of the obligation and the prevailing market rate of interest. When market rates go up, lower coupon issues decline in value to a market price below par. If the issue carries a coupon comparable to the market interest rate, its market value will correspond to its original principal value.

The final intrinsic provision is whether the issue is a "bearer bond" or a "registered" issue. With the former type, which is the more common, the holder, or bearer, is the owner. The issuer keeps no account of transfers in ownership, and interest is obtained by "clipping coupons" and sending them to the issuer for payment. Such payment is usually handled through local commercial banks in a routine, systematic manner. The issuers of registered bonds keep track of owners of record and, at the time of principal or interest payment, simply pay the owner of record by check.

Types of Issues

In contrast to common stock, issuers of bonds can have many different types outstanding at a single point in time. Generally, one type of bond is differentiated from another by the type of collateral behind the issue. Bonds can be distinguished as either senior or junior securities. The former are generally thought of as "secured bonds," that is, they are backed by a legal claim on some specified property of the issuer. For example, "mortgage bonds" are secured by real assets, and "Equipment Trust Certificates," which are popular with railroads and airlines, indicate a senior claim on the equipment of the railroad or airline.

Unsecured (junior) bonds are issues backed only by the promise of the issuer to pay interest and principal on a timely basis. There are several classes of unsecured bonds. One is a "debenture," which is simply a bond secured by the general credit of the issuer. In addition, there are "subordinated debentures" that represent a claim on income that is subordinated (or secondary) to the claim of another debenture bond. "Income issues" represent the most junior type because interest on these need to be paid only to the extent to which income is earned. They entail no legally binding requirement to pay interest on a periodic basis. While they are unusual in the corporate sector, they are a very popular municipal issue, and are referred to as "revenue bonds".

Finally, an issue could be a "refunding" type which means that one bond is prematurely retired by paying off its principal from the proceeds of the sale of another issue. The second issue remains outstanding after the refunding operation. Thus, such terms as "first and refunding" refer to refunding obligations. A refunding bond can take either a junior or senior position, depending upon whether it is secured or not. The type of issue has only a marginal effect on comparative yield because it is the credibility of the issuer that basically determines the quality of the obligation. In fact, a study of corporate bond price behavior found that the collateral of the obligation, or lack of it, did not become important until the issue approached default.[2] Usually, collateral and security only influence yield differentials when such senior/junior positions affect the quality ratings given to a bond by agencies such as Moody's, S&P, or Duff and Phelps.

Indenture Provisions

The indenture is the contract between the issuer and the bond holder specifying the legal conditions that must be met by the issuer. Most of the provisions are of little interest to bond investors because the trustee (i.e., the organization or institution acting in behalf of the bondholders) sees to it that all of the provisions are met, including the timely and orderly distribution of interest and principal.

However, investors should be aware of a few popular indenture provisions, especially the "call features." There are three types of call provisions: (1) the bond can be "freely callable," which means that the issuer can retire the bond at any time within its life given a notification period of, usually, 30 to 60 days; (2) the obligation can be "noncallable," which means that the issuer *cannot* retire the bond prior to its maturity; and (3) it may have a "deferred call" feature, stipulating that the obligation cannot be called for a certain length of time after the date of issue (recently the most popular time period has been between five and ten years). At the end of the deferred call period, the issue becomes freely callable. The investor should also be aware of the "call premium," the added cost the issuer must pay to the bondholder for prematurely retiring the bond.

In lieu of a call feature, a bond may contain a "refunding" provision which is exactly like the call feature *except that* it only prohibits (or allows) one thing: the retirement of an issue from the proceeds of a lower coupon refunding bond. This means that the obligation can still be called and prematurely retired for any reason other than refunding! If a firm has excess cash, for example, the issue could carry a nonrefunding provision but still be retired prior to maturity. In fact, during 1975 this occurred when many issuers did not refund their obligations but, instead, simply retired these costly high-coupon issues early because they had the cash and viewed the action as a viable investment opportunity.

Another important provision is the "sinking fund" feature which specifies how the bond will be amortized (or repaid) over its life. While most issues require some form of sinking fund provisions, a number of industrial obligations and government issues do not. In these cases, all or most of the issue is payable at maturity, and no attempt is made to systematically retire these obligations over their life. Such provisions have an effect on comparative yields at date of issue, but little subsequent effect on comparative price behavior.

There are many different types of sinking fund provisions. For example, util-

---

[2]W. Braddock Hickman, *Corporate Bond Quality and Investor Experience* (Princeton, NJ: Princeton University Press, 1958).

ity issuers often employ provisions actually giving them the right to use the periodic sinking fund to either acquire outstanding bonds *or increase the capital assets of the firm.* This is known as an "improvement" fund and requires an annual
sinking fund of at least one percent of the *total* bonds outstanding. The size of the
sinking fund can be a percentage of a given issue or of the *total* debt outstanding.
Moreover, it can be a fixed or variable sum, stated on a dollar or percentage basis. The amount of the issue that must be repaid before maturity ranges
from a nominal sum to 100 percent, and the payments may commence at the
end of the first year or be deferred for as long as five to ten years from date of
the issue.

Like a call or refunding provision, the sinking fund feature also carries a
nominal call premium, perhaps one percent or less. Unlike call or refunding features, however, a sinking fund provision must be carried out regardless of interest
rate behavior or other market conditions. Therefore, there is a small risk for investors in a sinking fund bond that the bond issue could be called on a random
basis. Such random public calls have been fairly rare because most bonds have
been trading at a discount (i.e., at a price below par) and are retired for sinking
fund purposes by having the issuer or trustee negotiate with a big institutional
holder to buy back the necessary amount of bonds at a price slightly above the
current market price.

Bond Rates of Return

The rate of return on a bond is computed in the same way as the rate of return
on stock or any asset; it is determined by the beginning and ending price and the
cash flows during the holding period. The major difference between stocks and
bonds is that the interim cash flows (i.e., the interest) are specified for bonds, while
the dividends on stock are not contractual. Therefore, the rate of return for a
bond will be:

$$R_{i,t} = \frac{P_{i,t+1} - P_{i,t} + Int_{i,t}}{P_{i,t}}$$

where:

$R_{i,t}$ = the rate of return for bond i during period t

$P_{i,t+1}$ = the market price of bond i at the end of period t

$P_{i,t}$ = the market price of bond i at the beginning of period t

$Int_{i,t}$ = the interest payments on bond i during period t.

It is important to recognize that the only fixed and known factor is the interest
payments, which are specified by contract. The beginning price will be determined by market forces, which we will discuss. The ending price will likewise be
determined by market forces prevailing at the time of sale unless the bond is held
to maturity, in which case the investor will receive the par value. The point is,

there can be large price variations in bonds which provide opportunities for an investor in bonds to experience capital gains or losses during different holding periods. Because of substantial interest rate volatility since the 1960s, there have been large price fluctuations in bonds. As a result, the capital gain or loss segment of the total return has been the major factor determining the rates of return on bonds.

Determination of Bond Price

The price of a bond is determined by the coupon that the issue carries, the length of its term to maturity, and the prevailing market interest rate on the bond referred to as its *yield*. While the next chapter contains the detailed mathematics of bond price behavior, it is important at this point to gain a basic understanding of how the price of bonds is determined. As we will show, given the coupon and maturity for a bond, the price is determined by the market interest rate on the bond (i.e., by the yield required). Therefore, bond price behavior over time is determined by how market interest rates change over time.

As discussed in Chapter 8, the price (value) of a bond is determined like that of any other financial asset; it is the present value of the expected cash flows from the asset. In the case of a bond, we know what the promised cash flows are, so the only unknown is the required rate of return. As an example, assume you want to determine the price of a $1,000 par-value bond with a 10 percent coupon that matures in ten years. Assuming annual interest payments are made, this implies that the expected cash flows will be $100 a year (.10 times $1,000) for ten years and $1,000 at the end of ten years. Given this information, it is necessary to know the required market yield on this bond. Assume you are told the required yield is 12 percent. As discussed in Chapter 8, the value of the bond is:

$100 × 5.650 (the present value of a ten-year   = $565.00
annuity at 12 percent)

$1,000 × .322 (the present-value factor for ten   =   322.00
years at 12 percent)

                                   Total Present Value $887.00

Therefore, the market price for this bond should be $887.00 or 88.7 percent of par. Obviously, because the market yield on this bond is above its coupon rate, the bond is selling at a discount from par.

Assume that over the next year, market interest rates decline and the market yield on this bond declines to 8 percent. At this point it is a nine-year bond (nine years to maturity) and the market price would be as follows:

$100 × 6.247 (the present value of a nine-year = $ 624.70
annuity at 8 percent)

$1,000 × .500 (the present-value factor for nine   =   500.000
years at 8 percent)

                                   Total Present Value $1,124.70

Therefore, the market price for this bond would be $1,124.70 or 112.47 of par. Now, because the market yield is below the coupon rate, the bond is selling at a premium relative to its par value. The rate of return for an investor who owned the bond during this year was as follows:

$$R_{i,t} = \frac{\$1,124.70 - 887.00 + 100.00}{887.00}$$

$$= \frac{237.70 + 100.00}{887.00}$$

$$= \frac{337.70}{887.00}$$

$$= .3807 = 38.07\%$$

Two important points regarding this example:

1. There was a substantial price change because of the change in market interest rates which affected the required market yield on this bond.

2. The rate of return received by the investor who held the bond during this year was mainly due to the change in price that occurred during the holding period.

Because bonds are so closely tied to market interest rates, the price of an issue actually depends on its prevailing *yield*. In practice, therefore, the yield of an issue is determined *first,* and then the dollar price of the obligation is derived. This is because a wide diversity of coupons and maturities exist in the market at any point in time, and the yield-based computation serves as an effective equalizer, allowing market-makers to systematically account for variations in coupon and/or maturity in the pricing of an issue. To appreciate the complexity of trying to directly price issues with different coupons and maturities, all one has to do is quickly glance at the bond quote page of the *Wall Street Journal* or *Barron's* and observe the myriad different combinations of coupons and maturities.

While bond price volatility is directly affected by the magnitude of movement in interest rates, price is more than a simple function of interest rates, because different bonds react differently to changes in these rates. Specifically, for a given change in market rates, price will vary according to the coupon and maturity of the issue, and bonds with longer maturities and/or lower coupons will respond most vigorously to a given change.[3] Other factors likewise cause differences in price volatility, including the call feature, but they are typically much less important. Even so, to the extent that they affect comparative rates of return, such factors certainly should not be ignored.

---

[3]This relationship among bond price volatility and maturity and coupon is discussed in detail in Chapter 15.

Bond Yields

Because the concept of yield is critical to the mechanics of bond pricing, it is important to differentiate among the types of yields. In the simplest sense, there are two: current yield and promised yield to maturity, or what is commonly known as "promised" yield. Current yield is the amount of current income that a bond provides (annual interest) relative to its prevailing market price. It is to a bond what dividend yield is to common stocks and has very little use in the bond valuation process. Promised yield, in contrast, is very important and is the yield upon which all bond prices are based! It encompasses interest income and price appreciation (or depreciation) in the valuation process, and total cash flow received over the life of the issue. Because it entails cash-flow timing, the promised yield computation is based on the present-value concept. Indeed, it is the same mathematical process as *internal rate of return* considered in the study of basic corporation finance. In discussing yield, the percentage point has been broken into 100 parts with each part being called a "basis point." Thus, a basis point is 1/100th of 1 percent and is a convenient means of depicting changes in yield or yield comparisons; e.g., a decline in yield from 8.5 percent to 8.0 percent is a 50-basis-point decline.

An Overview of Bond Market Structure

The market for fixed-income securities is gigantic and literally dwarfs the listed equity exchanges (NYSE, ASE, etc.). One reason is that corporations tend to issue bonds rather than common stock. For example, Federal Reserve figures indicate that, during 1980, out of 72.9 billion dollars in new corporate security issues, only about 20.4 billion (approximately 28 percent) were equity, which included preferred as well as common stock. Corporations do not issue common or preferred stock more frequently because the major source of equity financing for a firm is internally generated funds. Also, unlike the equity market, which is strictly corporations, the bond market has three substantial noncorporate sectors: the U.S. Treasury, several U.S. government agencies, and state and local governments. Federal Reserve figures reveal that, while recent corporate bond issues have been substantial, such volume has accounted for only 15–18 percent of *total* new bond issues! In 1980 the face value of corporate bonds issued was approximately 73 billion dollars, whereas the noncorporate sector added over 250 billion dollars in bonds to the market. Further evidence of the economic dimensions of the bond market can be gleaned from Table 14.1 which lists the dollar volume of par value outstanding for different types of bonds, as well as the annual net changes in new issues each year.

The Participants

There are five different types of issuers: (1) the U.S. Treasury, (2) various agencies of the U.S. government, (3) various state and local political subdivisions (known as municipalities), (4) corporations, and (5) institutional issuers.

	1970	1971	1972	1973	1974	1975	1976	1977	1978	1979
U.S. Treasury Obligations:										
Bills	87.90	97.50	103.90	107.80	119.70	157.50	164.00	161.10	161.70	172.60
Notes	101.20	114.00	121.50	124.60	129.80	167.10	216.70	251.80	265.80	283.40
Bonds	58.60	50.60	44.10	37.80	33.40	38.60	40.60	47.00	60.00	74.70
Total—Marketable Issues	247.70	262.10	269.50	270.20	282.90	363.20	421.30	459.90	487.50	530.70
Total—Nonmarketable Issues[a]	138.70	159.70	176.90	197.60	208.70	212.50	231.20	255.30	294.80	313.20
Grand Total	386.40	421.70	446.40	467.80	491.60	575.70	652.50	715.20	782.30	843.90
Corporates:										
Total	180.95	204.67	223.74	236.43	261.52	293.41	323.29	345.92	364.85(est)	385.10(est)
Municipals:										
Long Terms	123.50	139.90	154.00	167.30	179.20	196.10	213.90	232.90	250.70(est)	269.40(est)
Agency Issues:										
Federal Agencies[b]	9.3	12.5	11.1	11.55	12.72	19.05	22.42	22.76	23.49	24.72
Federally Sponsored[c]	8.3	35.7	51.3	60.04	76.66	78.63	81.43	89.71	113.58	138.58
Federal Financing Bank[d]	NA	NA	NA	NA	4.47	17.15	28.71	38.58	51.30	67.38
Total	17.6	48.2	62.4	71.59	93.85	114.83	132.04	151.05	188.37	230.68

Table 14.1   Total Amounts Outstanding (in billions of dollars, at year end)

[a]Includes: Securities issued to the Rural Electrification Administration and to state and local governments, depository bonds, retirement plan bonds, and individual retirement bonds.

[b]Includes: Defense Department, Export-Import Bank, FHA, GNMA, Postal Service, TVA, and U.S. Railway Association.

[c]Includes: Federal Home Loan Banks, Federal Home Loan Mortgage Corp., FNMA, federal land banks, federal intermediate credit banks, banks for cooperatives, Student Loan Marketing Association, and Farm Credit Banks.

[d]The FFB, which began operations in 1974, is authorized to purchase or sell obligations issued, sold, or guaranteed by other federal agencies. Because FFB incurs debt solely for the purpose of lending to other agencies, its debt is not included in the main portion of the table in order to avoid double counting.

Source: *Federal Reserve Bulletin*, various issues.

U.S. Treasury   The market for "treasuries" is the largest and the best known; it involves bonds, notes, and other debt instruments issued as a means of meeting the burgeoning needs of the U.S. government. These different types of debt instruments, along with obligations of several other issuers, will be reviewed in detail in the following section of this chapter.

Government Agencies   An important issuer, which has experienced the most rapid increase in size, is the United States Government through various agencies. These agencies represent political subdivisions of the government, though the securities are *not* direct obligations of the treasury. The agency market is composed of two types of issuers: government sponsored enterprises and federal agencies. Similar to treasuries, these securities are issued under the authority of an act of Congress, and the proceeds are used to finance many of the legislative mandates of that body. A number of these obligations carry guarantees of the U.S. Government, and, therefore, effectively represent the full faith and credit of the U.S. Treasury although they are not direct obligations of the government. Moreover, some have unusual interest payment provisions and tax features. But, in general, tax exposure of "agencies" is like that of treasury issues; while they are subject to the usual IRS federal tax provisions on interest and capital gains, the interest income is *free* from state and local levies. This is an important feature to investors because it can obviously increase the net return. Finally, another important feature is that the market yield of agency obligations is generally above that attainable from treasuries. Therefore, agencies represent a way to increase returns with only marginal differences in risk.

Corporations   The major nongovernmental issuer of debt is, of course, the corporate sector. Corporate bonds represent obligations of firms domiciled in the United States, Canada, and a few foreign countries. The market for corporate bonds is commonly subdivided into several segments: *industrials* (the most heterogeneous of the groups), *public utilities* (the dominant group in terms of volume of new issues), *rails and transportation* bonds, and *financial* issues (including those issued by banks, finance companies, and holding companies). The corporate sector probably provides the greatest diversity in types of issues and quality. In effect, the issuer can range from the highest investment-grade firm, such as American Telephone and Telegraph or IBM, to a high-risk firm that is relatively new or one that has experienced a default on its debt securities.

Municipalities   This debt issue is unlike any of the preceding three sectors. The major difference is that *interest income* on municipal obligations (which includes the issues of states, school districts, cities, or any other type of political subdivision such as a state university) is not subject to federal income tax. In contrast, however, *capital gains* on these issues based on price changes after the original issue are subject to normal federal income taxes. Moreover, with the exception of Puerto Rican issues, the obligations enjoy exemption from state and local taxes *when they are issues of the state or locality in which the investor resides.* That is, while a California issue would not be taxed in California, its interest income would be subject to state tax if the investor happens to reside in New York. The interest income of Puerto Rican issues enjoys total immunity from federal, state, and local taxes. Another distinguishing feature of municipal bonds is that the issues typically are serial obligations. Finally, while revenue obligations are rare in other sectors of the market, they are popular with some municipal issuers and account for a substantial portion of the municipal market.

Institutions   The final group are institutional obligations which are marketed by a variety of private, nonprofit institutions like schools, hospitals, and churches. These securities represent only a minute segment of the market, although they have some features that many investors would find fairly attractive. Unfortunately, because of the small size of these issues and the fact that the issuers are local there is a very thin, almost nonexistent, secondary market for these issues. Hence, most of the activity in the institutional segment of the market is centered in new issues. Many of the issuers are affiliated with a religious order (Roman Catholic—affiliated organizations have traditionally dominated the market). Likewise, hospital issues have been the preponderant type of obligation. Theses issues are sometimes referred to as "heart bonds" because of their emotional appeal, and some investors consider these investments charitable activities in support of a church or local hospital. However, the credit ratings on most of these issues is quite high because there have been very few defaults. At the same time, the yields have been above those on comparable corporate obligations which makes them attractive investments for those willing to accept the low liquidity characteristic.

Participating Investors

All sorts of individual and institutional investors, with myriad investment objectives, participate in the fixed-income security market because they feel that these securities yield competitive risk-adjusted rates of return. While numerous wealthy individual investors participate in this market, they still represent a relatively minor portion. Most individuals are discouraged by the sophistication required and the minimum denominations of most issues. Institutional investors dominate the bond market, typically accounting for 90–95 percent of the trading.[4] Of course, different segments of the market are more institutionalized than others. For example, the agency market is heavily institutional whereas individuals play a significant role in the municipal sector. Institutions have a substantial influence on the behavior of market yields because of the magnitude of their involvement. The size of their transactions is fairly substantial, often millions of dollars. It is not unusual for a few institutions (three or four) to acquire 70–80 percent of a $50–$100 million new issue. In contrast, large financial institutions have almost no interest in institutional bonds because of their lack of liquidity.

[4]Sidney Homer, "The Historical Evolution of Today's Bond Market," *Journal of Portfolio Management* 1 (1975): 6–11.

These institutional bonds are typically acquired by individuals and local banks with an interest in the community.

A variety of different institutions regularly invest a substantial proportion of their resources in the bond market. *Life insurance companies* are heavy investors in corporate bonds and, to a lesser extent, in treasury and agency securities; *commerical banks* invest substantial sums in the municipal market, as well as in government and agency issues; *property and liability insurance companies* are heavy investors in municipal obligations, as well as in treasuries; *private and government retirement and pension funds* are heavily committed to corporates, and also invest in treasuries and agencies. Finally *mutual funds,* because of their traditional equity orientation, have seldom considered bonds and fixed-income securities as an investment outlet, though attitudes are changing as various types of bond mutual funds attract the investing public. As the above review suggests, certain types of institutions tend to favor certain types of issues. There are two factors affecting these preferences: (1) the tax liability of the investing institution; (2) the nature of the liability that the institution assumes in relation to its depositors or clients. For example, commercial banks are subject to normal taxation and have fairly short-term liability structures. As a result, they favor short- to intermediate-term municipals. Life insurance companies and pension funds are virtually tax-free institutions with long-term commitments, so they prefer high-yielding long-term corporate bonds. Such institutional investment practices affect the supply of loanable funds and interest rate changes over short-run periods.

Investment and Trading Opportunities

Fixed-income securities are useful for investors who require current income, although an investor with a more speculative, shorter term investment horizon can also find abundant trading opportunities. An important dimension of recent bond investment has been high interest rates that provide attractive competitive returns, while the volatility of yields presents capital gains opportunities.

In contrast to the equity market, the bond market is primarily a new-issue (primary) market. As a result, the secondary market for seasoned securities is relatively thin and lacking in trading activity. Fortunately, some segments have fairly active secondary markets, including the treasury market, which does provide liquidity. Likewise, agencies are fairly actively traded in the secondary market, as are public utilities within the corporate market. In contrast, the municipal and institutional bond secondary markets are much less active. In fact, it is almost impossible for individual investors without access to specialized institutional publications to keep abreast of the price activity of municipal holdings because quotes do not appear regularly in the popular financial media. The cause of this illiquidity is that new municipal issues are relatively small, with total par values of less than $15–$20 million. In addition, because most municipals are serial obligations, the total issue is actually subdivided into a series of smaller issues, which compounds the size problem.

The trading of bonds is also unlike that followed with equity shares which are mainly traded on organized exchanges (i.e., the NYSE, the ASE, etc.). For example, commercial banks are popular dealers in government, agency, and municipal securities. Moreover, the trust departments of large commercial banks often act as secondary market dealers in the corporate OTC sector. While national and regional brokerage firms are active in marketing new issues, they only trade listed bond issues in the secondary market, and the listed issues only represent a small portion of total activity. Thus, there are few transactions in the secondary bond market because order placement and execution are carried out by specialized investment houses.

Because of the generally low level of liquidity, care must be exercised by trading-oriented investors to ensure that a substantial purchase or sale order can be executed rapidly. An investor who wishes to buy 50 bonds of a particular corporate issue (and this is certainly not a large order) may discover that normal volume in this issue amounts to fewer than 10 bonds a week. Clearly, it would be very time consuming to fill the order and probably equally time consuming to dispose of the position at the end of the investment horizon. With this time lag, substantial changes in yield and price could occur. Because such changes may seriously alter holding-period returns, you should consider an issue's trading volume before investing in it.

Bond Ratings

Agency ratings are an integral part of the bond market. Most fixed-income securities in the corporate, municipal, and institutional markets are regularly evaluated and rated by one or more agencies. The exceptions are bonds considered too small to rate and certain industry categories like bank issues (known as "non-rated" bonds). The rating agencies include two well-known firms, Moody's and Standard & Poor's, a third, much smaller agency, Fitch's Rating Service, and a recent addition to the rating services, Duff and Phelps, Inc. The two large firms along with Duff and Phelps dominate the corporate and municipal sectors, while the major rating service for institutional issues is Fitch.

Bond ratings are a very important service in the market for fixed-income securities because they provide the fundamental analysis for thousands of issues.[5] The rating agencies conduct extensive analyses of the intrinsic characteristics of the issuing organization and of the issue to determine the default risk for the investor and inform the market of their analysis through their ratings. Thus, in contrast to the situation with common stock, with bonds, the rating agencies have performed the fundamental analysis for the investor. Given the large, highly qualified staffs of the rating agencies, the general consensus is that additional analysis would only yield marginal insight regarding the intrinsic value or strength of an issue.

[5]Irwin Ross, "Higher Stakes in the Bond-Rating Game," *Fortune,* April 1976, pp. 132–140.

The primary question in bond analysis is not necessarily the growth prospect of the firm, but, rather, the ability of the firm to service a fixed amount of debt over the life of a given issue. Such an emphasis requires less attention be paid to highly uncertain expectations and forecasts and more concern with available data regarding the historical and current financial position of the company. Fortunately, the agencies have done an admirable job, although rare mistakes happen.[6] If anything, the rating services tend to be overly conservative as indicated by a study which suggests that risk of default has actually been *over*estimated by the market, resulting in unnecessarily high risk premiums given the default possibility.[7]

Because investors rely so heavily on agency ratings, it follows that there should be some concrete evidence to support the relationship between bond ratings and the quality of the issue. A study by Horrigan[8] concluded that the accounting data and financial ratios of the firm were, indeed, imbedded in corporate bond ratings. A subsequent study[9] found that bond ratings tend to vary directly with profitability, size, and earnings coverage, while they move inversely with financial leverage and earnings instability. The results of these and other empirical studies[10] clearly demonstrate that agency ratings are far more than the qualitative judgments of analysts.

The ratings assigned to bonds at the time of issue are important in terms of the marketability and effective interest rate of the issue. Generally, Moody's and S&P will give a particular bond the same rating. However, there can be "split ratings," i.e., different ratings from each service for one bond. Seasoned issues are also regularly reviewed to ensure that the assigned rating is still valid. While most issues will carry a given rating for an extended period of time (often over the life of the issue), it is not uncommon for some issues to experience revisions in their assigned ratings. Revisions can be either upward or downward and are usually done in increments of one rating grade.[11] Finally, although it may appear that the firm is receiving the rating, it is actually the issue that gets the grade. As a result, a firm can have outstanding issues with two different ratings. It is possible for senior securities to carry one rating and junior issues to be assigned one grade lower.

The agencies assign letter ratings, depicting what they view as the risk of default of an obligation. Letter ratings range from AAA to D. Table 14.2 specifies the various ratings that can be assigned to issues by the two major services. Ex-

---

[6]Hickman, *Corporate Bond Quality.*

[7]Gordon Pye, "Gauging the Default Premium," *Financial Analysts Journal* 30 (1974): 49–52.

[8]James O. Horrigan, "The Determination of Long-Term Credit Standing with Financial Ratios," *Empirical Research in Accounting: Selected Studies,* 1966, Supplement to *Journal of Accounting Research* 4: 44–62.

[9]Thomas F. Pogue and Robert M. Soldofsky, "What's in a Bond Rating?" *Journal of Financial and Quantitative Analysis* 4 (1969): 201–208.

[10]See, for example: Richard R. West, "An Alternative Approach to Predicting Corporate Bond Ratings," *Journal of Accounting Research* 8 (1970): 118–125; and George E. Pinches and Kent A. Mingo, "A Multivariate Analysis of Industrial Bond Ratings," *Journal of Finance* 28 (1973): 1–18.

[11]Bond rating changes and bond market efficiency are discussed in Chapter 15.

	Moody's	Standard & Poor's	Definition
High Grade	Aaa	AAA	The highest rating assigned to a debt instrument indicating an extremely strong capacity to pay principal and interest. Bonds in this category are often referred to as "gilt edge" securities.
	Aa	AA	High-quality bonds by all standards with strong capacity to pay principal and interest. These bonds are rated lower primarily because the margins of protection are not as strong as those for Aaa and AAA.
Medium Grade	A	A	These bonds possess many favorable investment attributes but elements may be present which suggest a susceptibility to impairment given adverse economic changes.
	Baa	BBB	Bonds regarded as having adequate capacity to pay principal and interest but certain protective elements may be lacking in the event of adverse economic conditions which could lead to a weakened capacity for payment.
Speculative	Ba	BB	Bonds regarded as having only moderate protection of principal and interest payments during both good and bad times.
	B	B	Bonds that generally lack characteristics of other desirable investments. Assurance of interest and principal payments over any long period of time may be small.
Default	Caa	CCC	Poor quality issues that may be in default or in danger of default.
	Ca	CC	Highly speculative issues that are often in default or possessing other marked shortcomings.
	C		The lowest rated class of bonds. These issues can be regarded as extremely poor in investment quality.
		C	Rating given to income bonds on which no interest is being paid.
		D	Issues in default with principal and/or interest payments in arrears.

Table 14.2   Bond Ratings

Adapted from: *Bond Guide* (New York: Standard & Poor's Corporation, monthly); *Bond Record* (New York: Moody's Investors Services, Inc., monthly). Reprinted by permission.

cept for the slight variation in designations, the meaning and interpretation is basically the same. The top four ratings are generally considered to be "investment-grade" securities. The next level of securities is known as "speculatives" and include the BB and B rated obligations.[12] The last group is the C and D categories, which are generally either income obligations or revenue bonds, many of which are trading "flat" (they are in arrears with regard to interest payments).

---

[12]Michael D. Joehnk and James F. Nielsen, "Return Risk Characteristics of Speculative Grade Bonds," *Quarterly Review of Economics and Business* 15 (1975): 35–43.

In the case of DDD-through D-rated obligations, the issues are in outright default, with the ratings indicating the bond's relative salvage value. Moody's also identifies the better quality *municipals* within the A and Baa categories as A1 and Baa1, respectively.

Market Rates of Return

Interest rate behavior is probably the most important variable to the investment-grade bond investor. Figures 14.1 and 14.2 illustrate different important characteristics of bond market interest rates. The first shows comparative yields in different market sectors and indicates that *there is not a single market rate* applicable to all segments of the bond market. Each segment of the market has its own, somewhat unique, level. Those shown are just three of the many different rates that exist in the market at any given point in time. For example, the corporate rate could be broken down into different segments of the corporate market (such as industrials, public utilities, and rails) and each of these could be further subdivided according to different quality levels (Aaa through Baa). Observe that, generally, the various market segments tend to move together, a common characteristic in investment-grade securities. In fact, previous studies have indicated that correlations *within* a wide variety of short-, intermediate-, and long-term yield series nearly always exceeded 90 percent.

Another important aspect to bond investors is how interest rates have performed historically, as shown in Figure 14.2. The data span more than 50 years and include the average behavior of one representative segment of the market: corporate investment-grade securities. Behavior in the first half of the period differs significantly from that in the second half and indicates why investors have recently found the bond market to be an attractive investment outlet. Prior to the mid-60s, the bond market was fairly stable, and there were few opportunities for aggressive investing. After the mid-60s, interest rates moved to highly competitive levels, and the substantial swings in interest rates have provided opportunities for capital-gains-oriented investors.

Bond Investment Risks

The typical bond investor is exposed to the same risk that any other investor faces. The important risks for bond holders include: (1) interest rate, (2) purchasing power, (3) liquidity or marketability, and (4) business.

The most important of these is interest-rate risk which is a function of the variability of bond returns (prices) caused by changes in the level of interest rates. Because of the relationship between bond prices and interest rates, no segment of the market, except perhaps for the highly speculative issues, is free of this important and powerful force. The price stability of investment-grade securities is mainly a function of interest rate stability and, therefore, interest-rate risk.[13]

---

[13] Frank K. Reilly and Michael D. Joehnk, "Association Between Market-Determined Risk Measures for Bonds and Bond Ratings," *Journal of Finance* 31 (1976): 1387–1403.

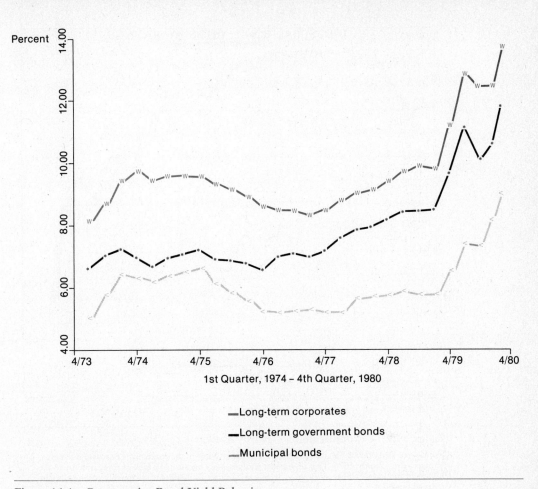

Figure 14.1   Comparative Bond Yield Behavior

Source: *Bond Record* (New York: Moody's Investors Services, Inc., monthly). Reprinted by permission.

Purchasing-power risk is linked to inflation and the loss of purchasing power over time. While purchasing power may decline over time with a given level of inflation, what is important to bond investors is the effect of inflation on yields and prices. While the level of inflation affects the promised yield, changes in the rate of inflation (or inflation expectations) lead to changes in the level of interest rates and thereby to changes in the prices of seasoned issues.

Marketability risk has to do with the liquidity of the obligation and the ease with which an issue can be sold at the prevailing market price. Smaller issues and those with inactive secondary markets will often experience marketability difficulties and are, therefore, subject to such risk.

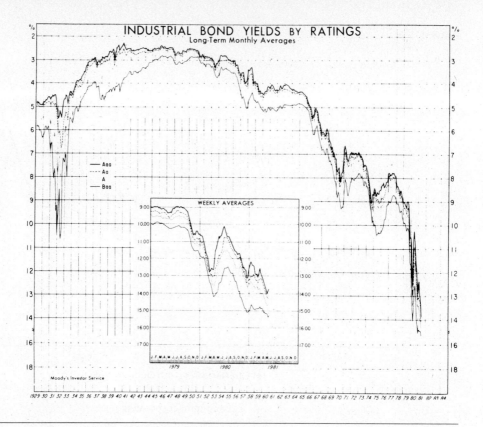

Figure 14.2   Corporate Bond Yields by Ratings

Note: As of December 1976, railroad bonds were removed from the combined Corporate Averages, retroactive to January 1974. This adjustment was necessary because of a lack of comparability to the Industrial and Public Utility averages, reflecting the limited availability of reasonably current coupon railroad bonds.

Source: *Bond Record* (New York: Moody's Investors Services), March 1981. Reprinted by permission.

Finally, business risk is the risk of default because of the financial and operating risks of the issuer. Such risks are only relevant for corporate, municipal, and institutional obligations. Generally, the ratings assigned by the various agencies reflect differences in business risk, and the ratings, in turn, influence the promised yields (the lower the default risk, the higher the agency rating and the lower the prevailing yield to maturity).

Default risk and marketability risk have an insignificant effect on price behavior because they only affect prevailing *levels* of yields. In contrast, interest-rate risk and purchasing-power risk can have dramatic effects on the price behavior of an obligation over time.

Alternative Investment Vehicles

Numerous sectors that exist within the bond market are characterized by fundamentally different issuers, the major categories of which include: the U.S. Treasury and government agencies, municipalities, corporations, and institutions. This section is a brief review of some of the popular issues available in these market sectors.

Treasury and Agency Issues

The dominant fixed-income market is that for U.S. Treasury obligations. Acting on behalf of the United States Government, and with the backing of its full faith and credit, the U.S. Treasury issues treasury bills (T-bills), which are for less than one year. The treasury also issues long-term obligations in one of two forms: government notes, which have maturities of 10 years or less; and treasury bonds, with maturities of more than 10 years (current maximum maturities go to about 25 years).

Treasury obligations come in denominations of $1,000 and $10,000, although a few older issues carry $500 par values, and are either in registered or bearer form. The interest income from the U.S. government securities is subject to federal income tax but *exempt* from state and local levies. Such obligations are popular with individual and institutional investors because they possess substantial liquidity.

Short-term T-bills differ from notes and bonds in terms of how the payments are made. Treasury bills are sold at a discount from par to provide the desired yield (the return is the difference between the purchase price and the par at maturity). In contrast, government notes and bonds carry semiannual coupons (similar to those on almost all other bonds) that specify the nominal yield of the obligation.

While government notes and bonds are similar to other straight-debt issues in most respects, they do have some unusual features. First, the deferred call features on treasury issues is unusually long and is generally measured relative to the *maturity* date of the issue, rather than from date of issue. For example, many treasury issues carry a deferment feature that expires five years *prior* to the *final* maturity date.

Also, certain government issues provide a tax break to investors because they can be used, at par, to pay federal estate taxes. It is possible, therefore, for an investor to acquire a treasury bond at a substantial discount which his estate can subsequently use at par to pay estate taxes. Such bonds have been given a nickname, "flower bonds." Although *new* flower bonds can no longer be issued, there are still approximately a dozen such issues available in the market. Most of these carry $2\frac{3}{4}$–$4\frac{1}{2}$ percent coupons, and have maturities that range between 1982 and 1998. This is advantageous to the investor because the lower the coupon, the better the price discount, and the more assurance of price appreciation at "time of departure." Recent revisions in estate tax laws that increased the size of an estate exempt from taxes have reduced the demand for such issues. At the same time, the available supply has declined because, as these flower bonds are used, they are retired by the government. Therefore, prices have been maintained and the yields on these bonds are consistently below those of other treasury issues of comparable maturity.

Government Agency Issues

Agency issues are obligations issued by the U.S. Government through some political subdivisions such as a government agency or a government-sponsored corporation. While there are only six government-sponsored enterprises, there are over two-dozen federal agencies. Table 14.3 lists selected characteristics of the more popular government-sponsored and federal agency obligations. It includes recent size of the market, typical minimum denominations, tax features, and the availability of bond quotes. (The issues in the table are only meant to be representative of the wide variety of different obligations available to the investor and not an exhaustive list.) Generally, agency issues are similar to those of other issuers.[14] Interest is usually paid semiannually, principal is due in full at maturity, and the minimum denominations vary between $1,000 and $10,000, although there are exceptions. These obligations are unusual because they are *not* direct issues of the treasury, yet they carry the full faith and credit of the United States Government. Moreover, unlike government obligations, some of the issues are subject to state and local income tax, while some are specifically exempt from such levies.[15]

Except for the fact that they are of high quality and involve special tax provisions, agency obligations are not unique. However, one agency issue offers particularly attractive investment opportunities: GNMA ("Ginnie Mae") pass-through certificates, which are obligations of the Government National Mortgage Association.[16] These bonds represent an undivided interest in a pool of federally insured mortgages. The bondholders receive monthly, rather than semiannual, payments from Ginnie Mae, and these payments include both principal and interest because they represent a pass through of the mortgage payments made by the original borrower (the mortgagee) to Ginnie Mae. This is why the bond has come to be known as a pass-through obligation.

---

[14]For expository purposes, we will no longer distinguish between federal agency and government-sponsored obligations; instead, the term "agency" shall apply to either type of issue.

[15]Federal National Mortgage Association (Fannie Mae) debentures, for example, are subject to state and local income tax, whereas the interest income from Federal Home Loan Bank bonds is exempt. In fact, a few issues are even exempt from *federal* income tax as well, e.g., Public Housing bonds.

[16]For a more extensive discussion of mortgage-backed securities, see: "Mortgage Securities Make It Big On Wall Street," *Savings and Loan News* 98 (1977): 33–35; and Donald Moffitt, "Ginnie Mae Pass-Throughs Offer High Yields Plus Safety for Cautious Savers," *Wall Street Journal* 18 September 1978, p. 38; *Mortgage-Backed Bond and Pass-Through Symposium*, Financial Analysts Research Foundation, Charlottesville, Virginia, 1980.

The pass throughs carry coupons that are somewhat related to the interest charged on the pool of mortgages. Also, because part of the cash flow represents return of capital (i.e., the principal part of payment), that portion is tax-free. The interest income is subject to federal, state, and local taxes. The issues are marketed in minimum denominations of $25,000, which eliminates some individual investors from this market. They come with maturities of 25 to 30 years, but generally have an average life of only 12 years because, as pooled mortgages are paid off, payments and prepayments are passed through to the investor. This also implies, however, that unlike the case with other issues, the monthly payment is *not* fixed.

Municipal Obligations

Municipal bonds are issued by states, counties, cities, and other political subdivisions. Basically, municipalities issue two distinct types of bonds: (1) general-obligation bonds and (2) revenue issues. General obligation bonds (GOs) are essentially backed by the full faith and credit of the issuer and its taxing power. Revenue bonds, in turn, are serviced by the income generated from specific revenue-producing projects of the municipality, for example, bridges, toll roads, municipal coliseums, public utility and water works, etc. As might be expected, revenue bonds generally provide higher returns to investors than GOs do, because the default risk inherent in the revenue obligations is greater. A revenue bond is like a general-obligation bond except that, should a municipality fail to generate sufficient income from a project used to secure a revenue bond, it has *no* legal debt-service obligation until the income becomes sufficient.

Another feature of municipal bonds, particularly the general obligations, is that they tend to be issued on a serial basis. Most GOs are set up this way so that the issuer's cash flow requirements will be steady over the life of the obligation. Therefore, the principal portion of the total debt-service requirement generally begins at a fairly low level and builds up over the life of the obligation. In contrast, revenue obligations are mostly term issues, so the major portion of the issue's total principal value is not due until the final maturity date or last few dates. In fact, even if a revenue issue is serial, it is generally set up so that the serial portion amortizes a relatively small amount of the bond (perhaps 10–25 percent), with the majority of the obligation due at or near final maturity. As an example, see the $32.4 million Cook County, Illinois Hospital Revenue Bond issue in Figure 14.3. Note that this is a combination serial bond ($2,545,000) and a term bond ($29,860,000) due in 2013.

The most important feature of municipal obligations is, of course, that the interest payments are exempt from federal income tax, as well as taxes in the locality and state in which the obligation was issued. This means that people in different income brackets find municipal bonds to be of varying attractiveness. The investor can convert the *tax-free yield* of a municipal to an equivalent *taxable* yield using the following equation:

Type of Security	Minimum Denomination	Form	Life of Issue	Tax Status	How Interest is Earned
Government Sponsored:					
Banks for Cooperatives (Co-ops)	$5,000	Bearer	6 months to (currently) 3½ years	Fed.: Taxable State: Exempt Local: Exempt	Interest bearing; 360-day year
Federal Intermediate Credit Banks (FICBs)	$5,000	Bearer	9 months to 4 years	Fed.: Taxable State: Exempt Local: Exempt	Interest bearing; 360-day year
Federal Home Loan Bank	$10,000	Bearer	1 to 20 years	Fed.: Taxable State: Exempt Local: Exempt	Semiannual interest payments
Federal Home Loan—Mortgage-backed bonds	$25,000	Registered or Bearer	12 to 25 years	Fed.: Taxable State: Taxable Local: Taxable	Semiannual interest payments
Mortgage Corporation—Participation certificates (FHLMC)	$100,000	Registered	15 to 30 years	Fed.: Taxable State: Taxable Local: Taxable	Monthly interest payments
Federal Land Banks (FLBs)	$1,000	Bearer	1 to 10 years	Fed.: Taxable State: Exempt Local: Exempt	Semiannual interest payments
Federal National Mortgage Association (FNMA) Discount notes	$5,000[a]	Bearer	30 to 270 days	Fed.: Taxable State: Taxable Local: Taxable	Discounted 360-day year
Secondary-market notes and debentures	$10,000	Registered or Bearer	3 to 25 years	Fed.: Taxable State: Taxable Local: Taxable	Semiannual interest payments

Issuer	Minimum Purchase	Form	Maturity	Tax Status	Interest
Federal Agencies: Export-Import Bank (Exim Bank)	$5,000	Registered or Bearer	3 to 7 years	Fed.: Taxable State: Taxable Local: Taxable	Semiannual interest payments
Farmers Home Administration (FHDA) (notes)	$25,000	Registered or Bearer	4 to 15 years	Fed.: Taxable State: Taxable Local: Taxable	Annual interest payments
Federal Housing Administration (FHA)	$50,000	Registered	1 to 40 years	Fed.: Taxable State: Taxable Local: Taxable	Semiannual interest payments
Government National Mortgage Association — Mortgage backed and participation	$25,000	Registered or Bearer	1 to 25 years	Fed.: Taxable State: Taxable Local: Taxable	Semiannual interest payments
(GNMA) Modified Pass-Through	$25,000	Registered	1 to 25 years (12-year average)	Fed.: Taxable State: Taxable Local: Taxable	Monthly interest payments
Tennessee Valley Authority (TVA)	$1,000	Registered or Bearer	3 to 25 years	Fed.: Taxable State: Exempt Local: Exempt	Semiannual interest payments
U.S. Postal Service	$10,000	Registered or Bearer	25 years	Fed.: Taxable State: Exempt Local: Exempt	Semiannual interest payments
Other: Federal Financing Bank	$10,000	Registered or Bearer	1 to 20 years	Fed.: Taxable State: Exempt Local: Exempt	Semiannual interest payments

Table 14.3 Agency Issues: Selected Characteristics

aMinimum Purchase Requirement of $50,000

Source: Adapted from: David M. Darst, *The Complete Bond Book* (New York: McGraw-Hill, Inc., 1975), pp. 274–283. Copyright © 1975 by McGraw-Hill, Inc. Reprinted by permission.

In the opinion of Bond Counsel, interest on the Series 1981 Bonds is exempt under existing law from Federal income taxes. The interest on the Series 1981 Bonds is not exempt from present Illinois income taxes.

New Issue

$32,405,000

Cook County, Illinois

Hospital Revenue Bonds, Series 1981
(Grant Hospital Project)

Dated: June 1, 1981   Due: June 1, as shown below

$2,545,000 Serial Bonds

Principal Amount	Due	Interest Rate	Principal Amount	Due	Interest Rate	Principal Amount	Due	Interest Rate
$160,000	1984	8¾ %	$210,000	1987	9½ %	$310,000	1991	10½ %
180,000	1985	9	235,000	1988	9¾	340,000	1992	10¾
195,000	1986	9¼	255,000	1989	10	380,000	1993	11
			280,000	1990	10¼			

$29,860,000 11⅞% Term Bonds due 2013

Price of all Bonds: 100%

(Accrued interest to be added)

Bonds may or may not be available from the account members or others at the indicated price.

The Series 1981 Bonds are offered when, as and if issued and received by the Underwriters, subject to prior sale, withdrawal or modification of the offer without notice and to the approval of legality of the Series 1981 Bonds by Hopkins & Sutter, Chicago, Illinois, Bond Counsel. Certain legal matters will be passed upon for the County by its Special Counsel, Chapman and Cutler, Chicago, Illinois, for the Hospital by its General Counsel, Gardner, Carton & Douglas, Chicago, Illinois, and for the Underwriters by their Counsel, Willkie Farr & Gallagher, New York, New York. It is expected that the Bonds in definitive form will be available for delivery to the Underwriters in New York, New York on or about June 25, 1981. Copies of the Official Statement may be obtained from such of the undersigned as may legally offer these securities under applicable securities laws.

Dillon, Read & Co. Inc.

A. G. Becker
Warburg Paribas Becker

Bache Halsey Stuart Shields
Incorporated

Bear, Stearns & Co.

Blyth Eastman Paine Webber
Incorporated

Alex. Brown & Sons   Clayton Brown & Associates, Inc.

Donaldson, Lufkin & Jenrette
Securities Corporation

Drexel Burnham Lambert
Incorporated

Ehrlich-Bober & Co., Inc.

The First Boston Corporation

Glickenhaus & Co.   Goldman, Sachs & Co.

E. F. Hutton & Company Inc.

Kidder, Peabody & Co.
Incorporated

Lazard Frères & Co.

Lehman Brothers Kuhn Loeb
Incorporated

Merrill Lynch White Weld Capital Markets Group
Merrill Lynch, Pierce, Fenner & Smith Incorporated

John Nuveen & Co.
Incorporated

Refco Partners

L. F. Rothschild, Unterberg, Towbin   Salomon Brothers

Shearson Loeb Rhoades Inc.

Smith Barney, Harris Upham & Co.
Incorporated

Thomson McKinnon Securities Inc.

Weeden Municipal Securities
Div. of Moseley, Hallgarten, Estabrook & Weeden Inc.

Wertheim & Co., Inc.

Dean Witter Reynolds Inc.

Bacon, Whipple & Co.   Robert W. Baird & Co.
Incorporated

Berghoff, Marsh & Company
Incorporated

William Blair & Company   Blunt Ellis & Loewi
Incorporated

Butcher & Singer Inc.

Channer Newman Securities Company   The Chicago Corporation   Columbian Securities, Inc.

A. G. Edwards & Sons, Inc.   Fahnestock & Co.   Hutchinson, Shockey, Erley & Co.

The Illinois Company
Incorporated

Legg Mason Wood Walker
Incorporated

Mesirow & Company

The Ohio Company   Oppenheimer & Co., Inc.

Rodman & Renshaw, Inc.

R. Rowland & Co.   Sauerman, Morter & Sauerman, Inc.
Incorporated

Securities Corporation of Iowa

Van Kampen Filkin & Merritt Inc.

M. B. Vick & Company

Burton J. Vincent, Chesley & Co.

Ziegler Securities, Inc.

June 4, 1981

Figure 14.3   An Example of a Municipal Bond Offering

$$TY = \frac{i}{(1-t)}$$

where:

TY = equivalent taxable yield

i = coupon rate of the municipal obligations

t = marginal tax rate of the investor.

(Note that TY can also be used to find the yield of treasury and/or agency obligations whenever state and local taxes are an issue.) An investor in the 30 percent marginal tax bracket would find that a 5 percent municipal yield is equivalent to a 7.14 percent fully taxable yield according to the following calculations:

$$TY = \frac{.05}{(1-.3)} = .0714$$

This conversion is essential because the tax-free yield is presumed to be the major motive for investing in municipal bonds. As a result the marginal tax rate is a *primary* concern in determining whether municipals are a viable investment vehicle. As a rough rule of thumb, you must be in the 30–35 percent tax bracket before municipal bonds offer yields that are competitive with those from fully taxable bonds because before-tax municipal yields are substantially *lower* than returns available from fully taxable issues, such as corporates. However, only the interest is tax-free; any capital gains are treated in the normal way.

Pollution Control Revenue Bonds   Most issues of municipal bonds are fairly standard and, as a result, seldom offer issue-oriented opportunities. One notable exception is pollution control revenue bonds which are actually disguised forms of *corporate* obligations. The debt-service funds for these bonds are derived through leases, or other similar payment pledges, made between a municipality and a business firm, such as a public utility. To illustrate, in December 1977, Marshall County, West Virginia issued $50 million of term revenue bonds, due in 2007, secured with a long-term payment pledge from the Ohio Power Company. Congress maintained that our environment has to be cleaned up, and this financing vehicle was provided as a means to help corporations meet the gigantic expense and also to encourage industrial development in smaller communities.[17]

Pollution control issues are very popular in the new-issues market because an investor is often able to increase his yield relative to GOs and possibly improve his risk of default. Also, these issues enjoy a fairly active secondary market.

---

[17] These bonds are not to be confused with industrial development revenue bonds, which were popular in the 50s and 60s. In fact, they became so popular that there was some pressure to restrict their use by limiting the amount a community could issue.

Municipal Bond Guarantees   These are another unusual, and growing feature of the municipal bond market. They provide the bondholder with the assurance of a third party *other than the issuer* that the principal and interest payments will be promptly made. The third party provides an additional source of collateral. The guarantees are actually a form of insurance placed on the bond at date of issue and are *unrevocable* over the life of the issue. The issuer purchases the insurance for the benefit of the investor and the municipality benefits from the lower issue costs and increased marketability.

In 1975, four states and two private organizations provided municipal bond guarantees. The states included: California, which guarantees certain forms of health facilities; New Hampshire, which guarantees school and sewage bonds; Minnesota, which guarantees any general obligations; and Michigan, which guarantees GO school bonds. There are two private guarantors that provide bond insurance throughout the country, rather than within a particular state. The first is a consortium of four large insurance companies that market their product under the name of Municipal Bond Insurance Association (MBIA). The second is a subsidiary of a large Milwaukee-based private insurer known as American Municipal Bond Insurance Corporation (AMBAC). Both of the private guarantors will insure either general-obligation or revenue bonds issued for any purpose. To qualify for private bond insurance, the issue must carry an S&P rating of triple-B or better. Because MBIA enjoyed a triple-A rating from Standard & Poor's, it initially captured more of the market than AMBAC did. In late 1979, AMBAC signed a reinsurance agreement with 14 large insurance companies, and Standard & Poor's indicated that they will now automatically give an AAA rating to any bond insured by AMBAC. This feature is expected to help AMBAC.[18] A purported effect of the private guarantee is that such issues enjoy a more active secondary market and, therefore, greater liquidity, although such claims have not been documented.

Corporate Bonds

Corporate bonds are one of two categories of *private* issues and represent the most significant segment.[19] Utilities dominate the corporate market. The other important segments include industrials (which rank second to utilities and include everything from mining firms to multinational oils to retail concerns), rail and transportation issues, and financial issues. This market includes debentures, first-mortgage issues, convertible obligations, bonds with warrants, subordinated debenture bonds, income bonds (similar to municipal revenue bonds), collateral trust bonds (typically backed by financial assets), equipment trust certificates, and mortgage-backed bonds.

---

[18]For a discussion of this feature and the bond insurance industry, see Maureen Bailey, "Triple-A Rating," *Barron's*, 31 December 1979.

[19]The other category is institutional bonds issued by hospitals, churches, etc. They will be discussed in the following section.

If we ignore equity-related securities, equipment trust certificates, and mortgage-backed bonds, the above list of obligations varies essentially according to the type of collateral behind the bond. Most issues have semiannual interest payments, sinking funds, and a single maturity date. Maturities range from 25 to 40 years, with public utilities generally on the longer end and industrials preferring the 25- to 30-year range. Nearly all corporate bonds carry deferred call provisions that range from 5 to 20 years. The length of the deferment tends to vary directly with the level of the interest rates (i.e., the higher the prevailing interest rate level, the more likely an issue will carry a 7- to 10-year deferment). On the other hand, "corporate notes," which normally carry maturities of from 5 to 7 years, are generally noncallable. Notes are popular with virtually all issuers, and tend to increase in popularity during periods of higher interest rates because issuers prefer to *avoid* long-term obligations during such periods.

Generally, the average yields for industrial bonds will be the lowest of the three major sectors, followed by utility returns, with yields on rail and transportation bonds generally being the highest. The differential in yield between utilities and industrials is simply a matter of demand for loanable funds. Because utilities dominate the market in terms of the supply of bonds, yields on these securities must rise to attract the necessary demand.

Corporate issues are popular with individual and institutional investors because of the availability of such issues and their relatively attractive yields. *Established* firms have very low default records, leading many investors to consider corporate bonds a means of attaining higher returns without assuming abnormal risk.

Equipment Trust Certificates

Several corporate issues contain unusual features. One is the equipment trust certificate issued by railroads (which are the biggest issuers of these obligations), airlines, and other transportation concerns. The proceeds are used to purchase equipment (freight cars, railroad engines, and airplanes) that serves as collateral for the equipment trust issue. Equipment trust issues generally carry maturities that range from one year to a maximum that seldom exceeds 15 to 17 years. The fairly short maximum maturities are popular because of the nature of the collateral. Equipment is subject to substantial wear and tear and tends to deteriorate rapidly.

Equipment trust certificates appeal to investors because of their *attractive yields,* and also because they have a record of very few defaults. Equipment trust certificates do not enjoy the same visibility and acceptance that other forms of corporate bonds do, but they have active secondary markets and attractive liquidity.

Mortgage-Backed Bonds

Another unusual form of corporate debt initiated in September 1977 is the mortgage-backed bond. These issues are marketed by commercial banks, savings and loan associations, and mortgage lenders, and are exactly like the GNMA pass-through certificates. They are backed by a pool of mortgages which provide the collateral for the bonds. These securities differ because they are *not* backed by the full faith and credit of the U.S. Government but, instead, carry the insurance of a third party, usually a private mortgage insurance company that provides insurance against defaults on the mortgages in the pool. The biggest private mortgage insurer for these bonds is the MGIC Investment Corporation discussed previously.[20]

Variable-Rate Notes

These were available in Europe for decades but were not introduced in this country until the summer of 1974, and became popular while interest rates were high. The typical variable-rate note possesses two unique features:

1. After the first 6–18 months of the issue's life, during which a minimum rate is often guaranteed, the coupon "floats," so that every 6 months it is pegged at a certain amount, usually one percent above a stipulated short-term rate (normally defined as the preceding three week's average 90-day T-bill rate).

2. After the first year or two, the notes are redeemable at par, at the *holder's* option, usually at six-month intervals.

Thus, such notes represent a long-term commitment on the part of the borrower, yet provide the lender with all the markings of a short-term obligation. Such obligations are available to investors in minimum denominations of $1,000. Because of the unusual features of such obligations, variable-rate notes could be attractive to yield-conscious, liquidity-oriented investors. However, although the six-month redemption feature provides liquidity, the variable rates can subject the issue to wide swings in semiannual coupons.[21]

Institutional Bonds

By far the smallest sector of the bond market is that for institutional issues such as hospital bonds. Even though these obligations have a virtually spotless default record, they offer returns of 100–150 basis points above comparably rated corporates because most institutional obligations do *not* enjoy an active secondary market! Offsetting such a handicap are many benefits in addition to the extra returns. For example, the obligations are issued on a serial basis with relatively short maximum maturities (seldom exceeding 15 to 18 years). Unlike most other serial bonds, institutional obligations generally call for *semiannual* maturities within the serial structure. Finally, they typically have deferred call features.

---

[20]A conference on these bonds was held by the Boston Society of Security Analysts in December 1979. For a copy of the proceedings contact Institute of Chartered Financial Analysts, University of Virginia, P.O. Box 3665, Charlottesville, Virginia 22903. Also see Richard G. Marcis, "Mortgage-Backed Securities," *Federal Home Loan Bank Board Journal,* November 1978.

[21]See Jill Bettner, "Once Stodgy Municipal Bonds, Going Modern, Now Offer Flexible Yields, Shorter Maturities," *Wall Street Journal,* 8 December 1980, p. 44.

Obtaining Information on Bonds

As might be expected, the data needs of bond investors are considerably different from those of stockholders. For one thing, fundamental intrinsic analysis is far less important because of the widespread reliance on rating agencies for in-depth analysis of the risk of default. In fact, except in the case of speculative-grade bonds and questionable revenue obligations, most fixed-income investors rely on the rating agencies to determine the default risk of an obligation. Some very large institutions employ in-house analysts to confirm assigned agency ratings or to uncover marginal incremental return opportunities. Given the vast resources that these institutions invest each year, the rewards of only a few more basis points can be substantial and the institutions enjoy economies of scale in research. Finally, because of an increasing demand for an independent appraisal of bond ratings, several private firms have established research houses that concentrate on bonds.[22]

So what type of information do bond investors require? In addition to information on risk of default, they need: (1) information on market and economic conditions and (2) information on intrinsic bond features. Market and economic information allows investors to stay abreast of the general tone of the market, overall interest-rate developments, and yield-spread behavior between different market sectors. Bond investors also require information on certain bond characteristics such as call features and sinking-fund provisions that can affect comparative yield and price behavior.

Where do bondholders find such information? Some is readily available in such popular publications as *The Wall Street Journal, Barron's, Business Week, Fortune,* and *Forbes,* which were discussed in Chapter 6. In addition, bond investors are regular users of other publications, many specifically dealing with bonds. We will deal with some of the more representative ones, but *not* with the numerous "financial services" that are available at varying costs. Two popular sources of bond data are the *Federal Reserve Bulletin* and the *Survey of Current Business,* which were also described in Chapter 6.

Treasury Bulletin   This includes average yields on long-term treasury, corporate, and municipal bonds as well as graphs of monthly average yields on new double-A corporate bonds, treasury bonds, and municipal bonds. The bulletin is published monthly.

The Standard & Poor's Bond Guide   This is published monthly and presents a condensed review of pertinent financial and statistical information. This was likewise described in Chapter 6. Moody's has a comparable publication available to investors titled *Moody's Bond Record.* (Nearly all bond publications produced by Standard & Poor's have counterparts marketed by Moody's.)

---

[22]Reba White, "Is Credit Analysis a Growth Industry?" *Institutional Investor* 10 (1976): 57–58; Robert J. Cirino, "Building a Fixed-Income Boutique," *Institutional Investor* 12 (1978): 35–36.

Moody's Bond Survey   This is published weekly and provides information on current conditions in the economy and their possible effects on bond markets. Recent and prospective taxable bond offerings are listed along with information such as assigned agency rating, offering date, amount of offer, name and type of issue, call price, re-offering price and yield, and recent bid price and yield. For each of the *major* government, agency, corporate, and municipal obligations coming to the market, *detailed* information is provided on bond features, indenture provisions, and corporate or municipal finances. This is a valuable source of information to bond investors because it provides information on all three categories of bonds. Standard & Poor's has a similar publication titled *Fixed Income Investor*.

Moody's Manuals   These include the *Municipal and Government Manual, The Bank and Financial Manual, Industrial Manual, OTC Industrial Manual, Transportation Manual*, and *Public Utility Manual*. These publications were described in Chapter 6 and are a primary source of fundamental information pertaining to the risk of default, but also contain data on various features of each outstanding issue.

Investment Dealers Digest   This provides extensive information on new issues and new-issue market activity, sections dealing with reviews of various segments of the bond market, and the market outlook. Detailed new-issue information is published weekly including extensive data on the features of bond issues currently in underwriting. The digest also contains the most extensive list of pending and recent issues available, which is helpful in obtaining insight into future demand for loanable funds and the effects of such demand on interest rates.

Sources of Bond Quotes

The above list includes sources intended to fill three needs of investors: evaluating risk of default, staying abreast of market and interest rate conditions, and obtaining information on specific bonds. Another important data need is *current* market information, i.e., bond quotes and prices. Unfortunately, many of the prime sources are simply not widely distributed. For example, *Bank and Quotation Record* is a valuable, though not widely circulated, source that provides a summary of price information on a monthly basis for government and agency bonds, a large number of listed and OTC corporate issues, municipals, and many money-market instruments. Quotes on municipal bonds are only available through a fairly costly publication, used by many financial institutions, titled *The Blue List*. It contains over 100 pages of price quotes for municipal bonds, municipal notes, and industrial development and pollution-control revenue bonds. Daily information on all publicly traded treasury issues, most important agency obligations, and many corporate issues is published in *The Wall Street Journal*. Similar data is available on a weekly basis in *Barron's*. While the list is fairly extensive for treasury and agency obligations, corporate bond quotes in

The Wall Street Journal/Barron's include only listed obligations which represent a minor portion of the total market. In addition to these published sources, major market dealers maintain firm quotes on a variety of issues that are available to clients and/or cooperating institutions.

Interpreting Bond Quotes

Essentially, all bonds are either quoted on the basis of yield or price. When they are quoted on the basis of price, the quote is always interpreted as a *percent of par*. For example, a quote of 98½ is not interpreted as $98.50, but 98½ percent of par. The dollar price can then be derived from the quote, given the par value. If par is $5,000 on a particular municipal bond, then the price of an issue quoted at 98½ would be $4,925. Actually, the market follows three systems of bond pricing: one system for corporates, another for governments (this includes both treasuries and agency obligations), and a third for municipals.

Corporate Bond Quotes

Figure 14.4 is a listing of corporate bond quotes and NYSE bond quotes which appeared in *The Wall Street Journal* of Wednesday, May 27, 1981. The data pertains to trading activity on May 26. Several quotes have been designated for illustrative purposes. The first is an AT&T (American Telephone and Telegraph) issue and is representative of most corporate prices. In particular, the "7⅛s03" indicates the coupon and maturity of the obligation; in this case, the AT&T issue carries a 7⅛ percent coupon and matures in 2003. The small "s" between the coupon and maturity is interpreted as "series" and has no real meaning. The next column provides the *current* yield of the obligation and is found by comparing the coupon to the current market price; e.g., a bond with an 8 percent coupon selling for 95 would have an 8.4 percent current yield. The next column is the volume of $1,000 par value bonds traded that day. The next columns indicate the high, low, and closing quote, which is followed by the net change in close from the last day the issue was traded. In this case, the issue went down by ⅛ of a point or $1.125 (since that is ⅛ of one percent of $1,000). The second quote, for the BoM bond, has one unique feature that makes a very significant difference. A small letter "f" follows the maturity date of the obligation; this means that the issue is trading "flat." Simply stated, the issuer is not meeting interest payments on the obligation. Therefore, the coupon of the obligation may be inconsequential. The next two bonds (3 and 4) are both TVA obligations traded on the NYSE. The first TVA is the 7 percent of 97 and is pointed out because of the small letter "r" which follows the maturity date. This letter specifies a *registered* issue. There is an unusual aspect to the 7.35 series of 98 (number 4)—a capital B behind the maturity date which defines the issue series more exactly because there are several 7.35-98s outstanding.

All fixed-income obligations, with the exception of preferred stock, are traded on an *accrued interest basis*. The prices pertain to principal value only and exclude interest that has accrued to the holder since the last interest payment

42

THE WALL STREET JOURNAL, Wednesday, May 27, 1981

CORPORATION BONDS
Volume $18,300,000

New York Exchange Bonds

Tuesday, May 26, 1981

Total Volume $18,490,000

	Domestic		All Issues	
	Tues	Fri	Tues	Fri
Issues traded	844	779	853	789
Advances	434	343	440	349
Declines	237	270	239	272
Unchanged	173	166	174	168
New highs	19	14	19	14
New lows	36	31	38	32

SALES SINCE JANUARY 1

1981	1980	1979
$1,858,259,000	$1,994,363,000	$1,343,826,000

Dow Jones Bond Averages

	—1979—		—1980—		—1981—				- - -TUESDAY- - -					
	High	Low	High	Low	High	Low			—1981—		—1980—		—1979—	
	86.10	73.35	76.61	60.96	65.78	58.37	20 Bonds	59.70	+ .73	72.02	− .26	84.39	+ .28
	88.60	72.40	78.63	59.40	66.18	56.48	10 Utilities	58.90	+ .92	73.76	− .52	85.50	+ .34
	84.28	74.25	74.92	61.55	69.33		10 Industrial	60.51	+ .55	70.28		83.28	+ .22

Figure 14.4 omitted detailed bond quotation columns

Figure 14.4   Sample Bond Quotations

Source: *The Wall Street Journal*, May 27, 1981. Reprinted by permission of *The Wall Street Journal*.

date. The actual price of the bond will exceed the quote listed because accrued interest must be added. With the AT&T $7^{1}/_{8}$ percent issue, if two months have elapsed since interest was paid, then the current holder of the bond is entitled to $^{2}/_{6}$ (or $^{1}/_{3}$) of the normal semiannual interest payment. More specifically, the $7^{1}/_{8}$ percent coupon provides semiannual interest income of \$35.625. The investor who held the obligation for two months beyond the last interest payment date is entitled to $^{1}/_{3}$ of that \$35.625 in the form of accrued interest. There will be added to the price of \$850 an accrued interest value of \$11.87.

Treasury and Agency Bond Quotes

Figure 14.5 illustrates the quote system used with treasury and agency issues. These quotes are like those customarily used for other over-the-counter securities because they contain both bid and ask prices, rather than high, low, and close. Looking first at the U.S. Treasury bond quotes, observe the small "n" behind the maturity date indicating that the obligation in question is actually a treasury *note*. All other obligations in this section are, of course, treasury bonds. The first quote selected for discussion is the 7 percent issue. The security identification is slightly different from that used with corporates because it is not necessary to list the issuer. Instead, the usual listing indicates the coupon, the year of maturity, the *month* of maturity, and any information on the call feature of the obligation. For example, the 7 percent issue carries a maturity of 1993–98; this means that the issue has a deferred call feature until 1993 (and is thereafter freely callable), and a (final) maturity date of 1998. The bid/ask figures are then provided and are also stated as a percent of par. Unlike the current-yield figure used with corporate issues, yield to maturity or *promised* yield is used with all other issues including treasuries, agencies, and municipals.

Quote 2 is an $8^{3}/_{8}$ percent obligation of 1995–00 which demonstrates the basic difference in the price system of governments (i.e., treasures and agencies). The bid quote is 67.6 and the ask is 67.14. Governments are traded in thirty-seconds of a point (rather than eighths), and the figures to the right of the decimal indicate the number of thirty-seconds in the fractional bid or ask. The bid price is actually $67^{6}/_{32}$ and the ask is $67^{14}/_{32}$ percent of par.

The securities listed below the treasury-bond section are for U.S. Treasury Bills.

Municipal Bond Quotes

The final illustration, Figure 14.6, pertains to municipal bond quotes and is drawn from *The Blue List of Current Municipal Offerings* for Monday, May 1, 1978. As can be seen, *The Blue List* provides daily quotes on municipal bonds ordered according to states and alphabetically within states. The information provided for each issue is: the amount of bonds being offered (in thousands of dollars), the name of the security, the coupon rate, the maturity (which includes month, day, and year), the yield and price, and finally, the dealer offering the bonds. Bond quote 1 is \$25,000 worth of Highland Park obligations. These are 3.375 percent coupon bonds that mature on September 1, 1986, and are part of

Treasury Issues

* * *

Bonds, Notes & Bills

Tuesday, May 26, 1981

Mid-afternoon Over-the-Counter quotations; sources on request.

Decimals in bid-and-asked and bid changes represent 32nds; 101.1 means 101 1/32. a-Plus 1/64. b-Yield to call date. d-Minus 1/64. n-Treasury notes.

Treasury Bonds and Notes

	Rate	Mat. Date		Bid	Asked	Bid Chg.	Yld.
	9¾s,	1981	May n	99.26	99.30	+ .2	16.55
	6¾s,	1981	Jun n	98.30	99.2	+ .4	16.73
	9⅛s,	1981	Jun n	99.5	99.9	+ .3	16.52
	9⅜s,	1981	Jul n	98.14	98.18	+ .3	17.23
	7s,	1981	Aug	97.8	97.24	− .8	17.36
	7⅝s,	1981	Aug n	97.22	97.26	+ .6	17.66
	8⅜s,	1981	Aug n	97.24	97.28	+ .5	18.07
	9⅝s,	1981	Aug n	97.26	97.30	+ .5	17.57
	6¾s,	1981	Sep n	96.10	96.14	+ .3	17.62
	10⅛s,	1981	Sep n	97.16	97.20	+ .6	17.21
	12⅝s,	1981	Oct n	98.4	98.8	+ .4	16.89
	7s,	1981	Nov n	95.19	95.23	+ .5	16.90
	7¾s,	1981	Nov n	95.30	96.2	+ .6	16.84
	12⅛s,	1981	Nov n	97.20	97.24	+ .6	16.93
	7¼s,	1981	Dec n	94.24	94.28	+ .7	16.66
	11⅜s,	1981	Dec n	97	97.4	+ .8	16.66
	11½s,	1982	Jan n	96.23	96.27	+ .10	16.59
	6⅛s,	1982	Feb n	93.6	93.14	+ .4	16.10
	8¼s,	1990	May	74.10	75.10	+ .9	12.98
	10¾s,	1990	Aug n	85.21	85.29	+ .19	13.47
	13s,	1990	Nov n	96.24	96.28	+ .24	13.60
	14½s,	1991	May n	104.15	104.17	+ .27	13.65
	4¼s,	1987-92	Aug	84.10	85.10	+ .14	6.07
	7¼s,	1992	Aug	65.10	66.10	+ 1.2	13.05
	4s,	1988-93	Feb	84.10	85.10	+ .16	5.74
	6¾s,	1993	Feb	63	64	+ .12	12.75
	7⅞s,	1993	Feb	67.6	67.22	+ .24	13.42
	7½s,	1988-93	Aug	65	66	+ .24	13.17
	8⅝s,	1993	Aug	71.6	71.14	+ 1.10	13.45
	8⅝s,	1993	Nov	71.2	71.10	+ 1.2	13.43
	9s,	1994	Feb	73.3	73.11	+ 1.6	13.42
	4⅛s,	1989-94	May	84.10	85.10	+ .16	5.75
	8¾s,	1994	Aug	71.2	71.18	+ 1.2	13.40
	10⅛s,	1994	Nov	79.17	79.25	+ 1.11	13.35
	3s,	1995	Feb	84.10	85.10	+ .16	4.44
	10½s,	1995	Feb	81.20	81.28	+ 1.2	13.43
	10⅜s,	1995	May	80.22	80.30	+ 1.2	13.43
	12⅝s,	1995	May	94.8	94.16	+ 1.18	13.49
	11½s,	1995	Nov	87.20	87.28	+ 1.20	13.42
1→	7s,	1993-98	May	63.8	64.8	+ 1.6	11.97
	3½s,	1998	Nov	84	85	− .8	4.78
	8½s,	1994-99	May	69.12	69.28	+ 1.4	12.82
	7⅞s,	1995-00	Feb	64	64.8	+ 1.22	13.00
2→	8⅜s,	1995-00	Aug	67.6	67.14	+ .12	13.03
	11¾s,	2001	Feb	88.28	89.4	+ 1.23	13.32
	13⅛s,	2001	May	98.1	98.9	+ 1.13	13.37
	8s,	1996-01	Aug	64.24	65	+ .28	12.91
	8¼s,	2000-05	May	65.28	66.12	+ 1.8	12.78
	13⅞s,	2006	May	104.27	104.31	+ 1.3	13.20
	7⅝s,	2002-07	Feb	63	63.8	+ 1.11	12.40
	7⅞s,	2002-07	Nov	65	65.8	+ .24	12.36
	8⅜s,	2003-08	Aug	67.4	67.12	+ .24	12.65
	8¾s,	2003-08	Nov	69.3	69.11	+ .7	12.81
	9⅛s,	2004-09	May	71.17	71.25	+ .13	12.87
	10⅜s,	2004-09	Nov	80.22	80.30	+ .20	12.91
	11¾s,	2005-10	Feb	89	89.8	.....	13.21
	10s,	2005-10	May	77.21	77.29	+ 1.19	12.94
	12¾s,	2005-10	Nov	97.2	97.10	+ .28	13.11

n– Treasury notes.

U.S. Treas. Bills

Mat. date	Bid Discount	Asked Discount	Yield	Mat. date	Bid Discount	Asked Discount	Yield
				9-17	15.74	15.54	16.56
-1981-				9-24	15.67	15.47	16.53
5-28	15.42	15.02	0.00	10- 1	15.40	15.28	16.37
6- 4	16.98	16.70	16.99	10- 8	15.31	15.21	16.34
6-11	16.99	16.71	17.05	10-15	15.15	15.01	16.16
6-18	17.14	16.84	17.24	10-22	15.10	14.96	16.16
6-25	16.74	16.66	17.22	10-29	15.10	14.96	16.20
7- 2	16.44	16.26	17.22	11- 5	14.99	14.87	16.15
7- 9	16.48	16.28	16.83	11-12	14.98	14.88	16.21
7-16	16.43	16.25	16.85	11-19	14.96	14.84	16.22
7-23	16.39	16.17	16.82	12- 3	14.95	14.83	16.26
7-30	16.34	16.12	16.82	12-31	14.79	14.69	16.13
8- 6	16.07	16.01	16.75	-1982-			
8-13	16.05	15.97	16.76	1-28	14.48	14.30	15.75
8-20	16.05	15.99	16.84	2-25	14.42	14.22	15.75
8-27	15.93	15.87	16.76	3-25	14.13	13.97	15.56
9- 3	15.86	15.66	16.58	4-22	14.07	13.91	15.61
9-10	15.82	15.62	16.59	5-20	13.95	13.89	15.73

Figure 14.5 Sample Quotes for Treasury and Agency Issues

Source: *The Wall Street Journal,* May 27, 1981. Reprinted by permission of *The Wall Street Journal* © Dow Jones & Company, Inc., 1981. All rights reserved.

a series of bonds that came out with this particular serial obligation. The $25,000 in bonds are being offered by Newhard, Cook and Co. at a yield of 5.25 percent. Municipals are the only segment of the bond market that regularly trade a major portion of the issues on the basis of *yield to maturity,* rather than percent of par. Indeed, an analysis of the page reveals that most obligations, particularly general-obligation bonds, are quoted on a yield basis. To determine the dollar price of

```
                                    MICHIGAN-CONTINUED
                                                                        (HARRIS TRUST & SAVING
                                                                        (FIRST N.B.OF CHICAGO
     1750(GENESEE COUNTY                    4.40      5/ 1/80      4.15((A.G.BECKER MUN S.INC.
         ( DTD 4/1/78  F/C 11/1/78  W.I.                                )(FIRST PENNCO SEC.
                                                                        (WALTERLEK&BROWN.INC.
                                                                        (AMER.N.B&T.  (CGO)
                                                                        (SMITH.HAGUE & CO.INC

        15 GENESEE COUNTY                    4.70      5/ 1/92      5.50  E.F.HUTTON & CO.(CGO.
         5 GENESEE COUNTY                    5         5/ 1/93      5.60  FIRST OF MICHIGAN CRP
         5 GLADSTONE AREA PUB.SCHS.          7.20      5/ 1/94  C88  5.85  E.F.HUTTON & CO.(CGO.
           (CA @ 103)
         5 GLADSTONE AREA PUB.SC      QUAL   7.40      5/ 1/05      6.20  FIRST OF MICHIGAN CRP
        25 GRAND RAPIDS BLDG. AU  P/C @ 104  6.60     11/ 1/93  C82  4.70  LOEB,RHOADES,HORN(NY)
         5 GRAND RAPIDS&KENT CO.JT.BLDG.AU.  5.50      8/ 1/01      5.80  LOEB,RHOADES,HORN(NY)
         5 GROSSE ILE TWP. S.D.             5.375      5/ 1/93      5.30  E.F.HUTTON & CO.(CGO.
        15 HAZEL PARK                        3.75      4/ 1/86      5.70  FIRST OF MICHIGAN CRP
  ① 25 HIGHLAND PARK                    3.375      9/ 1/86      5.25  NEWHARD,COOK & CO.
        15 HOLLAND SCHOOL DIST.      U.T.O.   5.75      1/ 1/98  C    5.60  WM.C.RONEY & CO.
        15 INGHAM CO.                         5.50     11/ 1/00      100  FIRST OF MICHIGAN CRP
        10 JACKSON COUNTY                     6.75     11/ 1/92  C87  5.45  LOEB,RHOADES,HORN(DET
           (CA @ 103)(Y/M 5.60)
         5 KENT COUNTY          W/S  G.O.     5.95     11/ 1/91      5.40  LOEB,RHOADES,HORN(DET
      + 100 KENT HOSP.FIN.AU.                 5.40      1/ 1/85      5.25  LISS,TENNER&GOLDBERG
      + 400 KENT HOSP.FIN.AU.                 5.70      1/ 1/87      5.55  LISS,TENNER&GOLDBERG
      + 100 KENT HOSP.FIN.AU.                 6         1/ 1/89      5.80  LISS,TENNER&GOLDBERG

       60(KENT HOSP.FIN.AU.                   6.15      7/ 1/91      5.80)(D.WITTER REYNOLD(DET)
         ( (BUTTERWORTH)                                                 )(MANLEY,BENNETT,MCDON

         5 LK.SUPERIOR ST.COLL.              7.125     9/15/02      6.75  LOEB,RHOADES,HORN(DET
        10 LITCHFIELD C.S.D.          QUAL   6.60      5/ 1/94  C86  5.40  LOEB,RHOADES,HORN(DET
           (CA @ 103)(Y/M 5.70)
        25 LIVONIA IND.DEV/REV.               6         4/ 1/97      73  LAIDLAW ADAMS&PECK(NY
           (ALLIED SUPERMARKETS)
      + 25 LIVONIA PUB.SCH.DIST.      QUAL   3.50      5/ 1/85      5.45  FIRST OF MICHIGAN CRP
        15 LUDINGTON S.D.                     5.25     11/ 1/98      6.10  FIRST OF MICHIGAN CRP
        50 MACKINAC BRIDGE AUTH.              4         1/ 1/94      101 1/2  BARR BROS. & CO.,INC.
        25 MACKINAC BRIDGE AUTH.              4         1/ 1/94      101  BONNIWELL & CO., INC.
        25 MACKINAC BRIDGE AUTH.              4         1/ 1/94      101  R.E.D.CHASE&PARTNERS
        25 MACKINAC BRIDGE AUTH.              4         1/ 1/94      101  F.B. COOPER & CO.,INC
        25 MACKINAC BRIDGE AUTH.              4         1/ 1/94      101  DONALDSON,LUFK,JENR.
        25 MACKINAC BRIDGE AUTH.              4         1/ 1/94      100 1/2  FIRST OF MICHIGAN CRP
        15 MACKINAC BRIDGE AUTH.              4         1/ 1/94      100 1/2  WEEDEN & CO.,INC.
  ②  3 MACKINAC BRIDGE AUTH.              5.25      1/ 1/94      100  F.B. COOPER & CO.,INC
        10 MACOMB CO.                         3.75      5/ 1/88      5.50  A.F. STEPP INVEST.INC

      + 50(MACOMB CO.                         3.75     11/ 1/90      6.00)(D.WITTER REYNOLD(DET)
                                                                        (MANLEY,BENNETT,MCDON

        10 MACOMB CO.                  G.O.   4.85      5/ 1/92      5.60  WM.C.RONEY & CO.
        25 MACOMB CO.            CA @ 102     5.75      5/ 1/95  C88  100  KIDDER,PEABODY(TOLEDO
        25 MARQUETTE WTR/SWR.RV.             5.75      7/ 1/01  C    100  KIDDER,PEABODY(TOLEDO
        15 MAYVILLE S.D.              QUAL    7.25      5/ 1/96      5.75  LOEB,RHOADES,HORN(DET
         5 MONROE SCH. DIST.          QUAL    5         5/ 1/88      4.70  FIRST OF MICHIGAN CRP
       200 MONROE COUNTY           SWR.D.    5.75     11/ 1/84      4.50  ROOSE,WADE (CLEVELAND
       700 MONROE CO.POLL.CTL.RV               6        6/ 1/03      6.25  MANLEY,BENNETT,MCDON
           (DETROIT ED.)
        10 MONROE CO.POLL.CTL.RV  CA @ 103    7         3/ 1/05  C87  6.35  LOEB,RHOADES,HORN(DET
           (DETROIT ED.)(Y/M 6.05)
        25 MONTABELLA COMM.S.D.              5.75      5/ 1/03      5.80  BECKER & COWNIE, INC.

                                                                        (FIRST OF MICHIGAN CRP
                                                                        (BLYTH,EASTMAN DILLON
      + 250(MUNISING P.S.D.                   5.95      5/ 1/00      100)(THE OHIO COMPANY
      + 325( DTD 4/1/78  U.T.O.    (85,240)  6         5/ 1/01-02   100-100)(PRESCOTT,BALL&TURBEN
      + 250(  F/C 11/1/78  W.I.               6         5/ 1/04      6.05)(LOEB,RHOADES,HORN(DET
      + 140(                                  6         5/ 1/07      6.10)(
                                                                        (BACHE HALSEY(CGO.TR.)
                                                                        (E.F.HUTTON & CO.(CGO.
                                                                        (PAINE,WEB,JACK,CURT.

        20 NORTHVILLE P.S.D.         QUAL    5.75      5/ 1/97      5.75  LOEB,RHOADES,HORN(DET
        50 NORTHVILLE P.S.D.                 5.80      5/ 1/98  C    5.60  FIRST OF MICHIGAN CRP
       150 NORTHVILLE P.S.D.                 5.80      5/ 1/99      5.70  VAN KAMPEN SAUERMAN
        10 NORTHVILLE P.S.D.         #2      3.75      5/ 1/86      5.50  LOEB,RHOADES,HORN(DET
        25 NOVI                       G.O.    4.60     10/ 1/85      4.85  BLYTH,EASTMAN(CHICAGO
      + 30 OAKLAND COUNTY                    6.25      5/ 1/83      4.70  E.F.HUTTON & CO.(CGO.
        15 OAKLAND COUNTY                    4.375      5/ 1/84      5.00  FIRST N.B.OF CHICAGO
        25 OAKLAND COUNTY                    6.25      5/ 1/84      4.95  NATL.BK. OF DETROIT
        25 OAKLAND COUNTY                    6.50      5/ 1/84      4.70  FOLGER,NOLAN,FLEM,DOU
        45 OAKLAND COUNTY                    6.50      5/ 1/84      4.75  LOEB,RHOADES,HORN(DET

                    MONDAY MAY 1, 1978                 PAGE 63
```

Figure 14.6   Quotes for Municipals

Source: *The Blue List of Current Municipal Offerings*, May 1, 1978. The Blue List, Division of Standard & Poor's. Reprinted by permission.

this issue, one would have to compute the present value of a 3.375 percent, 8.33-year bond that is yielding 5.25 percent.

The second issue $3,000 of the Mackinac Bridge Authority 5¼ percent of 94, is highlighted because the quote is stated as a percent of par. This is a customary pricing procedure with *term revenue issues*. Most of these bonds are quoted on a dollar basis, rather than on a yield basis—thus these are called "dollar bonds." Actually, the quote is still listed as a percent of par, rather than a dollar price, although the dollar figure is much easier to obtain for the Mackinac Bridge Authority than for the Highland Park issue.

Summary

The purpose of this chapter was to deal with the fundamental aspects of bonds to provide the necessary background for a discussion of bond valuation and investment strategies. We initially looked at the basic features of bonds with respect to interest, principal, and maturity.

Several key relationships were discussed in regard to price behavior. First, price is essentially a function of coupon, maturity, and prevailing market interest rates. Second, bond price volatility depends on coupon and maturity. In general, bonds with longer maturities and/or lower coupons respond most vigorously to a given change in market rates. Finally, other factors, including intrinsic characteristics, type of issue, and indenture provisions, must be considered.

Major benefits to investors included: high returns for nominal risk, potential for capital gains, certain tax advantages, and the opportunity for additional returns based on aggressive trading of bonds. Major concerns for the aggressive bond investor include secondary-market activity, investment risks, and interest-rate behavior.

Several popular issues available in the various market sectors were reviewed, with consideration given to liquidity, yield spreads, tax implications, and special features unique to each sector. The final section contained a discussion of the information needs of investors. In terms of default risk, most bond investors rely on agency ratings as their source of information. For additional information on market and economic conditions, and information on intrinsic bond features, individual and institutional investors rely on a host of readily available publications. Various examples of typical issue quotes were given with accompanying explanations.

Questions

1. How does a bond differ from other types of debt instruments?

2. Explain the difference between calling a bond and bond refunding.

3. Identify the three most important factors in determing the price of a bond. Describe the effect of each.

4. Given a change in the level of interest rates, what are the two factors that will influence the relative change in price for individual bonds and what is their impact?

5. Define two different types of bond yields.

6.   What factors determine whether a bond is "senior" or "junior"? Give examples of each type of bond.

7.   What is a bond indenture?

8.   Explain the differences in taxation of income from municipal bonds as opposed to U.S. Treasury bonds and corporate bonds.

9.   List several types of institutional participants in the bond market and explain what types of bond they are likely to purchase and why they purchase them.

10. Why should an investor be aware of the trading volume for a particular bond in which he is interested?

11. What is the purpose of bond ratings; what are they supposed to indicate?

12. What part does a bond's rating play in the evaluation of a bond for investment?

13. Demonstrate through an example the effects of interest-rate risk on the price of a bond.

14. An investor in the 35 percent tax bracket is trying to decide which of two bonds to purchase. One is a corporate bond, carrying an 8 percent coupon and selling at par. The other is a municipal bond, with a 5½ percent coupon, and it, too, sells at par. Assuming all other relevant factors are equal, which bond should the investor select?

15. Compare and contrast a corporate mortgage-backed bond with a Ginnie Mae pass-through certificate.

16. In the latter part of this chapter, a large number of sources of information on bonds were described and their contents discussed. Yet the statement was made earlier that "it is almost impossible for individual investors . . . to keep abreast of the price activity of municipal holdings." Discuss this apparent paradox, explaining how such a condition might exist.

17. Using various sources of information described in the chapter, name at least five bonds, rated B or better, that have split ratings.

18. Using various sources of information, select five bonds from those firms listed on the NYSE. Prepare a brief description of each bond, including such factors as its rating, call features, collateral, if any, interest dates, and refunding provisions.

References

Ahearn, Daniel S. "The Strategic Role of Fixed Income Securities." *Journal of Portfolio Management* (1975).

Baskin, Elba F., and Crooch, Gary M. "Historical Rates of Return on Investments in Flat Bonds." *Financial Analysis Journal* 24 (1968).

Bierman, Harold, and Hass, Jerome. "An Analytical Model of Bond Risk Differentials." *Journal of Financial and Quantitative Analysis* 10 (1975).

Brimmer, Andrew F. "Credit Conditions and Price Determination in the Corporate Bond Market." *Journal of Finance* 15 (1960).

Darst, David M. *The Handbook of the Bond and Money Markets.* New York: McGraw-Hill, 1981.

Fisher, Lawrence. "Determinants of Risk Premiums on Corporate Bonds." *Journal of Political Economy* 67 (1959).

Greenbaum, Mary. "Sorting Out the Floating Rate Securities." *Fortune,* 17 December 1979.

Hickman, W. Braddock. *Corporate Bond Quality and Investor Experience.* Princeton, NJ: Princeton University Press, 1958.

Homer, Sidney. "The Historical Evolution of Today's Bond Market." *Journal of Portfolio Management* 1 (1975).

Homer, Sidney, ed. *The Great American Bond Market.* Homewood, IL: Dow-Jones-Irwin, 1978.

Horrigan, James O. "The Determination of Long-Term Credit Standing with Financial Ratios." *Empirical Research in Accounting: Selected Studies,* Supplement to *Journal of Accounting Research* 4 (1966).

Joehnk, Michael D., and Nielsen, James F. "Return Risk Characteristics of Speculative Grade Bonds." *Quarterly Review of Economics and Business* 15 (1975).

Landsea, William F. "Agency Bonds in Liquidity Portfolios." *Mississippi Valley Journal of Business and Economics* 7 (1971–72).

Meyer, Kenneth, R. "The Dividends from Active Bond Management." *Journal of Portfolio Management* 1 (1975).

Pinches, George E., and Mingo, Kent A. "A Multivariate Analysis of Industrial Bond Ratings." *Journal of Finance* 28 (1973).

Pogue, Thomas F., and Soldofsky, Robert M. "What's in a Bond Rating?" *Journal of Financial and Quantitative Analysis* 4 (1969).

Pye, Gordon. "Gauging the Default Premium." *Financial Analysts Journal* 30 (1974).

Reilly, Frank K., and Joehnk, Michael D. "Association Between Market-Determined Risk Measures for Bonds and Bond Ratings," *Journal of Finance* 31 (1976).

Ross, Irwin, "Higher Stakes in the Bond-Rating Game." *Fortune,* April 1976.

"Say Hello To Tax-Free Bonds Funds," *Savings and Loan News* 98 (1977).

Schwarz, Edward W. *How To Use Interest Rate Futures Contracts.* Homewood, IL., Dow Jones-Irwin, 1979.

Sharpe, William F. "Bonds Versus Stocks: Some Lessons from Capital Market Theory." *Financial Analysts Journal* 29 (1973).

Thygerson, Kenneth J., and Parliment, Thomas J. "Mortgage Securities Make It Big On Wall Street." *Savings and Loan News* 98 (1977).

Van Horne, James C. *Financial Market Rates and Flows.* Englewood Cliffs, NJ: Prentice-Hall, 1978.

Weil, Roman. "Realized Interest Rates and Bondholder's Returns." *American Economic Review* 60 (1970).

West, Richard R. "An Alternative Approach to Predicting Corporate Bond Ratings." *Journal of Accounting Research* 8 (1970).

Martin L. Leibowitz

Martin L. Leibowitz is general partner and manager of the Bond Portfolio Analysis Group, Salomon Brothers. He received his B.A. and M.A. from the University of Chicago, and his Ph.D. in mathematics from New York University.

With Sidney Homer, a limited partner in Salomon Brothers and formerly the general partner in charge of the firm's bond market research department, Leibowitz co-authored a book on bonds titled Inside the Yield Book, which was jointly published in 1972 by Prentice-Hall and the New York Institute of Finance. This book has enjoyed widespread acceptance by academicians and practitioners. It is considered essential reading for those seriously involved in bond analysis and active bond portfolio management.

In 1974, Leibowitz authored Total After-Tax Bond Performance and Yield Measures. This Salomon Brothers publication was intended as a special supplement to Inside the Yield Book dealing with taxable bond portfolios.

Articles by Leibowitz have appeared in the Money Manager, Trusts and Estates, Euromoney, Pension and Welfare News, the Financial Analysts Journal, Banker's Magazine, The Financial Analysts Handbook, and The Journal of Portfolio Management.

In the publication, The Analysis of Intermediate Term Bond Financing, *Leibowitz explored the problem of the corporate (or government) issuer faced with choosing between an intermediate and a long maturity for a given debt financing situation. In 1976, his study on "Horizon Analysis for Managed Bond Portfolios" was published as a chapter in the book,* The Theory and Practice of Bond Portfolio Management.

For his paper, "Horizon Annuity: Linking the Growth and Payout Phase of Long-Term Bond Portfolios," *the Financial Analysts Federation presented Leibowitz* with the Graham & Dodd Award "in recognition of an outstanding feature article in the Financial Analysts Journal during the year of 1979."

His recent work includes studies of mortgage related securities, "Cash Flow Characteristics of Mortgage Securities," a series of works relating to the subject of bond immunization, and several studies developing a new approach to the analysis of financial futures. In another recent work, Leibowitz introduced the concept of a structured approach to active bond portfolio management in a paper titled "Contingent Immunization."

Sidney Homer

If one were to ask bond analysts and bond portfolio managers to name the individual who had done the most extensive research in bonds over the past 50 years and who was the most widely respected, it is very likely that the vast majority would select Sidney Homer. The choice seems obvious when one considers the several significant books written by Homer and the volume of research generated by Salomon Brothers during the years when Sidney Homer was in charge of the firms bond research department.

He is the author of A History of Interest Rates *(Rutgers University Press, 1963), which deals with interest rates for 40 countries over 40 centuries (2,000 B.C. to 1976). The book was revised in 1978. Homer also wrote* The Bond Buyers Primer *(1968) and was the co-author with Richard I. Johannesan of* The Price of Money *(Rutgers University Press, 1969). His most widely read book is* Inside the Yield Book *(co-authored with Martin Leibowitz & published by Prentice-Hall in 1972). This book has become essential reading for bond analysts and active bond portfolio managers. It is widely used in university courses and is a required text for the Chartered Financial Analysts (CFA) program. His most recent book is* The Great American Bond Market *(Dow Jones-Irwin, 1979) which is a collection of speeches by Homer on the bond market and bond investment techniques.*

Sidney Homer was born in 1902 in West Chester, Pennsylvania. He received an A.B. degree in philosophy (magna cum laude) from Harvard College in 1923 and subsequently worked on Wall Street as a credit investigator for a bank, and then managed a statistical department and bond department for a brokerage firm prior to establishing a bond dealer firm (Homer & Co.). He managed the institutional investment department of Scudder, Stevens & Clark (investment counselors) before joining Salomon Brothers in 1961 where he became a general partner in charge of the bond market research department. He retired in 1971 and currently acts as a consultant to Salomon Brothers and other firms.

BOND VALUATION AND PORTFOLIO MANAGEMENT

⇒ 15 ⇐

Like any long-term investment, fixed-income securities are valued on the basis of their future stream of income. One purpose of this chapter is to explore the bond valuation process and to identify the important determinants of bond price and yield. This includes an analysis of the causes of bond price volatility. It is recognized that successful bond investment involves far more than the ability to value individual bonds. The fact is, you must use economic and market data to formulate viable portfolio policies and investment strategies. Alternative bond investors, with different risk profiles, follow one of several portfolio strategies that we consider, ranging from buy-and-hold to sophisticated bond swapping. Finally, we consider the implications of Capital Market Theory on bond portfolio management and the question of bond market efficiency.

Fundamentals of the Bond Valuation Process

Present-Value Model

Basically, the bond valuation process is similar to the procedures used with equity securities because the value of a bond is equal to the present value of expected cash flows. The only real difference is that the cash flow involved is the periodic interest payments and capital recovery. In a theoretical framework, the basic principles of bond valuation can be described in the following present-value model:

$$P = \sum_{t=1}^{n} C_t \frac{1}{(1+i)^t}$$

(15.1)

where:

n = the number of periods in the investment horizon, or what is more popularly known as term to maturity

C_t = the cash flow (periodic interest income and principal) received in period t, and

i   = the rate of discount (or market yield) for the issue.

Essentially, any fixed-income security can be valued on the basis of Equation (15.1), which provides an indication of what the investor expects to realize by holding the issue over a given investment horizon. In most cases, the holding period is assumed to be equal to the term to maturity of the obligation. As a result, the rate of discount represents the "promised" yield to maturity that can be earned by purchasing the obligation and holding it to its expiration date. Aggressive bond investors, however, normally do not hold obligations to maturity. Rather, the intent is to buy and sell the security prior to that point. Under such conditions, *"realized" yield* is a more important description of performance, and Equation 15.1 would represent an expected realized yield, rather than promised return.

The present-value model is attractive because it incorporates several important aspects of bond yields and prices. Current income is a facet of coupon receipts and is included in C_t. More important, we know that interest-rate behavior is a critical aspect of bond price performance, and this effect is incorporated in i, where the discount rate is the prevailing bond yield (described as promised yield to maturity) at a given point in time. Further, changes in interest rates affect the level of capital gains (or losses) that would be realized by an investor who buys and sells an issue prior to maturity,[1] and this impact is incorporated into the model within the cash flow component, C_t.

Another factor affecting capital gains in the model is the effect of changes in *yield spreads* over the investment horizon. These spreads are simply differences in yields that exist between different market sectors or types of issues. Yield spreads account for the subtle differences in performance owing to such aspects as differential call features, variations in coupons, and maturities, etc.

Bond valuation requires an evaluation of interest receipts, interest rates, changes in interest rates, and yield spreads. *The major problem facing a bond investor is determining interest-rate changes and yield-spread behavior.* Clearly, the coupon income and par value are specified and fixed. The only real concern is determining the risk of default, and much of that is handled by agency ratings. Moreover, if an investor is examining an obligation solely on the basis of promised yield, then prevailing available market rates define i. In contrast, the computation of *realized* yield assumes that the investment horizon is less than term to maturity, and this realized yield is directly related to the possibility of capital gains or losses. Further, the potential capital gains or losses depend upon interest rate changes and yield spreads.

The investor must not only understand those forces that affect the *level* of interest rates, but also must be able to project future interest rates. Once interest

---

[1]Indeed, for many aggressive investors, it is *the* major factor because their major objective is attractive capital gains.

rate levels have been evaluated, and anticipated *changes* in rates have been formulated, the investor must consider *differential* market rates, and that implies examination of yield spreads. That is, an evaluation of yield-spread behavior over the holding period will indicate that certain segments of the market will be more attractive because of their relative yield performance. In effect, yield-spread analysis considers interest-rate behavior for specific segments of the market. The importance of estimating interest-rate changes and yield-spread changes is greater for the investor engaged in extensive bond trading than for the buy-and-hold investor.

The subsequent discussion of the valuation process pertains to investment-grade securities that possess acceptable levels of interest rate sensitivity. Essentially, speculative-grade securities are less sensitive to interest rates and, given the importance of interest rates in the bond valuation process, the framework specified would be inappropriate for bonds that are not interest sensitive.[2]

The Mathematics of Bond Pricing and Yields

Basically there are five types of yields in bond-market trading vernacular: nominal yield, current yield, promised yield, yield to call, and realized yield. *Nominal yield* is the coupon rate a particular issue carries. A bond with an 8 percent coupon would have an 8 percent nominal yield. It is only significant because it provides a convenient way of describing the coupon characteristics of an issue.

Current yield (CY) is to bonds what dividend yield is to stocks, and is computed as:

$$CY = C_t/P_m \qquad\qquad (15.2)$$

where:

C_t = the annual coupon payment of the obligation

P_m = the current market price of the issue.

This yield indicates the relative level of current income provided by the obligation and is important to income-oriented investors. Unfortunately, it excludes an important component in the bond valuation process, capital recovery. A bond with an 11 percent coupon currently selling at 90 would have a current yield of 12.22%.

[2]For a more detailed discussion of the determinants of speculative-grade bond yields and price behavior, see Michael D. Joehnk, and James F. Nielsen, "Return and Risk Characteristics of Speculative Grade Bonds," *Quarterly Review of Economics & Business* 15 (1975): 35–43; and Elba F. Baskin and Gary M. Crooch, "Historical Rates of Return on Investments in Flat Bonds," *Financial Analysts Journal* 24 (1968): 95–97.

Promised Yield (Yield to Maturity)

Promised yield is *the* most important and widely used bond valuation model! Essentially, promised yield indicates the fully compounded rate of return offered to the investor at prevailing prices, assuming the investor *holds the obligation to maturity*. Also known as *yield to maturity*, it excludes any trading possibilities. The concept simply involves prevailing market prices, periodic coupon income, and par value (which, when related to prevailing market price, accounts for capital appreciation or depreciation). The actual yield to maturity is determined by finding that rate of interest that will discount all future cash flows to equal the current market price of the bond, assuming the bond is held to maturity. This is the same specification as the internal rate of return concept used in capital budgeting in corporate finance.

Like any present-value computation, promised yield has important reinvestment implications. In particular, the promised yield is the *required reinvestment rate* that the investor must subsequently earn on each of the interim cash flows (coupon receipts) to realize a return equal to the promised yield. This is directly related to compound value and is also known as "interest-on-interest."[3] The yield to maturity figure is the return promised so long as the issuer meets all interest and principal obligations on a timely basis *and the investor reinvests coupon income to maturity at a rate equal to the computed promised yield.* If a bond offers an 8 percent yield to maturity, the investor must reinvest coupon income at a rate equal to 8 percent to realize that return. If coupons are not reinvested, or if future investment rates during the life of the issue are less than the promised yield at purchase, then the *realized* yield earned will be *less* than the promised yield to maturity.

This important and often overlooked concept is fully developed in the excellent book by Homer and Leibowitz.[4] The importance of interest-on-interest varies directly with coupon and maturity; the higher the coupon and/or the longer the term to maturity, the more important is reinvestment. Figure 15.1 depicts the concept and the impact of interest-on-interest assuming an 8 percent, 25-year bond was bought at par to yield 8 percent. This chart shows that if you invested $1,000 today at a rate of 8 percent for 25 years and all the income were reinvested at 8 percent, you would have approximately $7,100 at the end of 25 years. To prove this, look up the compound value for 8 percent for 25 years (which is 6.8493) or 4 percent for 50 periods (this assumes semiannual compounding), which is 7.1073. The chart shows that this $7,100 is made up of $1,000 principal return, $2,000 of coupon payments over the 25 years ($80 a year for 25 years), and the rest ($4,100) is interest earned on the coupon payments at 8 percent. It is important to recognize that if you never reinvested any of the coupon payments, you would only have an ending wealth value of $3,000.

---

[3]Sidney Homer and Martin L. Leibowitz, *Inside the Yield Book* (Englewood Cliffs, NJ: Prentice-Hall, 1972), chapter 1.

[4]Op. cit.

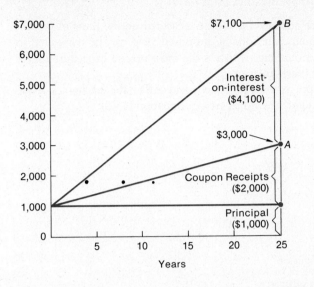

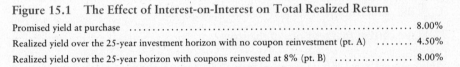

Figure 15.1   The Effect of Interest-on-Interest on Total Realized Return

Promised yield at purchase 8.00%

Realized yield over the 25-year investment horizon with no coupon reinvestment (pt. A) 4.50%

Realized yield over the 25-year horizon with coupons reinvested at 8% (pt. B) 8.00%

This ending wealth value relative to the beginning investment of $1,000 implies a *realized* yield of 4.5 percent (i.e., 4.5 percent is the rate that will discount $3,000 back to $1,000 in 25 years). Obviously if you had reinvested the coupon payments at some rate between 0 and 8 percent, your ending wealth position would have been above $3,000 and below $7,100 and, therefore, your realized return would be somewhere between 4.5 percent and 8 percent. Alternatively, if you were able to consistently reinvest the coupon payments at rates above 8 percent, your ending wealth position would be above $7,100 and your realized return would be above 8 percent.

Interestingly, during periods of very high interest rates, you will often hear investors talk about "locking-in" high yields. In many instances they do not realize that they are subject to "yield illusion" because they don't realize that to attain the high "promised" yield, they must reinvest all the coupon payments at the *very high yields that currently exist.* As an example, if you buy a 20-year bond with a promised yield to maturity of 15 percent, to *realize* the 15 percent yield you must be able to reinvest all the coupon payments at 15 percent over the next 20 years.

Approximate Promised Yield

Depending upon the accuracy desired, there are several procedures that can be used to compute promised yield. It can be computed on the basis of approximate yield, or, for slightly more accuracy, it can be measured on the basis of present value using annual compounding. Finally, promised yield can be computed in terms of semiannual compounding, which is the most precise procedure and is the procedure used in the marketplace.

Looking first at the approximate promised yield (APY), the mechanics of this measure are relatively straightforward as seen in Equation (15.3):

(15.3)

$$APY = \frac{C_t + \dfrac{P_p - P_m}{n}}{\dfrac{P_p + P_m}{2}}$$

where:

P_p = par value of the obligation

n = number of years to maturity

C_t = the *annual* coupon value of the obligation and

P_m = the current market price of the issue.

Approximate yield differs from current yield because it encompasses the impact of capital gain or loss on the annual income and on the base investment. Specifically, the numerator considers the annual coupon payment *plus* an annual capital gain or loss provision based upon the difference between the purchase price and the par value of the issue. The denominator estimates the average investment as the midpoint between the purchase price and the par value. The approximate yield assumes annual interest payments and is useful because it does not require iterations as the present-value computations of yield to maturity do.

Assume that we want to determine the approximate promised yield of an 8 percent bond, with 20 years remaining to maturity, and a current price of $900. The approximate promised yield of this bond is 8.95 percent as follows:

$$APY = \frac{80 + \dfrac{1000 - 900}{20}}{\dfrac{1000 + 900}{2}}$$

$$= \frac{80 + 5}{950}$$

$$= 8.95\%$$

The idea is that this bond will provide annual interest of $80 plus an annual capital gain of $5 on an average investment of $950.

Promised Yield: Annual Compounding

For even more accuracy, promised yield can be computed using the present-value model and annual compounding. Equation (15.4) shows this version of the promised-yield valuation model:

$$P_m = \sum_{t=1}^{n} \frac{C_t}{(1 + i)^t} + \frac{P_p}{(1 + i)^n} \qquad (15.4)$$

where all the variables are as described above. In this model the intent is to find that discount rate (i) that will equate the present value of the stream of coupon receipts (C_t and principal value (P_p), with the current market price of the obligation (P_m). As noted previously, the process of finding this discount rate is the same as finding the internal rate of return on an investment in corporate finance and requires a series of iterations or interpolations to arrive at the final solution. Using the same example as above, the intent is to find the discount rate that will equate the interest payments ($80 a year) and the principal payment at the end of 20 years to the current market price of $900. Using the approximate promised yield derived previously (8.95 percent), you might begin by discounting at 9 percent. This exercise would indicate a value of $908.68, so you would know the true yield must be above 9 percent to get a lower value. By moving up slowly or jumping to a higher discount rate (9.25), and interpolating, you would find that the promised yield is 9.11 percent as follows:

$$900 = 80 \sum_{t=1}^{20} \frac{1}{(1.0911)^t} + 1000 \frac{1}{(1.0911)^{20}}$$

$$= 80\,(9.0625) + 1000\,(.1750)$$

$$= 900$$

(Note in the above illustration that the values for $\frac{1}{1 + i}$ were obtained from present-value interest factor tables.)

A comparison of the results from Equation (15.4) with those obtained from the approximate promised-yield computation indicates a variation of 16 basis points in computed promised yield. As a rule, approximate yield tends to *understate* actual promised yield for issues trading at a discount, with the size of the differential varying directly with the length of the holding period; i.e., the greater n is, the bigger the difference will be. Note that with APY the *ranking* of yields based on Equation (15.3) will generally be identical to the rankings determined by more precise methods.

Promised Yield: Semiannual Compounding

For maximum accuracy, semiannual rather than annual, compounding should be used because the cash flow from bonds is semiannual. Even in those situations in which the cash flow occurs over something other than six-month intervals (for example, GNMA pass-throughs), semiannual compounding is still employed as a basis for yield valuation. Semiannual compounding can be calculated by altering Equation (15.4) as follows:

(15.5)

$$P_m = \sum_{t=1}^{2n} \frac{C_t/2}{(1 + i/2)^t} + \frac{P_p}{(1 + i/2)^{2n}}$$

where all the variables are as described above. The major adjustments include doubling the number of periods within the investment horizon, because each now covers six months rather than one year. Because coupons are received every six months, the value of C_t is halved. The promised yield with this method amounts to 9.09 percent. The mechanics of the calculation are identical to those in Equation (15.4), so an illustration is unnecessary. You can test your skills by using Equation (15.5) to arrive at the indicated yield.

Clearly, the improvement in accuracy (two basis points) is nowhere near as great as it was when we moved from approximate yield to Equation (15.4). Such improved accuracy would be necessary only for large investment sums and large bond portfolios. Notably, Equation (15.5) is the procedure used to determine published bond quotes.

Yield to Call

While promised yield to maturity is used most often, it is occasionally necessary to establish return on the basis of promised yield to call. Whenever a *premium bond* is quoted at a value equal to or greater than par plus one year's interest, yield to call should be computed in place of yield to maturity, because the marketplace bases its pricing on the most conservative (i.e., lowest) yield measure. Therefore, when bonds are trading at or above a certain dollar value, the yield to call will normally provide the lowest yield measure. The value at which the yield to call is appropriate is referred to as the "cross-over point" (or price) which approximates par plus one year's interest.[5] Implicitly, the market assumes that the obligation will *not* remain outstanding to maturity, but instead will be retired at the end of the deferred call period. Thus, what you want to do is derive the promised yield based on an investment horizon extending only to the call date. Yield to call becomes important when there are many high-yielding, high-coupon obligations issued that possess substantial levels of call risk.

Yield to call is calculated using variations of Equations (15.3), (15.4), or (15.5). If the approximate yield to call (AYC) were desired, then the investor would use the following variation of the approximate promised-yield computation:

---

[5]For an extended discussion of the derivation of the "cross over point," see Homer and Liebowitz, *Inside the Yield Book,* chapter 4.

$$AYC = \frac{C_t + \dfrac{P_c - P_m}{nc}}{\dfrac{P_c + P_m}{2}}$$ (15.6)

where:

P_c = the call price of the obligation (as noted above, this is generally equal to par value plus one year's interest)

nc = the number of years to first call date, and

all other variables in the model are as defined above. Observe that this model is comparable to approximate yield to maturity, except that P_c has replaced P_p (in Equation (15.3) and nc has replaced n.

As an illustration, assume an 8 percent, 20-year bond that is trading at 115 ($1,150) and has 5 years remaining to first call at a price of 108 ($1080). Using Equation (15.6), we see that:

$$AYC = \frac{80 + \dfrac{1080 - 1150}{5}}{\dfrac{1080 + 1150}{2}} = 5.92\%$$

The approximate yield to call of the obligation is 5.92 percent, and is derived under the assumption that the issue will be prematurely retired after five years at the call price of 108. You can compute the approximate promised yield to maturity of this issue to confirm that yield to call is the more conservative value. (Promised yield to maturity based on Equation (15.3), will equal 6.74 percent.)

Similar simple adjustments can be made in present-value models (15.4) and (15.5). For the annual-compounding approach, yield to call would appear as follows:

$$P_m = \sum_{t=1}^{nc} \frac{C_t}{(1 + i)^t} + \frac{P_c}{(1 + i)^{nc}}$$ (15.7)

where all the variables are described as above. For the semiannual approach to bond valuation, yield to call can be determined using the following model:

$$P_m = \sum_{t=1}^{2nc} \frac{C_t/2}{(1 + i/2)^t} + \frac{P_c}{(1 + i/2)^{2nc}}$$ (15.8)

where all the variables are described as above. The same two changes that were noted with the approximate method are used with the present-value methods; i.e., P_p (par value) is replaced by the call price of the issue (P_c), and the remaining life of the obligation is not term to maturity (n), but the number of years or semiannual periods to call (nc).

Realized Yield

The final measure is realized yield. Rather than assuming that the issue is bought and held to maturity (or first call), realized yield assumes that the investor is taking a trading position and intends to liquidate the bond prior to maturity (or first call) date. In essence the investor has a holding period (hp) that is less than n (or nc). The objective of realized yield is to determine the level of return attainable from trading bonds over relatively short investment horizons. The evaluation process considers the forecast value of the bond at date of liquidation, which is, of course, subject to normal levels of uncertainty. (This procedure is also used to measure *actual* realized yield earned in a completed buy-and-sell transaction.) Approximate realized yield (ARY/may be expressed as:

(15.9)
$$ARY = \frac{C_t + \dfrac{P_f - P_m}{hp}}{\dfrac{P_f + P_m}{2}}$$

where:

P_f = the future (selling) price of the issue

hp = the holding period of the issue, in years, and

all other variables are as defined above. Again, the same two variables change: the holding period (hp) is used instead of n, and P_f is used in lieu of P_p. Also note that P_f is a *computed value,* rather than a given contractual value. The computation of future price will be discussed in the section below.

Once hp and P_f are determined, approximate realized yield can be calculated. As an example, we will use an 8 percent, 20-year bond that you buy at $750 and anticipate selling two years later, after interest rates have, we hope, experienced a substantial decline, at a price of $900. Your realized yield would be:

$$ARY = \frac{80 + \dfrac{900 - 750}{2}}{\dfrac{900 + 750}{2}} = 18.79\%$$

The high return is the result of the expected realization of a substantial capital gains in a fairly short period of time.

In a comparable manner, the introduction of P_f and hp into the annual and semiannual compounding versions of yield provides the respective present-value versions of realized yield:

(15.10)
$$P_m = \sum_{t=1}^{hp} \frac{C_t}{(1 + i)^t} + \frac{P_f}{(1 + i)^{hp}}$$

and

$$P_m = \sum_{t=1}^{2hp} \frac{C_t/2}{(1 + i/2)^t} + \frac{P_f}{(1 + i/2)^{2hp}}$$ (15.11)

Because of the short holding period (i.e., small hp), the added accuracy of these measures is somewhat marginal. In fact, because the realized yield measures are based on expected price performance, and there is substantial uncertainty in such forecasts, either the approximate or annual compounding methods probably provide more than adequate levels of accuracy. In contrast, when realized yield is being computed for performance purposes, you should use the more accurate semiannual basis for compounding.

Bond Prices

There are two instances in which dollar bond prices are important. The first is with regard to realized yield; i.e., the determination of the future price of an issue (P_f). The second condition is when issues are quoted on a (promised) yield basis, as with municipals.

The dollar price can be derived using Equations (15.4) or (15.5) and simply solving for P_m. Consider a 10 percent bond with 25 years remaining to maturity that is quoted to yield 12 percent. Using the semiannual version of the model to price this issue:

$$P_m = 100/2 \sum_{t=1}^{50} \frac{1}{\left(1 + \frac{.120}{2}\right)} + 1000 \frac{1}{\left(1 + \frac{.120}{2}\right)^{50}}$$

$$= 50(15.7619) + 1000(.0543)$$

$$= \$788.10 + 54.30$$

$$= \$842.40$$

In contrast to current market price, anticipated future price (P_f) is computed when bond traders attempt to establish the expected realized yield performance of alternative issues. The determination of P_f is based on coupon (C_t) and par value (P_p), both of which are given. In contrast, the length of the holding period, and, therefore, the number of years remaining to maturity at date of sale and the expected prevailing market yield at time of sale (i) must be forecast by you. The real difficulty (and potential source of error) in specifying P_f lies in formulating hp and estimating i.

As an example, consider the 10 percent, 25-year bond discussed above. Assume that you bought this bond at about $842, which implies a yield to maturity of 12 percent. Based upon extensive analysis, you expect the market yield on this bond to decline to 8 percent in two years. Therefore, at this point you want to compute what the future price (P_f) will be of the bond to estimate your expected rate of return if you are correct. As noted, the two estimates you make are the holding period (2 years), which implies that the remaining life of the bond is 23 years, and the market yield of 8 percent. Using an annual model, the future price is:

$$P_f = 100 \sum_{t=1}^{23} \frac{1}{(1.08)} + 1000 \frac{1}{(1.08)^{23}}$$

$$= 100(10.3711) + 1000(.1703)$$

$$= \$1,037.11 + 170.30$$

$$= \$1,207.41$$

Further, your approximate annual return on this investment would be:

$$APY = \frac{100 + \dfrac{1,207 - 842}{2}}{\dfrac{1,207 + 842}{2}}$$

$$= \frac{100 + 182.50}{1,024.50}$$

$$= 27.57\%$$

For readers wishing to compute prices and yields on noninterest paying dates, this is basically a matter of interpolating using the prices or yields prevailing on the interest dates surrounding the desired date. For a detailed discussion of the procedure, refer to Homer and Leibowitz.[6]

Tax-Exempt Issues

Municipal bonds, treasury issues, and many agency obligations possess one common characteristic: their interest income is partially or fully tax-exempt. Recall that treasury and federal agency obligations are exempt from state and local taxation, while interest income on municipal obligations is exempt from federal and local levies.

Using promised yield as a basis of discussion, the tax status of an issue (including its ordinary income and capital-gains tax liability) can be included in the valuation model as follows:

(15.12)
$$P_m = \sum_{t=1}^{2n} \frac{C_{t/2}(1 - \tau)}{(1 + i/2)^t} + \frac{P_p - k(P_p - P_m)}{(1 + i/2)^{2n}}$$

---

[6]Homer and Leibowitz, *Inside the Yield Book*, chapter 13.

where:

τ = the investor's marginal tax liability on ordinary income

k = the investor's capital gains tax rate,

and the other terms are as defined above. While (15.12) provides a measure of *after-tax* promised yield, yield to call and realized yield can also be modified to readily accommodate the various tax effects (likewise, this applies to transactions that occur on noninterest payment dates).

In addition, the tax-adjusted models can be used when some of the issues are subject to normal taxation and others are totally tax-free. The valuation process itself adjusts for the specific tax liability of the obligation in generating after-tax yield (or price) because the specification of τ and k does not define the source or extent of tax liability. As a result, these variables should include appropriate federal, state, and/or local tax rates (depending, of course, on the tax exposure of the specific issue).

Undoubtedly, the most popular and one of the most often cited measures of performance for municipal issues is the "fully taxable equivalent yield" (FTEY). This is a simple adjustment for computing promised yields for those issues with tax-exempt features. The process involves adjusting a computed promised yield to reflect the rate of return that must be earned on fully taxable issues, such as corporates, to provide a yield equivalent to the fully or partially tax-exempt obligation. It is measured as:

$$FTEY = \frac{i}{1 - T}$$

(15.13)

where:

i = promised yield

T = the amount and type of tax *exemption* provided by the issue in question, and all other terms are defined earlier.

A caveat is in order, however. This simple computation is applicable only to par bonds or current-coupon obligations, such as new issues. In other words, the measure considers only interest income and, by ignoring capital gains, is inappropriate for issues trading at significant variations from par.

Yield Books

Bond value tables, commonly known as "bond books" or "yield books," are available to eliminate much of the mathematics from bond valuation. An illustration of a page from a yield book is provided in Figure 15.2. It is like a present-value interest factor table to the extent that a matrix of bond prices is provided relative to a stated coupon rate, various terms to maturity (on the horizontal

A **YEARS and MONTHS** **8%**

Yield	14-6	15-0	15-6	16-0	16-6	17-0	17-6	18-0
4.00	143.69	144.79	145.88	146.94	147.98	149.00	150.00	150.98
4.20	140.96	141.97	142.97	143.95	144.91	145.84	146.76	147.66
4.40	138.29	139.23	140.14	141.04	141.92	142.78	143.62	144.44
4.60	135.69	136.55	137.39	138.21	139.01	139.80	140.56	141.31
4.80	133.15	133.94	134.71	135.46	136.19	136.90	137.60	138.28
5.00	130.68	131.40	132.09	132.77	133.44	134.09	134.72	135.33
5.20	128.27	128.92	129.55	130.16	130.76	131.35	131.92	132.47
5.40	125.91	126.50	127.07	127.62	128.16	128.69	129.20	129.70
5.60	123.62	124.14	124.65	125.15	125.63	126.10	126.55	127.00
5.80	121.38	121.84	122.30	122.74	123.16	123.58	123.98	124.38
6.00	119.19	119.60	120.00	120.39	120.77	121.13	121.49	121.83
6.10	118.11	118.50	118.87	119.24	119.59	119.93	120.26	120.59
6.20	117.05	117.41	117.76	118.10	118.43	118.75	119.06	119.36
6.30	116.01	116.34	116.67	116.98	117.29	117.58	117.87	118.15
6.40	114.97	115.28	115.58	115.88	116.16	116.43	116.70	116.96
6.50	113.95	114.24	114.51	114.78	115.05	115.30	115.54	115.78
6.60	112.94	113.20	113.46	113.71	113.95	114.18	114.40	114.62
6.70	111.94	112.18	112.42	112.64	112.86	113.07	113.28	113.48
6.80	110.95	111.17	111.39	111.59	111.79	111.99	112.17	112.35
6.90	109.98	110.18	110.37	110.56	110.74	110.91	111.08	111.24
7.00	109.02	109.20	109.37	109.53	109.70	109.85	110.00	110.15
7.10	108.07	108.22	108.38	108.52	108.67	108.80	108.94	109.07
7.20	107.13	107.27	107.40	107.53	107.65	107.77	107.89	108.00
7.30	106.20	106.32	106.43	106.54	106.65	106.75	106.85	106.95
7.40	105.28	105.38	105.48	105.57	105.66	105.75	105.83	105.92
7.50	104.37	104.46	104.54	104.61	104.67	104.76	104.83	104.90
7.60	103.48	103.54	103.61	103.67	103.73	103.78	103.84	103.89
7.70	102.59	102.64	102.69	102.73	102.78	102.82	102.86	102.90
7.80	101.72	101.75	101.78	101.81	101.84	101.87	101.90	101.92
7.90	100.85	100.87	100.87	100.88	100.90	100.91	100.93	100.94
8.00	100.00	100.00	100.00	100.00	100.00	100.00	100.03	100.00
8.10	99.16	99.14	99.13	99.11	99.10	99.09	99.07	99.06
8.20	98.32	98.29	98.26	98.24	98.21	98.18	98.16	98.14
8.30	97.50	97.45	97.41	97.37	97.33	97.29	97.26	97.22
8.40	96.68	96.62	96.57	96.51	96.46	96.41	96.37	96.32
8.50	95.88	95.81	95.74	95.67	95.61	95.55	95.49	95.43
8.60	95.08	95.00	94.91	94.84	94.76	94.69	94.62	94.56
8.70	94.29	94.20	94.10	94.01	93.93	93.85	93.77	93.69
8.80	93.52	93.41	93.30	93.20	93.10	93.01	92.92	92.84
8.90	92.75	92.63	92.51	92.40	92.29	92.19	92.09	92.00
9.00	91.99	91.86	91.73	91.61	91.49	91.38	91.27	91.17
9.10	91.24	91.09	90.96	90.82	90.70	90.57	90.46	90.35
9.20	90.50	90.34	90.19	90.05	89.91	89.78	89.66	89.54
9.30	89.76	89.60	89.44	89.29	89.14	89.00	88.87	88.74
9.40	89.04	88.86	88.69	88.53	88.38	88.23	88.09	87.96
9.50	88.32	88.13	87.96	87.79	87.62	87.47	87.32	87.18
9.60	87.61	87.42	87.23	87.05	86.88	86.72	86.56	86.42
9.70	86.91	86.71	86.51	86.32	86.15	85.98	85.81	85.66
9.80	86.22	86.01	85.80	85.61	85.42	85.24	85.08	84.91
9.90	85.54	85.31	85.10	84.90	84.70	84.52	84.35	84.18
10.00	84.86	84.63	84.41	84.20	84.00	83.81	83.63	83.45
10.20	83.53	83.28	83.05	82.82	82.61	82.41	82.21	82.03
10.40	82.23	81.97	81.72	81.48	81.25	81.04	80.84	80.64
10.60	80.96	80.68	80.42	80.17	79.93	79.71	79.50	79.29
10.80	79.72	79.43	79.15	78.89	78.64	78.41	78.19	77.98
11.00	78.50	78.20	77.91	77.64	77.37	77.14	76.91	76.70
11.20	77.31	77.00	76.71	76.43	76.15	75.90	75.67	75.45
11.40	76.15	75.83	75.52	75.22	74.96	74.70	74.46	74.23
11.60	75.02	74.68	74.37	74.07	73.79	73.53	73.28	73.04
11.80	73.90	73.56	73.24	72.94	72.65	72.38	72.13	71.89
12.00	72.82	72.47	72.14	71.83	71.54	71.26	71.00	70.76

8% **YEARS and MONTHS** **B**

Yield	18-6	19-0	19-6	20-0	20-6	21-0	21-6	22-0
4.00	151.94	152.88	153.81	154.71	155.60	156.47	157.32	158.16
4.20	148.54	149.40	150.25	151.08	151.89	152.68	153.46	154.22
4.40	145.24	146.03	146.80	147.56	148.29	149.02	149.72	150.41
4.60	142.05	142.76	143.46	144.15	144.82	145.47	146.11	146.74
4.80	138.95	139.60	140.23	140.85	141.45	142.05	142.62	143.19
5.00	135.94	136.52	137.10	137.65	138.20	138.73	139.25	139.76
5.20	133.02	133.54	134.06	134.56	135.05	135.52	135.99	136.44
5.40	130.18	130.65	131.11	131.56	132.00	132.42	132.84	133.24
5.60	127.43	127.85	128.26	128.66	129.04	129.42	129.79	130.14
5.80	124.76	125.13	125.49	125.84	126.18	126.51	126.84	127.15
6.00	122.17	122.49	122.81	123.11	123.41	123.70	123.98	124.25
6.10	120.90	121.20	121.50	121.78	122.06	122.33	122.59	122.84
6.20	119.65	119.93	120.21	120.47	120.73	120.98	121.22	121.46
6.30	118.42	118.68	118.93	119.18	119.42	119.65	119.87	120.09
6.40	117.21	117.45	117.68	117.91	118.13	118.34	118.55	118.75
6.50	116.01	116.23	116.45	116.66	116.86	117.05	117.24	117.43
6.60	114.83	115.04	115.23	115.42	115.61	115.79	115.96	116.13
6.70	113.67	113.86	114.04	114.21	114.38	114.54	114.70	114.85
6.80	112.53	112.69	112.86	113.01	113.17	113.31	113.46	113.59
6.90	111.40	111.55	111.70	111.84	111.97	112.11	112.23	112.36
7.00	110.29	110.42	110.55	110.68	110.80	110.92	111.03	111.14
7.10	109.19	109.31	109.42	109.54	109.64	109.75	109.85	109.94
7.20	108.11	108.21	108.31	108.41	108.50	108.60	108.68	108.77
7.30	107.04	107.13	107.22	107.30	107.38	107.46	107.54	107.61
7.40	105.99	106.07	106.14	106.21	106.28	106.35	106.41	106.47
7.50	104.96	105.02	105.08	105.14	105.19	105.25	105.30	105.35
7.60	103.94	103.99	104.04	104.08	104.12	104.16	104.20	104.24
7.70	102.93	102.97	103.00	103.04	103.07	103.10	103.13	103.16
7.80	101.94	101.96	101.99	102.01	102.03	102.05	102.07	102.09
7.90	100.96	100.98	100.99	100.99	101.01	101.01	101.02	101.04
8.00	100.00	100.00	100.00	100.00	100.00	100.00	100.00	100.00
8.10	99.05	99.04	99.03	99.02	99.01	99.00	98.99	98.98
8.20	98.11	98.09	98.07	98.05	98.03	98.01	97.99	97.98
8.30	97.19	97.16	97.13	97.10	97.07	97.04	97.01	96.99
8.40	96.28	96.24	96.20	96.16	96.12	96.08	96.05	96.02
8.50	95.38	95.33	95.28	95.23	95.19	95.14	95.10	95.06
8.60	94.49	94.43	94.37	94.32	94.26	94.21	94.16	94.12
8.70	93.62	93.55	93.48	93.42	93.36	93.30	93.24	93.19
8.80	92.76	92.68	92.60	92.53	92.46	92.40	92.34	92.28
8.90	91.91	91.82	91.74	91.66	91.58	91.51	91.44	91.38
9.00	91.07	90.98	90.89	90.80	90.72	90.64	90.56	90.49
9.10	90.24	90.14	90.04	89.95	89.86	89.78	89.70	89.62
9.20	89.43	89.32	89.21	89.11	89.02	88.93	88.84	88.76
9.30	88.62	88.51	88.40	88.29	88.19	88.09	88.00	87.91
9.40	87.83	87.71	87.59	87.48	87.37	87.27	87.17	87.08
9.50	87.05	86.92	86.79	86.68	86.57	86.46	86.36	86.26
9.60	86.27	86.14	86.01	85.89	85.77	85.66	85.55	85.45
9.70	85.51	85.37	85.24	85.11	84.99	84.87	84.76	84.66
9.80	84.76	84.62	84.48	84.34	84.22	84.10	83.98	83.87
9.90	84.02	83.87	83.72	83.59	83.46	83.33	83.21	83.10
10.00	83.29	83.13	82.98	82.84	82.71	82.58	82.45	82.34
10.20	81.86	81.69	81.53	81.38	81.24	81.10	80.97	80.85
10.40	80.46	80.28	80.12	79.96	79.81	79.67	79.53	79.40
10.60	79.10	78.92	78.74	78.58	78.42	78.28	78.13	78.00
10.80	77.78	77.59	77.41	77.24	77.08	76.92	76.78	76.64
11.00	76.49	76.29	76.11	75.93	75.76	75.61	75.46	75.31
11.20	75.23	75.03	74.84	74.66	74.49	74.33	74.17	74.03
11.40	74.01	73.80	73.61	73.42	73.25	73.08	72.93	72.78
11.60	72.82	72.61	72.41	72.22	72.04	71.87	71.71	71.56
11.80	71.66	71.44	71.24	71.05	70.87	70.70	70.53	70.38
12.00	70.53	70.31	70.10	69.91	69.72	69.55	69.39	69.25

Figure 15.2   A Yield Book

Source: Reproduced with permission from Expanded Bond Values Publication #83, pp. 879–880, copyright 1970 Financial Publishing Co., Boston, Mass.

axis), and promised yields (on the vertical axis). Such a table allows the user to readily determine either promised yield or price. Observe in situation A that a $17\frac{1}{2}$ year, 8 percent bond, yielding 10 percent would carry a price of 83.63. Likewise, in situation B, a 20-year issue priced at 109.54 would yield 7.10 percent. As might be expected, access to computers via office and portable terminals has substantially reduced the need for and use of yield books. For our purposes though, it is essential that the detailed mechanics and subtleties of the various yield and price models be fully understood so that the dimensions of promised yield, yield to call, realized yield, and bond prices are appreciated.

Determinants of Bond Yields and Yield Spreads

The value of a bond is equal to the present value of its future cash flow stream. An important dimension of the bond valuation model is the rate at which the future cash flows are discounted. In the promised-yield version of the model, this rate reflects prevailing market interest rates and indicates the importance of interest rates in the bond valuation process. It follows that bond managers must constantly evaluate the current level of market interest rates and expected changes in these rates.

This book takes a practical view of the role of interest rates in the bond investment decision. While the assessment of interest rates is absolutely essential to the attainment of attractive bond portfolio returns, the development of interest rate formulations is a complex economic matter that often involves extensive econometric modeling, a task we shall leave to the professional economist. Instead, our goal as bond investors and bond portfolio managers should be to continually monitor current and expected interest-rate behavior in an informal fashion by considering the major determinants of interest rates. A bond portfolio manager can assess the *major* dimensions of interest-rate behavior on his own, and will typically rely on economic services for more detailed insight into the structure and behavior of market rates provided by many large bond-portfolio-management firms.

Fundamental Determinants of Interest Rates

According to published market sources, average interest rates for long-term corporate bonds in March 1980 amounted to almost 14 percent. Three months later, these rates had declined to about 11 percent, and by December 1980 they had risen to over 14 percent. Obviously during the period of declining rates, many bond investors obtained very attractive rates of return on their bonds. In sharp contrast, during the period of rising interest rates, many bond investors suffered losses in their bond portfolios. Clearly, this indicates the importance of monitoring interest rates. Similar to the model in Chapter 1, the level of interest rates (r) can be specified according to the following conceptual model:

$$r = RFR + I + RP \tag{15.14}$$

where:

$$RFR = \text{the "real" risk-free rate of interest}$$

$$I = \text{the expected rate of inflation}$$

$$RP = \text{the risk premium.}$$

This simple equation is a complete statement of the complex nature of interest rate behavior. The difficult part is *forecasting* changes in the rate of inflation and in the risk premium over time, as well as in other economic conditions that affect interest rate levels. That it is very difficult to accurately forecast interest rates has been well documented.[7]

In essence, interest rates can be viewed as being related to economic and issue characteristics:

$$r = f \text{ (economic forces + issue characteristics)}$$
$$= (RFR + I) + RP$$

This rearranged version of Equation (15.14) facilitates a more thorough discussion of the fundamental determinants of interest rates.[8]

The pure rate of interest (RFR) is the economic cost of money, and represents the opportunity cost necessary to compensate individuals for forgoing consumption. As discussed in Chapter 1, this real RFR is determined by the economy's long-run rate of growth and, as such, represents the economy's basic opportunity rate on investments.

Inflation is the other economic dimension of interest rates. The *level of inflation* (I) is added to the risk-free rate (RFR) to specify a general *market-based* level of interest. For example, if the RFR is 3 percent, and expected inflation is $5\frac{1}{2}$ percent, then it follows that the market-based (nominal) risk-free rate of interest (r) would equal approximately $8\frac{1}{2}$ percent. Given the stability of the RFR, it is clear that *the wide swings in r experienced in the past decade or so can largely be attributed to swings in real or perceived inflation.* This nominal risk-free rate can also be influenced in the short run by changes in the supply and demand for funds caused by economic shifts, e.g., changes in monetary policy, the fiscal environment (deficits, etc.), or corporate demand due to the business cycle.

Interest rates (r) are also influenced by issue characteristics. The *risk premium* (RP) component of r is directly associated with the characteristics of the issue and issuer. Whereas the economic forces (the risk-free rate and inflation) reflect a market- or system-wide level of interest rates, issue characteristics are

[7]Oswald D. Bowlin and John D. Martin, "Extrapolations of Yields Over the Short Run, Forecast or Folly?" *Journal of Monetary Economics* 1 (1975): 275–488, and Stephen F. Leroy, "Interest Rates and the Inflation Premium," *Monthly Review,* Federal Reserve Bank of Kansas City, May 1973, pp. 11–18.

[8]For an excellent and extensive exploration of interest rates and interest rate behavior, the reader should see James C. Van Horne, *Financial Market Rates and Flows* (Englewood Cliffs, NJ: Prentice-Hall, 1978).

unique to individual securities or market sectors. Thus, the differences in the yields of corporate and treasury issues are *not* caused by economic forces, but by differential issue characteristics, i.e., differences in the risk premium.

There are three major components within the risk premium that should be considered by bond investors and portfolio managers:

1. quality differential (or risk of default)

2. term to maturity, which can affect rate uncertainty as well as yield and price volatility

3. indenture provisions (including collateral, call features, and sinking fund provisions).

Of the three, quality and maturity considerations are the most important and dominate the risk premium.

Quality Considerations   These reflect the risk of default, which is largely reflected in agency ratings. The matter of quality is primarily the ability of the issuer to service the debt which lowers the risk of default. Quality considerations mean yield differentials will exist between differently rated issues. For example, AAA-rated obligations possess lower risk of default than BBB obligations do and, therefore, provide lower yield.

There is substantial empirical support for the position that quality-derived risk premiums are largely dependent upon the intrinsic characteristics of the issuer.[9] Note, however, that quality-based yield premiums are also influenced by prevailing economic conditions. Specifically, the *size of the risk premiums* changes over the business cycle; it increases during recessions as investors value quality and vice versa during expansions.[10]

Maturity   This also affects the risk premium because it affects the level of uncertainty assumed by the investor as well as price and yield volatility. As discussed in the following section on the term structure of interest rates, there is generally a positive relationship between the term to maturity of an issue and the level of interest rates.

Bond Indenture Provisions   These are the final risk premium determinants. Relevant aspects include the amount of collateral provided, the call feature, and sinking fund provisions. Collateral provides capital protection to the investor on those rare occasions of corporate insolvency and forced liquidation,[11] and distinguishes a mortgage bond from a debenture obligation. Collateral can influence

[9]See, for example, Lawrence Fisher, "Determinants of Risk Premiums on Corporate Bonds," *Journal of Political Economy* 67 (1959): 217.

[10]For a detailed discussion of these changes, see Van Horne, *Financial Market Rates*, chapter 6.

[11]Harold G. Fraine and Robert H. Mills, "Effect of Defaults and Credit Determination on Yields of Corporate Bonds," *Journal of Finance* 16 (1961): 423–434.

an agency rating; differences of several basis points are common for comparably rated issues that differ only in terms of collateral provisions.

The call feature is perhaps the most influential bond indenture provision. Other things being equal, the greater the call-risk protection provided, the lower the market yield of the obligation, particularly for new issues and current coupon obligations.[12] Clearly, a ten-year deferred call feature provides more call risk protection than, say, a freely callable provision does, and, therefore, should logically result in lower yield. This call protection becomes especially important during periods of high interest rates.

The final indenture provision affecting the risk premium is the sinking fund feature. The sinking fund provision reduces the investor's risk and results in lower yield for two reasons. First, a sinking fund reduces default risk by providing for orderly debt service and systematic reduction of outstanding principal. Second, sinking funds provide support for the bond because of added demand and also a more liquid secondary market because of the increased trading.

Term Structure of Interest Rates

The term structure of interest rates (or the "yield curve" as it is more popularly known) is a static function that relates *term* to maturity to *yield* to maturity at *a given point in time*. Thus, it represents a cross section of yields for a category of bonds that *are comparable in all respects but maturity*. The quality of the issues must be held constant, as should coupon, call feature, and perhaps even industry category. One can derive different yield curves for treasury issues, government agencies, prime-grade municipals, AAA utilities, and so on.[13]

As an example, consider Figure 15.3. The yield curve is constructed for a sample of U.S. Treasury obligations. Yield-to-maturity information on a variety of comparable treasury issues is obtained from *The Wall Street Journal*. These promised yields are represented on the graph by the several plotted points. After the yields are plotted, the yield curve itself is drawn.

All yields curves, of course, do not have the same shape as Figure 15.3. Quite the contrary, for, while yield curves per se are static in nature, *their behavior over time is quite fluid!* As a result, the shape of the yield curve can undergo dramatic alterations. In particular, it can follow one of the four patterns shown in Figure 15.4. The ascending curve is the most common and tends to prevail when interest rates are at low or modest levels. The declining yield curve is relatively uncom-

[12]Frank C. Jen and James E. Wert, "The Value of the Deferred Call Privilege," *National Banking Review* 3 (1966): 369–378; and Michael D. Joehnk and James E. Wert, "The Call-Risk Performance of the Discounted Seasoned Issue," *Mississippi Valley Journal of Business and Economics* 9 (1973–1974): 1–15.

[13]See, for example, J. Huston McCulloch, "Measuring the Term Structure of Interest Rates," *Journal of Business* 44 (1971): 19–31; William T. Carleton and Ian A. Cooper, "Estimation and Uses of the Term Structure of Interest Rates," *Journal of Finance* 31 (1976): 1067–1084; and Burton G. Malkiel, *The Term Structure of Interest Rates* (Princeton, NJ: Princeton University Press, 1966).

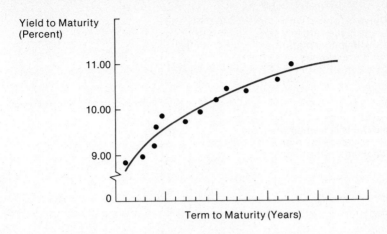

Figure 15.3   Construction of a Yield Curve

mon and tends to exist when rates are at relatively high levels. The humped yield curve occurs when interest rates are extremely high and about to retreat to more normal levels. Finally, there is the flat yield curve which rarely exists for any period of time. In all of the illustrations, the slope of the line tends to level off after 15 years. This is common market behavior. After a point ($\cong$ 15 years), promised yield differentials that exist with longer maturities tend to be rather insignificant, especially relative to the spreads that occur at the shorter end.

While the effects of term to maturity on comparative promised yield (r) are obvious from examining the various shapes of the term structure, it is *not* equally clear why the term structure assumes different shapes. Fortunately, there is an extensive body of theoretical and empirical literature available to help explain the shape of yield curves. Three major theories are available: the expectations hypothesis, the liquidity preference hypothesis, and the segmented-market hypothesis.[14]

Expectations Hypothesis

According to this theory, the shape of the term structure is explained by the interest rate expectations of market participants. More specifically, *any long-term rate is simply the geometric mean of current and future one-year rates expected to prevail over the horizon of the issue.*

[14]For a more extensive discussion of the alternative theories of the term structure of interest rates, see Burton G. Malkiel, *Term Structure of Interest Rates: Theory, Empirical Evidence and Applications* (New York: McCaleb-Seiler, 1970); and Van Horne, *Financial Market Rates.*

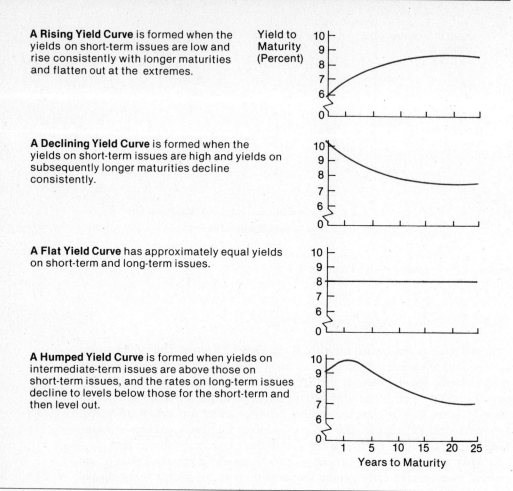

A Rising Yield Curve is formed when the yields on short-term issues are low and rise consistently with longer maturities and flatten out at the extremes.

A Declining Yield Curve is formed when the yields on short-term issues are high and yields on subsequently longer maturities decline consistently.

A Flat Yield Curve has approximately equal yields on short-term and long-term issues.

A Humped Yield Curve is formed when yields on intermediate-term issues are above those on short-term issues, and the rates on long-term issues decline to levels below those for the short-term and then level out.

Figure 15.4   Types of Yield Curves

In essence, a series of intermediate- and long-term rates are part of the term structure, each of which, in turn, is a reflection of the geometric average of current and expected one-year rates. Under such conditions, the equilibrium long-term rate is clearly that which the long-term investor would expect to earn through successive investments in short-term securities over an investment horizon equal to the maturity of the longer term issue.

The expectations theory can account for any shape of yield curve. If short-term rates are expected to rise in the future, then the yield curve will be ascending; if short-term rates are expected to fall, then the long-term rates will lie below the short-term rates and the term structure will descend. Similar explanations can be made for flat and humped yield curves. Consider the following example of how the expectations hypothesis can explain the shape of the term structure of interest rates.

tR₁ = 5¹/2%   This is the one-year rate of interest prevailing at period t (now).

t+1R₁ = 6%   This is the one-year rate of interest expected to prevail during period t+1 (next year).

t+2R₁ =7¹/2%   This is the one-year rate of interest expected to prevail during period t+2 (two years from now).

t+3R₁ = 8¹/2%   This is the one-year rate of interest expected to prevail during period t+3 (three years from now).

Based upon this information, it is possible to compute the rate on a one-year bond (given), and a two-, three-, or four-year bond (designated R_2, R_3, R_4) as follows:

$_tR_1$ = 5.50% (given)

$_tR_2$ = (.055 + .06)/2 = 5.75%

$_tR_3$ = (.055 + .06 + .075)/3 = 6.33%

$_tR_4$ = (.055 + .06 + .075 + .085)/4 = 6.88%

In the above illustration (which uses the arithmetic average as an approximation of the geometric mean), the yield curve is upward sloping because, at present, investors expect *future* short-term rates to be above current short-term rates. This is not how the term structure is formally constructed. It is constructed as demonstrated in Figure 15.3 with regard to prevailing promised yields for issues with different maturities. Rather, the expectations hypothesis attempts to explain *why* the yield curve is upward sloping, downward sloping, humped, or flat by explaining the type of expectations implicit in various term structures. The evidence is fairly substantial (and convincing) that the expectations hypothesis is a workable and (somewhat) practical explanation of the term structure.[15] Because of its documentation, relative simplicity, and intuitive appeal, the expectations hypothesis of the term structure of interest rates is rather widely accepted.

Liquidity Preference

This theory holds that long-term securities should provide higher returns than short-term obligations do, because rational investors are willing to pay a price premium (i.e., accept lower yields) on short maturity obligations to avoid the risk of principal volatility of the long maturity obligation. The liquidity preference theory contends that given the uncertainty which exists in the real world, short-term issues should be more desirable than longer maturities because they can easily be converted into cash should unforeseen events occur.

The liquidity preference theory argues that, in the absence of market anom-

[15]See for example, David Meiselman, *The Term Structure of Interest Rates* (Englewood Cliffs, NJ: Prentice-Hall, 1962); and Franco Modigliani and Richard Sutch, "Innovations in Interest Rate Policy," *American Economic Review: Papers and Proceedings* 56 (1966): 178–197.

alies, the yield curve should be upward sloping and any other shape should be viewed as a temporary aberration. This theory can be considered an extension of the pure expectations hypothesis because, following from the liquidity preference hypothesis, it can be contended that future short-term rates will be higher than expectations due to the liquidity premium. While a pure liquidity preference theory has received some empirical support, the combined expectations–liquidity preference theory has probably received more support than either theory alone, i.e., the yield curve shows a definite upward bias.[16]

Segmented-Markets Theory
The segmented-markets theory is an intuitive theory that has not received very much empirical support, but enjoys wide acceptance among market practitioners.

The theory—also known as preferred habitat, the institutional theory, or the hedging-pressure theory—asserts that different groups of institutional investors have different maturity needs, which lead them to confine their security selections to specific maturity segments of the term structure. Thus, it is argued that the term structure is ultimately a function of the investment policies of major financial institutions.

Financial institutions tend to structure their investment policies in line with such things as their tax environment, liability structure, and the level of earnings demanded by savers and depositors. Therefore, commercial banks invest in short- to intermediate-term municipal bonds, and life insurance firms go for long-term corporate bonds.

In fact, in its strongest form, the segmented-market theory holds that the maturity preferences of different investors and borrowers are so strong that they would *never* purchase securities outside of their preferred maturity range to take advantage of yield differentials. As a result, advocates of this hypothesis argue that the short and long maturity markets are effectively segmented, and yields are determined solely by supply and demand *within* each market maturity segment.

Trading Implications of the Term Structure
Information on maturity behavior can be used to formulate yield expectations by simply observing the shape of the term structure; e.g., if the shape is humped, then historical evidence suggests that interest rates are most likely about to undergo a broad-based decline. Ardent expectations theorists would suggest that one need *only* examine the prevailing yield curve to obtain some idea of what interest rates should do in the future.

A more significant use of the term structure involves formulating predictions of the future shape of the term structure, along with interest rates, to assess yield volatility by maturity sector. Such an analysis allows those maturity segments

---

[16]See Reuben A. Kessel, *The Cyclical Behavior of the Term Structure of Interest Rates,* National Bureau of Economic Research Occasional Paper 91 (Washington, D.C., 1965), and Phillip Cagan, ed., Essays on Interest Rates (New York: Columbia University Press for the National Bureau of Economic Research, 1969).

that offer the greatest yield and, therefore, potential price appreciation, to be identified.

Yield Spreads

Another important dimension of interest-rate behavior is yield spreads. Basically, *a yield spread is a difference in promised yield, which exists at any given point in time, between different bond issues or segments of the market.* These differences are issue or market specific and, thus, are additive to the rates determined by economic forces (RFR + I). Yield spreads are caused by quality differentials, different maturities, and unique call features. These variables lead to different promised yields for different types of securities.

A yield spread may be either positive or negative, depending upon whether a particular bond provides a promised yield to maturity in excess of (or less than) that offered on an alternative issue. Moreover, *the magnitude or direction of these yield spreads changes over time.* A yield spread "narrows" whenever the differences in yield become smaller, and it "widens" as the difference becomes greater.

Table 15.1 provides average data on a variety of past yield spreads. Yield spreads change due to changing levels of interest rates and variations in investor perceptions of risk. Four major factors account for the existence of various yield differentials:

1. different *segments* of the bond market (e.g., governments vs. agencies, or governments vs. corporates),

2. different *sectors* of the same market segment (e.g., prime-grade municipals vs. good-grade municipals, or AA utilities vs. BAA utilities, or AAA industrials vs. AAA public utilities),

3. different *coupons* within a given market segment/sector (e.g., current-coupon governments vs. deep-discount governments, or new AA industrials vs. seasoned AA industrials), and

4. different *maturities* within a given market segment/sector (e.g., short agencies vs. long agencies, or 3-year prime municipals vs. 25-year prime municipals).

Whether yield spreads are a result of segment, sector, coupon, and/or maturity differences, they exist because there are different market rates associated with different types of bonds. A bond investor should evaluate yield-spread *changes* because they influence price behavior and comparative realized-yield performance over a given investment horizon. If (in the absence of yield spreads) two issues undergo an identical 150-basis-point change in yield over an equal investment horizon, then, other things being equal, there would be nothing to make one preferable to the other as an investment. If the yield spread change over time is greater for one than for the other, then the issue that enjoyed the larger drop in yield would provide the superior realized yield (because of its greater price volatility).

Comparisons[a]	1969	1970	1971	1972	1973	1974	1975[b]
Short Govts: Long Govts	+56	+70	−4	+10	+23	+22	+75
Short Munies: Long Munies	+77	+150	+192	+157	+95	+100	+166
Long Govts: Long Corps	+119	+162	+173	+172	+75	+132	+131
10-Yr Govts: 10-Yr Agencies	+55	+70	+80	+53	+45	+85	+83
Long Munies: Long Corps	+172	+202	+217	+234	+254	+337	+296
10-Yr Munies: 10-Yr Agencies	+191	+256	+256	+261	+273	+301	+259
Long Prime Munies: Long Good Munies	+20	+15	+20	+10	+10	+10	+10
Long Aa Utils: Long Baa Utils	+112	+75	+93	+53	+79	+191	+354
Long Aa Utils: Long Aa Ind'ls	−26	−48	−44	−28	−29	−50	−49
Long Discounted Corps: Long Curr. Cpn Corps	+60	+86	+58	+42	+37	+108	+81

Table 15.1   Selected Mean Yield Spreads (reported in basis points)

The yield spreads are based on average market rates (monthly observations) existing for each of the respective market sectors; the "short" maturities are 3–5 years while the "long" maturities are 20–25 years; unless otherwise noted, the municipals are rated as prime grade, while the corporates are represented by Aa public utilities.

[a] The yield spreads are reported using the bond sector listed first as the benchmark, e.g., a + yield spread with the "Short Govts: Long Govts" comparison means the latter type of issue is providing the higher average market yield.

[b] The 1975 data include observations through the first six months—January through June.

Source: Michael D. Joehnk, "The Effects of Yield Spreads on Comparative Bond Price Behavior," *Financial Planner* 6 (1977): 35. Reprinted by permission.

In summary, an analysis of yield spreads and potential changes in spreads will allow you to capitalize on temporary yield-spread anomalies and to gain the most from anticipated major swings in market rates.

Bond Price Volatility

Numerous variables can affect yield behavior and are, therefore, important to price-conscious bond investors. Price volatility, however, is not linked solely to yield behavior. So what causes the variations in price? Burton Malkiel used the bond valuation model to demonstrate that the market price of a fixed-income security is ultimately a function of four factors: (1) the par value of an obligation, (2) the issue's coupon, (3) its years to maturity, and (4) the prevailing market rate.[17] Malkiel showed that the following relationships exist between yield changes and bond-price behavior:

1. Bond prices move inversely to bond yields.

2. For a given change in market yield, changes in bond prices are greater for longer term maturities; i.e., bond price volatility is *directly* related to term to maturity.

3. The amount of maturity-derived price volatility (percentage of price change) increases at a diminishing rate as term to maturity increases.

4. Price movements resulting from equal absolute increases or decreases in yield are not symmetrical because a decrease in yield raises bond prices by more than a corresponding increase in yield lowers prices.

5. The higher the coupon of the issue, the smaller will be the percentage of price fluctuation for a given change in yield; i.e., bond price volatility is *inversely* related to coupon.

Thus, price volatility is a function of the percentage of change in yield, the issue's coupon, the term to maturity of the obligation, the level of yields, and the direction of yield change. However, while both the level and direction of change in yields may be interesting variables to consider, they do not provide concrete trading strategies. This is not true of the other variables. Any time price volatility is sought (or avoided), the percentage of change in yield must be of paramount importance. Attention can then shift to the two variables within the selection process over which investors have control: coupon and maturity. As yields change, these two variables have a dramatic effect on comparative bond-price volatility.

[17]Burton G. Malkiel, "Expectations, Bond Prices, and the Term Structure of Interest Rates," *Quarterly Journal of Economics* 76 (1962): 197–218.

Some Trading Strategies

Given that these two variables (coupon and maturity) are the major factors influencing price volatility, it is possible to consider some basic portfolio changes that you should attempt for a given change in market interest rates. Specifically, if you expect a major *decline* in market interest rates, you know that bond prices will increase, and you want to own a portfolio of bonds with the *maximum price volatility* so that you will enjoy *maximum* capital gains from the change in interest rates. The previous discussion indicates that you should attempt to build a portfolio of *long maturity bonds* with *low coupons*. Such a portfolio should provide maximum price appreciation for a given decline in market interest rates.

In contrast, if you expect an *increase* in market interest rates, you know that bond prices will decline, and you want a portfolio with *minimum price volatility* (i.e., you want to minimize the capital losses from the increase in interest rates). In this instance you would want to change your portfolio to *short maturity bonds* with *high coupons*. As discussed above, this combination should provide minimal price volatility for a change in market interest rates.

The Concept of Duration

Because the price volatility of a bond varies inversely with the coupon and directly with the term to maturity, it can be difficult to balance these two factors when selecting bonds. It would obviously be desirable to have a composite measure that considered both of these factors. Fortunately, such a measure was developed over 40 years ago by F. R. Macaulay,[18] and is known as the "duration" of a security. Macaulay showed that duration was a more appropriate measure of the time element of a bond than term to maturity because it takes into account not only the ultimate recovery of capital at maturity, but also the size and timing of coupon payments that occur prior to final maturity. *Duration is defined as the weighted average time to full recovery of principal and interest payments.* Using annual compounding, we can define duration (D) as:

(15.15)
$$D = \frac{\displaystyle\sum_{t=1}^{n} \frac{C_t(t)}{(1 + i)^t}}{\displaystyle\sum_{t=1}^{n} \frac{C_t}{(1 + i)^t}}$$

where:

t = the time period in which the coupon and/or principal payment occurs

C_t = the interest and/or principal payment that occurs in period t

i = the market yield on the bond.

---

[18]Frederick R. Macaulay, *Some Theoretical Problems Suggested by the Movements of Interest Rates, Bond Yields, and Stock Prices in the United States Since 1856* (New York: National Bureau of Economic Research, 1938).

The denominator in Equation (15.15) is the price of an issue as determined by the present-value model. The numerator is the present value of all cash flows weighted according to the length of time to receipt.

At first glance, the formula above for computing duration may look rather forbidding. The following example, which sets forth the specific computations for two bonds, indicates the procedure and also will highlight some of the properties of duration. Consider the following two sample bonds:

	Bond A	Bond B
Face Value	$1,000	$1,000
Maturity	10 yrs.	10 yrs.
Coupon	4%	8%

Assuming annual interest payments and an 8 percent market yield on the bonds, duration is computed as shown in Table 15.2. This example indicates the following characteristics of duration:

1. When a bond has coupons, the duration of the bond will always be less than the term to maturity because duration gives weight to these interim payments.

2. A bond with a *larger* coupon will have a *shorter* duration because more of the total cash flows come earlier in the form of interest payments; i.e., the 8 percent bond has a shorter duration than the 4 percent bond.

3. A bond with no coupon payments (i.e., a pure discount bond like a treasury bill) will have duration *equal* to term to maturity. In this case, the only payment is made at maturity, so the only flow is at maturity.

4. There is generally a positive relationship between term to maturity and duration; i.e., all else the same, *a bond with longer term to maturity will have a higher duration*. Note that the relationship is not direct because, as maturity increases, the present value of the principal declines in value.

5. All else the same, *the higher the market yield, the lower the duration*. As an example, in Table 15.2, if the market yield had been 12 percent rather than 8 percent, the duration would have been about 7.75 and 6.80 rather than 8.12 and 7.25.

This concept can be very useful to you in bond portfolio management because it combines the properties of maturity and coupon mentioned earlier. Duration is positively related to term to maturity and inversely related to coupon. It has been shown, both theoretically and empirically, that bond price movements *will vary proportionally* with duration. *The percentage of change in bond price is equal to the change in yield times duration.* As an example, if yields decline by one percent (100 basis points), a bond with a duration of ten years will increase in price by approximately 10 percent. Thus, *maximum price variation* is achieved with

Bond A

(1) Year	(2) Cash Flow	(3) PV at 8%	(4) PV of Flow	(5) PV as % of Price	(6) (1) × (5)
1	$ 40	0.9259	$ 37.04	0.0506	0.0506
2	40	0.8573	34.29	0.0469	0.0938
3	40	0.7938	31.75	0.0434	0.1302
4	40	0.7350	29.40	0.0402	0.1608
5	40	0.6806	27.22	0.0372	0.1860
6	40	0.6302	25.21	0.0345	0.2070
7	40	0.5835	23.34	0.0319	0.2233
8	40	0.5403	21.61	0.0295	0.2360
9	40	0.5002	20.01	0.0274	0.2466
10	1,040	0.4632	481.73	0.6585	6.5850
Sum			$731.58	1.0000	8.1193

Duration = 8.12 Years

Bond B

(1) Year	(2) Cash Flow	(3) PV at 8%	(4) PV of Flow	(5) PV as % of Price	(6) (1) × (5)
1	$ 80	0.9259	$ 74.07	0.0741	0.0741
2	80	0.8573	68.59	0.0686	0.1372
3	80	0.7938	63.50	0.0635	0.1906
4	80	0.7350	58.80	0.0588	0.1906
5	80	0.6806	54.44	0.0544	0.2720
6	80	0.6302	50.42	0.0504	0.3024
7	80	0.5835	46.68	0.0467	0.3269
8	80	0.5403	43.22	0.0432	0.3456
9	80	0.5002	40.02	0.0400	0.3600
10	1,080	0.4632	500.26	0.5003	5.0030
Sum			$1000.00	1.0000	7.2470

Duration = 7.25 Years

Table 15.2   Computation of Duration (assuming 8 percent market yield)

the *longest* duration.[19] These and other characteristics of duration are shown in Table 15.3.

While bond-price variation tends to move proportionally with duration, Table 15.3 demonstrates that there are numerous ways to achieve a given duration measure. Thus, if you anticipate a decline in interest rates and want to capture maximum capital gains by increasing the duration of your bond portfolio,

[19]A generalized proof of this is contained in Michael H. Hopewell and George Kaufman, "Bond Price Volatility and Term to Maturity: A Generalized Respecification," *American Economic Review* 63 (1973): 749–753.

Years to maturity	Various coupon rates			
	.02	.04	.06	.08
1	0.995	0.990	0.985	0.981
5	4.756	4.558	4.393	4.254
10	8.891	8.169	7.662	7.286
20	14.981	12.980	11.904	11.232
50	19.452	17.129	16.273	15.829
100	17.567	17.232	17.120	17.064
∞	17.167	17.167	17.167	17.167

Table 15.3   Bond Duration in Years for a Bond Yielding 6 Percent Under Different Terms

Source: L. Fisher and R. L. Weil, "Coping with the Risk of Interest Rate Fluctuations: Returns to Bondholders from Naive and Optimal Strategies," *Journal of Business* 44 (October 1971): 418. Copyright © 1971 by The University of Chicago Press. Reprinted by permission of The University of Chicago Press.

there are several maturity/coupon combinations that would provide the desired price performance. The duration concept has become increasingly popular because it is the convenient way of incorporating the time element of a security in terms of *both* coupon and term to maturity, and it is useful for the active bond trader in structuring his portfolio to take advantage of changes in market yields. For example, if you expect a decline in market yields, you should increase the average duration of your bond portfolio to experience maximum price volatility and vice versa.

Portfolio Immunization

In contrast to an investor who wants to maximize the return from his bond portfolio by changing duration in anticipation of changes in market interest rates, there are some investors who do not want to play the trading game, but simply want to be assured of a specified return for a predetermined investment period, e.g., a 10 percent annual return over the next five years. The problem in this regard is that market interest rates change, and this can influence the *price* of your securities, and these changes also affect your *reinvestment rates*. Fortunately, these two risks work in opposite directions: when interest rates decline there are *positive* price effects (bond prices increase), but *negative* reinvestment effects (your reinvestment rate declines).

Because of the conflict between price and reinvestment risk, it is maintained that, to "immunize" fixed-income investments to subsequent changes in market rates, these two risks must be balanced so that they completely offset one another. Balancing occurs only when an investment horizon is equal to a bond's measure of duration. *When duration equals the planning period, interest rate risk is minimized.* Thus, an investor with a five-year horizon should not necessarily seek an issue with five years to maturity, but should seek issues with maturity/coupon combinations that provide a *duration* of approximately 5.0.[20]

In summary, the concept of duration has implications for both aggressive and conservative bond investors. It is an important idea that conveniently encompasses the coupon *and* maturity dimensions of bond price behavior.[21]

Bond Trading Strategies

To understand bond trading strategies and bond portfolio management requires knowledge of various bond investment techniques. Our discussion involves three basic strategies: (1) buy-and-hold; (2) forecast interest rates; and (3) bond swaps.

Buy-and-Hold

This is the simplest strategy and is obviously not unique to bond investors. It involves finding an issue with desired quality, coupon levels, term to maturity, and important indenture provisions, such as call feature. The buy-and-hold-investor does not consider trading in and out of positions to achieve attractive returns. Rather, because of his risk-return preferences, he seeks modest returns with little risk. Buy-and-hold investors also tend to look for vehicles with maturities (or duration) that approximate their stipulated investment horizon to reduce price and reinvestment risk.

Many bond investors follow a *modified* version of the buy-and-hold strategy. That is, an investment is made in an issue with the intention of holding it until the end of the investment horizon. However, such investors actively look for opportunities to trade into more desirable positions.

Whether the investor follows a strict, or a modified, buy-and-hold approach, the key ingredient is finding investment vehicles that possess attractive features such as maturities and yields.

Investment Selection Based on Forecast Interest-Rate Behavior

This approach to bond investment is perhaps the riskiest strategy because it involves relying on uncertain forecasts of future interest-rate behavior as a guide to restructuring a bond portfolio. This strategy entails preserving capital when an increase in interest rates is anticipated, and achieving attractive capital gains

---

[20]For a detailed derivation and test of this concept, see Lawrence Fisher and Roman L. Weil, "Coping with the Risk of Interest-Rate Fluctuations: Returns to Bondholders from Naive and Optimal Strategies," *Journal of Business* 44 (1971): 408–431; and G. O. Bierwag and George C. Kaufman, "Coping with the Risk of Interest Rate Fluctuations: A Note," *Journal of Business* 50 (1977): 364–370.

[21]For a more extensive discussion of duration see Van Horne, *Financial Market Rates,* chapter 5; R. W. McEnally, "Duration as a Practical Tool for Bond Management," *Journal of Portfolio Management* 3 (1977): 53–57; and Frank K. Reilly and Rupinder Sidhu, "The Many Uses of Bond Duration," *Financial Analysts Journal* 36 (1980): 58–72.

when interest rates are expected to decline. Such objectives are usually attained by altering the maturity structure of the portfolio, i.e., shortening the maturity (duration) of the bonds in the portfolio when interest rates are expected to increase, and lengthening the average maturity (duration) when a decline in yields is anticipated.

The risk in such portfolio restructuring is largely a function of maturity alterations. When the portfolio manager shortens his maturities to preserve capital, he could sacrifice substantial income and the opportunity for capital gains. Similarly, when the investor anticipates a decline in rates, his risk is great because the coupon at this point in the interest rate cycle is normally reduced as maturity increases. Therefore, the investor is sacrificing current income (by investing in lower coupon bonds), and exposing the portfolio to substantial price volatility (with an unexpected increase in yields).

An investor who anticipates an increase in interest rates would reduce his maturity structure by acquiring high-yielding, short-term obligations such as treasury bills. It is important to consider income and also *liquidity* because, when the rate change has occurred, it is desirable to *quickly* shift positions. When investors anticipate a decline in interest rates, the basic rule is to *lengthen maturities* (duration) because the longer the duration, the greater the price volatility. *Liquidity* is also important because the investor wants to be able to close out the position *quickly* when the drop in rates has been completed.

Given the constraints of duration and liquidity, the investor attempts to determine the most attractive market segments and issues. The object is to find the market segment that promises the greatest price reaction to the decline in interest rates.

In any investment strategy based on a decline in interest rates, *interest sensitivity* is critical so high-grade securities (e.g., Baa through Aaa) should be used. Likewise treasuries and agencies might be attractive because they are also very interest sensitive. In fact, the higher the quality of the obligation, the more sensitive it is to interest-rate behavior.

Bond Swaps

This is perhaps the most intriguing of the various investment strategies. *Bond swaps involve liquidating a current position and (simultaneously) buying a different issue in its place.* An investor holds a particular bond in his portfolio and is offered another bond with similar attributes except that it offers the chance for improved return.

Swaps can be executed to increase current yield, to increase yield to maturity, to take advantage of shifts in interest rates or realignments of yield spreads, to improve the quality of a portfolio, or for tax purposes. While some swaps are highly sophisticated and require a computer, most are fairly simple transactions with obvious goals and risks. They go by such names as "profit takeouts," "substitutions swaps," "intermarket spread swaps," or "tax swaps." While some swaps involve low risk (such as the pure yield pickup swap), others entail substantial risk (the rate-anticipation swap). Regardless of the risk involved, all swaps are intended *as a means of portfolio improvement.*

Most swaps involve several different types of risk. One obvious risk is that the market will move against the investor while the swap is "outstanding." Interest rates may move up over the holding period and cause the investor to incur a loss. Another risk is that yield spreads may not respond in the anticipated fashion, thus offsetting the benefits of the bond swap. If the new bond is not a true substitute, even if expectations and interest rate formulations are correct, the swap may be unsatisfactory because the *wrong* issue was selected. Finally, if the workout time is longer than anticipated, the realized yield might be less than expected.

These risks will become more obvious as we examine several types of popular bond swaps. Three of the more popular potential swaps are briefly reviewed below.[22]

The Pure Yield Pickup Swap

A yield pickup swap is basically long-term and involves little or no estimation of market rates. An investor swaps out of a low coupon bond into a comparable higher coupon bond to realize an automatic and instantaneous increase in current yield and promised yield.

An example of a pure yield pickup swap begins with an investor who currently holds a 30-year Aa rated 10 percent issue that is trading at 12.40 percent. Assume that the investor is offered a comparable 30-year Aa rated obligation bearing a 13 percent coupon priced to yield 13 percent. The investor would report (and realize) some book loss if he bought the original issue at par, but he is also able to simultaneously improve current yield and yield to maturity if the new obligation is held to expiration date.

The investor need not predict rate changes and the swap is not based on any imbalance in yield spread. It is simply a matter of seeking out higher yields through a bond swap. Quality and maturity stay the same, as do all other factors *except coupon.*

Substitution Swap

The substitution swap is generally short-term, relies heavily on interest rate expectations, and is subject to definite risk. The procedure assumes a short-term imbalance in yield spreads that is expected to be corrected in the near future in issues which are perfect substitutes for each other. The investor might hold a 30-year, 12 percent issue that is yielding 12 percent, and be offered comparable 30-year, 12 percent bonds that are yielding 12.20 percent. The issue offered will trade at a price less than $1,000. Thus, for every issue sold, the investor can buy more than one of the offered obligations.

---

[22]For additional information on these and other types of bond swaps, the reader is directed to Homer and Leibowitz, *Inside the Yield Book;* and Martin L. Leibowitz, "How Swaps Can Pay Off," *Institutional Investor* 7 (1973): p. 49.

The expectation is that the yield-spread imbalance will be corrected because the yield on the offering bond will *decline* to the level of the issue that the investor now holds. Thus, the investor will realize capital gains by switching out of his current position into the higher yielding obligation.

While there are only modest differential rewards in *current* income, it is clear that, as the yield imbalance is corrected, attractive capital gains can be earned causing a handsome differential in *realized* yield. The workout time is important in realizing as high a differential return as possible.

At the end of the workout time, the investor has an improved capital position, which can be used for a subsequent swap or investment transactions. Of course, many of the typical risks are present in this swap. In addition to the pressure of workout time, the market could move *against* the investor, the yield spread may *not* be temporary, and the issue may *not* be a viable swap candidate if the spread exists because the issue is of a lower quality.

Tax Swap

The "tax swap" is a relatively simple procedure that involves no projections and few risks. The concept rests on the existence of tax laws and of *realized capital gains* in some other part of the portfolio. Assume you held $100,000 of corporate bonds for a period of two years and, at the time of liquidation, sold the securities for $150,000. As a result you have a capital gain of $50,000. One way to eliminate the tax liability of that capital gain is to review your portfolio for any issues that may have comparable long-term capital losses. If you found another long-term investment of $100,000 that presently has a current market value of $50,000, you could execute a tax swap to establish the $50,000 capital loss. By offsetting this capital loss and the comparable capital gain, you will enjoy *reduced income taxes*.

Municipal bonds are considered particularly attractive tax swap candidates because an investor can *increase his tax-free income* and still use the capital loss (which is subject to normal federal and state taxation) to *reduce capital gains tax liability*. Once the capital gain and capital loss have been established and used to offset each other, it is necessary to find a comparable issue to replace the one sold. While this could pose a problem, it is relatively easy in the bond market because there are numerous issues with varying coupons, maturities, etc. Tax swaps are common at year end, as investors establish capital losses. Also remember that the capital loss *must* occur in the *same taxable year* that the capital gain does.

This bond swap is slightly different from other swap transactions because it does not rest upon temporary market anomalies. Rather, it exists solely because of tax statutes.

Bond Portfolio Construction

Some or all of the various investment strategies discussed are ultimately used in bond portfolio management. The bond portfolio, in effect, reflects your invest-

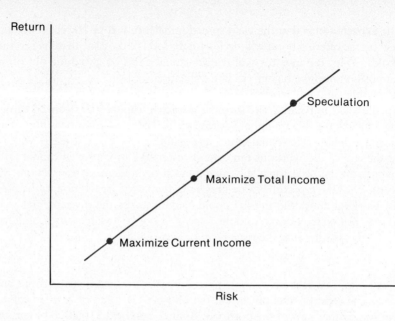

Figure 15.5   Characteristic Line: Bond Portfolios

ment objectives.[23] We should expect *portfolio objectives* to remain fairly fixed over time, but *investment strategies* to vary with prevailing conditions in the capital market. The idea is to capture as many of the beneficial attributes of a market as possible by altering the investment strategies while keeping in mind portfolio objectives.

Portfolio options vary from maximizing current income to speculation and short-term trading. Tactics vary according to the type of income sought. While our discussion is limited to three basic types of portfolios, it is possible to construct a portfolio that falls anywhere along the portfolio objective continuum by emphasizing one strategy over another.

The various bond portfolios can be visualized as points along an upward sloping line on which the portfolio that maximizes current income would be at the lowest point because it has low risk and promises the lowest yield. Farther up we would encounter the portfolio that seeks to maximize total income by maximizing *long-term* coupon income and capital gains and is willing to assume a modest amount of risk. Finally, speculation, which entails substantial risk, offers the highest level of expected return. These portfolio relationships can be seen in Figure 15.5. You can alter your position on the capital line by changing investment tactics and strategies.

---

[23]Of course, when dealing in an institutional framework, the objectives and constraints of the portfolio would be defined by the legal and operating requirements of the institution and/or by the wishes of its clients.

Maximizing Current Income

Given this portfolio objective, generating regular and sizable cash flows is of paramount importance. Such might be the objective of a retired couple, or a college endowment fund that requires a high cash flow for operating purposes, or part of an insurance company or pension fund portfolio that must provide a substantial amount of money to beneficiaries. In all of these cases the investor requires *a high level of current cash flow,* safety of principal, and certainty of cash flow. These objectives reduce or eliminate the possibility of lowering bond quality to attain higher returns.

The actual construction of a current-income portfolio will generally take one of three forms with regard to maturity considerations: maturities might be concentrated in one particular sector; they could follow a laddered approach in which approximately equal amounts of the portfolio are allotted to the various maturity segments; or you may use a barbell tactic, putting part of the capital into short maturities and the remainder into long-maturity bonds and ignoring everything in between.

Once maturity questions are resolved, you should consider other factors of importance, including call-risk protection (you want to lock-in high returns for a maximum period); tax implications given your unique tax situation; and quality desires as related to risk of default.

Buy-and-hold would probably be the strategy employed by income-oriented investors. Investment selections based on forecast interest-rate behavior would likely be unpopular with such investors who would use forecasts only in timing their investments.

Speculation and Short-Term Trading

The objective of the speculator is to attain substantial capital appreciation in as little time as possible. This type of portfolio management requires *extensive knowledge* of interest-rate behavior, yield spreads, market characteristics, and issue features. Given short-term interest-rate expectations, a speculator uses his extensive knowledge of the markets and alternative investment vehicles to derive maximum capital gains (when rates are expected to fall), and reap maximum returns while preserving capital (when rates move up).

There is only one maturity strategy followed by speculative or trading portfolio managers: maturity concentration. Securities are selected on the basis of forecast interest rates, and occasional bond swaps are made. This portfolio approach is appealing to highly aggressive investors, to certain mutual funds or pension funds that seek relatively high yields, and to common trust funds offered in the trust departments of progressive commercial banks.[24]

When interest rates are expected to *fall,* the short-term trader searches for

[24]Daniel S. Ahearn, "The Strategic Role of Fixed Income Securities," *Journal of Portfolio Management* 1 (1975): 12–16.

substantial capital gains. Margin trading is often used to magnify available returns by increasing the leverage of the investment. After the decline in rates has occurred, the bond speculator takes his profit and moves to the sidelines, awaiting the next major swing. Thus, as interest rates *level off,* or begin to *rise,* the trader assumes a more defensive position with short-term securities.

One feature of speculating in bonds is somewhat unique in the realm of capital markets. Short-term trading in the quest of substantial capital gains is usually done with *high-grade investment securities.* The securities involved are almost always A rated and above, and are often agency and treasury obligations. Thus, risk of default is *not* a factor in the transaction. Quality obligations are employed because a high degree of interest sensitivity is needed to take advantage of the price behavior that accompanies swings in interest rates.

Maximizing Total Income

Basically, this middle-of-the-road approach involves a bit of speculation, and a bit of current-income optimization. The investment portfolio designed to maximize total income is constructed on the belief that *either* source of return (current coupon income or capital gains) is welcome. Moreover, the portfolio takes a *long-term* outlook and generally involves a fairly aggressive investment posture.

Total-income portfolio managers would probably select securities based on anticipated interest-rate behavior, would likely use bond swaps, would often employ modified buy-and-hold approaches, and, when conditions were right, would use short-term trading strategies to improve returns. In effect, these managers actively seek *all* these sources of bond income (coupons, interest-on-interest, and capital gains).

No particular maturity strategy dominates the total-income portfolio, just as no specific investment strategy dominates the portfolio. This portfolio approach appeals to both individuals and institutions because it tends to avoid extremes. The total-income portfolio approach is very challenging and requires a high degree of investor knowledge and sophistication about the bond market, the effect of different issue characteristics, and trading tactics.

Portfolio Implications

The high level of interest rates that has prevailed since the latter part of the 1960s has provided increasingly attractive returns to bond investors, while the wide *swings* in interest rates that have accompanied the high levels of market yield have provided capital gains opportunities for the more aggressive portfolio managers. An important consideration for portfolio managers, therefore, is the proper role of fixed-income securities in an efficient market.

Bonds in a Total Portfolio Context

A more attractive market environment, along with more aggressive and sophisticated management tactics, have enhanced the investment role of fixed-income securities. In fact, when viewed in an efficient market context, the performance of fixed-income securities has improved even more than indicated by returns alone because bonds offer substantial diversification benefits in fully managed portfolios. In an efficient market, some combination of stocks and bonds should provide a superior risk-adjusted return compared to one composed solely of either taken alone, assuming low correlation between stocks and bonds. An article by Sharpe[25] confirmed that stock returns were superior to bond yields over his test period of 1938–1971. In addition, his results showed that, due to the favorable covariance between bonds and equities, the addition of fixed-income securities to an equity portfolio vastly improved the return per unit of variability measure. Therefore, *there are significant diversification advantages to fixed-income securities*.

Bonds and Capital Market Theory

Modern capital market theory contends that, when financial assets are evaluated in terms of risk-return characteristics, an upward sloping market line will occur; i.e., greater return is accompanied by greater risk. Financial assets that characteristically exhibit high levels of return logically possess higher levels of risk. Compared to other market vehicles, fixed-income securities have traditionally been viewed as low risk, and, therefore, the rates of return demanded by investors have been correspondingly modest.

Clearly the risk-return behavior of fixed-income securities, in terms of yield for bonds of different quality, is compatible with traditional capital market theory. Capital market theory, however, also relates the risk-return behavior of fixed-income securities to that of *other* types of financial assets. Because fixed-income securities are considered to be relatively conservative investments, we would expect long-term bonds to be on the lower end of a graph that related rate of return and risk. A study by Soldofsky and Miller examined the comparative risk-return characteristics of 14 classes of long-term securities.[26] Government bonds, various grades of corporate bonds, preferred stock, and common stock were compared in terms of their risk-premium behavior. Figure 15.6 shows the basic findings of the study, and confirms the a priori expectations because bonds behaved in line with capital market theory. A study comparing corporate and government bonds to common stocks and treasury-bill obligations likewise in-

---

[25]William F. Sharpe, "Bonds vs. Stocks: Some Lessons from Capital Market Theory," *Financial Analysts Journal* 29(1973): 74–80.

[26]Robert M. Soldofsky and Roger L. Miller, "Risk Premium Curves for Different Classes of Long-Term Securities, 1950–1966," *Journal of Finance* 24(1969): 429–446.

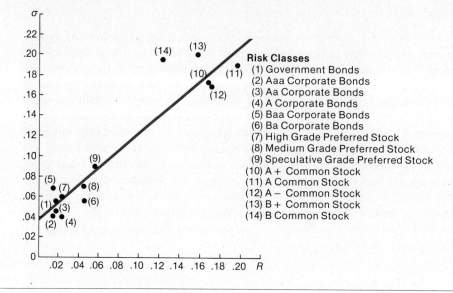

Figure 15.6   Risk-Premium Curve[a] 1950–1966

[a]Minimum Term to Maturity on Bonds is 15 Years.

Equation for Least Squares Regression Line is $y = .035 + .8783 \times R^2 = .90992$

.Source: Robert M. Soldofsky and Roger L. Miller, "Risk Premium Curves for Different Classes of Long-Term Securities, 1950–1966," *Journal of Finance*, Vol. 4, No. 2 (June, 1969). Reprinted by permission.

dicated that the long-run risk-return behavior was as expected. Treasury bills provided the lowest risk-return profile, followed by government bonds, corporate bonds, and finally, the most risky alternative, common stocks.[27]

Of course, such behavior is the reason for the diversification benefits of fixed-income securities. Because bonds have risk-return profiles that are different from those of equity securities, they provide viable diversification opportunities. As Sharpe noted, while there is some correlation in the return behavior of stocks and bonds, the "amount of such correlation by no means eliminates the advantages to be obtained from holding both types of investments."[28]

Bond Market Efficiency

The efficient capital market hypothesis contends that market prices "fully reflect" all information so that consistently superior performance on the part of investors

[28]Sharpe, "Bonds vs. Stocks," p. 77. Sharpe's analysis also uncovered risk-return behavior for stocks vs. bonds similar to that observed in Figure 15.6.

[27]Roger G. Ibbotson and Rex A. Sinquefield, *Stocks, Bonds, Bills and Inflation: The Past (1926–1976) and the Future (1977–2000)* (Financial Analysts Research Foundation, 1977).

is largely unattainable. Two versions of the efficient market hypothesis are examined in the context of fixed-income securities, the weak and the semi-strong theories.

The weak form assumes that security prices fully reflect all market information and maintains that price movements are independent events, and, therefore, *historical* price information is largely useless in predicting *future* price behavior. Although there has been limited empirical research on bond market efficiency, the studies that considered the weak form have provided convincing evidence supporting price efficiency.

The vehicle for studying the efficiency of bond prices has been the ability of investors to *forecast interest rates*. Such studies are logical because of the effects that interest rates have on price behavior and of the prominent position that interest-rate expectations occupy in bond portfolio management. If interest rates can be forecast with high degree of certainty, so, too, can future price behavior. Several studies[29] reached the same conclusion; interest-rate behavior *cannot* be consistently forecast with a high degree of accuracy! In fact, one study goes so far as to suggest that the best forecast is no forecast at all. Thus, it is clear that if interest rates cannot be forecast, then neither can bond prices using historical information which supports the weak form efficient market hypothesis.

The semi-strong efficient market hypothesis asserts that current prices fully reflect *all public knowledge* and that efforts to obtain and evaluate such information are largely unproductive. Three studies on the information content of *bond ratings* did not question the accuracy of agency ratings, but were directed toward examining the information value of bond rating *changes*.[30] Efficient market proponents contend that a rating change should have no effect on bond prices because the information is not new, but is already a factor in the current price of the issue. The results of the tests of the semi-strong form of bond market efficiency were mixed but generally supportive, indicating that bond prices typically adjusted *prior* to the rating change.

What does documentation of market efficiency imply regarding bond swaps and yield spreads? By their very nature, bond swaps suggest the existence of some degree of market inefficiency. If temporary anomalies exist within or between market segments, then such occurrences afford alert investors the opportunity for extraordinary returns. The widespread occurrence of profitable swap opportunities suggests that underlying price irregularities are neither rare nor random events. An increase in yield through a quality bond swap that results in *reduced* agency rating certainly does *not* imply any market inefficiency because the swap

---

[29]See, for example, Michael J. Prell, "How Well Do the Experts Forecast Interest Rates?" *Monthly Review*, Federal Reserve Bank of Kansas City, September-October 1973, pp. 3–13; Bowlin and Martin, "Extrapolation of Yields Over the Short-Run: Forecast or Folly," *Journal of Monetary Economics* 1 (1975): 275–288; R. Roll, *The Behavior of Interest Rates* (New York: Basic Books, 1970).

[30]Steven Katz, "The Price Adjustment Process of Bonds to Rating Reclassifications: A Test of Bond Market Efficiency," *Journal of Finance* 29(1974): 551–559; George W. Hettenhouse and William L. Sartoris, "An Analysis of the Informational Value of Bond-Rating Changes," *Quarterly Review of Economics and Business* 16(1976): 65–78; George E. Pinches and Clay Singleton, "The Adjustment of Stock Prices to Bond Rating Changes," *Journal of Finance* 33(1978): 29–44.

is totally compatible with efficient market theories, i.e., the greater the risk, the greater the return. However, to derive improved return through a swap based on temporary price anomalies, as in a substitution swap, does imply some degree of market inefficiency.

Such opportunities for abnormal profits may be caused by the *institutional* nature of the market and the resulting *market segmentation*. In effect, it may be largely artificial constraints, regulations, and statutes that lead to the opportunity to executive profitable bond swaps.

Yield spreads, on the other hand, are indications of high degrees of market efficiency because they reflect equilibrium yield rates that are based on differential standards of risk, quality, and other issue characteristics. In effect, their existence is totally rational. A triple-A corporate *should* yield less than an A-rated obligation does because it possesses a different risk-return profile. The existence of yield spreads is rational, and the sizes of such spreads are determined in a highly efficient manner.

In light of the forgoing discussion, the logical question is: Are bonds viable portfolio candidates? Based on the evidence and discussion, the answer has to be affirmative. Fixed-income securities provide beneficial covariance features, attractive competitive yields, and nominal risk. Moreover, they can be employed in numerous trading strategies to attain a variety of portfolio objectives.

Summary

The concept of bond valuation is essentially the same as that for equity pricing; i.e., it involves the present value of all future cash flows accruing to the investor. The present-value model incorporated several important dimensions of bond yields and prices, including coupon receipts, interest rates, and interest-rate changes. *The major problem facing the bond analyst is estimating expected changes in interest-rate and yield-spread behavior.* Once these factors have been evaluated, the next step is to select the optimal coupon, maturity, and call feature.

The next part of the chapter reviewed the mathematics of bond pricing, including the five basic types of yields: nominal yield, current yield, promised yield, yield to call, and realized yield. The concept of interest-on-interest, or coupon reinvestment, was discovered to be an extremely important factor in calculating realized yield.

Because of the importance of the discount rate, we examined the fundamental determinants of interest rates: the risk-free rate, a risk premium, and an inflation premium. Consideration was then given to the term structure of interest rates, i.e., yield-curve analysis. The four basic patterns of yield curves were examined with theoretical explanations given for the different shapes based on the expectations hypothesis, the liquidity preference hypothesis, and the segmented-markets hypothesis. Trading strategies were developed using yield-curve analysis and related changes in the yield curve.

Subsequently, we saw that bond price volatility was a function of the percentage of change in yield, the coupon of the issue, the term to maturity, the level of yields, and the direction of yield changes. Because trading strategies based on price volatility emphasize the percentage of yield change caused by coupon and maturity, the concept of duration was developed to incorporate these two factors. In the second half of this chapter, we looked at three basic investment strategies available to bond investors: the simple buy-and-hold approach; an interest rate forecasting approach; and bond swaps. We also addressed bond portfolio construction based on risk-return tradeoffs. Three major types of bond portfolios were reviewed along with some popular investment strategies used with each type.

The final section reviewed the role of fixed-income securities in an efficient market. Historical returns for equities and fixed-income securities were compared, and we reviewed the risk-return tradeoff for fixed income securities. Finally, the efficiency of the bond market was discussed in terms of weak and semi-strong tests.

Questions

(Note: In all bond valuation problems, assume a par value of $1,000.)

1. What are the crucial assumptions an investor makes when he calculates promised yield? Why are they crucial to the computation?

2. An investor purchases a bond with a nominal yield of 6 percent for $800. If the bond has 20 years to maturity, find promised yield by
    a. the approximate method
    b. present-value method, assuming annual interest payments
    c. present-value method, assuming semiannual interest payments.

3. A bond is currently quoted at $1,100 and has a current yield of 6.36 percent. The remaining life of the bond is 15 years, but it has 3 years remaining on a deferred call feature.
    a. Calculate promised yield using:
    (1) approximate method
    (2) present-value method, assuming annual payments.
    b. Calculate yield to call, assuming a call premium equal to one year's interest, using:
    (1) approximate method
    (2) present-value method, assuming annual payments.

4. An investor purchases a bond during a period of high yields. He pays $800 for a $7^{3}/4$ percent bond, expecting rates to drop over the next three years to the point at which the value of the bond would increase to $1,050. However, interest rates edge slightly upward, so that when he sells the bond three years later, he actually receives $750 for it.
    a. Calculate the realized yield the investor *anticipated* using the approximate method.
    b. Calculate the actual yield he *realized,* using the approximate method.

5. A bond with a 7 percent coupon and 10 years to maturity is selling to yield 9 percent. What is its price?

6. A new 20-year bond with an 8 percent nominal yield and paying an annual coupon is priced to yield 10 percent. An investor purchasing the bond expects that, 2 years from now, yields on comparable bonds will have declined to 9 percent. Calculate his realized yield using the approximate method if he expects to sell the bond in 2 years.

7.   a. Define the variables included in the following model:

$$r = (RFR, RP, I)$$

b. Comment on the appropriateness of the model, given the information that the firm whose bonds you are considering is not expected to break even this year.

8. Using the most current information available, construct a graph depicting the term structure of interest rates for Aaa-rated corporate bonds. (See Figure 15.3 for an example.)

9. Of the three hypotheses mentioned in the text, which one do you feel best explains the reasons for a "yield curve"? Defend your choice.

10. Construct a chart demonstrating current ranges of yields for bonds in the top three ratings. For example, you might want to randomly select three or four bonds in each rating category and show the average yield on each group, as well as the spread for each group.

11. Compute the duration of a 10-year bond with a 7 percent coupon, annual payments, and yielding 8 percent. Show all work.

12. Explain the difference between a pure buy-and-hold strategy and a modified buy-and-hold strategy.

13. Briefly define the following bond swaps: pure yield pickup swap, substitution swap, and tax swap.

14. What are two primary reasons for investing in deep-discounted bonds?

15. Speculating in common stocks often requires the purchase of low-quality stocks in anticipation of wide price movements. The same investment objective of buying bonds that have wide price movements requires bonds of the highest qualities. Explain why the latter is true.

16. Comment on the efficiency of the bond market with respect to tests of both the weak and semi-strong form EMH.

17. Explain how bonds could be attractive additions to a portfolio in spite of the higher historical yields of common stock.

18. What is meant by a laddered approach to portfolio construction?

19. Assume that over the next year you expect a large decline in market interest rates, would you attempt to increase or decrease the duration of your bond portfolio? Explain your decision.

References

Ahearn, Daniel S. "The Strategic Role of Fixed Income Securities." *Journal of Portfolio Management* 1 (1975).

Baskin, Elba F., and Crooch, Gary M. "Historical Rates of Return on Investments in Flat Bonds." *Financial Analysts Journal* 24 (1968).

Bierwag, G. O., Kaufman, G. G., Schweitzer, R. and Toeus, A. "The Art of Risk Management in Bond Portfolios," *Journal of Portfolio Management* 7 (1981).

Bowlin, Oswald D., and Martin, John D. "Extrapolations of Yields Over the Short Run; Forecast or Folly?" *Journal of Monetary Economics* 1 (1975).

Burton, John S., and Toth, John R. "Forecasting Secular Trends in Long-Term Interest Rates." *Financial Analysts Journal* 30 (1974).

Cagan, Phillip, ed. *Essays on Interest Rates.* New York: Columbia University Press for the National Bureau of Economic Research, 1969.

Carter, Andrew M. "Value Judgments in Bond Management." *Bond Analysis and Selection.* Financial Analysts Research Foundation, 1977.

Conard, Joseph W., and Frankena, Mark W. "The Yield Spread Between New and Seasoned Corporate Bonds," *Essays on Interest Rates* 1 (1969).

Dietz, Peter O., Fogler, Russell and Rivers, Anthony V. "Duration, Nonlinearity, and Bond Portfolio Performance," *Journal of Portfolio Management* 7 (1981).

Ederington, Louis H. "The Yield Spread on New Issues of Corporate Bonds." *Journal of Finance* 27 (1974).

Feldstein, Martin, and Eckstein, Otto. "The Fundamental Determinants of the Interest Rate." *Review of Economics and Statistics* 52 (1970).

Fisher, Lawrence. "Determinants of Risk Premiums on Corporate Bonds." *Journal of Polticial Economy* 67 (1959).

Fisher, Lawrence, and Weil, Roman L. "Coping with the Risk of Interest-Rate Fluctuations: Returns to Bondholders from Naive and Optimal Strategies." *Journal of Business* 44 (1971).

Hickman, W. Braddock. *Corporate Bond Quality and Investor Experience.* National Bureau of Economic Research. Princeton, NJ: Princeton University Press, 1958.

Homer, Sidney, and Leibowitz, Martin L. *Inside the Yield Book.* Englewood Cliffs, NJ: Prentice-Hall, 1972.

Jen, Frank C., and Wert, James E. "The Value of the Deferred Call Privilege." *National Banking Review* 3 (1966).

Joehnk, Michael D., and Nielsen, James F. "Return and Risk Characteristics of Speculative Grade Bonds." *Quarterly Review of Economics & Business* 15 (1975).

Joehnk, Michael D., and Wert, James E. "The Call-Risk Performance of the Discounted Seasoned Issue." *Mississippi Valley Journal of Business and Economics* 9 (1973–1974).

Johnson, Ramon E. "Term Structure of Corporate Bond Yields As a Function of Risk of Default." *Journal of Finance* 22 (1967).

Katz, Steven. "The Price Adjustment Process of Bonds to Rating Reclassifications: A Test of Bond Market Efficiency." *Journal of Finance* 29 (1974).

Kessel, Reuben A. *The Cyclical Behavior of the Term Structure of Interest Rates.* Occasional Paper 91 Washington, D.C., National Bureau of Economic Research, 1965.

Leibowitz, Martin L. "How Swaps Can Pay Off." *Institutional Investor* 7 (1973).

Lindvall, John R. "New Issue Corporate Bonds, Seasoned Market Efficiency and Yield Spreads." *Journal of Finance* 32 (1977).

Macauley, Frederick R. *Some Theoretical Problems Suggested by the Interest Rates, Bond Yields and Stock Prices in the United States Since 1856.* New York: National Bureau of Economic Research, 1938.

Malkiel, Burton G. "Expectations, Bond Prices, and the Term Structure of Interest Rates." *Quarterly Journal of Economics* 76 (1962).

Malkiel, Burton G. *The Term Structure of Interest Rates: Theory, Empirical Evidence, and Applications.* New York: McCaleb-Seiler, 1970.

Meiselman, David. *The Term Structure of Interest Rates.* Englewood Cliffs, NJ: Prentice-Hall, 1962.

Percival, John. "Corporate Bonds in a Market Model Context." *Journal of Business Research* 2 (1974).

Pinches, George E., and Singleton, Clay. "The Adjustment of Stock Prices to Bond Rating Changes." *Journal of Finance* 33 (1978).

Rea, John D. "The Yield Spread Between Newly Issued and Seasoned Corporate Bonds." *Monthly Review,* Federal Reserve Bank of Kansas City, June 1974.

Reilly, Frank K., and Joehnk, Michael D. "The Association Between Market-Determined Risk Measures For Bonds and Bond Ratings." *Journal of Finance* 31 (1976).

Reilly, Frank K., and Sidha, Rupindner, "The Many Uses of Bond Duration," *Financial Analysts Journal* 36 (1980).

Roll, R. *The Behavior of Interest Rates.* New York: Basic Books, 1970.

Sharpe, William F. "Bonds vs. Stocks: Some Lessons from Capital Market Theory." *Financial Analysts Journal* 29 (1973).

Soldofsky, Robert M., and Miller, Roger L. "Risk Premium Curves for Different Classes of Long-Term Securities, 1950–1966." *Journal of Finance* 24 (1969).

Van Horne, James C. "Called Bonds: How Does the Investor Fare?" *Journal of Portfolio Management* 6 (1980).

Van Horne, James C. *Financial Market Rates and Flows.* Englewood Cliffs, NJ: Prentice-Hall, 1978.

Weil, Roman L. "Macaulay's Duration: An Appreciation." *Journal of Business* 46 (1973).

Williams, Arthur III. "The Bond Market Line: Measuring Risk and Return," *Journal of Portfolio Management* 6 (1980).

ANALYSIS OF
ALTERNATIVE INVESTMENTS

PART·FOUR

The previous sections gave you the background necessary to deal with investments and a presentation of valuation principles and practices generally applied to common stock. The third section considered the evaluation and management of bonds. In this section we complete our discussion of investment alternatives by analyzing several investment instruments that will provide you with a wider range of risk-return possibilities.

In Chapter 16 we discuss stock options which have become very popular specifically because you can use them in a very aggressive, speculative investment program or consider them for a portfolio that would involve less risk than a pure stock portfolio does. We consider how they evolved, what they are, and how to evaluate them.

Chapter 17 contains material on warrants and convertible securities. These securities are very useful for issuing companies in terms of reducing the cost of capital because they are attractive for investors. Warrants have appeal because of the leverage involved, while convertible securities are desirable because they typically provide downside protection and good upside potential. Besides con-

sidering their general attributes, we consider how these securities should be analyzed and when they are optimal investments.

In Chapter 18 we consider two areas that have typically not received much attention in discussions of investments: commodities and financial futures. The general feeling is that commodities are different from stocks and bonds. Contrary to this idea, we begin the chapter with a discussion of how commodities and stocks are the same and subsequently discuss specific trades. Financial futures are relatively new. They were only introduced in 1976, and the substantial increase in trading volume in them began in 1979 and 1980. Besides discussing how they are traded, we consider who can use them and how to use them. Finally, we give examples of several typical transactions.

The last chapter in this section is concerned with investment companies and the role they can play in an investor's portfolio. It is argued that there is almost an infinite variety of funds available to meet almost every need. The objective of the chapter is to help you understand what funds are available, how to investigate them, and how to use them in your overall portfolio.

Fischer Black

Fischer Black is a professor of finance at MIT's Sloan School of Management. In his work it is assumed that individuals and firms are constantly seeking to take advantage of any profit opportunities. This has led him to study diverse subjects, including options markets, futures markets, business cycles, monetary theory, financial accounting, international economics, and public finance.

In empirical work, he feels his most important contribution was developing, with Michael Jensen and Myron Scholes, the "portfolio method" for testing the effects of various factors on expected returns. This method is intended to avoid the tendency inherent in other econometric procedures of overstating the significance of relationships.

The most important of his widely accepted theoretical papers was co-authored with Myron Scholes and dealt with option pricing. This classic paper (Journal of Political Economy: May/June, 1973) contained a valuation formula that is universally used by practitioners and academicians. All subsequent work in options begins with this formulation as a base. In addition, several authors have suggested valuation formulas for other assets based on the principles behind the B-S option pricing model. Professor Black also feels the paper showing that pension funds should be invested entirely in bonds is very important (Financial Analysts Journal: July/August, 1980).

His papers on monetary theory, business cycles, and international economics have not yet been widely accepted, but he feels they are more important than the option pricing and pension fund papers.

Recently, he has written papers suggesting that consumption taxes dominate income taxes, and that earnings are better related to value rather than to change in value.

Perhaps the work that had the biggest impact on the business world was done as a consultant to Wells Fargo Bank with Myron Scholes and led to the creation of the first index funds.

Fischer Black was born in Washington, D.C. on January 11, 1938. He received his A.B. in physics from Harvard College in 1959 and his Ph.D. in applied mathematics from Harvard University in 1964. Prior to his appointment at MIT, he was a Professor of Finance at the University of Chicago and Director of the Center for Research in Security Prices (CRSP).

Myron S. Scholes

Myron Scholes has authored or co-authored significant papers in several areas of investments and corporate finance. Clearly the most significant is the classic Black-Scholes paper on option pricing, "The Pricing of Options and Corporate Liabilities," Journal of Political Economy *(May/June 1973). An article from his dissertation was one of the first major studies that examined the price impact of large trades. "The Market for Securities: Substitution Versus Price Pressure and the Effects of Information on Share Prices,"* Journal of Business *(April 1972). His paper with Beaver and Kettler is widely cited on*

the factors that influence beta: "The Association Between Market Determined and Accounting Determined Risk Measures," Accounting Review *(October 1970). Several of his studies have empirically tested the capital asset pricing model: "The Capital Asset Pricing Model: Some Empirical Tests," (with Fischer Black and Michael Jensen), and "Rates of Return in Relation to Risk: A Re-Examination of Some Recent Findings," both from* Studies in the Theory of Capital Markets *(New York: Praeger Publishers, 1972), edited by Michael Jensen. There have also been studies testing the option pricing model.*

His recent efforts have been in the area of executive compensation and the impact of taxes: "Dividends and Taxes," (with Merton Miller) Journal of Financial Economics (December 1978), and "Executive Compensation, Taxes and Incentives," (with Merton Miller) in Financial Economics: Essays in Honor of Paul Cootner (Englewood Cliffs, N.J.: Prentice-Hall, 1981), edited by Katherine Cootner and William Sharpe.

Myron Scholes was born July 1, 1941, in Timmins, Ontario, Canada. He received his B.A. in economics from McMaster University in 1962, an M.B.A. from the University of Chicago in 1964; and his Ph.D. from the University of Chicago in 1969. He taught for several years at Massachusetts Institute of Technology before returning to the University of Chicago in 1973. Scholes has done extensive consulting with financial institutions and business firms on portfolio management, option pricing, and the evaluation of information on security prices. He was director of the Center for Research in Security Prices (CRSP) at the University of Chicago from 1976–1980. Currently he is professor of finance at the University of Chicago and research associate at the National Bureau of Economic Research.

Robert C. Merton

Robert C. Merton is one of several individuals who have made major contributions to the theory of finance and investments utilizing training in mathematics and economics. Specifically, Professor Merton received his B.S. in Engineering Mathematics from Columbia University in 1966, his M.S. in Applied Mathematics from California Institute of Technology in 1967, and his Ph.D. in Economics from Massachussetts Institute of Technology (MIT) in 1970.

Merton has extended earlier theoretical work in the area of warrants, options, and debt. His major contribution in these works has been the introduction of continuous-time models of uncertainty. His published works include, "Lifetime Portfolio Selection Under Uncertainty: The Continuous-Time Case," Review of Economics and Statistics (August 1969); "A Complete Model of Warrant Pricing that Maximizes Utility," with Paul Samuelson, Industrial Management Review, (Winter 1969); "Optimum Consumption and Portfolio Rules in a Continuous-Time Model," Journal of Economic Theory December 1971); "Theory of Rational Option Pricing," Bell Journal of Economics and Management Science (Spring 1973); "On the Pricing of Corporate Debt,"

Journal of Finance *(May 1974); "Option Pricing when Underlying Stock Returns are Discontinuous,"* Journal of Finance Economics *(January-February 1976); "The Impact on Option Pricing of Specification Error in the Underlying Stock Price Returns,"* Journal of Finance *(May 1976); "On the Pricing of Contingent Claims and the Modigliani-Miller Theorem,"* Journal of Financial Economics *(November 1977); "The Returns and Risks of Alternative Call Option Portfolio Investment Strategies," coauthored with Myron Scholes and M. Gladstein,* Journal of Business *(April 1978); "The Returns and Risk of Alternative Put Option Portfolio Investment Strategies," also coauthored with Scholes and Gladstein,* Journal of Business *(forthcoming); "On Market Timing and Investment Performance Part I: An Equilibrium Theory of Value for Market Forecasts,"* Journal of Business *(July 1981).*

Professor Merton was born on July 31, 1944 in New York City. After receiving his Ph.D. at MIT in 1970, he became an Assistant Professor of Finance at that institution. He was appointed associate professor in 1973 and became a full professor in 1974. Currently he is the J.C. Penney Professor of Management at MIT.

STOCK OPTIONS

⇒ 16 ⇐

Options give the holder the right to buy or sell a security at a specified price during a designated period of time (usually from three to nine months). There are two specific types: *call options* give the owner the right to *purchase* a given number of shares; *put options* give the holder the right to *sell* a given number of shares. Put and call options have been available to investors on the OTC market for a number of years, but have only become widely accepted and used as an investment vehicle since the Chicago Board Options Exchange (CBOE) was established. As a result of actions by the CBOE and, later, other stock exchanges that began to list options, there has been a large volume of options trading by individual and institutional investors. Another major reason for the increased interest in options is that they provide a substantial range of investment alternatives for all types of potential investors from the most speculative to the very conservative.

Recent History of Options Trading

For a number of years it has been possible to buy and sell put and call options in the over-the-counter market via individual investment firms that were members of the Put and Call Association. Through the individual firms in this association, investors could negotiate specific put and call options on given shares of stock. The arrangements were very flexible and also somewhat disorganized. An investor who wanted to buy an option on a stock would go to one of these dealers and indicate the stock involved and the time period he was interested in. The dealer would find an interested seller and the parties would then negotiate individually on the price of the options. Because secondary trading in options was limited, it was usually difficult to sell an option prior to maturity.

The environment changed dramatically when the CBOE was established on

April 26, 1973 and began trading options on 16 stocks. The options exchange made numerous innovations in the trading of options on listed securities, such as:

1. *The creation of a central marketplace* with regulatory, surveillance, disclosure, and price dissemination capabilities.

2. *The introduction of a Clearing Corporation* as the guarantor of every CBOE option. Standing as the opposite party to every trade, the Clearing Corporation enables buyers and sellers of options to terminate their positions in the market at any time by making any offsetting transaction.

3. *The standardization of expiration dates* (most CBOE options expire in January, April, July, and October, others in February, May, August, and November) and *the standardization of exercise prices* (the price per share at which the stock can be acquired upon exercise of the option).

4. *The creation of a secondary market.* While an option is a contract guaranteeing the owner the right to buy or sell stock at the agreed upon price, the majority of option buyers sell their options on the exchange either for a profit or to reduce loss. Before option exchanges were established, the buyers and sellers of over-the-counter options were essentially committed to their positions until the expiration date if the option was not exercised.

Operation of the CBOE

Readers are well aware of how a market is made on the New York and other stock exchanges. The specialist is at the center of the stock market and has two functions: (1) as a broker who maintains the limit-order book and (2) as a market-maker who buys and sells for his own account to ensure the operation of a "fair and orderly" market for investors. Recall the concern because the specialists had monopoly information in the form of the limit-order book and also a monopoly position as the sole market-makers in certain securities. One might therefore expect stock specialists to derive above-average returns, which they do.

Apparently the CBOE was aware of the potential problems of the stock exchange arrangement and attempted to avoid them. The limit-order book on the CBOE is handled by an individual (a "board broker") who is *not* a market-maker, so the two functions are separate. The board broker handles the limit-order book and accepts *only* public orders on the book. In addition, the limit-order book *is public!* Above the trading post there is a video screen that gives figures for the last trade, the current bid and ask for each of the options, and the limit orders on the book. The other major difference is that *there are competing market-makers for all options.* These members can *only* trade for themselves and are not allowed to handle public orders. As an example, there are four members of the CBOE who are specifically designated as primary market-makers for IBM. Each of the market-makers is assigned three or four "primary" options and another three or four options for which they are "secondary" market-makers. They are required to concentrate 70 percent of their trading activity in their pri-

		Number of Stocks Listed	
Exchange	Starting Date	Calls	Puts
Chicago Board Option Exchange (CBOE)	April 26, 1973	119	64
American Stock Exchange	January 13, 1975	81	77
Philadelphia Exchange	June 29, 1975	50	48
Pacific Exchange	April 9, 1976	37	21
Midwest Exchange[a]	December 10, 1976		
	TOTAL	287	210

Table 16.1   Options Listed on Exchanges (As of April 1981)
[a]Merged with CBOE on June 2, 1980.

mary issues. Similar to the stock exchange specialist, they are expected to provide liquidity for individual and institutional investors. Given the existence of several market-makers for each option, one would expect more funds to be available for trading, and superior markets because of the added competition.

The third category of CBOE members are floor brokers who execute all types of orders for their customers. These floor brokers are very similar to the floor brokers on stock exchanges.

Volume of Trading

The CBOE started with options on 16 stocks. This number was gradually increased and other exchanges were established during 1975 and 1976 as shown in Table 16.1. As of 1981, the various exchanges combined had call options on over 250 stocks. Initially, all option trading on the exchanges was in call options. As of June 1, 1977, the SEC allowed each of the exchanges to begin trading in five put options, and there was a "freeze" on adding any more. The freeze was lifted during 1980 and there are currently puts on about 200 stocks.

As one might expect, the options are on stocks of large companies that enjoy active secondary markets. In fact, the criterion for listing an option is the trading activity of the underlying stock.

The growth in trading volume has been phenomenal. During the first full month of trading on the CBOE (May 1973), the number of contracts traded totaled about 31,000. By early 1981, the total number traded on all five exchanges for each month consistently exceeded six million. The annual totals are contained in Table 16.2, as well as a breakdown for the individual exchanges. The figures reflect the larger volume in call options compared to put options. This can be explained by the fact that most of the puts are relatively new, and by the general tendency of investors to buy long rather than sell short (i.e., the purchase

A. Call Contracts (thousands)

Year	CBOE		AMEX		Phila		Pacific		Midwest[a]		Total
	No.	%	No.	%	No.	%	No.	%	No.	%	No.
1977	23,583	63.0	9,655	25.8	2,002	5.3	1,704	4.6	497	1.3	37,441
1978	30,743	58.7	13,644	26.1	3,010	5.7	2,929	5.6	2,041	3.9	52,367
1979	29,918	53.5	16,505	29.5	4,527	8.1	3,118	5.6	1,847	3.3	55,915
1980	42,941	53.5	25,104	31.3	6,686	8.3	4,410	5.5	1,111	1.4	80,252

B. Put Contracts (thousands)

Year	CBOE		AMEX		Phila		Pacific		Midwest[a]		Total
	No.	%	No.	%	No.	%	No.	%	No.	%	No.
1977	1,257	57.2	423	19.3	192	8.7	222	10.1	103	4.7	2,197
1978	3,979	63.7	841	13.5	296	4.7	640	10.2	489	7.8	6,245
1979	5,250	64.6	964	11.9	423	5.2	736	9.0	762	9.4	8,133
1980	9,954	60.0	4,103	24.7	1,051	6.3	1,076	6.5	408	2.5	16,592

Table 16.2   Number of Put and Call Contracts Traded and Percent of Contracts Traded on Different Exchanges

[a]Midwest Options Exchange merged with CBOE on June 2, 1980

of a call is based upon a bullish outlook, while you would buy a put if you were bearish on a stock).

The exchange breakdown reflects the initial dominance of the CBOE, which has declined, but apparently has stabilized at a strong 55 percent of call volume after the merger with the Midwest Exchange.

Competing Markets for Options

When the ASE established trading in options in January 1975, it was with 15 stocks that *were not* being traded on the CBOE. The point is that originally there was a very conscious effort by the exchanges *not* to establish competing markets, and this practice was continued when the Philadelphia Exchange began trading in options.

This changed late in 1976 when the ASE established a market in MGIC which was then traded on the CBOE. In February 1977, the ASE started a market in National Semiconductor, a very active issue on the CBOE.[1] The response

[1]For an extended discussion of what transpired, see Kevin J. Hamilton, "Options: The Dual Trading War," *Institutional Investor* 11(1977): 30–32; and Jonathon R. Laing and Richard E. Rustin, "Options Trading War May Afford a Preview of a National Market," *Wall Street Journal,* 27 May 1977, p. 1.

by the CBOE was to begin trading in six ASE issues: Merrill Lynch, Digital Equipment, Burroughs, Disney, Du Pont, and Tandy. The competition appeared to reduce the spread for these issues and increase their liquidity. There was a major effort by members of both exchanges to draw volume in the competitive issues because many brokerage houses did not check both markets when placing an order, but would select one of them as the "primary" exchange for an issue and channel all orders for the issue to this exchange.

The competition bothered the other exchanges that did not want their issues dual listed on either of these exchanges. In addition, all of the existing exchanges were concerned over the potential competition from the NYSE, which had applied for permission to establish an options market in early 1977. During late 1977 the increasing competition stopped abruptly when the SEC ruled that no further options could be added to any exchanges while trading practices on the exchanges were being investigated. All exchanges were frozen and the NYSE was not allowed to begin trading. In 1980, the "freeze" was lifted and there was an increase in the total number of options listed from about 220 to 287. Further, there has not been an increase in dual listed options. Most important, as of late 1981, the NYSE has still not established an options exchange.

Terminology

Given the unique nature of the options market, it is hardly surprising to find that it has developed its own terminology.

The Option Premium   This is the price paid for the option itself. It is what a buyer must pay for the ability to acquire the stock at a given price during some period in the future. The average premium on a newly issued option when the market price of the stock in question is close to the option price is typically about 10 percent of the value of the stock. The premium on a six-month option to buy a stock for $30, when the stock is selling for about $30, would be about $3.

The standard *option contract* is for 100 shares of a common stock referred to as the *underlying security*. As an example, a call option contract on IBM would be an option to buy 100 shares of IBM common stock. The price in the financial press is a per share price.

The Exercise Price   (Striking Price) This is the price at which the stock can be acquired. If the stock is currently selling for $38 a share, the option might specify an exercise price of $40 a share, meaning that the holder of the option can buy the stock for $40 for the duration of the option. The intervals for exercise prices are determined by the price of the stock involved. For stocks selling under $50, the exercise prices are set at $5 intervals: e.g., $35, $40, $45. For stocks selling between $50 and $200, they are set at $10 intervals: e.g., $60, $70, $80. Finally, for stocks selling for over $200 a share, the intervals are $20: e.g., $220, $240, $260. The initial exercise prices are set at the interval closest to the current market price of the stock. In a case of a stock selling for $43 at the time the option is established, the exercise price would be set at $45. If the stock declines to $41 a share, another option would be established at $40 a share. In contrast, if the price increased to $48 a share, an option would be established at $50. Therefore, when you look in the paper and a stock has options at numerous prices, it is an indication that the price has moved over a wide range during the recent past.

The Expiration Date   This is the date on which the option expires or the last date on which the option can be exercised. In July the exchange might establish a September option which means that the holder of this option can purchase the stock at any time between July and September when the option expires. The expiration dates are designated by month, while the actual date of expiration is *the Saturday following the third Friday of each month that is specified*. A September option would expire on the close of business on the Saturday following the third Friday in September. Actual trading in the option would cease at the close of the market on the third Friday.

Beyond these basic items of terminology, there are three general phrases used extensively in the trade. One of them is the term *"in the money option,"* which is an option with a *market price for the stock that is in excess of the exercise price for the option.* Assume that the exercise price of an option was $30 and the stock was currently selling for $34 a share. This would be an "in the money option" meaning that the market price ($34) exceeded the exercise price ($30) and so the option had an intrinsic value of at least $4 a share. The *"out of the money option"* has *an exercise price above the market price for the stock.* An example would be an option with an exercise price of $30 for a stock that is currently selling at $22 a share. In this instance, an investor may be willing to pay something for the option based on the *possibility* of the stock price increasing. The option itself has no intrinsic value because it provides the ability to buy a stock for $30 a share at a time when it is possible to buy the stock in the open market at only $22. The price you are willing to pay for an "out of the money" option is referred to as its *time value* because you are paying for the ability to acquire the stock at this price for the remaining time to maturity. Finally, an *"at the money option"* is one with a striking price approximately equal to the market price for the stock.

A Sample Quotation

Referring to Figure 16.1, assume that in May 1981, you were considering acquiring a call option in IBM. As shown in the right column, the stock is currently priced at $55^3/8$. The arrow (1) indicates that you could buy a "IBM July 50" for $7^1/8$. This means that you would pay $7.125 a share for the right to buy a share of IBM at $50 a share between the time of the purchase and the expiration of the option during the third week in July. This is an "in the money" option; it has an intrinsic value of $5^3/8$. If you wanted an option that expired in January 1982, it would cost $11 a share; the extra $3.875 is the cost of the additional six months.

You could also acquire an "IBM July 65" (arrow 2) for $5/16$($0.3125) a share. This is an "out of the money option" because the option exercise price of $65 exceeds the current market price of $55.375. The investor may be willing to pay

Listed Options Quotations

Friday, May 22, 1981

Closing prices of all options. Sales unit usually is 100 shares. Security description includes exercise price. Stock close is New York or American exchange final price. p-Put option. o-Old shares.

Chicago Board

Option &		price	– Jun – Vol.	Last	– Sep – Vol.	Last	– Dec – Vol.	Last	N.Y. Close
Apache		20	28	2¾	116	4	a	a	22½
Apache		25	100	7-16	42	1⅞	1	3	22½
Apach o		20	5	2¾	a	a	b	b	22½
Apach o		23⅜	a	a	5	2⅜	b	b	22½
Apach o		26⅝	a	a	6	1¼	b	b	22½
BrisMy		50	42	4⅝	a	a	a	a	53¾
BrisMy	p	50	30	¼	1	1¼	a	a	53¾
BrisMy		60	10	⅛	35	1⅜	a	a	53¾
BrisMy	p	60	12	6	a	a	a	a	53¾
Bruns		10	10	9⅝	10	9¾	a	a	19⅞
Bruns		15	77	5	69	5⅜	4	5¾	19⅞
Bruns		20	164	¾	144	1 13-16	12	2⅜	19⅞
Bruns	p	20	3	¾	a	a	a	a	19⅞
Bruns		25	b	b	33	½	8	⅞	19⅞
Chamln		20	5	5⅛	a	a	b	b	25⅛
Chamln		25	88	⅝	20	1¾	a	a	25⅛
Chamln		30	a	a	22	⅜	3	¾	25⅛
Chamln		35	a	a	23	⅛	a	a	25⅛
Coastl		40	5	5⅛	8	7⅝	a	a	44½
Coastl		45	7	2 3-16	7	5⅜	a	a	44½
Coastl		50	11	13-16	10	3⅛	b	b	44½
CompSc		15	5	8¾	a	a	a	a	23¼
CompSc		20	68	3¾	140	5¼	a	a	23¼
CompSc	p	20	4	1-16	10	½	a	a	23¼
CompSc		25	65	⅝	61	2	44	3	23¼
CompSc		30	9	1-16	b	b	b	b	23¼
CornGl		60	a	a	a	a	2	10½	66⅞
CornGl	p	60	35	3-16	3	1¼	1	1¾	66⅞
CornGl		70	39	⅝	7	3¼	a	a	66⅞
CornGl	p	70	17	3⅝	a	a	a	a	66⅞
CornGl		80	a	a	a	a	2	1½	66⅞
Dow Ch		30	117	2⅝	29	4	2	4⅞	32¼
Dow Ch	p	30	302	3-16	43	¾	34	1	32¼
Dow Ch		35	202	¼	136	1 5-16	46	2¼	32¼
Dow Ch	p	35	154	2¾	24	3⅛	1	3	32¼
Dow Ch		40	11	1-16	53	⅜	29	⅞	32¼
Esmark		50	2	18½	a	a	a	a	67¾
Esmark	p	50	a	a	5	½	7	1⅛	67¾
Esmark		60	5	7¾	1	11½	a	a	67¾
Esmark	p	60	62	⅛	a	a	11	2¼	67¾
Esmark		70	32	1½	14	4½	13	7	67¾
Esmark	p	70	3	3¼	a	a	a	a	67¾
Evans		20	23	2⅞	6	3¾	a	a	22¾
Evans		25	35	3-16	17	13-16	7	1½	22¾
Evans		30	2	1-16	b	b	b	b	22¾
Ford		15	a	a	54	8¼	b	b	23
Ford		20	68	3	60	4¼	8	5¼	23
Ford	p	20	54	⅛	8	9-16	a	a	23
Ford		25	132	¼	125	1½	44	2 7-16	23
Ford		30	2	1-16	92	7-16	10	⅞	23
Ford	p	30	a	a	2	7⅜	a	a	23
FptMcM		35	25	3⅝	12	5⅝	2	7	37⅝
FptMcM	p	35	62	½	3	1½	10	2	37⅝
FptMcM		40	147	⅞	184	3⅛	35	4⅝	37⅝
FptMcM	p	40	3	3	1	4	a	a	37⅝
FptMcM		33⅜	6	4¾	16	6¾	3	8	37⅝
FptMcM	p	33⅜	36	¼	a	a	10	1⅞	37⅝
FptMcM		39	238	1⅜	9	3⅝	a	a	37⅝
FptMcM	p	39	16	2¼	a	a	a	a	37⅝
FptMcM		44⅝	44	3-16	28	1⅝	a	a	37⅝
Gen El		50	7	15⅝	b	b	b	b	65⅜
Gen El		55	44	10¾	a	a	b	b	65⅜
Gen El		60	428	5⅞	192	7⅝	14	8½	65⅜
Gen El	p	60	170	3-16	51	1	4	1⅞	65⅜
Gen El		70	303	¼	88	1⅝	2	2⅞	65⅜
Gen El	p	70	a	a	1	5	1	5½	65⅜
G M	p	40	10	1-16	a	a	b	b	53¼
G M		45	66	8¾	9	9⅞	b	b	53¼
G M	p	45	36	1-16	61	½	b	b	53¼
G M		50	672	4¼	84	6⅜	35	7¾	53¼
G M	p	50	909	½	100	1¾	40	2⅝	53¼
G M		60	1784	⅛	359	1 7-16	50	2⅞	53¼
G M	p	60	422	6¾	156	7¼	23	7⅝	53¼
G M	p	70	180	17	b	b	b	b	53¼
Glf Wn		15	249	3⅛	39	3¾	59	4⅛	18
Glf Wn		20	993	¼	389	1 1-16	274	1 9-16	18
HughTl		70	51	8½	25	13½	a	a	77⅞
HughTl	p	70	288	¼	56	1⅜	14	2⅞	77⅞
HughTl		80	560	1 13-16	36	6	25	10⅛	77⅞
HughTl	p	80	518	3	52	5½	a	a	77⅞
HughTl		90	146	⅛	91	2⅜	15	5¾	77⅞
HughTl	p	90	26	12	2	12¼	a	a	77⅞
HughTl		100	a	a	14	⅝	b	b	77⅞
I T T		30	6	1¾	19	2⅞	10	3¾	31⅛
I T T	p	30	56	7-16	29	⅞	5	1⅛	31⅛
I T T		35	27	⅛	17	11-16	14	1⅜	31⅛
K mart		15	57	7⅛	a	a	a	a	22⅛
K mart		20	295	2¼	129	3	7	3¾	22⅛
K mart		25	77	⅛	23	11-16	14	1⅜	22⅛
Kenn C		25	2	30½	a	a	b	b	55⅝
Kenn C		30	4	26¼	1	26	b	b	55⅝
Kenn C		35	15	21⅜	a	a	b	b	55⅝
Kenn C	p	35	123	⅛	23	5-16	b	b	55⅝
Kenn C		40	15	16⅝	9	17¾	b	b	55⅝
Kenn C	p	40	345	5-16	12	¾	b	b	55⅝
Kenn C		45	a	a	2	13½	b	b	55⅝
Kenn C	p	45	973	11-16	170	1⅜	b	b	55⅝
Kenn C		50	667	8¼	178	9½	18	9⅝	55⅝
Kenn C	p	50	984	1⅝	176	2⅝	12	2⅞	55⅝
Kenn C		60	960	1⅛	572	1¾	992	1⅞	55⅝
Kenn C	p	60	504	4⅝	452	4⅞	13	5⅛	55⅝

Option &		price	– Jul – Vol.	Last	– Oct – Vol.	Last	– Jan – Vol.	Last	Close	
FedExp		70	329	3⅜	78	6¾	53	10	66⅞	
FedExp	p	70	102	6¼	15	8	2	8¾	66⅞	
F N M		10	70	⅜	374	⅞	180	1½	8⅞	
F N M		15	26	1-16	46	3-16	13	7-16	8⅞	
Fluor		35	12	5	1	7½	3	9¼	39	
Fluor	p	35	33	⅜	33	1⅛	15	1⅜	39	
Fluor		40	73	2	22	4⅛	159	5⅞	39	
Fluor	p	40	33	2⅛	1	3	7	3¾	39	
Fluor		45	194	¾	61	2¼	125	3¾	39	
Fluor	p	45	a	a	45	6½	6	7	39	
Fluor		50	120	¼	32	1⅛	5	2⅛	39	
Fluor	p	50	2	10¾	10	10¾	a	a	39	
Fluor		60	6	1-16	15	⅜	b	b	39	
Fluor		70	3	1-16	b	b	b	b	39	
Gt Wst		15	40	1⅜	a	a	1	3	15⅝	
Gt Wst		20	35	¼	6	¾	25	1	15⅝	
Halbtn		60	24	5¼	13	7	2	10½	62⅝	
Halbtn	p	60	22	1½	a	a	a	a	62⅝	
Halbtn		65	11	2½	b	b	b	b	62⅝	
Halbtn	p	65	114	4¼	b	b	b	b	62⅝	
Halbtn		70	176	⅞	533	2½	3	5	62⅝	
Halbtn	p	70	25	8	a	a	1	8½	62⅝	
Halbtn	p	75	25	13	b	b	b	b	62⅝	
Halbtn		80	10	⅛	7	15-16	500	2¼	62⅝	
Homstk		45	129	14½	a	a	b	b	58¼	
Homstk	p	45	294	3-16	79	¾	b	b	58¼	
Homstk		50	180	10	54	12½	19	13½	58¼	
Homstk	p	50	771	⅝	775	2⅛	8	2½	58¼	
Homstk		60	702	3½	165	6⅝	61	8½	58¼	
Homstk	p	60	289	3⅞	87	5¾	117	6¾	58¼	
Homstk		70	956	1 1-16	179	3⅜	177	5	58¼	
Homstk	p	70	34	11½	a	a	a	a	58¼	
Homstk		80	459	⅜	b	b	b	b	58¼	
Homstk	p	80	1	22	b	b	b	b	58¼	
Homstk		90	528	⅛	b	b	b	b	58¼	
Hou OM		45	113	⅞	2	2 1-16	a	a	27¾	
Hou OM	p	45	30	5⅜	4	5⅝	a	a	27¾	
Hou OM		50	30	¼	5	1¼	a	a	27¾	
Hou OM	p	50	a	a	1	10	a	a	27¾	
Hou OM		60	4	1-16	a	a	a	a	27¾	
HOiSgl		35	1	8	b	b	b	b	27¾	
HOiSgl		40	4	3⅞	b	b	b	b	27¾	
HOiSgl		45	16	1⅞	a	a	b	b	27¾	
HOiSgl	p	45	31	1¾	a	a	b	b	27¾	
HOiSgl		50	106	⅜	5	1¼	b	b	27¾	
HOiSgl	p	50	30	7½	a	a	b	b	27¾	
HOiSgl		60	a	a	10	½	b	b	27¾	
I N A		45	a	a	6	3¼	a	a	44⅞	
I N A		50	a	a	a	a	15	2	44⅞	
I B M		50	275	7⅛	129	9⅜	52	11	55⅜	←1
I B M	p	50	623	5-16	342	13-16	183	1¼	55⅜	
I B M		60	1573	1 5-16	398	3⅜	132	4¾	55⅜	
I B M	p	60	1122	4⅝	277	4¾	230	5¼	55⅜	
I B M		65	635	5-16	422	1⅝	95	3	55⅜	←2
I B M	p	65	487	9½	108	9¾	166	9⅝	55⅜	
I B M		70	439	1-16	166	11-16	b	b	55⅜	
I B M	p	70	312	14½	31	14⅝	b	b	55⅜	
I B M		75	33	1-16	b	b	b	b	55⅜	←3
In Har		15	14	2¼	53	3¼	6	4	16⅜	
In Har	p	15	198	9-16	100	1⅛	28	1⅜	16⅜	
In Har		20	32	½	131	1¼	8	1 15-16	16⅜	
In Har	p	20	20	3¾	4	4	2	4½	16⅜	
In Har		25	276	1-16	23	¼	b	b	16⅜	
In Min		45	a	a	10	4¾	a	a	44	
In Min		50	5	⅝	2	2½	5	4	44	
In Min		60	7	¼	a	a	b	b	44	
In Pap		45	15	2½	a	a	a	a	45⅜	
In Pap	p	45	20	1½	a	a	5	2½	45⅜	
In Pap		50	32	11-16	5	1⅞	5	2 11-16	45⅜	
In Pap	p	50	a	a	5	5¼	a	a	45⅜	
John J		30	21	6⅜	a	a	b	b	36⅜	
John J		33⅜	35	3½	a	a	16	5⅝	36⅜	
John J	p	33⅜	27	5-16	a	a	a	a	36⅜	
John J		35	b	b	1	3½	a	a	36⅜	
John J		36⅝	69	1½	11	3⅛	a	a	36⅜	
John J	p	36⅝	a	a	3	1 15-16	a	a	36⅜	
John J		40	38	½	27	1 13-16	3	3	36⅜	
John J	p	40	16	3⅞	15	4¾	a	a	36⅜	
Kerr M		60	1	14¼	23	16⅞	4	18	73⅞	
Kerr M	p	60	11	1-16	a	a	a	a	73⅞	
Kerr M		70	133	6⅛	3	9¾	a	a	73⅞	
Kerr M	p	70	52	1 7-16	a	a	a	a	73⅞	
Kerr M		80	157	1¾	51	4¼	2	6⅝	73⅞	
Kerr M	p	80	12	6¼	a	a	a	a	73⅞	
Kerr M		90	26	¼	b	b	b	b	73⅞	
Kerr M	p	90	2	16	b	b	b	b	73⅞	
Merck		70	10	22¾	a	a	b	b	90	

Figure 16.1 Quotations from Chicago Board Options Exchange

Source: *Wall Street Journal,* May 25, 1981. Reprinted by permission of The Wall Street Journal,

this $0.3125 based upon an expectation that the price of IBM will approach or exceed $65 by the third week in July.

It is also possible to buy or sell a put option in IBM. In this case, all those with prices below $55.375 are "out of the money" and the only "in the money" put is the $70 option (arrow 3). It is "in the money" because it allows the owner to *sell* a stock with a market value of 55³/8 for $70. Its intrinsic value is therefore at least $14.625. Again, the longer term put option has greater value.

Alternative Trading Strategies

With the introduction of put options, the number of strategies available to an investor has become enormous and the range of complexity is substantial. In this section, we will not attempt to cover all the strategies, but will limit our discussion to the major alternatives and refer you to articles and books that describe the more sophisticated techniques. Most trading involves the basic strategies discussed in this chapter. Also, to understand the more sophisticated strategies, it is necessary to understand the basic techniques because the more advanced methods build upon these.

Buying Call Options

Investors buy call options because they expect the price of the underlying stock to increase during the period prior to the expiration of the option. Given this expectation, the purchase of an option will yield a large return on a small dollar investment. When considering the purchase of a call option, there are several alternatives available in terms of the exercise price relative to the market price. One can purchase an out of the money option, an at the money option, or an in the money option. Probably the riskiest is an out of the money option because it is clearly possible to lose everything that has been invested if the stock price does not rise enough to equal or exceed the exercise price. At the same time, the rate of return can be very large and the initial investment is the lowest of the three alternatives.

Consider the following example (without taking commissions or taxes into account):[2] In June, when Avon is selling for $55 a share, an Avon October 60 call option is selling for $2 a share. Assuming you expect a sharp increase in the price of Avon during the next four months, you would pay $200 for the option. If you are correct, and the Avon stock goes to $65 (an 18 percent increase in price) within this period, the option will become an in the money option and have an intrinsic value of $5, and it could sell for more if there is any time left to the option. At this point, you could sell the option for at least $500 and enjoy a *150 percent*

---

[2]In all these examples, we ignore comissions and taxes to simplify the computations. This allows us to concentrate on the major impact but does *not* imply that these factors are not very important in the ultimate investment decision.

return on the option during a period when the increase in stock price was only *18 percent*. This comparison of returns reflects the leverage available in options. If the stock price never got above 60, the option would be worthless when it expired and you would lose the full $200. Note that your *maximum* loss was $200 irrespective of what happened to the stock. This points out the other major advantage to call options (besides leverage)—loss limit.

You could also acquire an in the money option on the stock. This differs from the out of the money option in that a larger investment is required because the option has an intrinsic value *and* a time value and does not have as much potential leverage. At the same time, the price of the underlying stock does not have to increase much for you to enjoy a return. Assume that in June when Avon stock is selling for 55, you buy a Avon October 50 at $6^3/4$. This option has an intrinsic value of $5 and a time value of about $1.75. In the near future, assume the stock goes to $59. The option will then have an intrinsic value of $9 and, even if the time value declines to $1, the option should be selling for about $10. Therefore, on a 7.3 percent increase in the stock price (59 vs. 55), the option has a return of 53.8 percent (10 vs. $6^1/2$). If the stock price declined to below 50, you would lose the full investment. If the price declined but was still above 50, the option would only have its intrinsic value at expiration and your gain or loss would be figured accordingly.

Writing Covered Call Options[3]

In contrast to buying call options, which is considered quite speculative, a strategy of writing call options is generally considered to be quite conservative. An option writer enters into a contract to deliver 100 shares of a stock at a predetermined exercise price during some specified time interval. When a writer enters into such a contract ("sells a call"), he can either own the stock (sell a covered option) or not own the stock (sell an uncovered, "naked," option). The option writer is typically looking for extra income from the stock (the premium he receives). The premium also give him some downside protection. At the same time, the option writer gives *up* a certain amount of upside potential on the stock if it rises above the exercise price and is called away.

Assume that in June you acquired 100 shares of Avon stock at $55 a share. You could sell an Avon October 60 for about $2 a share (sell a "covered" option). This would give you extra income ($200) or you could consider it as downside protection because your *net* price is now $53 ($55 − $2). If the stock does not change price between the middle of June and October (approximately four months), you have an additional $200 that you would not have had otherwise (a 3.6 percent return during the four-month period). If the stock increases to 61 and is called away, you have sold it at a profit of $5 per share and you still have

---

[3]For further readable discussions of writing strategies, see *The Merrill Lynch Guide to Writing Options* (New York: Merrill Lynch, Pierce, Fenner and Smith, 1981); and *Call Option Writing Strategies* (Chicago: The Chicago Board Options Exchange, 1975)

the premium. Your return (before dividends) during the period was $7 (a $2 premium plus the $5 capital gain), which would be 12.7 percent for the four months (7/55). As noted, if the stock goes to $65, you have given up the gain above $60 because of the option. Therefore, you are protected on the downside by the lower net price, but also restricted on the upside by the exercise price. If an option writer wants to get out of his contract, all he has to do is *buy* a comparable call option on the exchange and the two contracts cancel each other. This is referred to as a *closing purchase transaction* which liquidates the previous option.

Writing Options in Different Markets

Your option writing strategy should differ depending upon the general market environment (stable, rising, declining) and your outlook for the stock. If the market is *very stable* you would simply continue to sell options over time as a supplement to your dividend income. The only unique aspect of this arrangement would be that, if the option is an out of the money option or an at the money option, you would want to consider closing out your position (buying an option to offset your written option) prior to expiration so you can sell another one sooner. This strategy is based on the assumption that the option price gets pretty low near its maturity because it has no intrinsic value and its time value declines. Therefore, the cost of closing the position out is small and you can sell another option *sooner* so that your *annualized* return will increase.

If the market is *declining,* the sale of a call somewhat offsets the decline in price (i.e., the net cost of the stock is lower). After the stock has declined along with the market, the investor must decide whether he still wants to own the stock. If he does, he should write another call at a lower price. Assume you bought a stock at $58 and sold a 60 call. The stock then declines to 53. If you still want to own the stock, you would sell another call at 55, which would provide further income to offset the price decline.

Finally, assume that the stock price *increases* because of a market rise or for internal reasons. Again you must decide whether you want to continue to own the stock or let it be called away. Assume you bought the stock at $45, sold a $50 option, and the stock subsequently went to $52. If you are satisfied with the $5 capital gain plus the premium received, you might allow the stock to be called away and put the money into another stock. In contrast, if you feel there is further potential in the stock, you could simply buy back your $50 option and sell another at $55. You would have lost on the repurchase of the first option, but you would have made it up on the sale of the second option and you still own the stock.

Call Option Spreads

In contrast to simply buying or selling a call option, it is possible to enter into a spread and do both. The purpose is to reduce the risk of a long or short position in the option for a stock. There are two basic types of spread. A *price spread* (or vertical spread) involves buying the call option for a given stock, time, and price, and selling a call option for the same stock and time at a different price, e.g., buy an Avon October 50 and sell an Avon October 60. A *time spread* (or horizontal spread) involves buying and selling an option for the same stock and price, but the time differs, e.g., buying an Avon October 50 and selling an Avon January 50.

Bullish Spreads

These are spreads that you would consider if you were bullish on the underlying stock. Assume you are optimistic regarding the outlook for Avon (currently selling for 55) and want to enter into a price spread that will reduce the risk of such a transaction. The situation is as follows regarding October options (numbers rounded):

Avon 50 October   7
Avon 60 October   2

Because you are bullish, you would buy the Avon 50 and sell the Avon 60 for a net cost of 5 ($500) which is also your maximum loss. Assuming you are correct, and the stock goes from 55 to 65, the October 50 would be worth about 15 (only its intrinsic value) and the October 60 would sell for about 6 (a slight premium over intrinsic value). If you closed out both positions, you would obtain the following results:

October 50: bought at 7, sold at 15 —gain 8
October 60: sold at 2, bought at 6 —loss 4
Overall   —gain 4

If the stock had declined dramatically, your maximum loss would have been $500 even though both options were worthless when they expired. You should recognize that your maximum gain was also $500. Specifically, at some high stock price, the difference in the value of the options will be 10 which indicates a gross profit of $1,000 less the $500 initial cost.

Bearish Spreads

If an investor is bearish on a stock or on the market, he would buy the higher priced option and sell the lower priced option. Returning to Avon, you would:

Sell October 50 at 7
Buy October 60 at 2

This would generate an immediate gain of $500. If you are correct, and the stock declines to below 50, both options will be worthless when they expire and you will have the $500 return. If you were wrong, and the stock goes to 65 as discussed under the bullish spread, you would have the following:

October 50: sold at 7, bought at 15—loss 8
October 60: bought at 2, sold at 6 —gain 4
Overall   —loss 4

This loss of $400 compares favorably with possible loss of $800 or much more if you did not have some offset from the spread. At some very high price the two options will have a difference of 10, so your maximum loss is $500 ($1,000 gross loss less $500 gain on original transaction).

There are numerous other potential transactions for almost any possible set of risk-return desires. This discussion served only to introduce you to the basic transactions that are used in other strategies.[4]

In summary, this discussion of alternative call option investment strategies supports the statement made in the introduction to this chapter that options provide a wide range of risk-return possibilities. The alternatives ranged from very speculative purchases of call options which involve tremendous leverage and from which your returns can vary from large positive values to a negative 100 percent (complete loss). Alternatively, option spreads provide definite limits to gains and losses. Finally, an investor who sells covered call options on common stock owned will experience less variability of return on the stock because of the option; i.e., the option premium will offset any loss on the stock and limit any gain if the stock is called away.

The subsequent discussion of strategies that include put options expands the possibilities even further.

Buying Put Options

There are several major reasons for acquiring a put option on a stock. The most obvious is that you expect a particular stock to decline in price and you want to profit from this decline. As will be shown, the purchase of a put option allows you to do this with the benefits of leverage and yet provides protection because it limits the potential loss if your expectations regarding a price decline in the stock are wrong. In addition, it will be of benefit if you already own a stock and do not want to sell it at the present time although you feel it might decline in the near term. In this case, it is possible to buy a put option on the stock you own as a "hedge" against the decline; you will offset the decline in the stock with an increase in value of the put option. Finally, you might want to acquire a very

---

[4]A more extensive discussion is contained in George M. Frankfurter, Richard Stevenson, and Allan Young, "Option Spreading: Theory and an Illustration," *Journal of Portfolio Management* 5 (1979): 59–63, and in M. J. Gambala, R. Rosenfeldt, and P. L. Cooley, "Spreading Strategies in CBOE Options: Evidence on Market Performance," *Journal of Financial Research* 1 (1978): 35–44.

volatile stock with a good long-term outlook. While you feel confident of the long-run, you are uncertain about what might happen in the near term. In such a case, you could acquire the stock and also a put option for the short-term. If there is near-term weakness in the stock you would make money on the put as an offset to the stock decline.

Consider an example of a standard put acquisition. As of December, General Motors stock is selling for $52 but you feel it could decline. A June 50 put option for GM is selling for $3. Assume you purchase this option and by March GM stock declines to $44. At this time, your put option will have a minimum value of $6 ($50 − 44) and probably some value above this because there are still three months remaining before it expires. Assuming a price of 7, you could sell it and realize a *gain* of $4 (before commission) which is a 133 percent return on the option (7 − 3/3) during a period when the stock *declined* by 15 percent (8/52). Alternatively, assume that you were wrong and the stock did not decline below 50, or, in fact, increased in price. In this instance the put option expires worthless and your loss was *limited* to the $300 you paid for the option.

Assume the same set of events except that you owned the stock at $52 and thought the stock might experience some near-term weakness, but you did not want to sell it and then buy it back again. In this instance, if the stock declined to 44, you would have experienced an $800 loss in the value of your stock position, but you would have a gain of $400 on the put option as a partial offset.

Selling Put Options

When you sell (write) a put option you become obligated to buy a stock at a specified price during some time period. For accepting this obligation you receive a premium. An obvious reason for writing such an option is to increase the return on your portfolio during a period when you expect stock prices to rise. As an example, assume that currently Eastman Kodak stock is 49 and you expect the stock price to rise over the next six months. An EK six-month put of 50 is priced at $3\frac{1}{2}$. If you sell this put option, you receive $350 premium and, if the stock goes to 55 as you expect, the put option expires worthless and you have the extra $350.

In contrast, if you are wrong and EK declines to 45, the put option may go to about 6, if there is any time left. In this example, you will lose $250 ($600 cost less the $350 premium received) when you buy it back. Alternatively, you may be called upon to actually buy 100 shares of EK at 50 which entails paying $5,000 for stock only worth $4,500 before commissions.

Another very interesting strategy that you can use is to sell a put option as a means of acquiring stock that you want at a price below the current market price. Rather than placing a limit buy order below the market, you can sell a put at a striking price below the current market price. As an example, assume you want to buy IBM, but you think it is a little too high at its current price of 55. It is possible for you to sell an IBM 50 put option due in about six months for $1\frac{1}{4}$. If the stock declines as you expect to below 50, you will be called upon to buy 100 shares at

50, but your effective cost will only be 48³/₄ because of the premium you received. The outcome is that you own IBM as you wanted and at an effective price to you of $6 below the original market price. Alternatively, if the stock increased in price you would miss the profits, but you have the $125 premium.

Again it is possible to see the additional investment opportunities made available by put options. They may be used by a speculative investor who expects a price decline and wants to take advantage of the leverage of the put. Alternatively, they can be used by a very conservative investor who wants to hedge his current stock position. Finally, they can be used as a means to acquire a desirable stock at a lower effective price.

Valuation of Call Options

There are five figures needed to calculate the value of an American call option,[5] assuming the stock does not pay a dividend (this assumption will later be dropped): (1) the stock price, (2) the exercise price, (3) the time to maturity, (4) the interest rate, and (5) the volatility of the underlying stock.

Market Price–Exercise Price
The relationship between stock price and option valuation should be obvious from our earlier discussion. The relationship between these two prices is important because it determines whether the option is in the money and, therefore, whether the option has an intrinsic value, or whether it is out of the money and hence has only speculative (time) value. In addition, some of the other variables are influenced by the relationship between the market price and the exercise price.

Time to Maturity
A major component of the value of an option is its time to maturity. All other factors being equal, *the longer the time to maturity, the greater the value of the option* because the span of time during which gains are possible is longer. The longer option allows investors to reap all benefits of a shorter option and also provides added time after the short option has expired. It appears that this time value of the option is greatest when the market price and exercise price are the same. If the market price is below the exercise price (out of the money) it will take some of the time before the market price reaches the exercise price and the option begins to have intrinsic value. If the option is significantly in the money, for a given increase in the stock price, the percent of gain would be less than it would be when the market and exercise prices are almost equal. Therefore, an investor who acquires an at the money option pays less than he would for an in the

---

[5]An American call option can be exercised at *any time* prior to the expiration date; a European option can only be exercised *on* the expiration date.

money option, and will experience a larger percentage gain if the stock price increases.

The Interest Rate

When an investor acquires an option, he buys control of the underlying stock for a period of time, but his downside risk is limited to the cost of the option. On the upside, he has the potential to gain at an accelerating rate because of the leverage involved. The option is therefore similar to buying on margin, except that there is no explicit interest charge. The higher the market interest rate, the greater the saving from using options, and the greater the value of the option. Therefore, there is a *positive* relationship between the market interest rate and the value of the call option.

Volatility of Underlying Stock Price

In most cases, one considers a high level of stock price volatility an indication of greater risk and, therefore, this reduces value, all other factors being equal. In the case of call options on a stock, the opposite is true; there is a *positive* relationship between the volatility of the underlying stock and the value of the call option. This is because, with greater volatility, there is greater potential for gain on the upside, and the downside protection of the option is also worth more.

Derivation of Valuation Formula

Black and Scholes developed a formula for deriving the value of American call options in a classic article published in 1973,[6] which was later refined by Merton under less restrictive assumptions.[7] The resulting formula is set forth and demonstrated in the appendix to this chapter. As discussed in the appendix, although the formula appears rather forbidding it is noteworthy that almost all the required inputs are directly observable in the market. Further, although the calculations are rather difficult, there are a number of available computer programs that will expedite the process. These programs are available for several handheld calculators.

Efficiency of Options Markets

A study by Galai tested the efficiency of the CBOE shortly after it was established.[8] There are two phases to the tests of market efficiency. In the first, Galai considered whether a specified trading rule can be used to separate profitable

---

[6]Fischer Black and Myron Scholes, "The Pricing of Options and Corporate Liabilities," *Journal of Poltical Economy* 81 (1973): 637–654.

[7]Robert C. Merton, "The Theory of Rational Option Pricing," *Bell Journal of Economics and Management Science* 4 (1973): 141–183.

[8]Dan Galai, "Tests of Market Efficiency on the Chicago Board Options Exchange," *Journal of Business* 50 (1977): 167–195.

from unprofitable investments. The second phase determined whether it is possible to use the trading rule to generate above-normal risk-adjusted profits *in the real-world environment.* The analysis also examined changes in efficiency over time. The data were daily prices for each option on the CBOE from April 26, 1973 to November 30, 1973 (152 trading days).

Galai's main conclusions were: (1) the trading strategies based on the Black-Scholes (B-S) model performed well when the trades used the prices based on the B-S model versus the market prices. (2) The market did not seem perfectly efficient because some of the returns to market-makers from a realistic trading rule, i.e., where trading costs were considered, were positive. When transactions costs were considered, almost all positive returns disappeared. This means these above-normal returns are *not* available to the public. (3) The results did *not* generally indicate that the market became more efficient over time based upon an analysis of the first half of the sample period versus the second half. The whole test was conducted during the period shortly after the establishment of the CBOE, so the last conclusion may be somewhat premature.

Analysis of Investor Experience with Options

Several studies examined investor experience with options prior to the establishment of the CBOE.[9] The results of these early studies were mixed regarding the returns on the options compared to those from a stock portfolio. A more recent study by Dawson considered some of the problems in carrying out a program of continuous option writing and concluded that both return and risk are reduced.[10] A companion study by Grube, Panton, and Terrell likewise noted the reduction in return and variability from investing in covered call options, and also recognized the impact of such investment on turnover and transactions costs.[11]

A study by Merton, Scholes, and Gladstein is probably the most complete in terms of results and also in relating the results to expectations based upon factors that determine the value of call options.[12] They presented the results of a simulation for a group of 130 stocks that have options traded on the CBOE and for the 30 stocks in the Dow-Jones Industrial Average. The simulation involved the risk and returns for a fully covered call option program as compared to returns from owning the stock alone during the period July 1963 to December 1975.

In terms of the variability of returns, the results were generally consistent with our previous discussion. The returns from the deeply out of the money op-

[9]George W. Hettenhouse and Donald Puglisi, "Investor Experience with Put and Call Options," *Financial Analysts Journal* 31 (1975): 53–58; Richard C. Katz, "The Profitability of Put and Call Option Writing," *Industrial Management Review* 5 (1963): 205–213.

[10]Frederic S. Dawson, "Risks and Returns in Continuous Option Writing," *Journal of Portfolio Management* 5 (1979): 58–63.

[11]R. Corwin Grube, Don B. Panton, and J. Michael Terrell, "Risks and Rewards in Covered Call Positions," *Journal of Portfolio Management* 5 (1979): 64–68.

[12]Robert C. Merton, Myron S. Scholes, and Mathew L. Gladstein, "A Simulation of the Returns and Risk of Alternative Option Portfolio Investment Strategies," *Journal of Business* 51 (1978): 183–242.

tion strategies were more volatile than those from the other option categories. At the same time, *all option strategies were less volatile than a pure stock position* which experienced higher volatility and higher returns.

The authors contended that the investor who writes options against a portfolio of stocks will reduce his risk at the expense of also reducing his rate of return. Because the expected value of the option is heavily dependent on the expected volatility of the underlying stock, if an analyst can do a superior job of estimating the return volatility of the stock, then it should be possible for him to select overpriced options. The returns from consistently selling these overpriced options should be above normal on a risk-adjusted basis. *The crucial talent is the ability to do a superior job of estimating the variance of the individual security.*

Summary

Our discussion began with the recent history of options trading, starting with the establishment of the CBOE in April 1973. The reasons for the growth and expansion of this market segment were reviewed and we discussed the growing competition between exchanges dealing in options. The basic terminology for options was presented and quotations explained. This was followed by a discussion of alternative trading strategies, including the purchase and sale of call options under different market conditions, the use of call spreads under various market expectations, and the purchase or sale of put options.

A section on the valuation of call options dealt with the major variables that influence the value of a call option and the direction of the effect.

The chapter concluded with a discussion of studies of the efficiency of the options market and option investing returns and risk. The efficiency study by Galai indicated that the market was apparently not completely efficient when it was first established, but there are indications that this has changed. Recent studies on the return from and risk of selling covered options consistently indicated that the returns and risks were lower with options than with pure stock investing and also emphasized the importance of being able to estimate the variance of the underlying stock.

Questions

1. Define a call option; a put option.

2. How is the CBOE different from the original over-the-counter option market? Discuss the major factors that differentiate them.

3. What are the factors that motivate an exchange to begin trading in an option? Are you surprised that the ASE began to compete with the CBOE on certain options? Why or why not?

4. Define the following terms:
   a. premium
   b. exercise price
   c. expiration date
   d. in the money option
   e. at the money option
   f. out of the money option

5. Differentiate between selling a fully covered call and a "naked" call. Give an example of why the sale of an uncovered call is much riskier.

6. There are five variables that you need to estimate the value of a call option. List and discuss each of them and indicate *why* each is important and how it influences the value; e.g., when this value increases it causes an increase in the value of the option because . . . .

7. It has been contended that the sale of a fully covered option is a *conservative* investment strategy. Explain why this is so in terms of the possible distribution of returns from such a strategy. Use an example if it will help.

8. Assume you are bullish on the outlook for the stock market. Look up a four- to six-month option that is at the money in *The Wall Street Journal*. Assume the stock increases by 15 percent. Indicate approximately what will happen to your option and compute the percentage return on the option purchase.

9. Describe a time "spread" and a price "spread." Discuss why investors engage in spreads. Is the risk higher or lower than that for simply writing a call option?

10. Pick out a stock option on the CBOE and discuss what you would do to write a *bullish* price spread.
    a. Describe what will happen if the stock price increases by 20 percent.
    b. Describe what will happen if the stock declines by 20 percent.

11. Select an option listed on the American Stock Exchange and discuss how you would enter into a price spread assuming you were *bearish* on the stock.
    a. Describe what will happen if the stock price increases by 25 percent.
    b. Describe what will happen if the stock price declines by 30 percent.

12. Assume that you are generally bearish on common stocks and so you buy an IBM six-month put at 50 when the stock is 52. The put contract costs you $200. IBM subsequently goes to 55. What is your rate of return? What if IBM went to 45?

13. Assume that you want to buy Eastman Kodak, but feel that at its current level of 51 it is somewhat overpriced. Currently a six-month EK 50 put is selling for $3. Describe how you would use this put to accomplish your goal of buying EK if the stock declined to 45. What would happen if you sold a put and the stock rose to $54?

14. According to the Galai study, how do you test for the efficiency of the options market? Why would this test be considered a semi-strong test? Explain.

References

Articles and Pamphlets

Are Call Options For You? Chicago: Chicago Board Options Exchange, 1977.

Black, Fischer. "Fact and Fantasy in the Use of Options." *Financial Analysts Journal* 31 (1975).

Black, Fischer, and Scholes, Myron. "The Pricing of Options and Corporate Liabilities." *Journal of Political Economy* 81 (1973).

Black, Fischer, and Scholes, Myron. "The Valuation of Option Contracts and a Test of Market Efficiency." *Journal of Finance* 27 (1972).

Boness, A. J. "Elements of a Theory of Stock Option Value." *Journal of Political Economy* 72 (1964).

Bookstaber, Richard, and Clarke, Roger. "Options Can Alter Portfolio Return Distributions." *Journal of Portfolio Management* 7 (1981).

Boyle, Phelim, and Ananthanarayanan, A. L. "The Impact of Variance Estimation in Option Valuation Models." *Journal of Financial Economics* 5 (1977).

Brody, Eugene D. "Options and the Mathematics of Defense." *Journal of Portfolio Management* 1 (1975).

Buying Puts, Straddles and Combinations. Chicago: Chicago Board Options Exchange, 1977.

Chiras, D. P., and Manaster, "The Information Content of Option Prices and a Test of Market Efficiency." *Journal of Financial Economics* 5 (1978).

Cox, J. C.; Ross, S. A.; and Rubinstein, M. "Option Pricing: A Simplified Approach." *Journal of Financial Economics* 6 (1979).

Cox, John C., and Ross, Stephen A. "The Valuation of Options for Alternative Stochastic Processes." *Journal of Financial Economics* 3 (1976).

Dawson, Frederic S. "Risks and Returns in Continuous Option Writing." *Journal of Portfolio Management* 5 (1979).

Frankfurter, George M.; Stevenson, Richard; and Young, Allan. "Option Spreading: Theory and an Illustration." *Journal of Portfolio Management* 5 (1979).

Galai, Dan. "Characterization of Options." *Journal of Banking and Finance* 14 (1977).

Galai, Dan, and Masulis, Ronald W. "The Option Pricing Model and the Risk Factor of Stock." *Journal of Financial Economics* 3 (1976).

Gombola, M. J.; Roenfeldt, R.; and Cooley, P. L. "Spreading Strategies in CBOE Options: Evidence on Market Performance." *Journal of Financial Research* 1 (1978).

Gould, J. P., and Galai, D. "Transaction Costs and the Relationship Between Put and Call Prices." *Journal of Financial Economics* 1 (1974).

Grube, R. Corwin; Panton, Don B.; and Terrel, J. Michael. "Risks and Rewards in Covered Call Positions." *Journal of Portfolio Management* 5 (1979).

Hettenhouse, George W., and Puglisi, Donald. "Investor Experience with Put and Call Options." *Financial Analysts Journal* 31 (1975).

Katz, Richard C. "The Profitability of Put and Call Option Writing." *Industrial Management Review* 5 (1963).

Klemkosky, Robert C. "The Impact of Option Expirations on Stock Prices." *Journal of Financial and Quantitative Analysis* 8 (1978).

Klemkosky, R., and Resnick, B. "Put-Call Parity and Market Efficiency." *Journal of Finance* 34 (1979).

Latané, Henry A., and Rendleman, Richard J., Jr. "Standard Deviations of Stock Price Ratios Implied in Option Prices." *Journal of Finance* 31 (1976).

Merton, Robert C. "The Relationship Between Put and Call Option Prices: Comment." *Journal of Finance* 28 (1973).

Merton, Robert C. "The Impact on Option Pricing of Specification Error when the Underlying Stock Returns are Discontinuous." *Journal of Financial Economics* 3 (1976).

Merton, Robert C. "The Theory of Rational Option Pricing." *Bell Journal of Economics and Management Science* 4 (1973).

Merton, Robert C.; Scholes, Myron S.; and Gladstein, Mathew L. "A Simulation of the Returns and Risk of Alternative Option Portfolio Investment Strategies." *Journal of Business* 51 (1978).

Option Spreading. Chicago: Chicago Board Options Exchange, 1975.

Option Writing Strategies. Chicago: Chicago Board Options Exchange, 1975.

Parkinson, Michael. "Option Pricing: The American Put." *Journal of Business* 50 (1977).

Pounds, Henry M. "Covered Call Option Writing: Strategies and Results." *Journal of Portfolio Management* 4 (1978).

Pozen, Robert C. "The Purchase of Protective Puts by Financial Institutions." *Financial Analysts Journal* 34 (1978).

Puglisi, Donald J. "Rationale for Option Buying Behavior: Theory and Evidence." *Quarterly Review of Economics and Business* 14 (1974).

Reback, Robert. "Risk and Return in CBOE and AMEX Option Trading." *Financial Analysts Journal* 31 (1975).

Rendleman, Richard J., Jr. "Optimal Long-Run Option Investment Strategies." *Financial Management* 10 (1981).

Rogalski, Richard J. "Variances in Option Prices in Theory and Practice." *Journal of Portfolio Management* 4 (1978).

Ross, Stephen. "Options and Efficiency." *Quarterly Journal of Economics* 42 (1976).

Rubinstein, Mark. "The Valuation of Uncertain Income Streams and the Pricing of Options." *Bell Journal of Economics and Management Science* 7 (1976).

Schmalensee, Richard, and Trippi, Robert R. "Common Stock Volatility Expectations Implied by Option Premia." *Journal of Finance* 33 (1978).

Scholes, Myron. "Taxes and the Pricing of Options." *Journal of Finance* 31 (1976).

Slivka, Ronald T. "Call Option Spreading." *Journal of Portfolio Management* 7 (1981).

Smith, Clifford W., Jr. "Option Pricing: A Review." *Journal of Financial Economics 3 (1976).*

Stoll, Hans R. "The Relationship Between Put and Call Option Prices." *Journal of Finance* 24 (1969).

Tax Considerations in Using CBOE Options. Chicago: Chicago Board Options Exchange, 1975.

Understanding Options. Chicago: Chicago Board Options Exchange, 1977.

Wellemeyer, Marilyn. "The Values in Options." *Fortune,* November 1973.

Books

Auster, Rolf. *Option Writing and Hedging Strategies.* Hicksville, NY: Exposition Press, 1975.

Bokron, Nicholas. *How to Use Put and Call Option.* Springfield, MA: John Magee, 1975.

Clasen, Henry, Jr. *Dow-Jones-Irwin Guide to Put and Call Options.* rev. ed. Homewood, IL: Dow-Jones-Irwin, 1978.

Gastineau, Gary. *Stock Options Manual.* 2nd ed. New York: McGraw-Hill, 1979.

Gross, LeRoy. *The Stockbroker's Guide to Put and Call Option Strategies.* New York: Institute of Finance, 1974.

Keynes, Milton. *Put Options.* Englewood Cliffs, NJ: Cliffs Financial Publishing, 1976.

Malkiel, Burton, and Quandt, Richard. *Strategies and Rational Decisions in the Securities Options Market.* Cambridge, MA: M.I.T. Press, 1969.

Noddings, Thomas C. *CBOE Call Options: Your Daily Guide to Portfolio Strategy.* Homewood, IL: Dow-Jones-Irwin, 1975.

Pihlblad, Leslie H. *On Options.* New York: Perghing & Co., 1975.

Rosen, Lawrence R. *How to Trade Put and Call Options.* Homewood, IL: Dow-Jones-Irwin, 1974.

Rubinstein, Mark (assisted by John C. Cox). *Option Markets.* Englewood Cliffs, NJ: Prentice-Hall, 1980.

Appendix A to Chapter 16

Specification and Application of the Black-Scholes Option Pricing Model

In this appendix we will set forth the Black-Scholes (B-S) valuation formula and identify the variables involved. Subsequently, we will discuss what is involved in implementing the formula. Finally, we will give an example of the formula's application.

The basic valuation formula that has resulted from the work of B-S and Merton is as follows:[1]

$$Po = [P_s] [N(d_1)] - [E] [antiln(-rt)] [N(d_2)]$$

where:

Po = the market value of the call option

P_s = the current market price of the underlying common stock

$N(d_1)$ = the cumulative density function of d_1 as defined below

E = the exercise price of the call option

r = the current annualized market interest rate for prime commercial paper

t = the time remaining before expiration (in years, e.g., 90 days = .25)

$N(d_2)$ = the cumulative density function of d_2 as defined below:

$$d_1 = \left[\frac{\ln(P_s/E) + (r + .5\sigma^2)t}{\sigma(t)^{1/2}} \right]$$

$$d_2 = d_1 - [\sigma(t)^{1/2}]$$

where:

$\ln(P_s/E)$ = the natural logarithm of (P_s/E)

σ = the standard deviation of the annual rate of return on the underlying stock.

---

[1]Fischer Black and Myron Scholes, "The Pricing of Options and Corporate Liabilities," *Journal of Political Economy* 81(1973): 637–654; Robert C. Merton, "The Theory of Rational Option Pricing," *Bell Journal of Economics and Management Science* 4(1973): 141–183.

Implementing the Formula

Although the formula appears quite forbidding, almost all the required data are observable. The major inputs are: current stock price (P_s), exercise price (E), the market interest rate (r), the time to maturity (t), and the standard deviation of annual returns (σ). The *only* variable that is not observable is the volatility of price changes as measured by the standard deviation of returns (σ). Therefore, this becomes the major factor to be estimated and is the variable that will cause a difference in the estimated market value for the option. Black, in a subsequent article, made several observations regarding this estimate.[2] First, he noted that knowledge of past price volatility should be helpful, but *more* is needed because *the volatility for individual stocks changes over time.* This should not come as a surprise. A stock's volatility can change either because the market's volatility changes and the stock's beta is constant, or the market's volatility is constant and the individual stock's beta changes over time. Finally, it is possible for both variables to change. Therefore, given a historical estimate of the stock's volatility, the analyst should concentrate on determining the *direction* of the change; will the stock's volatility increase or decrease during the period prior to expiration? Given the variables determining volatility, one should first consider the future direction of *market* volatility; is there any reason to expect an increase or decrease in market volatility in the short run? Second, what do you expect to happen to the stock's beta in the future? This could be affected by industry factors or internal corporate variables, e.g., any future changes in business risk, financial risk, or liquidity.

The other variable that requires some attention is the interest rate. The idea is to use a rate that corresponds to the term of the option. The most obvious is the rate on prime commercial paper which is quoted daily in *The Wall Street Journal* for different maturities ranging from 30, 60, and 90 to 240 days.

To demonstrate the formula, consider the following example. All the values except stock price volatility are observable. In the case of volatility, the historical measure is given, but it is also assumed that the analyst expects the stock's volatility to increase.

An Example of Option Valuation Variables

P_s = \$36.00

E = \$40.00

r = .10 (the rate on 90-day prime commercial paper)

t = 90 days—.25 year

Historical σ = .40

Expected σ = .50 (analysts expect an increase in stock beta because of a new debt issue)

---

[2]Fischer Black, "Fact and Fantasy in the Use of Options." *Financial Analysts Journal* 31 (1975): 36–41.

$$d_1 = \left[\frac{\ln (36/40) + (.10 + .5(.4)^2).25}{.4(.25)^{1/2}} \right]$$

$$= \left[\frac{-.1054 + .045}{.2} \right]$$

$$= -.302$$

$$d_2 = -.302 - [.4(.25)^{1/2}]$$

$$= -.302 - .2$$

$$= -.502$$

$$N(d_1) = .3814$$

$$N(d_2) = .3079$$

$$P_0 = [P_s] [N(d_1)] - [E] [\text{antiln} (-rt)] [N(d_2)]$$

$$= [36] [.3814] - [40] [\text{antiln} (-.025)] [.3079]$$

$$= 13.7304 - [40] [0.9753] [.3079]$$

$$= 13.7304 - 12.0118$$

$$= 1.7186$$

Table 16A.1   Calculation of Option Value ($\sigma = .40$)

Table 16A.1 contains the detailed calculations for the option assuming the historical volatility ($\sigma = .40$). Table 16A.2 contains the same calculations except that we assume volatility is higher ($\sigma = .50$).

These results indicate the importance of estimating stock-price volatility; given a 25 percent increase in volatility (.50 vs. .40), there is a 36 percent increase in the value of the option. Because everything else is observable, this variable will differentiate estimates. Given its importance, the variable has been dealt with in several studies. Boyle and Ananthanarayanan examined the impact on how the variance was estimated on the value derived using the B-S model.[3] They concluded that almost all the estimations were subject to a bias. In contrast, rather than consider what variance estimate should be inserted, two related studies by Latané and Rendleman,[4] and Schmalensee and Trippi[5] showed that the B-S model could be used to derive the variances implied by the market, given the actual option prices and all the other known values included in the model. Both studies showed that, in many cases, these implied variances were better predictors of future variances than other methods based solely on past return data. It was noted that there was substantial instability in these implied variances over time. Con-

[3]Phelim Boyle and A. L. Ananthanarayanan, "The Impact of Variance Estimation in Option Valuation Models," *Journal of Financial Economics* 5(1977): 375–387.

[4]Henry A. Latané and Richard J. Rendleman, Jr., "Standard Deviations of Stock Price Ratios Implied in Option Prices," *Journal of Finance* 31(1976): 369–381.

[5]Richard Schmalensee and Robert R. Trippi, "Common Stock Volatility Expectations Implied by Option Premia," *Journal of Finance* 33(1978): 129–147.

$$d_1 = \left[\frac{1n\ (36/40) + (.10 + .5(.5)^2).25}{.5(.25)^{1/2}} \right]$$

$$= \frac{-.1054 + .05625}{.25}$$

$$= -.1966$$

$$d_2 = -.1966 - [.5(.25)^{1/2}]$$

$$= -.1966 - .25$$

$$= -.4466$$

$$N(d_1) = .4199$$

$$N(d_2) = .3275$$

$$P_0 = [36]\ [.4199] - [40]\ [antiln - .025]\ [.3275]$$

$$= 15.1164 - [40]\ [0.9753]\ [.3275]$$

$$= 15.1164 - 12.7764$$

$$= 2.34$$

Table 16A.2   Calculation of Option Value ($\sigma = .50$)

sistent with this, Black and Scholes found that the actual variance during a certain time period (which is obviously not observable prior to the period) is a more useful input to their model than estimates based on past data are.[6]

---

[6]Fischer Black and Myron Scholes, "The Valuation of Option Contracts and a Test of Market Efficiency," *Journal of Finance* 27(1972): 399–417.

WARRANTS AND

CONVERTIBLE SECURITIES

⇛ 17 ⇚

In previous chapters we examined a number of investment instruments including common stocks, bonds, and options. In this chapter, we will consider some other instruments beginning with common stock warrants which, while similar to call options, have some unique features that make them appealing to investors *and* to the companies that issue them. Subsequently, we will discuss convertible securities which are really a hybrid that is essentially a fixed-income security which has an option to convert the security to common stock. Specifically, we will examine convertible bonds that have the characteristics of both bonds and common stocks, and convertible preferred stocks which are a combination of preferred stock and common stock.

Warrants

A warrant is an option to buy a stated number of shares of common stock at a specified price at any time during the life of the warrant. You will probably recognize that this definition is quite similar to the description of a call option. However, there are several important differences. First, the life of a warrant is much longer than the term of a call option. At the time of issue, the typical call option on the CBOE has a term to expiration that ranges from three to nine months. In contrast, a warrant generally has an original term to maturity of at least two years, and many are much longer (there are a few perpetual warrants). A second major difference is that *warrants are issued by the company issuing the stock*. As a result, when an investor exercises the warrant and buys stock, the stock involved is acquired *from the company*, and the proceeds from the sale are new capital that goes to the issuing firm.

In general, warrants are used by companies as "sweeteners" for bond issues or other stock issues because they are options that could have value if the stock price increases as expected. The price of the stock or bond will be higher because the warrant is attached. At the same time, the warrant can provide a major source of new equity capital for the company. Investors are generally interested in warrants due to leverage possibilities that we will discuss. At the same time, you should recognize that warrants do *not* pay dividends and the holder has *no* voting rights. In addition, the investor must determine that the warrant offers some protection to the warrant holder against dilution in the case of stock dividends or stock splits. In such cases, either the exercise price is reduced or the number of shares that can be acquired is increased.

Example of Warrants

Consider the following hypothetical example. The Bourke Corporation is going to issue $10 million in bonds but knows that, within the next five years, it will also need an additional $5 million in new external equity (in addition to expected retained earnings). One way to make the bond issue more attractive and also, possibly, sell the stock, is to attach warrants to the bonds. If Bourke common stock is currently selling at $45 a share, the firm may decide to issue five-year warrants that will allow the holder to acquire the company's common stock at $50 a share. Because it wishes to raise $5 million, it must issue warrants for 100,000 shares ($5 million ÷ $50). Assuming the bonds will have a par value of $1,000, the company will sell 10,000 bonds and each bond will have 10 warrants attached to it. (We are assuming each warrant is for one share.) Assume the company is successful and the market price on the common stock reaches $55 a share over the five years. At this point the warrants will have an intrinsic value of $5 each ($55 − $50), and all the warrants should be exercised prior to their expiration. As a result, the company can sell 100,000 shares of common stock at $50 a share. The company pays no explicit commission cost, but does have administrative costs.

Other actual examples of outstanding warrants are listed in Figure 17.1 which is a page from the *R.H.M. Survey of Warrants, Options & Low-Price Stocks*. For each of the warrants included, there is an indication of the number of shares involved, the exercise terms (price and expiration date), the year of expiration, (if the warrant is not perpetual), and the current price of the common stock and the warrant. As an example, consider the Greyhound Corporation 1983 warrant. The specification in the table indicates that the warrants are for 6,140,000 common shares and each warrant allows the holder to buy one share of Greyhound common stock from the company for $23.50 a share at any time up until May 14, 1983. As of mid-1981, the common stock was selling on the NYSE at $17.25 per share and the warrant (which was likewise listed on the NYSE) was selling for $2.62. We will discuss the specific pricing of the warrant in the following subsection. At this point you should be aware of the numerous

THE R·H·M SURVEY
of WARRANTS·OPTIONS & LOW-PRICE STOCKS

VOL. XXX, No. 15   April 17, 1981

TDD.	OUTSTDG 000	NAME	EXERCISE TERMS	YEAR EXPR.	RECOM.	PRICES COM.	WT.
		Warrants on Listed Stocks					
S-O	320	APL Corp.	14.00 to 12-31-88	1988		6.87	.87
S-A	100	Alleghany Corp.	3.75	perp.		31.50	28.00
S-O	190	Allied Products	1.5shs. @tot. of 58.00 to 7-1-83 SS	1983		9.25	.31
S-S	5,000	Amer. Airlines Inc.	14.00 to 4-1-84 (See Ft. Note 7)	1984		16.75	6.37
S-A	833	Amer. Bdcstg. Cos.	1.50 shs. @ 16.00/sh. to 1-2-82	1982		32.00	22.25
S-A	1,000	Atlas Corp.	31.25	perp.		18.25	7.12
A-O	350	Audiotronics Corp. '85	10.35 to 1-20-83; 12.42 to 1-21-85	1985		7.12	1.31
S-S	1,050	Bache Group Inc.	18.50 to 10-31-85	1985		31.75	13.37
S-A	480	Braniff Airways	3.1827 shs. @22.94/sh. to 12-1-86 SS	1986		5.00	3.50
A-O	400	Buildex Inc. '82	10.00 to 3-31-82	1982		4.75	N.A.
S-O	875	Caesars World '85	24.50 to 8-1-85 SS	1985		12.12	3.12
S-S	3,750	Charter Company (The)	10.00 to 9-1-88 SS (See Ft. Note 12)	1988		12.12	7.25
S-S	5,000	Chrysler Corp. '85	13.00 to 6-15-85 (See Ft. Note 10)	1985		6.37	3.00
S-S	2,000	City-Inv.-GDV	1.02 shs. @ 27.70/sh. to 7-15-83	1983		14.50	1.62
S-S	420	CommonwealthEdison"A"	30.00 to 4-30-81; 1/3 sh. at anytime	–		18.12	6.00
S-S	310	CommonwealthEdison"B"	30.00 to 4-30-81; 1/3 sh. at anytime	–		18.12	6.00
A-PB	95	Consol. Oil & Gas "B"	2shs.@tot.of14.15to12-31-81SS(Ft.Note6)	1981		16.62	20.00
A-O	500	Custom Alloy Corp. '85	.5 sh. @14.00to12-17-81(aft.11-18-81)	1985		13.75	2.56
A-O	275	Damson Oil Corp. '83	14.715 to 3-31-83	1983		16.00	7.50
A-O	275	Data Access Systems	1.1 shs. @ total of 8.00 to 8-31-81	1981		16.50	9.00
S-P	603	Diversified Ind. Inc.	9.25 to 5-14-83	1983		4.37	1.50
S-O	2,200	Eastern Air June '87	10.00 to 6-1-87	1987		10.37	4.75
S-S	4,500	Eastern Air Oct. '87	10.00 to 10-15-87 SS	1987		10.37	5.12
S-O	430	Emhart Corp. '82	1.506878shs. @25.88/sh. to 7-24-82 SS	1982		36.62	17.00
A-A	1,655	Fed-Mart Corp. '81	14.00 to 9-5-81	1981		12.50	.43
S-P	76	Financial Corp. of Amer.	2.70 shs. @ 6.30/sh. to 10-31-81 SS	1983		18.25	31.50
S-S	2,200	First Pennsylvania	20.00 to 5-8-83	1983		4.50	.62
A-A	576	Frontier Airlines	9.99 to 3-1-87 SS	1987		23.87	15.62
S-O	672	Fuqua Ind. "1983"	1.14 shs. @ 38.16/sh. to 12-31-83 SS	1983		14.87	1.62
S-O	260	Golden Nugget Inc. '89	25.00 to 7-1-89 SS	1989		32.00	18.37
A-O	592	Goldfield Corp.(The)'84	1.12 to 12-31-84	1984		1.87	1.00
S-A	1,500	Goodrich (B. F.) Co.	30.00 to 8-15-81	1981		26.25	2.50
S-O	650	Government Employ.Ins.	2.08 shs. GEICO @24.00/sh. to 8-1-83	1983		19.87	6.18
S-S	6,140	Greyhound Corp.	23.50 to 5-14-83	1983	Buy	17.25	2.62
S-O	1,150	Greyhound Corp.'84"C"	30.00 to 5-15-84	1984	Buy	17.25	1.50
P-O	420	Hardwicke Co's. '84	15.00 to 7-12-84	1984		8.87	1.00
A-PB	403	Horn & Hardart	6.00 to 11-23-81	1981		12.25	6.75
A-O	750	Instrument Systems '81	1.034 shs. @ 38.67/sh. to 5-28-81	1981		1.12	.08
A-O	150	Integrated Resources	6.00 to 6-1-83	1983		17.37	11.37
A-O	720	Kenai Corp.	21.333 to 7-15-85	1985		23.12	10.00
S-A	200	Kidde Inc.	1sh.Series"C"Cv.Pfd.at90.00to4-29-81	1981		56.50	.03
A-O	550	Lundy Elec. & Sys.	(See Footnote 8)	1983		10.25	2.50
S-S	4,968	Mattel Inc.	4.00 to 4-5-86	1986		9.50	6.50
S-O	550	Modern Merchandising	4.20 to 6-1-82	1982		11.00	7.18
S-O	529	Puritan Fashions	5.75 to 8-1-81	1981		12.50	6.75
S-PB	737	Reliance Group "1987"	15.86 to 7-1-87 SS	1987		75.87	61.12
S-O	457	Republic Airlines '81	2.1 shs. @ 2.86/sh. to 7-1-81	1981		8.75	10.87
A-A	750	Resorts International	53.00 to 8-1-84 (Class A)	1984	Buy	29.25	5.37

(Continued on Page 824)

PUBLISHED WEEKLY BY R.H.M. ASSOCIATES, INC.
© 1981 R.H.M. Associates

-821-

417 NORTHERN BLVD., GREAT NECK, NEW YORK 11021
$120 PER ANNUM, $68 HALF-YEAR
+ Postage   + Postage

Figure 17.1   The R.H.M. Survey of Warrants, Options, and Low-Price Stock

Page from R.H.M. Survey of Warrants, Options and Low-Price Stocks, April 17, 1981. Reprinted with permission.

firms that have warrants, the numerous expiration dates, and the wide range of stock prices relative to exercise prices for the warrants.

Valuation of Warrants

The value of a warrant is determined in a manner similar to that used for call options because the only difference to the investor is the longer term. (An investor does not care whether he has the option to buy the stock from another investor or directly from the firm.) As was true with a call option, you should consider two components of the warrant price: the intrinsic value and the "speculative" value (sometimes referred to as the "premium"). The latter is based upon the leverage involved and the time value of the warrant. The intrinsic value of the warrant is determined by the difference between the market price of the common stock and the warrant exercise price as follows:

Intrinsic Value = (Market Price of Common Stock − Warrant Exercise Price) × Number of Shares each warrant entitles the owner to purchase.

This determines the intrinsic value of a warrant, assuming that the market price exceeds the warrant exercise price. As an example, in Figure 17.1, the Alleghany Corporation warrant has an exercise price of $3.75, and the common stock is currently selling for $31.50. Therefore, this warrant has an intrinsic value of $27.75 (31.50 − 3.75), because it allows the holder to purchase one share of common stock at a price lower than the market price.

Alternatively, if the warrant exercise price exceeds the market price of the common stock, the warrant has zero intrinsic value (a negative value is meaningless). An example of this is the Greyhound warrant discussed previously. In that instance the exercise price is $23.50, but the stock is only selling for $17.25 in the market. Thus, at that point in time, the Greyhound warrant had no intrinsic value.

In addition, a warrant has speculative value (i.e., premium value) due to its other characteristics. As was the case with a call option, an important feature of a warrant is the *leverage* it provides; i.e., the value of the warrant increases and declines by larger percentages than the value of the underlying stock fluctuates. As an example, assume a stock is selling for $48, and there is a warrant for the stock with an exercise price of $50. Assume the warrant is selling for $3 based upon its speculative value. (This warrant currently has no intrinsic value because the exercise price is above the market price.) If the stock goes to $55 (a 15 percent increase), the warrant will go to *at least* $5 because this is its intrinsic value. Thus, while the stock price increased by about 15 percent (55 − 48/48), the warrant increased by *at least* 67 percent (5 − 3/3). If there were some speculative value (premium), the increase in the price of the warrant would even be larger. Note that an indication of the amount of leverage can be derived by examining the stock price/warrant price relationship (ratio). *The larger this stock price/warrant price ratio, the greater the leverage effect.* The example given in Table 17.1

	Time				
	T	T+1	T+2	T+3	T+4
Stock Price	$22	$ 30	$ 40	$50	$60
Warrant Price	$ 2	$ 10	$ 20	$30	$40
Stock Price/Warrant Price Ratio	11	3	2	1.67	1.5
Percentage Change (Stock Price)		36.4	33.3	25.0	20.0
Percentage Change (Warrant Price)		400.0	100.0	50.0	33.3

Table 17.1   Differences in Leverage as Shown by Stock Price/Warrant Price Ratio

assumes that the warrant has an exercise price of $20 and sells at its theoretical value over time. The example demonstrates the relationship between the stock price/warrant price ratio and the different percentage changes in stock price and warrant price.

As shown, *the greater the ratio of stock price to warrant price, the greater the leverage of the warrant in terms of the percentage change in the warrant price for a given percentage change in the stock price.* Note that this leverage works both ways; for a given *decline* in the stock price, the warrant price would decline by more. Because investors in warrants typically find this leverage factor a positive attribute, the greater the stock price/warrant price ratio, the greater the speculative value of the warrant.

A major factor determining the price of a warrant, like the price of a call option, is the *length of time to maturity* (the longer the term, the greater the value). Because of their long term to expiration, warrants will typically have value even when they are deep out of the money. For example, a warrant with an exercise price of $50 will have time value even though the stock is selling for $40. As noted, this is a major factor distinguishing warrants from call options which are typically for less than nine months. As can be seen from Figure 17.1, warrants generally do not expire for 2—5 years, and there are some perpetual warrants.

Another important factor in warrant valuation is the volatility of the stock's price. The more volatile the stock price, the greater the probability of a positive move above the exercise price, and the greater the value of the warrant, as was true with the value of call options. One would not expect this factor to be very important in the valuation of a warrant on AT&T stock, but it could result in a large speculative value for stocks with high price volatility. A warrant would also be adversely affected by the payment of a dividend because this is subtracted from the total value of a firm, and the warrant holder does not receive the dividend.

Once an investor has analyzed a stock and decided that it could experience an increase in value over the next several years, he should find out whether the firm has any warrants outstanding, because this might allow him to control a large amount of the stock for a fairly long period (possibly several years) for a modest investment.[1]

In summary, the main determinants of the value of a warrant are:

1. The *intrinsic value* of the warrant based upon the difference between the market price of the stock and the exercise price times the number of shares per warrant.

2. The *speculative value* of the warrant (referred to as the premium value), which is a function of the following factors:

a. The potential *leverage* the warrant provides, which is a function of the ratio of the stock price to the warrant price. The greater the potential leverage, the larger the premium.

b. The *length of time to maturity*. The longer the time to maturity, the larger the premium.

c. The *price volatility* of the underlying stock. The greater the price volatility of the stock, the larger the premium.

d. The *dividend* paid by the stock. This is an inverse relationship; the larger the dividend, the smaller the premium.

Warrant Strategies

For the investor who is considering investing in warrants as part of an overall program, the following considerations should be kept in mind:

1. The ultimate success of the warrant depends on *the success of the stock*. Remember that the leverage factor works both ways. Therefore, you should be bullish on the stock and consider the warrant as a means to maximize the return from this stock.

2. *Diversification* is as important with warrants as with other investments. Therefore, if you decide to get involved in warrants you should probably consider the acquisition of a number of them if they are available on desirable stocks.

3. Given a diversified portfolio of warrants with higher leverage characteristics, it is important to *"cut your losses short and let the profits run."* This strategy is used with any leveraged investment, such as options or commodities. Success involves having several *small* losses, but a few *very big* winners: three warrants that provide returns in excess of 100 percent can easily compensate for five or six that lose 25–30 percent.

4. The *most desirable warrants* are generally those that have very little intrinsic

[1]For a further discussion on warrant pricing, see John P. Shelton, "The Relation of the Price of a Warrant to the Price of Its Associated Stock," *Financial Analysts Journal* 23(1967): 88–99. For an analysis of warrant hedging, see Moon K. Kim and Allan Young, "Rewards and Risks from Warrant Hedging," *Journal of Portfolio Management* 6(1980): 65–68.

value so the stock price/warrant price ratio is large and the leverage is high. In addition, you probably want a warrant with a minimum of two years remaining to maturity, and preferably three or four years. Also, the more volatile the stock price, the better (i.e., a beta above 1.2). These recommendations presuppose that the warrant has the standard protective features against dilution, call, etc. The final question is whether the speculative premium is reasonable given these characteristics. This can only be determined at a point in time based upon a comparison of alternative warrants as related to the underlying stock. As stated initially, you are ultimately betting on the underlying stock.

5. The search for desirable warrants can take one of two forms. The first is to simply engage in the three-step analysis process and finish with a list of good companies from desirable industries. As this point, given the stock list, check a warrant reference service like the *R.H.M Survey* to see whether any of these stocks have outstanding warrants that have the desirable characteristics mentioned above. An alternative approach is to initially examine a number of warrants listed in a service such as R.H.M and select several that apparently have most of the desirable characteristics mentioned above. Given this list of desirable warrants, you must analyze the issuing companies and their industries to see whether the stocks are desirable. The author's implicit preference is for the first approach that simply views warrant selection as part of the total investment process rather than as an end in itself.

Convertible Securities

A convertible security is one that gives the holder the right to convert one type of security into a stipulated amount of another type of security at the investor's discretion. Typically, but not invariably, the security is convertible into common stock, but it could be into preferred stock, or into a special class of common stock. The most popular convertible securities are convertible bonds and convertible preferred stock.

Convertible Bonds

A convertible bond is usually a subordinated[2] fixed-income security that can be converted into a stated number of shares of common stock of the company that issued the bond. The initial conversion price is generally above the current price of the common stock. Assume a company's common stock is selling for $36 a share. The company might decide to sell a subordinated convertible bond that matures in 20 years and is convertible into common stock at $40 a share. If the bonds are $1,000 par value, this would mean the bond is convertible into 25 shares of common stock (1,000 ÷ 40). Because convertible bonds are generally

---

[2]Subordinated means that the claims of the bondholders are junior to the claims of other debenture holders in terms of interest and claims on assets of the firm in the event of default.

considered to be an attractive investment (for reasons to be discussed), the interest rate on them is typically below the required return on the firm's straight debentures. In this case, assume an 8 percent coupon.

Advantages to Issuing Firms

Issuing convertible bonds is considered desirable for a company for several reasons. First, as stated, the interest cost is lower than it is on straight debt, and the extent of the saving on interest depends upon the growth prospects of the firm. In most cases, it is a minimum of one-half percent (50 basis points) and can be much higher. This differential in interest cost exists even though convertible bonds are riskier than straight debentures are because they are subordinated. The subordination feature has led bond rating agencies to consistently rate subordinated issues one class lower than a firm's straight debentures.[3] Therefore, the interest rate savings over a comparably rated bond are even more than the 50–100 basis points suggested.

Another advantage is that these bonds are "potential common stock." The bondholder may decide to convert on his own, or the firm will make it possible to force conversion in the future by including a call feature on the bonds. This "future common" feature may be desirable for a firm that currently needs equity for an investment, but does not want to issue common stock directly because of the potential dilution before the investment begins generating earnings. After the investment generates earnings, the stock price should rise above the conversion value, and the firm can force conversion by calling the bond. To understand how a firm forces conversion, consider the example of the bond convertible into stock at $40 a share (25 shares of common stock). Assume that the bond is callable at 108 percent of par ($1,080), and that two years after the issue was sold the common stock had gone from $36 to $45 a share because earnings have risen. Given the conversion feature, the bond has a *minimum* market value of $1,125 (25 × $45). At this point, if the firm decides that it wants to get the convertible bond off the balance sheet, it would simply issue a call for the bonds at 108 ($1,080). All the bondholders should convert their bonds because the stock they would receive in exchange is worth $1,125.

Advantages to Investor

We have mentioned that convertible bonds have special features that cause them to have coupon rates substantially below what you would expect on the basis of the quality of the issue. The reason for this lower rate is that there are significant advantages to investing in convertible bonds. Specifically, *they provide the upside potential of common stock, and the downside protection of a bond.* The upside potential can be seen from the example above. The bond is convertible into 25 shares of common stock, so, as soon as the price of the common stock exceeds

[3]See George E. Pinches and Kent A. Mingo, "A Multivariate Analysis of Industrial Bond Ratings," *Journal of Finance* 28(1973): 1–18.

$40 a share, the price of the bond should move in concert with the price of the common stock because the bond has intrinsic value (conversion value) above its par value.[4] At this point, as long as the stock goes up in value, the price of the bond will increase by *at least* the increase in conversion value. In most cases, the bond price will be above its conversion value because it offers downside protection, and the interest payments on the bond may exceed the dividend payments for the potential common stock (as will be explained shortly).

The convertible bond has downside protection because, irrespective of what happens to the stock, the price of the bond will not decline below what it would be worth as a straight bond. To continue our example, assume that this 8 percent subordinated bond is rated A by the rating services. (The company's regular debentures are rated AA.) Also assume that the firm's earnings decline so that the price of common stock declines to $25 a share. At this point, the bond has a conversion value of $625 (25 × $25). Would you expect the bond to decline to $625? The answer is probably no because it still has value as a bond. (This is an example of what is sometimes referred to as a bond's *investment value*.) The bond is an A-rated security with an 8 percent coupon. If we assume that this is an 18-year bond and comparable A-rated bonds are currently selling to yield 9 percent, the price of this bond will decline below par, but will *not* decline to $625. In this case, the price will decline to about $938.80 (.9388 of par.)[5] While the stock price declined about 30 percent (from $36 to $25), the bond price would only decline about 6 percent (from $1,000 to $938.80).

In addition to the upside potential-downside protection they offer, convertible bonds are also desirable because they typically have *higher current returns than common stock does*. Assume that the stock had an annual dividend of $1.50 a share. This would be a 3.75 percent yield on a $40 stock or 4.17 percent on a $36 stock, which is reasonable, but the total current income from the potential common shares would be less than what the investor would get from the bond. Total dividends on the 25 shares of stock would be $37.50 a year (25 × $1.50), compared to the interest income of $80 a year from the bond (.08 × $1,000). Obviously, the bond would be preferable until the dividend on the stock was raised to $3.20 a share ($80 ÷ 25). Even then, the bond would probably be preferred because it offers downside protection, and because the $80 interest is contractual, while the $80 dividend could be reduced if earnings decline. Therefore, you would probably wait until the common stock dividend reached $3.50 or $4.00 a share before you would convert to take advantage of the higher yield.

An advantage that has been lost is the potential for leverage on convertible bonds. Prior to the 1970s, investors could borrow on convertible bonds at about the same rate that they could borrow on straight debentures (about 80 percent). This made it possible to invest in convertibles with little cash and use the interest

---

[4]The conversion value is equal to the bond's conversion ratio (25 in this example) times the current market price of the stock.

[5]This is the price of an 18-year, 8 percent coupon bond priced to yield 9 percent.

on the bond to partially offset the interest on the loan. Currently, the margin on convertible bonds is the same as the margin on common stock.

Convertible bonds are, therefore, a desirable investment alternative because they offer upside potential, downside protection, and, typically, higher current income than common stocks offer. This yield advantage is especially true for issues of growth companies that pay low dividends and have substantial potential for price increases. In such cases, institutional investors are willing to accept substantially lower interest on a convertible bond than they accept on straight bonds.

Analysis of Convertible Bonds

Because a convertible bond is actually a hybrid of a bond and common stock, it is necessary to consider both aspects of the security. Specifically, the first part of a valuation analysis should consider the issue as a straight bond; i.e., what should be the yield and implied price of the bond if it were *not* a convertible security? This analysis will indicate your downside risk if the stock declined to the point where the security *only* had value as a straight bond.

As an example, consider the 5½ percent convertible bonds issued by Caterpillar Tractor Company due in 2000. These bonds are A-rated by Standard & Poor's and are convertible into 19.8 shares of common stock until maturity. In terms of the straight bond, it would be necessary to determine what the present going rate would be on an A-rated bond with about 17 years to maturity. If the current yield to maturity on such bonds were about 12 percent, this would imply a straight bond price of approximately $541 (the present value of this bond at 12 percent). You should compare this bond value price to the current market price of the bond to determine the price risk of the bond. If we assume the bond is currently selling for 104 of par based upon its conversion value (which we will discuss shortly), this would imply a 48 percent price risk (1040 − 541/1040). An obvious question you must ask is whether you are willing to accept this much downside risk.

The second part of the analysis is concerned with an evaluation of the bond in terms of its *stock* value; i.e., what is its upside potential due to the conversion factor? This requires that you consider the conversion terms of the bond and the conversion parity of the bond compared to the current market price of the stock. The conversion terms indicate how many shares you would receive if you converted the bond into common stock. In the Caterpillar Tractor example, the conversion terms specify that each $1,000 bond can be converted into 19.80 shares of stock. Given this information, you can compute *the conversion parity price of the bond which is equal to the purchase price of the convertible bond divided by the number of common shares into which it is convertible.* Assuming that the Caterpillar convertible bonds were selling for 104, this would imply a conversion parity price of $52.52 ($1,040 ÷ 19.8). You should compare this conversion parity price to the current market price of the common stock to determine how much the common stock must increase before the bond must increase. In the case of Caterpillar, assume that when the bond was selling for 104 and had a conversion parity price of 52.52, the common stock was selling for 51 on the NYSE. This indicates a parity price premium over market price of only 3 percent. Put another way, the common-stock price only has to increase 3 percent before the bond price would be justified in terms of its conversion value. Obviously, *the smaller this parity price premium, the more desirable is the bond.*

Beyond considering the current position, you should estimate the future *potential* for the common stock. What do you expect the Caterpillar common stock to sell for during your investment horizon period? If you expect the stock to go to $60 a share, your upside potential is approximately 14 percent. Specifically, if the stock goes to $60 a share, the bond will sell for *at least* $1,188 ($60 × 19.8), which is a 14 percent increase from $1,040.

Finally, you should consider the differential income from holding the stock compared to the bond. The bond has a 5½ percent coupon which indicates $55 a year in interest and a current yield of 5.3 percent at the price of 104 (55/1,040). In contrast, the stock is paying a dividend of $2.10 per share which is a 4.2 percent dividend and indicates a total dividend payment on the 19.8 shares of $44.58. Therefore, at this time, the current income from the bond exceeds the current income from the potential stock.

In summary, the analysis indicates the following characteristics of this bond. First, there is a fairly *large downside risk* on the bond as a straight bond because of its low coupon while interest rates are high. Alternatively, there is a *very small premium* of conversion parity price compared to the market price. This means that almost any increase in the common stock will be reflected in the price of the convertible bond. Note that you expect about a 14 percent increase in the value of the bond during your investment period. Finally, the yield on the bonds exceeds the dividend yield on the stock. At this point, the investor must decide whether the purchase of the bond is an appropriate way to take advantage of the outlook for the stock. One obvious consideration is the comparative returns on the two alternatives during your investment period. Let us assume this is one year. As stated, the current stock price is $51 and you expect it to go to $60. This information along with the dividend of $2.10 a share implies the following return on the stock:

$$R_{i,t} = \frac{EP - BP + Div}{BP}$$

$$= \frac{60.00 - 51.00 + 2.10}{51.00}$$

$$= \frac{11.10}{51.00}$$

$$= 21.76\%$$

where:

$R_{i,t}$ = the rate of return on security i during period t

EP = ending price

BP = beginning price

Div = dividend paid during the period.

If the stock goes to $60, the conversion value of the bond will be $1,188, and this information along with the interest of $55 implies the following return on the convertible bond as a minimum:

$$R_{i,t} = \frac{1188 - 1040 + 55}{1040}$$

$$= \frac{203}{1040}$$

$$= 19.52\%$$

As stated, this is a minimum because it assumes that the convertible bond will sell only at its conversion value without a premium. If it maintained its 3 percent premium, it would sell for about $1,224, and the rate of return would be 22.98 percent:

$$R_{i,t} = \frac{1224 - 1040 + 55}{1040}$$

$$= \frac{239}{1040}$$

$$= 22.98\%$$

In this case, it is difficult to make an obvious choice on the basis of the expected returns alone because they are quite similar and depend upon the assumed premium. The bond might be considered to have somewhat less downside risk because of the higher yield, but this is not obvious given the low straight-bond value for the security.

Sources of Information

A rather complete list of convertible bonds and information regarding these bonds is contained in the convertible bond section of the *Standard & Poor's Bond Guide*. A sample page is contained in Figure 17.2. Another source is *Moody's Bond Record* which contains a section with information on convertible bonds similar to the one in the *Bond Guide*. A service that provides analysis beyond the statistical information is the *Value Line Options and Convertibles*. This service indicates whether it feels the bond is under or overvalued and the expected impact on the bond of various changes in the underlying stock, i.e., its upside potential and downside protection.

XVI   **STANDARD & POOR'S CORPORATION**

CONVERTIBLE BONDS Issue, Rate, Interest Dates and Maturity	Outst'dg Mil.-$	B o n d	S&P Qual- ity Rating	Conv. Ex- pires	Shares per $1,000 Bond	Price per Share	Div. Income per Bond	1981 RANGE Hi Lo	Curr Bid Sale(s) Ask(A) Lo	Curr. Return	Yield to Mat	Stock Value of Bond	Conv. Parity	STOCK DATA Curr. P/E Price Ratio	Yr. End	Earnings Per Share 1979 1980	Last 12 Mos	1980 Di- lu'n
•Wean United.........5⅝s Ms 1993	25.9	R	B-	1993	41.67	24.00	66.20	56 43	‡43	12.7	16.7	22⅞	10%	‑5⅞	d Dc	0.05 d0.13 d0.13	n/r
•Wells Fargo Mtg/Eq¼s mN 1989	30.8	R	NR	1989	39.95	25.03	79.90	11¾%	106¾%	3.04	2.33	106⅜	31	‑3⅝	5 Je	-5.73 △3.10 3.68	n/r
Wells Fargo Mkg/Eq12s mN 2005	30.0	R	BBB+	2005	39.95	25.03	79.90	110¼%	103	11.6	5.41	77⅝	25⅞	‑19%	6 Je	-5.93 △2.10 3.07	n/r
•West Pt-Pepperell7⅞s aO15 2000	21.6	R	A-	2000	26.06	38.375	83.39	132 109	127¼	6.07	5.41	127¼	49	‑49	6 Au	5.66 9.32 9.25	8.35
•Western Air Lines..5⅝s Fa 1993	23.6	R	D	1993	36.58	11.55		96¾% 74	‡94	5.59	5.97	92	10%	‑10%	d Dc	2.99 d2.46 d1.92	n/r
‡Western Bancorp...7⅞s fA 2004	100	R	AA-	2004	27.21	36.75	50.07	109 96	108½	6.68	6.53	108⅜	39⅞	‑39%	7 Dc	-5.68 6.01 6.01	n/r
‡Western Union.....5¼s fA 1997	62.6	R	B	1997	15.15	66.00	21.21	55 48¾	‡50	10.5	12.5	35¼	33	‑23%	13 Dc	d0.34 1.80 1.80	n/r
‡Westport Co........6¾s jD 1991	2.32	R	NR	1991	47.62	21.00		47 45	46	14.6	18.6	24⅛	9%	‑5%	8 Dc	d0.83 A d0.49 d0.88	n/r
•White Consol Ind...4½s 3aO 1992	4.68	R	BBB-	1992	38.87	25.73	58.31	135 93	‡135	4.07	2.04	139%	34¾	‑35%	8 Dc	4.87 3.94 4.39	3.90
White Motor⁴.......5¾s Ms 1993	6.75	R	D	1993	24.18	41.35		35 28	29		Flat	6	12	‑2%	14 Dc	0.67 d9.00 d6.17	n/r
Whittaker Corp...4⅜s Mn15 1987	0.69	R	NR	1987	58.82	17.00	82.35	294¾ 166¾	293%	1.62		293⅛	49%	‑49%	12 Dc	3.28 3.90 4.02	3.70
•Whittaker Corp......4⅞s jJ 1988	6.25	R	B+	1988	21.28	47.00	29.79	104 62¾	103	4.37	4.00	106¾	48%	‑49%	12 Dc	3.28 3.90 4.02	3.70
•Wickes..............5⅝s Mn 1994	11.7	R	BB-	1994	22.00	45.45	22.88	54¾ 44¾	‡49%	10.3	13.4	35¼	22%	‑16	14 Ja	3.49 0.83 1.16	n/r
•Will Ross...........9s Mn 1999	19.1	R	BB-	1999	44.15	22.65	45.92	86¾% 76	‡84	10.7	11.0	70%	19	‑16	14 Ja	3.49 0.83 1.16	n/r
•Will Ross...........4⅞s mS 1987	4.04	R	A	1987	32.22	31.04	16.75	103% 81	103%	4.09	3.55	103%	32%	‑32%	14 Ja	▲1.60 2.05 2.08	n/r
•Will Ross...........5⅝s fA 1989	11.4	R	A	1989	22.75	43.96	11.83	80 72¾	‡76¾	6.89	9.49	73%	33%	‑32%	16 Dc	▲2.05 2.08	n/r
•Will Ross...........4⅞s mS 1992	22.0	R	B+	1992	21.82	45.83	11.35	73 66¾	71⅞	6.28	8.45	70%	32%	‑32%	16 Dc	▲1.60 2.08	n/r
•Wilshire Oil,Tex....6s mS 1995	2.31	R	A	1995	164.47	6.08		242 200	209%	2.86		209%	12%	‑12%	33 Dc	0.23 0.39 0.35	n/r
•Witco Chemical...4⅞s jD15 1993	12.5	R	A	1993	30.00	33.33	48.00	78 78	84%	5.31	6.27	84%	28%	‑28%	13 Dc	4.83 4.50 3.99	4.22
•Wometco Enterp5½s Ms15 1994	5.63	R	BBB-	1994	96.99	10.31	46.56	220 155	223%	2.46		223%	23	‑23	14 Dc	A1.48 1.56 1.70	1.50
♦Work Wear.........4¾s mS 1985	1.00	R	NR	1985	¶11.93	⁷83.82	23.14	71½ 70	67	7.09	15.6	39%	56%	‑33%	3 Sp	4.86 A5.33 5.09	n/r
•Wyle Laboratories...5⅞s fA 1988	10.2	R	B+	1988	68.68	14.56	27.47	89¾ 78¾	78¾	6.69	9.45	71%	11%	‑10%	11 Ja	1.50 1.16 0.94	1.07
•Wyly Corp²........7¾s Ms15 1995	13.2	R	CCC	1995	5.52	181.00		57 51½	52¾		7%	7%	‑14	27 Dc	0.41 0.50 0.51	n/r
•Wyoming Bancorp..7¾s mS 1996	7.95	R	NR	1996	100.81	9.92	80.65	196 180	194	.774		194	19%	‑19%	8 Dc	2.07 2.34 2.10	2.10
Xerox Corp²........5s AnDec 1988	73.6	R	C	1988	6.76	148.00	20.28	69 64	64%	2.75	12.4	36%	95%	‑54	3 Mr	6.69 7.33 7.44	n/r
•Xerox Corp.........6s mN 1995	129	R	AA-	1995	10.87	92.00	32.61	80 72¾	‡73¾	8.14	9.35	58%	67%	‑54	7 Dc	6.69 7.33 7.44	7.44
•Zayre Corp.........5⅜s jD15 1994	45.0	R	BBB-	1994	45.00	100.00	10.00	80 73	‡77¾	6.87	8.82	74%	30%	‑29%	8 Ja	3.30 3.42 3.73	3.19
•Zenith Radio.......8¾s mS12 1995	50.0	R	BB-	2005	45.00	150.00	36.49	92¾ 79	‡97%	7.58	8.67	97%	21	‑25%	15 Dc	2.84 3.36	n/r
•Zurn Indus.........5⅜s mS 1994	16.4	R	BBB-	1994	35.09	28.50		87½ 79	91	6.32	6.78	88%	25%	‑25%	8 Mr	2.84 1.27 3.27	2.98

Uniform Footnote Explanations—See Page XVI. Other: ¹Plan name chg to First Interstate Bancorp. ²Was HNC Mtge R I. ³Due Oct 23. ⁴Filed bankruptcy Chap XI.
⁵Subsid of & conv. into Searle (G.D.) & Co. ⁶Assumed by & data of ARA Services. ⁷Conv into ARA Services. ⁸Paid int arrears 4-3-78. ⁹Offered outside U.S. prin&int pay in U.S.$.

EXPLANATION OF COLUMN HEADINGS AND FOOTNOTES

MARKET Unlisted except where symbols • or ♦ are used.
•–New York Stock Exchange ♦–American Stock Exchange

ISSUE TITLE Name of Bond at time of offering; otherwise issue footnoted with name change of obligor. Minor changes with old title indicated in brackets, i.e.
#Prin & int payable in U.S. funds §Int. and/or prin. in default.

FORM OF BOND: Letters are used to indicate form of bond: C–Coupon only;
CR–Coupon or Registered, interchangeable; R–Registered only.

CONVERSION EXPIRES: Footnote keyed to bottom of page when conversion price changes during life of the privilege; also noted on conversion price.
⊚ Indicates a change in next 12 months. a–No fractional shs. issued upon conversion; settlements in cash.

DIVIDEND INCOME PER BOND: If $1,000 Bond were converted, the annual amount of dividends expected to be paid by the company on the stock based on most recent indication of annual rate of payment.
t–15% or 10% Canadian funds less 15% or 10% non-residence tax.

STOCK VALUE OF BOND: Price at which bond must sell to equal price of stock i.e., number of shares received on conversion times price of the stock

CONVERSION PARITY: Price at which stock must sell to equal bond price, i.e., price of bond divided by number of shares received on conversion.

P-E RATIO: (Price-Earnings Ratio) Represents market valuation of any $1 of per share earnings: i.e., the price of the stock divided by estimated or latest 12 months per share earnings.

EARNINGS: In general, are per share as reported by company. **FOR YEAR INDICATED:** Fiscal years ending prior to March 31 are shown under preceding year. Net operating earnings are shown for **banks**; net earnings before appropriation to general reserve for **savings & loan associations**; net investment income for **insurance companies**; **railroads**' earnings are reported to ICC. **Foreign** issues traded **ADR** are dollars per share, converted at prevailing exchange rate. Specific footnotes used:

△Excl extra-ord income   j–Currency at origin
▲Incl extra-ord income   ‑Partial Year
□Excl extra-ord charges   ↑New Year Earns
■Incl extra-ord charges   p–Preliminary
● Excl tax credits   b–Before depletion
        d–Deficit   p̂–Pro forma
        E–S&P Estimate   p̂–Fully diluted
                n/r–Not reported

LAST 12 Mos. indicates earnings through period indicated by superior number preceding figure, for Jan. for Feb. etc. Figure without superior number indicates fiscal year end.

DILUTION: Earnings on a fully diluted basis, as reported in accordance with Accounting Principles Board opinions.

Figure 17.2   Sample Page: Standard & Poor's Bond Guide

Convertible Preferred Stock

Convertible preferred stock is similar to convertible bonds in that it is a combination of a preferred stock issue and common stock. Beyond the conversion privileges, these issues typically have the following characteristics:

1. they are cumulative but not participating (i.e., the dividend cumulates if it is not paid, but the holders do not participate in earnings beyond the dividend),

2. they have no sinking fund or purchase fund,

3. they have a fixed conversion rate,

4. there is generally no waiting period before conversion can take place, and

5. the conversion privilege does not expire.[6]

As pointed out by Pinches, most convertible preferred stock was issued in connection with mergers as a way of providing income and yet not diluting the common equity of the acquiring firm.

Although preferred stock and convertible preferred stock have not been a major source of new financing, there are a number of convertible preferred issues outstanding for the interested investor.

Analysis of Convertible Preferred Stock

Because convertible preferred stock is likewise a hybrid security involving preferred stock and common stock, the valuation analysis, like that of a convertible bond, involves two steps. As an example, consider the FMC Corporation convertible preferred stock issue. This particular cumulative preferred stock issue pays an annual dividend of $2.25 a share. The stock is rated BBB, is listed on the NYSE, and is convertible into 1.25 shares of common stock. As of early 1981, the common stock was selling for $32 a share and the $2.25 convertible preferred stock was $40.50 a share.

In terms of a pure preferred stock issue, it would appear to have a fair amount of downside risk. At this time, most straight preferred stock issues were yielding between 12 and 14 percent compared to the yield on the FMC stock of 5.6 percent. Even using the conservative 12 percent would indicate a straight preferred stock price of $18.75 ($2.25/.12). This represents about a 54 percent decline from the prevailing market price of $40.50. Obviously, the stock is selling on the basis of its conversion value which is $40 (1.25 × $32).

As for the convertible preferred stock, you can derive a conversion parity value for the stock by dividing the current market price of the preferred stock by the conversion ratio. In this case, the conversion parity is $32.40 ($40.50/1.25).

---

[6]George E. Pinches, "Financing With Convertible Preferred Stock, 1960–1967," *Journal of Finance* 25 (1970): 61.

This indicates a very small difference from the prevailing common stock price of $32. Put another way, the convertible preferred stock is priced almost exactly in terms of its conversion value, which means the convertible preferred stock price will move almost exactly in line with the common stock price.

Given this price relationship, you should examine the income relationship between the common and preferred stock. The common stock was paying an annual dividend of $1.60 a share which indicates a dividend yield of 5 percent (1.60/32.00). In contrast, the preferred stock pays an annual dividend of $2.25 which indicates a 5.6 percent yield.

This would indicate that the convertible preferred stock has almost the same downside risk and upside potential as the common stock because it is selling for almost exactly its conversion value which is substantially above its pure preferred stock value. The only difference is that the current yield on the convertible preferred stock is a little higher than the yield on the common stock.

Summary

The purpose of this chapter was to consider two sets of investments not considered previously. Warrants were described and the several major similarities and differences between warrants and call options were discussed. We also considered the factors that influenced the valuation of these instruments.

Two types of hybrid securities were also considered: convertible bonds and convertible preferred stock. Following a discussion of the advantages of these securities to the issuing corporation and the investor, we set forth the valuation analysis procedure which involves evaluating both components of these securities: the value of the security as a straight bond or preferred stock and its conversion value, i.e., its common stock value.

Note that all of these investment instruments provide *additional* opportunities for you *after* you have already evaluated a firm and decided to invest in it. Following such a decision, the question becomes *how* should I invest in this firm? Clearly, if warrants or convertible securities are available, they should be considered.

Questions

1. What are two major differences between a warrant and a call option?

2. What advantage does a warrant have over a listed call option from the standpoint of a corporation?

3. What advantage does a warrant have compared to a listed call option for an investor?

4. Define the intrinsic value of a warrant. Give an example of a warrant with positive intrinsic value.

5. Discuss briefly three factors that influence the speculative value of a warrant (i.e., the premium over intrinsic value).

6. As an investor, would you want a high or low stock price/warrant price ratio? Explain why.

7. The Raymond Corporation has a warrant outstanding that allows the holder to acquire two shares of common stock at $15.00 a share for the next three years. The stock is currently selling for $12.00 and the warrant is selling for $2.00.

   a. Compute the intrinsic value of the warrant. What difference does it make that the warrant is for two shares?

   b. Compute the speculative value (premium) of this warrant.

   c. Would you expect the premium to be greater if the stock was selling for $14.00? Why?

8. The Carson City Corporation (3C) has a warrant that allows the holder to acquire a share of stock for $30.00 until 1990. The stock is currently selling for $32.00 and the warrant is selling for $2.00.

   a. Compute the intrinsic value and the speculative value of this warrant.

   b. What is the leverage factor for this warrant?

   c. Assume the stock increases to $40.00 a share, what will be the percentage of change in stock price and in warrant price assuming the same premium on the warrant?

   d. Discuss how the answer in part c relates to your answer to part b.

9. Find a warrant listed on the American Stock Exchange (there will be a "wt" after the name).

   a. From one of several sources determine its exercise terms (price and expiration).

   b. Determine the warrant's intrinsic value and speculative value.

   c. What are its leverage characteristics?

10. Describe how a firm "forces conversion" of a convertible bond. What conditions must exist?

11. The Baron Corporation debentures are rated Aa by Moody's and are selling to yield 8.75 percent. Their subordinated convertible bonds are rated A by Moody's and are selling to yield 8.40 percent. Explain why this is so.

12. Describe the upside potential of convertible bonds. Why do convertible bonds also provide downside protection?

13. Assume a convertible bond's conversion value is substantially above par. Why would the bondholder continue holding the bond rather than converting?

14. The University Football Corporation (UFC) has outstanding a 6 percent subordinated convertible debenture, due in 10 years. The current yield to maturity on this bond, which is rated A, is 5 percent. The current yield on other A-rated bonds is 10 percent. This bond is convertible into 21 shares of common stock and callable at 106 of par, which is $1,000. The company's $10 par-value common stock is currently selling for $54.

   a. What is the straight-debt value of the convertible bond assuming semiannual interest payments?

b. What is the conversion value of this bond?

c. At present, what would you expect the approximate price of the bond to be? Why?

d. At the present time, could UFC get rid of this convertible debenture? Discuss *specifically* how they would do it.

References

Warrants

Ayres, Herbert F. "Risk Aversion in the Warrant Market." *Industrial Management Review* 5 (1963).

Hilliard, Jimmy E., and Leitch, Robert N. "Analysis of the Warrant Hedge in a Stable Paretian Market." *Journal of Financial and Quantitative Analysis* 12 (1977).

Kassouf, S. T. "Warrant Price Behavior: 1945–1964." *Financial Analysts Journal* 24 (1968).

Kim, Moon K., and Young, Allan. "Rewards and Risks from Warrant Hedging." *Journal of Portfolio Management* 6 (1980).

Legbo, Dick A., and Rogalski, Richard J. "Warrant Price Movements and the Efficient Market Hypothesis," *Journal of Finance* 30 (1975).

Miller, J. D. "Longevity of Stock Purchase Warrants." *Financial Analysts Journal* 27 (1971).

Pease, Fred. "The Warrant—Its Powers and Its Hazards." *Financial Analysts Journal* 19 (1963).

Rogalski, Richard J. "Trading in Warrants by Mechanical Systems." *Journal of Finance* 32 (1977).

Samuelson, Paul. "Rational Theory of Warrant Pricing." *Industrial Management Review* 6 (1965).

Shelton, John P. "The Relation of the Price of a Warrant to the Price of Its Associated Stock." *Financial Analysts Journal* 23 (1967) 2 parts.

Sprenkel, Case M. "Warrant Prices as Indicators of Expectations and Preferences." *Yale Economic Essays* 1 (1961).

Turov, Daniel. "Dividend Paying Stocks and Their Warrants." *Financial Analysts Journal* 29 (1973).

Turov, Daniel. "Warrants and Options." In *Financial Analysts Handbook,* vol. 1. Homewood, IL: Richard D. Irwin, 1975.

Van Horne, James C. "Warrant Valuation in Relation to Volatility and Opportunity Cost." *Industrial Management Review* 10 (1969).

Yesting, Kenneth L. "CD Warrants." *Financial Analysts Journal* 26 (1970).

Convertible Securities

Alexander, Gordon J., and Hover, Roger D. "Pricing in the New Issue Convertible Debt Market." *Financial Management* 6 (1977).

Brennan, M. J., and Schwartz, E. S. "Convertible Bonds: Valuation and Optimal Strategies for Call and Conversion." *Journal of Finance* 32 (1977).

Baumol, William J.; Malkiel, Burton G.; and Quandt, R. E. "The Valuation of Convertible Securities." *Quarterly Journal of Economics* 80 (1966).

Brigham, Eugene F. "An Analysis of Convertible Debentures: Theory and Some Empirical Evidence." *Journal of Finance* 21 (1966).

Frank, Werner G., and Kroncke, Charles D. "Classifying Conversions on Convertible Debentures Over Four Years." *Financial Management* 3 (1974).

Frank, Werner G., and Weygandt, Jerry J. "Convertible Debt and Earnings Per Share: Pragmatism vs. Good Theory." *Accounting Review* 45 (1970).

Frank, Werner G., and Weygandt, Jerry J. "A Prediction Model for Convertible Debentures." *Journal of Accounting Research* 9 (1971).

Frankle, A. W., and Hawkins, C. A. "Beta Coefficients for Convertible Bonds." *Journal of Finance* 30 (1975).

Ingersoll, Jonathon E., Jr. "A Contingent-Claims Valuation of Convertible Securities." *Journal of Financial Economics* 4 (1977).

Jennings, Edward H. "An Estimate of Convertible Bond Premiums." *Journal of Financial and Quantitative Analysis* 9 (1974).

Lewellen, Wilbur G., and Racette, George A. "Convertible Debt Financing," *Journal of Financial and Quantitative Analysis* 8 (1973).

Meyer, Anthony, H. "Designing a Convertible Preferred Issue." *Financial Executive* 36 (1968).

Noodings, Thomas C. *The Dow-Jones Irwin Guide to Convertible Securities.* Homewood, IL: Richard D. Irwin, 1973.

Pinches, George E. "Financing with Convertible Preferred Stock, 1960–1967." *Journal of Finance* 25 (1970).

Poensgen, Otto H. "The Valuation of Convertible Bonds." *Industrial Management Review* 7 (1965); and 7 (1966).

Soldofsky, Robert M. "Yield-Risk Performance of Convertible Securities." *Financial Analysts Journal* 27 (1971).

Soldofsky, Robert M. "The Risk-Return Performance of Convertibles," *Journal of Portfolio Management* 7 (1981).

Vinson, Charles E. "Rates of Return on Convertibles: Recent Investor Experience." *Financial Analysts Journal* 26 (1970).

Walter, James E., and Que, Augustin V. "The Valuation of Convertible Bonds," *Journal of Finance* 28 (1973).

Weberman, Ben. "The Case for Convertibles." *Forbes,* 16 April 1979.

COMMODITIES AND
FINANCIAL FUTURES

≫ 18 ≪

When most individuals consider the subject of investments, they think in terms of securities investments—basically stocks and bonds. While these investment instruments typically constitute the bulk of most investment portfolios, the discussion in Chapter 2 pointed out the importance of considering a wide variety of investment alternatives because diversification is important to your overall investment objectives and a knowledge of diverse investments may point toward new opportunities for you. Commodities trading and financial futures meet both of these criteria. As shown in Chapter 2, the correlation between commodity prices and stock and bond prices is quite low, so you could envision commodity trading as a means to further diversify your overall investment portfolio. At the same time, the subsequent discussion will indicate that commodities trading provides a wide range of investment opportunities, from relatively conservative hedging transactions carried out by farmers or food processors to fairly high-risk speculative transactions from which the short-run returns can be very large positive or negative values. Financial futures, while similar to commodity futures contracts, involve financial instruments.

Because of the inherent belief that futures trading is very unique and somewhat specialized, it is considered important to begin the chapter with a discussion of the similarities and differences between trading in common stocks and trading in futures. In the process, you should become familiar with some of the details of futures trading. Following a discussion of commodity quotations, we will discuss specific commodity trading techniques in detail including various hedging techniques and examples of various speculative trading transactions. We will have a similar presentation for financial futures.

Some Basic Concepts of Commodities Trading

Before we discuss specific similarities and differences between stocks and commodities, we should consider some basic concepts related to commodities trading. An important one is that there are two distinct types of contracts in commodities: *cash* contracts and *futures* contracts. A cash contract is for the immediate delivery of a commodity. It is used by food processors or others who need the commodity now to fulfill an order; i.e., a flour producer would purchase wheat in the cash market to fulfill a flour contract. A futures contract is an agreement that involves delivery of a specified amount of a stated commodity at a designated time in the future (if the contract is not liquidated before it reaches maturity). As an example, a July futures contract for wheat requires the delivery of 5,000 bushels of wheat in July.

Almost all of our discussion will be concerned with the purchase and sale of futures contracts. You should be aware that very few futures contracts ever mature in the sense that the delivery is made. In about 97 percent of the cases, the futures contract is "liquidated" by an offsetting transaction; e.g., if you previously *bought* a July wheat contract, you liquidate it (or close it out) by *selling* a July wheat contract.

Most futures contracts are bought and sold as a means of hedging or speculating and there is never any intention of taking delivery. In fact, it is not necessary to take delivery. Once contracts are offset they cancel each other out and that is the end of it. Only if a contract is held to maturity (about 3 percent of investors do this) will the commodity be delivered. Put another way, every futures contract does *not* have a cash crop behind it. Ultimately, the actual cash crop will be sold in the spot market.

An important relationship between cash and futures contracts is the "basis." The basis is the difference between the cash price of a commodity and the futures prices of the same commodity. As an example, if the current cash price for wheat is $2.70 a bushel and the price for July wheat is $2.80 a bushel, the "basis" for July wheat is 10 cents. As we will discuss, the basis is not a constant, and changes in the basis can work to your advantage or disadvantage.

There are other terms and concepts unique to commodities trading that are discussed in the Glossary at the end of this chapter.

Given this background, let us consider some specific similarities and differences between stock and commodity trading.

Similarities in Stock and Commodity Trading Practices

1. For both areas of investment there are highly organized exchanges. This is in contrast to other investment alternatives such as real estate, coins, or stamps, for which the trading markets are highly fragmented on a geographical basis.

2. Trading on a given exchange is limited to specified stocks or commodities. Just as the New York and American Stock Exchanges will only allow trading in "listed" stocks, each of the commodity exchanges limits trading to specified commodities.

3. Only "members" can trade on an exchange (stock or commodity), either for themselves or for others.

4. The mechanics of buying and selling stocks or commodities are quite similar. In both cases, you give an order to your local broker, who then sends it to the floor of the exchange where a member of the exchange executes the order through the stock specialist or in the appropriate commodities pit.

5. With the exception of the OTC segment of the stock market, both markets are basically auction markets. This use of the auction process is in contrast to the functioning of other investment markets in which trading is mainly carried out on a negotiated basis.

6. There is substantial similarity in the types of orders on the exchanges. In both "market" orders, stop orders, and limit orders are frequently used.

7. Because they have highly organized exchanges and communication networks, both areas of investment enjoy substantial liquidity. This ability to turn investments into cash almost instantaneously at a fairly certain price contrasts sharply with the situation for other investments.

8. In both areas some investors base their decisions on the "fundamentals" of supply and demand, and there are "chartists" who are mainly, and almost totally, dependent upon past price movements for indications of future price movements.

Differences in Stock and Commodity Trading Practices

1. One of the major differences is that there is much greater leverage in commodity trading. While the current margin requirement on stocks is 50 percent, the requirements on commodity futures range between 10 and 20 percent. Not only is more leverage available for trading commodities, but it is also universally used, while in stocks leverage is rather limited. In addition, not all common stocks are eligible for margin trading, while it is possible to buy all commodities on margin.

2. There are interest charges on the money borrowed to acquire stocks, but there are no interest charges on the difference between the total value and the margin for a commodity future contract. The reason is that the commodity contract is a *future* contract, and, therefore, no funds are required until the date on which the contract is actually scheduled for delivery. In fact, what is referred to as margin in commodity trading is really a "good faith" deposit to protect the commodity broker.

3. While there is a commission charged for the purchase and another charged for the sale of the stock, commissions on commodities are only paid on a completed contract (purchase and sale). The commissions also tend to be smaller in terms of the total value of the contract.

4. Stock prices are free to fluctuate without limit. In contrast, there is a daily limit on the amount of change in price allowed each commodity, and once a given commodity reaches this limit, trading in it cannot take place beyond the limit price.

5. One of the major problems facing the stock market in recent years has been the stock certificate and the stock transfer procedure. This is not a problem in commodity trading because there are no certificates and transferring is done through the Commodity Clearing Corporation.

6. In the stock market, there is a clearing corporation but there are also dealers on each side of the trade, one buying, one selling. In the commodities market, the clearing corporation actually takes the other side in all transactions, either buying or selling directly. In commodities, the transaction between two brokers or traders takes place in the pit. After the transaction, each party reports to his own clearinghouse which makes sure that the orders match and charges each broker accordingly. Once this is done, the brokers have no connection to each other, but only to the clearing corporation that handles all subsequent closing trades directly and settles with the customer. It is the clearing corporation that eventually records the fact that a sale was offset with a purchase and thereby "closed out."

7. In the stock market, you specifically sell the stock you bought or buy the stock you sold short to complete a transaction. In commodities, you simply engage in an opposite transaction, and the two individual transactions cancel each other out through the clearing corporation.

8. Even though there are organized exchanges in both areas, there are no specialists in commodities. When a trade is desired, a member of the commodity exchange simply goes to the appropriate "pit", makes it known that he has an order, and all interested traders respond.

9. When an investor wants to sell a stock short, it cannot be done on a down tick; he must wait until there is a trade at the previous price or an up tick (an increase). There is no such tick requirement for commodity short selling; you simply sell a contract you did not buy previously.

10. Trading in commodities is simpler than stock trading because there are no dividends to worry about and nothing similar to stock splits. As a result, the price changes reflect all rates of return.

11. About five percent of trading in the NYSE is in odd lots (sales or purchases of less than 100 shares). In contrast, there are typically no odd lot contracts available in commodity trading on the major exchanges. Because of the substantial leverage available, it is typically not necessary. Still, there are "mini" contracts on some smaller exchanges.

12. There are differences in sources of information. While the major source of information about specific firms is the company itself, the principal source of information for major commodities is the U.S. Department of Agriculture. Because of this, there is less of a problem with "inside information" in commodities because the government is scrupulous about any possible leaks.

13. Many of the previously mentioned differences produce a substantially different "typical" holding period for the two investment alternatives. The holding period for commodities seldom exceeds 90 days and, generally, cannot exceed a year because the contracts are deliverable within that period. In contrast, stocks can be held almost indefinitely and the average holding period is probably close to a year.

14. There are differences in the normal unit of trading. In the case of stocks, the normal unit of trading is a round lot which is almost always 100 shares. In contrast, commodities are traded on the basis of "contracts," and what is involved in a contract differs dramatically between commodities. As shown in Figure 18.1, the type of contract is listed at the top of each commodity entry; e.g., a wheat contract on the CBT (Chicago Board of Trade) is for 5,000 bushels, while a contract of fresh eggs on the CME (Chicago Mercantile Exchange) is 22,500 dozen eggs.

15. There are differences in price volatility and even greater differences in the volatility of rates of return. Commodity prices are generally more volatile than stock prices because of the nature of the information affecting the price, which includes the impact of weather and international demand. In addition to basic price volatility, the rates of return actually experienced by an investor in commodities will be more volatile due to the substantial leverage caused by buying on margin (i.e., the investor is only required to put up a small percentage of the value of the contract as a good faith deposit).

Commodity Quotations

Prior to discussing specific commodity trading procedures, it seems appropriate that we should briefly consider the information contained in the commodity quotations section of the newspaper. Figure 18.1 is an example of the "Futures Prices" section appearing daily in the *Wall Street Journal*. This section lists all the major commodities traded on all the principal exchanges (the example does not include the full section). The commodities are divided into the following groups:

1. grains and feeds
2. livestock and meat
3. foods and fiber
4. metals
5. wood
6. financial.

For each commodity, the listing indicates where the commodity is traded (e.g., CBT is the Chicago Board of Trade) and the standard contract for the commodity (e.g., the contract for corn on the CBT is for 5,000 bushels). Finally the heading indicates what the quotes are for, e.g., cents per bushel or cents per pound. In the case of wheat, a quote of 406 means $4.06 per bushel. The left-hand column indicates when the contracts come due and this obviously differs by commodity depending upon the normal growing season; naturally most of them

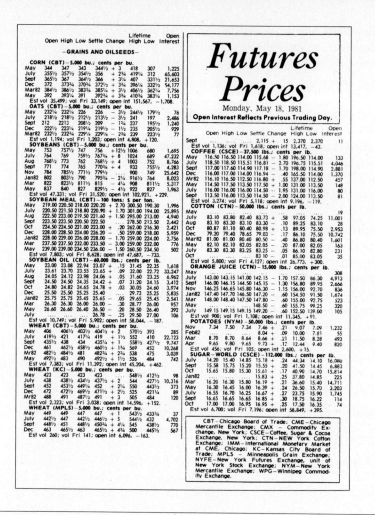

Figure 18.1   Commodity Quotations in The Wall Street Journal

Source: *Wall Street Journal*, May 19, 1981. Reprinted by permission of The Wall Street Journal, © Dow Jones & Company, Inc., 1981. All rights reserved.

are due during the summer months. The subsequent columns indicate the daily movements in the commodity contract: the opening transaction, the high and low transaction for the day, and the final transaction (settle) of the day. The change column indicates the price change from the previous day's settle price. The season's high and low indicates the range of prices for this contract since it began trading. The open interest is the number of contracts that have not been closed out. At the bottom, there is an estimated volume of trading in all contracts for the day, the total open interest for all months of contracts, and the change in this total open interest from the previous day.

Trading Commodity Futures

Individuals involved in commodities trading can be categorized initially into one of two groups: hedgers or speculators. Hedgers enter into a futures contract to offset another risk. This will be dealt with more fully below. In contrast, a speculator is attempting to derive a rate of return on the purchase and sale of the commodity in line with the risk he accepts in the transaction. In this regard, the speculator is like the typical common stock investor who buys stock when he expects a price increase, and sells stock short if he expects a price decline.

Hedging Transactions

As stated, an individual enters into a hedge transaction to reduce the risk of loss from price fluctuations. The standard procedure is to take the position opposite to the one that you are already in; i.e., you become long and short in the commodity at the same time. Long means you currently own the commodity; short means you do not own it; i.e., to sell short means you sell something you do not own. There are two standard examples: the farmer hedging his crop and a processor of commodities who wants to hedge an order for future delivery.

Consider the example of a farmer who is growing corn. As of June he expects that he will harvest about 20,000 bushels in August. In June, the September futures for corn are selling for 294 ($2.94 a bushel). If the farmer feels that $2.94 is a reasonable price and does not want to gamble on possibly higher *or* lower prices at the time of harvest, he can *sell* futures contracts to hedge his current long position; i.e., the farmer is basically long in the crop that he owns and is going to harvest. Therefore, by selling a futures contract in that commodity he has offset his own long position. For our example, assume that he only wants to hedge part of his position, so he sells two September corn contracts for 10,000 bushels (half his expected crop). Let us now consider what happens if the price of corn goes up or down between June and August when he harvests the 10,000 bushels of corn. To simplify the example, we will not consider commissions and other transactions costs.

If the price of corn decreases to $2.80 a bushel between June and August, the farmer will *lose* on his harvested crop relative to what he expected to receive (which is what he was concerned about), but will *gain* a comparable amount on the contract he sold short as shown below.

Revenue from cash crop:	10,000 × $2.80 =	$28,000
Sale of 2 contracts at $2.94 =	$29,400	
Purchase of 2 contracts at $2.80 =	$28,000	
Gain on short sale		$ 1,400
Total revenue (before transactions costs)		$29,400

By entering into the hedge the farmer has assured himself of the $2.94 a bushel because what he loses on the cash market he gains in the futures market.

If the price of corn *increases* to $3.05 a bushel between June and August, the opposite occurs. In this instance, the farmer will *gain* on his cash crop relative to what he expected to receive, but will *lose* on his futures contract as shown below.

$$
\begin{aligned}
&\text{Revenue from cash crop:} \quad 10,000 \times \$3.05 = \$30,500 \\
&\text{Sale of 2 contracts at } \$2.94 = \qquad \$29,400 \\
&\text{Purchase of 2 contracts at } \$3.05 = \underline{\$30,500} \\
&\qquad \text{Loss on short sale} \qquad\qquad\qquad \$(1,100) \\
&\text{Total revenue (before transaction costs)} \qquad \$29,400
\end{aligned}
$$

In this instance the farmer has likewise assured himself of $2.94 a bushel and thereby *foregone the added gain* due to the price rise. It is just this sort of possibility that causes some farmers to avoid using the futures market as a means to hedge some or all of their crop. It must be recognized that, when they do not hedge, they are basically speculators in the commodity because, by definition, they are long in the commodity that they are growing.

It should be recognized that it is seldom possible to completely hedge a position because of transactions costs and differential price movements. Specifically, there are going to be commissions on the futures transaction that will add to the loss or detract from the gain. Still, this commission will be small compared to the gain or loss on a large crop. In addition, futures prices may not move completely with the cash price, and this could mean you will not get a complete offset. As an example, consider the first case in which the cash price declined to $2.80 a bushel. If we assume that the September futures contract only declined to $2.82 a bushel, the gain on the short sale would have only been $1,200 so you would not have a complete offset.

A second group that consistently enters into hedging positions is commodity processors who are basically forced to be short some required commodity due to the nature of their business. Consider the example of a flour producer who signs a contract in April with a food processing firm to deliver a certain amount of flour the following July. Because the contract is for July delivery, the price quoted will be based upon the July wheat price. Assume that the flour is going to require the type of wheat sold on the Kansas City Board of Trade (the type of wheat traded on each of the exchanges differs—hard red winter wheat; soft red winter wheat, etc.—and each of these wheats is used to produce a flour that has different uses). At the time the contract is signed, the price for a July Kansas City wheat contract is 440 ($4.40 a bushel). Therefore, the commodity processor will quote a price for the flour that assumes he will buy the wheat required at $4.40 a bushel. If the contract requires 20,000 bushels of wheat, once the contract is signed the processor is basically short 20,000 bushels of Kansas City wheat at $4.40 a bushel; i.e., he has agreed to deliver flour that will require 20,000 bushels of wheat and he does not own the wheat. To hedge his position he would immediately *buy* four July wheat contracts on the Kansas City Exchange. Assume that between April and June (when the processor must buy the wheat in the cash market to fulfill his flour contract) the price of wheat has increased to $4.75 a bushel. The processor's costs will be as shown below:

Cost of 20,000 bushels at $4.75 = $95,000
Cost of 2 contracts at $4.40 = $88,000
Sale of 2 contracts at $4.75 = $95,000
Gain on futures contracts $ 7,000
Net cost of wheat for flour contract $88,000

As shown, although the processor had to pay more for his cash wheat than the contract price, he made a profit on his futures contract. As a result, his *net* cost was $88,000, or $4.40 a bushel, which is consistent with his contract.

In contrast, assume that the price of wheat declined from $4.40 to $4.20, the processor's costs will be as shown below:

Cost of 20,000 bushels at $4.20 = $84,000
Cost of 2 contracts at $4.40 = $88,000
Sale of 2 contracts at $4.20 = $84,000
Loss on futures transaction $ (4,000)
Total cost of wheat for flour contract $88,000

In this instance, the processor did not have to pay as much for the wheat, but lost on his futures transaction so that the total cost was $88,000, or $4.40 a bushel. Again, one might say that he would have been better off in this case if he had not entered into the futures contract because he would have made more on the flour contract. The fact is, this would have required the processor to *speculate* on the future price of wheat. The whole point of the hedge was to *avoid* speculation. The processor wants to make his income from processing the wheat and does *not* want to be required to accept the possible *price* risk related to his basic commodity. The use of the hedge has allowed him to avoid this price risk.

Again, the hedge may not work perfectly due to transaction costs involved in the futures investment and also to the fact that prices in the cash market and futures market may not move perfectly together.

Why Speculate in Commodities?

As mentioned, besides using the futures market to hedge a position, an investor can speculate in commodities futures. The reasons for entering into speculative commodity transactions are similar to the reasons for investing in other investment instruments. Specifically, you want to either reduce the risk involved in your overall portfolio while holding expected return constant, or attempt to increase your return for a given level of risk. There is potential for risk reduction in commodities trading because the prices and returns on commodities are not very highly correlated with those in other securities markets (i.e., stocks and bonds). You will recall from Chapter 2 that the correlation between commodity prices and stock prices was about 0.29. Therefore, although the total variability of commodity returns is rather high, the movements are not related to your other investments so the variance of your *total* portfolio could be reduced.

As the examples will show, there is the potential for large rates of return on your investment in a short period of time with commodities because of the substantial leverage involved. Therefore, for the investor with the time, temperament, and discipline required for commodities investing, the rewards can be substantial. After we have considered several examples of potential commodity trades, we will discuss some common rules that a speculator in commodities should keep in mind.

Speculative Transactions

In the case of speculation, it is necessary to consider what commodities to deal in and what approach you will use in analysis. Regarding what commodities to consider, a quick analysis of the *Wall Street Journal* will indicate that there are about 30 different commodities that can be traded in a wide range of categories (e.g., grains, foods, metals). At the same time, it is clear that few traders ever attempt to trade more than 5 or 6 at a time because of the diverse nature of the markets and the difference in supply and demand analysis factors. Trying to analyze and trade wheat, orange juice, and pork bellies would be like trying to analyze industrials, railroads, and banks at the same time. Therefore, you would normally concentrate on commodities within a given group (e.g., corn and soybeans) or between groups that might be related (e.g., corn and livestock).

After you have selected a limited number of commodities that you want to trade, you must decide how you are going to go about making your trading decisions. Similar to stock investors, commodity investors are basically divided between fundamentalists and technicians. *Fundamentalists* attempt to analyze changes in the supply and demand for the commodity. Factors influencing supply would include the amount of acreage planted, the weather during the growing season in the major areas for the crop in question, and the carry-over of the crop from the previous season. Regarding demand, the analyst would consider the domestic demand for the product based upon secular population growth, and also demand for animal feed. In addition, a growing aspect of demand is that from *foreign* countries. Hence, it is necessary to consider foreign supply and demand for the commodity and its residual impact on our market.

Some investors adhere to *technical analysis;* i.e., that future price movements can be predicted on the basis of past price changes and volume changes, and some investors consider a combination of fundamental and technical analysis. It appears that there is a stronger preference for the technical approach in commodity analysis than there is in stock analysis, although there is a fair amount of empirical support for random changes in commodity prices.[1]

At this point, let us consider some examples, assuming you have made your decision regarding the commodity you are going to trade and your method of analysis.

Long on Soybeans   Assume you have become interested in soybeans and, based upon your analysis, you expect soybean prices to increase over the next six months (from January to July). Therefore, you want to be long in July soybeans and decide to buy two contracts (10,000 bushels). After making your decision, you call your commodities broker and place a market order for two July soybean contracts. Like a common stock transaction, your order is transmitted to the firm's representative on the floor of the Chicago Board of Trade (CBT), and this floor broker proceeds to the soybean pit and calls out that he wants to buy two July contracts. After bargaining with several other brokers or traders, he completes the transaction at 660 ($6.60 a bushel). If we assume that the current margin on soybeans at the CBT is 15 percent, it would be necessary to send the broker $9,900 (.15 × $66,000). Because each contract is for 5,000 bushels, each one-cent change in the price of soybeans is worth $50 per contract, or $100 to you because you control two contracts.

After the purchase, the investor can enter a stop-loss order, as is done with stocks, or simply watch the market closely. One difference between trading stocks and commodities is that limits are placed on the daily price changes of each commodity. These limits ensure that no major price change occurs due to an unexpected catastrophe. The idea is that the limit allows time for new investors or speculators to enter the market.

Assume that in March, the price of July soybeans has gone to $6.85 a bushel which is about where you expected them to go, so you decide to take your profit. You call your broker and tell him to close out your long July soybean position by *selling* two July soybean contracts on the market. Again, the broker contacts his representative on the floor of the CBT who sells two contracts at $6.85 a bushel. Your position is cleared and your return is as shown below:

Bought 2 July Contracts at $6.60 a bushel	$66,000
(you deposited 15 percent: $9,900)	
Sold 2 July Contracts at $6.85 a bushel	$68,500
Gross Profit	$ 2,500
Less estimated "round trip" commission ($30/contract)	$ 60
Net Profit	$ 2,440
Rate of return on amount committed:	
2,440/$9,900 = <u>24.6%</u>	

[1]Holbrook Working, "Prices of Cash Wheat and Futures at Chicago Since 1883," *Wheat Studies* 2 (1934): 75–134; Arnold B. Larson, "Measurement of a Random Process in Futures Prices," in *The Random Character of Stock Market Prices,* ed. Paul Cootner (Cambridge, Mass.: MIT Press, 1964), pp. 219–230.

Note that this 24.6 percent return was generated during a two-month period, which means the annualized return would be approximately six times as large. Also, consider the impact of leverage: you received a 24.6 percent return on your investment when the price of soybeans only increased by 3.8 percent ($6.85 versus $6.60).

Now consider the same investment, but assume that the price of soybeans does not rise but begins to decline during February. As do most commodity traders, assume that after the purchase you automatically put in a stop-loss order at $6.45 a bushel, which means that if soybeans ever hit this price the broker is instructed to put in a market sell order for you. The purpose is to ensure that you cut any losses short; i.e., the maximum loss should be approximately 15 cents a bushel. If the price declines to this level, the broker puts in a market sell, and let us assume that he sells the two contracts for $6.44 a bushel. (He is not able to get the $6.45 at that point.) Under these assumptions your results would be as follows:

Brought 2 July contracts at $6.60 a bushel (you deposited 15 percent: $9,900)	$66,000
Sold 2 July contracts at $6.44 a bushel	$64,400
Gross Loss	$ (1,600)
Less estimated "round trip" commission ($30/contract)	$ 60
Net Loss	$ (1,660)
Rate of return on investment:	
($1,660)/$9,900 = (16.8%)	

In this example you have a return of minus 16.8 percent in approximately one month, which would convert to an annual loss of about 12 times this number. Again, it is possible to see the impact of leverage. You experienced a negative return of 16.8 percent on your investment when soybean prices only declined 2.5 percent ($6.44 versus $6.60).

Short Pork Bellies   In contrast to being optimistic about soybeans, assume that, based upon your fundamental and/or technical analysis, you are pessimistic about the future price of pork bellies (uncured bacon). According to the quotation section, pork bellies are traded on the Chicago Mercantile Exchange (CME), and the standard contract is 38,000 pounds. In November you decide to sell three May pork-belly contracts that are selling for 44.00 (44 cents a pound). This means that each contract is worth $16,720 ($.44 × 38,000). In this instance, a one-cent change in the price of pork bellies changes the value of the contract by $380. To protect yourself if you are wrong, assume you put in a stop-gain order at 48 cents. Such an order means you want to buy three contracts to offset your prior sale if pork bellies reach this price. It is not certain that you will receive 48 cents, but it should be fairly close.

Assume that prices increase, your stop-gain order is enacted, and you sell at 48.5 cents a pound in February. Your return would be as follows:

Sale of 3 May Pork-Belly Contracts at 44¢/lb (you deposited 15 percent: $7,524)	$50,160
Purchase of 3 May Pork-Belly Contracts at 48.5¢/lb.	$55,290
Gross Loss	$ (5,130)
Less estimated "round trip" commission ($30/contract)	$ 90
Total Loss	$ (5,220)

Rate of return on investment: (5,220)/7,524 = (69.4%)

In this instance, pork bellies increased in price by 10.2 percent, and you experienced a negative rate of return of over 69 percent on your investment in three months.

These examples are meant to indicate the opportunities and risks involved in commodities trading as a speculator.

Basic Rules for Commodity Trading

A large brokerage firm devoted to commodities trading has run a series of ads containing rules for commodities trading.[2] The following is a composite list derived from these.

1. Have a basic money management plan that takes into account your financial needs and your risk preferences.

2. Establish your trading plans *before* engaging in any trading, and stick to your plan irrespective of short-run market changes. If you want to change your plan, only do so after reconsideration of all aspects of it and not when under pressure.

3. Your trading plan should be detailed in terms of specifying such factors as entry point, objective of the trade, and exit price. This includes extensive use of stop-loss or stop-gain orders that ensure that you maintain your discipline and do not allow yourself to get caught up in the emotion of the market.

4. In general, your trading plan should be an attempt to cut your losses short and let your profits run because most commodities traders lose on most trades but hope to make the losses up on a few big winners. Therefore, the key is to have a number of *small losses,* but a few *big gains.*

5. Select a broker whose psychology of trading is consistent with yours. In many instances, the best source of recommendation for a broker is another satisfied

[2]Conti Commodity Services, Inc., 1800 Board of Trade Building, Chicago, Illinois, 60604.

customer. In most cases, the main task of your broker is to protect you from yourself and your impulse not to stick to your plan.

6. Keep in constant contact with your broker so that when action is required you will not hesitate.

7. Be sure you begin with enough money to accomplish your plan. If not, you may not be able to stay through temporary setbacks; i.e., a string of small losses may wipe you out before you make a big gain.

Financial Futures

Futures contracts on various commodities have been in existence for many decades as a means of hedging against price changes in these commodities. Another set of futures contracts is relatively new: futures contracts on financial instruments such as government bonds and commercial paper. The basic idea and purpose of these contracts is the same as those for commodity contracts. Specifically, *a financial futures contract promises the delivery of a specified amount of a particular financial instrument at some future time.* As an example, if you buy a September treasury bond contract on the Chicago Board of Trade, this contract specifies that, if you hold it to maturity, you will receive $100,000 face value of 8 percent, 20-year U.S. Treasury bonds (the specific characteristics of the bonds are set forth for all contracts).

The reason for creating such futures contracts is the same as it is for commodities: *the futures contract allows participants in the market to hedge against price risk in the underlying instrument.* We will discuss some specific examples in a later section.

Examples of Financial Futures

Each contract is for a different amount, and the characteristics of the financial instrument are unique, as the following examples of contracts will show:

a. 90-Day U.S. Treasury Bill—this contract is for delivery of $1,000,000 in T-Bills.

b. One-Year U.S. Treasury Bill—$250,000.

c. Four-Year U.S. Treasury Note—this is for $100,000 of a 7% coupon security.

d. Long-Term U.S. Treasury Bond—this contract is for $100,000 of an 8%, 20-year bond.

e. GNMA pass-through certificates—$100,000.

A Brief History

While there have been financial futures contracts in existence since the early 1970s, the real acceptance of the contracts began in 1976 when the International

Monetary Market (IMM), a subsidiary of the Chicago Mercantile Exchange, initiated the 90-Day Treasury Bill contract. The T-bill contract was initiated in January of that year, and was followed by contracts in one-year T-bills in September 1978, and four-year treasury notes in July 1979. As one might expect, because this is a futures market, the Chicago Board of Trade (CBT) initiated a financial futures market with a long-term Treasury bond in August 1977 followed by GNMA Pass Throughs in September 1978 and a 4-6 year Treasury Note in June 1979.

Because of the exceptional growth in trading experienced by these two exchanges, other exchanges have initiated contracts, but the volume on these exchanges has been relatively light. Specifically, the New York Commodity Exchange (COMEX) began trading financial futures in 1979, but the volume is realtively small. In addition, the New York Futures Exchange (NYFE, pronounced "Knife") which is part of the New York Stock Exchange, was started in 1980, but apparently is not enjoying very large volume.[3] While it appears that the Chicago markets are currently the strongest and most active, there are numerous exchanges anxious to enter the field with a variety of financial instruments including a futures contract for a common stock index like the S&P 500.[4]

An Example of Growth

While it is not possible to document the growth in trading of all the contracts, it is informative to consider what has happened to the trading volume for treasury bond contracts on the Chicago Board of Trade since the contract was initiated in August 1977:

1977	32,101
1978	555,350
1979	33,870,680
1980	45,281,571

Number of Treasury Bond Contracts Traded on the Chicago Board of Trade
Source: Chicago Board of Trade

As of 1981, this particular contract (long-term treasury bonds) was the most active financial futures instrument.

---

[3]See Roger Lowenstein, "Commodities Trader Pushes a New Market for Financial Futures," *Wall Street Journal,* 29 December 1980, p. 1; "NYFE Seat Prices Hit Low Amid Uncertainty," *Wall Street Journal,* 30 March 1981, p. 28; "The Big Board Lays an Egg," *Dun's Review,* June 1981, p. 95.

[4]"An Explosion of Options and Futures," *Business Week,* 23 March 1981, p. 88.

Why the Growth?

Clearly the growth in trading of financial futures has been dramatic. An obvious question is why have financial futures become so popular? The explanation is based on the reason for the establishment of the contracts, i.e., the need to hedge the price risk of the underlying financial instruments. As noted earlier, the economic rationale for financial futures contracts is the same as the rationale for commodity futures contracts. Everyone is aware of the substantial price volatility of commodities such as wheat, corn, and soybeans. Given this price volatility, futures contracts allow processors and others to hedge their position. In the case of financial futures, the need for hedging has arisen due to *the increasing volatility of interest rates that has caused an increase in the price volatility of the financial instruments.* Because of greater interest rate volatility, several groups involved in the bond market need to protect themselves by hedging their current or future bond positions, as will be illustrated later. A demonstration of the volatility of interest rates is contained in the tables below that show the average T-bill rates for various years and the average rates during 1980:

1971	4.33	1976	4.98
1972	4.07	1977	5.27
1973	7.03	1978	7.19
1974	7.84	1979	10.07
1975	5.80	1980	11.43

Average Rate on Treasury Bills
Source: *Federal Reserve Bulletin,* various issues.

One can imagine what happened to bond prices during a period like 1972–1973, when rates increased by almost 75 percent, or during the period 1977–1980, when rates more than doubled.

An even more dramatic change occurred during 1980 as shown below:

1/80	12.00	5/80	8.58	9/80	10.77
2/80	12.86	6/80	7.07	10/80	11.62
3/80	15.20	7/80	8.06	11/80	13.73
4/80	13.20	8/80	9.13	12/80	15.49

Monthly Average of Rates on 90-Day T-Bills (1980)
Source: *Federal Reserve Bulletin,* various issues.

In this case, rates declined by 50 percent from March to June and then proceeded to more than double by December. While this is clearly an extreme example, it demonstrates that the bond market has become much more volatile, which in turn has prompted a large number of participants to consider the use of financial futures as a way to protect themselves against substantial price movements.

At the same time, such interest rate volatility is very appealing to speculators who are anxious to take the other side of the transaction and perceive the opportunity for substantial profits.[5]

Reading a Quote

The following is an example of a quote that would be contained in the *Wall Street Journal* for one of the financial futures.

						Yield		
	Open	High	Low	Settle	Change	Settle	Change	Open Interest
June	66−15	66−27	65−26	66−16	+14	12.631	−.085	49,636

Treasury Bonds (CBT) − $100,000; 32nd of 100%, 8%−20-year bond

As noted, treasury-bond contracts are traded on the CBT and are for $100,000 of 8 percent, 20-year bonds. The quotes are in 32nds which means that a quote of 66−15 is 66 and 15 thirty-seconds, or 66.46875. In this case, the settling price (the consensus of closing trades) is 66−16 which means that a bond with a par value of $100,000, an 8 percent coupon, and 20 years to maturity would sell for $66,500 for delivery in June. This price implies a yield to maturity of 12.631 on this bond. As shown, this settling price was 14/32 above the settling price the day before. In turn, this increase in price implied a decline in yield of .085 (i.e., the settling yield the day before was 12.716). The open interest indicates that there are 49,636 contracts for this particular period that have been bought or sold and remain outstanding for delivery. Similar to commodity futures, almost all of these will be offset before the expiration of the contracts.

The Clearing Corporation

All transactions are "cleared" through the clearing corporation which ensures that all payments are made on a daily basis for current transactions and for all outstanding (open) contracts. It is notable that following a trade between two parties, both of them settle with the clearing corporation; the clearing corporation is the opposite side in all trades. This ensures the integrity of all trades, i.e., ensures that either side can always offset the initial trade and receive his money.

Given this background, the following subsections deal with various trades in

[5]The impact is discussed in Sue Shellenbarger, "Boom in Financial Futures Trading Transforms Commodities Markets," *Wall Street Journal*, 23 March 1981, p. 23.

terms of who carries them out and gives examples of three types of trades: (1) short hedges, (2) long hedges, and (3) speculation.

Short Hedge

A short hedge involves the sale of a financial futures contract to hedge a current position in that financial instrument. The following examples of how various participants can use a short hedge will help you understand what is involved.

a. *A bond dealer* with an inventory of bonds can use a short hedge to avoid price risk in a volatile interest-rate market by selling interest-rate futures contracts against his inventory.

b. *An investment banker* can sell interest-rate futures contracts against a recent bond issue that is not completely sold out. A prime example of this was an IBM bond issued in October 1979 that suffered a major price decline shortly after the offering because of a change in Federal Reserve policy. Fortunately, investment bankers had sold futures contracts against part of the unsold offering, so the loss on the unsold issue was partially offset by a gain on the futures contracts.

c. *A bond portfolio manager* can sell futures contracts against a unique holding in the portfolio that is expected to decline. In this case, rather than sell the issue and then have to buy it back later, he would sell futures contracts against the issue and offset the expected loss by a gain on the futures sale.

d. *A bond portfolio manager* can enter into a short hedge as protection against a price decline when attempting to liquidate an illiquid issue. If he decides to sell off a large position, but knows that because the market for this bond is thin, it will take two weeks to sell it out. To protect himself against a price decline during this period, he could sell futures contracts against the position.

e. *A financial manager* for a corporation who is anticipating a bond financing could use financial futures to hedge against higher rates before the actual financing.

The following is an example of a fairly typical short-hedge transaction:

Intent: *Sell* futures contracts short against a cash position.

Cash	Futures	Basis
		(cash-future)
Nov. 1: You *own* $1 million of 15 yr., 8³/₈% U.S. Bonds @ 82−17 (Yld 10.45%) (Value: $825,312.50)	*Sell* 10 March Bond Futures Contracts at 80−09	+2-8
Mar. 3: You sell the 8³/₈% bonds at 70−26 (Yld 12.31%) (Value: $708,125)	Buy 10 March bond futures contracts at 66-29	+3-29
Loss: 11-23 per bond → $117,187.50	*Gain:* 13-12 per contract → $133,750	

Overall gain on hedge of $16,562.50 because basis moved in your direction.

Example of a Short Hedge

Long Hedge

A long hedge involves the purchase of financial futures contracts to offset adverse price movements related to the future purchase of the actual bonds (i.e., a future cash position). Long hedges are not as widespread as short hedges. The most obvious instance in which a long hedge would be useful would involve a portfolio manager who is expecting to receive some future cash flow that will be available to buy bonds. Given this expectation, if the portfolio manager feels that yields might decline between now and the time when the cash flows will arrive, it is possible to "lock-in" the higher yield through a long hedge, i.e., buy futures contracts on the bonds.

The following example of a long hedge shows how this would work:

Intent: *Buy* futures contracts against a future cash position

	Cash	Futures	Basis
			(cash-future)
June 1:	A 20-year treas. bond is currently yielding 12.45%. Price for 20-yr., 8¼% bond is 67-28 (current cost is $678,750)	*Buy* 10 Dec. bond futures contracts at 66-13	+1-15
Dec. 3:	Buy $1 million of 20-yr., 8¼% U.S. bonds at 83-23 (Yield: 10.03%) (Cost of $837,187.50)	Sell 10 Dec. Bond futures contracts at 81-22	+2-1
	Loss: $837,187.50 678,750.00 $\overline{$158,437.50}$	Gain: $81,687.50 66,406.25 $\overline{$15,281.25}$/contract $152,812.50 Total	

Overall loss on hedge of $5,625 because basis moved against you.

Example of a Long Hedge

Speculative Transactions

Investors can engage in speculative financial futures transactions when they anticipate a rise or decline in interest rates and want to buy or sell bonds to profit from this change. The use of futures contracts allows you to speculate on this expectation with a small capital outlay and derive all the benefits and/or risks of substantial leverage.

The following examples will demonstrate the large profit potential available because of the leverage; i.e., you control a large amount of bonds with a relatively small margin. As a result, a small change in price results in a large percentage gain *or* loss on your capital investment. Never forget—when there is a potential for a large gain there is *also* the potential for a large loss.

The final example is for a speculator who expects an increase in interest rates. This situation is somewhat unique because typically, if you are in such a

Outlook: You expect a decline in interest rates over the next three months.

April 1:   You *buy* a 90-day T-bill futures contract at 87 (13% discount). Your initial margin on this contract is $1,500. The contract unit is $1,000,000; a one-basis-point change on this contract is worth $25.

July 10:   You were *correct* and rates declined from 13% to 11%. You can *sell* your contract at 89 (11% discount). The 200-basis-point change is worth $5,000 (200 × $25). You have made $5,000 on an investment of $1,500.

Note: If you were wrong, and the rates had increased to 15%, you would have sold the contract for 85 and *lost* $5,000 on a $1,500 investment.

Example of a Speculative Trade

position, you do not have any way to make money on the expectation of a price decline. About all you can do is either avoid buying bonds or sell those you currently own. As shown, with futures contracts you can make money on the price decline.

Outlook: You expect an *increase* in interest rates over the next three months.

Sept. 1:   You *sell* a long-term treasury bond future at 89-00. Your initial margin on this contract is $2,000. The contract unit is $100,000; a one-basis-point change in this contract is worth $31.25.

Oct. 15:   You were correct and rates increase. As a result, the futures price declines to 86-00. You buy back the contract at 86-00. This offsets the original sale. The three-point change is equal to 96 32nds (3 × 32). The total gain is: 96 × 31.25 = $3,000.

This $3,000 gain is on an investment of $2,000.

Example of a Speculative Trade

Summary

This chapter has been concerned with trading in commodities and financial futures which is considered by many observers to be very different from trading stocks and bonds. In contrast, the initial section of this chapter was intended to point out the areas in which commodities and stock trading are very similar. Subsequently, we considered the several areas in which stocks and commodities differ and, in the process, discussed many characteristics of commodities trading.

The subsequent discussion set forth examples of commodity trading by the two major segments of the market: hedgers and speculators. It was noted that hedgers enter into commodity transactions to avoid risk, while speculators are willing to accept the risk to derive potentially large returns. The examples of alternative trades by speculators indicated the large potential gains *or* losses possible due to rapid price changes *and* the substantial leverage available in commodities trading.

The final section of the chapter was concerned with a new, fast-growing segment of the securities market: financial futures. We initially defined a financial futures contract and briefly described rapid growth of this market since it began in 1976. We considered the reason for this growth (i.e., an increase in interest rate volatility caused bond price variability). The final subsections considered alternative types of transactions (short hedges, long hedges, and speculation) used in financial futures trading and provided examples of each.

Questions

1. Discuss two areas in which trading commodities and trading common stocks are similar.

2. Discuss two differences in trading commodities and trading common stocks.

3. Discuss one advantage that commodities have over stocks; an advantage that stocks have over commodities.

4. Based upon prices listed in *The Wall Street Journal,* compute the value of a contract in soybeans for delivery in about six months (or a length of time close to this). Assuming a 15 percent margin, compute what you must deposit with your broker.

5. Given conditions in Question 4, compute your return if you buy the contract and prices increase by 10 percent. What is your return if prices decline by 10 percent?

6. Assume a margin of 10 percent and that you sell the soybean contract. What is your return if prices decline by 15 percent? What is your return if they rise by 8 percent?

7. What is the purpose of a stop-gain order? Give an example for a current three-month soybean meal contract.

8. You are a Kansas wheat farmer and in June decide to hedge 15,000 bushels of your August harvest. Using the September Kansas City contract shown in Figure 18.1, show what would happen if you did it and prices increased by 15 cents a bushel.

9. In January, July wheat on the Kansas City Board of Trade (KC) is selling for 484 ($4.84 a bushel). You are bullish on wheat and buy three contracts (15,000 bushels).

    a. Assuming a 15 percent margin, how much must you deposit with your broker?

b. In April, the price of wheat is 496. Assuming the commission is $30/contract, compute your annualized rate of return if you close out this contract. Discuss the impact of leverage on this trade.

c. Assume that in March the price of wheat is 475 and you feel you should close out your trade. Assuming a commission of $30/contract, compute the annualized rate of return on your investment. Discuss the impact of leverage.

10. In February you read reports about the number of cattle that will be coming to market over the next nine months and feel that cattle prices will probably decline from current levels. Therefore, you decide to sell two August live cattle contracts (40,000 lbs per contract) on the Chicago Mercantile Exchange (CME). Currently, the price of August live cattle is 71.00 (71 cents a pound). Given a margin of 15 percent on live cattle and a commission of $30 a contract:

a. Assume you put in a stop-gain order at 76 cents a pound and you get closed out at that price in June. Compute the rate of return on your investment for this trade. What is your annualized rate of return?

b. Assume cattle prices decline to 65 cents a pound in July and you decide to close out your position. Compute the annualized rate of return on your investment.

c. Compute your annualized rate of return for the conditions in part b if the margin were 10 percent rather than 15 percent. Discuss the difference in leverage effect between b and c.

11. You have been reading about the diversification benefits of gold as well as the returns enjoyed by some "gold bugs." In June, you decide to take the plunge and buy a March contract in gold (100 troy ounces) on the International Monetary Market (IMM) at the CME. March gold on the IMM is 665 ($665 an ounce), the margin on gold is 10 percent, and the commission is $30 a contract:

a. In September there is an outbreak in the Middle East and the price of March gold goes to 725. Compute the rate of return on your investment.

b. When you bought the gold contract in June you put in a stop-loss order at 655. In November, over the weekend, there are several very optimistic announcements by the government regarding the inflation outlook, interest rates, and peace in the Middle East. Gold closes down the limit for five days and the price goes right through your limit order to 640 before your broker can sell your contract. Compute the rate of return on your investment. Discuss the leverage involved.

References

Cootner, Paul H. "Common Elements in Futures Markets for Commodities and Bonds." *American Economic Review* 51 (1961).

Gold, Gerald. *Modern Commodity Futures Trading.* New York: Commodity Research Bureau, 1959.

Gould, Bruce G. *Dow-Jones Irwin Guide to Commodities Trading.* Homewood, IL: Dow-Jones Irwin, 1973.

Harlow, Charles V., and Teweles, Richard J. "Commodities and Securities Compared." *Financial Analysts Journal* 28 (1972).

Hieronymous, Thomas A. *Economics of Futures Trading.* New York: Commodity Research Bureau, 1971.

Labys, W. C., and Granger, C. W. J. *Speculation, Hedging and Commodity Price Forecasts.* Lexington, MA: Heath, Lexington Books, 1970.

Peck, Anne E. *Selected Writings on Futures Markets.* Vol. 1 and 2. Chicago: Chicago Board of Trade, 1977.

Schwarz, Edward W. *How to Use Interest Rate Futures Contracts.* Homewood, IL: Dow-Jones Irwin, 1979

Teweles, Richard J.; Harlow, Charles V.; and Stone, Herbert L. *The Commodity Futures Trading Guide.* New York: McGraw-Hill 1969.

Teweles, Richard J.; Harlow, Charles V.; and Stone, Herbert L. *The Commodity Futures Game—Who Wins, Who Loses? Why?* New York: McGraw-Hill, 1974.

Commodity and Financial Futures Glossary

Basis The spread or difference between the spot or "cash" price and the price of the future.

Buy In To cover or liquidate a sale.

Carrying Charges Those charges incurred in carrying the actual commodity, generally including interest, insurance, and storage.

Close The period at the end of the trading session during which all trades are officially declared as having been executed "at or on the close." The closing range is the range of actual sales during this period.

Cover The buying of a commodity or a financial instrument to offset sales previously made.

Current Delivery Delivery during the current month.

Day Orders Those limited orders that are to be executed on a specific day and are automatically cancelled at the close of that day.

Delivery Month The calendar month during which a futures contract matures.

Delivery Points Those locations designated by futures exchanges at which the commodity covered by a futures contract may be delivered in fulfillment of the contract.

Discount Commodity or bond prices that are below the future, deliveries at a lesser price than others (e.g., May price is below the July price), or a lesser price owing to quality differences.

Hedging Hedging is the sale of a futures contract against the physical commodity, an existing bond position, or its equivalent as protection against a price decline. Alternatively, it is the purchase of a futures contract against anticipated prices of the physical commodity or bond as protection against a price advance.

Life of Delivery (or Contract) The period between the beginning of trading in a particular futures contract and the expiration of that contract.

Liquidation Sale of a previously bought contract, otherwise known as long liquidation. It may also be the repurchase of a previously sold contract, generally referred to as short covering.

Margin The amount deposited by a client with his broker to protect the broker against losses on contracts being carried, or to be carried by the broker. A margin call is a request to deposit either the original margin at the time of the transaction, or to restore the margin to the "maintenance" levels required for the duration of the time the contract is held.

Opening Range/Closing Range In open auction with many buyers and sellers, commodities are often traded at several prices at the opening or close of the market. Buying or selling orders might be filled at any point within such a price range.

Open Interest The total of unfilled or unsatisfied contracts on either side of the market. In any delivery month, the short interest equals the long interest; in other words, the total number of contracts sold equals the total number bought.

Pit The designated location on the trading floor where futures trading in a specific commodity takes place.

Scalper A speculator operating on the trading floor who provides market liquidity by buying and selling rapidly, with small profits or losses, and who holds his position for a short time.

Settlement Price The daily price at which the clearing house clears all the day's trades in a given commodity; also the price established by the exchange to settle contracts unliquidated because of acts of God, such as floods or other causes.

Speculator One who attempts to anticipate price changes and, through market activities, profit from these changes.

Spot Commodity Goods available for immediate delivery.

Trading Limit The maximimum price change permitted for a single session. These limits vary in the different markets. After prices have advanced or declined to the permissible daily limits, trading automatically ceases unless, of course, offers appear at the permissible upper trading limit or bids appear at the permissible lower limit.

Volume of Trading The purchases or sales of a commodity future during a specified period.

INVESTMENT
COMPANIES

❧ 19 ❧

Throughout the book we have emphasized the importance of diversification. We have also discussed in detail the procedure for analyzing the aggregate market, alternative industries, and specific stocks in a search for above-average risk-adjusted rates of return. At the same time, it has been noted that it is difficult and requires a great deal of time to derive above-average returns in a world with relatively efficient capital markets. A very appealing alternative for many investors who do not have the time or inclination to do fundamental analysis is to acquire an interest in one or several investment companies that invest in the types of stocks or bonds that appeal to them. These investment companies provide *instant diversification* in a given investment area, and there are numerous different types of investment companies available. As a result, they offer a wide variety of well-diversified options in terms of risk and returns. Therefore, you should be aware of what investment companies are, how they operate, what types of investment companies there are, how they have performed in the past, and where to get information on them.

We will begin by defining investment companies in general, discussing their basic management organization, and describing the major types of companies. These different types, ranging from very conservative money market funds or bond funds to very aggressive common stock funds, are the subject of the second section. In the third section, we will discuss some studies that have examined the historical performance of mutual funds. The final section deals with sources of information on investment companies and lists some suggestions on how to go about selecting a portfolio of investment companies.

Investment Company Defined

An investment company is a pool of funds belonging to many individuals that is used to acquire a collection of individual investments such as stocks, bonds, and other publicly traded securities. As an example, 10 million shares of an investment company might be sold to the public at $10 a share, for a total of 100 million dollars. Assuming that this is a common-stock fund, the managers of the company might then invest the funds in the stock of companies like American Telephone and Telegraph, General Motors, IBM, Xerox, and General Electric. As a result, each of the individuals that bought shares of the investment company would own a percentage of the total portfolio of the investment company. In other words, they would have acquired shares of a diversified portfolio of securities. The value of the investor's shares depends upon what happens to the portfolio of assets acquired by the managers of the fund. If we assume no transactions are made, and the total market value of all the stocks in the portfolio increased to 105 million dollars, then the per share value of each of the original shares would be $10.50 ($105 million ÷ 10 million shares). This figure is referred to as the *net asset value* (NAV) and is equal to the total market value of all the assets of the fund divided by the number of shares of the fund outstanding.

Management of Investment Companies

The investment company is typically a corporation whose major assets are the portfolio of marketable securities. The *management* of the portfolio and most of the other administrative duties related to the company and its portfolio of securities are handled by a *separate* management company hired by the board of directors of the investment company. While this is the legal description, the actual management usually begins with a group of managers or an investment advisor who start an investment company and select a board of directors for the fund that will then hire the investment advisory firm as the fund manager. The contract between the investment company (fund) and the management company indicates the duties of the management company and the fee it will receive for these services. Major responsibilities of the management company include *research, portfolio management,* and *administrative duties* such as issuing securities and handling redemptions and dividends. The management fee is generally stated in terms of a percentage of the value of the fund. Fees typically range from one-quarter of one percent to one-half of one percent of the total value, with a sliding scale as funds get larger. As an example, assuming that a fund had a total market value of 200 million dollars and a one-half of one percent fee, the management company would receive $100,000 a year to perform all the duties mentioned. If the management company has to pay out less than $100,000 in salaries and other costs, it will make money. Because there are substantial economies of scale involved in money management, it is in the interest of the management company for the fund to get larger. If the fund grew to 500 million dollars, and the fee scale did not change, the management company would receive $250,000, and it is likely that management expenses would not increase very much because it does not cost much more to manage a 500 million dollar fund than it does a 200 million dollar fund.

Because of economies of scale in investment management, many management companies start *several* funds with different characteristics.[1] This allows the management group to appeal to many different types of investors, provides the investors witht the flexibility to switch between funds, and increases the total capital managed. We will discuss the ability of investors to switch between funds later in the chapter.

Open-End vs. Closed-End Funds

Investment companies are begun like any other company—by selling an issue of common stock to a group of investors. In the case of an investment company, the proceeds are used to purchase the securities of other publicly held companies rather than buildings and equipment. The difference between an open-end investment company (often referred to as a mutual fund) and a closed-end investment company is how they operate *after* the initial public offering is sold.

A closed-end investment company   operates like any other public firm in that its stock is bought and sold on the regular secondary market, and the market price of the investment company shares is determined by supply and demand. There are typically no further shares offered by the investment company, and it does *not* repurchase the outstanding shares on demand. There are *no* subsequent additions to the investment company unless it makes another public sale of securities. Also, there is *no withdrawal* of funds unless the investment company decides to repurchase its stock, which is quite unusual.

There are two prices of importance for shares of a closed-end investment company. The first is the *net asset value* (NAV) for the shares, which is computed as discussed earlier. The investment company's net asset value is computed twice a day, based upon prevailing market prices for the securities in the portfolio. The second price is the *market price* of the fund shares, which is determined by the relative supply and demand for investment company stock in the market. When buying or selling shares of a closed-end investment company, the investor pays this *market* price plus or minus a regular trading commission. It is very important to recognize that *the two prices (NAV and market price) are almost never the same!* The long-run historical relationship has been that the market price for closed-end investment companies is from 5 to 20 percent *below* the net asset value. Figure 19.1 contains a list of closed-end funds from *Barron's* (they are currently referred to as "Publicly Traded Funds"). As shown, only 3 of the 27 funds were selling at a premium over net asset value. A lingering question has been why these funds sell at a discount, and why the discounts differ between funds. Of even more importance are the returns available to investors from funds that sell at large discounts because, given the fact that an investor is acquiring a portfolio

[1]For an interesting discussion of cases in which insurance companies acquired management companies, see David Armstrong, "Were Mutual Funds Worth the Candle?" *Journal of Portfolio Management* 2(1976): 46–51.

```
┌─────────────────────────────────────────────┐
│                                               │
│  ████████                                     │
│  PUBLICLY TRADED FUNDS                        │
│  ████████                                     │
│                                               │
│              May 15, 1981                     │
│     Following is a weekly listing of unaudited│
│  net asset values of publicly traded invest-  │
│  ment fund shares, reported by the companies  │
│  as of Friday's close. Also shown is the clos-│
│  ing listed market price or a dealer-to-dealer│
│  asked price of each fund's shares, with the  │
│  percentage of difference.                    │
│                         N.A.   Stk    %       │
│                        Value  Price  Diff     │
│  Diversified Common Stock Funds               │
│  Adams Express         17.89  14    −21.7     │
│  Baker Fentress       102.16  78    −23.6     │
│  Gen'l Amer Inv        21.29  20⅜  − 4.3      │
│  Lehman                16.51  14½  −12.2      │
│  Madison               26.18  21⅜  −18.4      │
│  Niagara Share         22.26  22⅜  + 0.5      │
│  Overseas Sec           6.20   8⅝  +39.1      │
│  Source               27.56  23⅞  −13.4      │
│  Tri-Continental       29.73  21⅞  −26.4      │
│  US & Foreign          29.44  22⅛  −24.9      │
│  Specialized Equity and Convertible Funds     │
│  Am Gn Cv              31.81  28¾  − 9.6      │
│  bASA                  63.27  54⅛  −14.5      │
│  Bancroft Conv         29.49  23⅝  −19.9      │
│  Castle Conv           29.18  24¼  −16.9      │
│  Central Sec           11.76   8¾  −25.6      │
│  Chase Conv            15.26  12⅞  −15.6      │
│  Claremont             28.58  21½  −24.8      │
│  CLAS                 (−2.69) 13/16  .....    │
│  CLAS PFD              27.62   ....   ....     │
│  Cyprus                 .41    ¾   +82.9      │
│  Engex                 17.10  12    −29.8     │
│  Enrg Util             17.87  15¼  −14.7      │
│  Japan Fund            13.69  11    −19.6     │
│  Nautilus              36.60  30    −18.0     │
│  New American Fd       34.82  26    −25.3     │
│  Pete & Res            40.38  37¼  − 7.8      │
│  Prec Metal            18.66  16¾  −10.2      │
│     a-Ex-Dividend. b-As of Thursday's close.  │
│  z-Not available.                             │
└─────────────────────────────────────────────┘
```

Figure 19.1   Sample Quotations on Publicly Traded Funds

Source: *Barron's*, May 18, 1981. Reprinted by permission.

at a price below market value, the returns from such an investment would be expected to exceed average returns.[2]

Open-end investment companies   are funds for which shares continue to be bought and sold *after* the initial public offering is made. They stand ready to *sell* additional shares at the *net asset value* of the fund with or without a sales charge. In addition, open-end investment companies stand ready to buy back shares of the fund (redeem shares) at the *net asset value* at any time, with or without a redemption fee.

Open-end mutual funds have enjoyed substantial growth during the postwar period, as shown by the figures in Table 19.1. As can be seen, there was a steady

[2]Eugene J. Pratt, "Myths Associated with Closed-End Investment Company Discounts," *Financial Analysts Journal* 22(1966): 79–82; Julian L. Simon, "Does 'Good Portfolio Management' Exist?" *Management Science* 15(1969): B308–B319; Morris Mendelson, "Closed-End Fund Discounts Revisited," *The Financial Review* (1978): 48–72.

Year End	Number of Reporting Funds[a]	Assets (billions)	Year End	Number of Reporting Funds[a]	Assets (billions)
1945	72	$ 1.3	1965	170	35.2
1946	74	1.3	1966	182	34.8
1947	80	1.4	1967	204	44.7
1948	87	1.5	1968	240	52.7
1949	91	2.0	1969	269	48.3
1950	98	2.5	1970	361	47.6
1951	103	3.1	1971	392	55.0
1952	110	3.9	1972	410	59.8
1953	110	4.1	1973	421	46.5
1954	115	6.1	1974	416	34.1
1955	125	7.8	1975	390	42.2
1956	135	9.0	1976	404	47.6
1957	143	8.7	1977	427	45.0
1958	151	13.2	1978	444	45.0
1959	155	15.8	1979	448	49.3
1960	161	17.0	1980	458	58.4
1961	170	22.8			
1962	169	21.3			
1963	165	25.2			
1964	160	29.1			

Table 19.1   Open-End Investment Company Assets 1945–1980

[a]The figures are for "conventional" funds; money market funds are *not* included.

Source: *Mutual Fund Fact Book* (Washington, D.C.: Investment Company Institute, 1981). Reprinted by permission.

increase in the number of funds until 1973, followed by a decline in 1974 and 1975 due to mergers. The growth in the number of funds resumed in 1976 and continued through 1980. The market value of the assets of the funds has not grown as fast due to an overall decline in stock prices and redemptions by fund stockholders. Clearly, open-end funds account for a substantial portion of investment assets and provide a very important service for almost 9 million accounts.

Load vs. No-Load Open-End Funds
One distinction between open-end funds is whether they charge a sales fee when the fund is initially offered. In the case of a *load fund*, the offering price for a share is equal to the net asset value of the share *plus* a sales charge, typically 7.5–8.0 percent of the NAV. Therefore, assuming an 8 percent sales charge ("load"), an individual investing $1,000 in such a fund would only receive $920

worth of stock. In such cases, the funds generally do *not* charge a redemption fee, which means the shares can be redeemed at their net asset value. Therefore, the funds are typically quoted in the paper with a bid and ask price. The bid price is the redemption price and is equal to the net asset value of the shares. The ask price is the offering price and is equal to the net asset value divided by .92, assuming an 8 percent load. The percent of the load typically declines with the size of the order.

There is no initial sales charge on a *no-load fund,* so the shares are sold at their net asset value. In some instances, there is a small redemption charge on these funds (one-half of one percent). When examining the prices of mutual funds listed in *The Wall Street Journal,* the reader will see the bid price is listed as net asset value and, in the case of a no-load fund, in the offering price column, there is the designation NL (no-load). A number of no-load funds have been established in recent years. The mutual fund listing in *The Wall Street Journal* quotes about 110 no-load funds. A directory of such funds is available.[3]

Types of Investment Companies Based upon Portfolio Makeup

Common Stock Funds

Some funds invest almost solely in common stocks, as contrasted to those that invest in preferred stocks, bonds, etc. Within this category of common stock funds there are wide differences in terms of whether their emphasis is on the common stock of "growth" companies, or on the stock of companies in specific industries (e.g., Chemical Fund, Oceanography Fund), or in certain areas (e.g., Technology Fund). In some instances, funds will even concentrate their investments in given geographic areas (e.g., Northeast Fund). This would include *international* funds that concentrate their investments in foreign securities. These international funds are discussed extensively in Chapter 21. The point is, within the general category of common stock funds *there is a very wide variety of types of funds to suit almost any taste or investment desire.* Therefore, the first decision an investor must make is whether he wants a fund that only invests in common stock, and if so, then he must consider the type of common stock desired.

Index Funds

As discussed in Chapter 7, index funds are investment funds set up to specifically match the performance of an aggregate stock market series such as the Standard & Poor's 500 Composite Index. Because research had indicated that many portfolio managers could not consistently generate risk-adjusted rates of return that were superior to those of the aggregate stock market, it was reasoned that it would be preferable to engage in "passive" investment management and simply invest in a portfolio that attempted to *match* the market portfolio. The result was

---

[3]No-Load Mutual Fund Association, Inc., Valley Forge, Pennsylvania, 19481.

the creation of index funds by banks and investment advisers that invested in a cross section of the common stocks in a particular stock market series. The goal of these "market" funds is to match, as closely as possible, the performance of the market series.

In addition to the creation of index funds for domestic stock indexes, banks have also developed bond index funds that attempt to match the performances of some aggregate bond series like the Salomon Bros. Index or the Kuhn Loeb Index. Finally, because of the interest in international diversification, there has been an attempt to derive an international stock index fund that will invest in the principal stocks of major foreign countries.

Balanced Funds

Balanced funds invest in a combination of common stocks *and* fixed-income securities which could include government bonds, corporate bonds, convertible bonds, or preferred stock. The idea is to balance the commitment of the fund and not restrict the portfolio to only one kind of security. Therefore, managers diversify outside of the stock market. The ratio of stocks to fixed-income securities will vary by fund, as stated in the prospectus for the fund. Given the balanced nature of these funds, one would expect them to have a beta factor of less than one, which means they would not rise as much as the aggregate stock market will rise during bull markets, but they also should not decline as much during bear markets.[4]

Bond Funds

As indicated by the name, bond funds are concentrated in various types of bonds in order to generate high current income with a minimum of risk. As is true of common stock funds, there is a difference in the bond investment policy of different funds. Some concentrate in only high-grade corporate bonds, while others hold a mixture of investment grades. Some portfolio managers may engage in more trading of the bonds in the portfolio. In addition to corporate bond funds, a change in the tax law in 1976 made it possible to establish *municipal bond funds*. A number of these funds have been established and provide investors with monthly interest checks that are exempt from federal income taxes (some of the interest may be subject to state and local taxes).

Money Market Funds

Another relatively recent addition to the universe of investment companies is money market funds. These funds were initiated during 1973, when interest rates on short-term money market securities were at record levels. Managers of these funds attempt to provide current income and safety of principal by investing in short-term securities such as treasury bills, bank certificates of deposit, bank acceptances, and commercial paper. The intent is to provide a diversified port-

[4]A recent article on these funds is Jill Bettner, "Stodgy Image of Old 'Balanced' Mutual Funds Could Change with Rally in Both Stocks, Bonds," *Wall Street Journal*, 29 June 1981, p. 42.

folio of such investments to investors who are concerned with liquidity and safety. Many conservative investors, who normally invest in savings accounts or savings and loan shares, switched into money market securities because the yields had risen substantially above the ceiling allowed banks and savings and loan associations. During 1980 and early 1981 the annualized return ranged between 14 percent and 17 percent for the typical money market fund. In addition, all of these are no-load funds and there is also no penalty for withdrawal at any time. Finally, as an option, most of them allow the holder to write checks against the account; typically a $500 minimum investment is required.[5]

As of the end of 1974, there were 15 money market funds worth $1.7 billion reporting to the industry's trade association. There was substantial growth in 1977 (to about $4 billion) and in 1978 (to over $7 billion), followed by explosive growth in 1979 and 1980. As of July 1981 there were 125 money market funds, and the total value of these funds was in excess of $127 billion.

Because of the interest in money market funds, the *Wall Street Journal* on Mondays carries a special section within the Mutual Fund section titled "Money Market Funds." This section indicates the average maturity of the portfolio for the various funds and the average current yield for these funds.

Breakdown by Fund Characteristics

The figures in Table 19.2 break down the funds in terms of how they market their funds and by investment objectives. Wholesale-retail means that these funds are sold through brokers, while direct selling means that the fund has its own sales force. The figures on methods of distribution attest to *the substantial growth of no-load funds* in absolute terms (they almost doubled during the period) and in relative terms; they increased from about 13 percent to almost 27 percent of the total. These figures reflect the creation of new no-load funds and the conversion of some load funds to no-load funds.

The breakdown by investment objective indicates a shift in investor emphasis and a response to this shift by the investment-company industry. While the aggressive growth funds have experienced some growth in absolute dollar value and as a percent of the total, there has been a notable movement from growth and income, and balanced funds into the income and bond funds. The data also reveal investor interest in the new municipal bond funds. Finally, one percent of the total is in option income funds that specialize in writing covered call options.

Dual Funds

Dual funds are special purpose closed-end funds that issue two classes of stock, income shares and capital shares. An investor in a dual fund indicates whether he wants the income shares or the capital shares. Holders of the income shares re-

---

[5]For a list of names and addresses of money market funds, write to Investment Company Institute, 1775 K Street N.W., Washington, D.C. 20006. A service that concentrates on money market funds is *Donoghue's Money Letter*, 770 Washington Street, Holliston, MA 01746. An analysis of performance is contained in Michael G. Ferri and H. Dennis Oberhelman, "How Well Do Money Market Funds Perform?" *Journal of Portfolio Management* 7 (1981): 18–26.

	1976		1977		1978		1979	
	Dollars	%	Dollars	%	Dollars	%	Dollars	%
Total Net Assets	47,581.8	100.0	45,049.2	100.0	44,979.7	100.0	49,297.1	100.0
Method of Distribution								
Wholesale-Retail	30,088.4	63.2	25,745.1	57.1	25,684.7	57.1	26,233.8	53.2
Direct Selling	10,168.3	21.4	9,136.9	20.3	8,852.2	19.7	8,720.2	17.7
No-Load	6,026.9	12.7	8,988.8	20.0	9,407.4	20.9	13,047.2	26.5
Other	1,298.2	2.7	1,178.4	2.6	1,035.4	2.3	1,295.9	2.6
Investment Objective								
Aggressive Growth	2,202.7	4.6	2,212.5	4.9	2,329.9	5.2	2,964.8	6.0
Growth	13,855.8	29.1	11,652.7	25.9	11,380.9	25.3	13,010.4	26.4
Growth and Income	18,233.3	38.3	16,098.1	35.7	15,237.9	33.9	16,462.3	33.4
Balanced	4,898.6	10.3	4,108.9	9.1	3,722.5	8.3	3,438.0	7.0
Income	4,589.6	9.7	4,364.3	9.8	4,557.8	10.1	4,542.1	9.2
Bond	3,255.5	6.8	3,999.3	8.8	4,700.2	10.4	5,086.5	10.3
Municipal Bond	546.3	1.2	2,276.3	5.1	2,631.6	5.9	3,324.0	6.7
Option Income	(a)	—	337.1	0.7	418.9	0.9	469.0	1.0

Table 19.2   Total Net Assets by Fund Characteristics

(a) Did not exist prior to 1977.

Sources: *Mutual Fund Fact Book* (Washington, D.C.: Investment Company Institute, 1980). Reprinted by permission.

	Capital Shares Price	NAV Capital Shares	% Difference
Gemini	35¼	42.93	−17.9
Hemisphere	3⅞	3.10	+25.0
Income and Cap	11¾	13.07	−10.1
Leverage	29⅜	31.83	− 7.7
Putnam Duo Fund	15½	17.41	−11.0
Scudder Due-Vest	14⅜	16.06	−10.5
Scudder D-V Exch	33	41.21	−19.9

Table 19.3   Dual Purpose Funds Friday, June 19, 1981

Following is a weekly listing of the unaudited net asset value of dual purpose, closed-end investment funds' capital shares as reported by the companies as of Friday's close. Also shown is the closing listed market price or the dealer-to-dealer asked price of each fund's capital shares, with the percentage of difference.

Source: *Barron's Weekly,* June 22, 1981, p. 98. Reprinted by permission.

ceive a stated dividend income from *all* investments, but they give up potential capital gain. Investors in the capital shares do not receive any income during the life of the fund, but receive the capital value of *all* the shares at the end of the life of the fund.

Problems can arise for these funds if they are not balanced in terms of the proportion of income to capital appreciation stocks. Additional problems can arise if stock prices decline, in which case the income required on the remaining capital is above normal expectations.[6] The data in Table 19.3 indicate the status of some of the funds as of June 1981. Like the closed-end fund, these funds sell at deep discounts from their NAV.[7]

Performance of Investment Companies

A number of studies have examined the historical performance of mutual funds for a variety of reasons. One is that the funds are a prime example of what can be accomplished by professional money managers. Another very important

[6]See John P. Shelton, Eugene F. Brigham, and Alfred E. Hofflander, Jr., "An Evaluation and Appraisal of Dual Funds," *Financial Analysts Journal* 23(1967): 131–139; and James A. Gentry and John R. Pike, "Dual Funds Revisited," *Financial Analysts Journal* 24(1968): 149–157.

[7]For a recent analysis and evaluation of dual funds, see Robert H. Litzenberger and Howard B. Sosin, "The Structure and Management of Dual Purpose Funds," *Journal of Financial Economics* 4(1977): 203–230; idem, "The Performance and Potential of Dual Purpose Funds," *Journal of Portfolio Management* 4 (1978): 56–68; idem, "The Theory of Recapitalizations and the Evidence of Dual Purpose Funds," *Journal of Finance* 32 (1977): 1433–1456; and Julian J. Nagdeman, "Double Play," *Barron's,* 18 June 1979, p. 11.

reason is that data on the funds are available for lengthy periods of time. Consequently, two of the three major portfolio evaluation techniques were derived in connection with a study of mutual fund performance. These alternative measures of portfolio performance are discussed in detail in Chapter 23. The following discussion concentrates on the overall results as they apply to an investor.

Sharpe Study

Sharpe derived a composite performance measure that considered returns and risk and used this measure to evaluate the performance of 34 open-end mutual funds during the period 1944–1963.[8] For the total period, the performance of only 11 of the 34 funds was superior to that of the DJIA. Sharpe compared the ranks of the various funds during the first part of the sample period (1944–1953) to the rank during the second half (1954–1963) to predict performance of the funds. The results indicated some relationship between past and future performance of the funds, but it was generally concluded that past performance in terms of the performance measure was *not* the best predictor of future performance. An analysis of the relationship between fund performance and the fund's expense ratio indicated that *good performance was associated with low expense ratios*. On the other hand, there was only a slight relationship between size and performance. Notably, there was some consistency in the risk measure over time for alternative funds. Finally, the analysis of *gross* performance, when expenses were added back, indicated that 19 of the 34 funds did better than the DJIA. The author concluded:

it appears that the average mutual fund manager selects a portfolio at least as good as the Dow-Jones Industrials, but that the results actually obtained by the holder of mutual fund shares (after the costs associated with the operations of the fund have been deducted) fall somewhat short of those from the Dow-Jones Industrials.[9]

Jensen Study

A study by Jensen developed a composite portfolio evaluation technique that likewise considered returns adjusted for risk differences and used this measure to evaluate 115 open-end mutual funds during the period 1945–1964.[10] For the full period Jensen examined returns *net* of expenses (i.e., after deducting the costs of operating the fund) and *gross* of expenses (i.e., the expenses are added back each year). The analysis of net returns indicated that 39 funds (34 percent) had above-average returns adjusted for risk, while 76 (66 percent) experienced abnormally

---

[8]William F. Sharpe, "Mutual Fund Performance," *Journal of Business* 39(1966): supplement 119–138.

[9]Sharpe, "Mutual Fund Performance," p. 137.

[10]Michael C. Jensen, "The Performance of Mutual Funds in the Period 1945–1964," *Journal of Finance* 23(1968): 389–416.

poor returns. Using gross returns, 48 funds (42 percent) had above-average results, and 67 (58 percent) had below-average results. The results for gross returns indicate the forecasting ability of all the funds, because they do not penalize the funds for operating expenses. All the funds have to do is cover the brokerage commissions. On the basis of these results and other extensive tests of subgroups, Jensen concluded:

The evidence on mutual fund performance discussed above indicates not only that these 115 mutual funds were on average *not able to predict security prices well enough to outperform a buy-the-market-and-hold policy, but also that there is very little evidence that any* individual *fund was able to do significantly better than that which we expected from mere random chance.*[11]

Mains Comment   A comment by Mains on the Jensen study questioned several of the estimates made by Jensen that apparently biased the results against the mutual funds.[12] To test the effect of these estimates, Mains examined the performance of 70 funds (all in the Jensen sample) using monthly rates of return for the ten year period 1955–1964 and adjusted for the biases. The author contended that, after the Jensen results are corrected for several biases, the performance of the funds on a net-return basis is neutral. Further, on the basis of gross returns, the results indicate that the majority of fund managers demonstrated above-average performance owing either to stock selection or timing ability.

Carlson Study

Carlson examined the overall performance of mutual funds during the period 1948–1967, with an emphasis on analyzing the effect of the market series used and the difference in results depending on the time period.[13] An analysis of performance relative to the market indicated that the results were heavily dependent upon which market series is used: the S&P 500, the NYSE composite, or the DJIA. For the total period, almost all the fund groups outperformed the DJIA, but only a few had *gross* returns that were better than those for the S&P 500 or the NYSE composite. Using net returns, *none* of the groups did better than the S&P 500 or the NYSE composite. An analysis of various ten-year subperiods showed that the relative results were clearly dependent on the time interval examined.

The author also analyzed the factors related to performance during this period. Although there was consistency over time for return or risk taken alone, there was *no* consistency in the risk-adjusted performance measure. Less than

---

[11]Ibid., p. 415.

[12]Norman E. Mains, "Risk, the Pricing of Capital Assets, and the Evaluation of Investment Portfolios: Comment," *Journal of Business* 50(1977): 371–384.

[13]Robert S. Carlson, "Aggregate Performance of Mutual Funds, 1948–1967," *Journal of Financial and Quantitative Analysis* 5(1970): 1–32.

one-third of the funds that experienced above-average performance during the first half did so in the second half, and consistency *declined* over time.

Carlson also analyzed performance relative to size, expense ratios, and a new-funds factor. The results indicated *no* relationship with size or the expense ratio, although there was a relationship between performance and a measure of new cash into the fund. Finally, an analysis of 8 no-load funds compared to the other 74 funds indicated that the no-load funds experienced superior performance. This conclusion was tentative because the sample was limited.

McDonald Study

A study by McDonald examined the performance of 123 mutual funds relative to the stated objective of each fund.[14] The results indicated a positive relationship between objectives and risk measures, i.e., risk increased as objectives became more aggressive. In addition, rates of return generally increased with aggressiveness, and, as expected, there was a positive relationship between return and risk. The relationship between objective and *risk-adjusted* performance indicated that the more aggressive funds experienced the superior results, although only one-third of the funds did better than the aggregate market.

Klemkosky on Consistency

Klemkosky examined the consistency of results for 158 mutual funds for the period 1968–1975 by analyzing the rank order of performance over different two-year and four-year periods.[15] The results indicated some consistency between four-year periods, but relatively low consistency between adjacent two-year periods. Therefore, the author recommends caution in using past performance to predict future performance of mutual funds.

Summary of Performance Studies

Except for the slightly diverse results derived by Mains after extensive adjustments, the results for all the studies are quite consistent. Specifically, they indicate that, if you do *not* consider the expenses of running the funds (i.e., consider gross returns), about half the funds do better than the market and half do worse than the market, which is what you would expect with random selection. In contrast, if you consider expenses (i.e., subtract expenses to arrive at *net* returns) only about one-third of the funds do better than the market and two-thirds do worse. Further, good performance is *not* consistent within a given fund.

[14]John G. McDonald, "Objectives and Performance of Mutual Funds, 1960–1969," *Journal of Financial and Quantitative Analysis* 9(1974): 311–333.

[15]Robert C. Klemkosky, "How Consistently Do Managers Manage?" *Journal of Portfolio Management* 3(1977): 11–15.

Implications of Performance Studies

Assume that you had your own personal portfolio manager and consider the functions you would want him to perform for you. Some of these we talked about in the chapter on efficient markets. The list would probably include:

1. determine your risk-return preferences and develop a portfolio that will be consistent with your desires;

2. diversify the securities in your portfolio to eliminate unsystematic risk;

3. control your portfolio to maintain diversification and ensure that you remain in your desired risk class. At the same time, allow flexibility so you can shift between investment instruments if you desire;

4. attempt to derive a risk-adjusted performance record that is superior to aggregate market performance. This can be done by either consistently selecting undervalued stocks or by proper timing of market swings. Some investors, assuming that they have other diversified investments, may be willing to sacrifice diversification for this superiority;

5. administer the account, keep records of costs, provide timely information for tax purposes, and reinvest dividends, if desired.

The reader will recognize that most of the performance studies discussed above were concerned with number four—risk-adjusted performance. Still, it seems appropriate to consider all of the functions to put performance in perspective.

The first function, determining your risk preference, is *not* performed by mutual funds. However, once you have determined what you want, it is clear that the industry provides a large variety of funds that can meet almost any goal in the area of marketable securities. The empirical studies indicated that *the funds were generally consistent in meeting their stated goals;* i.e., the risks and returns *were* consistent with the stated objectives.

The second function is to diversify your portfolio to eliminate unsystematic risk. One of the major benefits of mutual funds is *instant diversification*. This is especially beneficial to the new, small investor who does not have the resources to acquire 100 shares of 10 or 12 different issues and thereby reduce unsystematic risk. With most mutual funds, it is possible to start with about $1,000 and acquire a portfolio of securities that is correlated about .90 with the market portfolio (about 90 percent diversified). Therefore, while there is a range of diversification, *most funds provide excellent diversification* especially if they state this as an objective.

The third function is to maintain diversification and keep you in your desired risk class. Mutual funds have been quite good in terms of the stability of diversification. This is not too surprising because, once you have a reasonably well-diversified portfolio, it is difficult to change its makeup substantially. Further, the evidence is quite strong regarding the consistency of the risk class. Recall that even the studies that indicated there was not much consistency in risk-adjusted performance did generate results that indicated *consistency in risk alone*.

Finally, on the flexibility to change investment instruments, the initiation of a number of funds by a given management company helps accomplish this goal. For a small service charge (five to ten dollars), or no charge, these investment groups will typically allow an investor to shift between their funds simply by calling the fund. Therefore, it is possible to shift from an aggressive stock fund to a money market fund for much less than it would cost you if you did it yourself.

The fourth function is to provide risk-adjusted performance that is superior to that of the aggregate market (i.e., naive buy-and-hold). I am sure the reader will not be surprised when I conclude that the news on this function is not very good. A reasonable summary of the evidence is that, on average, the results achieved by portfolio managers through their ability to select securities or time the market are *about as good as* or only *slightly better* than would be achieved with a buy-and-hold policy. This conclusion is based upon evidence using *gross* returns. Unfortunately, the evidence regarding *net* returns, which is what the investor receives, indicates that the majority of funds do *not* do as well as a buy-and-hold policy. A reasonable estimate is that the shortfall in performance is about one percent a year, which is roughly the average cost of expenses and commissions. For the investor who would like to find one of the superior funds, the news is likewise not very encouraging. Most studies show a lack of consistency in performance over time except among funds that consistently do *not* perform well. Apparently, if the poor performance is due to excessive expenses, this state of affairs will continue, so such funds should be avoided. In general, an investor should *not* expect to consistently enjoy superior risk-adjusted returns from investment in a mutual fund.

The final objective is administration of the account. This is a major benefit of most mutual funds, because they provide automatic reinvestment of dividends at no charge and consistently provide a record of total cost. Further, each year they supply a statement that indicates the dividend income and capital gain distribution for tax purposes.

Most investors have a set of functions they want their portfolio manager to perform. *Typically, mutual funds can help the investor accomplish four of the five at a cost, in terms of time and money, lower than it would be if they did it on their own.* Unfortunately, the price of this is about one percent a year in loss of performance. The studies we discussed did not take into account the sales load of many funds, which also detracts from performance. An obvious way to avoid this loss is to acquire a no-load fund. The limited evidence to date indicates that the performance of no-load funds is about equal to that of the load funds.

Sources of Information

Given the wide variety of types and number of funds available, it is important to be able to determine the performance of various funds over time and to derive some understanding of their goals and management philosophies.

Daily quotations on a large number of open-end funds are contained in *The Wall Street Journal*. A more comprehensive weekly list of quotations and the dividend income and capital gain for the past 12 months are carried in *Barron's*, which also includes a quarterly update on performance over the past ten years for a number of funds. *Barron's* contains a list of closed-end funds with current net asset values, current market quotes on the funds, and indicated percent of difference between the two figures. (See Figure 19.1 for an example of these quotes.) As mentioned, the market price is typically about 5–20 percent below the net asset value. Finally, for those interested in dual funds, *Barron's* contains a list of seven dual funds, giving their current net asset value, market quotation, and the percent of difference between the two. The discounts on these funds are generally close to 15 percent.

The major source of comprehensive historical information is an annual publication issued by Arthur Wiesenberger Services titled, *Investment Companies*. This book is published each year and currently contains vital statistics for over 535 mutual funds, arranged alphabetically. The description of each fund includes: a brief history, investment objectives and portfolio analysis, statistical history, special services available, personnel, advisers and distributors, sales charges, and a hypothetical $10,000 investment charted over ten years for major funds. A sample page for the Technology Fund is contained in Figure 19.2. In addition, the Wiesenberger book contains a summary table that lists the annual rates of return and price volatility for a number of funds. Recently, Wiesenberger has added two additional services. Every three months the firm publishes *Management Results* which is an update on the long-term performance of over 400 mutual funds, arranged alphabetically according to the investment objective of the fund. Every month the firm also publishes *Current Performance and Dividend Record* which contains the dividend and short-run performance of over 400 funds. The funds are listed alphabetically with the objective indicated.[16]

Another source of analytical historical information on funds is *Forbes*, a biweekly financial publication that usually contains information about individual companies and their investment philosophies. In addition, the magazine conducts an annual survey of mutual funds in August. A sample page is contained in Figure 19.3. As shown, the survey not only considers recent and ten-year returns, but also indicates sales charges and the annual expense ratio for each fund.

Because of the interest in mutual funds, United Business Service Company publishes a semimonthly service called *United Mutual Fund Selector*. Each issue contains several articles on specific mutual funds or classes of mutual funds (e.g., municipal bond funds). The first issue each month contains a four-page supplement titled, "Investment Company Performance Comparisons," that gives recent and historical changes in NAV for load and no-load funds. A sample page is contained in Figure 19.4.[17]

[16]These services are currently published by Wiesenberger Investment Companies Services, 210 South Street, Boston, Massachusetts, 02111.

[17]This service is available from United Business Service Company, 210 Newbury St., Boston, Massachusets, 02116.

TECHNOLOGY FUND, INC.

Organized in 1948 as Television Fund, Technology Fund became Television-Electronics Fund in 1951 and adopted its present name in January 1968. On December 10, 1976, the name of the fund's adviser (then Supervised Investors Services, Inc.) was changed to Kemper Financial Services, Inc., a wholly owned subsidiary of Kemper Corp., an insurance and financial services holding company.

Under the policy revised in early 1968, the fund invests primarily in securities of companies expected to benefit from technological advances and improvements in such fields as aerospace, astrophysics, chemistry, electricity, electronics, geology, mechanical engineering, metallurgy, nuclear physics and oceanography. Management may, however, seek investment opportunities in virtually any industry in which they may be found. An advisory board provides information of a technical nature relating to new inventions and developments.

At the end of 1979, the fund had 94.8% of its assets in common stocks, highest level of such calendar year-end investments in the past 20 years. A major proportion of the year-end portfolio was concentrated in five industry groups: energy & related services (23.1% of assets), electronic data processing & instruments (13.2%), aerospace (11.6%), electrical & electronic components

(10.7%), and transportation (5.7%). The five largest individual investments were Schlumberger and Boeing Co. (each 5.9% of assets), American International Group (4.9%), Intel Corp. (4.3%), and Teledyne (3.8%). The rate of portfolio turnover during the latest fiscal year was 39.2% of average assets. Unrealized appreciation was 33.9% of calendar year-end assets.

Special Services: An open account system serves for accumulation and automatic dividend reinvestment. Minimum initial investment is $100; subsequent investments must be at least $25. Income dividends are invested at net asset value. Plan payments may be made by way of pre-authorized checks against the investor's checking account. Arrangements may be made for payroll deduction. A monthly or quarterly withdrawal plan is available without charge to accounts worth $5,000 at the offering price; payments may be of any designated amount. Shares may be exchanged for those of other funds in the Kemper Financial group without service fee. Tax-deferred retirement plans are available for corporations and the self-employed, as well as Individual Retirement Account plans. A one-time account reinstatement privilege is available to redeeming shareholders within a specified time.

Statistical History

		AT YEAR-ENDS					% of Assets in			ANNUAL DATA				
Year	Total Net Assets ($)	Number of Share-holders	Net Asset Value Per Share ($)	Offer-ing Price ($)	Yield (%)	Cash & Equiv-alent	Bonds & Pre-ferreds	Com-mon Stocks	Income Div-idends ($)	Capital Gains Distribu-tion ($)	Expense Ratio (%)	Offering Price ($) High	Low
1979	427,059,368	58,190	10.17	11.11	2.3	4	1	95	0.26	0.43	0.60	11.45	8.86
1978	375,341,562	63,590	8.26	9.03	2.7	2	14	84	0.25	0.20†	0.62	9.67	6.56
1977	358,694,594	70,491	7.14	7.80	2.5	8	2*	90	0.20	0.10	0.60	8.31	7.17
1976	432,029,805	77,716	7.58	8.28	2.3	3	6*	91	0.19	—	0.59	8.42	6.82
1975	416,490,321	86,336	6.20	6.78	2.8	6	3*	91	0.19	—	0.64	7.42	5.12
1974	338,514,102	91,141	4.67	5.12	3.5	12	3*	85	0.18	—	0.67	7.01	4.66
1973	489,644,043	96,032	6.21	6.81	2.2	8	2*	90	0.15	—	0.59	8.47	6.30
1972	665,133,022	100,312	7.66	8.39	1.6	6	4*	90	0.14	0.36	0.56	9.24	8.02
1971	667,760,452	106,008	7.47	8.14	2.1	5	6*	89	0.18	0.30	0.54	9.02	7.06
1970	617,992,236	109,703	6.91	7.53	2.6	10	6	84	0.20	0.10	0.59	8.12	5.80
1969	631,010,166	108,777	7.34	8.00	2.3	13	6	81	0.20	0.74	0.54	9.95	7.75

* Includes a substantial proportion in convertible issues.   † Includes $0.01 short-term capital gains.

Directors: John Hawkinson, Pres.; Thomas R. Anderson, Vice President; David W. Belin; Lewis A. Burnham; Russell H. Matthias; Harry C. De Muth; Earl D. Larsen; Matthew W. Powers; Christian G. Schmidt; Reuben Thorson. Advisory Board: Dr. William L. Everitt; Dr. Frederick E. Terman; Dr. Jerome B. Wiesner.
Investment Adviser: Kemper Financial Services, Inc. Compensation to the Adviser is ½ of 1% annually of average daily net assets on first $215 million; 0.375% on the next $335 million; 0.30% on the next $250 million; and 0.25% on all assets over $800 million.
Custodian and Transfer Agent: United Missouri Bank of Kansas City N.A., Kansas City, MO 64141.
Shareholder Service Agent: Data-Sys-Tance, Inc., Kansas City, MO 64141.

Distributor: Kemper Financial Services, Inc., 120 South La Salle Street, Chicago, IL 60603.
Sales Charge: Maximum is 8½% of offering price; minimum is 1% at $1 million. Reduced charges begin at $10,000 and are applicable to combined purchases of the fund and other of the Kemper Mutual Funds.
Dividends: Income dividends are paid in cash or shares quarterly in the months of February, May, August and November. Capital gains, if any, are paid optionally in shares or cash in November.
Shareholder Reports: Issued quarterly. Fiscal year ends October 31. Current prospectus effective in March.
Qualified for Sale: In all states and DC.
Address: 120 South LaSalle St., Chicago, IL 60603.
Telephone: (312) 346-3223.

An assumed investment of $10,000 in this fund, with capital gains accepted in shares and income dividends reinvested, is illustrated below. The explanation on Page 153 must be read in conjunction with this illustration.

TECHNOLOGY FUND, INC.

Cost of Investment January 1, 1970 $10,000

(Initial Net Asset Value $9,150)

— Total Return.
--- Value of Original Shares.

December 31, 1979

*Includes Value of Shares Accepted as Capital Gains $3,115; Reinvested Income Dividends $4,484.

$20,280 Total Value of Investment*

$12,681 Value of Original Shares

	1970	1971	1972	1973	1974	1975	1976	1977	1978	1979		Dollar amounts of distributions reinvested: Capital Gains	Income Dividends
Value of Shares Initially acquired Through Investment of $10,000	$8,616	$9,314	$9,551	$7,743	$5,823	$7,731	$9,451	$8,903	$10,299	$12,681	1970	$ 127	$ 252
											1971	398	237
											1972	510	197
Value of Shares Resulting From Reinvestment of Capital Gains and Income Dividends (Cumulative)	416	1,125	1,873	1,729	1,549	2,379	3,242	3,589	4,988	7,599	1973	—	225
											1974	—	278
											1975	—	303
											1976	—	312
											1977	170	338
											1978	355	442
Total Return	9,032	10,439	11,424	9,472	7,372	10,110	12,693	12,492	15,287	20,280	1979	809	486
											Total	$2,369	$3,070

Results Taking Capital Gains in SHARES and Income Dividends in CASH		Results Taking All Dividends and Distributions in CASH	
Initial Investment At Offering Price, January 1, 1970	$10,000	Initial Investment At Offering Price, January 1, 1970	$10,000
Value as of 12/31/79 of Shares Initially Acquired	$12,681	Total Value, December 31, 1979	$12,681
Value of Shares Accepted as Capital Gains Distributions	$ 2,683#	Distributions From Capital Gains	$ 1,858
Total Value, December 31, 1979	$15,364	Dividends From Investment Income	$ 2,419
Total Dividends PAID From Investment Income	$ 2,651		

\# Dollar Amount of these distributions at the time shares were acquired: $2,021

Figure 19.2   Sample Page from *Investment Companies*

1981 Fund Ratings

Performance in UP markets	in DOWN markets	Stock funds (load)	Average annual total return 1968-81	Latest 12 months return from capital growth	return from income dividends	Total assets 6/30/81 (millions)	% change '81 vs. '80	Maximum sales charge	Annual expenses per $100
		Standard & Poor's 500 stock average	5.7%	14.9%	4.9%				
		Forbes stock fund composite	5.8%	25.2%	3.4%				
		Forbes balanced fund composite	4.7%	3.0%	8.3%				
		Forbes bond and preferred stock fund composite	3.6%	−13.4%	12.5%				
		Stock funds (load) *Group averages*	5.6%	24.6%	3.7%				
D	D	Affiliated Fund	7.5%	14.8%	6.2%	$1,736.5	10.5	7.25%	$0.38
A	B	AMCAP Fund	10.0	26.3	3.8	254.1	91.2	8.50	0.80
•C	•A	American Birthright Trust	—*	14.8	none	129.7	77.2	8.50	1.32
B	B	American General Comstock Fund[1]	10.0	33.0	4.3	179.5	39.7	8.50	0.90
B	F	American General Enterprise Fund	4.2	44.2	1.0	605.0	20.9	8.50	0.75
A+	•C	American General Pace Fund[2]	—*	51.7	2.7	59.6	210.4	8.50	1.05
•B	•C	American General Venture Fund	—*	34.5	2.9	60.4	205.1	8.50	1.12
C	A	American Growth Fund	8.4	14.8	5.1	28.2	26.5	7.25	1.49
C	B	American Insurance & Industrial Fund	9.6	13.1	6.3	15.1	5.6	8.50	1.00
D	•D	American Leaders Fund	—*	9.1	7.9	48.1	0.4	6.50	1.37
D	B	American Mutual Fund	9.1	22.7	4.7	508.0	30.5	8.50	0.54
C	C	American National Growth Fund	8.0	23.0	4.3	57.7	41.4	8.50	0.79
D	F	Anchor Growth Fund	0.1	23.9	4.4	139.0	7.3	8.50	0.65
D	C	Axe-Houghton Stock Fund	4.4	25.2	1.4	122.4	64.7	8.50	0.88
B	•D	BLC Growth Fund	—*	37.0	2.3	14.6	40.4	8.50	1.04
D	•B	BLC Income Fund	—*	25.3	5.2	16.4	32.3	8.50	0.94
C	C	Broad Street Investing Corp	7.9	20.3	4.8	377.0	17.1	7.25	0.45
C	D	Bullock Fund	6.4	17.5	4.0	140.4	5.5	8.50	0.78
C	D	The Cardinal Fund	4.5	16.2	4.0	13.5	4.7	8.50	0.93
C	D	Century Shares Trust	6.5	16.9	4.6	71.9	10.8	7.25	0.99
B	F	CG Fund	5.7	23.4	3.9	152.2	28.8	7.50	0.68
A+	A	Charter Fund	13.5	26.2	3.1	40.6	60.5	8.50	1.35
B	C	Chemical Fund	6.2	21.2	3.0	1,032.6	20.0	8.50	0.62
•B	F	Colonial Growth Shares	2.8	24.5	2.1	67.0	11.1	8.50	1.18
C	F	Common Stock Fund State Bond & Mortgage Co	3.1	17.3	3.2	33.8	5.3	8.50	1.15
D	D	Commonwealth Fund Indenture Trust Plans A & B	2.8	5.5	7.8	10.2	−5.6	7.50	0.40
D	C	Commonwealth Fund Indenture of Trust Plan C	4.2	6.5	6.5	35.4	0.6	7.50	0.75
D	D	Composite Fund	4.8	24.6	3.8	26.0	21.5	7.00	0.91
C	C	Corporate Leaders Tr Fund Certificates, Series "B"	6.7	14.8	6.3	49.6	7.1	†	0.10
C	D	Country Capital Growth Fund	3.7	26.0	2.7	47.0	16.3	7.50	0.85
D	C	Decatur Income Fund	8.4	13.6	6.3	376.3	29.5	8.50	0.69
D	D	Delaware Fund	6.0	25.5	4.1	255.9	7.8	8.50	0.77
D	D	Delta Trend Fund	2.2	46.9	2.7	10.3	27.2	8.50	1.60
D	C	Diversified Fund of State Bond and Mtge Co	6.1	12.7	4.9	7.4	17.5	8.50	1.00
D	C	Dividend Shares	5.1	11.0	5.4	251.8	1.7	8.50	0.80
C	C	The Dreyfus Fund	6.4	26.8	3.9	1,752.2	15.9	8.50	0.74
B	•C	The Dreyfus Leverage Fund	—*	9.4	4.4	322.4	1.9	8.50	1.00
		Eaton & Howard Funds							
A	F	Growth	4.2	41.3	1.0	36.5	21.7	7.25	0.95
D	F	Stock	1.1	7.2	4.7	73.2	−5.6	7.25	0.67
A+	F	Fairfield Fund	3.2	48.3	0.6	32.8	36.7	8.50	1.13
•B	•B	Fidelity Destiny Fund	—*	33.4	2.9	233.1	48.0	‡	0.75
A+	D	Fidelity Magellan Fund[3]	13.0	67.9	2.7	104.4	161.7	2.00	1.23
C	•F	First Investors Discovery Fund	—*	48.2	0.3	6.0	42.9	8.50	1.50
A	F	First Investors Fund for Growth	3.7	31.3	2.2	69.9	16.3	8.50	1.01
D	C	First Investors Natural Resources Fund[4]	2.5	−4.8	10.0	11.1	−9.0	8.50	1.30
D	B	First Investors Option Fund	3.4	14.3	4.7	81.8	97.1	7.25	1.10
C	C	Founders Mutual Fund	4.5	16.3	4.5	132.8	5.1	4.00	0.52

• Fund rated for two periods only; maximum allowable rating A. *Fund not in operation for full period. †Fund not currently selling new shares; existing shares traded over-the-counter. ‡ Available only through contractual plan. [1]Formerly Comstock Fund. [2]Formerly Pace Fund. [3]Formerly Magellan Fund. [4]Formerly First Investors Fund.

Figure 19.3   Sample Fund Page from *Forbes*

Source: Reprinted by permission of *Forbes* Magazine from the August 31, 1981 issue.

UNITED Mutual Fund Selector

Investment Company Performance Comparisons

Change in Net Asset Value •   NO-LOAD FUNDS   % Change in Net Asset Value •

Fund	6 Mos 1981	6 Mos 1980	6 Mos 1979	6 Mos 1978	6 Mos 1977	5 Years 1976-80
• Acorn Fund	+ 2.1	+ 2.9	+ 24.7	+ 10.6	+ 15.4	+ 326
ADV Fund	- 3.3	+ 6.4	§	§	§	§
Afuture Fund	+ 4.9	+ 9.9	- 15.4	+ 11.5	- 3.1	+ 168
Alpha Fund	+ 16.1	+ 6.3	+ 12.3	+ 5.2	- 4.0	+ 89
Am. Investors Fund	+ 3.6	+ 12.0	+ 36.2	+ 13.3	+ 8.6	- 249
Armstrong Associates	+ 0.5	+ 7.2	+ 6.8	- 19.4	+ 2.8	- 234
Babson Funds:						
Income Trust	0.0	+ 8.6	+ 6.1	0.0	+ 2.2	+ 21
• Investment	- 3.5	+ 5.6	+ 8.4	+ 5.2	- 6.8	+ 73
Beacon Hill Mutual	+ 1.0	+ 2.6	+ 3.5	- 7.5	- 2.2	+ 65
• Boston Company Fund	+ 5.9	+ 6.9	+ 10.4	+ 4.9	- 5.7	+ 8.3
Bull & Bear Group:						
Capamerica Fund	- 3.5	+ 3.5	+ 4.9	+ 5.1	+ 0.9	+ 121
Capital Shares	- 4.4	+ 7.5	+ 23.2	- 10.6	+ 5.3	+ 266
Golconda Investors	- 13.2	+ 24.7	+ 27.3	NA	NA	+ 171
Columbia Growth Fund	+ 1.7	+ 4.1	+ 16.0	- 11.0	- 0.3	+ 164
Companion Fund	+ 5.9	+ 5.9	+ 11.5	- 4.5	- 6.4	+ 108
Constellation Growth	- 5.3	+ 11.8	+ 23.5	+ 24.5	- 4.4	+ 347
Dodge & Cox Stock Fund	+ 0.9	+ 6.4	- 11.9	+ 6.1	- 3.3	+ 98
Drexel Burnham Fund	- 1.8	+ 9.5	+ 9.9	+ 6.2	- 2.3	+ 120
Dreyfus Group:						
Number Nine	- 2.6	+ 15.5	+ 21.7	+ 21.3	- 3.2	+ 286
Special Income	- 2.0	+ 6.2	- 11.7	+ 1.4	+ 5.0	+ 69
Third Century	+ 7.6	+ 24.1	+ 27.5	- 13.8	+ 11.5	+ 237
• Evergreen Fund	+ 4.0	+ 11.4	+ 18.8	+ 28.4	+ 12.4	+ 481
Evergreen Total Return	+ 7.7	+ 9.6	- 13.2	§	§	§
Fidelity Group Funds:						
Asset Invest. Tr	+ 14.0	+ 9.2	+ 13.0	§	§	§
Contrafund	+ 9.5	+ 1.9	+ 15.5	+ 8.4	- 6.6	+ 109
Corporate Bond	- 0.7	+ 7.6	+ 5.7	- 0.1	+ 2.2	+ 29
• Equity-Income	+ 9.0	+ 11.0	+ 21.3	+ 11.6	+ 5.7	+ 181
Fund	- 0.7	+ 7.1	+ 8.7	+ 5.4	- 0.5	+ 104
Government Securities	+ 3.0	+ 9.6	§	§	§	§
High Income	+ 4.5	+ 7.2	+ 8.9	+ 2.9	§	§
Puritan Fund	+ 9.0	+ 8.7	+ 10.7	+ 3.8	+ 2.9	- 89
Thrift Trust	+ 4.5	+ 10.7	+ 5.3	+ 1.1	+ 1.5	+ 56
Trend Fund	- 1.8	- 0.5	+ 12.9	+ 8.7	- 1.6	+ 103
Financial Programs:						
Dynamics	+ 6.7	+ 4.7	+ 21.5	+ 10.2	+ 9.0	+ 154
Industrial	- 10.6	+ 7.3	- 19.3	+ 4.7	+ 4.0	+ 144
• Industrial Income	- 4.9	+ 6.5	+ 12.9	+ 4.5	+ 4.4	+ 130
44 Wall Street	- 1.2	- 6.1	+ 35.2	+ 32.1	+ 4.7	+ 432
Founders Group Funds:						
Growth Fund	+ 1.7	+ 8.3	+ 13.3	+ 7.5	- 3.8	+ 132
Income	+ 10.6	+ 5.0	+ 12.7	+ 2.2	- 1.0	+ 92
Special Fund	+ 0.1	+ 6.4	+ 22.8	+ 10.8	+ 9.0	+ 230
Fd. for U.S. Gov. Sec	- 2.4	+ 6.0	+ 5.4	- 0.8	+ 0.9	+ 13
Funds, Inc.:						
Commerce Income Shs	- 2.2	+ 7.4	+ 7.8	- 0.6	- 2.1	+ 67
Pilot Fund	- 1.2	0.0	+ 11.2	+ 3.6	+ 1.4	+ 112
G.T. Pacific Fund	- 21.5	+ 6.9	- 14.1	+ 29.7	§	§
Gateway Option Income	+ 3.8	+ 4.6	+ 9.3	+ 4.0	§	§
General Electric S&S	- 1.2	+ 3.8	- 10.6	+ 4.5	- 5.3	+ 61
General Securities	+ 5.1	+ 9.8	+ 8.4	- 8.7	0.0	+ 114
Growth Industry Shares	+ 7.2	+ 8.3	+ 13.5	+ 12.8	- 6.8	+ 143
Hamilton Income	+ 6.6	+ 4.8	+ 12.7	+ 6.3	- 0.5	+ 122
Hartwell Growth Fund	- 2.7	+ 7.8	- 12.2	+ 15.9	+ 1.7	- 317
Hartwell Leverage Fund	+ 1.4	+ 14.4	+ 15.1	- 14.0	+ 10.1	+ 427
Herold Fund	- 1.1	+ 14.1	+ 11.6	+ 7.6	- 0.2	- 102
Horace Mann Fund	+ 1.8	+ 5.2	- 11.3	+ 5.1	- 4.5	+ 82
Istel Fund	- 4.4	+ 16.4	- 19.5	+ 7.3	- 1.4	- 115
Ivy Fund	+ 4.8	+ 13.2	+ 17.5	+ 3.6	- 7.2	+ 101
Janus Fund	+ 13.3	+ 3.9	+ 8.5	+ 12.4	+ 1.6	+ 197
Lexington Group:						
Growth	+ 4.7	+ 4.4	+ 13.4	+ 24.1	+ 7.1	+ 237
Research	+ 6.0	+ 6.4	+ 9.3	+ 4.1	- 4.5	+ 96

Fund	6 Mos 1981	6 Mos 1980	6 Mos 1979	6 Mos 1978	6 Mos 1977	5 Years 1976-80
Lindner Fund	+ 27.0	+ 6.3	+ 21.9	+ 23.0	NA	+ 304
Loomis-Sayles Funds:						
Capital Development	+ 9.8	+ 5.1	+ 7.5	+ 19.3	+ 0.3	+ 158
Mutual	+ 2.8	+ 7.0	+ 7.5	+ 3.6	- 3.7	+ 51
• Mathers Fund	+ 1.5	+ 12.7	+ 21.1	- 14.1	+ 6.8	+ 259
• Mutual Shares	+ 8.8	+ 2.4	+ 22.6	+ 15.6	+ 12.3	+ 258
Nat'l Aviation & Tech.	+ 8.4	+ 0.7	+ 3.3	+ 26.5	- 3.5	+ 182
National Industries	- 18.4	+ 2.2	+ 10.2	+ 2.8	- 1.6	+ 134
Neuberger & Berman:						
• Energy Fund	- 7.7	+ 12.5	+ 20.7	+ 3.1	+ 6.4	+ 196
• Guardian Mutual	- 1.9	+ 4.8	+ 16.5	+ 6.7	+ 1.5	+ 151
Liberty Fund	+ 3.4	+ 4.4	+ 11.1	+ 2.2	- 1.7	+ 32
Manhattan Fund	- 4.6	+ 5.9	+ 8.9	+ 5.3	- 8.3	+ 95
• Partners Fund	+ 4.0	+ 10.7	+ 19.4	+ 12.2	- 5.9	+ 200
Schuster Fund	+ 8.3	+ 6.9	+ 14.3	+ 13.2	+ 7.8	+ 189
Newton Growth Fund	+ 4.9	+ 6.4	+ 9.0	+ 7.1	- 0.7	+ 123
Newton Income	+ 0.5	+ 6.3	+ 3.9	- 1.2	- 4.5	+ 14
Nicholas Fund	+ 15.6	+ 6.2	+ 14.8	+ 19.0	+ 5.8	+ 224
Northeast Investors:						
• Trust	+ 4.8	+ 10.8	+ 5.2	- 0.6	+ 3.8	+ 26
• Nova Fund	+ 8.7	§	§	§	§	§
Omega Fund	- 10.1	+ 10.1	+ 24.4	+ 2.7	+ 8.1	+ 201
One-Hundred Fund	+ 7.2	+ 4.7	+ 6.1	+ 13.1	- 1.1	+ 138
One William Street	+ 2.7	+ 5.2	+ 15.3	+ 6.1	- 3.6	+ 101
Penn Square Mutual	+ 8.3	+ 7.3	+ 13.9	+ 5.4	- 1.0	+ 95
Pennsylvania Mutual	+ 11.2	- 2.2	+ 22.3	+ 23.3	+ 8.4	+ 253
Planned Investment Fund	+ 8.2	+ 8.4	+ 16.8	+ 4.4	- 2.2	+ 97
T. Rowe Price Funds:						
• Growth Stock	- 4.3	+ 4.4	+ 5.0	+ 8.5	- 7.4	+ 67
International	+ 6.0	+ 4.86	§	§	§	§
• New Era	- 7.8	+ 12.4	+ 23.4	+ 2.9	- 3.2	+ 202
New Horizons	+ 0.6	+ 6.5	+ 10.5	+ 19.9	+ 1.4	+ 218
• New Income	+ 0.7	+ 7.0	+ 4.5	+ 1.0	+ 3.6	+ 37
PRO Services:						
• Medical Technology	+ 3.7	+ 5.9	§	§	§	§
PRO Fund	+ 3.1	- 2.2	+ 15.8	+ 18.6	+ 7.1	+ 105
Rainbow Fund	+ 10.7	+ 7.8	- 18.4	+ 5.8	+ 14.0	- 149
Revere Fund	- 2.0	+ 5.1	+ 15.3	+ 0.2	+ 3.5	+ 120
SAFECO Group:						
Equity Fund	+ 4.8	+ 5.8	+ 15.2	+ 10.3	+ 1.8	- 148
Growth Fund	+ 5.3	+ 0.9	+ 10.1	+ 16.2	+ 7.2	+ 279
Scudder Funds:						
Common Stock	- 8.2	+ 6.0	+ 7.2	+ 7.5	- 1.7	+ 124
Development	+ 15.1	+ 7.7	+ 13.1	+ 31.3	+ 7.9	+ 279
Income Fund	- 0.5	+ 6.2	+ 6.4	0.0	+ 0.4	+ 28
International	- 3.1	+ 14.1	+ 5.4	- 12.3	- 2.1	+ 89
Special Fund	+ 4.8	+ 5.6	+ 10.0	+ 17.2	- 0.5	+ 170
Selected Funds:						
American Shares	- 1.1	+ 7.5	+ 7.4	+ 1.1	0.0	+ 62
Special Shares	- 1.7	+ 4.8	- 13.4	+ 3.0	- 7.0	+ 69
• Sequoia Fund	+ 15.1	- 0.3	+ 5.2	+ 17.2	+ 4.7	+ 217
• Sherman Dean Fund	+ 15.1	+ 50.3	+ 15.1	+ 39.3	+ 14.8	+ 220
State Farm Balanced	- 2.4	+ 3.4	+ 15.2	+ 6.6	+ 0.7	+ 111
State Farm Growth	+ 3.0	+ 2.7	- 21.3	+ 9.4	+ 1.3	+ 187
Steadman Funds:						
American Industry	- 10.1	- 0.6	+ 14.5	+ 3.8	+ 4.3	+ 81
Associated Fund	0.0	+ 1.0	+ 7.2	+ 0.9	+ 3.6	+ 52
Investment	- 5.5	+ 4.4	+ 7.9	- 3.4	+ 1.3	+ 85
Oceanographic						
Technology & Growth	- 11.4	+ 2.6	+ 18.7	- 3.6	+ 3.1	+ 117
Stein Roe & Farnham:						
Balanced Fund	- 6.2	+ 5.7	+ 9.9	- 2.6	- 4.3	+ 71
Capital Opportunities	- 11.8	+ 18.1	- 23.4	+ 7.9	- 3.3	+ 302
Stock Fund	- 13.8	+ 12.6	+ 12.1	+ 3.8	- 6.3	+ 133
Stratton Growth Fund	- 4.3	+ 1.4	- 14.7	+ 10.7	+ 4.5	+ 136
Tudor Fund	+ 8.9	+ 4.4	+ 8.1	+ 19.4	+ 0.8	+ 189
20th Century Growth	- 2.1	+ 3.5	+ 19.4	+ 35.1	+ 2.8	+ 597

See page 102 for footnotes

Figure 19.4   Sample Page from United Mutual Fund Selector

Source: *United Mutual Fund Selector* (a division of United Business Service) 210 Newbury Street, Boston, MA, July 19, 1981, p. 99.

Selecting an Investment Company

Given an appreciation of what investment companies can do for you, a natural question is, how do I go about selecting one? Following are some of the questions you should ask yourself and a potential procedure to follow:

1. Determine your objective or objectives for the money you want to invest. The objective(s) will depend on the rest of your portfolio and your overall investment objective, and can range from safety and high liquidity to high risk and growth.

2. For each objective, consider what kind of an investment company would be best. If you want safety and liquidity, you would probably consider a money market fund or a high-grade bond fund. Alternatively, if you are looking for a high-risk, aggressive investment, you might consider a pure common stock fund that concentrates in growth companies or small firms. If you are in a high tax bracket you might consider a municipal bond fund.

3. Given the general type of fund desired, use one of the summary evaluation services like the *United Market Fund Selector* to spot investment companies that fit your needs. This step will probably generate a list of at least 20 investment companies.

4. Examine the long-run and the recent short-run performance of each of these funds. This information is available in the *Selector,* in the annual *Forbes* issue, or in a recent edition of *Barron's* that contains a quarterly review. You are looking for a group of funds that *typically* enjoys returns above average for the risk level involved. As noted, very few funds are able to consistently beat the market, but you want one that can do it occasionally and does not do a very poor job during the bad years. Note that *Forbes* ranks funds in terms of performance in up and down markets. This exercise should reduce the number of potential companies to fewer than ten.

5. Look up each of these funds in the Weisenberger publication *Investment Companies.* The write-up provides a detailed discussion of each of the funds including overall investment philosophy and some of the largest holdings. There is also a plot of their value over the past ten years. Finally, there is a listing of portfolio breakdown and past expense ratios. Based upon this analysis, your potential universe will probably be down to fewer than six funds.

6. Using the address or phone number provided in *Investment Companies,* write or call to get a copy of the fund's prospectus. This prospectus will include all the information discussed previously and the original cost of and a recent market price for the fund's portfolio. At this point you can get a better feel for the philosophy of the managers and determine whether their philosophy is consistent with yours; i.e., do they invest in the kind of securities you would buy if you had the time and inclination to invest on your own?

7. At this point, you should be down to two or three companies. The determining factor might be whether it is a load or no-load fund. Unless the load fund is clearly superior, you would probably be better off investing in a no-load and saving the 7–8 percent charge. Alternatively, if the load fund does have superior results and fills your other needs, it might be worth the load; especially if you are planning to hold the investment for several years.

8.   Another factor to consider if all else is fairly constant is: does the company belong to a "family" of mutual funds? Owning a company within a "family" of funds can be advantageous if you want to shift to another fund due to a change in needs or objectives. As an example, assume you initially bought an aggressive growth fund and decide you should shift to a balanced fund. If your fund is part of a family, you probably can shift to the balanced fund with a phone call, at little or no cost to you.

9.   Except in rare cases, you should probably sign up for automatic reinvestment of dividends and capital gains to derive the benefits of compounding your gains. This also saves you from the problem of doing your own reinvesting.

10. Once you have made the investment, be sure to keep track of how your fund is doing relative to the competition and always look for funds that do a better job consistently and meet your objectives. If you find one that seems better, you can switch your investment or put *new* money into the alternative fund. Remember, there is nothing wrong with a diversified portfolio of funds.

Summary

The purpose of this chapter was to describe the general characteristics of investment companies and discuss the historical performance of mutual funds. The first section defined investment companies and discussed typical management arrangements. A breakdown of types of investment companies, including closed-end, open-end, load, no-load, and dual funds, was then considered. This was followed by a discussion of the wide variety of funds available. Almost any investment objective or combination of objectives can currently be matched by some set of investment companies.

The latter half of the chapter was a discussion of the results of a number of studies examining the historical performance of mutual funds. Most of the studies indicated that less than half the funds did as well as the aggregate market did on a risk-adjusted basis using net returns, while the results with gross returns generally indicated an average risk-adjusted return about equal to the market's, with about half the funds doing better than the market did. There were also some studies that indicated performance was superior when gross returns were considered. Following a discussion of the implications of the results for an individual investor, the chapter concluded with a discussion of sources of information on mutual funds.

Questions

1. How do you compute the net asset value of an investment company?

2. Discuss the difference between an open-end investment company and a closed-end investment company.

3. What are the two prices of importance to a closed-end investment company? How do these prices typically differ?

4. What is the difference between a load and no-load fund?

5. What are the differences between a common stock fund and a balanced fund? How would you expect their risk and return characteristics to compare?

6. Why would anyone buy a money market fund?

7. What is the purpose of dual funds? What are some potential problems for these funds? What has been the typical relationship between NAV and market price?

8. Do you care about how well a mutual fund is diversified? Why or why not?

9. Why is the stability of risk for a mutual fund important to an investor? Discuss. What is the empirical evidence in this regard—i.e., is the risk measure for mutual funds generally stable?

10. Do you feel the performance of mutual funds should be judged on the basis of return alone or on a risk-adjusted basis? Why? Discuss using examples.

11. Define the net return and gross return for a mutual fund. Discuss how you would compute each of these.

12. a. As an investor in a mutual fund, is net return or gross return relevant to you? Discuss why.

b. As an investigator attempting to determine the ability of mutual fund managers to select undervalued stocks or project market returns, which return is relevant: net or gross? Discuss why.

13. Based upon the numerous tests of mutual fund performance, you are convinced that only about half of them do better than a naive buy-and-hold policy. Does this mean you would forget about investing in them? Why or why not?

14. a. You are told that Fund X experienced above-average performance over the past two years. Do you think it will continue over the next two years? Why or why not?

b. You are told that Fund Y experienced consistently poor performance over the past two years. Would you expect this to continue over the next two years? Why or why not?

15. Assume that you see advertisements for two mutual funds which indicate that the investment objectives of the funds are consistent with yours.

a. Indicate where you would go to get a quick view of how these two funds have performed over the past two or three years.

b. Where would you go to get more in-depth information on the funds, including an address so you can write for a prospectus?

References

Bogle, John C. "Mutual Fund Performance Evaluation." *Financial Analysts Journal* 26(1970).

Carlson, Robert S. "Aggregate Performance of Mutual Funds, 1948–1967." *Journal of Financial and Quantitative Analysis* 5(1970).

Ferri, Michael G., and Oberhelman, H. Dennis. "How Well Do Money Market Funds Perform?" *Journal of Portfolio Management* 7 (1981).

Friend, Irwin; Blume, Marshall; and Crockett, Jean. *Mutual Funds and Other Institutional Investors.* New York: McGraw-Hill, 1970.

Friend, Irwin; Brown, F. E.; Herman, Edward S; and Vickers, Douglas. *Mutual Funds.* Report of the Committee on Interstate and Foreign Commerce, 87th Congress, 2d session, 28 August 1962.

Gaumnitz, Jack E. "Appraising Performance of Investment Portfolios." *Journal of Finance* 25(1970).

Gentry, James A., and Pike, John R. "Dual Funds Revisited." *Financial Analysts Journal* 24(1968).

Greeley, Robert E. "Mutual Fund Management Companies." *Financial Analysts Journal* 23(1967).

Horowitz, Ira. "A Model for Mutual Fund Evaluation." *Industrial Management Review* 6(1965).

Horowitz, Ira. "The Reward-to-Variability Ratio and Mutual Fund Performance." *Journal of Business* 39(1966).

Horowitz, Ira, and Higgins, Harold B. "Some Factors Affecting Investment Fund Performance." *Quarterly Review of Economics and Business* 3(1963).

Investment Companies. Boston, MA: Arthur Wiesenberger Services, published annually.

Jensen, Michael C. "The Performance of Mutual Funds in the Period 1945–1964." *Journal of Finance* 23(1968).

Litzenberger, Robert H., and Sosin, Howard B. "The Performance and Potential of Dual Purpose Funds." *Journal of Portfolio Management* 4(1978).

Litzenberger, Robert H., and Sosin, Howard B. "The Structure and Management of Dual Purpose Funds." *Journal of Financial Economics* 4(1977).

Litzenberger, Robert H., and Sosin, Howard B. "The Theory of Recapitalizations and the Evidence of Dual Purpose Funds." *Journal of Finance* 32(1977).

Levy, Haim, and Sarnat, Marshall. "The Case for Mutual Funds." *Financial Analysts Journal* 28(1972).

McDonald, John G. "Objectives and Performance of Mutual Funds, 1960–1969." *Journal of Financial and Quantitative Analysis* 9(1974).

Mills, Harlan D. "On the Measurement of Fund Performance." *Journal of Finance* 25(1970).

"Mutual Funds Make a Comeback." *Dun's Review,* February 1978.

Netter, Joseph, II. "Dual-Purpose Funds." *Financial Analysts Journal* 23(1967).

Pratt, Eugene J. "Myths Associated with Closed-End Investment Company Discounts." *Financial Analysts Journal* 22(1966).

Sharpe, William F. "Mutual Fund Performance." *Journal of Business* 39(1966), supplement.

Shelton, John P.; Brigham, Eugene F; and Hoffflander, Alfred E. "An Evaluation and Appraisal of Dual Funds." *Financial Analysts Journal* 23 (1967).

Simonson, Donald G. "The Speculative Behavior of Mutual Funds." *Journal of Finance* 27(1972).

Treynor, Jack L. "How to Rate Management of Investment Funds." *Harvard Business Review* 43(1965).

Treynor, Jack L., and Mazuy, Kay K. "Can Mutual Funds Outguess the Market?" *Harvard Business Review* 24(1966).

Williamson, Peter J. "Measuring Mutual Fund Performance." *Financial Analysts Journal* 28(1972).

Glossary of Mutual Fund Terms

Accumulation Plan (Periodic Payment Plan) Enables an investor to purchase mutual fund shares periodically in large or small amounts, usually with provisions for the reinvestment of income dividends and capital gains distributions in additional shares.

Adviser The organization employed by a mutual fund to give professional advice on its investments and management of its assets.

Asked or Offering Price The price at which a mutual fund's shares can be purchased. The asked or offering price means the net asset value per share plus, at times, a sales charge.

Automatic Reinvestment The option available to mutual fund shareholders whereby fund income dividends and capital gains distributions are automatically put back into the fund to buy new shares and thereby build up holdings.

Balanced Fund A mutual fund which has an investment policy of "balancing" its portfolio, generally by including bonds, preferred stocks, and common stocks.

Bid or Redemption Price The price at which a mutual fund's shares are redeemed (bought back) by the fund. The bid or redemption price usually means the net asset value per share.

Bond Fund A mutual fund with a portfolio consisting primarily of bonds. The emphasis of such funds is normally on income rather than growth.

Bookshares A modern share recording system that eliminates the need for mutual fund share certificates but gives the fund shareowner a record of his holdings.

Broker-Dealer (or Dealer) A firm that retails mutual fund shares and other securities to the public.

Capital Gains Distributions Payments to mutual fund shareholders of gains realized on the sale of the fund's portfolio securities. These amounts usually are paid once a year.

Capital Growth An increase in the market value of a mutual fund's securities which is reflected in the net asset value of fund shares. This is a specific long-term objective of many mutual funds.

Closed-End Investment Company Unlike mutual funds (known as "open-end"), closed-end companies issue only a limited number of shares and do not redeem them (buy them back). Instead, closed-end shares are traded in the securities markets, with supply and demand determining the price.

Common Stock Fund A mutual fund with a portfolio consisting primarily of common stocks. The emphasis of such funds is usually on growth.

Contractual Plan A program for the accumulation of mutual fund shares in which the investor agrees to invest a fixed amount on a regular basis for a specified number of years. A substantial portion of the sales charge applicable to the total investment is usually deducted from early payments.

Conversion Privilege (Exchange Privilege) Enables a mutual fund shareholder to transfer his investment from one fund to another within the same fund group if his needs or objectives change, sometimes with a small transaction charge.

Custodian The organization (usually a bank) that holds in custody and safekeeping the securities and other assets of a mutual fund.

Diversification The mutual fund policy of spreading investments among a number of different securities to reduce the risks inherent in investing.

Dollar-Cost Averaging Investing equal amounts of money at regular intervals regardless of whether the stock market is moving upward or downward. This reduces average share costs in periods of lower securities prices and number of shares in periods of higher prices.

Exchange Privilege See Conversion Privilege.

Growth Fund A mutual fund with the primary investment objective of growth of capital. Invests principally in common stocks with growth potential.

Growth-Income Fund A mutual fund with the aim of providing for a degree of both income and long-term growth.

Income Dividends Payments to mutual fund shareholders of dividends, interest, and short-term capital gains earned on the fund's portfolio securities after deduction of operating expenses.

Income Fund A mutual fund with the primary investment objective of current income rather than growth of capital. It invests in stocks and bonds normally paying higher dividends and interest.

Individual Retirement Account A retirement program for individuals who are not covered under employer or government retirement plans. An individual may contribute and deduct from his or her income tax an amount up to the lesser of 15 percent of compensation or $1,500. An individual retirement account may be funded with mutual fund shares.

Investment Adviser See Adviser.

Investment Company A corporation, trust, or partnership in which investors may pool their money to obtain professional management and diversification of their investments. Mutual funds are the most popular type of investment company.

Investment Objective The goal (e.g., long-term capital growth, current income, etc.) that an investor or a mutual fund pursues.

Keogh Plan A retirement program for self-employed individuals and their employees based on tax-saving provisions. A Keogh plan may be funded with mutual fund shares.

Liquid Asset Fund See Money Market Fund.

Management Fee The amount paid by a mutual fund to the investment adviser for its services. The average cost to the shareholder industry-wide is about one-half of one percent of his investment a year.

Money Market (Cash Management) Fund A mutual fund that invests primarily in short-term instruments, such as instruments issued or guaranteed by the U.S. Government or its agencies and instrumentalities, bank certificates of deposit, bankers' acceptances, and commercial paper. The fund's primary objective is current income.

Municipal Bond Fund A mutual fund that invests in a broad range of tax-exempt bonds issued by states, cities, and other local governments. The interest obtained from these bonds is passed through to shareowners free of federal tax. The fund's primary objective is current income.

Mutual Fund An investment company that ordinarily stands ready to buy back (redeem) its shares at their current net asset value; the value of the shares depends on the market value of the fund's portfolio securities at the time. Also, mutual funds generally continuously offer new shares to investors.

Net Asset Value Per Share The market worth of a mutual fund's total resources (securities, cash, and any accrued earnings) after deduction of liabilities, divided by the number of shares outstanding.

No-Load Fund A mutual fund selling its shares at net asset value without the addition of sales charges.

Open-End Investment Company The more formal name for a mutual fund, indicating that it continuously offers new shares to investors and redeems them (buys them back) on demand.

Payroll Deduction Plan An arrangement whereby an employee may accumulate shares in a mutual fund by authorizing his employer to deduct and transfer to a fund a specified amount from his salary at stated times.

Periodic Payment Plan See Accumulation Plan.

Prospectus A booklet describing the mutual fund and offering its shares for sale. It contains information required by the Securities and Exchange Commission on such subjects as the fund's investment objectives and policies, services, investment restrictions, officers and directors, how shares can be bought and redeemed, its charges, and its financial statements.

Qualified Retirement Plan A private retirement plan that meets the rules and regulations of the Internal Revenue Service. Contributions to a qualified retirement plan are in almost all cases tax deductible and earnings on such contributions are always tax sheltered until the investor retires.

Redemption Price The amount per share the mutual fund shareholder receives when he cashes in his shares (also known as "bid price"). The value of the shares depends on the market value of the fund's portfolio securities at the time.

Reinvestment Privilege A service provided by most mutual funds for the automatic reinvestment of a shareholder's income dividends and capital gains distributions in additional shares.

Sales Charge An amount charged to purchase shares in most mutual funds. Typically the charge is 8.5 percent of the initial investment. The charge is added to the net asset value per share in determining the offering price. (Some funds, which do not have salesmen, have no sales charge and are called "no-load" funds.)

Specialty Fund A mutual fund specializing in the securities of certain industries, special types of securities, or in regional investments.

Split Funding A program that combines the purchase of mutual fund shares with the purchase of life insurance contracts or other investment instruments.

Transfer Agent The organization employed by a mutual fund to prepare and maintain records relating to the accounts of fund shareholders.

Underwriter (Principal Underwriter) The organization that acts as the distributor of a mutual fund's shares to broker-dealers and the public.

Variable Annuity A contract under which an annuity is purchased with a fixed number of dollars that are converted into a varying number of accumulation units. At retirement, the annuitant is paid a fixed number of monthly units which are converted into a varying number of dollars. The value of both accumulation and annuity units varies in accordance with the performance of a portfolio invested in equity securities.

Variable Life Insurance An equity-based life insurance policy in which the reserves may be invested in common stocks. The death benefit is guaranteed never to fall below the face value, but it could increase if the value of the securities increased. There may be no guaranteed cash surrender value under this kind of policy.

Voluntary Plan A flexible accumulation plan in which there is no definite time period or total amount to be invested.

Withdrawal Plans Many mutual funds offer withdrawal programs whereby shareholders receive payments from their investments at regular intervals. These payments typically are drawn from the fund's dividends and capital gains distributions, if any, and from principal, to the extent necessary.

PORTFOLIO THEORY
AND APPLICATION

PART·FIVE

After considering a number of individual investment instruments, your final task is to combine these assets into a portfolio that reflects your risk and return preferences. You will also want to be able to evaluate your own performance, or that of your investment manager, in selecting a portfolio. The material in this section is intended to help you in this final phase of your investment program.

Chapter 20 contains a detailed discussion of basic portfolio theory as developed by Harry Markowitz. The intent is to ensure that you understand all phases of the theory, beginning with the basic concepts of covariance and correlation. The subsequent discussion of alternative portfolios is heavily illustrated with detailed problems.

Building upon basic portfolio theory, several authors extended it into what is referred to as the Capital Asset Pricing Model (CAPM), which, as shown in Chapter 21, can be used in the pricing of individual capital assets. Numerous examples are given that illustrate the implications of the theory for selection of undervalued and overvalued stocks.

Chapter 22 is an application of portfolio theory to a rather unique set of investments: securities of firms in foreign countries. We consider the logic behind international diversification, and the empirical evidence in favor of such diversification for optimal portfolio construction. Finally, we consider the problems international diversification involves, and how it can be accomplished through one of several international mutual funds.

The final chapter is concerned with helping you to evaluate the performance of your portfolio. Whether you make all of your own decisions or employ a professional portfolio manager (e.g., either an investment counselor or an investment company) it is important that you take the time to determine whether the risk-adjusted performance of your portfolio is worth the time you spend on it or the money you pay someone else to manage it. The discussion in Chapter 23 will help you evaluate portfolio performance and also deals with the information available from some professional evaluation services.

Harry M. Markowitz

In every field of study it is possible to look back and identify a person or event that caused a major change in the direction or development of the field. In investments it is clear that the seminal work by Harry Markowitz on portfolio theory changed the field more than any other single event. His Ph.D. dissertation written at the University of Chicago dealt with portfolio selection and in it he developed the basic portfolio model. A brief presentation of the model was published in the Journal of Finance *in 1952. Subsequently, a complete presentation of the theory and its implementation was published in* Portfolio Selection: Efficient Diversification of Investments, *published by* John Wiley and Sons in 1959 and by Yale University Press in 1972. Because of this work, Markowitz is referred to as the father of modern portfolio theory, and much subsequent research has been based on this development.

Markowitz designed the SIMSCRIPT and SIMSCRIPT II programming languages. He is author with B. Hausner and H. Karr, of: SIMSCRIPT: A Simulation Programming Language (Prentice-Hall, 1963); The SIMSCRIPT II Programming Manual, with P. Kiviat and R. Villanueva (Prentice-Hall, 1969); and an article on SIMSCRIPT in The Encyclopedia of Computer Science and Technology (Marcell-Decker, 1979).*

His study on sparse matrices, "The Elimination Form of the Inverse and Its Application to Linear Programming," published in Management Science, 1957, spawned extensive work on sparse matrix techniques and is currently used in large linear programming codes.

Other work includes the modeling of industry-wide and economy-wide production relationships, economic behavior under uncertainty, and quadratic programming, as in Studies in Process Analysis: Economy-Wide Production Capabilities, edited by Manne and Markowitz (John Wiley & Sons, 1963); "Utility of Wealth," Journal of Finance, 1952; "The Optimization of a Quadratic Function Subject to Linear Constraints," Naval Research Logistics Quarterly, 1956.

Harry Markowitz was born in Chicago, Illinois on August 24, 1927. He received his M.A. in economics in 1950 and his Ph.D. in economics in 1954 from the University of Chicago. He worked for the RAND Corporation from 1950 to 1952 and 1961 to 1962; was Technical Director of CACI, Inc. 1962–1968; portfolio manager and then president of Arbitrage Management Company 1969–1972. He is currently a research staff member of IBM's T.J. Watson Research Center.

PORTFOLIO THEORY

❧ 20 ❧

Previously we discussed the basic concepts of investing and valuation theory applied to a number of diverse assets: stocks, bonds, options, warrants, and commodities. At this point it is necessary to consider how you should *combine* these assets into a portfolio that will provide you with a combination of risk and return that is optimum for you; i.e., one that will provide the highest potential rate of return for a given level of risk, or that will minimize the amount of risk for a given level of return. Prior to the 1960s investors typically constructed their portfolios in a rather ad hoc fashion. Specifically, investors or portfolio managers knew that they should diversify their investments to reduce the risk of the portfolio. Unfortunately, there was no very rigorous measure of risk available, so they did not know exactly what they were trying to reduce. In addition, when investors diversified, they knew they should invest in "different" assets, but they were not certain of which characteristic should be different. This ad hoc approach to portfolio construction changed during the 1950s when Harry Markowitz developed what is called *portfolio theory*.[1] This theory implied a measure of risk and also indicated how this risk measure is computed for a portfolio of assets. The derivation of the portfolio risk formula indicates *how* to combine different assets in a portfolio; i.e., what is important when combining different assets.

The purpose of this chapter is to explain portfolio theory step-by-step so that you will understand the basic portfolio risk formula and recognize what is important when you are combining different assets. At times the formulas may appear forbidding, but all of them will be explained and numerous examples presented so that you can appreciate the impact of various assumptions.

---

[1]Harry Markowitz, "Portfolio Selection," *Journal of Finance* 7 (1952): 77–91; and idem, *Portfolio Selection—Efficient Diversification of Investments* (New York: John Wiley & Sons, 1959).

An Optimum Portfolio

One basic assumption of portfolio theory is that investors want to maximize the returns from their portfolio of investments for a given level of risk (uncertainty). It is important to recognize that the portfolio you are considering should include *all* of your assets and liabilities, not only stocks or even only marketable securities, but also such items as your car, house, and other less marketable assets like coins, stamps, antiques, furniture, thoroughbred race horses, etc. The full spectrum of your assets must be considered because the returns from all of these assets interact and *this interaction in the rates of return is important.* Hence a good portfolio is *not* simply a collection of individually good assets.

An Assumption: Risk Aversion

It is also assumed that *investors are basically risk averse,* which simply means that, given a choice between two assets with equal rates of return, an investor will select the asset with the lower level of risk. Evidence that most investors are risk averse is provided by the fact that they purchase various types of insurance including life insurance, car insurance, and hospital and accident insurance. Insurance is basically a current certain outlay of a given amount to guard against an uncertain possibly larger outlay in the future. People who purchase insurance are willing to pay to avoid the uncertainty of the future regarding these items. In other words, they want to avoid the risk of a potentially large future loss. Further evidence of risk aversion is the difference in promised yield for different grades of bonds that are supposedly of different risk classes. The required rate of return (promised yield) increases as you go from AAA (the lowest risk class) to AA to A, etc. This means that investors require a higher rate of return to accept higher risk.

The foregoing does not imply that everybody is risk averse, or that investors are completely risk averse regarding all financial commitments. Not everybody buys insurance for everything and there are some people who have no insurance against anything, either by choice or because they can't afford it. In addition, some individuals buy insurance and also gamble at race tracks or in Las Vegas where it is known that the expected returns are negative, which means that participants are willing to pay for the excitement of the risk involved. This combination of risk preference and risk aversion can be explained by a utility function that is not completely concave or convex, but is a combination of the two that depends upon the amount of money involved. Friedman and Savage speculate that such is the case for people who like to gamble for small amounts (in lotteries or nickel slot machines), but insure themselves against large losses like fire or accidents.[2]

However, most investors committing large sums of money to developing a

---

[2]Milton Friedman and Leonard J. Savage, "The Utility Analysis of Choices Involving Risk," *Journal of Political Economy* 56 (1948): 279–304.

portfolio of earning assets are risk averse. This means that there should be a positive relationship between expected return and expected risk.

While there is a difference in the specific definitions of risk and uncertainty, for our purposes, and in most financial literature, the two terms are used interchangeably. In fact, one way to define risk is as *the uncertainty of future outcomes.* An alternative definition might be, *the probability of an adverse outcome.*

Markowitz Portfolio Theory

In the 1950s and early 1960s a large segment of the investment community talked about risk, but there was no measurable specification for the term. One aspect of the portfolio model is that it required investors to quantify their risk variable. The basic portfolio model, developed by Harry Markowitz, derived the expected rate of return for a portfolio of assets and an expected risk measure. Markowitz showed that the variance of the rate of return was a meaningful measure of risk under a reasonable set of assumptions and derived the formulas for computing the variance of the portfolio. This portfolio variance formulation indicated the importance of diversification for reducing risk, and showed how to properly diversify. The Markowitz model is based on several assumptions regarding investor behavior:

1. Investors consider each investment alternative as being represented by a probability distribution of expected returns over some holding period.

2. Investors maximize one-period expected utility and possess utility curves that demonstrate diminishing marginal utility of wealth.

3. Individuals estimate risk on the basis of the variability of expected returns.

4. Investors base decisions solely on expected return and risk; i.e., their utility curves are a function of expected return and variance (or standard deviation) of returns only.

5. For a given risk level, investors prefer higher returns to lower returns. Similarly, for a given level of expected return, investors prefer less risk to more risk.

Under these assumptions, *a single asset or portfolio of assets is considered to be "efficient" if no other asset or portfolio of assets offers higher expected return with the same (or lower) risk, or lower risk with the same (or higher) expected return.*

One of the best-known measures of risk is the *variance or standard deviation of expected returns.* It is a statistical measure of the dispersion of returns around the expected value; i.e., a larger value indicates greater dispersion, all other factors being equal. The idea is that the more disperse the returns, the greater the uncertainty of those returns in any future period. Another measure of risk is the *range of returns* based upon the assumption that a larger range of returns, from the lowest to the highest, means greater uncertainty regarding future expected returns.

In contrast to using measures that analyze any deviation from expectations, some feel that the investor should only be concerned with *returns below expectations*—deviations below the mean value. A measure that only considers such adverse deviations is the semivariance. An extension of this measure would be *deviations below zero* or negative returns. Both measures implicitly assume that investors want to minimize their regret from below-average returns. It is implicit that investors would welcome positive returns or returns above expectations, so these are not considered when measuring risk. Similarly, Zinbarg proposed the use of *negative opportunity returns* as a measure of risk. Negative opportunity returns are returns below the risk-free rate of return.[3]

Although there are numerous potential measures of risk, we begin with the variance or standard deviation of returns because this measure is somewhat intuitive, and it is a correct risk measure for most investors.

Portfolio Return

The expected rate of return for a portfolio of assets is simply the weighted average of the expected rates of return for the individual assets in the portfolio. The weights are the proportion of total value for the asset. The expected return for a hypothetical individual asset is computed as shown in Table 20.1. In this example, we assume that we have estimated equal probabilities for all the potential returns.

The expected return for an individual asset with the set of potential returns and probabilities used in the example would be 11 percent. The expected return for a hypothetical four-asset portfolio is shown in Table 20.2.

The expected return for the total portfolio would be 11.5 percent. The effect of adding or dropping any security from the portfolio would be easy to determine, given the new weights based on value, and the expected returns for each of the assets. This computation of the expected return for the portfolio can be generalized as follows:

$$E(Rport) = \sum_{i=1}^{n} W_i R_i$$

Variance (Standard Deviation) of Returns

It was mentioned earlier that we would be using the variance, or the standard deviation of returns, as the measure of risk (the reader will recall that the standard deviation is the square root of the variance). Therefore, at this point we will

---

[3]Edward D. Zinbarg, "Modern Approach to Investment Risk," *Financial Executive* 41 (1973): 44–48.

Probability	Potential Return (%)	Expected Return (%)
.25	.08	.0200
.25	.10	.0250
.25	.12	.0300
.25	.14	.0350
		$E(R) = .1100$

Table 20.1   Computation of Expected Return for Individual Risky Asset

Weight (W_1) (% of Portfolio)	Expected Security Return R_i	Expected Portfolio Return ($W_i \times R_i$)
.20	.10	.0200
.30	.11	.0330
.30	.12	.0360
.20	.13	.0260
		$E(Rport) = .1150$

Table 20.2   Computation of the Expected Return for a Portfolio of Risky Assets

demonstrate the computation of the standard deviation of returns for an individual asset. Subsequently, after a discussion of some other statistical concepts we will consider the determination of the standard deviation for a *portfolio* of assets.

The variance or standard deviation is a measure of the variation of possible rates of return (R_i) from the expected rate of return [$E(R_i)$] as follows:

$$\text{Variance } (\sigma^2) = \sum_{i=1}^{n} [R_i - E(R_i)]^2 P_i$$

where P_i is the probability of the possible rate of return (R_i).

$$\text{Standard Deviation } (\sigma) = \sqrt{\sum_{i=1}^{n} [R_i - E(R_i)]^2 P_i}$$

The computation of the variance and standard deviation for the individual risky asset in Table 20.1 is set forth in Table 20.3.

Prior to discussing the derivation of the risk of the portfolio, it is necessary for you to understand two basic concepts in statistics: covariance and correlation.

Potential Return (R_i)	Expected Return $E(R_i)$	$R_i - E(R_i)$	$[R_i - E(R_i)]^2$	P_i	$[R_i - E(R_i)]^2 P_i$
.08	.11	−.03	.0009	.25	.000225
.10	.11	−.01	.0001	.25	.000025
.12	.11	.01	.0001	.25	.000025
.14	.11	.03	.0009	.25	.000225
Variance (σ^2) = .00050					.000500
Standard Deviation (σ) = .02236					

Table 20.3   Computation of the Variance for an Individual Risky Asset

Covariance of Returns—Discussion and Example

Covariance is a measure of the degree to which two variables "move together" over time. In portfolio analysis, we usually are concerned with the covariance of *returns* rather than that of prices or some other variable.[4] If the covariance between the returns for two assets is positive, this indicates that the returns tend to move in the same direction at the same time; if the covariance is negative, it indicates that the returns tend to move in opposite directions. The *magnitude* of the covariance depends upon the variances of the individual return series, as well as on the relationship between the series.

Figure 20.1 contains a time-series plot of the monthly rates of return for two stocks: Avon and IBM. Although it appears that the two return series moved together during some months, in other months it appears that the returns moved in opposite directions. The purpose of the covariance measure is to provide an *absolute* measure of their movement together over time.

For two assets, i and j, the covariance of monthly rates of return is defined as:

$$Cov_{ij} = E\{[R_i - E(R_i)][R_j - E(R_j)]\}$$

$$= \frac{1}{12} \sum_{i=1}^{12} [R_i - E(R_i)][R_j - E(R_j)]$$

As can be seen, if the rates of return for one stock are above its mean during a given period, and the returns for the other stock are likewise above its mean dur-

---

[4]Returns, of course, can be measured in a variety of ways, depending upon the type of asset being considered. The reader will recall that we defined returns in Chapter 1 as
$$R_t = \frac{EV - BV + CF}{BV},$$
where EV is ending value, BV is beginning value, and CF is the cash flow during the period.

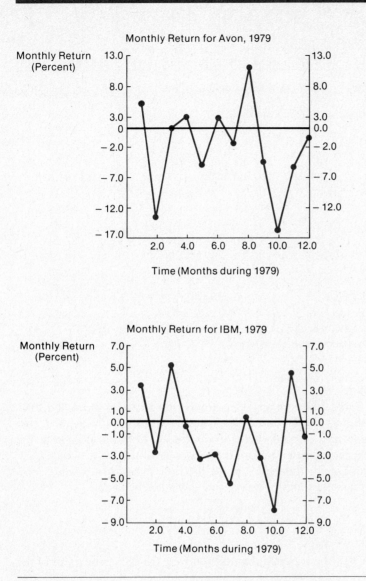

Figure 20.1   Time-Series Plot of Returns for Avon and IBM

ing this same period, then the *product* of these deviations from the mean will be positive (i.e., the covariance will be some large positive value). In contrast, if, during a given month, the return on Avon was above its mean and the return on the IBM stock was below its mean, the product of these deviations would be negative. If this contrary movement happened consistently, the covariance between the rates of return would be a large negative value.

	Closing Prices[a]		Monthly Return (%)				
	Avon	IBM[a]	Avon (R_j)	IBM (R_j)	$R_i - E(R_i)$	$R_j - E(R_j)$	$[R_i - E(R_i)][R_j - E(R_j)]$
12/78	$50^3/_4$	$74^5/_8$	—	—	—	—	—
1/79	$53^1/_2$	$77^1/_8$	5.4	3.4	7.2	4.5	32.40
2/79	$46^1/_4$	75	−13.6	−2.8	−11.8	−1.7	20.06
3/79	$46^3/_4$	$78^7/_8$	1.1	5.2	2.9	6.3	18.27
4/79	$48^1/_4$	$78^5/_8$	3.2	−0.4	5.0	0.7	3.50
5/79	$45^7/_8$	76	− 4.9	−3.3	− 3.1	−2.2	6.82
6/79	$47^1/_4$	$73^7/_8$	3.0	−2.8	4.8	−1.7	− 8.16
7/79	$46^5/_8$	$69^3/_4$	− 1.3	−5.6	0.5	−4.5	− 2.25
8/79	$51^7/_8$	70	11.3	0.4	13.1	1.5	19.65
9/79	$49^5/_8$	$67^3/_4$	− 4.3	−3.2	− 2.5	−2.1	5.25
10/79	$41^5/_8$	$62^3/_8$	−16.1	−7.9	−14.3	−6.8	97.24
11/79	$39^1/_2$	$65^1/_4$	− 5.1	4.6	− 3.3	5.7	−18.81
12/79	$39^3/_8$	$64^3/_8$	− 0.3	−1.3	1.5	−0.2	− 0.30
		E(R) =	− 1.8%	−1.1%			Σ = 173.67

Table 20.4   Computation of Covariance of Returns for Avon and IBM
[a]All prices adjusted for 4-for-1 split in June 1979.

As an example, Table 20.4 contains data on monthly prices for Avon and IBM common stock during 1979. For simplicity, we have ignored dividends in this example, although they normally would be included. Without looking at the figures, one might expect the returns for the two stocks to show a reasonably low covariance because of the differences in the products these firms produce (cosmetics and computers). Monthly returns were computed by taking:

$$R_{it} = \frac{P_{it} - P_{i,t-1}}{P_{i,t-1}}$$

and similarly for R_{jt}. The expected returns E(R) were the arithmetic mean of the monthly returns:

$$E(R_i) = \frac{1}{12} \sum_{t=1}^{12} R_{it} \text{ and } E(R_j) = \frac{1}{12} \sum_{t=1}^{12} R_{jt}$$

All figures (except those in the last column) were rounded to the nearest tenth of one percent. As shown in Table 20.4, the average monthly return on Avon was −1.8 percent and the average monthly return for IBM was −1.1 percent.

From the table we can compute the covariance as follows:

$$Cov_{ij} = \frac{1}{12} (173.67) = 14.472$$

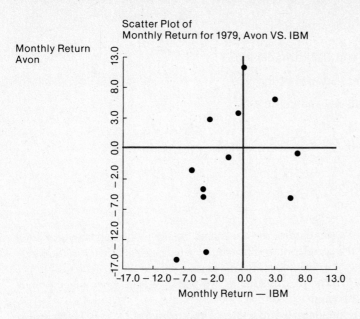

Figure 20.2   Scatter Plot of Monthly Returns for Avon and IBM

Interpretation of a number like 14.472 is difficult; i.e., is 14 high or low for co-variance? We know the relationship is generally positive, but it is not possible to be more specific.

Figure 20.2 shows a scatter diagram with paired values of R_{it} and R_{jt} plotted against each other. This plot demonstrates the linear nature and strength of the relationship.

Covariance and Correlation

Covariance is affected by the variability of the two return series. Therefore, interpreting a number such as the 14.472 computed in the previous section is difficult because, if the two individual series were very volatile, 14 might not indicate a very strong positive relationship. In contrast, if the two series were very stable, a value of 14 could be relatively large. Obviously, what you want to do is to "standardize" this covariance for the individual variability of the two return series. This is done in the following relationship:

$$r_{ij} = \frac{Cov_{ij}}{\sigma_i \sigma_j}$$

where:

r_{ij} = the correlation coefficient of returns

σ_i = the standard deviation of R_{it}

σ_j = the standard deviation of R_{jt}

$$\sigma_i{}^2 = E\{[R_{it} - E(R_i)]^2\} = \sum_{t=1}^{N} [R_{it} - E(R_i)]^2 \frac{1}{N}$$

$$\sigma_j{}^2 = E\{[R_{jt} - E(R_j)]^2\} = \sum_{t=1}^{N} [R_{jt} - E(R_j)]^2 \frac{1}{N}$$

As shown, when we standardize the covariance by the individual standard deviations, we derive the correlation coefficient (r_{ij}) which can only vary in the range -1 to $+1$. A value of $+1$ would indicate a perfect positive linear relationship between R_i and R_j; i.e., the returns for the two stocks would move together in a completely linear manner.

To derive this standardized measure of the relationship, it is necessary to compute the standard deviation for the two individual series. We already have the values for $R_{it} - E(R_i)$ and $R_{jt} - E(R_j)$ in Table 20.4. We can square each of these values and sum them as is done in Table 20.5.

Thus:

$$\sigma_i^2 = \frac{1}{12} (652.88) = 54.406$$

and

$$\sigma_j^2 = \frac{1}{12} (176.73) = 14.728$$

Therefore:

$$\sigma_i = \sqrt{54.406} = 7.376\%$$
$$\sigma_j = \sqrt{14.728} = 3.838\%$$

Thus, the correlation coefficient between returns for Avon and IBM is:

$$r_{ij} = \frac{Cov_{ij}}{\sigma_i\sigma_j} = \frac{14.472}{(7.376)(3.838)} = 0.51$$

As noted, a correlation of $+1.0$ would indicate perfect positive correlation, a value of -1.0 would mean that the returns moved in a completely opposite direction, while a value of zero would mean that there is no linear relationship between the returns. That is, they are uncorrelated from a statistical standpoint; this does not mean that they are independent. The value of $r_{ij} = 0.51$ is significant but

	Avon		IBM	
	$R_{it} - E(R_i)$	$[R_{it} - E(R_i)]^2$	$R_{jt} - E(R_j)$	$[R_{jt} - E(R_j)]^2$
1/79	7.2	51.84	4.5	20.25
2/79	−11.8	139.24	−1.7	2.89
3/79	2.9	8.41	6.3	39.69
4/79	5.0	25.00	0.7	0.49
5/79	− 3.1	9.61	−2.2	4.84
6/79	4.8	23.04	−1.7	2.89
7/79	0.5	0.25	−4.5	20.25
8/79	13.1	171.61	1.5	2.25
9/79	− 2.5	6.25	−2.1	4.41
10/79	−14.3	204.49	−6.8	46.24
11/79	− 3.3	10.89	5.7	32.49
12/79	1.5	2.25	−0.2	0.04
		$\Sigma = 652.88$		$\Sigma = 176.73$

Table 20.5 Computation of Standard Deviation of Returns for Avon and IBM

not very high compared to the correlation between some stocks within industries where the correlations exceed 0.85.

Given this understanding of the concepts of covariance and correlation, it is now possible to consider the formula for computing the standard deviation of returns for a portfolio of assets. It is necessary to be able to compute the standard deviation because this is the measure of risk we will use. As noted, the derivation of the formula for computing the standard deviation of a portfolio of assets was accomplished by Harry Markowitz.[5]

Standard Deviation of a Portfolio

Earlier we set forth the formula for the expected return for a portfolio of assets and showed that the expected return of the portfolio was simply the weighted average of the expected returns for the individual assets in the portfolio; the weights were the percentage of value of the portfolio. (See the example in Table 20.2.) Under such conditions, it is very easy to see the impact on the portfolio's expected return of adding or deleting an asset. Based upon this, one might assume that it is possible to derive the standard deviation of the portfolio in the same manner, i.e., by computing the weighted average of the standard deviations for the individual assets. The fact is, this is *not* correct! When Markowitz derived the general formula for the standard deviation of a portfolio it was as follows:[6]

[5]Markowitz, "Portfolio Selection," and idem, *Portfolio Selection: Efficient Diversification.*

[6]For the detailed derivation of this formula the reader is referred to Markowitz, *Portfolio Selection: Efficient Diversification.*

$$\sigma_{port} = \sqrt{\sum_{i=1}^{N} W_i^2 \sigma_i^2 + 2 \sum_{i=1}^{N} \sum_{j=1}^{N} W_i W_j Cov_{ij}}$$

where:

σ_{port} = the standard deviation of the portfolio

W_i^2 = the weights of the individual assets in the portfolio, where weights are determined by the proportion of value in the portfolio

σ_i^2 = the variance of asset i

Cov_{ij} = the covariance between the returns for assets i and j.

In words, this formula indicates that the standard deviation for the portfolio is a function of the weighted average of the individual variances (where the weights are squared), plus two times *the weighted covariances between all the assets in the portfolio.* The point is, the standard deviation for the portfolio encompasses not only the variances, but *also* the covariances between pairs of individual securities. Further, it can be shown that, in a portfolio with a large number of securities, this formula can be stated as the summation of weighted covariances. This means that the important factor to consider when adding an asset to a portfolio with a number of other assets is *not* the individual asset's variance, but *its average covariance with all the other assets in the portfolio.* In the following examples we will consider the simple case of a two-asset portfolio. It is important to see the impact of different covariances on the total risk (standard deviation) of the portfolio.

The Two-Asset Portfolio

Examining the simplest case, in which only two assets are combined to form a portfolio, serves to illustrate the computations involved and to help explain the characteristic shape of the efficient frontier. Because the Markowitz model assumes that any asset, or portfolio of assets, can be described by only two parameters, the expected return and expected standard deviation of returns, the following could be applied to two *individual* assets with the indicated parameters and correlation coefficients, or to two *portfolios* of assets with the same indicated parameters and correlation coefficients.

Equal Risk and Return—Changing Correlations

Consider first the case in which both assets have the same expected return and expected standard deviation of return. As an example, let us assume:

$$E(R_1) = .20 \qquad E(\sigma_1) = .10$$

$$E(R_2) = .20 \qquad E(\sigma_2) = .10$$

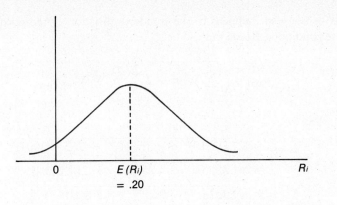

Figure 20.3 Normally Distributed Returns

If the returns were normally distributed, the distribution of each asset's returns would appear as shown in Figure 20.3. At first glance, it might appear that identical $E(R_i)$ and $E(\sigma_i)$ would imply that

$$E(R_{port}) = .20, \text{ and } E(\sigma_{port}) = .10$$

regardless of the correlation between the returns of assets 1 and 2. While this *is* true of *expected portfolio return* (as can easily be verified by reference to the equation for computing expected returns), it is *not* true of expected portfolio standard deviation, unless the returns are perfectly positively correlated, as in the following example. To see the effect of different covariances (i.e., we assume different levels of correlation between the two assets), consider the following set of examples where the two assets have equal weights in the portfolio (i.e., $W_1 = .50$; $W_2 = .50$). Therefore, the only value that will change in each example is the correlation between the returns for the two assets. Recall that:

$$Cov_{ij} = r_{ij}\sigma_i\sigma_j$$

Thus, consider the following alternative correlation coefficients and attendant covariances. The covariance will be equal to: $(r_{1,2})(.10)(.10)$ because both standard deviations are .10.

a. $r_{1,2} = 1.00$ $Cov_{1,2} = (1.00)(.10)(.10) = .01$

b. $r_{1,2} = 0.50$ $Cov_{1,2} = .005$

c. $r_{1,2} = 0.00$ $Cov_{1,2} = .000$

d. $r_{1,2} = -0.50$ $Cov_{1,2} = -.005$

e. $r_{1,2} = -1.00$ $Cov_{1,2} = -.01$

Now let us see what happens to the standard deviation of the portfolio under these five conditions. Recall that:

$$\sigma_{\text{port}} = \sqrt{\sum_{i=1}^{N} W_i^2 \sigma_i^2 + 2 \sum_{i=1}^{N} \sum_{j=1}^{N} W_i W_j \text{Cov}_{ij}}$$

Thus in case (a):

$$\sigma_{\text{port(a)}} = \sqrt{(.5)^2(.10)^2 + (.5)^2(.10)^2 + 2(.5)(.5)(.01)}$$
$$= \sqrt{(.25)(.01) + (.25)(.01) + 2(.25)(.01)}$$
$$= \sqrt{(.0025) + (.0025) + (.50)(.01)}$$
$$= \sqrt{(.0050) + (.0050)}$$
$$= \sqrt{.01}$$
$$= .10$$

As shown, in this case the returns for the two assets are perfectly positively correlated, so the standard deviation for the portfolio *is* the weighted average of the individual standard deviations, and there is no real benefit to combining the two assets; they are like one asset already because their returns move together. Now consider case (b) where $r_{1,2}$ equals 0.50.

$$\sigma_{\text{port(b)}} = \sqrt{(.5)^2(.10)^2 + (.5)^2(.10)^2 + 2(.5)(.5)(.005)}$$
$$= \sqrt{(.0025) + (.0025) + (.50)(.005)}$$
$$= \sqrt{(.0050) + (.0025)}$$
$$= \sqrt{.0075}$$
$$= .0866$$

As can be seen by comparison to the previous example, case (a), the only term that changed in the computation was the last term (i.e., $\text{Cov}_{1,2}$), which changed from .01 to .005. The ultimate result was that the standard deviation declined by about 13 percent from .10 to .0866. Note that *the expected return did not change* because it is simply the weighted average of the individual expected returns; i.e., it is equal to 0.20 in both cases.

In the third example (c):

$$\sigma_{\text{port(c)}} = \sqrt{(.5)^2(.10)^2 + (.5)^2(.10)^2 + 2(.5)(.5)(0.00)}$$
$$= \sqrt{(.0025) + (.0025) + (.5)(0.00)}$$
$$= \sqrt{.0050}$$
$$= .0707$$

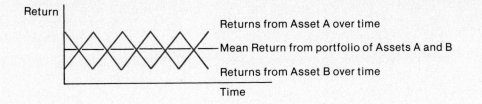

Figure 20.4   Time Pattern of Returns for Two Assets with
Perfect Negative Correlation

Again, the only term that changed was the covariance which became zero because the correlation was zero. The result is that the standard deviation declined 18 percent from case (b) to .0707. The expected return for this case remains at 0.20 percent.

The result for case (d), where $r_{1,2} = -0.50$ is as follows:

$$\sigma_{\text{port(d)}} = \sqrt{(.5)^2(.10)^2 + (.5)^2(.10)^2 + 2(.5)(.5)(-0.50)}$$
$$= \sqrt{(.0025) + (.0025) + (.5)(-0.0050)}$$
$$= \sqrt{(.0050) + (-0.0025)}$$
$$= \sqrt{.0025}$$
$$= 0.05$$

In this case, the covariance term is *negative*, so it reduces the variance terms. As a result, the portfolio standard deviation is only half the size it was when the correlation was +1.00.

The final case where the correlation between the two assets is −1.00 indicates the ultimate benefits of diversification.

$$\sigma_{\text{port(e)}} = \sqrt{(.5)(.10) + (.5)(.10) + 2(.5)(.5)(-1.00)}$$
$$= \sqrt{(.0025) + (.0025) + (.5)(-0.01)}$$
$$= \sqrt{(.0050) + (-0.0050)}$$
$$= \sqrt{0}$$
$$= 0$$

In this final case, the covariance term exactly offsets the individual variance terms, and so the overall standard deviation of the portfolio is zero. *This would be a risk-free portfolio.* A graph of such a pattern is contained in Figure 20.4.

The result of perfect negative correlation is that the mean return for the two securities combined over time is equal to the mean for each of them, and there is

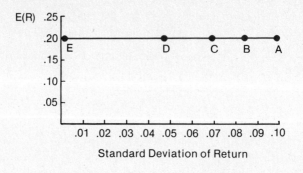

Figure 20.5   Plot of Risk-Return for Portfolios with Different Correlations

no variability of returns for the portfolio. Returns above and below the mean for each of the assets are *completely offset* by the return for the other asset, so there is no variability in total returns for the portfolio; it is a riskless portfolio because there is no uncertainty of returns. The combination of two assets that are completely negatively correlated provides the maximum benefits of diversification— it eliminates risk.

The graph in Figure 20.5 shows the difference in the risk-return posture for these five cases. As noted, the only impact of the change in correlation is that the standard deviation of a portfolio that contains the two assets changes. As we combine assets that are not perfectly correlated, we do *not* affect the expected return of the portfolio, but we are able to *reduce the risk* of the portfolio (its standard deviation) until we reach the ultimate combination in which there is perfect negative correlation and we *eliminate* risk.

Combining Stocks with Different Returns and Risk

The previous discussion indicated what happens when we combined two assets with the same expected return and standard deviation, and the only difference was the correlation coefficient (covariance) between the assets. In this section we will consider two assets (or portfolios) that have different expected rates of return and individual standard deviations and show what happens when we vary the correlations between them. We will assume the following:

Stock	$E(R_i)$	W_i	σ_i^2	σ_i
1	.10	.50	.0049	.07
2	.20	.50	.0100	.10

We will briefly consider the same set of correlation coefficients as previously, with a different set of covariances as follows:

Case	Correlation Coefficient	Covariance $(r_{ij}\sigma_i\sigma_i)$
a	+1.00	.0070
b	+0.50	.0035
c	0.00	.0000
d	−0.50	−.0035
e	−1.00	−.0070

Because we are assuming that the proportion (weights) in all cases is the same (.50−.50), the expected return in *all* instances will be:

$$E(R_{port}) = .5(.10) + .5(.20)$$

$$= .15$$

The standard deviation for case (a) will be:

$$\sigma_{port(a)} = \sqrt{(.5)^2(.07)^2 + (.5)^2(.10)^2 + 2(.5)(.5)(.0070)}$$

$$= \sqrt{(.25)(.0049) + (.25)(.01) + (.5)(.0070)}$$

$$= \sqrt{(.001225) + (.0025) + (.0035)}$$

$$= \sqrt{.007225}$$

$$= .085$$

Again it is shown that *in case of perfect positive correlation, the standard deviation of the portfolio is the weighted average of the standard deviations of the individual assets:*

$$(.5)(.07) + (.5)(.10) = .085$$

Obviously, as we changed the weights, the standard deviation would change in a linear fashion. This property is emphasized because it is important in the discussion of the Capital Asset Pricing Model (CAPM) in the following chapter.

For cases (b), (c), (d), and (e), the standard deviation for the portfolio would be as follows:[7]

$$\sigma_{port(b)} = \sqrt{(.001225) + (.0025) + (.5)(.0035)}$$

$$= \sqrt{(.003725) + (.00175)}$$

$$= \sqrt{.005475}$$

$$= .07399$$

---

[7]In all of the following examples, we will skip some steps because the reader is aware that only the last term changes. The reader is encouraged to work out the individual steps to ensure understanding of the computational procedure.

$$\sigma_{\text{port}(c)} = \sqrt{(.001225) + (.0025) + (.5)(.00)}$$

$$= \sqrt{.003725}$$

$$= .0610$$

$$\sigma_{\text{port}(d)} = \sqrt{(.001225) + (.0025) + (.5)(-.0035)}$$

$$= \sqrt{(.003725) + (-.00175)}$$

$$= \sqrt{.001975}$$

$$= .0444$$

$$\sigma_{\text{port}(e)} = \sqrt{(.003725) + .5(-.00700)}$$

$$= \sqrt{(.003725) - (.0035)}$$

$$= \sqrt{.000225}$$

$$= .015$$

Note that in this set of examples, with perfect negative correlation the standard deviation of the portfolio is not zero. This is because the different examples have equal weights, but the individual standard deviations are not equal. As shown elsewhere, it is possible to derive the weights that would give zero standard deviation under these conditions.[8]

Figure 20.6 shows the results for the two individual assets and the portfolio of the two assets under the assumption of different correlation coefficients as set forth in cases (a) through (e). As before, the expected return does not change because the proportions are all set at .50–.50, so all the portfolios lie along the horizontal line at the return R = .15.

Changing Weights

If we changed the weights of the two assets for a given correlation coefficient, we would derive a set of combinations which trace out an ellipse that would start at stock two, go through the 50–50 point and end at stock one. To show this, consider case (c) in which the correlation coefficient is zero (this eases the computation), and we change the weights as follows:

Case	W_1	W_2	$E(R_i)$
f	.20	.80	.18
g	.40	.60	.16
h	.50	.50	.15
i	.60	.40	.14
j	.80	.20	.12

[8]See Frank K. Reilly, *Investment Analysis and Portfolio Management*, (Hinsdale, IL: Dryden Press, 1979), p. 569.

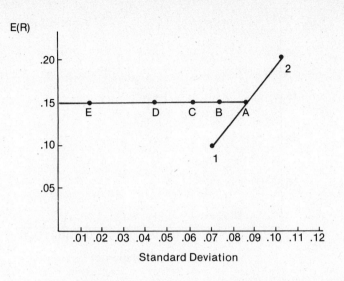

Figure 20.6   Plot of Risk-Return for Portfolios with Different Correlations

In cases (f), (g), (i), and (j) the standard deviations would be (we already know the σ for portfolio h):

$$\sigma_{port(f)} = \sqrt{(.20)^2(.07)^2 + (.80)^2(.10)^2 + 2(.20)(.80)(.000)}$$
$$= \sqrt{(.04)(.0049) + (.64)(.01) + (0)}$$
$$= \sqrt{(.000196) + (.0064)}$$
$$= \sqrt{.006596}$$
$$= .0812$$

$$\sigma_{port(g)} = \sqrt{(.40)^2(.07)^2 + (.60)^2(.10)^2 + 2(.40)(.60)(.00)}$$
$$= \sqrt{(.16)(.0049) + (.36)(.01) + (0)}$$
$$= \sqrt{.000784 + .0036}$$
$$= \sqrt{.004384}$$
$$= .0662$$

$$\sigma_{port(i)} = \sqrt{(.60)^2(.07)^2 + (.40)^2(.10)^2 + 2(.60)(.40)(.00)}$$
$$= \sqrt{(.36)(.0049) + (.16)(.01) + 0}$$
$$= \sqrt{(.001764) + (.0016)}$$
$$= \sqrt{.003364}$$
$$= .0580$$

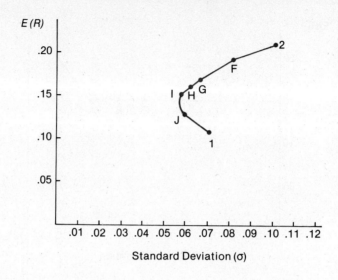

Figure 20.7   Plot of Portfolio Risk-Return for Different Weights When $r_{ij} = 0.00$.

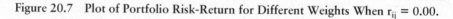

$$\sigma_{\text{port}(j)} = \sqrt{(.80)^2(.07)^2 + (.20)^2(.10)^2 + 2(.80)(.20)(.00)}$$

$$= \sqrt{(.64)(.0049) + (.04)(.01) + 0}$$

$$= \sqrt{(.003136) + (.0004)}$$

$$= \sqrt{.003536}$$

$$= .0595$$

Therefore, the alternative weights, assuming the same correlations, indicate the following risk-return combinations:

Case	W_1	W_2	$E(R_i)$	$E(\sigma_{\text{port}})$
f	.20	.80	.18	.0812
g	.40	.60	.16	.0662
h	.50	.50	.15	.0610
i	.60	.40	.14	.0580
j	.80	.20	.12	.0595

A graph of what these combinations provide in terms of return and risk is contained in Figure 20.7. It would be possible to derive a complete curve by simply varying the weights by small increments.

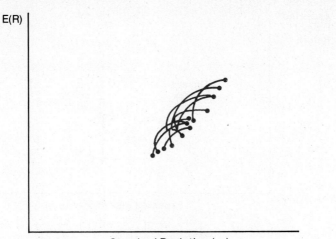

Figure 20.8   Graph of Numerous Portfolio Combinations from Set of Available Assets

As noted, the amount of curvature in the graph will depend upon the correlation between the two assets or portfolios. In the case where $r_{ij} = +1.00$, the combinations would lie along a straight line between the two assets. If we draw the possible combinations when we assumed that $r_{ij} = -1.00$, the graph would be more curved than the one in Figure 20.7, and would actually touch the vertical line with some combination (i.e., the risk would be zero).

If we examined a number of assets and derived the curves assuming all the possible weights, we would have a graph as shown in Figure 20.8, if we only considered combinations of two assets and portfolios.

The envelope curve that contains the best of all these possible combinations is referred to as the *efficient frontier*. Specifically, *the efficient frontier is that set of portfolios that has the maximum return for every given level of risk, or the minimum risk for every level of return.* An example of such a frontier is contained in Figure 20.9. As can be seen, the set of portfolios on the efficient frontier dominates all the portfolios *beneath* the frontier. Specifically, every portfolio *on* the frontier has either higher return for equal risk or lower risk for equal return than some portfolio beneath the frontier. As an example, portfolio A dominates portfolio C because it has an equal return but substantially less risk. Portfolio B dominates portfolio C because it has equal risk but a higher expected rate of return. Because of the benefits of diversification among assets that are not perfectly correlated, we would expect the efficient frontier to be made up of *portfolios,* with the possible exception of the two end points (i.e., the highest return asset and the lowest risk asset).

It was postulated that investors would determine where they wanted to be along the frontier based upon their utility function and attitude toward risk. They

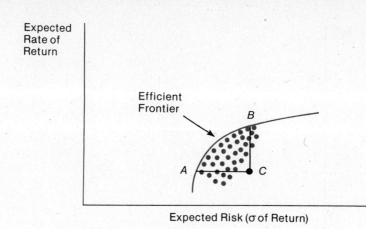

Figure 20.9   Efficient Frontier for Alternative Portfolios

would select some portfolio on the efficient frontier based upon their risk preferences. No portfolio on the efficient frontier is dominated by any other portfolio on the efficient frontier. They all have different return and risk measures, and returns increase with risk.

The Efficient Frontier and Investor Utility

Once the efficient frontier has been determined for portfolios formed from the securities under consideration, the investor has a choice to make. The efficient frontier will show him the portfolio that offers the highest attainable expected return for each attainable risk level (or the lowest attainable risk for each attainable expected return level). However, as Figure 20.9 shows, the shape of the efficient frontier for risky assets is generally such that one has to tolerate more and more risk to achieve higher returns. The slope of the efficient frontier

$$\frac{\Delta E(R_{port})}{\Delta E(\sigma_{port})}$$

decreases steadily as you move up the curve. This implies that taking on the same amount of added risk, as you move up the efficient frontier, will add progressively *less* of an increment in expected return.

The utility curves for an individual specify the tradeoffs he is willing to make between expected return and risk. An investor's utility curves are used in conjunction with the efficient frontier to determine which *particular* efficient portfolio is the best, given these risk-return preferences. Two investors will not choose the same portfolio from the efficient set unless their utility curves are identical. In Figure 20.10, two sets of utility curves have been drawn, along with the efficient

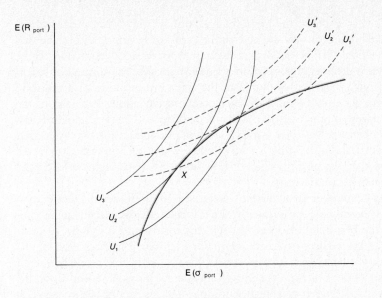

Figure 20.10   Choice of the Optimal Risky Portfolio

frontier. The curves labeled U_1 are for a very risk-averse investor (with $U_3 > U_2 > U_1$). These curves are quite "steep," indicating that the investor will not tolerate much additional risk to obtain additional returns. The investor is indifferent to any $E(R),E(\sigma)$ combinations along a specific utility curve (e.g., U_1).

The curves labeled $U_1'(U_3' > U_2' > U_1')$ are for a less risk-averse investor. He is willing to tolerate a bit more risk to get a higher expected return, and thus will choose a portfolio with higher risk and expected return than will the investor whose preferences are described by U_1, U_2, and U_3.

The *optimal portfolio* is the efficient portfolio with the highest utility. This will be found at *the point of tangency between the efficient frontier and the curve with the highest possible utility for a given investor.* For the more conservative investor, the highest utility is at the point where the curve U_2 just touches the efficient frontier, X in Figure 20.10. The other investor, because he is less risk averse, would choose portfolio Y, which has both higher expected returns and higher risk than portfolio X. Thus, given their respective attitudes toward risk and return, it is perfectly logical that these two investors will choose different portfolios from the efficient set.

Summary

The purpose of this chapter has been to present the basic Markowitz portfolio model in detail. Initially, we considered the assumption that investors are risk averse, followed by a consideration of alternative measures of risk and the observation that, at this point, the preferred measure of risk is the standard deviation of expected return. It was shown that the expected return of a portfolio was simply the weighted average of the expected return for the individual assets in the portfolio. After a detailed discussion and demonstration of the concept of covariance and correlation, it was shown that the standard deviation of a portfolio was a function not only of the individual standard deviations, but *also* of the covariance between all the pairs of assets in the portfolio. The impact of different correlation coefficients was shown with a series of examples using two assets that had equal return and risk, and also for a series where the assets had different returns and risk. It was also possible to show how different weights would yield a curve of potential combinations.

Assuming a number of available assets and a multitude of combination curves, it was shown that the efficient frontier is the envelope curve that encompasses all of the best combinations; i.e., the efficient frontier is that set of portfolios that has the highest expected return for each given level of risk, or the minimum risk for each given level of return. Finally, given this set of dominant portfolios, the investor is expected to select a specific portfolio based upon the point of tangency between the efficient frontier and his highest utility curve. It is recognized that, because alternative investors have different utility functions in terms of their tradeoff between return and risk, they will have different points of tangency and, therefore, they can logically select different portfolios.

Given this understanding of basic portfolio theory, it is possible to consider the Capital Asset Pricing Model (CAPM) which is an extension of portfolio theory. The CAPM is an equilibrium asset pricing model. Consideration of the CAPM is the subject of the following chapter.

Questions

1. Why do most investors hold diversified portfolios?

2. What is covariance and why is it important in portfolio theory?

3. Why do most assets of the same type show positive covariances of returns with each other? Would you expect this to be true of covariances of returns between *different* types of assets (e.g., returns on treasury bills and General Motors common stock, or commercial real estate)? Why or why not?

4. What is the relationship between the covariance and the correlation coefficient? Why is the correlation coefficient considered more useful?

5. You are considering two assets with the following characteristics:

$$E(R_1) = .15 \qquad E(\sigma_1) = .10 \qquad W_1 = .5$$
$$E(R_2) = .20 \qquad E(\sigma_2) = .20 \qquad W_2 = .5$$

Compute the mean and standard deviation of two portfolios if $r_{1,2} = .40; -.60$. Plot the two portfolios for a risk-return graph.

6. Explain why the efficient frontier takes its characteristic shape.

7. Draw a properly labeled graph of the Markowitz efficient frontier. Describe in exact terms what the efficient frontier is. Discuss the concept of dominant portfolios.

8. Assume you want to run a computer program to derive the efficient frontier for your feasible set of stocks. What information must you provide for the program; i.e., what are your inputs?

9. Why are investor's utility curves important in portfolio theory?

10. Explain how the optimal portfolio for a given investor is chosen. Will it always be a diversified portfolio, or could it be a single asset? Explain your answer.

References

Evans, John L., and Archer, Stephen H. "Diversification and the Reduction of Dispersion: An Empirical Analysis." *Journal of Finance* 24(1968).

Fisher, Lawrence. "Using Portfolio Theory to Maintain an Efficiently Diversified Portfolio." *Financial Analysts Journal* 28(1972).

Francis, Jack C., and Archer, Stephen H. *Portfolio Analysis*. 2d ed. Englewood Cliffs, NJ: Prentice-Hall, 1979.

Friedman, Milton, and Savage, Leonard J. "The Utility Analysis of Choices Involving Risk." *Journal of Political Economy* 56(1948).

Gaumnitz, Jack E. "Maximal Gains from Diversification and Implications for Portfolio Management." *Mississippi Valley Journal of Business and Economics* 6(1971).

Hagin, Robert. *Modern Portfolio Theory*. Homewood, IL: Dow-Jones-Irwin, 1979.

Markowitz, Harry. "Markowitz Revisited." *Financial Analysts Journal* 32(1976).

Markowitz, Harry. "The Optimization of Quadratic Function Subject to Linear Constraints." *Naval Research Logistics Quarterly* 3(1956).

Markowitz, Harry. "Portfolio Selection." *Journal of Finance* 7(1952).

Markowitz, Harry. *Portfolio Selection: Efficient Diversification of Investments*. New York: John Wiley & Sons, 1959.

Martin, A. D., Jr. "Mathematical Programming of Portfolio Selections." *Management Science* 1(1955).

Pogue, Gerald A. "An Extension of the Markowitz Portfolio Selection Model to Include Variable Transaction Costs, Leverage Policies, and Short Sales." *Journal of Finance* 25(1970).

Marshall E. Blume

Marshall Blume has been a major contributor in the testing and application of the Capital Asset Pricing Model (CAPM). Some of the initial work was a product of his dissertation at the University of Chicago, "Measurement of Portfolio Performance Under Uncertainty," later published in the American Economic Review *(September 1970). Probably his most widely quoted study was, "On the Assessment of Risk,"* Journal of Finance *(April 1971) which was a detailed analysis of the betas for stocks on the NYSE. Subsequent studies that tested the model include: "A New Look at the Capital Asset Pricing Model,"* Journal of Finance *(March 1973); "Price, Beta, and Exchange Listing,"* Journal of Finance *(May 1973); "Risk, Investment Strategies and the Long-Run Rates of Return,"* Review of Economics and Statistics *(August 1974); Betas and their Regression Tendencies,"* Journal of Finance *(June 1975); "Two Tiers—But How Many Decisions?,"* Journal of Portfolio Management *(Spring 1976); "The Comparative Efficiency of Various Portfolios,"* Journal of Finance *(May 1980); and "Stock Returns and Dividend Yields: Some More Evidence,"* Review of Economics and Statistics, *(November 1980).*

Blume was born in Chicago, Illinois, on March 31, 1941. He received his S.B. degree from Trinity College in 1963, an M.B.A. in 1965, and a Ph.D. in 1968, both from the University of Chicago. He has been managing editor of the Journal of Finance *and associate editor of the* Journal of Financial and Quantitative Analysis. *At present, Blume is an associate editor of the* Journal of Financial Economics. *Currently, he is the Howard Butcher Professor of Finance and associate director of the Rodney L. White Center for Research at The Wharton School of Economics, the University of Pennsylvania.*

William F. Sharpe

If Harry Markowitz is the father of modern portfolio theory, William Sharpe should probably be designated as one of the fathers of the Capital Asset Pricing Model, (CAPM) as a result of his article "Capital Asset Prices—A Theory of Market Equilibrium Under Conditions of Risk," (Journal of Finance, *September 1964). There were several other articles published shortly after the Sharpe paper that likewise developed the theory, but the Sharpe article has been the most widely read and quoted. In a subsequent study of mutual fund performance he derived a risk-adjusted portfolio performance measure that is widely used and is discussed in Chapter 23.*

William F. Sharpe is Timken Professor of Finance at the Stanford University Graduate School of Business. He joined the Stanford faculty in 1970, having previously taught at the University of Washington and the University of California at Irvine.

Professor Sharpe has published articles in a number of professional journals, including the Financial Analysts Journal, The Journal of Business, The Journal of Finance, The Journal of Financial Economics, The Journal of Financial and Quantitative Analysis, The Journal of Portfolio Management, *and* Management Science.

He has also written five books: with Jacob; An Introduction to Computer Programming Using the BASIC Language (The Free Press, 1967, 1971, and 1979); The Economics of Computers (Columbia University Press, 1969); Portfolio Theory and Capital Markets (McGraw-Hill, 1970); An Introduction to Managerial Economics (Columbia University Press, 1973); and Investments (Prentice-Hall, 1978).

Professor Sharpe was born in Cambridge, MA on June 16, 1934. He received his A.B. in economics from the University of California at Los Angeles (UCLA) in 1955, his M.A. and Ph.D. in economics from UCLA in 1956 and 1961.

Professor Sharpe is past president of the American Finance Association, a trustee of the College Retirement Equities Fund, and has served as a consultant for a number of corporations and investment organizations.

CAPITAL MARKET
THEORY

≫ 21 ≪

Capital market theory builds on portfolio theory, and so, in this chapter, we will basically begin where the Markowitz efficient frontier ended. It is assumed that the set of risky assets has been examined, and that the aggregate efficient frontier has been derived. Further, it is assumed that you and all other investors want to maximize your utility, so you will choose a portfolio of risky assets on the efficient frontier at a point where your utility map is tangent to the frontier as shown in Figure 20.10. When you act in this manner, you are referred to as a Markowitz efficient investor. The purpose of capital market theory is to extend portfolio theory to a model that can be used to price all risky assets. The final product is the Capital Asset Pricing Model (CAPM) that will indicate how you determine the required rate of return for all risky assets.

In this chapter, we will initially consider some of the assumptions required to derive the model. Subsequently we will discuss the concept of a risk-free asset, its properties relative to a portfolio of risky assets, and how this allows us to derive a linear relationship between the expected return on an asset and the risk involved. This analysis also implies the existence of a simple, unique risk measure for all risky assets. We will show in detail how this risk measure is computed for an individual asset, and how this model can be used to select undervalued, overvalued, and properly valued securities.

As was the case in the last chapter, there are a number of equations required to properly develop the theory. These will be explained and detailed examples of the computations given. As a result, you should finish the chapter with a good understanding of this very important theory and how to derive the relevant risk measures and to apply the theory to your own investments.

Assumptions of Capital Market Theory

Because capital market theory builds upon the Markowitz protfolio model, this theory requires all of the assumptions discussed in relation to the Markowitz model, but they are expanded as follows:

1. *All investors are Markowitz efficient investors who want to be somewhere on the efficient frontier.* The exact location on the efficient frontier will depend upon the risk-return function of the investor and will differ among investors.

2. *It is possible for investors to borrow or lend any amount of money at the risk-free rate of return (RFR).* Clearly, it is always possible to lend money at the nominal risk-free rate by buying risk-free securities such as government T-bills. It is not always possible to borrow at this risk-free rate, but we will see that assuming a higher borrowing rate does not change the results very much.

3. *All investors have homogeneous expectations; i.e., all investors estimate identical probability distributions for future rates of return.* Again, this assumption can be relaxed, and, as long as expectations are not vastly different, the effect is minor.

4. *All investors have the same one-period time horizon, e.g., one month, six months, one year.* The model will be developed for one hypothetical period, but it is acknowledged that the results could be affected by a different assumption and an investor would have to derive risk measures that are consistent with his horizon.

5. *All investments are infinitely divisible; i.e., it is possible to buy or sell fractional shares of any asset or portfolio.* This assumption simply allows us to discuss the various investment alternatives as continuous curves. Changing this assumption would have little impact on the theory.

6. *There are no taxes or transaction costs involved in buying or selling assets.* This is a reasonable assumption in a number of instances. Specifically, there are many investors who do not have to pay taxes (e.g., pension funds, religious groups), and the transactions costs for most financial institutions is less than one percent on most financial instruments. Again, the relaxation of this assumption modifies the results, but does not change the basic thrust.

7. *There is no inflation or change in interest rates, or inflation is fully anticipated.* This is a reasonable initial assumption and can be modified.

8. *Capital markets are in equilibrium.* This means that we begin from a state in which all assets are properly priced in terms of the risk involved.

You may feel that some of these assumptions are unrealistic and wonder how useful a theory can be that is based on them. In this regard, two points are important. First, as discussed above, we will see that many of these assumptions can be relaxed with minor impact on the model and no change in the main implications or conclusions. Second, a theory should *not* be judged on the basis of the assumptions it involves, but on *how well it explains and helps us predict behavior in the real world.* Specifically, if we can develop a model that includes these assumptions, and the model helps us explain the rates of return on a wide variety of risky assets, the theory is very useful. Put another way, the important test of the model is *how well it works.* If the model works with these unrealistic assumptions, it simply means that the factors assumed away were really not very important in attaining the ultimate objective—determining the required rate of return for risky assets. In this regard, after presenting the model, we will briefly review some of the studies that have empirically tested the model.

The Initial Development

The major factor in developing capital market theory was the introduction of the concept of a risk-free asset. Specifically, following the development of the Markowitz portfolio model, several authors considered what would happen if we assumed the existence of a risk-free asset that, by definition, would have zero variance. It will be shown that such an asset would have zero correlation with all other risky assets. Such an asset would yield the risk-free rate of return (RFR) and would be on the vertical axis of a portfolio graph. Assuming the existence of a risk-free asset made it possible to extend the Markowitz portfolio theory and to derive a generalized theory of capital asset pricing under conditions of uncertainty. This development has generally been attributed to William Sharpe, but similar independent derivations were made by Lintner and Mossin.[1] (Because of this parallel development, the reader may see the reference to the Sharpe-Lintner-Mossin (SLM) Capital Asset Pricing Model.) Given its importance to the model, we will begin with a discussion of the risk-free asset, and consider the effect of combining a risk-free asset with other risky assets.

Risk-Free Asset

We have defined a *risky* asset as one about which *there is uncertainty regarding the future return.* Further, we have measured this uncertainty by the variance or standard deviation of returns. *A risk-free asset is one for which there is no uncertainty regarding the expected rate of return;* i.e., the standard deviation of returns is equal to zero ($\sigma_{RF} = 0$). Such an asset should provide a rate of return that is consistent with this characteristic, and this return should be equal to the long-run real growth rate of the economy, with short-run liquidity having some effect. In other words, the RFR is approximately equal to the long-run real growth rate of the economy.

[1]See William F. Sharpe, "Capital Asset Prices: A Theory of Market Equilibrium Under Conditions of Risk," *Journal of Finance* 19 (1964): 425–442; John Lintner, "Security Prices, Risk and Maximal Gains from Diversification," *Journal of Finance* 20 (1965): 587–615; and J. Mossin, "Equilibrium in a Capital Asset Market," *Econometrica* 34 (1966): 768–783.

Covariance with the Risk-Free Asset

The reader will recall that the covariance between two sets of returns is equal to:

$$Cov_{ij} = \sum_{i=1}^{n} (R_i - E(R_i))\ (R_j - E(R_j))/n$$

Because the returns for the risk-free asset are certain, $\sigma_{RF} = 0$, which means $R_i = E(R_i)$ during all periods. Consequently, when computing the covariance of the risk-free asset with that of *any* risky asset or portfolio of assets, the expression for the risk-free asset will always be equal to zero (i.e., $R_i - E(R_i) = 0$)/ and the product will equal zero. Therefore, *the covariance between any risky asset or portfolio of risky assets and a risk-free asset is zero.*

Combining the Risk-Free Asset and a Risky Portfolio

At this point, an important question to consider is, what happens to the average rate of return and standard deviation when a risk-free asset is combined with a portfolio of risky assets such as exists on the Markowitz efficient frontier?

Expected Return   Similar to the expected return for a portfolio of two risky assets, *the expected return is the weighted average of the two returns* as follows:

$$E(R_{port}) = W_{RF}(RFR) + (1 - W_{RF})E(R_i)$$

where:

W_{RF} = the proportion of the portfolio invested in a risk-free asset

$E(R_i)$ = the expected rate of return on risky portfolio i.

Standard Deviation   Recall from Chapter 20 that the expected variance for a two-asset portfolio is:

$$E(\sigma^2_{port}) = W_1^2\sigma_1^2 + W_2^2\sigma_2^2 + 2W_1W_2r_{12}\sigma_1\sigma_2$$

Substituting the risk-free asset for security one, and the risky asset portfolio for security two, this formula would become:

$$E(\sigma^2_{port}) = W_{RF}^2\sigma_{RF}^2 + (1 - W_{RF})^2\sigma_i^2 + 2W_{RF}(1 - W_{RF})r_{RFi}\sigma_{RF}\sigma_i$$

We know that the variance of the risk-free asset is zero (i.e., $\sigma_{RF}^2 = 0$) and the correlation between the risk-free asset and any risky asset, i, is also zero (i.e., $r_{RF,i} = 0$). Therefore, any component of the formula that has either of these terms will equal zero and the formula will become:

$$E(\sigma^2_{port}) = (1 - W_{RF})^2\sigma_i^2$$

The standard deviation is:

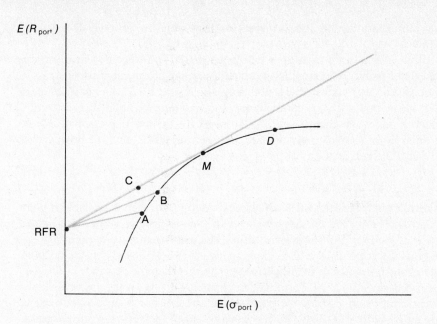

Figure 21.1   Portfolio Possibilities Combining the Risk-Free Asset and Risky Portfolios on the Efficient Frontier

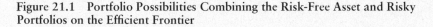

$$E(\sigma_{\text{port}}) = \sqrt{(1 - W_{\text{RF}})_i^2\sigma^2}$$

$$= (1 - W_{\text{RF}})\,\sigma_i$$

Therefore, the standard deviation of a portfolio that combines the risk-free asset and a portfolio of risky assets is *the linear proportion of the standard deviation of the risky asset portfolio.*

And, *both* the expected return *and* the standard deviation of return for such a portfolio are *linear* combinations, which means the alternative portfolio returns and risks are represented by a *straight line* between the two assets. A graph depicting portfolio possibilities when the risk-free asset is combined with alternative risky portfolios on the Markowitz efficient frontier is contained in Figure 21.1.

It is possible to attain any point along the straight line RFR–A by investing some portion of your portfolio in the risk-free asset (W_{RF}) and the remainder ($1 - W_{\text{RF}}$) in the risky asset portfolio at point A on the efficient frontier. This set of portfolio possibilities dominates all risky asset portfolios below point A because there is a portfolio along the line RFR–A that has equal variance but a higher rate of return than the portfolio on the original efficient frontier. Likewise, it is possible to attain any point along the line RFR–B by investing in some combination of the risk-free asset and the risky asset portfolio at point B. Again, these combinations dominate all portfolio possibilities below point B (including line RFR–A).

It is possible to draw further lines from the RFR to the efficient frontier at higher and higher points until you reach the point of tangency which is set at point M. The set of portfolio possibilities along line RFR–M dominates *all* portfolios below point M. You could attain a risk and return combination at point C (which is midway between the RFR and point M) by investing one-half of your portfolio in the risk-free asset (lending money at the RFR) and the other half in the risky portfolio at point M.

A Leveraged Portfolio

An investor may want to attain a higher expected return than is available at point M and also be willing to accept higher risk. One alternative would be to invest in one of the risky asset portfolios on the efficient frontier above point M, e.g., the portfolio at point D. A second alternative is to add *leverage* to the portfolio by *borrowing* money at the risk-free rate and investing the proceeds in the risky asset portfolio at point M. Assuming an investor does this, what effect will it have on the return and risk for the portfolio? If the investor is able to *borrow* an amount equal to *50 percent* of his original wealth, W_{RF} is not a positive fraction, but a negative 50 percent (i.e., $W_{RF} = -0.50$). The effect on the expected return for the portfolio is as follows:

$$E(R_{port}) = W_{RF}(RFR) + (1 - W_{RF})E(R_m)$$
$$= -0.50(RFR) + (1 - (-0.50))E(R_m)$$
$$= -0.50(RFR) + 1.50E(R_m)$$

As shown, the return will increase in a *linear* fashion along the line RFR–M because the gross return increases by 50 percent, but it is necessary to pay interest (at the RFR) on the money borrowed. As an example, assume that the E(RFR) = .06 and $E(R_m)$ = .12, then the return to the leveraged portfolio would be:

$$E(R_{port}) = -0.50(.06) + 1.5(.12)$$
$$= -.03 + .18$$
$$= .15$$

The effect on the standard deviation of the leveraged portfolio is similar.

$$E(\sigma_{port}) = (1 - W_{RF})\sigma_m$$
$$= (1 - (-0.50))\sigma_m = 1.50\sigma_m$$

Therefore, *both return and risk increase in a linear fashion along the original line RFR–M*, and this extension dominates everything below the line on the original efficient frontier. Thus, this "new" efficient frontier is the straight line from the RFR tangent to point M. This line is referred to as the *capital market line (CML)* and is shown in Figure 21.2.

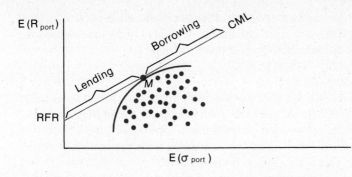

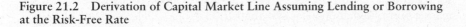

Figure 21.2   Derivation of Capital Market Line Assuming Lending or Borrowing at the Risk-Free Rate

As was shown in the discussion of portfolio theory, when two assets were *perfectly correlated*, the set of portfolio possibilities between them was on a straight line. Therefore, because it is a straight line, *all the portfolios on the CML are perfectly positively correlated*. This positive correlation is also intuitive because, as shown, all the portfolio possibilities on the CML are a combination of risky portfolio M and either borrowing or lending at the risk-free rate, so all variability is caused by the variability of the M portfolio. The only difference is the *magnitude* of the variability because of the proportion of the risky asset in the total portfolio.

The Market Portfolio

Because portfolio M is the tangent portfolio that gives the highest portfolio possibility line, everybody will want to invest in this risky asset portfolio and borrow or lend to be somewhere on the CML. Because *all* investors want this portfolio of risky assets as part of their total portfolio, *all* risky assets *must* be in this portfolio. If a risky asset were not in this portfolio, it would have no demand and, therefore, no value. Because the market is in equilibrium, *all assets are included in this portfolio in proportion to their market value*. If this were not true, prices would adjust until the value of the asset was consistent with its proportion in portfolio M. If a higher proportion of an asset than was justified by its value was included in portfolio M for any reason, the excess demand for this asset would cause an increase in its price until its value was consistent with the proportion. This portfolio of all risky assets is referred to as the *market portfolio*.

The market portfolio does *not* include only common stocks, but *all* risky assets such as bonds, options, real estate, coins, stamps, etc. Since the market portfolio contains *all* risky assets, it is a *completely diversified* portfolio. Because of this, all unsystematic risk of individual assets in the portfolio is diversified away in the M portfolio, i.e., the "unique" risk of one asset is off set by the "unique" variability of the other assets in the portfolio. The only risk is the systematic risk caused by macroeconomic variables that influence all risky assets. This systematic risk is measured by the standard deviation of returns of the market portfolio. This market variability (systematic risk) can change over time as the macroeconomic variables that affect the valuation of risky assets change.[2]

Measure of Diversification

All portfolios on the CML are perfectly positively correlated, which means that all portfolios on the CML are perfectly correlated with the market portfolio. This implies a *measure of complete diversification*.[3] Specifically, a portfolio that is completely diversified will be perfectly correlated with the market portfolio (i.e., $R^2 = + 1.00$). This is also logical because *complete diversification requires the elimination of all unsystematic risk* and, if all that is left is systematic risk, such a completely diversified portfolio should be perfectly correlated with the market portfolio that only has systematic risk.

Separation Theorem

Given the existence of the CML, everyone should invest in the *same* risky asset portfolio, the M portfolio. The only difference among individual investors should be in the *financing* decision they make, which depends upon their risk preferences. If you are relatively risk averse, you will lend some part of your portfolio at the RFR (i.e., you will buy some risk-free securities), and invest the remainder in the market portfolio. For example, you might invest in the portfolio combination at point A in Figure 21.3. In contrast, if you prefer more risk, you will borrow funds at the RFR and invest everything in the market portfolio. As a result, you will invest in a portfolio combination such as the one at point B which provides more risk and greater return than the market portfolio. The CML becomes the efficient frontier of portfolios, and investors decide where they want to be along this efficient frontier, as shown in Figure 21.3. This division of the *investment decision and the financing decision* is referred to as the separation theorem and was developed by James Tobin.[4] Specifically, to be somewhere on this CML, which is the efficient frontier, you initially make an investment decision, to invest in the market portfolio, M. Subsequently, based upon your risk preferences, you make a separate financing decision (i.e., whether to borrow or lend) to attain the preferred point on the CML (e.g., A or B).

Risk in a CML World

The relevant risk measure for risky assets is *their covariance with the M portfolio*. This covariance with the market portfolio is referred to as the stock's *sys-*

---

[2]For an analysis of changes in stock market volatility and causes of changes, see John M. Wachowicz and Frank K. Reilly, "An Analysis of Changes in Aggregate Stock Market Volatility," (Paper delivered at the Midwest Finance Association Meeting, Chicago, IL: April 1979); and "An Analysis of Factors that Influence Aggregate Stock Market Volatility," (Paper delivered at the Southern Finance Association Meeting, Atlanta, GA, November 1979).

[3]James Lorie, "Diversification: Old and New," *Journal of Portfolio Management* 1 (1975): 25–28.

[4]James Tobin, "Liquidity Preference as Behavior Towards Risk," *Review of Economic Studies* 25 (1958): 65–85.

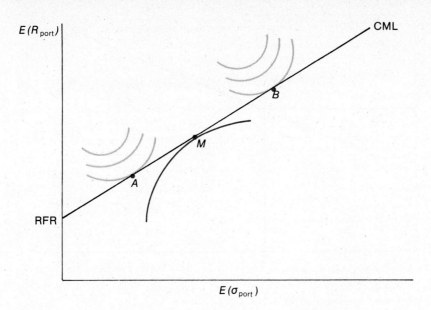

Figure 21.3   Choice of Optimal Portfolio Combinations on the CML

tematic risk. One can see why it is this covariance that is important if one considers the following:

1. In the Markowitz portfolio discussion it was noted that the relevant risk consideration for a security being added to a portfolio is its average covariance with all other assets in the portfolio. Because the only relevant portfolio is the M portfolio, the only important consideration for any individual risky asset is its average covariance with all the stocks in the M portfolio, or simply *the asset's covariance with the market portfolio.* This, then, is the relevant risk measure for an individual risky asset.

2. Alternatively, because all individual risky assets are a part of the M portfolio, one can describe individual asset returns in relation to the returns for the M portfolio with the following linear model:

$$R_{it} = a_i + b_i R_{mt} + e$$

where:

R_{it} = return for asset i during period t

a_i = constant term for asset i

b_i = slope coefficient for asset i

R_{mt} = return for M portfolio during period t

e = random error term.

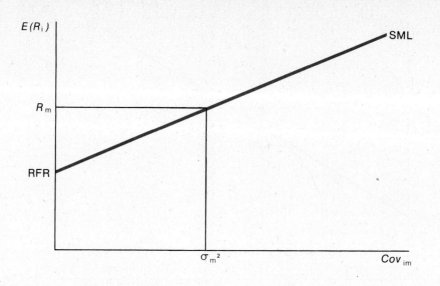

Figure 21.4   Graph of Security Market Line

Its variance of returns could be described as:

$$\mathrm{Var}(R_{it}) = \mathrm{Var}(a_i + b_i R_{mt} + e)$$

$$= \mathrm{Var}(a_i) + \mathrm{Var}(b_i R_{mt}) + \mathrm{Var}(e)$$

$$= 0 + \mathrm{Var}(b_i R_{mt}) + \mathrm{Var}(e)$$

but $\mathrm{Var}(b_i R_{mt})$ is the variance due to the variance of the market return which is referred to as *systematic* variance. $\mathrm{Var}(e)$ is the residual variance, which is the variance of return for the individual asset that is *not* related to the market portfolio. It is also referred to as *unsystematic* variance or "unique" variance because it is caused by the unique features of the asset. Therefore:

$$\mathrm{Var}(R_{it}) = (\text{Systematic Variance}) + (\text{Unsystematic Variance})$$

We know that all unsystematic variance is *eliminated* in a completely diversified portfolio such as the market portfolio. Therefore, *the unsystematic variance is not relevant to investors,* and they should not expect to receive added returns for assuming this risk. *The only variance that is relevant is the systematic variance* that *cannot* be diversified away because it is attributable to macroeconomic factors that affect *all* risky assets.

Security Market Line

Because the relevant risk measure for an individual risky asset is its covariance with the market portfolio (Cov_{im}), we can draw the risk-return relationship as shown in Figure 21.4.

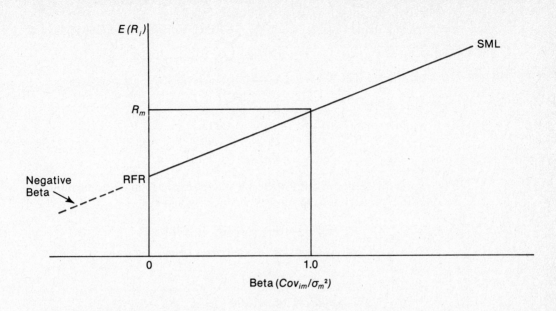

Figure 21.5   Graph of Security Market Line with Normalized Systematic Risk

The market return (R_m) should be consistent with its own risk, which is the covariance of the market with itself. The reader will recall that the covariance of any asset with itself is its variance $Cov_{ii} = \sigma^2_i$. Therefore, the covariance of the market with itself is the variance of the market rate of return (i.e., $Cov_{mm} = \sigma^2_m$). The equation for this line is:

$$E(R_i) = RFR + \frac{R_m - RFR}{\sigma^2_m} (Cov_{im})$$

$$= RFR + \frac{Cov_{im}}{\sigma^2_m} (R_m - RFR)$$

but $Cov_{im} / \sigma^2_m = $ beta (β_i), so this can be stated

$$E(R_i) = RFR + \beta_i (R_m - RFR)$$

Beta is a *normalized* measure of systematic risk; the covariance of any asset i with the market portfolio (Cov_{im}) is normalized by the market portfolio covariance. Therefore, if β_i is above 1.0, the asset has higher risk than the market has. Now the SML graph can be expressed as shown in Figure 21.5.

Determining Expected Return

Therefore, the expected rate of return for a risky asset is determined by the RFR plus a risk premium that is a function of the *systematic* risk of the asset (β_i), and the prevailing market risk premium (R_m − RFR). Consider the following example stocks:

Stock	Beta
A	0.70
B	1.00
C	1.15
D	1.40
E	−0.30

If we expect the economy's RFR to be .08 and the expected market return (R_m) to be .14, the expected return for these four stocks would be:

$$E(R_i) = RFR + \beta_i (R_m - RFR)$$

$$E(R_a) = .08 + 0.70 (.14 - .08)$$

$$= .122 = 12.2\%$$

$$E(R_b) = .08 + 1.00 (.14 - .08)$$

$$= .14 = 14\%$$

$$E(R_c) = .08 + 1.15 (.14 - .08)$$

$$= .149 = 14.9\%$$

$$E(R_d) = .08 + 1.40 (.14 - .08)$$

$$= .164 = 16.4\%$$

$$E(R_e) = .08 + (-0.30) (.14 - .08)$$

$$= .08 - .018$$

$$= .062 = 6.2\%$$

As stated, these are the expected (required) rates of return that these stocks should provide based upon the systematic risk of each stock. Stock A has lower risk than the aggregate market, so an investor should not expect (require) a return from it as high as the return on the market portfolio of risky assets. In this instance, one should expect a return of 12.2 percent. In case B, the stock has systematic risk equal to the market (beta = 1.00), so the rate of return expected should likewise be equal to the expected market return (.14). Stocks C and D have systematic risk greater than the market, and so are expected to provide returns consistent with this risk. Finally, stock E is an asset that not only has systematic risk that is below the market risk, but has a *negative* beta (which is quite rare in practice). As a result, the expected return on this stock is *below* the RFR.

In equilibrium, *all* assets and *all* portfolios of assets should plot on the SML. That is, all assets should be priced such that their expected (required) rate of return is consistent with their systematic risk. Any security that plots *above* the SML would be considered *underpriced* because its estimated return would be above what is required in terms of its systematic risk. In contrast, assets that plot *below* the SML would be considered *overpriced* because their estimated return is below the return required for an asset having that expected systematic risk. In a market that is completely efficient and in equilibrium, one would not expect to find any assets that plot off the SML. Alternatively, if the market is generally efficient, but not completely efficient, it might be possible to find certain assets that are somewhat mispriced because not *everyone* is aware of *all* the relevant information for the asset. As discussed in the efficient markets chapter, the function of a superior analyst is to derive estimates of value and rates of return that are consistently superior to the aggregate market's evaluation and also different from the consensus estimate, so that the returns derived will be above average on a risk-adjusted basis.

Determination of Undervalued and Overvalued Assets

Now that we have determined the rate of return that an investor should expect or require for a specific risky asset using the SML, it is possible to compare this required return to the rate of return that is projected over some future investment horizon to determine whether we should invest in a given asset or not. Such an evaluation requires an *independent* estimate of the return outlook for the security done using either fundamental or technical analysis techniques. To understand what is involved in such a determination, let us consider the following example for the five assets discussed in the previous section.

Assume that there are five stocks being followed by analysts in a major trust department. Based upon extensive fundamental analysis such as discussed in Chapters 8–12, the analysts report the following price and dividend outlooks for the stocks:

Stock	Current Price (P_t)	Expected Price (P_{t+1})	Expected Dividend (D_{t+1})	Estimated Future Rate of Return
A	25	27	1.00	12.0%
B	40	42	1.25	8.1%
C	33	40	1.00	24.2%
D	64	65	2.40	5.3%
E	50	55	—	10.0%

Table 21.1 summarizes the relationship between the required rates of return based on systematic risk and the estimated future rate of return based upon the current price, the future price, and the dividend outlook.

When these values are plotted on the SML, they would appear as shown in Figure 21.6. As shown, stock A is almost exactly on the line and so is considered

Stock	Beta	$E(R_i)$	Estimated Return	Estimated Return minus $E(R_i)$	Evaluation
A	0.70	12.2	12.0	− 0.2	Properly Valued
B	1.00	14.0	8.1	− 5.9	Overvalued
C	1.15	14.9	24.2	9.3	Undervalued
D	1.40	16.4	5.3	−11.1	Overvalued
E	−0.30	6.2	10.0	3.8	Undervalued

Table 21.1   Comparison of Required Rate of Return to Estimated Rate of Return

properly valued. Alternatively, stocks B and D are considered overvalued because you would not expect to receive a rate of return during the coming period that is consistent with the risk involved. Therefore, they both plot below the SML. In contrast, stocks C and E are expected to provide rates of return greater than what is required based upon their systematic risk; i.e., both stocks plot above the SML.

Assuming that you had faith in the ability of your analyst to forecast estimated values and, therefore, estimated returns, you would buy stocks C and E and you would sell stocks B and D, possibly selling them short if you are aggressive in this regard. Finally, you would probably take no action on stock A because it is expected to provide a return about in line with its systematic risk.

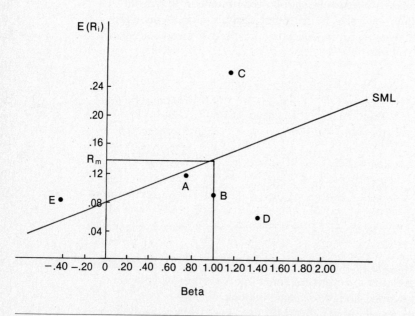

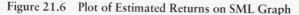

Figure 21.6   Plot of Estimated Returns on SML Graph

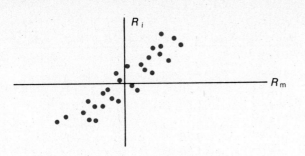

Figure 21.7   Scatter Plot of Rates of Return

The Characteristic Line

How do you compute the systematic risk for an asset? The systematic risk input for an individual asset is derived from the following regression model that is referred to as the asset's characteristic line with the market portfolio:

$$R_{it} = a_i + B_i R_{mt} + e$$

where:

R_{it} = the rate of return for asset i during period t

R_{mt} = the rate of return for the market portfolio during period t

a_i = the constant term or intercept of the regression which equals $\bar{R}_i - B_i \bar{R}_m$

B_i = the slope coefficient for the regression which is equal to Cov_{im}/σ_m^2.

The characteristic line is the line of best fit through a scatter plot of rates of return for the individual risky asset and for the market portfolio of risky assets over some designated past period, as shown in Figure 21.7.

In practice the number of observations used and the time interval employed varies. As an example, Value Line Investment Services derives the characteristic line for stocks using the most recent five years of *weekly* rates of return (i.e., 260 weekly observations). Alternatively, Merrill Lynch, Pierce, Fenner and Smith, Inc., provides betas based upon the recent five-year period using *monthly* rates of return.[5] The point is, there is no theoretically correct time interval and period of analysis. It becomes a tradeoff between using enough observations to eliminate the impact of random rates of return, and yet not going so far back in time (e.g., 15 or 20 years) that the issuing company may have changed dramatically

---

[5]A comparison of the estimates is contained in Meir Statman, "Betas Compared: Merrill Lynch vs Value Line," *Journal of Portfolio Management* 7 (1981): 41–44.

Mo./Yr.	Month-End Price	R_{m+}	R_{IBM+}^a	$R_{mt} - \overline{R_m}$	$R_{IBM+} - \overline{R_{IBM}}^a$	$(R_{mt} - \overline{R_m})(R_{IBM+} - \overline{R_{IBM}})$
	S&P 500					
12/78	96.11	—	—	—	—	—
1/79	99.93	3.97	3.40	2.93	4.50	13.185
2/79	96.28	−3.65	−2.80	−4.69	−1.70	7.973
3/79	101.59	5.52	5.20	4.48	6.30	28.224
4/79	101.76	0.17	−0.40	−0.87	0.70	−0.609
5/79	99.08	−2.63	−3.30	−3.67	−2.20	8.074
6/79	102.91	3.87	−2.80	2.83	−1.70	−4.811
7/79	103.81	0.87	−5.60	−0.17	−4.50	0.765
8/79	109.32	5.31	0.40	4.27	1.50	6.405
9/79	109.32	0.00	−3.20	−1.04	−2.10	2.184
10/79	101.82	−6.86	−7.90	−7.90	−6.80	53.720
11/79	106.16	4.26	4.60	3.22	5.70	18.354
12/79	107.94	1.68	−1.30	0.64	−0.20	−0.128
	E(R)=	1.04	−1.10%			133.336

Table 21.2   Computation of Beta Coefficient for IBM During 1979 Relative to S&P 500

$\text{Cov}_{IBM,M} = 133.336/12 = 11.111$

$\sigma_M^2 = \Sigma(R_{Mt} - \overline{R_M})^2/N$

$\qquad = 165.4148/12 = 13.785$

$\beta_{IBM} = 11.111/13.785 = .806$

$\sigma_M = \sqrt{13.785} = 3.713$

$r_{IBM,M} = \dfrac{\text{Cov}_{IBM,M}}{\sigma_{IBM}\ \sigma_M} = \dfrac{11.111}{(3.838)(3.713)} = \dfrac{11.111}{14.250} = .780$

$\alpha = \overline{R}_{IBM} - \beta_{IBM}\overline{R}_M$

$\qquad = -1.10 - .806(1.04)$

$\qquad = -1.10 - 0.84$

$\qquad = -1.94$

[a]Computed in Chapter 20.

in the interim. It is important to remember that you are using the historical data to help you estimate the *future* beta for the asset.

Also, there is no obviously available portfolio series that contains all the risky assets in the economy. Therefore, most investigators use the Standard & Poor's 500 Composite Index as a proxy for the market portfolio. The stocks in this index have a large proportion at the total market value of stocks, and it is a value-weighted series.

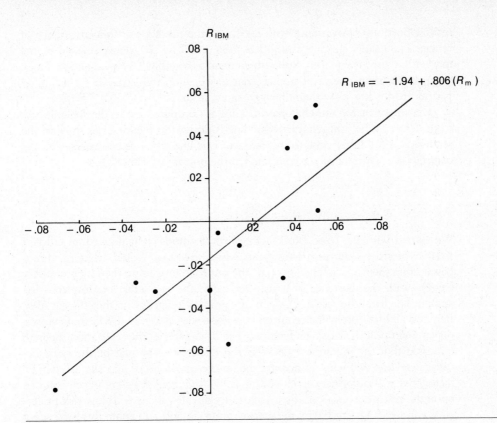

Figure 21.8   Scatter Plot of IBM and S&P 500 with Characteristic Line for IBM

An Example Computation

To demonstrate how one goes about deriving the characteristic line for a specific risky asset, consider the following computation of the characteristic line for IBM based upon the monthly rates of return during 1979. Twelve is probably not enough observations, but it should provide a good example. As is often done, we will use the S&P 500 Index as a proxy for the market portfolio.

The actual monthly price changes for IBM and the S&P 500 Index during 1979 are computed using the closing prices for the last day of each month; e.g., the return for January 1979 is the percentage change from the closing price on December 30, 1978 to the closing price on January 30, 1979. These data are contained in Table 21.2. A scatter plot of the rates of return is contained in Figure 21.8. During most months, IBM had returns that were generally consistent with the aggregate market returns. As shown in Table 21.2, there were only three instances in which one series experienced a return above or below its mean while the other series was not likewise above or below its mean. As a result, almost all the products are positive and the covariance between IBM and the market is positive. To derive an index of systematic risk, we compare this covariance to the market portfolio's covariance with itself, i.e., the market portfolio's variance of return. The results indicate a ratio less than one. The covariance divided by the market variance is equal to .806, which means that IBM's systematic risk index (beta) is less than one. This implies that based upon this analysis for a limited period, IBM is less risky than the aggregate market is.

The intercept for the characteristic line is computed using the formula set forth before. When this characteristic line is drawn on Figure 21.8, most of the scatter plots fall fairly close to the characteristic line which is consistent with the correlation coefficient of .78 computed at the bottom of Table 21.2.

Portfolio Management With a CAPM

We started with the basic Markowitz portfolio model that derived an efficient frontier of risky asset portfolios from which investors would select portfolios based upon their utility functions (i.e., the portfolio tangent to their highest utility curve). With the existence of a risk-free asset, the new efficient frontier is the straight line from the risk-free asset to the point of tangency on the efficient frontier, and all investors will attempt to be somewhere along the CML that evolves, depending upon their risk preferences. The discussion of the separation theorem indicated that the investment decision for all investors should be the same because everyone will want to acquire the market portfolio of all risky assets. The factor that will differ between investors is the *financing* decision, which is based upon the risk preferences of the investor. Specifically, those with low risk preference will select a point below the market portfolio and will attain this by *lending* part of their portfolio at the risk-free rate and putting the rest in the market portfolio. In contrast, those who are looking for high return and risk will *borrow* money at the risk-free rate and invest it in the market portfolio to attain a point above the market portfolio.

Two practical questions arise. First, how do you acquire the market portfolio of risky assets? Second, assuming that you cannot use leverage (i.e., borrow), how do you attain a high-risk portfolio? Regarding the first question, there really is no such portfolio containing not only common stocks but also bonds, real estate, coins, stamps, antiques, and the multitude of other risky assets. What one generally assumes is that you can acquire a diversified portfolio of some of these assets that would be highly correlated with this mythical market portfolio. As an example, it *is* possible to acquire well-diversified portfolios of common stock through large, balanced mutual funds (as described in Chapter 19). As shown, these mutual fund portfolios are generally very highly correlated with the S&P 500 Index. It is likewise possible to acquire diversified portfolios of municipal, government, and corporate bonds through fixed-income mutual funds (see Chapter 17). Finally, REIT's, discussed in Chapter 2, provide a diversified portfolio of real estate. The acquisition of a diversified portfolio of assets like coins, stamps, and antiques is more difficult, but this is not expected to drastically affect the implementation because the market value of these assets is generally small compared to the value of stocks, bonds, and real estate. Thus the returns on these available assets would be dominant. In addition, it is generally assumed that during most periods the returns for these various assets are positively (although not perfectly) correlated.

Regarding the second question: what happens to investors who cannot borrow and leverage their portfolio? The obvious answer is that they can construct a diversified portfolio of high-risk assets rather than a completely diversified portfolio that is equal to the market portfolio. As an example, if I want my portfolio to have a beta of 1.30 and I cannot borrow to attain this risk level, I would simply acquire a portfolio that had a weighted average beta of 1.30 rather than 1.00. This would require avoiding low beta assets and concentrating on assets with betas of 1.20, 1.30, etc. While it is more difficult to diversify with such a portfolio due to the concentration in one segment of the risk spectrum, diversification is certainly possible by acquiring more securities.

Empirical Tests of the CAPM

In the discussion of the assumptions of capital market theory it was pointed out that a theory should *not* be judged on the basis of its assumptions, but on how well it is able to explain the relationships that exist in the real world. While there have been numerous tests of the CAPM, there are two major questions that should concern us. The first involves the stability of the measure of systematic risk, i.e., the stability of beta. Given that beta is our principal risk measure, it is important to know whether it is possible to use past betas as estimates of future betas. The second question is basic to the theory: is there a positive linear relationship as hypothesized between beta and the rate of return on risky assets?

Stability of Beta

While numerous studies have considered this question, two older articles are noteworthy and two recent articles provide useful insights. One by Levy examined weekly rates of return for 500 stocks on the NYSE during the period 1960–1970.[6] The author concluded that the risk measure was not stable for individual stocks over fairly short periods (52 weeks). Alternatively, when stocks were put into portfolios, the stability of the portfolio betas increased dramatically. Further, the larger the portfolio (e.g., 25 or 50 stocks) and the longer the period (over 26 weeks), the more stable the beta of the portfolio. Specifically, the correlation of 25- and 50-stock portfolio betas over 26-week periods averaged above .91. He also noted a tendency for the betas to regress toward the mean; high beta portfolios had a tendency to decline over time toward unity (1.00), while low beta portfolios tended to increase over time toward unity.

A study by Blume likewise examined the stability of beta for all common stock listed on the NYSE over the period January 1926 through June 1968.[7]

---

[6]Robert A. Levy, "On the Short-term Stationarity of Beta Coefficients," *Financial Analysts Journal* 27 (1971): 55–62.

[7]Marshall E. Blume, "On the Assessment of Risk," *Journal of Finance* 26 (1971): 1–10.

Besides providing some very interesting descriptive statistics on beta, he carried out an extensive analysis of the stability of beta. The correlation of beta for individual stocks during adjoining periods was quite good, .60 to .73. Similar to Levy's findings, the stability was shown to increase substantially for portfolios of 20 or more stocks; i.e., the correlation ranged from .93 to .98. He also found a tendency for regression toward one.

A study by Tole proposes a different measure of stability and likewise suggests the importance of large portfolios to generate stable estimates.[8] Finally, a study by Carpenter and Upton indicates that it is necessary to consider the volume of trading during the period of estimation.[9]

In summary, these studies and others that examined the same question have generally indicated that the beta for *individual* securities is not very stable, but the beta for *portfolios* of securities is extremely stable over short- and long-run periods. Given that most investors are concerned with a portfolio of assets, these results are very encouraging in terms of using beta as a measure of the future risk of a portfolio.

Relationship Between Systematic Risk and Return

As stated, the ultimate question regarding the CAPM is whether it is useful in explaining the returns on risky assets. Is there a positive linear relationship between the systematic risk for risky assets and the rates of return on these assets? A study by Sharpe and Cooper generally provided support for a *positive* relationship, although it was not completely linear.[10] Specifically, they put stocks into risk classes based upon their systematic risk (beta) and examined the average rates of return for each of the risk classes. The returns increased with risk class except for the very highest risk classes where there was a tendency for the *returns to level off* and decline slightly. They also showed that the betas for portfolios were stable. Therefore, it was possible to derive the average beta for a portfolio based upon historical betas, and the return during a subsequent period was generally consistent with the risk.

In contrast, a study by Douglas did not find a strong positive relationship between return and covariance with the market portfolio.[11] A study by Miller and Scholes indicated some biases in the Douglas study, but could not fully explain the poor relationship.[12] Finally, a study by Black, Jensen, and Scholes found a positive relationship between systematic risk and return, but the pattern did not

---

[8]Thomas M. Tole, "How to Maximize Stationarity of Beta," *Journal of Portfolio Management* 7 (1981): 45–49.

[9]Michael D. Carpenter and David E. Upton, "Trading Volume and Beta Stability," *Journal of Portfolio Management* 7 (1981): 60–64.

[10]William F. Sharpe and Guy M. Cooper, "Risk-Return Classes of New York Stock Exchange Common Stocks: 1931–1977," *Financial Analysts Journal* 28 (1972): 46–54.

[11]G. W. Douglas, "Risk in the Equity Markets: An Empirical Appraisal of Market Efficiency," *Yale Economic Essays* 9 (1969): 3–48.

[12]M. H. Miller and M. Scholes, "Rates of Return in Relation to Risk: A Reexamination of Some Recent Findings," in *Studies in the Theory of Capital Markets,* (New York: Praeger, 1976).

completely conform to that indicated by the SML for the period.[13] Specifically, it appeared that the low-risk securities achieved returns that were above expectations, while the high-risk securities received returns lower than those implied by the SML.[14] In summary, the empirical evidence indicates a positive relationship as hypothesized by the theory, but the relationship is not completely linear.[15]

Summary

Following a consideration of the assumptions of capital market theory, we defined a risk-free asset and showed that the correlation and covariance of any asset with the risk-free asset is zero. Given this relationship, it was demonstrated that any combination of an asset or portfolio with the risk-free asset generated a linear return and risk function. Therefore, when you combine the risk-free asset with any risky asset on the Markowitz efficient frontier, you derive a set of straight-line portfolio possibilities, with the dominant line the one that is tangent to the efficient frontier. This dominant line is referred to as the capital market line (CML), and all investors should want to be somewhere along this line depending upon their risk preferences. Because all investors want to invest in the risky portfolio at the point of tangency, this portfolio, referred to as the market portfolio, must contain all risky assets in proportion to their relative values. Moreover, the investment decision and the financing decision can be separated because, while everyone will want to invest in the market portfolio, each of them will differ in financing decisions (i.e., lending or borrowing) which are based upon risk preferences.

Given the CML and the dominance of the market portfolio, it was shown that the relevant risk measure for an individual risk asset is its covariance with the market portfolio, i.e., its systematic risk. When this covariance is normalized by the covariance for the market portfolio, we can derive the well-known beta measure of systematic risk. With the beta coefficient it is possible to construct a security market line (SML) that relates expected return to beta. All individual securities and portfolios should plot on this SML. This means one can determine the expected (required) return on a security based upon its systematic risk. Alternatively, assuming markets for all securities are not completely efficient, we

---

[13]F. Black, M. C. Jensen, and M. Scholes, "The Capital Asset Pricing Model: Some Empirical Tests," in *Studies in the Theory of Capital Markets*, ed. M. C. Jensen (New York: Praeger, 1976).

[14]A study that suggests an alternative reason for the problem is James M. Johnson and Howard P. Lanser, "Dividend Risk Measurement and Tests of the CAPM," *Journal of Portfolio Management* 7 (1981): 50–54.

[15]An excellent review of theory and empirical work is Michael C. Jensen, "Capital Markets: Theory and Evidence," *Bell Journal of Economics and Management Science* 3 (1972): 357–398. More recent reviews are contained in Stephen A. Ross, "The Current Status of the Capital Asset Pricing Model (CAPM)," *Journal of Finance* 33 (1978): 885–890. Barr Rosenberg, "The Capital Asset Pricing Model and the Market Model," *Journal of Portfolio Management* 7 (1981): 5–16.

demonstrated how undervalued and overvalued securities can be identified. We included an example of how to calculate the characteristic line for an individual risky asset and thereby compute its beta coefficient. We concluded with a discussion of several empirical studies related to the CAPM. The studies on the stability of beta indicated that individual betas were not very stable, but portfolio betas were *very* stable. Regarding the relationship between beta and rates of return, the results indicated a positive relationship, but it was not completely linear.

Questions

1. Define a risk-free asset.

2. What is the covariance between a risk-free asset and a portfolio of risky assets? Explain your answer.

3. Why is the set of points between the risk-free asset and a portfolio on the Markowitz efficient frontier a straight line? Explain.

4. What happens to the Markowitz efficient frontier when you assume the existence of a risk-free asset and combine this with alternative risky asset portfolios on the Markowitz efficient frontier? Draw a graph to show this and explain it.

5. Show graphically and explain why the line from the RFR that is tangent to the efficient frontier is the dominant set of portfolio possibilities.

6. It has been shown that the Sharpe capital market line (CML) is tangent to one portfolio on the Markowitz efficient frontier. This portfolio at the point of tangency is referred to as portfolio M. What stocks are in this portfolio and why are they in it? Be precise in your discussion.

7. Discuss leverage and indicate what it does to the CML.

8. Why is the CML considered the "new" efficient frontier?

9. Define complete diversification in terms of capital market theory.

10. How would you *measure* the extent of diversification of a portfolio? Discuss the rationale for this answer.

11. Discuss why in a world with a CML, the investment decision and the financing decision are separate.

12. Given the Sharpe capital market line, what is the relevant measure of risk for an individual security? Why is this the relevant risk measure? Be very precise and complete in your discussion.

13. It is contended that the total variance of returns for a security can be broken down into "systematic" variance and unsystematic, or "unique", variance. Describe what is meant by each of these terms.

14. In a Capital Asset Pricing Model (CAPM) there is systematic and unsystematic risk for an individual security. Which is the relevant risk variable in a

CAPM framework and why is it relevant? Why is the other risk variable not relevant?

15. Draw a properly labeled graph of the security market line (SML) and explain it. How does the SML differ from the CML?

16. a Assume that you expect the economy's rate of inflation to be 3 percent and, in line with this, you expect the RFR to be .06 and the market return (R_m) to be .12. Draw the SML.

b. Now assume that you expect an increase in the rate of inflation from 3 percent to 6 percent. What effect would you expect this to have on your RFR and R_m? Draw another SML on the same graph used for part a.

c. Draw the SML on the same graph if you expect the RFR to be .09 and the R_m to be .17. How does this SML differ from that derived in part b? Explain what has transpired.

17. You expect the RFR to be .10 and the market return (R_m) to be .14. Compute the expected return for the following stocks, and plot these on an SML graph.

Stock	Beta	$E(R_i)$
U	.85	
N	1.25	
D	−0.20	

18. You ask a stockbroker what his firm's research department expects for these three stocks. The broker responds with the following information:

Stock	Current Price	Expected Price	Expected Dividend
U	22	24	0.75
N	48	51	2.00
D	37	40	1.25

Plot your estimated returns on the graph from Question 17 and indicate what action you would take with regard to these stocks. Discuss your decision.

19. Select a stock from the NYSE and collect the month-end prices for the latest 13 months in order to compute 12 monthly percentages of price changes (ignore dividends). Do the same for the S&P 500 series. Plot these on a graph and draw a *visual* characteristic line of best fit (the line which minimizes the deviations from the line). Compute the slope of this line *from the graph*.

20. Given the returns derived in Question 19, compute the beta coefficient using the formula and techniques employed in Table 20.2. How many negative products did you have for the covariance? How does this computed beta compare to the visual beta derived in Question 19?

21. Select a stock that is listed on the ASE and plot the returns during the last 12 months relative to the S&P 500. In general, would you expect this stock to have a higher or lower beta than the NYSE stock? Explain your answer.

22. Given the returns for the ASE stock in Question 21, plot the stock returns relative to monthly rates of return for the ASE Index and draw a *visual* line of best fit. Does the slope of this line differ from that derived in Question 21? If so, how can you explain this? Hint: Consider the formula for the beta coefficient and what changes between Question 21 and 22.

References

Blume, Marshall E. "On the Assessment of Risk." *Journal of Finance* 26 (1971).

Fama, Eugene F. "Risk, Return and Equilibrium." *Journal of Political Economy* 79 (1971).

Hagin, Robert. *Modern Portfolio Theory.* Homewood, IL: Dow-Jones-Irwin, 1979.

Jensen, Michael C. "Capital Markets: Theory and Evidence." *Bell Journal of Economics and Management Science* 3 (1972).

Lindahl-Stevens, Mary. "Some Popular Uses and Abuses of Beta." *Journal of Portfolio Management* 4 (1978).

Lintner, John. "Security Prices, Risk and Maximal Gains from Diversification." *Journal of Finance* 20 (1965).

Modigliani, Franco, and Pogue, Gerald A. "An Introduction to Risk and Return." *Financial Analysts Journal* 30 (1974) 2 parts.

Mossin, J. "Equilibrium in a Capital Asset Market." *Econometrica* 34 (1966).

Mossin, J. "Security Pricing and Investment Criteria in Competitive Markets." *American Economic Review* 59 (1969).

Rosenberg, Barr. "The Capital Asset Pricing Model and the Market Model." *Journal of Portfolio Management* 7 (1981).

Ross, Stephen A. "The Current Status of the Capital Asset Pricing Model (CAPM)." *Journal of Finance* 33 (1978).

Sharpe, William F. "Capital Asset Prices: A Theory of Market Equilibrium Under Conditions of Risk." *Journal of Finance* 19 (1964).

Tobin, James. "Liquidity Preference as Behavior Towards Risk." *Review of Economic Studies* 25 (1958).

INTERNATIONAL DIVERSIFICATION

⇥ 22 ⇤

By now, you should be fully aware of the importance of diversification for reducing the risk of the portfolio and also that the important factor when selecting an asset for diversification purposes is the covariance of the asset with all other assets in the portfolio. Further, with the CAPM it is shown that the relevant covariance is that between the asset and the market portfolio of *all risky assets in the economy.* In the search for investment assets that have low covariance with the market portfolio, increasing attention has been paid to international capital markets because of the *a priori* expectation that the covariance between international securities and United States securities should be very low. Hence, you should consider adding such investments to a portfolio composed of domestic stocks.

Because of the growing importance of international investments to individuals and institutions, this chapter will deal with the topic in some detail. Initially, we will consider *why* international diversification should be beneficial; i.e., what is the rationale for expecting significant benefits from international diversification? Subsequently we will discuss the results of several studies that have examined the historical relationships between the returns for U.S. securities and foreign securities. The results of these studies will indicate whether international diversification would have been useful for a U.S. investor.

Given the apparent benefits of international diversification, it is important to consider some of the obstacles involved. We conclude the chapter with a consideration of available mutual funds that invest specifically in foreign securities. You will see that there are a variety of readily available investments that provide the benefits of international diversification.

Why International Diversification?

Because the objective of diversification is to reduce the overall variance of a portfolio, one must ask why foreign securities should be expected to have low covariance with a portfolio of U.S. risky assets. Although the market portfolio used in the CAPM is *theoretically* supposed to contain all risky assets available, the investor is typically concerned with risky assets in the United States. Further, it has been noted on several occasions that almost all empirical studies of the CAPM have used the Standard & Poor's 500 Composite Index as a proxy for the market portfolio. This is a gross understatement of the market portfolio because the S&P 500 Index only includes common stocks and almost all of them are stocks listed on the NYSE. Given this orientation, it can be demonstrated that foreign securities *should* be included in domestic portfolios. The true market portfolio should be a *total world portfolio* to derive the maximum benefits of diversification.

This discussion leads us back to our assumption of low covariance between the returns for domestic and foreign securities. To see why this expectation is reasonable, one should consider the basic dividend valuation formula

$$P = \frac{D_1}{K - g}$$

The relevant variables are expected dividend (D_1), the required rate of return (K), and the expected growth rate for dividends (g). It is contended that these variables differ significantly between countries and for different securities in the various countries. Because K and g are the most important variables, we will concentrate on them.

Differences in the Required Rate of Return (K)

K is a function of the economy's risk-free rate of return, the expected inflation in the economy, and a risk premium for the uncertainty involved. Therefore, let us consider each of these components in terms of how they would differ for a foreign country compared to those for the U.S.

The Risk-Free Rate   It has been shown that the risk-free rate is basically determined by the real growth rate in the economy and, in the short-run, by tightness or ease in the capital markets. Different countries have experienced different rates of growth during the past several decades. Examples include the high rate of growth in Japan and Germany. The point is, these rates of growth in different countries are *not synchronized*. Further, there are differences in the short-run ease or tightness in the capital markets in different countries. Therefore, one would expect differences in the *level* of the RFR and also somewhat independent *changes* in the RFR for various countries.

Differences in the Rates of Inflation   We have talked extensively about the impact of the rate of inflation on the required rate of return on all assets and specifically about how inflation has affected securities in the U.S. In fact, it is probably safe to say that inflation has been the most important variable influencing asset valuation during the last decade. The crucial question in terms of international diversification is whether the level of inflation is generally the same around the world, and more important, whether *changes* in the rate of inflation are cor-related. If these changes are correlated, then required rates of return would gen-erally move together and security prices would be related. Obviously, such a scenario would reduce the utility of international diversification. In contrast, if changes in the rates of inflation are typically unique, then returns for securities in various countries would not be correlated, and international diversification would be useful.

To get a feeling for whether rates of inflation should be related it is necessary to consider the factors that cause inflation. Specifically, inflation is generally de-scribed as either demand-pull (excess demand) or cost-push. In turn there is some controversy regarding whether excess demand inflation is fueled by monetary policy or fiscal policy. Without entering into this discussion, it is enough to recog-nize that generally *both* the monetary policy and the fiscal policy of a country are determined by internal factors, and, therefore, the specification and implementa-tion of policy directives should typically be independent among countries. Further, the impact of any monetary or fiscal stimulus will differ between coun-tries depending upon the current state of the country's economy in terms of un-employment, etc. Regarding cost-push inflation, again the impact will depend upon the state of the economy and the power of various economic units, e.g., unions. Again, this inflationary impact will differ between countries.

The point is, while the basic causes of inflation may be reasonably universal, there are major differences in these causes in alternative countries. Therefore, one should expect differences in the level of inflation and relatively independent *changes* in the rate of inflation for different countries. Because of the major im-pact that inflation has on the required rate of return, this discussion would imply substantial independence in K and consequent *independence* in security returns due to changes in K.

Differences in Risk Premiums   The risk premium can either be estimated using internal characteristics (business risk, financial risk, and liquidity risk) or external market risk (covariance with the market portfolio). Because this discussion is concerned with why the covariance with the market portfolio should be low, it is appropriate to consider the relationship among the internal characteristics. Be-cause we are interested in *changes* in stock prices (as they affect rates of return), we will consider whether *changes* in the relevant risk variables are independent.

Recall that business risk is a function of sales volatility and operating lever-age. One would therefore generally expect *changes* in business risk for firms in different countries to be unique because the factors that affect domestic sales, such as fiscal policy and monetary policy, are independent, and so changes in sales volatility should also be relatively independent. Similarly, the degree of operating leverage (DOL) is a function of how close a firm is operating to its break-even point. Again, because sales are generally independent, the DOL will be unique and changes in this variable for firms in different countries should not be con-sistently related. Therefore, because changes in sales volatility and changes in operating leverage are not related, you should *not* expect changes in business risk to be related.

Financial risk is a function of the proportion of debt in the financial structure, and is typically measured in terms of the debt/total capital ratio or interest coverage. Firms within an economy typically determine how much debt to employ based upon the tax laws (the higher the corporate tax rate, the greater the tax advantage of debt versus equity), earnings stability (with greater stability it is possible to employ more debt), and the expected rate of inflation (a higher rate of inflation would prompt more firms to become net debtors). These factors that determine the desired level of financial leverage are generally independent, and *changes* in these factors are unique. Therefore, *changes* in the level of financial risk for different countries should be relatively independent.

Liquidity risk is the uncertainty regarding the ability to buy or sell an asset quickly at a known price. The liquidity of an asset is a function of the number of investors who own and trade the asset, i.e., the volume of trading in the asset. In turn, the amount of trading in common stocks or other financial assets is influenced by the general economic climate in a country and, again, one would not expect consistency between countries. This expectation is borne out by differences in trading volume on different national exchanges. For example, there have been instances in which trading in Japan was extremely heavy while volume on U.S. exchanges was relatively light. Therefore, because trading-volume changes are unique, we should expect changes in liquidity risk to be independent for different countries.

Summary Regarding Required Rate of Return

As noted, there are three determinants of the required rate of return on securities: the economy's risk-free rate, the expected rate of inflation, and the risk premium for alternative assets. A specific analysis of each of these factors indicated that *changes* in each of these variables in different countries were generally determined by internal factors that were *independent* between countries. Therefore, one can conclude that *changes in the required rate of return for securities in various countries will not be highly correlated, and in many cases the changes could be relatively independent.* If other factors are held constant, and the required rate of return on foreign securities experiences changes that are independent of changes in the required return on U.S. securities, then the resulting rates of return on U.S. and foreign securities should have small covariance or correlation.

It should be noted that the level of covariance between two countries will depend upon the relationship between the economies involved. As an example, one would probably expect a fairly high correlation between U.S. and Canadian securities because the economies are highly related. In contrast, the U.S. economy has a very weak relationship to those of some third world countries, so one would expect a weak correlation between stock returns.

Independent Changes in the Growth Rate

It can similarly be argued that the major factors determining the growth rate (g) are generally independent between countries. You will recall that the growth rate is a function of the retention rate and the return on equity. One would expect changes in the retention rate to vary between countries based upon differences in their tax structure, the investment opportunities in the country, and the availability of external capital in the country's capital markets. Because all of these factors differ between countries and change independently, changes in the retention rate should be unique to a given nation. The return on equity (ROE) is determined by equity turnover and the profit margin. The equity turnover, in turn, is heavily influenced by sales growth, retention policy, and changes in the debt-equity financing ratio. All of these factors differ between countries. The profit margin depends upon such factors as capacity utilization, unit labor cost, inflation, exports, and imports. Again, the two major factors are capacity utilization and unit labor cost, and both of these are clearly variables that are internal to the economy. Therefore, changes in these variables for alternative nations should be relatively independent.

Therefore, almost all of the determinants of growth are unique and differ for different countries. Moreover, *changes* in these variables are generally determined by internal conditions, and these conditions are expected to be independent. Similar to the changes in K, the degree of independence in these growth factors will vary depending upon the economic ties between the countries. Because changes in these growth variables cause changes in security prices, the resultant price changes should likewise be relatively independent.

Why International Diversification?

In this section we employed the basic dividend valuation model to help us determine whether international diversification makes sense. An analysis of the two major determinants of value (K and g) indicated that both variables are heavily influenced by the macro-economic organization and management of the economy. Moreover, the major decisions that generally affect a country's economy are made by an internal group concerned with a country's well-being. As such, most of the decisions are independent of circumstances in other countries. Therefore, changes in both K and g should be independent between countries or have low correlation. As a result, price changes should be relatively independent and the covariance between returns for securities in *different* countries should be much lower than the covariance of returns for securities *within* a country.

Empirical Studies of International Diversification

Since 1968, a number of studies have examined the effect of international diversification empirically and attempted to answer questions regarding the real benefits of such diversification.

Grubel Studies

One of the first studies by Herbert Grubel showed the benefits of international diversification by analyzing monthly rates of return (adjusted for changes in ex-

	Per cent Per Annum (1)	Standard Deviation (2)	Correlation (R) with USA (3)
USA	7.54	47.26	1.0000
Canada	5.95	41.19	0.7025[a]
United Kingdom	9.59	65.28	0.2414[a]
West Germany	7.32	94.69	0.3008[a]
France	4.27	49.60	0.1938[a]
Italy	8.12	103.33	0.1465
Belgium	1.09	37.56	0.1080
Netherlands	5.14	86.34	0.2107[a]
Japan	16.54	92.52	0.1149
Australia	9.44	34.87	0.0585
South Africa	8.47	61.92	−0.1620

Table 22.1   Rates of Return and Standard Deviation from Investing in Foreign Capital Markets: 1959–1966

[a]Statistically significant at the 5 percent level.

Source: Herbert G. Grubel, "Internationally Diversified Portfolios: Welfare Gains and Capital Flows," *American Economic Review* 58 (1968): 1304. Reprinted by permission.

change rates) for 11 major countries during the period 1959–1966.[1] The rates of return, standard deviation, and correlation with the U.S. index are shown in Table 22.1.

Japan had the highest rate of return during the period, but also one of the largest standard deviations. More important though, this index had very low correlation with the U.S. index (.1149), indicating that securities from Japan would be a good addition to a portfolio composed of U.S. securities. Australia had the lowest correlation (.0585) with the U.S. index, and the South African index had a *negative* correlation (−.1620). This negative correlation is probably caused by heavy involvement in gold mining. One would expect securities from these foreign indexes, except Canada, to be excellent additions to a domestic portfolio.

Grubel derived hypothetical portfolios using data from all 11 countries. The results clearly showed that *diversification among the assets from the 11 countries permitted investors to attain higher rates of return or lower variance than would be attained with a portfolio of only U.S. stocks.*

A subsequent study by Grubel and Fadner considered three questions concerning international diversification.[2] The first was an analysis of diversification

[1]Herbert G. Grubel, "Internationally Diversified Portfolios: Welfare Gains and Capital Flows," *American Economic Review* 58 (1968): 1299–1314.

[2]Herbert G. Grubel and Kenneth Fadner, "The Interdependence of International Equity Markets," *Journal of Finance* 26 (1971): 89–94.

within a country compared to diversification *between* countries. The results indicated that diversification *between* countries was much more effective, and that
the correlations were influenced by the proportion of importing and exporting
between countries. (The more trade between countries the higher is the correlation, and the less effective the diversification.) The second question concerned
the differences in correlation for different holding periods. The results indicated
that correlation increased with the holding period, which implies some reduction
in the benefits of international diversification with longer holding periods. Finally,
the authors found little difference in results for returns adjusted for exchange
rates versus unadjusted returns because exchange rates were relatively stable
during the period studied.

Levy-Sarnat Study
A study by Levy and Sarnat examined the potential benefits of international
diversification by analyzing returns for 28 countries during the period 1951–
1967.[3] They found a wide range of returns and standard deviations for alternative countries, and when they derived efficient frontiers from different groups of
countries they found *the best frontier was derived with all 28 countries included.*

Lessard Study
Lessard examined rates of return for four Latin American countries (Colombia,
Chile, Argentina, and Brazil) during the period 1958 to 1968.[4] An analysis of returns indicated that stocks within a country with an undeveloped capital market
have a large common component; i.e., they are highly correlated. In contrast, the
market component for each country was generally *independent* of the market
component for other countries, which implies *large gains from international
diversification.* Note that this implies benefits from investing in developing countries in a single geographical area; the benefits would clearly be even better for a
U.S. investor diversifying with these countries, because the relationship between
the U.S. and any of these developing countries would be almost nonexistent.

French Mutual Funds
McDonald examined the investment performance of internationally diversified
portfolios by analyzing the performance of French mutual funds for the period
1964–1969.[5] French funds were analyzed because they represent a range of investment in both domestic French stocks and foreign stocks, with most foreign
securities listed on the NYSE. Also, the funds are typically managed by French
banks that have superior access to company information. The results supported
the concept of international diversification because the fund composed only of

---

[3]Haim Levy and Marshall Sarnat, "International Diversification of Investment Portfolios," *American
Economic Review* 60 (1970): 668–675.

[4]Donald R. Lessard, "International Portfolio Diversification: A Multivariate Analysis for a Group of Latin
American Countries," *Journal of Finance* 28 (1973): 619–633.

[5]John G. McDonald, "French Mutual Fund Performance: Evaluation of Internationally Diversified
Portfolios," *Journal of Finance* 28 (1973): 1161–1180.

	Adjusted	Unadjusted			Adjusted	Unadjusted
Australia	.137	.161	Japan		.092	.076
Austria	.027	.020	Netherlands		.344	.349
Belgium	.205	.232	Switzerland		.242	.245
Canada	.634	.643	United Kingdom		.096	.125
France	.107	.097	West Germany		.163	.171
Italy	.002	.021				

Table 22.2   Correlations of Weekly Rates of Return Between U.S. and Other Countries: 1963–1972

Source: O. Maurice Joy, Don Panton, Frank K. Reilly, and Stanley A. Martin, "Comovements of Major International Equity Markets," *The Financial Review* (1976).

French stocks had the lowest performance ratio, while the fund with the *most* international diversification had the highest performance ratio.

Joy et al. Study

A study by Maurice Joy and others considered the relationship among major international equity markets and also analyzed *changes* in these relationships over time during the period 1963–1972.[6] The correlations between the U.S. and each of the countries for unadjusted and adjusted returns are contained in Table 22.2. As shown, *most of the correlations are very low.* This supports previous studies which contended that *there are substantial risk reduction possibilities through international diversification.* During this period there was also little difference between the results with adjusted and unadjusted rates of return.

The authors also found a significant difference among the correlations which means that it is important to determine the specific intercountry relationship, e.g., the rather high correlation of the U.S. with Canada compared to the low correlation with Italy or Japan. They also determined that *the relationships change over time,* and there was a *small positive trend* in the correlations which means that the benefits of diversification may not be as great, but *the trend was very gradual.*

Morgan Guaranty Analysis

A presentation by Joel Swanson for Morgan Guaranty Trust Company contains data for some major countries during the period 1969–1978.[7] Table 22.3 contains the total rates of return, standard deviations, and correlation coefficients for these countries and the S&P 500.

As shown, the rates of return from foreign securities were often higher than

[6]O. Maurice Joy, Don B. Panton, Frank K. Reilly, and Stanley A. Martin, "Comovements of Major International Equity Markets," *The Financial Review* (1976): 1–20.

[7]Joel Swanson, *Investing Internationally to Reduce Risk and Enhance Return* (New York: Morgan Guaranty Trust Company, 1979).

Country	Total Rates of Return (Adjusted)	Standard Deviation of Rates of Return	Correlation Coefficient with U.S.
France	2.5	24.8	.37
Germany	11.8	19.1	.30
Japan	18.1	25.0	.28
Switzerland	11.1	22.5	.45
United Kingdom	0.7	32.0	.44
United States	2.1	16.9	—

Table 22.3   Rates of Return, Standard Deviations, and Correlation Coefficient for Foreign Countries and S&P 500: 1969–1978

Source: *Investing Internationally to Reduce Risk and Enhance Return,* (New York: Morgan Guaranty Trust Company, 1979).

those from U.S. portfolios. At the same time, the standard deviation of the U.S. portfolio was consistently lowest. Still, because of the relatively low correlations, the impact of diversification on a *world portfolio* is quite positive as shown in Table 22.4.

As shown, during this period, the world index provided not only a *higher* rate of return, but also a *lower* level of risk. This would imply that, with international diversification, the efficient frontier would not only move to the left to reflect lower risk, but also move up due to the higher return.

Conclusions and Implications

Based upon the results of the several studies discussed, it is possible to derive several major conclusions regarding the usefulness of international diversification, and to derive some implications of these findings.

	1969–73	1974–78
Rates of Return (Price Only)		
U.S. Index	3.34	3.56
World Index	6.40	5.14
Standard Deviation of Return		
U.S. Index	13.9	17.6
World Index	13.4	14.9

Table 22.4   Differential Return and Risk From Domestic Versus World Portfolios

Source: *Investing Internationally to Reduce Risk and Enhance Return,* (New York: Morgan Guaranty Trust Company, 1979).

Level of Correlation   The results consistently indicate a *much lower* level of correlation between the stocks of *different* countries than for stocks *within* a country. This implies that there are substantial benefits to be derived from international diversification, as was demonstrated in several of the articles discussed.

It was also shown that *the correlation differs between countries* depending upon their level of development and the level of interdependence of their economies. The relationship between less developed countries and highly developed countries is clearly less than average simply because the undeveloped countries have unique economic problems such that their economies do not move together, and the rates of return on their stocks are not associated. Therefore, for purposes of diversification, such undeveloped countries are excellent candidates for investment. The correlations were not stable over time, so it is not possible to simply use past correlations to develop future portfolios. It will also be necessary to adjust the portfolios over time to reflect expected changes in the relationships.

Finally, there have been results that indicate a positive trend in some of the correlations. This would imply that there will be less benefit derived from international diversification in the future. The trend is gradual and is not positive for all combinations. This means that you should examine each country on an individual basis and make an appropriate decision based upon the past relationship, recent trends, and your assessment of the future relation between the countries involved.

Obstacles to International Diversification

Previous studies have generally indicated that the benefit of international diversification stems from the low correlation between foreign and domestic stocks. Even though international investment may involve some problems owing to the instability of relationships between the securities, these are relatively minor and no more of a problem than dealing with unstable betas for individual U.S. stocks. Therefore, given the clear advantages of international diversification and the limited theoretical problems, why do individuals and institutions in the U.S. not invest more in foreign securities? The chief obstacle is the fact that international capital markets are clearly not perfect. As discussed, the major characteristics of perfect markets are complete and costless information, zero transaction costs, and complete liquidity.

Availability of Information
A *set* of obstacles to foreign investment are subsumed under this general heading. The first is the *availability of information* on individual companies, industries, and economies. American investors take for granted an enormous set of data that is simply not available in many other countries, especially in some less developed nations. The numerous sources of economic data, including organizations like the Federal Reserve System and the Commerce Department, simply do not exist in

many foreign countries. Further, we have a number of private sources of industry data, companies like Standard & Poor's, Moody's, Value Line, and industry trade associations that do not exist elsewhere. Finally, analysts in the U.S. are almost overwhelmed each year by annual reports and quarterly reports. Again, *almost none* of this is available in *most* foreign countries. For analysts and portfolio managers accustomed to a plethora of information, it is difficult to make decisions under these conditions.

There is a further problem of *interpretation of the data* received because reporting standards in many countries are different from those used here. Investors often complain about the different accounting techniques used by American firms, techniques that can seriously affect reported income. These differences are minor compared to the variations employed in many foreign countries. What, then, does the analyst do with the Japanese or German earnings figure to make it comparable to a U.S. figure?

Finally, there are timing problems because of *reporting lags*. How long will it take until figures are publicly available? In many instances, the lag is substantial compared to what it is in the U.S. Further, once figures are available, it may be a while until they are reported in the U.S. Clearly, this reporting lag could be very important in the price adjustment process.

Liquidity

Liquidity is generally defined as the ability to buy or sell an asset quickly without the price changing significantly from what it was during a previous transaction, assuming no new information has entered the market. In earlier chapters we have discussed this concept extensively regarding how liquidity affects an investment's required rate of return. Liquidity is important for any investment and is especially crucial to large institutional investors who need to establish major positions in an investment if it is going to be worthwhile. Unfortunately, the liquidity of most foreign stocks is *substantially below* that of most U.S. stocks listed on an exchange. Although there are some stocks with good trading volume and liquidity, *the great majority of foreign stocks experience only limited trading and substantial volatility*. Therefore, while a number of foreign stocks could be acquired by individuals, only a *very limited* number of foreign stocks have the necessary liquidity to be considered by institutional investors.

Transaction Costs

One must also consider the above-average transaction costs involved in a foreign trade. These include commission costs (that will probably be above average), transfer taxes, and all the other costs involved in placing the order and securing the certificate.[8]

Notably, there has been a major change in the attitude of U.S. pension funds

[8]An article by Anna Marjos indicates that many of these problems have declined in recent years with the growth of American Depository Receipts (ADRs). See Anna Majos, "How to Invest Abroad," *Barron's* 24 July 1978, p. 9.

toward foreign investing. While they generally recognize the problems involved, they feel that the potential benefits in terms of higher returns and lower risk through diversification are worth the effort.[9]

Alternatives to Direct Investment

Assume that an investor acknowledges that it is a good idea to invest in foreign securities and yet is also aware of the problems; what alternatives are available? For an individual investor an obvious solution would be to purchase shares in an investment company that specializes in foreign securities.[10] Doing it this way would solve the problem of lack of information because professionals are involved who are familiar with the countries and their markets. This does not mean that the funds will do above average relative to an index for these countries, but they should do about average, and the investor should still derive the benefits of diversification. This approach should also reduce the liquidity problem because many of the funds available are open-end funds that will reacquire shares at their net asset value. The few closed-end funds appear to enjoy relatively active markets on exchanges (e.g., the Japan Fund is listed on the NYSE).

The following section is a listing of most of the mutual funds investing in foreign securities as determined by the author. This brief description should not be construed as a recommendation by the author, but is set forth as an aid to the reader interested in this aspect of investment. In all cases, there is an address you can write for the latest prospectus and other information. Note that almost all of these international funds concentrate their portfolios in one country or geographic area. However, several of them are almost wholly concerned with gold or other precious metals. Therefore, it might be necessary to invest in *several* of these international funds to derive the full benefits of world diversification.

Canadian Fund, Inc.
One Wall Street
New York, NY 10005
This is an *open-end* fund that seeks long-term capital growth by investing in companies expected to benefit from any growth or development in Canada. It is a *load* fund.

International Investors Incorporated
122 East 42nd Street
New York, NY 10017
This is an *open-end* fund that has concentrated its investments in *gold mining shares*. Because approximately three-quarters of the Free World's output of gold

---

[9]See Lawrence Rout, "Many Pension Funds are Looking Overseas for New Investments," *Wall Street Journal* 24 May 1979, p. 1; and Daniel Hertzberg, "Pension Managers Invest More Overseas, Aware of Risks but Hopeful About Profits," *Wall Street Journal* 2 July 1981, p. 36.

[10]For a discussion of the attraction to individuals, see Jill Bettner, "Foreign Stocks Catch on with Small Investors; Gains are Bigger Lure than Diversification," *Wall Street Journal* 20 April 1981, p. 36. For a discussion of international funds, see Laurie Cohen, "International Stock Funds Attracting American Investors," *Chicago Tribune* 19 May 1981, p. 3.

is produced in South Africa, about 60 percent of the company's net assets (as of the end of 1980), were securities of South African issue, although the fund also has significant investments in Canadian gold mines. Under normal conditions, the company expects to have at least two-thirds of the value of its assets in foreign securities. It is a *load* fund.

The Japan Fund, Inc.
One Rockefeller Plaza
New York, NY 10020
This is a *closed-end* fund that invests in a diversified portfolio of common stocks of leading Japanese companies. Shares of this fund are listed on the New York Stock Exchange and may be bought or sold like any other stock. The commission would be the standard commission for any purchase on the NYSE.

Kemper International Fund, Inc.
120 South LaSalle Street
Chicago, IL 60603
This is an *open-end* fund that intends to invest more than 80 percent of its funds in non-United States issuers. It is a *load* fund.

Nomura Capital Fund of Japan, Inc.
100 Wall Street
New York, NY 10005
This is an *open-end* fund that primarily invests in equities of Japanese corporations. Under normal conditions at least 80 percent of the fund's assets will be invested in Japanese common stocks and convertible bonds. It is a *load* fund.

G. T. Pacific Fund, Inc.
601 Montgomery Street
Suite 1400
San Francisco, CA 94111
This is an *open-end* fund that invests principally in *Japanese securities.* Under normal conditions at least 80 percent of the fund's assets will be invested in Japanese equity instruments. It is a *no-load* fund.

Putnam International Equities Fund, Inc.
265 Franklin Street
Boston, MA 02110
This is an *open-end* fund that invests up to 70 percent of its assets in securities traded in *several foreign markets.* It is a *load* fund.

Research Capital Fund, Inc.
155 Bovet Road
San Mateo, CA 94402
This is an *open-end* fund that concentrates in securities of issuers engaged in *mining, processing or dealing in gold or other precious metals such as silver, platinum, and palladium.* The fund expects to invest a substantial portion of its assets in securities issued by companies domiciled and operating outside the U.S.; i.e., about 50 percent of their assets are expected to be invested in foreign securities. It is a *load* fund.

Scudder International Fund, Inc.
345 Park Avenue, at 51st Street
New York, NY 10022
This is an *open-end* fund that invests in equity securities in established *companies outside the U.S. and in economies with growth prospects.* The countries represented as of 1980 were Australia, Canada, France, Germany, Netherlands, Hong Kong, Japan, South Africa, Switzerland, and the United Kingdom. It is a *load* fund.

So Gen International Fund, Inc.
620 Fifth Avenue
New York, NY 10020
This is an *open-end* fund that invests in U.S. and foreign securities. As of the end of 1980, non–U.S. securities constituted about 30 percent of the total value of the portfolios. It is a *load* fund.

Strategic Investments Fund, Inc.
10110 Crestover Drive
Dallas, TX 75229
This is an *open-end* fund that invests in the equity securities of established companies engaged in the *exploration, mining, processing, fabrication, and distribution of natural resources.* As of October 1980, management expected that most assets would be invested in *gold mining companies.* Because most gold production is in foreign countries, management anticipates that at least 50 percent of the fund's investments will be in securities of foreign issuers. This is a *load* fund.

Templeton Growth Fund, Ltd.
155 University Avenue
Toronto, Ontario M5H 3B7
CANADA
This is an *open-end* fund that seeks long-term growth through investments in stocks and debt obligations of companies and governments of *any* nation. As of April 1980, the fund held securities from seven different nations as follows: United States (56.6 percent); Canada (20.3 percent); Japan (7.2 percent); Australia (4.4 percent); The Netherlands (2.8 percent); South Africa (0.5 percent); Hong Kong (0.1 percent); and 8 percent short-term obligations. It is a *load* fund.

Templeton World Fund, Inc.
41 Beach Drive, S.E.
St. Petersburg, FL 33701
This is an *open-end* fund that seeks long-term growth by investing in companies and governments of *any* nation. As of October 1980, the fund held securities from five different nations as follows: United States (62.3 percent); Canada (12.5 percent); Australia (4.5 percent); Japan (3.3 percent); Netherlands (2.8 percent); and 14.6 percent short-term obligations. This is a *load* fund.

United Services Fund, Inc.
110 East Byrd Boulevard
Universal City, TX 78148
This is an *open-end* fund that invests virtually all of its funds in foreign precious metals stocks, mainly *gold mining stocks*. Because most of the companies invested in are in foreign countries (e.g., Republic of South Africa), as of June 1980, approximately 97 percent of the fund's assets were invested in foreign securities. This is a *no-load* fund.

Lehman Multi-Currency Assets Fund, Inc.
55 Water Street
New York, NY 10041
This is a *no-load*, undiversified, open-end investment company whose primary investment objective is to seek a high, stable rate of return by investing in high-quality, interest-bearing obligations and money market instruments denominated in foreign currencies as well as in U.S. dollars. The minimum initial investment is $25,000.

Summary

This chapter was concerned with an analysis of the benefits and potential problems involved in international diversification. Our initial discussion considered the reasons that there should be a relatively low level of correlation between securities from different countries, based upon the dividend valuation model. Because almost all of the relevant valuation variables are not related, one should not expect the rates of return to be correlated.

The subsequent section contained a discussion of several studies that empirically examined the concept. The results consistently indicated that international diversification should be beneficial, although the correlations between countries change over time. There was also some evidence of an increase in the correlations among securities from various countries, but the trend was small and did not apply to all countries.

Although there are theoretical and empirical reasons for international diversification, it is clear that it is not without problems. The main obstacles are the availability of information, the reliability of the information received, the time lag in getting the information, a substantial liquidity problem with many securities, and higher transaction costs.

An alternative to direct investment by individuals is acquiring shares of an investment company that concentrates in foreign stocks. To aid readers, a number of funds that invest in foreign securities were listed and briefly discussed. It was noted that most of these funds either concentrated in a geographical area or were basically concerned with gold and precious metals. Therefore, to derive a truly international portfolio, it is necessary to acquire shares in several of these funds.

Questions

1. What is the purpose of international diversification? Why should portfolio managers invest in foreign securities?

2. Discuss in some detail why international diversification should work. Specifically, why would you *expect* low correlation in the rates of return for domestic and foreign securities?

3. Would you expect a *difference* in the correlation of returns between U.S. and various foreign securities? Why? Be specific.

4. Using a source of international statistics, compare the percentage changes in the following economic data for Japan, West Germany, Italy, Canada, and the U.S. for a recent year:

    a. aggregate output (GNP)

    b. inflation

    c. corporate earnings

    d. money supply growth

What were the differences, and which country or countries differed most from the U.S.?

5. Using a recent edition of *Barron's,* examine the weekly percentages of change in the stock price indexes for Japan, West Germany, Italy, Canada, and the U.S. For each of three weeks, which foreign series moved most closely with the U.S. series; which series was most divergent from the U.S. series? What would this indicate to you regarding international diversification?

6. What were the empirical findings regarding changes in the correlations *over time* between the stock price series for various countries? What are the implications of these results for a portfolio manager interested in international diversification?

7. Would you expect there to be a trend in the correlations between U.S. stock price series and the stock price series for different countries? Why or why not, and what would influence such a trend?

8. Assuming you are told that there has been a small increase in the correlations between the securities market in the U.S. and other countries, what does this mean to you as a portfolio manager?

9. Briefly discuss the major problems involved in international diversification. Which of the problems is greatest for individuals; which is most important to institutions? Why?

10. Aside from direct investment in foreign stocks, what alternatives are available?

11. Select two of the mutual funds discussed in the chapter and look them up in the Weisenberger *Investment Company* book. During the past five years, how have they done on a year-to-year basis compared to the DJIA?

References

Bergstrom, Gary L. "A New Route to Higher Returns and Lower Risks." *Journal of Portfolio Management* 2 (1975).

Garrone, Francois, and Solnik, Bruno. "A Global Approach to Money Management." *Journal of Portfolio Management* 2 (1976).

Grubel, Herbert G. "Internationally Diversified Portfolios: Welfare Gains and Capital Flows." *American Economic Review* 58 (1968).

Grubel, Herbert G., and Fadner, Kenneth. "The Interdependence of International Equity Markets." *Journal of Finance* 26 (1971).

Joy, O. Maurice; Panton, Don; Reilly, Frank K.; and Martin, Stanley. "Comovements of Major International Equity Markets." *The Financial Review* (1976).

Lessard, Donald, R. "International Portfolio Diversification: A Multivariate Analysis for a Group of Latin American Countries." *Journal of Finance* 28 (1973).

Levy, Haim, and Sarnat, Marshall. "International Diversification of Investment Portfolios." *American Economic Review* 60 (1970).

McDonald, John G. "French Mutual Fund Performance: Evaluation of Internationally Diversified Portfolios." *Journal of Finance* 28 (1973).

Marjos, Anna. "How to Invest Abroad." *Barron's,* 24 July 1978.

Solnik, Bruno H. "Why Not Diversify Internationally Rather Than Domestically?" *Financial Analysts Journal* 30 (1974).

Swanson, Joel. *Investing Internationally to Reduce Risk and Enhance Return.* New York: Morgan Guaranty Trust Company, 1979.

Michael C. Jensen

Professor Jensen gained initial recognition through an article based on his Ph.D. dissertation written at the University of Chicago in 1968, dealing with evaluating the performance of mutual funds: "The Performance of Mutual Funds in the Period 1945–1964," Journal of Finance (May 1968). Not only was it one of the most thorough studies of fund performance, but it also included a new composite measure of investment performance that considered returns adjusted for the portfolio's risk level as determined in the context of the CAPM.

Subsequently, Jensen was one of the co-authors in the famous FFJR stock split study: "The Adjustment of Stock Prices to New Information," International Economic Review (February 1969). He also authored a widely read article that reviewed the theory and empirical work in capital market theory, "Capital Markets: Theory and Evidence," Bell Journal of Economics and Management Science (Autumn 1972). He also edited a book of readings in capital market theory, Studies in the Theory of Capital Markets (New York: Praeger Publishers, 1972), and wrote two important articles in the collection, "The Foundation and Current State of Capital Market Theory," and "The Capital Asset Pricing Model: Some Empirical Tests," (with Fischer Black and Myron Scholes). An article that he wrote on agency theory (co-authored with W. H. Meckling): "Theory of the Firm: Managerial Behavior, Agency Costs and Ownership Structure," Journal of Financial Economics (1976), is widely quoted and has stimulated substantial interest in this topic.

In addition to extensive research, he was the founding editor of the Journal of Financial Economics, which is one of the leading journals in finance. Professor Jensen was born in Rochester, Minnesota, on November 30, 1939. He received an A.B. in Economics from Macalester College in 1962, an MBA from the University of Chicago in 1964, and a Ph.D. from the University of Chicago in 1968. Currently, Michael Jensen is professor of finance and director of the Managerial Economics Research Center at the University of Rochester.

Richard Roll

Richard Roll did some of his early work in the area of bonds but is best known for his recent work questioning the usefulness of some popular portfolio evaluation techniques because of problems with deriving a proxy for the market portfolio. This latter work has caused substantial debate among both academicians and portfolio managers who have been evaluated using techniques implied by the Capital Asset Pricing Model. The articles that sparked the controversy include "A Critique of the Asset Pricing Theory's Tests," Journal of Financial Economics (1977); "Ambiguity When Performance is Measured by the Security Market Line," Journal of Finance (September 1978); "Performance Evaluation and Benchmark Errors, I and II," Journal of Portfolio Management (Summer 1980; Winter 1981).

Roll is currently professor of finance at UCLA and vice-president of MRR, Inc. After working on the Saturn moon rocket as an aeronautical engineer, he returned to school and received a Ph.D. from the University of Chicago in 1968. His doctoral dissertation won the 1969 Irving Fisher award as the best American dissertation in economics. He was a member of the faculty at Carnegie-Mellon University from 1968–1973, and he taught in Belgium and France from 1973 to 1976. Since 1976, he has been at UCLA.

He has published two books and several articles in professional journals devoted to finance, statistics, and economics. With MRR, Inc., he has been a consultant to numerous corporations, government agencies, and law firms.

EVALUATION OF PORTFOLIO PERFORMANCE

➤ 23 ➤

It is important for investors to evaluate the performance of their investment portfolios whether they do their own analysis or have it done by a professional money manager. If you do your own analysis, you will find that it is difficult and time consuming to analyze and select securities for a portfolio. In this case, you must determine whether the time and effort were well spent in terms of the results. Alternatively, if you are paying a professional money manager (e.g., through a mutual fund or an investment counselor), it is important for you to evaluate his performance and determine whether the results justify the cost of the service.

This chapter is concerned with what is involved in evaluating the performance of a portfolio. Initially, we will consider what is required of a portfolio manager and discuss how performance was evaluated before portfolio theory and the CAPM were developed. This is followed by a discussion of three major portfolio performance evaluation techniques that consider return and risk (referred to as *composite performance measures*). We subsequently consider how to derive the needed inputs for an individual portfolio and then examine the application of these performance measures for a group of investment companies. Finally, because of the development of these performance evaluation techniques and the concern of many individuals and institutions with performance, several firms have been established to help portfolio managers evaluate their own performance and also help customers evaluate other portfolio managers, i.e., help pension funds evaluate the performance of several of their portfolio managers. Therefore, we conclude with a discussion of what information is provided by these services.

What is Required of a Portfolio Manager?

When evaluating the performance of a portfolio manager, two major factors should be considered:

1. the ability to derive above-average returns for a given risk class

2. the ability to diversify (eliminate all unsystematic risk from the portfolio).

In terms of return, the first requirement is obvious, but the necessity of considering *risk* in this context was not always immediately apparent. Risk was typically not considered prior to the 1960s, when work in portfolio theory showed its significance. In terms of modern theory, superior risk-adjusted returns can be derived *either* through superior timing or superior stock selection. If a portfolio manager can do a superior job of predicting market turns, he can alter his portfolio composition to anticipate the expected changes in the market. Specifically, if a portfolio manager expected a strong, rising market, he would shift his portfolio into high-beta securities to take maximum advantage of the increase, or borrow money and leverage his portfolio if that were allowed. In contrast, if the manager projected a market decline, he would shift the portfolio into very low-beta securities and also put a larger proportion into short-term money market instruments to avoid negative market returns; a relatively low return on short-term government securities is clearly superior to a *negative* return on stocks during a market decline. Obviously, if a portfolio manager could consistently make these moves, he would derive higher returns during bull markets and smaller negative returns during bear markets. As a result, he would show an overall higher average return. Further, because the portfolio avoided large market declines, the risk would also be lower.

Alternatively, if a portfolio manager and his analysts are able to consistently select undervalued securities for a given risk class, the portfolio should likewise provide above-average risk-adjusted rates of return. Obviously, this implies that the portfolio manager has "superior" analysts working for him and that he recognizes this. In terms of the discussion in Chapter 21 on capital market theory, this implies that the analysts are able to consistently select securities that plot above the security market line (SML).

The second factor to consider in evaluating a portfolio manager is his ability to diversify completely. The market only pays returns on the basis of systematic (market) risk. Therefore, investors should not expect to receive returns for assuming unsystematic risk, because this nonmarket risk can be eliminated in a diversified market portfolio of risky assets. Investors, consequently, want their portfolio to be completely diversified, which means eliminating unsystematic risk. The level of diversification can be judged on the basis of the correlation between the portfolio returns and the returns for a market portfolio; a completely diversified portfolio is perfectly correlated with the market portfolio, which is, in turn, completely diversified.

It is important to be constantly aware of these two requirements of a portfolio manager because some portfolio evaluation techniques that we will discuss take into account one requirement and not the other, and one evaluation technique implicitly takes both into account, but does not differentiate between them.

Composite Performance Measures

Initially, investors evaluated portfolios almost entirely on the basis of the rate of return. They were clearly aware of the notion of risk and uncertainty, but did not know how to quantify risk, so they could not consider it explicitly. Developments in portfolio theory in the early 1960s enabled investors to quantify risk in terms of the variability of returns, but there was still no composite measure; it was necessary to consider both factors separately. This is basically the approach used in several early studies.[1] The idea was to put portfolios into similar risk classes based upon some measure of risk such as variance of return, and then to directly compare the rates of return for alternative portfolios *within* a risk class.

Measures of Performance

The Treynor Measure

The first composite measure of portfolio performance (including risk) was developed by Jack Treynor in an article in the *Harvard Business Review*.[2] Treynor recognized that one of the major problems in evaluating portfolio managers was deriving a means of measuring the risk for a portfolio. He contended that there were two components of risk: risk produced by general market fluctuations, and risk resulting from unique fluctuations in the particular securities in the portfolio. To identify the first risk (market fluctuations as related to the portfolio), Treynor introduced the *characteristic line* which defines the relationship between the rates of return for a portfolio over time and the rates of return for an appropriate market portfolio. He noted that the *slope* of the characteristic line measures the *relative volatility* of the fund's returns in relation to aggregate market returns. In current terms, this slope is the fund's beta coefficient. The higher the slope, the more sensitive the fund is to market returns and the greater its market risk.

The deviations from the characteristic line indicate *unique* returns for the fund relative to the market. These unique portfolio returns are attributable to the unique returns on individual stocks in the portfolio. *If* the fund is properly diversified, these unique returns for individual stocks should *cancel out*. Therefore, deviations from the characteristic line are an indication of the ability of the portfolio manager to properly diversify. The higher the correlation of the fund with the market, the less the unique risk and the better diversified the portfolio.

Given that the risk measure is the systematic risk of the portfolio (i.e., beta), the performance measure proposed (designated T) indicates the rate of return

---

[1]Irwin Friend, Marshall Blume, and Jean Crockett, *Mutual Funds and Other Institutional Investors* (New York: McGraw-Hill, 1970).

[2]Jack L. Treynor, "How to Rate Management of Investment Funds," *Harvard Business Review* (1965): 63–75.

earned above the risk-free rate relative to this risk measure during a designated time period as follows:[3]

$$T_i = \frac{R_i - RFR}{B_i}$$

where:

T_i = the Treynor portfolio performance measure for portfolio i during a designated time period.

R_i = the average rate of return for portfolio i during a given time period.

RFR = the average rate of return on a risk-free investment during a specified time period.

B_i = the slope of portfolio i's characteristic line which indicates the portfolios's relative volatility and its systematic risk.

With this specification, the larger the T value, the more preferable the fund is for *all* investors, irrespective of their risk preferences. One can view the numerator of this ratio ($R_i - RFR$) as the *risk premium* and the denominator as the measure of risk. Therefore, the total expression indicates the fund's *return per unit of risk* and, obviously, all risk-averse investors would prefer to maximize this value. The risk variable is *systematic risk* and, as such, indicates nothing about diversification. In fact, this formulation implicitly assumes that the portfolios are perfectly diversified so that systematic risk is the relevant risk measure. When this T value for a fund is compared to a similar measure for the aggregate market, this measure indicates whether the fund would plot above the SML. Specifically, the T value for the aggregate market is as follows:

$$T_m = \frac{R_m - RFR}{B_m}$$

Note that this expression where B_m equals 1.0 (the market's beta) is the slope of the SML. Therefore, if a fund has a higher T value than the market portfolio, it would plot above the SML, and this would be considered superior risk-adjusted performance. To demonstrate this, consider the following example: Assume that during the most recent ten-year period, the average annual rate of return on an aggregate market portfolio (e.g., the S&P 500) was 14 percent (R_m = .14) and the average rate of return on government T-bills was 8 percent (RFR = .08). Assume that you are the administrator of a large pension fund that has been divided among three money managers during the past ten years. Currently, it is

---

[3]The terms used in the formula differ from those used by Treynor but are consistent with our earlier discussion.

time to renew your investment management contracts with all three money managers, and you must decide how they have performed. Without going into how the numbers have been derived (this will be done in a later section), assume you are given the following results:

Investment Manager	Average Annual Rate of Return	Beta
Z	.12	0.90
B	.16	1.05
Y	.18	1.20

Based upon this information, you can compute T values for the market portfolio and for each of the individual portfolio managers as follows:

$$T_m = \frac{.14 - .08}{1.00} = .060$$

$$T_z = \frac{.12 - .08}{0.90} = .044$$

$$T_b = \frac{.16 - .08}{1.05} = .076$$

$$T_y = \frac{.18 - .08}{1.20} = .083$$

These results would indicate that investment manager Z not only ranked the lowest of the three managers, but did not do as well as the aggregate market did. In contrast, the performance by both B and Y was superior to the market portfolio, and manager Y did somewhat better than B. In terms of the SML, both of their portfolios plotted above the line. The specific plot is shown in Figure 23.1.

Note that this measure of performance is *not* affected by changing the RFR. The computed T values may change, but the *ranking* of the funds relative to each other and compared to the market portfolio will *not* change. The reader is encouraged to demonstrate this by substituting a higher or lower RFR rate into the example (Hint: if you use .06 you will get $T_m = .080$; $T_z = .066$; $T_b = .095$; $T_y = .100$.)

Also, it is possible to get *negative* T values. This can happen with very poor performance or very good performance with a low-risk portfolio. An example of poor performance would be a portfolio that had an average rate of return lower than the risk-free rate and a positive beta. As an example, for the case

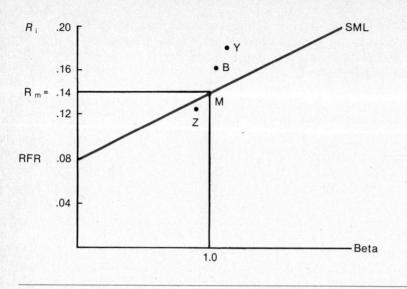

Figure 23.1   Plot of Performance on SML (T Measure)

above assume that a fourth portfolio manager (X) had a portfolio beta of 0.50, but the average rate of return was only .07. The T value would be:

$$T_x = \frac{.07 - .08}{0.50} = -.02$$

Obviously, this performance would plot below the SML in Figure 23.1.

In contrast, it is possible to conceive of a case in which the portfolio might have a *negative* beta and an average rate of return above the risk-free rate of return. This would likewise result in a negative T value but would indicate very *superior* performance. As an example, assume that a portfolio manager invested heavily in gold-mining stocks during a period of great political and economic uncertainty. Because gold has typically had a negative correlation with most stocks, it is possible the portfolio beta would be negative. If you were examining a period during which gold prices increase in value due to the uncertainty, it is possible that the returns on this portfolio could be quite good. Extending our example, assume that our "gold bug" portfolio had a beta of −0.20 and yet experienced an average rate of return of 10 percent. The T value would then be:

$$T = \frac{.10 - .08}{-.20} = -.100$$

While the T value is −.100, you can see that if you plotted this on our graph it would indicate a position substantially *above* the SML in Figure 23.1. In the case of negative betas, the T value can give confusing results. Therefore, it is preferable to either plot the portfolio on an SML graph or compute the expected return using the SML equation and compare the expected return to the return actually experienced; i.e., determine whether the actual return was above or below expectations. In the example above, the expected return would have been:

$$E(R_i) = RFR + B_i (R_m - RFR)$$
$$= .08 + (-.20) (.06)$$
$$= .08 - .012$$
$$= .068$$

When this expected return is compared to the 10 percent actually earned it is clear that the portfolio manager did a superior job.

The Sharpe Measure

Sharpe likewise conceived of a composite performance measure to evaluate the performance of mutual funds.[4] The measure followed closely his earlier work on the Capital Asset Pricing Model (CAPM), specifically the capital market line (CML). The Sharpe measure (designated S) is stated as follows:

$$S_i = \frac{R_i - RFR}{SD_i}$$

where:

S_i = the Sharpe portfolio performance measure for portfolio i during a designated time period.

R_i = the average rate of return for portfolio i during a specified time period

RFR = the average risk-free rate that prevailed during the time period

SD_i = the standard deviation of the rate of return for portfolio i during the time period.

As can be seen, this composite measure of performance is the same as the Treynor measure except that the risk measure is the *total* risk (the standard deviation of returns) rather than only *systematic* risk (beta). Because the numerator is the risk premium earned on the portfolio, this measure indicates *the return per unit of total risk*. Given that we are talking about total risk, in terms of capital market theory this performance measure examines portfolios compared to the CML while the Treynor measure employs the SML.

Consider the following examples that use the Sharpe measure. Again assume that $R_m = .14$ and RFR = .08. In addition, you are told that the standard deviation of the annual rate of return for the market portfolio over the past 10 years was 20 percent (i.e., $SD_m = .20$). Now you want to examine the performance of the following portfolios:

---

[4]William F. Sharpe, "Mutual Fund Performance," *Journal of Business* 39 (1966): 119–138.

Portfolio	Average Annual Rate of Return	Standard Deviation of Return
B	.13	.18
O	.17	.22
P	.16	.23

The Sharpe measure for these portfolios would be as follows:

$$S_m = \frac{.14 - .08}{.20} = 0.300$$

$$S_B = \frac{.13 - .08}{.18} = 0.278$$

$$S_O = \frac{.17 - .08}{.22} = 0.409$$

$$S_P = \frac{.16 - .08}{.23} = 0.348$$

In this case, the B portfolio had the lowest return per unit of total risk and also did not perform as well as the aggregate market portfolio. In contrast, portfolios O and P experienced performance that was superior to the aggregate market, and O did better than P.

Given the results for the market portfolio during this period, it is possible to draw the CML that apparently prevailed. If we then plot the results for B, O, and P on this graph as shown in Figure 23.2, we see that portfolio B plots below the line, while the O and P portfolios are above the line, indicating superior performance.

Treynor Versus Sharpe Measure

The Sharpe measure uses the standard deviation of returns as the measure of risk, while the Treynor measure employs beta (systematic risk). The Sharpe measure, therefore, implicitly evaluates the portfolio manager on the basis of return performance, but *also* takes into account how well diversified the portfolio was during this period. If a portfolio is perfectly diversified (does not contain any unsystematic risk), the two measures would give identical rankings because the total variance of the portfolio would be the systematic variance. If a portfolio is poorly diversified, it is possible for it to have a high ranking on the basis of the Treynor measure, but a much lower ranking on the basis of the Sharpe measure. Any difference should be directly attributable to the poor diversification of the portfolio. Therefore, the two measures provide *complementary* but *different* information and *both measures should be derived.* As pointed out by Sharpe, if one is dealing with a well-diversified group of of portfolios, such as mutual funds, the two measures will provide very similar rankings.

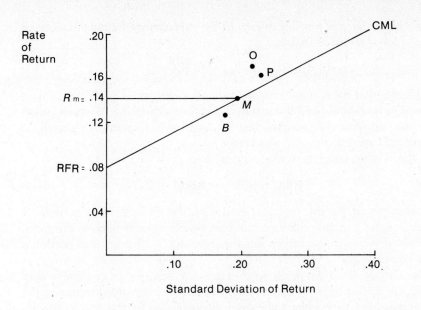

Figure 23.2   Plot of Performance on CML (S measure)

The Jensen Measure

The Jensen measure is similar to the measures already discussed in that it is based upon the Capital Asset Pricing Model (CAPM).[5] All versions of the CAPM indicate the following expression for the expected one-period return on any security or portfolio:

$$E(R_j) = RFR + B_j[E(R_m) - RFR]$$

where:

$E(R_j)$ = the expected return on security or portfolio j

RFR = the one-period risk-free interest rate

B_j = the systematic risk for security or portfolio j

$E(R_m)$ = the expected return on the market portfolio of risky assets.

Each of the expected returns and the risk-free return are different for different periods. Therefore, we are concerned with the time series of expected rates of return for security j or portfolio j. Moreover, assuming that the asset pricing model

[5]Michael C. Jensen, "The Performance of Mutual Funds in the Period 1945–1964." *Journal of Finance* 23 (1968): 389–416.

is empirically valid, it is possible to express the expectations formula in terms of *realized* rates of return as follows:

$$R_{jt} = RFR_t + B_j[R_{mt} - RFR_t] + U_{jt}$$

This indicates that the *realized* rate of return on a security or portfolio during a given time period should be a linear function of the risk-free rate of return during the period, plus some risk premium that is a function of the security's systematic risk during the period, plus a random error term.

If the risk-free return is subtracted from both sides we have:

$$R_{jt} - RFR_t = B_j[R_{mt} - RFR_t] + U_{jt}$$

This indicates that the risk premium earned on the jth security or portfolio is equal to B_j times a market risk premium plus a random error term. In this form, one would not expect an intercept for the regression if all assets and portfolios were in equilibrium.

Alternatively, if certain portfolio managers *are* superior either because they can forecast market turns or they consistently select undervalued securities, the risk premium they experience will exceed those implied by this market model. Specifically, a superior portfolio manager will have consistent positive random error terms; i.e., his actual returns will consistently be above expected returns. To detect and measure this superior performance, it is necessary to allow for an intercept (i.e., a nonzero constant) that will take account of the positive residuals. The positive residuals will cause a positive intercept. If we allow a nonzero constant, the earlier equation becomes:

$$R_{jt} - RFR_t = \alpha_j + B_j[R_{mt} - RFR_t] + U_{jt}$$

Given this equation, the α_j indicates whether the portfolio manager is superior or inferior in market timing or stock selection. If he is superior, the α will be a *significant positive value* because of all the positive residuals. In contrast, if the portfolio manager is *inferior,* his actual returns will consistently be *lower* than expectations based upon the market model and he will have negative residuals. In such a case, the nonzero constant would be a *significant negative value,* indicating that the manager consistently underperformed the market on a risk-adjusted basis. Finally, if a portfolio manager has no forecasting ability and yet he is not clearly inferior, his performance will be equal to that of a naive buy-and-hold policy. In terms of the equation, his actual returns will typically match those expected based upon the market model; his residual returns will generally be randomly positive and negative. In this case, the constant term would be *insignificantly different from zero,* indicating that the manager basically matched the market on a risk-adjusted basis.

This measure is very useful because it allows you to determine whether the abnormal returns are *statistically significant* (positive or negative). Also, the α represents the average incremental rate of return on the portfolio per unit of time which is attributable to the manager's ability to derive above-average returns *adjusted for risk*. These superior risk-adjusted returns can be caused by the fact that the manager is good at predicting market turns, or because he has the ability to forecast the behavior of prices of individual issues in the portfolio.

The Jensen formulation requires a different RFR to be used for each time interval during the sample period. If one is examining the performance of a fund manager for over a ten-year period using yearly intervals, it is necessary to examine the annual returns for the fund for each year, less the return on risk-free assets for each year, and to relate this to the annual return on the market portfolio less the same risk-free rate. This contrasts with other techniques that examine *the average returns for the total period* for all variables (the fund, the market, and the risk-free asset). Also, the Jensen measure, like the Treynor measure, does *not* evaluate the ability of the portfolio manager to diversify, because it only examines risk premiums in terms of *systematic* risk. When evaluating the performance of a group of well-diversified portfolios like mutual funds, this is probably a fairly legitimate assumption. In Jensen's analysis of mutual fund performance, it was shown that assuming complete diversification was valid because the correlations of the funds with the market typically exceeded .90.

Application of Performance Measures

To demonstrate how one applies these measures, we selected 20 open-end mutual funds for which data was available for the 15-year period 1966–1980. The specific results for the first fund (Affiliated Fund, Inc.) are contained in Table 23.1. The returns are the total returns for each year computed as follows:

$$R_{it} = \frac{EP_{it} + Div_{it} + Cap.\ Dist._{it} - BP_{it}}{BP_{it}}$$

where:

R_{it} = total return on fund i during year t

EP_{it} = ending price for fund i during year t

Cap. Dist.$_{it}$ = capital gain distributions made by fund i during year t

Div_{it} = dividend payment made by fund i during year t

BP_{it} = beginning price for fund i during year t.

As computed, these returns do not take into account any sales charge by the funds. Given the fund's results for each year, and the aggregate market (represented by the S&P 500), it is possible to compute the composite measures presented at the bottom of the table. As shown, the arithmetic average annual rate of return for Affiliated was above that for the market (9.05 vs 8.10), and the fund's beta was below 1.00 (0.883). Therefore, the Treynor measure for the fund was *above* the same measure for the market (3.035 vs 1.730). Likewise, the standard deviation of returns was below the market's (17.32 vs 18.23), so the Sharpe measure for the fund was also above the measure for the market (.155 vs .095).

Year	R_{it}	R_{mt}	RFR_t	$R_{it} - RFR_t$	$R_{mt} - RFR_t$
1966	−6.53	−9.98	4.85	−11.38	−14.83
1967	21.97	23.73	4.29	17.68	19.44
1968	17.13	10.81	5.34	11.79	5.47
1969	−14.60	−8.32	6.67	−21.27	−14.99
1970	1.67	3.51	6.39	−4.72	−2.88
1971	8.03	14.12	4.33	3.70	9.79
1972	11.54	18.72	4.07	7.47	14.65
1973	−5.81	−14.51	7.03	−12.84	−21.54
1974	−15.62	−26.03	7.84	−23.46	−33.87
1975	38.45	36.92	5.80	32.65	31.12
1976	33.20	23.64	4.98	28.22	18.66
1977	−6.99	−7.16	5.27	−12.26	−12.43
1978	2.88	6.39	7.19	−4.31	−0.80
1979	27.39	18.19	10.07	17.32	8.12
1980	23.01	32.48	11.43	11.58	21.05

Table 23.1   Example of Computation of Portfolio Evaluation Measures Using Affiliated Fund, Inc.

$\overline{R}_i = 9.05$ $\sigma_i = 17.32$ $B_i = 0.883$ $R_{im}^2 = .858$

$\overline{R}_m = 8.10$ $\sigma_m = 18.23$ $\overline{RFR} = 6.37$

$T_i = 3.035$ $S_i = .155$

$T_m = 1.730$ $S_m = .095$

$\overline{(R_{it} - RFR_t)} = 2.68$ $\overline{(R_{mt} - RFR_t)} = 1.80$

Finally, the regression of the fund's annual risk premium ($R_{it} - RFR_t$) and the market's annual risk premium ($R_{mt} - RFR_t$) indicated a positive intercept (constant) value of 1.151 that was not statistically significant. If the value were significant, it would have indicated that Affiliated, on average, earned a risk-adjusted annual rate of return that was about one percent above the market average.

Overall Results

An analysis of the overall results in Table 23.2 indicates that they are generally consistent with the findings of earlier studies, even though our sample selection was rather casual because it was only made for demonstration purposes. The mean return for all the funds was quite close to the market return (9.25 vs 8.10). If *only* the rate of return was considered, 12 of the 20 funds performed better than the market did.

The R^2 for a portfolio with the market fund can be used as a measure of diversification, and the closer it is to 1.00, the more perfectly diversified it is. Al-

	Return	σ	Beta	R^2	Sharpe[a]	Treynor[a]	Jensen[a]
1. Affiliated Fund, Inc.	9.05	17.32	.883	.858	.155(10)	3.035(10)	1.151 (12)
2. Anchor Growth Fund, Inc.	4.90	22.18	1.032	.680	−.066(18)	−1.424(18)	−3.253 (18)
3. Dividend Shares, Inc.	7.45	14.88	.727	.898	.073(15)	1.486(15)	− .290 (15)
4. Energy Fund, Inc.	11.99	21.23	.982	.725	.265 (3)	5.723 (2)	3.921 (5)
5. Fidelity Fund, Inc.	8.05	15.81	.849	.933	.106(13)	1.979(13)	.216 (13)
6. Fundamental Investors, Inc.	4.59	17.34	.920	.913	−.103(19)	−1.935(19)	−3.371[b](20)
7. Guardian Mutual Fund	11.62	18.16	.930	.876	.289 (2)	5.645 (3)	3.642[b] (6)
8. Istel Fund, Inc.	11.84	18.85	.788	.533	.290 (1)	6.942 (1)	4.682 (4)
9. Lexington Research Fund, Inc.	7.82	20.20	1.031	.826	.072(16)	1.406(16)	−3.366 (19)
10. Mass. Investors Growth Stock Fund	8.76	19.45	.907	.709	.123(11)	2.635(11)	8.161 (1)
11. Oppenheimer Fund, Inc.	8.99	21.44	1.066	.821	.122(12)	2.458(12)	1.318 (11)
12. Philadelphia Fund, Inc.	10.82	19.12	.971	.858	.233 (5)	4.583 (7)	2.772 (7)
13. T. Rowe Price Growth Stock Fund	7.54	19.50	.983	.808	.060(17)	1.190(17)	− .626 (16)
14. The Putnam Growth Fund, Inc.	9.45	18.74	.978	.888	.164 (8)	3.149 (9)	1.392 (10)
15. Scudder Special Fund, Inc.	10.89	27.75	1.311	.709	.163 (9)	3.448 (8)	2.252 (9)
16. Security Equity Fund, Inc.	13.30	27.11	1.252	.684	.256 (4)	5.535 (4)	4.764 (3)
17. Sigma Investment Shares, Inc.	7.87	18.30	.994	.958	.082(14)	1.509(14)	− .219 (14)
18. Technology Fund, Inc.	10.85	20.74	1.031	.851	.216 (6)	5.264 (5)	2.700 (8)
19. Value Line Special Situations Fund	14.62	40.82	1.670	.545	.202 (7)	4.940 (6)	5.306 (2)
20. Wellington Fund, Inc.	4.68	13.43	.700	.920	−.126(20)	−2.414(20)	−2.901[b](17)
Means	9.25	20.62	1.000	.800	.129	2.758	1.413
S&P 500	8.10	18.23	1.000	1.000	.095	1.730	.000
90-day T-Bill Rate	6.37	2.13	—	—			

Table 23.2   Performance Measures for 20 Selected Mutual Funds: 1966–1980

[a]Rank in parentheses

[b]Significant at .05 level

though the average R^2 is reasonably good at .800, the range is quite large, from .533 to .958. This indicates that a number of these funds are not well diversified.

The two risk measures (standard deviation and beta) likewise show a wide range, but are generally consistent with expectations. Specifically, 14 of the 20 funds had a standard deviation that was larger than the market's, and the mean standard deviation was also larger (20.62 vs 18.23). This larger standard deviation is consistent with the lack of complete diversification. Only seven of the funds had a beta above 1.00, but the average beta was equal to one.

The performance of individual funds was very consistent for alternative measures. Using the Sharpe measure, 13 of the 20 funds had a higher value than the market did; using the Treynor measure, 14 of the 20 funds experienced performance above the market's, while the Jensen measure indicated that 13 of the 20 had positive intercepts, but only one of the positive intercepts was statistically significant. The mean values for all of the composite measures were above the figure for the aggregate market. These results indicate that, on average, this sample of funds outperformed the market during this time period.

Relationship Among Performance Measures

Previously, we discussed the relationship between the Treynor measure and the Sharpe measure of performance. We noted that the main difference between these two was that the Treynor measure examined the excess rate of return per unit of *systematic* risk (beta), while the Sharpe measure derived the excess rate of return per unit of *total* risk (standard deviation of return). Therefore, when the analysis involved portfolios that were well diversified so that total risk approached systematic risk, the measures should provide similar rankings. It was subsequently pointed out that the Jensen measure likewise was based on the CAPM and related actual returns to expected returns based on the fund's *systematic* risk. Therefore, you should expect this measure to provide rankings similar to the other two measures, especially for well-diversified portfolios.

An analysis of the relative rankings using the three measures generally confirms that they provide almost identical rankings as indicated by the ranks shown in parentheses. A more exact measure can be provided by a rank correlation that relates ranks rather than exact values. The specific rank correlations for the funds in Table 23.2 are:

Sharpe = Treynor: .975

Sharpe = Jensen: .913

Treynor = Jensen: .909

Therefore, while the alternative measures give similar rankings, it is still recommended that you generally *employ all three measures* because they provide somewhat different information regarding performance, risk, and the significance of the differential performance. As discussed in a subsequent section, there are several commercial portfolio performance evaluation services available that typically provide all of this information, as well as information regarding specific competitive managers. Because of the importance of performance, the tendency is to provide substantial detail.

Application of Evaluation Techniques

The answers generated using these performance measures are only as good as the data inputs. Therefore it is necessary to be careful in computing the rates of return and take proper account of all inflows and outflows. More important, it is necessary to use judgment in the evaluation process. Just as Rome was not built in a day, it is not possible to properly evaluate a portfolio manager on the basis of performance over a quarter or even a year. The evaluation should extend over a number of years and cover *at least* a full market cycle. This will make it possible to determine whether there is any difference in performance during rising or declining markets.[6]

Measurement Problems

As noted, the portfolio performance measures discussed are all basically derived from the CAPM. As such, they depend upon the notion of a "market portfolio" that is the point of tangency on the Markowitz efficient frontier. Obviously, this implies that the market portfolio is an efficient portfolio. We also acknowledged earlier in the book that it contained all risky assets in the economy and that it was a completely diversified portfolio. The problem arises in finding a real world proxy for this theoretical market portfolio. As noted on several occasions earlier in the text, the "typical" proxy used is the Standard & Poor's 500 Index because it is a fairly diversified portfolio of stocks and the sample is market value weighted, which is how a true market portfolio should be. The point is, the assets included in the portfolio are *only* common stocks and most of them are from the NYSE. It does not include the many other risky assets that theoretically should be considered (e.g., bonds, real estate, coins, stamps, antiques, etc.).

This lack of completeness has always been recognized, but has not been highlighted to any extent until the publication of several articles by Richard Roll. Specifically, Roll was the first to recognize the problem with the proxy that is used for the market portfolio. He rigorously worked out the implications of this problem in terms of measuring portfolio performance. The articles began appearing in 1977 and initiated a major controversy regarding the usefulness of the CAPM.[7] While it is not possible to present a detailed discussion of Roll's critique, we can consider his major point regarding the measurement of the mar-

---

[6]In this regard, see Robert G. Kirby, "You Need More than Numbers to Measure Performance," paper presented at Institute of Chartered Financial Analysts seminar in Chicago on April 2, 1976.

[7]Richard Roll, "A Critique of the Asset Pricing Theory's Tests," *Journal of Financial Economics* 4 (March 1977): 129–176. Richard Roll, "Ambiguity When Performance is Measured by the Securities Market Line," *Journal of Finance* 33 (September 1978) 1051–1069. Richard Roll, "Performance Evaluation and Benchmark Error 1," *Journal of Portfolio Management* 6 (Summer 1980): 5–12. Richard Roll, "Performance Evaluation and Benchmark Errors II," *Journal of Portfolio Management* 7 (Winter 1981): 17–22.

ket portfolio. Roll refers to this as a benchmark error—i.e., when evaluating portfolio performance, various techniques employ the market portfolio as the benchmark in determining superior or inferior performance. We also use this proxy of the market portfolio to derive beta measures which then are used as our risk measures. Roll shows in several ways that if the proxy used for the "true" market portfolio is not a truly efficient portfolio, then the betas derived are not true betas, and the security market line that is derived may not be the true SML—i.e., it could have a higher slope. Therefore, it is shown that a portfolio which is plotted above the SML by using a poor benchmark (market portfolio proxy) could actually plot below the true SML that is derived by using the true market portfolio. A shift of a portfolio based upon a change in its beta against the true market portfolio could also occur.

The important point is this: the benchmark problems that Roll analyzed does not negate the value of the CAPM in terms of its usefulness as a normative model of equilbrium pricing. The theory is still correct and viable; the problem is a *measurement problem* when attempting to implement the theory in measuring portfolio performance. This simply means it is necessary to find a better proxy for the market portfolio or be aware that it is necessary to adjust measured performance for these benchmark errors. In fact, in one of his later articles, Roll makes several suggestions in this regard.[8]

Description of Major Commercial Portfolio Performance Services

Because of the interest in the area, its complexity, and the importance of comparing performance to that of other firms, a number of firms have established services that evaluate the performance of selected institutions that provide the required data. In this section, we discuss the major services and the specific data they provide for their clients.

A. G. Becker Funds Evaluation Service[9]

This service attempts to indicate the overall performance of an investment fund and also provide insights into the reasons for the performance. In this regard, the annual report is organized into seven parts that deal with interrelated aspects of the fund's performance.

Part 1 *Introduction*   provides an overview of the performance of the equity and bond market during the period so you can determine the impact of market conditions on your fund's performance.

---

[8]Richard Roll, "Performance Evaluation and Benchmark Errors II," *Journal of Portfolio Management* 7 (Winter 1981): 17–22.

[9]A. G. Becker & Co., Inc., Funds Evaluation and Planning Services, First National Plaza, Chicago, Illinois 60603.

Part 2 *Asset Deployment*   identifies sources of growth or decline in your fund's assets and considers current income, capital gain or loss, and external growth due to new funds put in or withdrawn. In addition, there is an analysis of how your assets are allocated among equity, debt, and cash equivalents. These proportions over time are compared to the commitment of assets by the other funds in the Becker data base.

Part 3 *Measuring Total Fund Performance*   compares the performance of your total fund to comparable performance of the Becker background population. Specifically, the average annual total return for a number of time periods (ten years to one year), the income rate of return, and the variability of quarterly rates of return are considered. In each instance, charts indicate how your performance compares, in percentiles, to the total universe.

Part 4 *Evaluating Equity Portfolio Results*   provides measures of total rate of return, dividend rate, and variability of quarterly rate of return. In addition to these overall measures, they examine the purchase and sale turnover and compare this to those of other funds, the market sensitivity of your fund (i.e., its beta), and its diversification characteristics (i.e., its R^2 with the market portfolio).

Part 5 *Evaluating Bond Portfolio Results*   indicates the total rates of return earned on your bond portfolio during different periods on an absolute basis and also relative to the total Becker population. They also indicate the income rate of return on the bonds and the variability of the quarterly rates of return over time. Finally, they measure rates of return on all fixed-income securities (bonds, convertibles, cash equivalents, and private placements) for individual years and for various multiyear periods.

Part 6 *Investment Policy*   The purpose of this section is to help you judge whether the portfolio manager is carrying out your stated policy and how well he is performing compared to others with a similar policy. Therefore, the analysis considers the range of performance of funds with similar policy-related attributes: e.g., your rate of return compared to the rates of return for funds with a similar equity commitment, variability of quarterly returns, or dividend return.

Part 7 *Ranks and Measures*   contains a summary of the fund's performance in terms of annualized returns (dollar weighted and time weighted) for each of the portfolio segments (equities, bonds, etc.). This is done for total periods, individual years, and market cycles. In all instances the fund is ranked relative to all the funds in the Becker population.

Computer Directions Advisors (CDA)[10]
Computer Directions Advisors, Inc. has a standard six-page report that they will provide for any fund or any segment of a fund. The following information is contained in the basic report. (It is possible to request further analysis.)

---

[10]Computer Directions Advisors, Inc., 8750 Georgia Avenue, Silver Spring, Maryland 20910.

Page 1   contains time-weighted and dollar-weighted rate of return measures for your fund during selected fiscal periods (one year, three years, five years, since inception). There are comparable returns for a number of equity funds including the S&P 500, the DJIA, bank pooled funds, insurance company accounts, and other mutual funds. There are also fixed-income indexes such as Salomon Bros. hi-grade corporates, S&P AA corporates, bank-pooled funds, insurance company accounts, mutual bond funds, and U.S. T-Bills. Finally, there are balanced indexes of stocks and bonds.

Page 2   contains time-weighted rates of return for your fund over recent market cycles compared to the performance for all the indexes considered on page one.

Page 3   contains a cost of living comparison of your fund to the value of the fund that is required to match changes in the cost of living as measured by the Consumer Price Index. In addition, for each quarter the excess or deficit of your fund's value compared to the required value is derived in dollar terms and as a percent of your fund.

Page 4   contains a detailed analysis of the fund's asset growth since its inception. Specifically, for each quarter beginning market value, contributions/withdrawals, profits/losses, and ending market value are listed along with a quarterly and cumulative percentage of growth figure.

Page 5   contains an analysis of the fund's rate of return during various fiscal periods compared to the fund's risk as measured by its beta since its inception. There is also an analysis of its diversification measured in terms of the fund's relationship with the S&P 500; i.e., its R^2 with the S&P 500. Finally, there is an analysis of the fund's risk-adjusted performance derived by comparing what the fund did during various periods to what you would expect it to do based upon beta and the prevailing security market line during the period. On the basis of this you can see whether the fund experienced risk-adjusted performance above or below expectations.

Page 6   contains unit values for your fund and the market index and computes quarterly rates of return for the two series over time.

Callan Associates, Inc.[11]

Callan Associates, Inc. has a number of services for pension fund investors including:

1. An *Investment Strategy Report* that contains the results of a survey done every six months to determine the economic and investment projections by a number of investment managers (approximately 100) and likely investment strategies based on their projections.

---

[11]Callan Associates, Inc., 601 California Street, San Francisco, California 94108.

2. *Portfolio Characteristic Review* measures the fundamental characteristics of the equity portfolio of a firm's various managers. Specifically, given the equity portfolio of one of your pension managers, this service calculates the basic *company characteristics* for the stocks involved (e.g., total assets, revenues, current ratio, market capitalization, etc.); the *growth characteristics* of these firms (e.g., profit margins, return on assets, return on equity, growth in assets, earnings, etc.); and *investment characteristics* (dividend yield, price-earnings ratio, number of holdings, value of holdings, etc.). The purpose is to help the pension fund understand the type of portfolio constructed by the manager so as to evaluate whether it is consistent with the stated objective.

3. *Asset Allocation Study for Pension Plans* attempts to help a pension plan reach its investment objective by helping it answer three questions: (1) which types of investments to use; (2) what should be the minimum quality of each investment type; and (3) what is the best combination of these investments. The answers to these questions suggest various investment strategies. Investment simulations are run to show the results for these alternatives and help the plan's sponsor make choices based upon more detailed information. They also help in the selection of investment managers and evaluation of investment results.

4. *Investment Measurement Service* contains some basic descriptive components on the makeup of the portfolio by the type of investment (equities, bonds, cash) and by manager. Asset growth, growth in total value, and cumulative results are also computed. Fund rate of return performance is set forth by manager and by type of investment for short and long-term periods (5–6 years) and compared to market indicator series for stocks and bonds. Returns are also analyzed over market cycles. Finally, results are compared to other data bases, e.g., bank pooled funds, insurance equity funds, etc., and each manager's results ranked against the total sample.

5. *Portfolio Audit Service* is a detailed listing of all transactions during a period (e.g., a quarter) that reconciles beginning assets, all inflows, purchases, sales, and ending asset position. This is done by industry and by individual stock purchase (indicating price paid relative to high and low for the day of purchase or sale, the ending position in the stock, and what brokerage firm was used for the transaction). There is also a detailed daily cash balance analysis.

Merrill Lynch, Pierce, Fenner & Smith, Inc.[12]
The total report titled "Investment Performance Analysis," is divided into nine sections as follows:

1. *Market Returns* includes total returns for equities (S&P 500 Index), bonds (Merrill Lynch Corporate and Government Master Index), and cash equivalents

---

[12]Merrill Lynch, Pierce, Fenner & Smith, Inc., One Liberty Plaza, 165 Broadway, New York, N.Y. 10080.

(90-day Treasury bills). This is provided annually and cumulatively for the last five years and also includes a measure of variability.

2. *Management Summary* presents the most important performance information and fund characteristics in the report. Returns are shown for the total portfolio and components and related to appropriate market series with rankings shown for the latest quarter, year, and five years. There is also an asset allocation breakdown.

3. *Fund Returns* contains a detailed listing of returns for the components of the portfolio relative to a market series. Specifically, for each quarter over the last five years they list the percentages in equities and the total return and a comparable return for the S&P 500. They do the same for bonds relative to the Merrill Lynch Bond Index, and the total portfolio is compared to a custom index that is a weighted average of the stock index, bond index, and T-bills and that matches the fund portfolio at the beginning of the quarter. Finally, they compute returns on "other assets" for which price information is not readily available.

4. *Comparisons* contains comparative returns for the total funds and components of the fund to various other groups of funds such as tax-exempt funds, bank commingled equity funds, bank commingled bond funds, and mutual funds. In each case they consider cumulative returns for each of the last four quarters and the last five years. There is also ranking of the fund and the comparable fund.

5. *Distribution of Results* contains a detailed report of results achieved by managed tax-exempt funds, bank commingled equity funds, mutual funds, and bond funds. The report includes annualized returns; equity characteristics (market sensitivity, a measure of stock selection performance, and a measure of diversification); asset allocation measures and a timing measure; and reward-to-variability ratios for equities, bonds, and total portfolios.

6. *Equity Portfolio Analysis* contains a detailed analysis of the performance of the equity section of the fund in which *what* the fund did and *why* it did it are determined. The point is, the performance of a fund is dependent on the market sensitivity of the fund (i.e., its beta or risk measure), its diversification, and the manager's stock selection ability. Therefore, they compute the fund's beta and also its R^2 with the market as a measure of diversification. Given the beta for a fund, it is possible to determine what the fund should do for a given market return (this is referred to as return due to the market). The difference between this return due to the market and the actual return indicates the stock selection ability of the manager. Finally, there is a detailed analysis of the characteristics of the stocks in the portfolio.

7. *Bond Portfolio Analysis* examines the cumulative returns for the bond portfolio relative to the Merrill Lynch Bond Index, and also relative to a number of other indexes that plot out a security market line for bonds. In addition, they compute the reward to variability for the fund. The reward is the return above the risk-free return, and variability is the standard deviation of excess return. This re-

ward to variability is compared to a similar measure for a number of bond indexes.

8. *Allocation of Assets* examines the long-run mix of equity, bonds, and cash (which is considered a *policy* decision) and also short-run changes in the mix over time (a *timing* decision). They examine the effect of asset allocation on portfolio returns by (1) showing the impact of a change in the long-run equity percent by 10 percent up or down; and (2) showing the effect of timing decisions by comparing actual returns to potential returns if the fund did not deviate from the long-run allocation. There is also a market cycle analysis which examines returns for the fund to other indexes during broad market cycles.

9. *Total Portfolio Analysis* compares the return for the total portfolio to a custom index that matches the portfolio mix of the fund. There is also an analysis of portfolio growth from firm contributions, and from investment returns. Finally, the value of the fund is compared to the growth in the Consumer Price Index and a constant growth of 6.5 percent.

Frank Russell Company, Inc.[13]

The Frank Russell Company has a performance measurement service, but it is considered only a small part of the total package of services available to the firm's limited clientele.[14] Specifically, unlike other firms that provide several individual services available to the public, Frank Russell only accepts clients on an ongoing basis and is limited to 40 of them, mainly in the pension fund area. In turn, the client pays a fee that is based on the size of the pension fund involved and thereafter receives *all* the services of Frank Russell as part of the arrangement (except a special audit service).

The services include helping a client set objectives for the fund and determine the optimum resource allocation consistent with the objectives. The heart of the procedure appears to be the help in *manager selection* for the client. In addition to having extensive quantitative information on the performance of various money managers, the analysts at Frank Russell spend a great deal of time personally interviewing and tracking money managers who are on their "approved" list and whom they recommend to their clients. The analysis of the money managers goes beyond quantitative performance to include whether they have a well-specified management style and whether their performance is consistent with this style.

After the selection of a money manager they measure the performance of a client's money manager over time on a risk-adjusted basis relative to other funds with similar objectives. While detailed examples are not available, it appears that the presentation is similar to that provided by A.G. Becker and Merrill Lynch.

Finally, the firm conducts a number of seminars for its clients to keep them

[13]Frank Russell Company, Inc., 1100 One Washington Plaza, Tacoma, WA 98402.

[14]See Julie Rohrer, "The King of the Pension Consultants," *Institutional Investor* 12 (1978): 44, 46, 48, 50, 160.

abreast of new developments in pension money management (e.g., real estate investment, options, securities lending, etc.).

Summary

This chapter was intended as a discussion of portfolio performance evaluation and of the several techniques that can be used in making such an evaluation. The first major goal of portfolio management is to derive rates of returns that equal or exceed the returns on a naively selected portfolio with equal risk. The second goal is to attain complete diversification. Prior to the development of capital market theory, portfolio managers were only judged on the basis of the rate of return they achieved, with no consideration of risk. Risk was later considered, but not in a very rigorous manner. Since 1965, three major techniques have been derived based upon the Capital Asset Pricing Model, which provide a *composite* measure of performance. The first was developed by Treynor to measure the excess returns earned per unit of *systematic* risk. The Sharpe measure indicates the excess return per unit of *total* risk. The third technique, developed by Jensen, likewise is used to evaluate performance in terms of the systematic risk involved, but the measure also makes it possible to determine whether the difference in risk-adjusted performance (good or bad) is statistically significant.

The application of the evaluation techniques to a selected sample of 20 mutual funds indicated the importance of considering both risk and return because the different funds presented a wide range of total risk and systematic risk. We also discussed how differences in diversification could influence the rankings generated using different performance measures. The rank correlations among the alternative measures were extremely high, ranging from about .90 to .97.

We discussed some general factors to consider when using the techniques including the consideration of nonquantitative factors and using an adequate period. There was also a consideration of some problems with using the techniques presented by Richard Roll. It was noted that these measurement problems do not negate the overall theoretical value of the CAPM or the portfolio evaluation measures—it is simply necessary to recognize that a measurement problem exists and attempt to adjust for it.

Following a discussion of the three major performance measures, we discussed five major commercial services that provide all the information generated using the three measures and additional detailed data on individual portfolio managers and their competitors.

It is important for investors to evaluate their own performance and the performance of hired managers. The various techniques discussed here provide theoretically justifiable measures, but they all differ slightly. The author feels strongly that *all the measures should be used* in the evaluation process because they provide different information. An evaluation of a portfolio manager should also be done *a number of times* over *different market environments* before a final judgment is reached.

Questions

1.   Assuming you are managing your own portfolio, do you think you should evaluate your own performance? Why or why not? Against what would you compare your performance?

2.   What are the two major factors that should be considered when evaluating a portfolio manager? What should the portfolio manager be trying to do?

3.   What can a portfolio manager do to try to derive superior risk-adjusted returns?

4.   What is the purpose of diversification according to the CAPM? How can you measure whether a portfolio is completely diversified? Explain why this measure makes sense.

5.   Prior to the development of composite portfolio performance measures, how could you evaluate portfolio performance, taking risk into consideration?

6.   Define the Treynor measure of portfolio performance. Discuss this measure in terms of what it indicates. (What does it measure?)

7.   Assume that during the past ten-year period the risk-free rate was 4 percent and three portfolios had the following characteristics:

Portfolio	Return	Beta
A	.11	1.10
B	.09	0.90
C	.14	1.20

Compute the T value for each portfolio and indicate which portfolio had the best performance. Assume you are told that the market return during this period was 10 percent; how did these managers fare relative to the market?

8.   Define the Sharpe measure of performance and discuss what it indicates.

9.   Assume the three portfolios in Question 7 have standard deviations of .14, .10, and .20 respectively. Compute the Sharpe measure of performance. Is there any difference in the ranking achieved using the Treynor versus the Sharpe measure? Discuss the probable cause.

10. Why is it suggested that both the Treynor and Sharpe measures of performance be employed? What additional information is provided by a comparison of the rankings achieved using the two measures?

11. Define the Jensen measure of performance and indicate whether it should produce results similar to those produced using the Treynor or Sharpe methods. Why?

References

Evaluation and Measurement of Investment Performance. Charlottesville, VA.: Seminars on Portfolio Management, Financial Analysts Research Foundation, 1977.

Fama, Eugene. "Components of Investment Performance." *Journal of Finance* 27 (1971).

Fielitz, Bruce, and Greene, Myron T. "Shortcomings in Performance Evaluation via MPT." *Journal of Portfolio Management* 6 (1980).

Friend, Irwin, and Blume, Marshall. "Measurement of Portfolio Performance Under Uncertainty." *American Economic Review* 60 (1970).

Friend, Irwin; Blume, Marshall; and Crockett, Jean. *Mutual Funds and Other Institutional Investors.* New York: McGraw-Hill, 1970.

Jensen, Michael C. "The Performance of Mutual Funds in the Period 1945–1964." *Journal of Finance* 23 (1968).

Jensen, Michael C. "Risk, the Pricing of Capital Assets, and the Evaluation of Investment Portfolios." *Journal of Business* 42 (1969).

Kim, Tye, "An Assessment of the Performance of Mutual Fund Management: 1969–1975." *Journal of Financial and Quantitative Analysis* 13 (1978).

Kon, Stanley J., and Jen, Frank C. "The Investment Performance of Mutual Funds: An Empirical Investigation of Timing, Selectivity, and Market Efficiency." *Journal of Business* 52 (1979).

Klemkosky, Robert C. "The Bias in Composite Performance Measures." *Journal of Financial and Quantitative Analysis* 8 (1973).

Klemkosky, Robert C. "How Consistently Do Managers Manage?" *Journal of Portfolio Management* 3 (1977).

Mains, Norman E. "Risk, the Pricing of Capital Assets, and the Evaluation of Investment Portfolios: Comment." *Journal of Business* 50 (1977).

Measuring the Performance of Pension Funds. Park Ridge, IL: Bank Administration Institute, 1968. A supplement, *Risk and the Evaluation of Pension Fund Performance,* was written by Eugene Fama.

Roll, Richard. "Ambiguity When Performance is Measured by the Securities Market Line," *Journal of Finance* 33 (1978).

Roll, Richard. "Performance Evaluation and Benchmark Errors I." *Journal of Portfolio Management* 6 (1980).

Roll, Richard. "Performance Evaluation and Benchmark Errors II." *Journal of Portfolio Management* 7 (1981).

Sharpe, William F. "Mutual Fund Performance." *Journal of Business* 39 (1966).

Treynor, Jack L. "How to Rate Management of Investment Funds." *Harvard Business Review* 43 (1965).

Williams, Arthur, III. *Managing Your Investment Manager.* Homewood, IL: Dow Jones-Irwin, 1980.

Appendix A to Chapter 23
How to Become a Chartered Financial Analyst

As mentioned in the section on career opportunities, the professional designation of Chartered Financial Analyst (CFA) is becoming a significant requirement for a career in investment analysis and/or portfolio management. For that reason, this appendix presents the history and objectives of the Institute of Chartered Financial Analysts and general guidelines for acquiring the CFA designation. If you are interested in the program, you can write to the Institute for more information.

The Institute of Chartered Financial Analysts was formed in 1959 and was incorporated under the laws of Virginia in 1962. It has its headquarters in Charlottesville, Virginia. The CFA candidate examinations were first offered in 1963. The ICFA has close ties with the University of Virginia, The Financial Analysts Federation, and The Financial Analysts Research Foundation.

The Institute is an autonomous professional organization composed of mem - bers who have been awarded the registered professional designation Chartered Financial Analyst (CFA). The Institute's Objectives are

To encourage and promote high standards of education and professional de- velopment in financial analysis,

To conduct and foster programs of research, study, discussion, and publishing that improve the practice of financial analysis,

To administer for CFA candidates a study and examination program with the threefold purpose of guiding analysts in mastering a professional body of knowledge, developing analytical skills, and testing the competency of financial investment analysts,

To award the professional designation, Chartered Financial Analyst (CFA), to persons who meet recognized standards of competency and stipulated standards of conduct for the professional practice of financial analysis, and

To sponsor and enforce a code of ethics and standards of professional conduct.

A college degree or equivalent is necessary to enter the program. No work experience per se is required to take any of the three examinations. To take the Level II and Level III examinations, the candidate should be a member of a Society of The Financial Analysts Federation. Although experience is no longer a specific requirement for the examinations, professional experience could help the indi- vidual answer questions on the Level II and Level III examinations. Before being awarded the Charter, the candidate must have at least four years' experience in financial analysis as related to investments. The professional conduct of a candi- date must conform to the Institute's code of ethics and standards of professional conduct.

The CFA Program is directed toward the professional development of financial and investment analysts and protfolio managers. The study program covers:

1. ethics and professional standards,
2. financial accounting,
3. fixed income securities analysis,
4. equity securities analysis, and
5. portfolio management.

The program requires the successful completion of three examinations of increas- ing difficulty. Examinations are taken in their numbered sequence, and only one examination may be taken in a given year. Regardless of educational background and professional experience, every candidate must successfully complete all three examinations. The examinations are given annually in early June at some 90 sites in the U.S., Canada, and abroad.

Members and candidates are typically employed in the investment field. From 1963 to 1981, a total of 6,780 charters have been awarded. Over 2,500 individuals are registered in the CFA Candidate Program. If you are interested in learning more about the CFA program, the Institute has a booklet that describes the program and includes an application form. The address is Institute of Chartered Financial Analysts, University of Virginia, P.O. Box 3668, Charlottesville, Virginia 22903.

Appendix A   Interest Tables

Table A.1   Present Value of $1: PVIF = $1/(1 + k)^t$

Period	1%	2%	3%	4%	5%	6%	7%	8%	9%	10%	12%	14%	15%	16%	18%	20%	24%	28%	32%	36%
1	.9901	.9804	.9709	.9615	.9524	.9434	.9346	.9259	.9174	.9091	.8929	.8772	.8696	.8621	.8475	.8333	.8065	.7813	.7576	.7353
2	.9803	.9612	.9426	.9246	.9070	.8900	.8734	.8573	.8417	.8264	.7972	.7695	.7561	.7432	.7182	.6944	.6504	.6104	.5739	.5407
3	.9706	.9423	.9151	.8890	.8638	.8396	.8163	.7938	.7722	.7513	.7118	.6750	.6575	.6407	.6086	.5787	.5245	.4768	.4348	.3975
4	.9610	.9238	.8885	.8548	.8227	.7921	.7629	.7350	.7084	.6830	.6355	.5921	.5718	.5523	.5158	.4823	.4230	.3725	.3294	.2923
5	.9515	.9057	.8626	.8219	.7835	.7473	.7130	.6806	.6499	.6209	.5674	.5194	.4972	.4761	.4371	.4019	.3411	.2910	.2495	.2149
6	.9420	.8880	.8375	.7903	.7462	.7050	.6663	.6302	.5963	.5645	.5066	.4556	.4323	.4104	.3704	.3349	.2751	.2274	.1890	.1580
7	.9327	.8706	.8131	.7599	.7107	.6651	.6227	.5835	.5470	.5132	.4523	.3996	.3759	.3538	.3139	.2791	.2218	.1776	.1432	.1162
8	.9235	.8535	.7894	.7307	.6768	.6274	.5820	.5403	.5019	.4665	.4039	.3506	.3269	.3050	.2660	.2326	.1789	.1388	.1085	.0854
9	.9143	.8368	.7664	.7026	.6446	.5919	.5439	.5002	.4604	.4241	.3606	.3075	.2843	.2630	.2255	.1938	.1443	.1084	.0822	.0628
10	.9053	.8203	.7441	.6756	.6139	.5584	.5083	.4632	.4224	.3855	.3220	.2697	.2472	.2267	.1911	.1615	.1164	.0847	.0623	.0462
11	.8963	.8043	.7224	.6496	.5847	.5268	.4751	.4289	.3875	.3505	.2875	.2366	.2149	.1954	.1619	.1346	.0938	.0662	.0472	.0340
12	.8874	.7885	.7014	.6246	.5568	.4970	.4440	.3971	.3555	.3186	.2567	.2076	.1869	.1685	.1372	.1122	.0757	.0517	.0357	.0250
13	.8787	.7730	.6810	.6006	.5303	.4688	.4150	.3677	.3262	.2897	.2292	.1821	.1625	.1452	.1163	.0935	.0610	.0404	.0271	.0184
14	.8700	.7579	.6611	.5775	.5051	.4423	.3878	.3405	.2992	.2633	.2046	.1597	.1413	.1252	.0985	.0779	.0492	.0316	.0205	.0135
15	.8613	.7430	.6419	.5553	.4810	.4173	.3624	.3152	.2745	.2394	.1827	.1401	.1229	.1079	.0835	.0649	.0397	.0247	.0155	.0099
16	.8528	.7284	.6232	.5339	.4581	.3936	.3387	.2919	.2519	.2176	.1631	.1229	.1069	.0930	.0708	.0541	.0320	.0193	.0118	.0073
17	.8444	.7142	.6050	.5134	.4363	.3714	.3166	.2703	.2311	.1978	.1456	.1078	.0929	.0802	.0600	.0451	.0258	.0150	.0089	.0054
18	.8360	.7002	.5874	.4936	.4155	.3503	.2959	.2502	.2120	.1799	.1300	.0946	.0808	.0691	.0508	.0376	.0208	.0118	.0068	.0039
19	.8277	.6864	.5703	.4746	.3957	.3305	.2765	.2317	.1945	.1635	.1161	.0829	.0703	.0596	.0431	.0313	.0168	.0092	.0051	.0029
20	.8195	.6730	.5537	.4564	.3769	.3118	.2584	.2145	.1784	.1486	.1037	.0728	.0611	.0514	.0365	.0261	.0135	.0072	.0039	.0021
25	.7798	.6095	.4776	.3751	.2953	.2330	.1842	.1460	.1160	.0923	.0588	.0378	.0304	.0245	.0160	.0105	.0046	.0021	.0010	.0005
30	.7419	.5521	.4120	.3083	.2314	.1741	.1314	.0994	.0754	.0573	.0334	.0196	.0151	.0116	.0070	.0042	.0016	.0006	.0002	.0001
40	.6717	.4529	.3066	.2083	.1420	.0972	.0668	.0460	.0318	.0221	.0107	.0053	.0037	.0026	.0013	.0007	.0002	.0001	*	*
50	.6080	.3715	.2281	.1407	.0872	.0543	.0339	.0213	.0134	.0085	.0035	.0014	.0009	.0006	.0003	.0001	*	*	*	*
60	.5504	.3048	.1697	.0951	.0535	.0303	.0173	.0099	.0057	.0033	.0011	.0004	.0002	.0001	*	*	*	*	*	*

*The factor is zero to four decimal places.

Table A.2   Present Value of an Annuity of $1 Per Period for n Periods:

$$PVIFA = \sum_{t=1}^{n} \frac{1}{(1+k)^t} = \frac{1 - \frac{1}{(1+k)^n}}{k}$$

Number of payments	1%	2%	3%	4%	5%	6%	7%	8%	9%	10%	12%	14%	15%	16%	18%	20%	24%	28%	32%
1	0.9901	0.9804	0.9709	0.9615	0.9524	0.9434	0.9346	0.9259	0.9174	0.9091	0.8929	0.8772	0.8696	0.8621	0.8475	0.8333	0.8065	0.7813	0.7576
2	1.9704	1.9416	1.9135	1.8861	1.8594	1.8334	1.8080	1.7833	1.7591	1.7355	1.6901	1.6467	1.6257	1.6052	1.5656	1.5278	1.4568	1.3916	1.3315
3	2.9410	2.8839	2.8286	2.7751	2.7232	2.6730	2.6243	2.5771	2.5313	2.4869	2.4018	2.3216	2.2832	2.2459	2.1743	2.1065	1.9813	1.8684	1.7663
4	3.9020	3.8077	3.7171	3.6299	3.5460	3.4651	3.3872	3.3121	3.2397	3.1699	3.0373	2.9137	2.8550	2.7982	2.6901	2.5887	2.4043	2.2410	2.0957
5	4.8534	4.7135	4.5797	4.4518	4.3295	4.2124	4.1002	3.9927	3.8897	3.7908	3.6048	3.4331	3.3522	3.2743	3.1272	2.9906	2.7454	2.5320	2.3452
6	5.7955	5.6014	5.4172	5.2421	5.0757	4.9173	4.7665	4.6229	4.4859	4.3553	4.1114	3.8887	3.7845	3.6847	3.4976	3.3255	3.0205	2.7594	2.5342
7	6.7282	6.4720	6.2303	6.0021	5.7864	5.5824	5.3893	5.2064	5.0330	4.8684	4.5638	4.2883	4.1604	4.0386	3.8115	3.6046	3.2423	2.9370	2.6775
8	7.6517	7.3255	7.0197	6.7327	6.4632	6.2098	5.9713	5.7466	5.5348	5.3349	4.9676	4.6389	4.4873	4.3436	4.0776	3.8372	3.4212	3.0758	2.7860
9	8.5660	8.1622	7.7861	7.4353	7.1078	6.8017	6.5152	6.2469	5.9952	5.7590	5.3282	4.9464	4.7716	4.6065	4.3030	4.0310	3.5655	3.1842	2.8681
10	9.4713	8.9826	8.5302	8.1109	7.7217	7.3601	7.0236	6.7101	6.4177	6.1446	5.6502	5.2161	5.0188	4.8332	4.4941	4.1925	3.6819	3.2689	2.9304
11	10.3676	9.7868	9.2526	8.7605	8.3064	7.8869	7.4987	7.1390	6.8052	6.4951	5.9377	5.4527	5.2337	5.0286	4.6560	4.3271	3.7757	3.3351	2.9776
12	11.2551	10.5753	9.9540	9.3851	8.8633	8.3838	7.9427	7.5361	7.1607	6.8137	6.1944	5.6603	5.4206	5.1971	4.7932	4.4392	3.8514	3.3868	3.0133
13	12.1337	11.3484	10.6350	9.9856	9.3936	8.8527	8.3577	7.9038	7.4869	7.1034	6.4235	5.8424	5.5831	5.3423	4.9095	4.5327	3.9124	3.4272	3.0404
14	13.0037	12.1062	11.2961	10.5631	9.8986	9.2950	8.7455	8.2442	7.7862	7.3667	6.6282	6.0021	5.7245	5.4675	5.0081	4.6106	3.9616	3.4587	3.0609
15	13.8651	12.8493	11.9379	11.1184	10.3797	9.7122	9.1079	8.5595	8.0607	7.6061	6.8109	6.1422	5.8474	5.5755	5.0916	4.6755	4.0013	3.4834	3.0764
16	14.7179	13.5777	12.5611	11.6523	10.8378	10.1059	9.4466	8.8514	8.3126	7.8237	6.9740	6.2651	5.9542	5.6685	5.1624	4.7296	4.0333	3.5026	3.0882
17	15.5623	14.2919	13.1661	12.1657	11.2741	10.4773	9.7632	9.1216	8.5436	8.0216	7.1196	6.3729	6.0472	5.7487	5.2223	4.7746	4.0591	3.5177	3.0971
18	16.3983	14.9920	13.7535	12.6593	11.6896	10.8276	10.0591	9.3719	8.7556	8.2014	7.2497	6.4674	6.1280	5.8178	5.2732	4.8122	4.0799	3.5294	3.1039
19	17.2260	15.6785	14.3238	13.1339	12.0853	11.1581	10.3356	9.6036	8.9501	8.3649	7.3658	6.5504	6.1982	5.8775	5.3162	4.8435	4.0967	3.5386	3.1090
20	18.0456	16.3514	14.8775	13.5903	12.4622	11.4699	10.5940	9.8181	9.1285	8.5136	7.4694	6.6231	6.2593	5.9288	5.3527	4.8696	4.1103	3.5458	3.1129
25	22.0232	19.5235	17.4131	15.6221	14.0939	12.7834	11.6536	10.6748	9.8226	9.0770	7.8431	6.8729	6.4641	6.0971	5.4669	4.9476	4.1474	3.5640	3.1220
30	25.8077	22.3965	19.6004	17.2920	15.3725	13.7648	12.4090	11.2578	10.2737	9.4269	8.0552	7.0027	6.5660	6.1772	5.5168	4.9789	4.1601	3.5693	3.1242
40	32.8347	27.3555	23.1148	19.7928	17.1591	15.0463	13.3317	11.9246	10.7574	9.7791	8.2438	7.1050	6.6418	6.2335	5.5482	4.9966	4.1659	3.5712	3.1250
50	39.1961	31.4236	25.7298	21.4822	18.2559	15.7619	13.8007	12.2335	10.9617	9.9148	8.3045	7.1327	6.6605	6.2463	5.5541	4.9995	4.1666	3.5714	3.1250
60	44.9550	34.7609	27.6756	22.6235	18.9293	16.1614	14.0392	12.3766	11.0480	9.9672	8.3240	7.1401	6.6651	6.2492	5.5553	4.9999	4.1667	3.5714	3.1250

Table A.3   Future Value of $1 at the End of n Periods: $FVIF_{k,n} = (1 + k)^n$

Period	1%	2%	3%	4%	5%	6%	7%	8%	9%	10%	12%	14%	15%	16%	18%	20%	24%	28%	32%	36%
1	1.0100	1.0200	1.0300	1.0400	1.0500	1.0600	1.0700	1.0800	1.0900	1.1000	1.1200	1.1400	1.1500	1.1600	1.1800	1.2000	1.2400	1.2800	1.3200	1.3600
2	1.0201	1.0404	1.0609	1.0816	1.1025	1.1236	1.1449	1.1664	1.1881	1.2100	1.2544	1.2996	1.3225	1.3456	1.3924	1.4400	1.5376	1.6384	1.7424	1.8496
3	1.0303	1.0612	1.0927	1.1249	1.1576	1.1910	1.2250	1.2597	1.2950	1.3310	1.4049	1.4815	1.5209	1.5609	1.6430	1.7280	1.9066	2.0972	2.3000	2.5155
4	1.0406	1.0824	1.1255	1.1699	1.2155	1.2625	1.3108	1.3605	1.4116	1.4641	1.5735	1.6890	1.7490	1.8106	1.9388	2.0736	2.3642	2.6844	3.0360	3.4210
5	1.0510	1.1041	1.1593	1.2167	1.2763	1.3382	1.4026	1.4693	1.5386	1.6105	1.7623	1.9254	2.0114	2.1003	2.2878	2.4883	2.9316	3.4360	4.0075	4.6526
6	1.0615	1.1262	1.1941	1.2653	1.3401	1.4185	1.5007	1.5869	1.6771	1.7716	1.9738	2.1950	2.3131	2.4364	2.6996	2.9860	3.6352	4.3980	5.2899	6.3275
7	1.0721	1.1487	1.2299	1.3159	1.4071	1.5036	1.6058	1.7138	1.8280	1.9487	2.2107	2.5023	2.6600	2.8262	3.1855	3.5832	4.5077	5.6295	6.9826	8.6054
8	1.0829	1.1717	1.2668	1.3686	1.4775	1.5938	1.7182	1.8509	1.9926	2.1436	2.4760	2.8526	3.0590	3.2784	3.7589	4.2998	5.5895	7.2058	9.2170	11.703
9	1.0937	1.1951	1.3048	1.4233	1.5513	1.6895	1.8385	1.9990	2.1719	2.3579	2.7731	3.2519	3.5179	3.8030	4.4355	5.1598	6.9310	9.2234	12.166	15.916
10	1.1046	1.2190	1.3439	1.4802	1.6289	1.7908	1.9672	2.1589	2.3674	2.5937	3.1058	3.7072	4.0456	4.4114	5.2338	6.1917	8.5944	11.805	16.059	21.646
11	1.1157	1.2434	1.3842	1.5395	1.7103	1.8983	2.1049	2.3316	2.5804	2.8531	3.4785	4.2262	4.6524	5.1173	6.1759	7.4301	10.657	15.111	21.198	29.439
12	1.1268	1.2682	1.4258	1.6010	1.7959	2.0122	2.2522	2.5182	2.8127	3.1384	3.8960	4.8179	5.3502	5.9360	7.2876	8.9161	13.214	19.342	27.982	40.037
13	1.1381	1.2936	1.4685	1.6651	1.8856	2.1329	2.4098	2.7196	3.0658	3.4523	4.3635	5.4924	6.1528	6.8858	8.5994	10.699	16.386	24.758	36.937	54.451
14	1.1495	1.3195	1.5126	1.7317	1.9799	2.2609	2.5785	2.9372	3.3417	3.7975	4.8871	6.2613	7.0757	7.9875	10.147	12.839	20.319	31.691	48.756	74.053
15	1.1610	1.3459	1.5580	1.8009	2.0789	2.3966	2.7590	3.1722	3.6425	4.1772	5.4736	7.1379	8.1371	9.2655	11.973	15.407	25.195	40.564	64.358	100.71
16	1.1726	1.3728	1.6047	1.8730	2.1829	2.5404	2.9522	3.4259	3.9703	4.5950	6.1304	8.1372	9.3576	10.748	14.129	18.488	31.242	51.923	84.953	136.96
17	1.1843	1.4002	1.6528	1.9479	2.2920	2.6928	3.1588	3.7000	4.3276	5.0545	6.8660	9.2765	10.761	12.467	16.672	22.186	38.740	66.461	112.13	186.27
18	1.1961	1.4282	1.7024	2.0258	2.4066	2.8543	3.3799	3.9960	4.7171	5.5599	7.6900	10.575	12.375	14.462	19.673	26.623	48.038	85.070	148.02	253.33
19	1.2081	1.4568	1.7535	2.1068	2.5270	3.0256	3.6165	4.3157	5.1417	6.1159	8.6128	12.055	14.231	16.776	23.214	31.948	59.567	108.89	195.39	344.53
20	1.2202	1.4859	1.8061	2.1911	2.6533	3.2071	3.8697	4.6610	5.6044	6.7275	9.6463	13.743	16.366	19.460	27.393	38.337	73.864	139.37	257.91	468.57
21	1.2324	1.5157	1.8603	2.2788	2.7860	3.3996	4.1406	5.0338	6.1088	7.4002	10.803	15.667	18.821	22.574	32.323	46.005	91.591	178.40	340.44	637.26
22	1.2447	1.5460	1.9161	2.3699	2.9253	3.6035	4.4304	5.4365	6.6586	8.1403	12.100	17.861	21.644	26.186	38.142	55.206	113.57	228.35	449.39	866.67
23	1.2572	1.5769	1.9736	2.4647	3.0715	3.8197	4.7405	5.8715	7.2579	8.9543	13.552	20.361	24.891	30.376	45.007	66.247	140.83	292.30	593.19	1178.6
24	1.2697	1.6084	2.0328	2.5633	3.2251	4.0489	5.0724	6.3412	7.9111	9.8497	15.178	23.212	28.625	35.236	53.108	79.496	174.63	374.14	783.02	1602.9
25	1.2824	1.6406	2.0938	2.6658	3.3864	4.2919	5.4274	6.8485	8.6231	10.834	17.000	26.461	32.918	40.874	62.668	95.396	216.54	478.90	1033.5	2180.0
26	1.2953	1.6734	2.1566	2.7725	3.5557	4.5494	5.8074	7.3964	9.3992	11.918	19.040	30.166	37.856	47.414	73.948	114.47	268.51	612.99	1364.3	2964.9
27	1.3082	1.7069	2.2213	2.8834	3.7335	4.8223	6.2139	7.9881	10.245	13.110	21.324	34.389	43.535	55.000	87.259	137.37	332.95	784.63	1800.9	4032.2
28	1.3213	1.7410	2.2879	2.9987	3.9201	5.1117	6.6488	8.6271	11.167	14.421	23.883	39.204	50.065	63.800	102.96	164.84	412.86	1004.3	2377.2	5483.8
29	1.3345	1.7758	2.3566	3.1187	4.1161	5.4184	7.1143	9.3173	12.172	15.863	26.749	44.693	57.575	74.008	121.50	197.81	511.95	1285.5	3137.9	7458.0
30	1.3478	1.8114	2.4273	3.2434	4.3219	5.7435	7.6123	10.062	13.267	17.449	29.959	50.950	66.211	85.849	143.37	237.37	634.81	1645.5	4142.0	10143
40	1.4889	2.2080	3.2620	4.8010	7.0400	10.285	14.974	21.724	31.409	45.259	93.050	188.88	267.86	378.72	750.37	1469.7	5455.9	19426	66520	•
50	1.6446	2.6916	4.3839	7.1067	11.467	18.420	29.457	46.901	74.357	117.39	289.00	700.23	1083.6	1670.7	3927.3	9100.4	46890	•	•	•
60	1.8167	3.2810	5.8916	10.519	18.679	32.987	57.946	101.25	176.03	304.48	897.59	2595.9	4383.9	7370.1	20555	56347	•	•	•	•

•FVIF > 99,999

Table A.4   Sum of an Annuity of $1 Per Period for n Periods:

$$FVIFA_{k,n} = \sum_{t=1}^{n} (1+k)^{t-1} = \frac{(1+k)^n - 1}{k}$$

Number of Periods	1%	2%	3%	4%	5%	6%	7%	8%	9%	10%	12%	14%	15%	16%	18%	20%	24%	28%	32%	36%
1	1.0000	1.0000	1.0000	1.0000	1.0000	1.0000	1.0000	1.0000	1.0000	1.0000	1.0000	1.0000	1.0000	1.0000	1.0000	1.0000	1.0000	1.0000	1.0000	1.0000
2	2.0100	2.0200	2.0300	2.0400	2.0500	2.0600	2.0700	2.0800	2.0900	2.1000	2.1200	2.1400	2.1500	2.1600	2.1800	2.2000	2.2400	2.2800	2.3200	2.3600
3	3.0301	3.0604	3.0909	3.1216	3.1525	3.1836	3.2149	3.2464	3.2781	3.3100	3.3744	3.4396	3.4725	3.5056	3.5724	3.6400	3.7776	3.9184	4.0624	4.2096
4	4.0604	4.1216	4.1836	4.2465	4.3101	4.3746	4.4399	4.5061	4.5731	4.6410	4.7793	4.9211	4.9934	5.0665	5.2154	5.3680	5.6842	6.0156	6.3624	6.7251
5	5.1010	5.2040	5.3091	5.4163	5.5256	5.6371	5.7507	5.8666	5.9847	6.1051	6.3528	6.6101	6.7424	6.8771	7.1542	7.4416	8.0484	8.6999	9.3983	10.146
6	6.1520	6.3081	6.4684	6.6330	6.8019	6.9753	7.1533	7.3359	7.5233	7.7156	8.1152	8.5355	8.7537	8.9775	9.4420	9.9299	10.980	12.135	13.405	14.798
7	7.2135	7.4343	7.6625	7.8983	8.1420	8.3938	8.6540	8.9228	9.2004	9.4872	10.089	10.730	11.066	11.413	12.141	12.915	14.615	16.533	18.695	21.126
8	8.2857	8.5830	8.8923	9.2142	9.5491	9.8975	10.259	10.636	11.028	11.435	12.299	13.232	13.726	14.240	15.327	16.499	19.122	22.163	25.678	29.731
9	9.3685	9.7546	10.159	10.582	11.026	11.491	11.978	12.487	13.021	13.579	14.775	16.085	16.785	17.518	19.085	20.798	24.712	29.369	34.895	41.435
10	10.462	10.949	11.463	12.006	12.577	13.180	13.816	14.486	15.192	15.937	17.548	19.337	20.303	21.321	23.521	25.958	31.643	38.592	47.061	57.351
11	11.566	12.168	12.807	13.486	14.206	14.971	15.783	16.645	17.560	18.531	20.654	23.044	24.349	25.732	28.755	32.150	40.237	50.398	63.121	78.998
12	12.682	13.412	14.192	15.025	15.917	16.869	17.888	18.977	20.140	21.384	24.133	27.270	29.001	30.850	34.931	39.580	50.894	65.510	84.320	108.43
13	13.809	14.680	15.617	16.626	17.713	18.882	20.140	21.495	22.953	24.522	28.029	32.088	34.351	36.786	42.218	48.496	64.109	84.852	112.30	148.47
14	14.947	15.973	17.086	18.291	19.598	21.015	22.550	24.214	26.019	27.975	32.392	37.581	40.504	43.672	50.818	59.195	80.496	109.61	149.23	202.92
15	16.096	17.293	18.598	20.023	21.578	23.276	25.129	27.152	29.360	31.772	37.279	43.842	47.580	51.659	60.965	72.035	100.81	141.30	197.99	276.97
16	17.257	18.639	20.156	21.824	23.657	25.672	27.888	30.324	33.003	35.949	42.753	50.980	55.717	60.925	72.939	87.442	126.01	181.86	262.35	377.69
17	18.430	20.012	21.761	23.697	25.840	28.212	30.840	33.750	36.973	40.544	48.883	59.117	65.075	71.673	87.068	105.93	157.25	233.79	347.30	514.66
18	19.614	21.412	23.414	25.645	28.132	30.905	33.999	37.450	41.301	45.599	55.749	68.394	75.836	84.140	103.74	128.11	195.99	300.25	459.44	700.93
19	20.810	22.840	25.116	27.671	30.539	33.760	37.379	41.446	46.018	51.159	63.439	78.969	88.211	98.603	123.41	154.74	244.03	385.32	607.47	954.27
20	22.019	24.297	26.870	29.778	33.066	36.785	40.995	45.762	51.160	57.275	72.052	91.024	102.44	115.37	146.62	186.68	303.60	494.21	802.86	1298.8
21	23.239	25.783	28.676	31.969	35.719	39.992	44.865	50.422	56.764	64.002	81.698	104.76	118.81	134.84	174.02	225.02	377.46	633.59	1060.7	1767.3
22	24.471	27.299	30.536	34.248	38.505	43.392	49.005	55.456	62.873	71.402	92.502	120.43	137.63	157.41	206.34	271.03	469.05	811.99	1401.2	2404.6
23	25.716	28.845	32.452	36.617	41.430	46.995	53.436	60.893	69.531	79.543	104.60	138.29	159.27	183.60	244.48	326.23	582.62	1040.3	1850.6	3271.3
24	26.973	30.421	34.426	39.082	44.502	50.815	58.176	66.764	76.789	88.497	118.15	158.65	184.16	213.97	289.49	392.48	723.46	1332.6	2443.8	4449.9
25	28.243	32.030	36.459	41.645	47.727	54.864	63.249	73.105	84.700	98.347	133.33	181.87	212.79	249.21	342.60	471.98	898.09	1706.8	3226.8	6052.9
26	29.525	33.670	38.553	44.311	51.113	59.156	68.676	79.954	93.323	109.18	150.33	208.33	245.71	290.08	405.27	567.37	1114.6	2185.7	4260.4	8233.0
27	30.820	35.344	40.709	47.084	54.669	63.705	74.483	87.350	102.72	121.09	169.37	238.49	283.56	337.50	479.22	681.85	1383.1	2798.7	5624.7	11197.9
28	32.129	37.051	42.930	49.967	58.402	68.528	80.697	95.338	112.96	134.20	190.69	272.88	327.10	392.50	566.48	819.22	1716.0	3583.3	7425.6	15230.2
29	33.450	38.792	45.218	52.966	62.322	73.639	87.346	103.96	124.13	148.63	214.58	312.09	377.16	456.30	669.44	984.06	2128.9	4587.6	9802.9	20714.1
30	34.784	40.568	47.575	56.084	66.438	79.058	94.460	113.28	136.30	164.49	241.33	356.78	434.74	530.31	790.94	1181.8	2640.9	5873.2	12940.	28172.2
40	48.886	60.402	75.401	95.025	120.79	154.76	199.63	259.05	337.88	442.59	767.09	1342.0	1779.0	2360.7	4163.2	7343.8	22728.	69377.	*	*
50	64.463	84.579	112.79	152.66	209.34	290.33	406.52	573.76	815.08	1163.9	2400.0	4994.5	7217.7	10435.	21813.	45497.	*	*	*	*
60	81.669	114.05	163.05	237.99	353.58	533.12	813.52	1253.2	1944.7	3034.8	7471.6	18535.	29219.	46057.	*	*	*	*	*	*

*FVIFA > 99,999

GLOSSARY OF
FINANCIAL TERMS *

Accelerated Depreciation   Depreciation methods that involve writing off the cost of an asset at a faster rate than the write-off under the straight-line method.

Accrued Interest   Interest accrued on a bond since the last interest payment was made. The buyer of the bonds pays the market price plus accrued interest. Exceptions include bonds that are in default and income bonds.

Advance-Decline Line   See Breadth of Market.

All or None Order   A market or limited price order that is to be executed in its entirety or not at all. Bids or offers on behalf of all or none orders may not be made in stocks, but may be made in bonds when the number of bonds is 50 or more.

Amortize   To liquidate on an installment basis; an amortized loan is one in which the principal amount of the loan is repaid in installments during the life of the loan.

Annual Report   The formal financial statement issued yearly by a corporation to its shareowners. The annual report shows assets, liabilities, earnings, how the company stood at the close of the business year and how it fared profitwise during the year.

Annuity   A series of payments of a fixed amount for a specified number of years.

Arrearage   Overdue payment; frequently, omitted dividend on preferred stocks.

Arbitrage   Process of buying and simultaneously selling the same or equivalent securities in different markets.

Assets   Everything that a corporation owns or that is due to it: cash, investments, money due it, materials and inventories, which are called current assets; buildings and machinery, which are known as fixed assets; and patents and goodwill, called intangible assets.

Attainable Set   All possible portfolios attainable within the constraint of the investor's funds.

---

*Most of the definitions are from *Glossary of Investment Language* (New York: New York Stock Exchange).

At the Close Order   A market order that is to be executed at or as near to the close as practicable.

At the Opening or at the Opening Only Order   A market or limit order that is to be executed at the opening of the market or not at all, and any such order or portion thereof not so executed is treated as cancelled.

Averages   Various ways of measuring the trend of securities prices, the most popular of which is the Dow-Jones average of 30 industrial stocks listed on the New York Stock Exchange.

Balloon Payment   When a debt is not fully amortized, the final payment is larger than the preceding payments and is called a "balloon" payment.

Bankruptcy   A legal procedure for formally liquidating a business carried out under the jurisdiction of courts of law.

Bear   Someone who believes the market will decline. (See Bull.)

Bear Market   A declining market.

Bearer Bond   A bond for which the owner's name is not registered on the books of the issuing company and which is payable to the holder (bearer). (See Registered Bond.)

Bid and Ask   Often referred to as a quotation or quote. The bid is the highest price anyone has declared that he wants to pay for a security at a given time; the ask is the lowest price anyone will take at the same time.

Big Board   A popular term for the New York Stock Exchange.

Block   A large holding or transaction of stock—typically considered to be 10,000 shares or more.

Blue Chip   Common stock in a company known nationally for the quality and wide acceptance of its products or services, and for its ability to make money and pay dividends.

Blue Sky Laws   A popular name for laws various states have enacted to protect the public against securities frauds. The term is believed to have originated when a judge ruled that a particular stock had about the same value as a patch of blue sky.

Bond   Negotiable promissory note of a corporation or public body.

Bond-Yield Table   Table of the average compound interest returns on bonds at various possible prices and coupon rates if the bonds are held to maturity.

Book   A notebook the specialist in a stock uses to keep a record of the buy and sell orders at specified prices, i.e., limit orders, in sequence of receipt, which are left with him by other brokers.

Book Value   An accounting term. The book value of a stock is determined from a company's records by adding all assets (generally excluding such intangibles as goodwill), then deducting all debts and other liabilities, plus the liquidation price of any preferred issues. The sum arrived at is divided by the number of common shares outstanding, and the result is the book value per common share. Book value of the assets of a company or a security may have little or no significant relationship to market value.

Breadth of Market   The cumulative index of the net differences between the number of price advances and declines.

Broker   An agent, often a member of a stock exchange firm or an exchange member himself, who handles the public's orders to buy and sell securities or commodities. For this service a commission is charged.

Brokers' Loans   Money borrowed by brokers from banks for a variety of uses. It may be used by specialists and odd-lot dealers to help finance inventories of stocks they deal in; by brokerage firms to finance the underwriting of new issues of corporate and municipal securities; to help finance a firm's own investments; and to help finance the purchase of securities for customers who prefer to use the broker's credit when they buy securities.

Bull   One who believes the market will rise. (See Bear.)

Call   (1) An option to buy (or "call") a share of stock at a specified price within a specific period; (2) the process of redeeming a bond or preferred stock issued before its normal maturity.

Call Loan   A loan that may be terminated or "called" at any time by the lender or borrower. Used to finance purchases of securities.

Call Premium   The amount in excess of par value that a company must pay when it calls a security.

Call Price   The price that must be paid when a security is called. The call price is equal to the par value plus the call premium.

Call Privilege   A provision incorporated into a bond or a share of preferred stock that gives the issuer the right to redeem (call) the security at a specified price.

Callable   A bond issue, all or part of which may be redeemed by the issuing corporation under definite conditions before maturity. The term also applies to preferred shares that may be redeemed by the issuing corporation.

Calling   The action of exercising the call privilege and redeeming securities prior to their maturity date.

Capital Gain or Capital Loss   Profit or loss from the sale of a capital asset. A capital gain, under current federal income tax laws, may be either short-term (12 months or less) or long-term (more than 12 months).

Capital Stock   All shares representing ownership of a business, including preferred and common stock.

Capital Structure   The permanent long-term financing of the firm represented by long-term debt, preferred stock, and net worth (net worth consists of capital, capital surplus, and earned surplus). Capital structure is distinguished from financial structure, which includes short-term debt plus all reserve accounts.

Capitalization   Total amount of the various securities issued by a corporation. Capitalization may include bonds, debentures, preferred and common stock, and surplus.

Cash Flow   Reported net income of a corporation plus amounts charged off for depreciation, depletion, amortization, and extraordinary charges to reserves, which are bookkeeping deductions and not paid out in actual dollars and cents.

Cash Sale   A transaction on the floor of the stock exchange which calls for delivery of the securities the same day. In "regular way" trades, the seller is to deliver on the fifth business day.

Certificate   The actual piece of paper that is evidence of ownership of stock in a corporation.

Central Certificate Service (CCS)   A department of the Stock Clearing Corporation that conducts a central securities certificate operation through which clearing firms effect security deliveries between each other via computerized bookkeeping entries, thereby reducing the physical movement of stock certificates.

Certainty Equivalents   The amount of cash that someone would require with certainty to make him indifferent to the choice between this certain sum and a particular uncertain, risky sum.

Chartist   A technical analyst who uses graphic presentations of stock prices to predict future stock prices.

Collateral   Securities or other property pledged by a borrower to secure repayment of a loan.

Collateral Trust Bond   A bond secured by collateral deposited with a trustee. The collateral is often the stocks or bonds of companies controlled by the issuing company but may be other securities.

Commercial Paper   Short-term promissory notes of a major corporation.

Commission   The broker's fee for purchasing or selling securities or property for a client.

Commission Broker   An agent who executes the public's orders for the purchase or sale of securities or commodities.

Common Size Statement   See Comparative Balance Sheet and Comparative Income Statement.

Common Stock   Securities that represent an ownership interest in a corporation. If the company has also issued preferred stock, both common and preferred stockholders have ownership rights, but the preferred normally has a prior claim on dividends and, in the event of liquidation, assets. Claims of both common and preferred stockholders are junior to claims of

bondholders or other creditors of the company. Common stockholders assume the greater risk, but generally exercise the greater control and may gain the greater reward in the form of dividends and capital appreciation.

Comparative Balance Sheet   A balance sheet in which each item is expressed as a percentage of the total assets or liabilities. Also referred to as a "common size statement."

Comparative Income Statement   An income statement in which each item is expressed as a percentage of total sales. Also referred to as a "common size statement."

Compound Interest   An interest rate that is applicable when interest in succeeding periods is earned not only on the initial principal but also on the accumulated interest of previous periods. Compound interest is contrasted to simple interest, in which returns are not earned on interest received.

Compounding   The arithmetic process of determining the final value of a payment or series of payments when compound interest is applied.

Confidence Index   The ratio of the yield on high-grade bonds to the yield on low-grade bonds.

Conglomerate   A corporation seeking to diversify its operations by acquiring enterprises in widely varied industries.

Consolidated Balance Sheet   A balance sheet showing the financial condition of a corporation and its subsidiaries.

Consolidated Tape   Under the Consolidated Tape Plan, the NYSE and ASE ticker systems became the "Consolidated Tape," Network A and Network B respectively, on June 16, 1975. Network A reports transactions in NYSE listed securities that take place on the NYSE or any of the participating regional stock exchanges and other markets. Each transaction is identified according to its originating market. Similarly, transactions in ASE listed securities, and certain other securities listed on regional stock exchanges, are reported and identified on Network B.

Constant Ratio Plan   A portfolio management plan which attempts to profit by adjusting stock-bond proportions by a fixed ratio.

Conversion price   The effective price paid for common stock when the stock is obtained by converting either convertible preferred stocks or convertible bonds. For example, if a $1,000 bond is convertible into 20 shares of stock, the conversion price is $50 ($1,000/20).

Conversion Ratio   The number of shares of common stock that may be obtained by converting a convertible bond or share of convertible preferred stock.

Convertible   A bond, debenture, or preferred share that may be exchanged by the owner for common stock or another security of the issuing firm.

Corner   Buying of a stock or commodity on a scale large enough to give the buyer, or buying group, control over the price. A person who must buy that stock or commodity, for example, one who is short, is forced to do business at an arbitrarily high price with those who obtained the corner.

Correspondent   A securities firm, bank, or other financial organization that regularly performs services for another in a place or market to which the other does not have direct access. Securities firms may have correspondents in foreign countries or on exchanges of which they are not members.

Coupon Bond   Bond with interest coupons attached. The coupons are clipped as they come due and are presented by the holder for payment of interest.

Coupon Rate   The stated rate of interest on a bond.

Coverage of Fixed Charges   The number of times available pretax earnings would cover bond interest and related charges.

Covering   Buying a security previously sold short.

Credit Balance   The unborrowed cash in an investor's margin account.

Cumulative Preferred   A stock having a provision that if one or more dividends are omitted, the omitted dividends must be paid before dividends may be paid on the company's common stock.

Cumulative Voting   A method of voting for corporate directors that enables the shareholder to multiply the number of his shares by the number of directorships being voted on and cast the total for one director or a selected group of directors. Cumulative voting is required under the corporate laws of some states, and is permitted in most others.

Curb Exchange   Former name of the American Stock Exchange, second largest exchange in the country. The term comes from the market's origin on a street in downtown New York.

Current Assets   Those assets of a company that are reasonably expected to be realized in cash, or sold, or consumed during the normal operating cycle of the business. These include cash, U.S. government bonds, receivables and money due usually within one year, and inventories.

Current Liabilities   Money owed and payable by a company, usually within one year.

Current Ratio   The ratio of a firm's current assets to its current liabilities.

Customers' Net Debit Balances   Credit of New York Stock Exchange member firms made avilable to help finance customers' purchases of stocks, bonds, and commodities.

Day Order   An order to buy or sell which, if not executed, expires at the end of the trading day on which it was entered.

Dealer   An individual or firm in the securities business acting as a principal rather than as an agent. Typically, a dealer buys for his own account and sells to a customer from his own inventory. The dealer's profit or loss is the difference between the price he pays and the price he receives for the same security. The dealer's confirmation must disclose to his customer that he has acted as a principal. The same individual or firm may function, at different times, either as broker or dealer.

Debenture   A promissory note backed by the general credit of a company and usually not secured by a mortgage or lien on any specific property.

Debit Balance   The amount of borrowed funds in an investor's margin account.

Deferred Call   The contractual inability of the bond issuer to redeem the bond for a specific period.

Depletion Accounting   Natural resources, such as metals, oils and gas, and timber, which can possibly be reduced to zero over the years, present a special problem in capital management. Depletion is an accounting practice consisting of charges against earnings based upon the amount of the asset taken out of the total reserves during the period for which accounting is made. A bookkeeping entry, it does not represent a cash outlay.

Depository Trust Company (DTC)   A central securities certificate depository through which members effect securities deliveries between each other via computerized bookkeeping entries which reduces the physical movement of stock certificates.

Depreciation   Normally, charges against earnings to write off the cost, less salvage value, of an asset over its estimated useful life.

Dilution   Reducing the actual or potential earnings per share by issuing more shares or giving options to obtain them.

Director   Person elected by shareholders to establish company policies. The directors appoint the president, vice-president, and all other operating officers. Directors decide, among other matters, if and when dividends shall be paid.

Discount   The amount by which a preferred stock or bond may sell below its par value.

Discount Rate   The rate used in the discounting process; sometimes called capitalization rate.

Discretionary Account   An account in which the customer gives the broker or someone else discretion, which may be complete or within specific limits, as to the purchase and sale of securities or commodities including selection, timing, amount, and price to be paid or received.

Discretionary Order   The customer empowers the broker to act on his behalf with respect to the choice of security to be bought or sold, a total amount of any securities to be bought or sold, and/or whether any such transaction shall be one of purchase or sale.

Diversification   Spreading investments among different companies in different fields. Another type of diversification is also offered by the securities of many individual companies because of the wide range of their activities. The important attribute is that returns over time are not correlated. In terms of modern portfolio theory, the elimination of all unsystematic ("unique") risk.

Dividend   The payment designated by the board of directors to be distributed pro rata among the shares outstanding. On preferred shares, it is generally a fixed amount. On common shares, the dividend varies with the fortunes of the firm.

Dividend Yield   The ratio of the current dividend to the current price of a share of stock.

Double Taxation   Short for double taxation of dividends. The federal government taxes corporate profits once as corporate income; any part of the remaining profits distributed as dividends to stockholders may be taxed again as income to the stockholder who receives it.

Dollar Cost Averaging   A system of buying securities at regular intervals with a fixed dollar amount. Under this system the investor buys by the dollars' worth rather than by the number of shares. If each investment is of the same number of dollars, payments buy more when the price is low and fewer when it rises. Thus temporary downswings in prices benefit the investor if he continues periodic purchases in both good and bad times, and the price at which the shares are sold is more than their average cost.

Dow Theory   A theory of market analysis based upon the performance of the Dow-Jones industrial and transportation stock price averages. The theory says that the market is in a basic upward trend if one of these averages advances above a previous

important high, accompanied or followed by a similar advance in the other. When the averages both dip below previous important lows, this is regarded as confirmation of a basic downward trend. The theory does not attempt to predict how long either trend will continue, although it is widely misinterpreted as a method of forecasting future action.

Dual Fund   A closed-end investment company with two classes of stock—an income-oriented class and capital gains-oriented class.

Earnings per Share   Total after-tax earnings, after preferred dividends, divided by the average number of common shares outstanding during the period.

EBIT   Abbreviation for "earnings before interest and taxes."

Efficient Frontier   The set of possible portfolios, each of which has the highest expected return for a given level of risk or the lowest risk for a given level of return.

Equipment Trust Certificate   A type of security, generally issued by a railroad, to pay for new equipment. Title to the equipment, such as a locomotive, is held by a trustee until the notes are paid off. An equipment trust certificate is usually secured by a first claim on the equipment.

Equity   The net worth of a business, consisting of capital stock, capital (or paid-in) surplus, earned surplus (or retained earnings), and occasionally, certain net worth reserves. Common equity is that part of the total net worth belonging to the common stockholders. Total equity would include preferred stock. The terms "common stock," "net worth," and "equity" are frequently used interchangeably.

Exchange Acquisition   A method of filling an order to buy a large block of stock on the floor of the exchange. Under certain circumstances, a member-broker can facilitate the purchase of a block by soliciting orders to sell. All orders to sell the security are lumped together and crossed with the buy order in the regular auction market. The price to the buyer may be on a net basis or on a commission basis.

Exchange Distribution   A method of disposing of large blocks of stock on the floor of the exchange. Under certain circumstances, a member-broker can facilitate the sale of a block of stock by soliciting and getting other member-brokers to solicit orders to buy. Individual buy orders are lumped together and crossed with the sell order in the regular auction market. A special commission is usually paid by the seller; ordinarily the buyer pays no commission.

Exchange Ratio   The ratio of the shares offered by the acquiring company for each share of the acquired company.

Ex-Dividend   A synonym for "without dividend." The buyer of a stock selling ex-dividend does not receive the recently declared dividend. Open buy and sell stop orders, and sell stop-limit orders in a stock on the ex-dividend date are ordinarily reduced by the value of that dividend. In the case of open stop-limit orders to sell, both the stop price and the limit price are reduced. Every dividend is payable on a fixed date to all shareholders recorded on the books of the company as of a previous date of record.

Ex-Rights   Without the rights. Corporations raising additional money may do so by offering their stockholders the right to subscribe to new or additional stock, usually at a discount from the prevailing market price. The buyer of a stock selling ex-rights is not entitled to the rights usually associated with stock ownership.

Extra   The short form of "extra dividend." A dividend in the form of stock or cash in addition to the regular or usual dividend the company has been paying.

Face Value   (sometimes referred to as par value). The value of a bond that appears on the face of the bond, unless the value is otherwise specified by the issuing company. Face value is ordinarily the amount the issuing company promises to pay at maturity. Face value is not an indication of market value.

Federal Funds   Interbank, overnight loans.

Financial Risk   The variability imparted to the earnings power of the operating entity because of the method of financing asset acquisition. Typically refers to fixed obligation securities—i.e., the larger the proportion of capital derived from bonds, the greater the financial risk.

Fiscal Year   A corporation's accounting year. Due to the nature of their particular business, some companies do not use the calendar year for their bookkeeping. A typical example is the department store which finds December 31 too early a date to close its books after the Christmas rush. For that reason many stores wind up their accounting year January 31.

Fixed Charges   A company's fixed expenses, such as bond interest, which it has agreed to pay whether or not earned, and which are deducted from income before earnings on equity capital are computed.

Flat   The price at which a bond is traded including consideration for all unpaid accruals of interest. Bonds in default of interest or principal are traded flat. Income bonds, which pay interest only to the extent earned, are usually traded flat. All other bonds are usually dealt in "and interest," which means that the buyer pays to the seller the market price plus interest accrued since the last payment date. When applied to a stock loan, flat means without premium or interest.

Floor Broker   A member of the stock exchange who executes orders on the floor of the exchange to buy or sell any listed securities.

Fundamental Research   Analysis of industries and companies based on such factors as sales, assets, earnings, products, markets, and management. The objective is to derive an "intrinsic value" for the asset and compare this to the current market price.

Funded Debt   Usually interest-bearing bonds or debentures of a company. Could include long-term bank loans. Does not include short-term loans and preferred or common stock.

General Mortgage Bond   A bond secured by a blanket mortgage on the company's property, but which is often outranked by one or more other mortgages.

General Obligation   A municipal bond secured by the full faith, credit, and taxing power of the municipality.

Gilt-edged   High-grade bond issued by a company that has demonstrated its ability to earn a comfortable profit over a period of years and pay its bondholders their interest without interruption.

Give-Ups   Controversial practice under which brokers deliver portions of their commissions on large securities transactions to other brokers as compensation for favors done for the customer by the latter brokers.

Good Delivery   Certain basic qualifications must be met before a security sold on the exchange may be delivered. The security must be in proper form to comply with the contract of sale and to transfer title to the purchaser.

Good 'Til Cancelled Order (GTC) or Open Order   An order to buy or sell which remains in effect until it is either executed or cancelled.

Goodwill   Intangible assets of a firm established by the excess of the price paid for the going concern over its book value.

Government Bonds   Obligations of the U.S. government, regarded as the highest grade issues in existence.

Growth Company   A company with prospects for future growth; a company whose earnings are expected to increase at a relatively rapid rate because it has the ability to invest funds at rates of return above the cost of capital.

Guaranteed Bond   A bond which has interest or principal, or both, guaranteed by a company other than the issuer. Usually found in the railroad industry when large roads, leasing sections of trackage owned by small railroads, may guarantee the bonds of the smaller road.

Guaranteed Stock   Usually preferred stock on which dividends are guaranteed by another company, under much the same circumstances as a bond is guaranteed.

Holding Company   A corporation that owns the securities of another, in most cases with voting control.

Hypothecation   The pledging of securities as collateral for a loan.

Inactive Post   A trading post on the floor of the New York Stock Exchange where inactive securities are traded in units of 10 shares instead of the usual 100-share lots.

Inactive Stock   An issue traded on an exchange or in the over-the-counter market in which there is a relatively low volume of transactions. Volume may be no more than a few hundred shares a week or even less.

On the New York Stock Exchange many inactive stocks are traded in 10-share units rather than the customary 100.

In-and-Out   Purchase and sale of the same security within a short period—a day, week, even a month. An in-and-out trader is generally more interested in day-to-day price fluctuations than in dividends or long-term growth.

Income Bond   Generally, a bond that involves a promise to pay interest only when earned.

Indenture   A written agreement under which debentures are issued setting forth maturity date, interest rate, and other terms.

Index   A statistical yardstick expressed in terms of percentages of a base year or years. An index is not an average.

Inflation   An increasing price level. Usually measured as the annualized increase in the Consumer Price Index (CPI).

Institutional Investor   An organization whose primary purpose is to invest its own assets or those held in trust by it for others. Includes pension funds, investment companies, insurance companies, universities, and banks.

Interest   Payments a borrower makes to a lender for the use of his money. A corporation pays interest on its bonds to its bondholders.

Interest-Rate Risk   The potential price change in a financial asset in response to a change in the interest rate.

Investment   The commitment of funds for a period of time that will provide returns to compensate the investor for the time period involved, the rate of inflation during the period, and the risk involved.

Investment Banker   Also known as an underwriter. He is the middleman between the corporation issuing new securities and the public. The usual practice is for one or more investment bankers to buy outright from a corporation a new issue of stocks or bonds. The group forms a syndicate to sell the securities to individuals and institutions. Investment bankers also distribute very large blocks of stocks or bonds—perhaps held by an estate.

Investment Counsel   One whose principal business consists of acting as investment adviser, and a substantial part of whose business consists of rendering investment supervisory services.

Investment Company   A company that uses its capital to invest in other companies. There are two principal types of investment companies: closed-end and open-end, which are referred to as mutual fund.

Legal List   A list of investments selected by various states in which certain institutions and fiduciaries, such as insurance companies and banks, may invest. Legal lists are often restricted to high-quality securities meeting certain specifications.

Leverage   The effect on the per-share earnings of the common stock of a company when large sums must be paid for bond interest or preferred stock dividends, or both, before the common stockholder is entitled to share in earnings. Leverage may be advantageous for the common when earnings are good, but may work against the common stock when earnings decline. When a company has common stock only, no leverage exists because all earnings are available for the common, although relatively large fixed charges payable for lease of substantial plant assets may have an effect similar to that of a bond issue.

Liabilities   All the claims against a corporation. Liabilities include accounts and wages and salaries payable, dividends declared payable, accrued taxes payable, and fixed or long-term liabilities such as mortgage bonds, debentures, and bank loans.

Lien A claim against property which has been pledged or mortgaged to secure the performance of an obligation. A bond is usually secured by a lien against specified property of a company.

Limit, Limited Order, or Limited-Price Order An order to buy or sell a stated amount of a security at a specified price, or at a better price, if obtainable after the order is represented in the trading crowd.

Liquidation The process of converting securities or other property into cash. The dissolution of a company, with cash remaining after sale of its assets and payment of all indebtedness being distributed to the shareholders.

Liquidity The ability to buy or sell an asset quickly with reasonably small price changes assuming no new information has entered the market. Liquidity is one of the most important characteristics of a good market.

Listed Security Security that is fully accepted for trading on a stock exchange.

Load The portion of the offering price of shares of open-end investment companies that covers sales commissions and all other costs of distribution. The load is incurred only on purchase, there being, in most cases, no charge when the shares are sold.

Locked In An investor is said to be locked in when he has a profit on a security he owns but does not want to sell because his profit would immediately become subject to a capital gains tax.

Long Signifies ownership of securities: "I am long 100 U.S. Steel" means the speaker owns 100 shares.

Management The board of directors, elected by the stockholders, and the officers of the corporation, appointed by the board of directors.

Manipulation An illegal operation. Buying or selling a security for the purpose of creating false or misleading appearance of active trading or for the purpose of raising or depressing the price to induce purchase or sale by others.

Margin The amount paid by the customer when he uses his broker's credit to buy a security. Under Federal Reserve regulations, the initial margin required in the past 20 years has ranged from 40 percent of the purchase price all the way to 100 percent.

Margin Call A demand upon a customer to put up money or securities with the broker. The call is made when a purchase is made and also if a customer's equity in a margin account declines below a minimum standard set by the exchange or by the firm.

Market Order An order to buy or sell a stated amount of a security at the most advantageous price obtainable after the order is represented in the trading crowd.

Market Price In the case of a security, the market price is usually considered the last reported price at which the stock or bond sold.

Matched and Lost When two bids to buy the same stock are made on the trading floor simultaneously, and each bid is equal to or larger than the amount of stock offered, both bids are considered to be on an equal basis. So the two bidders flip a coin to decide who buys the stock. Also applies to offers to sell.

Maturity The date on which a loan or a bond or debenture comes due and is to be paid off.

Member Corporation A securities

brokerage firm, organized as a corporation, with at least one member of the New York Stock Exchange who is a director and a holder of voting stock in the corporation.

Member Firm   A securities brokerage firm organized as a partnership and having at least one general partner who is a member of the New York Stock Exchange.

Merger   The formation of one company from two or more previously existing companies.

Money Market   Financial markets in which funds are borrowed or loaned for short periods. (The money market is distinguished from the capital market, which is the market for long-term funds.)

Money Market Fund   An investment company that primarily invests in very short-term instruments such as U.S. T-bills, corporate commercial paper, and certificates of deposit of U.S. and foreign banks.

Mortgage Bond   A bond secured by a mortgage on a property.

Municipal Bond   A bond issued by a state or a political subdivision, such as a county, city, town, or village. The term also designates bonds issued by state agencies and authorities. In general, interest paid on municipal bonds is exempt from federal income taxes.

Mutual Fund   See Investment Companies.

NASD   The National Association of Securities Dealers, Inc. An association of brokers and dealers in over-the-counter securities. The association has the power to expel members who have been declared guilty of unethical practices.

Negotiable   Refers to a security, the title to which is transferable by delivery.

Net Asset Value (NAV)   A term usually used in connection with investment trusts

and meaning net asset value per share. It is common practice for an investment trust to compute its assets daily, or even twice daily, by totaling the market value of all securities owned. All liabilities are deducted, and the balance divided by the number of shares outstanding. The resulting figure is the net asset value per share.

Net Change   The change in the price of a security from the closing price on one day to the closing price on the following day on which the stock is traded. In the case of a stock that is entitled to a dividend on one day, but is traded "ex-dividend" the next, the dividend is considered in computing the change. The mark $+1\frac{1}{8}$ means up $1.125 a share from the last sale on the previous day the stock traded.

Net Worth   The capital and surplus of a firm—capital stock; capital surplus (paid-in capital); earned surplus (retained earnings); and, occasionally, certain reserves. For some purposes, preferred stock is included; generally, net worth refers only to the common stockholder's position.

New Issue   A stock or bond sold by a corporation for the first time. Proceeds may be used to retire outstanding securities of the company, for new plant or equipment, or for additional working capital.

Noncumulative   A preferred stock on which unpaid dividends do not accrue. Omitted dividends are, as a rule, gone forever.

NYSE Common Stock Index   A composite index covering price movements of all common stocks listed on the "Big Board." It is based on the close of the market on December 31, 1965 as 50.00 and is weighted according to the market value for each issue.

Odd Lot   An amount of stock less than the established 100-share unit or 10-share unit of trading; from 1 to 99 shares for the great majority of issues, 1 to 9 for so-called inactive stocks.

Odd-Lot Dealer A member firm of the exchange that buys and sells odd lots of stocks. Odd-lot prices are geared to the auction market. On an odd-lot market order, the odd-lot dealer's price is based on the first round-lot transaction that occurs on the floor following receipt of the odd-lot order.

Odd-Lot Theory A technical approach to stock trading which maintains that the odd-lotter is consistently incorrect.

Off-Board This term may refer to transactions over-the-counter in unlisted securities, or to a transaction involving listed shares that was not executed on a national securities exchange.

Offer The price at which a person is ready to sell, as opposed to bid, the price at which one is ready to buy.

Option A right to buy or sell specific securities or properties at a specified price within a specified time. (See Puts and Calls.)

Orders Good Until a Specified Time A market or limited price order that is to be represented in the trading crowd until a specified time, after which such order or the portion thereof not executed is to be treated as cancelled.

Organized Security Exchanges Formal organizations have tangible, physical locations. Organized exchanges conduct an auction market in designated ("listed") investment securities. For example, the New York Stock Exchange is an organized exchange.

Overbought An opinion as to price levels. May refer to a security which has had a sharp rise or to the market as a whole after a period of vigorous buying, which, it may be argued, has left prices "too high."

Oversold An opinion—the reverse of overbought. It is believed that a security or the market has declined to an unreasonable level.

Over-the-Counter (OTC) A market for securities made up of securities dealers who may or may not be members of securities exchanges. Over-the-counter is mainly a market made over the telephone. Thousands of companies have insufficient shares outstanding, stockholders, or earnings to warrant application for listing on the N.Y. Stock Exchange. Securities of these companies are traded in the over-the-counter market among dealers who act either as principals or as brokers for customers. The over-the-counter market is the principal market for U.S. government bonds and municipal bonds and the stocks of banks and insurance companies.

Paper Profit An unrealized profit on a security still held. Paper profits become realized profits only when the security is sold.

Par In the case of a common share, par means a dollar amount assigned to the share by the company's charter. Par value may also be used to compute the dollar amount of the common shares on the balance sheet. Par value has little significance insofar as the market value of common stock is concerned. Many companies today issue no-par stock but give a stated per share value on the balance sheet. Par at one time was supposed to represent the value of the original investment behind each share in cash, goods, or services. In the case of preferred shares and bonds, however, par is important. It often signifies the dollar value upon which dividends on preferred stocks, and interest on bonds, are figured. The issuer of an 8 percent bond promises to pay that percentage of the bond's par value annually.

Participating Preferred   A preferred stock that is entitled to its stated dividend and, also, to additional dividends on a specified basis upon payment of dividends on the common stock.

Passed Dividend   Omission of a regular or scheduled dividend.

Payout Ratio   The percentage of earnings paid out in the form of dividends.

Penny Stocks   Low-priced issues, often highly speculative, selling at less than one dollar a share. Frequently used as a term of disparagement, although a few penny stocks have developed into investment-calibre issues.

Percentage Order   A market or limited price order to buy (or sell) a stated amount of a specified stock after a fixed number of shares of such stock have traded.

Point   In the case of shares of stock, a point means $1. In the case of bonds a point means $10, because a bond price is quoted as a percentage of $1,000. In the case of market averages, the word point means merely that and no more. A point in the DJIA is not equivalent to $1.

Portfolio   Holdings of securities by an individual or institution. A portfolio may contain the bonds, preferred stocks, and common stocks of various types of enterprises as well as other earning assets such as coins, stamps, real estate.

Preferred Stock   A class of stock with a claim on the company's earnings before payment may be made on the common stock and usually entitled to priority over common stock if the company liquidates. Usually entitled to dividends at a specific rate when declared by the board of directors and before payment of a dividend on the common stock and depending upon the terms of the issue.

Premium   The amount by which a preferred stock or bond sells above its par value. In the case of a new issue of bonds or stocks, premium is the amount the market price rises over the original selling price. Also refers to a charge sometimes made when a stock is borrowed to make delivery on a short sale. May also refer to the redemption price of a bond or preferred stock if it is higher than face value.

Present Discounted Value (PDV)   The value today of a future payment or payments, discounted at an appropriate rate.

Price-Earnings (P/E) Ratio   The current market price of a share of stock divided by earnings per share for a twelve-month period.

Primary Distribution   Also called primary offering. The original sale of a company's securities.

Prime Rate   The rate of interest commercial banks charge very large, strong corporations.

Principal   The person for whom a broker executes an order, or a dealer buying or selling for his own account. The term may also refer to a person's capital or to the face amount of a bond.

Proxy   Written authorization given by a shareholder to someone else to represent him and vote his shares at a shareholders' meeting.

Proxy Statement   Information the SEC requires to be given stockholders as a prerequisite to solicitation of proxies for a security subject to the requirements of the Securities Exchange Act.

Puts and Calls   Options that give the right to buy or sell a fixed amount of a certain stock at a specified price within a specified time. A put gives the holder the right to sell the stock, a call the right to buy the stock. Puts are purchased by those who think a stock may go down. A put obligates the seller to acquire the stock and pay the specified price to the owner of the option within the time limit of the contract. The price specified in a put or call is usually close to the market price of the stock at the time the contract is made. Calls are purchased by those who think a stock may rise. A call gives the holder the right to buy the stock from the seller of the contract at the specified price within a fixed period of time. Put and call contracts are written for 3, 6, or 9 months. If the purchaser of a put or call does not wish to exercise the option, the price he paid for the option becomes a loss.

Quick Ratio   The ratio of cash plus marketable securities and accounts receivable to current liabilities.

Quotation   Often shortened to "quote." The highest bid to buy and the lowest offer to sell a security in a given market at a given time. If you ask your broker for a "quote" on a stock, he may come back with something like "45$\frac{1}{4}$ to 45$\frac{1}{2}$." This means that $45.25 is the highest price any buyer wanted to pay at the time the quote was given on the floor of the exchange and that $45.50 was the lowest price any seller would take at the same time.

R²   The coefficient of determination, a statistic that indicates the degree of accuracy with which a regression explains actual observations.

Rally   A brisk rise following a decline in the general price level of the market or of an individual stock.

Random Walk   A theory which claims that stock price changes occur randomly and are independent of one another over time.

Ratio Analysis   Investment analaysis involving comparing a firm's balance sheet and income statement ratios to each other and to external data.

Ratio of Collateral to Debt   The number of times total stock margin debt is covered by total collateral value:

$$\frac{\text{Collateral Value}}{\text{Stock Margin Debt}} = \text{Ratio}$$

Record Date   The date on which one must be registered as a shareholder on the stock book of a company in order to receive a declared dividend or, among other things, to vote on company affairs.

Redemption Price   The price at which a bond may be redeemed before maturity, at the option of the issuing company. Redemption price also refers to the price the company must pay to call in certain types of preferred stock.

Refinancing   Same as refunding. New securities are sold by a company and the money is used to retire existing securities. The object may be to save interest costs, extend the maturity of the loan, or both.

Registered Bond   A bond that is registered on the books of the issuing company in the name of the owner, unlike a bearer bond. It can be transferred only when endorsed by the registered owner.

Registered Representative   Current name for the older term "customers' man." In a New York Stock Exchange member firm, a registered representative is a full-time employee who has met the requirements of the exchange in terms of background and knowledge of the securities business. Also known as an account executive or customer's broker.

Registered Trader   A member of an exchange who trades in stocks on the floor for an account in which he has an interest.

Registrar   Usually a trust company or bank

charged with the responsibility of preventing the issuance of more stock than was authorized by a company.

Registration   Before a public offering of new securities may be made by a company, or of outstanding securities by controlling stockholders either through the mails or by some other form of interstate commerce, the securities must be registered under the Securities Act of 1933. The registration statement is filed with the SEC by the issuer. It must include pertinent information relating to the company's operations, securities, management, and the purpose of the public offering. Securities of railroads under the jurisdiction of the Interstate Commerce Commission and certain other types of securities are exempted. On security offerings involving less than $300,000, less information is required.

Before a security may be admitted to dealings on a national securities exchange, it must be registered under the Securities Exchange Act of 1934. The application for registration must be filed with the exchange and with the SEC by the company issuing the securities. It must include pertinent information relating to the company's operations, securities, and management. Registration may become effective 30 days after the SEC receives certification from the exchange of approval of listing and registration, or sooner by special order of the commission.

Regression Analysis   A statistical procedure for predicting the value of one variable (dependent variable) on the basis of knowledge of one or more other variables (independent variables).

Regulation T   The federal regulation governing the amount of credit that may be advanced by brokers and dealers to customers for the purchase of securities.

Regulation U   The federal regulation governing the amount of credit that may be advanced by a bank to its customers for the purchase of listed stocks.

Relative Strength   A technical trading strategy that maintains today's strongest performing stocks relative to a market index will also be tomorrow's strongest performing stocks.

Reorganization   In bankruptcy the restructuring of a firm's capital structure and operating facilities under court protection.

Resistance Level   According to technicians, it is a price area where the stock price will turn down due to heavy supply from owners who bought the stock prior to a decline and are waiting for it to return to this level. It is also the upside ceiling a price must penetrate to indicate a significant change or move to a new equilibrium.

Revenue Bond   A municipal bond backed by the revenues of the project it financed.

Right   A short-term option to buy a specified number of shares of a new issue of securities at a designated "subscription" price from the company.

Risk Function   The relationship between the expected return and the associated risk.

Round Lot   A unit of trading or a multiple thereof. On the NYSE the unit of trading is generally 100 shares in stocks and $1,000 par value in the case of bonds. In some inactive stocks, the unit of trading is 10 shares.

Scale Order   An order to buy (or sell) a security that specifies the total amount to be bought (or sold) and the amount to be bought (or sold) at specified prices.

Seat   A traditional figure of speech referring to a membership on an exchange. Price and admission requirements vary by exchange.

SEC   The Securities and Exchange Commission, established by Congress to help protect investors. The SEC enforces the Securities Act of 1933, the Securities Exchange Act of 1934, the Trust Indenture Act, the Investment Company Act, the Investment Advisers Act, and the Public Utility Holding Company Act.

Secondary Distribution   Also known as a secondary offering. The redistribution of a block of stock some time after it has been sold by the issuing company.

Seller's Option   A special transaction on the NYSE that gives the seller the right to deliver the stock or bond at any time within a specified period ranging from not less than 6 business days to not more than 60 days.

Selling Against the Box   A method of protecting a paper profit. If an investor owns 100 shares of XYZ that has advanced in price, and he thinks the price may decline, he sells 100 shares short, borrowing 100 shares to make delivery. He retains in his security box the 100 shares that he owns. If XYZ declines, the profit on his short sale is exactly offset by the profit on the market value of the stock he has retained. He can close out his short sale by buying 100 shares to return to the person from whom he borrowed, or he can send the buyer the 100 shares he owns.

Serial Bond   An issue that matures at periodic stated intervals rather than on a single, specific date.

Short Covering   Buying stock to return stock previously borrowed to make delivery on a short sale.

Short Position   Stocks sold short and not covered as of a particular date. On the NYSE, a tabulation is issued a few days after the middle of the month listing all issues on the exchange in which there was a short position on the mid-month settlement date if 5,000 or more shares were involved or the short position had changed by 2,000 or more shares in the preceding month. This tabulation is based on reports of positions in member firms' books. Short position also means the total amount of stock an individual has sold short and has not covered as of a particular date. Initial margin requirements for a short position are the same as those for a long position. Proceeds from short sales are excluded entirely from this report. The initial margin required of the short seller, however, and profits and losses on short sales are reflected in stock-margin debt.

Short Sale   A person who believes a stock will decline and sells it, though he does not own any stock, has made a short sale. For instance, an investor instructs his broker to sell short 100 shares of ABC. His broker borrows the stock so that he can deliver the 100 shares to the buyer. Sooner or later the investor must cover his short sale by buying the same amount of stock he borrowed to return to the lender. If he is able to buy ABC at a lower price than he sold it for, his profit is the difference between the two prices, not counting commissions and taxes. But if he has to pay more for the stock than the price he received, that is the amount of his loss. (See also Selling Against the Box.)

Sinking Fund   Money regularly set aside by a company and used to redeem its bonds, debentures, or preferred stock.

SIPC   Securities Investor Protection Corporation which provides funds for use, if necessary, to protect customers' cash and securities which may be on deposit with an SIPC member firm in the event the firm fails and is liquidated under the provisions of the SIPC Act. SIPC is not a government agency but is a non-profit membership corporation created by an Act of Congress.

Special Bid   A method of filling an order to buy a large block of stock on the floor of the New York Stock Exchange. In a special bid, the bidder for the block of stock, a pension fund, for instance, will pay a special commission to the broker who represents him in making the purchase. The seller does not pay a commission. The special bid is made on the floor of the exchange at a fixed price that may not be below the last sale of the security or the current bid in the regular market, whichever is higher. Member firms may sell this stock for customers directly to the buyer's broker during trading hours.

Special Offering   Occasionally, a large block of stock becomes available for sale that, due to its size and the market in that particular issue, calls for special handling. A notice is printed on the ticker tape announcing that the stock will be offered for sale on the NYSE floor at a fixed price. Member firms may buy this stock for customers directly from the seller's broker during trading hours. The price is usually based on the last transaction in the regular auction market. If there are more buyers than stock, allotments are made. Only the seller pays a commission on a special offering.

Specialist   A member of an organized exchange like the New York Stock Exchange who has two functions: first, to maintain an orderly market, insofar as reasonably practicable, in the stocks in which he is registered as a specialist. In order to maintain an orderly market, the exchange expects the specialist to buy or sell for his own account, to a reasonable degree, when there is a temporary disparity between supply and demand. Second, the specialist acts as a broker's broker. When a commission broker on the exchange floor receives a limit order, say, to buy at $50 a stock then selling at $60, he cannot wait at the post where the stock is traded until the

price reaches the specified level. So he leaves the order with the specialist, who will try to execute it in the market if and when the stock declines to the specified price. At all times the specialist must put his customer's interests above his own.

Specialist Block Purchase   Purchase by a specialist for his own account of a large block of stock outside the regular exchange market. Such purchases may be made in the regular market within a reasonable time and at reasonable prices, and when the purchase by the specialist would aid him in maintaining a fair and orderly market.

Specialist Block Sale   Opposite of the specialist block purchase. Under exceptional circumstances, the specialist may sell a block of stock outside the regular market on the exchange for his own account at a price above the prevailing market. The price is negotiated between the specialist and the broker for the buyer.

Speculator   One who is willing to assume a relatively large risk in the hope of gain. His principal concern is to increase his capital rather than his dividend income. The speculator may buy and sell the same day or speculate in an enterprise that he does not expect to be profitable for years.

Split   The division of the outstanding shares of a corporation into a larger number of shares. A 3-for-1 split by a company with one million shares outstanding results in three million shares outstanding. Ordinarily, splits must be voted by directors and approved by shareholders.

Standard Deviation   A measure of dispersion within a probability distribution.

Standard Error of the Estimate   A measure of dispersion related to regression estimates, i.e., the dispersion around a regression line.

Stock Clearing Corporation   A subsidiary

of the New York Stock Exchange that acts as a central agency for clearing firms in providing a "clearance operation" through which transactions made on the floor are confirmed and balanced and, also, a "settlement operation" that handles the physical delivery of securities and money payments.

Stock Dividend   A dividend paid in securities rather than cash. The dividend may be additional shares of the issuing company, or shares of another company (usually a subsidiary) held by the company.

Stockholder of Record   A stockholder whose name is registered on the books of the issuing corporation.

Stop-Limit Order   A stop-limit order to buy becomes a limit order that can be executed at the limit price, or at a better price if obtainable, when a transaction in the security occurs at or above the stop price. A stop-limit order to sell becomes a limit order that can be executed at the limit price, or at a better price if obtainable, when a transaction in the security occurs at or below the stop price.

Stop Order   A stop order to buy becomes a market order when a transaction in the security occurs at or above the stop price. A stop order to sell becomes a market order when a transaction in the security occurs at or below the stop price. Because it becomes a market order when the stop price is reached, there is no certainty that the trade will be executed at that price.

Stopped Stock   Performance, in most cases by the specialist, of an order given him by a commission broker. For example, XYZ just sold at $50 a share. Broker A comes along with an order to buy 100 shares at the market price. The lowest offer is $50.50. Broker A believes he can do better for his client than $50.50, perhaps might get the

stock at $50.25. But he doesn't want to take a chance that he'll miss the market, that is, the next sale might be $50.50 and the following one even higher. So he asks the specialist if he will stop 100 at $1/2$ ($50.50). The specialist agrees. The specialist guarantees Broker A that he will get 100 shares at $50^{1/2}$ if the stock sells at that price. In the meantime, if the specialist or Broker A succeeds in executing the order at $50.25, the stop is called off.

Street Name   Securities held in the name of a broker instead of his customer's name are said to be carried in a "street name." This occurs when the securities have been bought on margin or when the customer wishes the security to be held by the broker.

Support Level   The downside price floor. It supposedly occurs after a stock has enjoyed a large runup. When the stock experiences weakness, technicians expect strong demand at this price from investors who missed the prior runup. If the price breaks through and goes below the support level, this is a bearish indication to technicians.

Switching   Selling one security and buying another.

Syndicate   A group of investment bankers who together underwrite and distribute a new issue of securities or large block of an outstanding issue.

Take–Over   The acquiring of one corporation by another—usually in a friendly merger but sometimes marked by a "proxy fight." In "unfriendly" take-over attempts, the potential buying company may offer a price well above current market values including new securities and other inducements to stockholders. The management of the subject company might ask for a better price, fight the take-over, or attempt to merge with another company.

Tax-Exempt Bonds   The securities of states, cities, and other public authorities specified under federal law, the interest on which is either wholly or partly exempt from federal income taxes.

Tax Selling   Sales made to realize gains or losses for income tax purposes.

Technical Analysis   A theory of stock prices that maintains that it is possible to predict future price movements based on past price changes.

Technical Indicator   A term applied to the various internal market factor indicators, as opposed to external forces such as earnings, dividends, political considerations, and general economic conditions. Some internal factors considered in appraising the market's technical position include the size of the short interest; whether the market has had a sustained advance or decline without interruption, a sharp advance or decline without interruption, a sharp advance or decline on small volume; and the amount of credit in use in the market.

Tender Offer   A public offer to buy shares from existing stockholders of one public corporation by another company under specified terms good for a certain time period. Stockholders are asked to "tender" (surrender) their holdings for stated value, usually at a good premium above the current market price, subject to the tendering of a minimum and maximum number of shares.

Term Structure   The relationship among the yields on bonds of equal quality but different maturities.

Thin Market   A market in which there are comparatively few bids to buy or offers to sell or both. The phrase may apply to a single security or to the entire stock market. In a thin market, price fluctuations between transactions are usually larger than they are when the market is liquid. A thin market

in a particular stock may reflect lack of interest in that issue or a limited supply of or demand for stock in the market.

Third Market   Trading of stock exchange listed securities in the over-the-counter market by non-exchange member brokers and all types of investors.

Ticker   The instrument that prints prices and volume of security transactions in cities and towns throughout the U.S. and Canada within minutes after each trade on the exchange floor.

Time Order   An order that becomes a market or limit-price order at a specified time.

Trader   One who buys and sells for his own account for short-term profit.

Trading Post   One of 18 horseshoe-shaped trading locations on the floor of the New York Stock Exchange at which stocks assigned to that location are bought and sold.

Transfer   This term may refer to two different operations. For one, the delivery of a stock certificate from the seller's broker to the buyer's broker and legal change of ownership, normally accomplished within a few days. For another, the recording of the change of ownership on the books of the corporation by the transfer agent.

Transfer Agent   A transfer agent keeps a record of the name of each registered shareowner, his or her address, and the number of shares owned, and sees that certificates presented to his office for transfer are properly cancelled and new certificates issued in the name of the transferee.

Transfer Tax   A tax imposed by New York State when a security is sold or transferred from one person to another. The tax is paid by the seller. There is no tax on the transfer of bonds.

Treasury Stock Stock issued by a company but later reacquired. It may be held in the company's treasury indefinitely, reissued to the public, or retired.

Turnover The volume of business in a security or in the entire market. If turnover on the NYSE is reported at 40 million shares on a particular day, 40 million shares changed hands. Odd-lot turnover is tabulated separately and ordinarily is not included in reported volume.

Turnover Rate The volume of shares traded in a year as a percentage of total shares listed on an exchange. It is also possible to compute the turnover rate for an individual company's stock which is the number of shares outstanding during the period. Finally, it is possible to compute the trading turnover for a portfolio of stocks which is the number of shares bought and sold as a percent of the average number of shares in the portfolio during the year.

Two-Dollar Broker Members on the floor of the NYSE who execute orders for other brokers having more business at that time than they can handle themselves, or for firms who do not have their exchange member-partner on the floor.

Unlisted A security not listed on a stock exchange.

Unlisted Trading Privileges On some exchanges a stock may be traded at the request of a member without any prior application by the company itself. The company has no agreement to conform with the standards of the exchange. Today, allowing a stock unlisted trading privileges requires SEC approval of an application filed by the exchange. The information in the application must be made available to the public by the exchange.

Uptick A term used to designate a transaction made at a price higher than the preceding transaction. Also called a "plus-tick." A stock may be sold short only on an uptick or on a "zero-plus" tick. A "zero-plus" tick is a term used for a transaction at the same price as the preceding trade but higher than the last price.

Conversely, a downtick, or "minus" tick, is a term used to designate a transaction made at a price lower than the preceding trade. A "zero-minus" tick is a transaction made at the same price as the preceding sale but lower than the last price.

Utility Function The relationship between the expected return and the satisfaction it generates.

Volume The number of shares traded in a security or an entire market during a given period.

Voting Right The stockholder's right to vote his stock in the affairs of his company. Most common shares have one vote each. Preferred stock usually has the right to vote when preferred dividends are in default for a specified period. The right to vote may be delegated by the stockholder to another person.

Warrant A certificate giving the holder the right to purchase securities at a stipulated price within a specified time limit or perpetually.

When Issued A short form of "when, as, and if issued." The term indicates a conditional transaction in a security authorized for issuance but not as yet actually issued. All "when issued" transactions are on an "if " basis, to be settled if and when the actual security is issued and the exchange or National Association of Securities Dealers rules the transactions are to be settled.

Wire House A member firm of an exchange maintaining a communications network linking either its own branch offices of correspondent firms, or a combination of such offices.

Working Capital   Refers to a firm's investment in short-term assets, e.g., cash, short-term securities, accounts receivable, and inventories. Gross working capital is defined as a firm's total current assets. Net working capital is defined as current assets minus current liabilities. If the term "working capital" is used without further qualification, it generally refers to gross working capital. Net liquid assets with which a firm does business are roughly measured as current assets minus current liabilities.

Working Control   Theoretically, ownership of 51 percent of a company's voting stock is necessary to exercise control. In practice,

effective control sometimes can be exerted through ownership, individually or by a group acting in concert, of less than 50 percent.

Yield   Figuring the yield of a bond to maturity calls for a bond yield table.

Yield Curve   The relationship among the yields of bonds of equal quality but different maturities.

Yield to Maturity   The annual discounted return to a bond, including any annual accumulation or amortization. The same as the internal rate of return (IRR) on the bond.

Yield Spread   The relationship among the yield on bonds of the same maturity but of different qualities or different industries— e.g., utilities vs industrials.

INDEX

685